The Econometric Analysis

of Time Series

LSE Handbooks in Economics

Series Editors:
F. A. Cowell
*Reader in Economics, London School of Economics and
   Political Science*
J. J. Thomas
*Lecturer in Economics, London School of Economics
   and Political Science*

Editorial Advisory Board:

A. B. Atkinson	C. A. Pissarides
M. J. Desai	K. Roberts
A. C. Harvey	N. Stern

This series is designed to present new work across the discipline of theoretical and applied economics. Written at a level suitable for advanced students and professional economists it will draw attention to new areas of economic enquiry, areas of contention and debate and the reporting of new research findings. The series will call on the expertise of one of the foremost groups of economists in the world and the authors will be drawn from a wide international base.

The Econometric Analysis
of Time Series

A C HARVEY

The London School of Economics

Second Edition

PHILIP ALLAN

New York   London   Toronto   Sydney   Tokyo   Singapore

First published 1981 by
Philip Allan

66 Wood Lane End, Hemel Hempstead,
Hertfordshire, HP2 4RG
A division of
Simon & Schuster International Group

Reprinted 1982, 1983, 1985, 1986, 1988
Second edition 1990

© A. C. Harvey 1981, 1990

Printed and bound in Great Britain by
BPCC Wheaton Ltd, Exeter

British Library Cataloguing in Publication Data

Harvey, A. C. (Andrew C.)
   The econometric analysis of time series. — 2nd Ed.
   1. Economics. Time Series. Analysis. Econometric models
   I. Title
   330'.01'51955

   ISBN 0-86003-085-7
   ISBN 0-86003-192-6 pbk

4 5   94 93

Contents

Preface   ix

List of Abbreviations   xii

1   Introduction   **1**

    1.1.   Estimation, Testing and Model Selection   1
    1.2.   Time Series Observations   7
    1.3.   Mathematical and Statistical Preliminaries   14
    1.4.   Asymptotic Theory   19
    1.5.   Time Series Analysis and Model Building   23
    1.6.   Econometric Models   33

2   Regression   **37**

    2. 1.   Linear Regression Models   37
    2. 2.   Least Squares Estimation   40
    2. 3.   Properties of the Ordinary Least Squares Estimator   44
    2. 4.   Generalised Least Squares   48
    2. 5.   Prediction   51
    2. 6.   Recursive Least Squares   52
    2. 7.   Residuals   56
    2. 8.   Test Statistics and Confidence Intervals   58
    2. 9.   Systems of Equations: Seemingly Unrelated Regression Equations   65
    2.10.   Multivariate Regression   72
    2.11.   The Method of Instrumental Variables   75
    2.12.   Autoregression   79

3   The Method of Maximum Likelihood   **84**

    3.1.   Introduction   84
    3.2.   Sufficiency and the Cramér – Rao Lower Bound   89
    3.3.   Properties of the Maximum Likelihood Estimator   93
    3.4.   Maximum Likelihood Estimation of Regression Models   95
    3.5.   Dependent Observations   104
    3.6.   Identifiability   111
    3.7.   Robustness   116

4   Numerical Optimisation   **122**

4.1.   Introduction   122
4.2.   Principles of Numerical Optimisation   123
4.3.   Newton – Raphson   130
4.4.   Maximisation of a Likelihood Function   133
4.5.   Two-Step Estimators   140
4.6.   Test Statistics and Confidence Intervals   143

5   Test Procedures and Model Selection   **146**

5.1.   Introduction   146
5.2.   Tests of Misspecification   150
5.3.   Classical Test Procedures: The Likelihood Ratio Test   160
5.4.   Wald Tests   166
5.5.   The Lagrange Multiplier Test   169
5.6.   Non-Nested Models   177
5.7.   Post-Sample Predictive Testing   181
5.8.   A Strategy for Model Selection   185

6   Regression Models with Serially Correlated Disturbances   **191**

6.1.   First Order Autoregressive Disturbances   191
6.2.   Comparison of Estimators   195
6.3.   Testing for First Order Autoregressive Disturbances   200
6.4.   Higher Order Autoregressive Disturbances   204
6.5.   Moving Average and Mixed Disturbances   207
6.6.   Tests Against Serial Correlation   210
6.7.   Prediction   213
6.8.   Systems of Equations   216
6.9.   ARCH Disturbances   219

7   Dynamic Models I   **225**

7.1.   Introduction   225
7.2.   Systematic Dynamics   232
7.3.   Estimation of Transfer Function Models with
       Independent Disturbances   238
7.4.   Serial Correlation   245
7.5.   Model Selection   246
7.6.   Trend and Seasonality   250
7.7.   Prediction and Forecasting   253
7.8.   Polynomial Distributed Lags   257

8   Dynamic Models II: Stochastic Difference Equations   **264**

8.1.   Introduction   264
8.2.   Estimation   267
8.3.   Testing for Serial Correlation   275
8.4.   Model Selection   280
8.5.   Error Correction Models and Co-Integration   289
8.6.   Systems of Equations   296
8.7.   Causality   303
8.8.   Exogeneity   309

9   Simultaneous Equation Models   **313**

    9.1.   Introduction   313
    9.2.   Identifiability   318
    9.3.   Maximum Likelihood Estimation   329
    9.4.   Two-Stage and Three-Stage Least Squares   332
    9.5.   Testing the Validity of Restrictions on the Model   340
    9.6.   Dynamic Models   342
    9.7.   Estimation and Identification of Dynamic Models   346
    9.8.   Forecasting, Prediction and Control   351

Appendix on Matrix Algebra   **359**

Tables   **361**

Answers to Selected Exercises   **369**

References   **371**

Subject Index   **380**

Author Index   **386**

Preface

As the title suggests, this book concentrates primarily on the econometric theory relating to time series data. However, because the initial chapters deal with general principles, there are few areas of the subject which are not touched on, either directly or indirectly. In fact, the topics covered correspond roughly to those which are included in the econometric theory course given to final year undergraduates at the London School of Economics.

The book may be regarded as a treatise on the statistical aspects of economic model building. There are three major themes. The first is concerned with the way in which recent advances in time series analysis have affected the development of a theory of dynamic econometrics. The second is concerned with setting out an integrated approach to the problems of estimation and testing based on the method of maximum likelihood. Because of the tremendous advances in computer technology and accompanying development of algorithms for numerical optimisation, such an approach is now feasible whereas fifteen years ago it was not. The final theme is the attempt to present a reasonably coherent strategy for model selection. Finding a suitable specification is the most difficult part of any exercise in econometric model building. Unfortunately this aspect of the subject is still in its infancy, and the material presented here represents only the beginnings of a solution.

Questions relating to the estimation, testing and specification of dynamic models which are not based on any behavioural theory are discussed in much greater detail in the companion volume, *Time Series Models*. On occasion reference will be made to this work as *TSM*. Although this present book is designed to be self-contained, a student wishing to study econometric theory in any depth would be well advised to become familiar with the material in *TSM*.

The emphasis in the text is on creating an understanding of the main ideas and concepts in econometrics, rather than in presenting a series of rigorous proofs. As a result, mathematical and statistical prerequisites are not unduly heavy. It is assumed that the reader has attended an introductory course in matrix algebra, but heavy matrix manipulations are avoided wherever possible. Certain key topics, such as matrix differentiation, are dealt with in the Introduction and the

Appendix. On the statistical side, it is assumed that the reader is familiar with the basic ideas of statistical inference and with regression.

Equations are numbered according to the section. The chapter number is omitted except when referring to an equation in another chapter. Examples are numbered within each section and are referenced in the same way as equations. Tables and figures are numbered consecutively throughout each chapter and are independent of the section in which they appear. The Notes at the end of each chapter are primarily for references not given in the text, and for further reading.

Certain sections are starred (*). These sections contain material which is more difficult or more esoteric, or both. They can be omitted without any loss of continuity, although for a graduate course most of them would be included.

The exercises at the end of each chapter are specifically designed to test the understanding of various points in the text. They should not be regarded as examination-type questions. The book by Phillips and Wickens *Exercises in Econometrics* provides an excellent source for further questions on the material presented here, as well as allowing the reader the opportunity to extend his knowledge on certain topics.

Bold face type-setting is not used in the text. As a general rule lower case letters denote scalars or vectors, while, with a few obvious exceptions, upper case letters denote matrices.

My understanding of econometrics has benefited considerably from discussions with colleagues at the LSE. In particular, the ideas of Denis Sargan and David Hendry have had a profound influence on my attitude to the subject, although they themselves are in no way responsible for the way in which I have expressed my views in this book. Similarly, all the colleagues and friends who were kind enough to comment on various draft chapters are exempt from blame for any blunders I may have committed. In this respect special thanks must go to Dick Baillie, James Davidson, Katarina Juselius and Hugh Wills.

The bulk of the manuscript was typed at LSE by Maggie Robertson and Sue Kirkbride, although Sue Pratt, Hazel Rice and Anne Usher also shared in the workload. Some of the earlier drafts were typed in Vancouver by Maryse Ellis. I'm grateful to them all for their efficiency in typing a difficult manuscript. Last, but by no means least, I would like to thank Lavinia Harvey for her help in typing, referencing and indexing.

London
March 1980

The second edition includes new material on a number of topics and several sections have been completely rewritten. I would like to thank the many colleagues and students whose comments and suggestions have led to improvements in the text.

Since the first edition appeared a wide range of econometric packages have become available for personal computers. The packages PC-GIVE by David Hendry and MICRO FIT by Bahram and Hashem Pesaran link in particularly well with the techniques and methodology described in this book.

London
March 1989

Abbreviations

Abbreviations used include:

ACF: autocovariance, or autocorrelation, function
AD: autoregressive distributed
AIC: Akaike Information Criterion
AR: autoregressive
ARCH: autoregressive conditional heteroscedasticity
ARIMA: autoregressive-integrated-moving average
ARMA: autoregressive-moving average
AN: asymptotically normal
BHHH: Berndt, Hall, Hall and Hausman
BLUE: best linear unbiased estimator
BLUP: best linear unbiased predictor
BLUS: best linear unbiased scalar
CES: constant elasticity of substitution
CSS: conditional sum of squares
CUSUM: cumulative sum
D−W: Durbin−Watson
ECM: error correction model
EWMA: exponentially weighted moving average
FIML: full information maximum likelihood
FIVE: full information instrumental variable efficient
GLS: generalised least squares
IV: instrumental variable
LIML: limited information maximum likelihood
LIVE: limited information instrumental variable efficient
LM: Lagrange multiplier
LR: likelihood ratio
LUS: linear unbiased scalar
MA: moving average
MAD: minimum absolute deviation
ML: maximum likelihood
MSE: mean square error
MMSE: minimum mean square estimator or estimate
MMSLE: minimum mean square linear estimator
MVB: minimum variance bound
MVUE: minimum variance unbiased estimator

NID(μ, σ^2): normally and independently distributed with mean μ and
          variance σ^2.
OLS: ordinary least squares
PDF: probability density function
P(S)D: positive (semi-)definite
SSE: sum of squared errors
SURE: seemingly unrelated regression equations
TSM: 'Time Series Models'
UMP: uniformly most powerful
URF: unrestricted reduced form
VAR: vector autoregression
VES: variable elasticity of substitution
WLS: weighted least squares
WS: wide sense
2SLS: two-stage least squares
3SLS: three-stage least squares

1
<u>Introduction</u>

1.1. Estimation, Testing and Model Selection

Econometrics is concerned with the estimation of relationships suggested by economic theory. This serves two purposes. Firstly, it allows economic hypotheses to be tested empirically. Secondly, it provides a framework for making rational and consistent predictions. These two objectives are, of course, closely related, since the ability to make successful predictions provides the crucial test of any theory.

Econometric models may be fitted to both time series and cross-section observations. A household budget survey provides an example of cross-sectional data and a typical economic hypothesis might concern the expenditure of households on a commodity such as food. Suppose that economic theory specifies a behavioural relationship in which expenditure on food depends on household income and the size of the family. If the relationship between these variables is taken to be linear, the model becomes

$$y = \delta + \beta_1 x_1 + \beta_2 x_2 \tag{1.1}$$

where y is household expenditure on food, x_1 is household income and x_2 is household size. Given estimates of the parameters, δ, β_1 and β_2, predictions of food expenditure for households not in the sample can be made on the basis of information about their income and size.

Estimates of the parameters in (1.1) can be obtained by the method of least squares. This may be justified on purely pragmatic grounds: an attempt is being made to fit the model as closely as possible to the observations. In carrying out this exercise, it is implicitly recognised that the relationship in (1.1) will not hold exactly for every household in the sample. However, the deterministic model makes no explicit allowance for these discrepancies. Thus, while the estimates of δ, β_1 and β_2 will clearly be different if they are computed from another sample, no attempt is made to assess the variability which can be expected. In a similar way no attempt is made to assess the margin

1

of error associated with predictions. It is therefore impossible to test economic hypotheses in any meaningful way using this model.

The solution to the above problem is to construct a statistical model. If a 'j' subscript indicates an observation on the jth household in a sample of size N, the statistical model suggested by (1.1) is

$$y_j = \delta + \beta_1 x_{1j} + \beta_2 x_{2j} + u_j, \qquad j = 1, \ldots, N \tag{1.2}$$

where u_j is a *disturbance* term. This represents the influence of all the variables excluded from the model, including unobservables such as individual tastes. The introduction of such a term allows y_j to be treated as a random variable. Conditional on the values of x_{1j} and x_{2j}, certain assumptions may be made concerning the distribution of y_j and it is these assumptions which complete the specification of the statistical, or stochastic, model.

Given the probability structure of the model, it becomes possible to deduce the properties of estimators and test statistics and to assess their value. The test statistics may be used to confront specific economic hypotheses with the empirical evidence presented by the data. More generally, they provide a guide to choosing between the different specifications suggested by economic theory. It is this interaction between economic theory and statistical inference which provides the key to successful work in applied economics. The purpose of the first five chapters of this book is to lay the statistical foundations for such work by examining the principles for the construction of efficient estimators and by considering the ways in which test statistics may be constructed and applied in model specification.

Estimation

For a model like (1.2), the method of ordinary least squares has a strong intuitive appeal. Indeed it can be justified on statistical grounds under very mild conditions regarding the distribution of the dependent variable. However, for many of the models encountered in econometrics, least squares is not an appropriate estimation technique. Econometric models typically consist of sets of equations which incorporate feedback effects from one variable to another. These are known as simultaneous equation systems. Treating the estimation of a single equation from such a system as an exercise in multiple regression will, in general, lead to estimators with poor statistical properties. Furthermore, even when a model can be conceived as a single equation, it will often be of a form which does not fit naturally into a regression framework. Some of the dynamic models which are applied to time series data fall into this category.

A more general approach to estimating the parameters of a statistical model is to apply the method of *maximum likelihood*. The essence of this approach is to write down the joint density function of the observations and then to treat it as a function of the unknown parameters. Interpreted in this way, it becomes a likelihood function which indicates the plausibility of different parameter values, given the particular set of observations obtained. The most plausible values are taken to be those which maximise the likelihood function. These are the maximum likelihood estimators and under suitable conditions they are statistically efficient. However, as a general rule, this property can be demonstrated only in large samples. Hence the discussion of some of the basic aspects of asymptotic theory to be found in Section 1.4.

A key feature of maximum likelihood estimation concerns the form of the distribution of the observations. Unless there is prior information to suggest otherwise, this is generally taken to be normal. In a regression model, the interpretation of the disturbance term as a composite of omitted variables means that the assumption of normality can, to some extent, be justified by the central limit theorem. A more pragmatic reason for its adoption is that the likelihood function is usually relatively easy to handle mathematically. However, if the normality assumption is inappropriate, the maximum likelihood estimator can have very poor properties, even though the remaining features of the model are correctly specified. This point is examined in Section 3.7, and a number of estimators which are *robust* to the form of the distribution are introduced. Although robust procedures are not widely used in econometrics at present, there is clearly a case for their adoption. Indeed the whole area of robustness deserves more attention. As a general concept, robustness concerns the sensitivity of particular estimation techniques to all the assumptions of the model, not just those concerned with the shape of the distribution.

The maximum likelihood estimators are generally obtained by differentiating the likelihood function with respect to the unknown parameters. Setting each of the derivatives equal to zero yields the likelihood equations. If these equations are non-linear, which is usually the case, they must be solved by an iterative procedure. At one time this was considered a serious drawback to maximum likelihood estimation. However, with the rapid advances in computer technology and the accompanying development of numerical optimisation procedures, these arguments have lost much of their force. This is not to say that maximising a likelihood function is now a straightforward affair. A number of pitfalls await the unwary and it is as well to have some understanding of what is involved in the optimisation procedures which are used. Thus, having described the statistical theory of maximum likelihood estimation in Chapter 3, various methods of computing the estimators are reviewed in Chapter 4. However, although Chapter 4 is devoted primarily to numerical methods, an important theoretical result emerges in Section 4.5. It is shown there that numerical procedures specifically geared towards maximum likelihood estimation can be used as the basis for constructing estimators which, although not iterative, are fully efficient. These are known as *two-step estimators* and such estimators are often proposed in econometrics without their relationship to maximum likelihood being made explicit.

Indeed, two-step estimators constructed on a relatively *ad hoc* basis often turn out not to have the desirable properties associated with maximum likelihood.

Although the stress in this book is on maximum likelihood, the method of least squares is dealt with at some length in Chapter 2. The material here covers the classical linear regression model, the generalised linear regression model and (non-simultaneous) systems of regression equations. The properties of ordinary least squares and generalised least squares estimators are established, and the method of *instrumental variables* introduced. As with least squares estimators, instrumental variable estimators use only information contained in the first two moments of the data. Nevertheless they can be extremely useful, particularly in large scale econometric models. Furthermore, instrumental variables estimates can often be used as starting values for maximum likelihood iterative procedures. From the theoretical point of view, the method of instrumental variables provides the framework for a unified treatment of certain estimation procedures in simultaneous equations systems. Such systems are discussed in Chapter 9. There, both two-stage and three-stage least squares are treated as instrumental variable estimators, and this interpretation then leads to the construction of similar estimators in more complex models.

Testing

In a classical linear regression model, tests of hypotheses may be based on the *t*- and *F*-statistics. These are described in Chapter 2, but in Chapter 5 it is shown that they may be developed within the more general framework of maximum likelihood. The basic test procedure is based on the likelihood ratio statistic, the null hypothesis being that certain restrictions on the model are valid. As with the maximum likelihood estimator, the likelihood ratio test has certain desirable statistical properties. However, it suffers from the disadvantage that the model must be estimated both with and without the restrictions implied by the null hypothesis. Fortunately, two alternative test procedures with similar statistical properties are available. These are the Wald and Lagrange multiplier tests. The Wald test requires only that the unrestricted model be estimated, whereas the Lagrange multiplier test is based on the restricted model.

The likelihood ratio, Wald and Lagrange multiplier tests form the basis of classical hypothesis testing. However, they cannot always be applied. When comparing two models, neither of which is a special case of the other, non-nested procedures must be employed. These procedures are also described in Chapter 5, although it is worth noting that they too are developed in a likelihood framework.

Methods for determining how well a model fits the data are also considered in Chapter 5. These are known as diagnostic checks, and include graphical procedures as well as formal test statistics. They are discussed primarily within the context of linear regression, although their application is much wider.

Model Selection

A strategy for model selection is developed in Chapter 5 and elaborated further in Chapter 8. The main points at issue concern the ways in which the formal test procedures and diagnostic checks can be used to arrive at the most appropriate specification. However, before considering the statistical basis for model selection, the fundamental question of what constitutes a 'good' model must first be answered. Seven criteria will be distinguished. These may be characterised as parsimony, identifiability, data coherency, data admissibility, theoretical consistency, predictive power, and encompassing.

Parsimony   The mechanisms by which economic variables are generated are invariably complex. When a model is constructed, it is not intended to be an accurate description of the real world. On the contrary, the aim is to simplify the underlying processes in such a way that only the essential features are brought out. In the words of Milton Friedman (1953, p. 14): 'A hypothesis is important if it explains much by little...'. Similar sentiments are expressed by Popper (1959, p. 142) when he says that: 'Simple statements...are to be prized more highly than less simple ones because they tell us more; because their empirical content is greater; and because they are better testable'.

From the statistical point of view, the key feature of a simple model is that it contains a small number of parameters. This is often known as the principle of parsimony, and it is well illustrated by (1.1). In explaining household expenditure on food, we are well aware of influences other than income and household size. Occupation, education, social class and age are all relevant factors, but in formulating (1.1) it is hypothesised that income and household size are the dominating influences. Very little explanatory power is lost by relegating the other factors to the disturbance term, but a good deal is gained by focusing attention on the variables which really matter.

Identifiability   A model is not identifiable if more than one set of parameter values is consistent with the data. This concept is fundamental to any statistical model and it is defined more precisely in Section 3.6. The main point to note for the moment is that if a model is not identifiable, the estimates cannot, in general, be interpreted in any meaningful way. In econometrics, identifiability is particularly important in connection with simultaneous equation models and a good deal of the discussion in Chapter 9 is concerned with rules for determining whether a given equation is identifiable. If it is not, there is no point in attempting to estimate it, even with a large number of observations.

Although identifiability is a precisely defined statistical concept, it is related to parsimony. As a general rule, the more parsimonious a model, the less likely it is to suffer from problems of identifiability.

Data Coherency   The object of building a model like (1.1) is to explain the movements in the dependent variable. If the model is at all successful, the prediction based on x_{1t} and x_{2t} should be reasonably close to the observed value, y_t, for all points in the sample. The goodness of fit of a regression model may be characterised by a measure such as the coefficient of multiple correlation, R^2, and similar criteria may be constructed for other classes of models. However, other considerations arise in determining whether the movements in a variable, or variables, are adequately captured by the model. In particular, the *residuals* from the fitted model should be approximately random. If they are not, there is some systematic aspect of behaviour which is not being picked up. The purpose of 'diagnostic checks' is basically to assess the adequacy of a model in this respect.

Data Admissibility   A model should be unable to predict values which violate definitional constraints. For example, some variables cannot be negative.

Theoretical Consistency   A fifth requirement of a good model is that it should be consistent with what is known *a priori*, irrespective of whether that knowledge stems from economic theory or common logic. In the case of (1.1), for example, an equation in which the coefficient of either x_1 or x_2 was negative would have to be viewed with suspicion.

Predictive Power   Another criterion for judging a model is the accuracy of its predictions. To quote again from Friedman (1953, p. 7): '...the only relevant test of the validity of a hypothesis is comparison of its predictions with experience'. It is important, therefore, to be clear about what is meant by predictive power in this context; in particular, it must be distinguished from the criterion of 'goodness of fit' within the sample.

In the cross-sectional example, (1.2), a model is specified and estimated on the basis of a sample of N observations. The accuracy of predictions within the sample is captured by a goodness of fit measure such as R^2. The important question, however, is whether the estimated model can predict food expenditure for households *outside* the sample, given the relevant information on income and household size. Success in this respect is much more convincing than the attainment of a good fit within the sample, since the preferred specification is being validated against a set of completely fresh observations.

Similar considerations apply in modelling time series. The usual strategy is to examine the accuracy of predictions for observations arising after the sample, i.e. in the *post-sample* period.

A number of criteria can be formulated for assessing predictive power outside the sample period. One obvious possibility is the sum of squares of the prediction errors, and this is the measure proposed at the end of Chapter 5. Once such a measure has been adopted, some operational content can be given to the idea that a model should be retained until it is confronted with an alternative which yields more accurate predictions.

Encompassing A model is said to encompass a rival formulation if it can explain the results given by the rival formulation. If this is the case, the rival model contains no information which could be used to improve the preferred model; see Mizon (1984). In order to be encompassing a model does not need to be more general than its rivals. Indeed, the notion of parsimonious encompassing is essential to avoid vacuous formulations.

1.2. Time Series Observations

The basic techniques of estimation, testing and specification are developed in Chapters 2 to 5. These techniques are applicable to both cross-section and time series problems. However, the main interest is in time series, and the last four chapters are primarily concerned with applying the methodology in this direction. The variable of interest, y_t, is observed at equally spaced intervals over the period $t = 1, \ldots, T$, together with a set of possible explanatory variables. Econometric theory is concerned with the issues surrounding the estimation and specification of a suitable model for explaining and predicting the behaviour of y_t. More generally y_t is a vector of observations and the model constructed takes the form of a system of equations.

The element of time introduces a new dimension into modelling. It raises important questions concerning the economic interpretation of a model, particularly with respect to equilibrium and steady-state growth, and it brings in a whole range of statistical considerations concerned with modelling variables which do not adjust instantaneously to changes in other variables. The models proposed in time series analysis form the statistical basis for the models used in dynamic econometrics.

Statics and Dynamics

The model

$$y_t = \beta x_t + u_t \tag{2.1}$$

is static. If x changes, y immediately responds and no further change takes place in y if x then remains constant. The system is therefore always observed in an equilibrium position.

A dynamic element may be injected into (2.1) by introducing lagged values of the explanatory variable. A very simple modification is

$$y_t = \beta_0 x_t + \beta_1 x_{t-1} + u_t \tag{2.2}$$

If x increases by one unit, the expected value of y increases immediately by β_0 units, but the full change of $\beta_0 + \beta_1$ units is only felt after one whole time period has elapsed.

An alternative way of introducing dynamic effects into a model is by means of a lagged dependent variable. Consider the specification

$$y_t = \alpha y_{t-1} + \beta x_t + u_t \tag{2.3}$$

where α and β are parameters. Suppressing the disturbance term and substituting repeatedly for lagged values of y gives

$$y_t = \beta x_t + \beta \alpha x_{t-1} + \beta \alpha^2 x_{t-2} + \ldots \tag{2.4}$$

Provided $|\alpha| < 1$, the influence of values of x in the remote past is negligible. In these circumstances the model has an equilibrium solution, since if x_t is constant at $x_t = \bar{x}$ the right hand side of (2.4) is an infinite geometric progression. On summing these terms the equilibrium value of y is given by

$$\bar{y} = \beta \bar{x} / (1 - \alpha) \tag{2.5}$$

If x changes, y moves gradually towards its new equilibrium level. The closer $|\alpha|$ is to one the more slowly this adjustment takes place.

Systems of Equations

A simple supply and demand model consists of three equations. The first is the supply curve, which determines the way in which the quantity supplied, q^s, responds to a change in price, p. The second is the demand curve, which relates the quantity demanded, q^D, to price, while the third is the market clearing condition. This is simply an identity which sets demand equal to supply.

Under the assumption that the demand and supply curves are both linear, a possible deterministic specification is:

$$q_t^S = \gamma_{11} p_t + \beta_{11} + \beta_{12}\, x_t \tag{2.6a}$$

$$q_t^D = \gamma_{21} p_t + \beta_{21} \tag{2.6b}$$

$$q_t^S = q_t^D \tag{2.6c}$$

It will be observed that supply is assumed to depend on another variable other than price. The variable x is unlike p and q in that it is not generated within the system. It is *exogenous* rather than *endogenous* and the significance of this distinction will become apparent in due course. The immediate point to note is that the three equations in (2.6) can be reduced to two. Setting $q_t^S = q_t^D = q_t$, yields

$$S: \ q_t = \gamma_{11} p_t + \beta_{11} + \beta_{12} x_t \tag{2.7a}$$

$$D: q_t = \gamma_{21} p_t + \beta_{21} \tag{2.7b}$$

If x_t is constant, the position of the supply curve is fixed, and it may be traced out from (2.6a). The demand curve may also be traced out and figure 1.1 shows the familiar supply and demand diagram of economic theory. The equilibrium solution is at the intersection of the demand and supply curves, and so long as x_t remains constant, this remains unchanged. Both q and p are endogenous, and once x_t is fixed, their values are jointly determined by the market clearing condition. In other words they are determined *simultaneously*. Thus although p_t appears on the right hand side of both equations, its status is exactly the same as q_t.

If x_t moves to a new level, the supply curve shifts to S' and a new equilibrium solution is obtained. Because the system in (2.6) is a static one, the movement to this new position takes place immediately, and no further movement takes place if the new level of x_t is maintained.

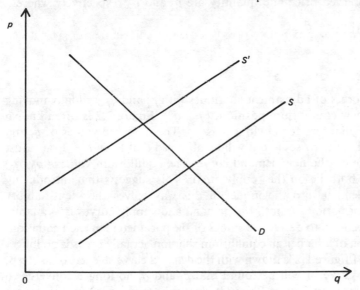

Figure 1.1   Demand and Supply Curves for Model 2.6

Each time x_t changes, a new equilibrium position is reached and values of p_t and q_t trace out the demand curve. However, the form of the supply curve cannot be determined on the basis of these observations. Even though the model is deterministic, there is a problem of identifiability.

If the exogenous variable were attached to the demand equation, rather than the supply equation, the supply curve would be traced out. However, the demand curve would not now be obtainable. Interestingly enough, this position can change in a dynamic model. Consider the following modification:

$$q_t^S = \gamma_{11} p_{t-1} + \beta_{11} \qquad (2.8a)$$

$$q_t^D = \gamma_{21} p_t + \beta_{21} + \beta_{22} x_t \qquad (2.8b)$$

$$q_t^S = q_t^D \qquad (2.8c)$$

The demand equation is still static, but the supply equation is dynamic insofar as the quantity supplied does not adjust instantaneously to a change in price. The consequences of this are shown in figure 1.2. Suppose that the market is initially in equilibrium at (p_0, q_0), but that at $t = 1$, the level of x changes to $\bar{x}$, causing the demand curve to shift outwards. The effect of this change is to increase price, but because the quantity supplied responds only to the price in the *previous* time period, q remains at q_0. Hence the immediate effect is to push the price up from p_0 to p_1, as shown on the diagram. In the next time period the quantity supplied is determined by the price, p_1. However, putting this quantity, q_2, on the market causes the price to fall and at time $t = 2$ the observed price and quantity are p_2 and q_2 respectively where

$$q_2 = \gamma_{11} p_1 + \beta_{11}$$

and

$$p_2 = q_2 - \beta_{21} - \beta_{22} \bar{x}$$

The above process of adjustment continues with p_t and $\dot{q}_t$ gradually moving towards the new equilibrium position, (p^*, q^*). Figure 1.2 is often known as a 'cobweb' diagram for obvious reasons. The observed values of q_t and p_t are marked with crosses and it will be observed that from $t = 1$ onwards, all of these lie on the new demand curve. The equilibrium values (p_0, q_0) and (p^*, q^*) both lie on the supply curve. This suggests that introducing a dynamic element into the model in this way solves the identifiability problem. Information on both the demand and supply curves is available, and this can be used to derive the values of the parameters in each equation.

The question of whether an equilibrium solution actually exists is no longer a trivial one. If figure 1.2 is drawn with the demand curve steeper, or as steep, as the supply curve, it will be found that p_t and q_t no longer converge to the new equilibrium solution. Translated into the terms of (2.8), this means that the condition

$$|\gamma_{21}| > \gamma_{11} \qquad (2.9)$$

must hold if the model is to be stable. (It is implicitly assumed that $\gamma_{11} > 0$ and $\gamma_{21} < 0$.) If model (2.8) were estimated and (2.9) did not hold, the appropriateness of the specification would have to be seriously questioned.

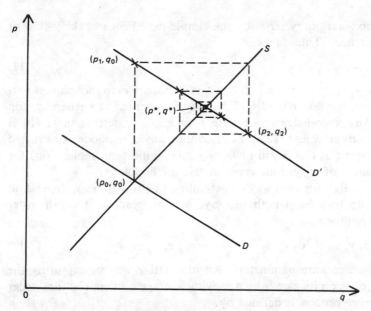

Figure 1.2   Cobweb Diagram for Model 2.8

The final point to note about this model concerns the availability of data. Suppose that (2.8) is a reasonable reflection of the way the market works when the time period is one month, but that the variables are only recorded every six months. If changes in x_t take place relatively infrequently, all that will tend to be observed is a series of equilibrium positions. Thus, in terms of the observation period, the model is effectively a simultaneous one, and the demand curve cannot be identified.

Time Series Models

A univariate time series model attempts to explain the behaviour of a variable, y_t, in terms of its own past. The most fruitful approach is to regard y_t as a stochastic process, in which the observations evolve over time according to certain probabilistic laws. The first order autoregressive model,

$$y_t = \phi y_{t-1} + \epsilon_t \tag{2.10}$$

is a simple example. The term ϵ_t denotes a sequence of uncorrelated disturbances with mean zero and constant variance.

If ϕ is less than one in absolute value, the observations generated by (2.10) fluctuate around a mean of zero. If, on the other hand, $|\phi|$ is greater than one, the model is explosive. A model which satisfies the condition $|\phi| < 1$ is said to be stationary. Stationarity is an important concept in time series modelling, although very few time series display the characteristics which it implies. Nevertheless, the theory surrounding stationary time series can often be applied to non-stationary series by the simple expedient of taking first or second differences. Thus suppose

$$\Delta y_t = \phi \Delta y_{t-1} + \epsilon_t \tag{2.11}$$

where $\Delta y_t = y_t - y_{t-1}$. If $|\phi| < 1$, Δy_t is stationary even though y_t is not.

The dynamic regression model, (2.3), may be regarded as a generalisation of (2.10). Any knowledge concerning estimation or testing in (2.10) is therefore directly relevant to (2.3). Furthermore, any other model constructed in the same spirit as (2.10) will obviously have important implications for the development of a dynamic econometric methodology.

The most straightforward way of extending (2.10) is to let y_t depend on past values up to a lag length of, say, p. This leads to the pth order autoregressive process

$$y_t = \phi_1 y_{t-1} + \phi_2 y_{t-2} + \cdots + \phi_p y_{t-p} + \epsilon_t \tag{2.12}$$

where $\phi_1, \ldots, \phi_p$ are parameters. An alternative way of capturing the dependence of y_t on its past is by a moving average model. The first order *moving average* process is defined by

$$y_t = \epsilon_t + \theta \epsilon_{t-1} \tag{2.13}$$

Although this is formulated in terms of two unobservable random disturbances, ϵ_t and ϵ_{t-1}, repeated substitution gives

$$y_t = - \sum_{j=1}^{\infty} (-\theta)^j y_{t-j} + \epsilon_t \tag{2.14}$$

provided that $|\theta| < 1$. Model (2.13) is therefore an autoregressive process with an infinite number of lags, but the coefficients, $\phi_1, \phi_2, \ldots$, are constrained so as to depend on only one parameter.

The different characteristics of autoregressive and moving average processes may be combined in a mixed model,

$$y_t = \phi_1 y_{t-1} + \cdots + \phi_p y_{t-p} + \epsilon_t + \theta_1 \epsilon_{t-1} + \cdots + \theta_q \epsilon_{t-q} \tag{2.15}$$

This is known as an *autoregressive-moving average* (ARMA) process, and it represents the most flexible class of models for univariate time series. Provided $\theta_1, \ldots, \theta_q$ satisfy certain constraints, (2.15) can be expressed as an autoregressive process in the same way as (2.13). By selecting a suitable model from the class of ARMA processes, y_t may be modelled in terms of its past using a minimum number of parameters.

The above considerations extend to multivariate time series. If y_t is a vector of observations, it may be modelled in terms of its own past by a *multivariate*, or *vector*, ARMA process,

$$y_t = \Phi_1 y_{t-1} + \cdots + \Phi_p y_{t-p} + \epsilon_t + \Theta_1 \epsilon_{t-1} + \cdots + \Theta_q \epsilon_{t-q}$$

$$\text{(2.16)}$$

The parameters are now contained within the square matrices, $\Phi_1, \ldots, \Phi_p, \Theta_1, \ldots, \Theta_q$, while ϵ_t is a vector of random disturbances. A pure autoregressive process

$$y_t = \Phi_1 y_{t-1} + \cdots + \Phi_p y_{t-p} + \epsilon_t \qquad\qquad \text{(2.17)}$$

is the easiest model to handle statistically. It is usually known as a *vector autoregression,* and abbreviated as VAR.

Data Generation

The cross-sectional model, (1.2), applies to a sample of N households selected at random. The basic assumption underlying statistical inference in such a model is that the sample obtained is simply one of an infinite number of possible samples. The whole exercise of drawing a sample and estimating parameters on the basis of it could be repeated as many times as we wished.

Similar considerations are adopted in modelling a time series. The observations are regarded as a single *realisation* from some underlying data generation process. Unlike the cross-sectional case, however, only one set of observations can ever be obtained in practice. Nevertheless it is possible to regard the underlying data generation process as being capable, in principle, of producing an infinite number of realisations over that same time period. It is on this basis that the properties of dynamic models are derived and statistical inferences made.

In a pure time series model, such as (2.10), this is all that needs to be said. The model generates a set of observations $y_1, \ldots, y_T$, the values of which depend on the random disturbances, $\epsilon_1, \ldots, \epsilon_T$, and on the initial value, y_0. For a regression model like (2.3) there is the additional complication of the explanatory variable. This can be regarded as fixed or stochastic. If it is fixed, the observed values would be reproduced if another set of observations on y were generated. If it is stochastic its values would change in repeated realisations, thereby introducing an additional source of variation into y_t. In a cross-sectional model, such as (1.2), it is fairly easy to visualise both fixed and stochastic explanatory variables: the survey could be repeated with the same households or with a completely different sample of households. For a dynamic model the distinction is less clear cut, but as a rule it is more reasonable to regard the explanatory variables as being stochastic. However, from the statistical point of view the distinction between stochastic and non-stochastic variables is often unimportant. If no information is lost by conditioning on an explanatory variable, i.e. by treating it as if it were fixed, that variable is said to be *exogenous*. Unless otherwise stated, an exogenous variable will be denoted by the symbol '*x*', as will a variable which truly can be considered fixed in repeated samples.

Prediction and Forecasting

Model (2.3) embodies a *behavioural* hypothesis in that it attempts to explain the movements in y_t in terms of the movements in x_t. A test of the validity of the theory linking y to x is made by comparing post-sample observations on y with the predictions made by equation (2.3) on the basis of post-sample observations on x. This is sometimes known as *ex post* prediction. It should be carefully distinguished from *ex ante* predictions, in which unconditional predictions of future values of y are made. An exercise of this kind requires predictions for future values of x.

Unconditional predictions are called *forecasts*. The use of the term prediction without any qualification implies that future values of the exogenous variables are known. Of course for pure time series models, such as (2.15), there is no distinction between conditional and unconditional predictions, and the terms forecast and prediction may be used interchangeably.

1.3. Mathematical and Statistical Preliminaries

It is assumed that the reader has a grounding in probability and statistical inference, and is familiar with calculus and matrix algebra. This section is merely intended to review certain key concepts in these areas and to introduce some notational conventions.

A familiarity with asymptotic theory is not taken for granted and Section 4 is devoted to a relatively heuristic introduction to the subject.

Matrix Algebra

A thorough understanding of the basic operations in matrix algebra, such as addition and inversion, is necessary. In addition, the reader should be aware of the concept of the trace of a matrix, i.e. the sum of the elements on the leading diagonal, and the definitions of a positive definite (p.d.) and positive semi-definite (p.s.d.) matrix. A symmetric matrix A is said to be p.d. if $x'Ax > 0$, where x is any vector such that $x \neq 0$; it is p.s.d. if $x'Ax \geq 0$. Kronecker (tensor) products are reviewed in the Appendix.

The factorisation of a p.d. matrix appears in the text in a number of places. If A denotes such a matrix it can always be factored as $A = L'L$, where

L is non-singular. One way of carrying out this factorisation is by means of the *Cholesky decomposition*. In this case L is lower triangular, with all the elements on the leading diagonal positive; see, for example, Wolfe (1978, pp. 275-277). An alternative formulation is $A = \bar{L}'D\bar{L}$, where $\bar{L}$ is a lower triangular matrix with ones in the leading diagonal and D is a diagonal matrix.

Vector and matrix differentiation play an important role in estimation and the following definitions will be used. If $f(x)$ is a function of an $n \times 1$ vector of variables, $x = (x_1, x_2, \ldots, x_n)'$, the $n \times 1$ vector of partial first derivatives is

$$\frac{\partial f}{\partial x} = \left(\frac{\partial f}{\partial x_1}, \frac{\partial f}{\partial x_2}, \ldots, \frac{\partial f}{\partial x_n} \right)' \tag{3.1}$$

The notation $\partial f/\partial x'$ indicates the row vector $(\partial f/\partial x)'$. The $n \times n$ matrix of second order derivatives is

$$\frac{\partial^2 f}{\partial x \partial x'} = \begin{bmatrix} \dfrac{\partial^2 f}{\partial x_1^2} & \dfrac{\partial^2 f}{\partial x_1 \partial x_2} & \cdots & \dfrac{\partial^2 f}{\partial x_1 \partial x_n} \\ \dfrac{\partial^2 f}{\partial x_2 \partial x_1} & \dfrac{\partial^2 f}{\partial x_2^2} & \cdots & \dfrac{\partial^2 f}{\partial x_2 \partial x_n} \\ \vdots & \vdots & & \vdots \\ \dfrac{\partial^2 f}{\partial x_n \partial x_1} & \dfrac{\partial^2 f}{\partial x_n \partial x_2} & \cdots & \dfrac{\partial^2 f}{\partial x_n^2} \end{bmatrix} \tag{3.2}$$

This matrix, which is known as the *Hessian*, is symmetric if the second order derivatives are continuous functions of the x's.

Some specific results on vector and matrix differentiation are given in the Appendix.

Random Variables and the Expectation Operator

The probability density function (p.d.f.) of a random variable, y, will be denoted by $p(y;\psi)$ where ψ is a vector of parameters. It will often be abbreviated to $p(y)$. The *expectation* of y is the mean of this distribution; if y is continuous over the range $-\infty < y < \infty$,

$$E(y) = \mu = \int_{-\infty}^{\infty} y p(y) dy \tag{3.3}$$

The variance is defined as

$$\text{Var}(y) = \sigma^2 = E[(y-\mu)^2] = \int_{-\infty}^{\infty} (y-\mu)^2 p(y)\,dy \qquad (3.4)$$

For some purposes it is only necessary, or desirable, to specify the mean and variance of a distribution. When this is the case, the abbreviation $y \sim WS(\mu, \sigma^2)$ is sometimes used; WS stands for wide sense.

A linear combination of two random variables is defined by $w_1 y_1 + w_2 y_2$ where w_1 and w_2 are fixed weights. If

$$y_1 \sim WS(\mu_1, \sigma_1^2) \qquad \text{and} \qquad y_2 \sim WS(\mu_2, \sigma_2^2)$$

then

$$E(w_1 y_1 + w_2 y_2) = w_1\mu_1 + w_2\mu_2 \qquad (3.5)$$

while

$$\text{Var}(w_1 y_1 + w_2 y_2) = w_1^2\sigma_1^2 + w_2^2\sigma_2^2 + 2w_1 w_2\,\text{Cov}(y_1, y_2) \qquad (3.6)$$

If the two variables are uncorrelated, $\text{Cov}(y_1, y_2) = 0$ and the last term in (3.6) disappears.

More generally we may consider the vector of random variables $y = (y_1, \ldots, y_n)'$. This has a multivariate distribution with mean vector

$$\mu = E(y) = \{\, E(y_1), E(y_2), \ldots, E(y_n)\,\}' \qquad (3.7)$$

and variance—covariance matrix

$$V = E\{\,(y - \mu)(y - \mu)'\,\} \qquad (3.8)$$

The matrix V, which is usually known simply as the *covariance matrix,* is p.d. provided that individual variances, which are the elements on the main diagonal, are strictly positive. Results (3.5) and (3.6) may be extended by defining an $m \times n$ matrix of fixed weights, W, and considering the properties of the $m \times 1$ vector of random variables $z = Wy$. If $y \sim WS(\mu, V)$, then

$$E(z) = W \cdot E(y) = W\mu \qquad (3.9)$$

while

$$\text{Var}(z) = E\{\, W(y-\mu)(y-\mu)'\,W'\,\} = WVW' \qquad (3.10)$$

The Normal Distribution

The density function for the normal distribution is

$$p(y;\mu, \sigma^2) = \frac{1}{\sigma\sqrt{2\pi}} \exp\left\{-\frac{1}{2}\frac{(y-\mu)^2}{\sigma^2}\right\} \qquad (3.11)$$

The distribution is completely specified once μ and σ^2 are given, and it is usual to summarise (3.11) by writing $y \sim N(\mu, \sigma^2)$. The *standard* normal distribution has $\mu = 0$ and $\sigma^2 = 1$.

If the $n \times 1$ vector $y = (y_1, \ldots, y_n)'$ has a multivariate normal distribution, the joint density of the variables depends on the mean vector, μ, and the covariance matrix, V, as defined in (3.7) and (3.8). The p.d.f. is

$$p(y; \mu, V) = (2\pi)^{-n/2} |V|^{-1/2} \cdot \exp \{-\tfrac{1}{2}(y - \mu)' V^{-1}(y - \mu)\}$$
(3.12)

where V must be p.d. As in the univariate case, the abbreviation, $y \sim N(\mu, V)$ can be adopted. If V is diagonal, $y_1, \ldots, y_n$ are mutually uncorrelated. Furthermore, the joint density function (3.12) can be decomposed as $p(y_1, \ldots, y_n) = p(y_1) \cdot p(y_2) \ldots p(y_n)$. Thus, if normal variables are uncorrelated, they are also independent.

A set of independent normally distributed random variables, $y_1, \ldots, y_T$ with mean μ and variance σ^2 will be indicated by writing $y_t \sim NID(\mu, \sigma^2)$, $t = 1, \ldots, T$.

By using the moment generating function of the normal distribution it can be shown that any linear combination of normal variables is itself normal. More generally, if $y \sim N(\mu, V)$ and $z = Wy$, where W is an $m \times n$ matrix, it follows that $z \sim N(W\mu, WVW')$. Note that W must have full row rank if WVW' is to be p.d.

A number of distributions are associated with the normal. If $y_1, \ldots, y_n$ are independent standard normal variates, it follows that $z = y_1^2 + y_2^2 + \ldots + y_n^2$ has a *chi-square* distribution with n degrees of freedom; i.e. $z \sim \chi_n^2$. Furthermore, if z and x are independent χ^2 variates with n and m degrees of freedom respectively, then $z + x \sim \chi_{n+m}^2$.

An important result links the χ^2 distribution to the multivariate normal. If y is an $n \times 1$ vector such that $y \sim N(\mu, V)$, then

$$(y - \mu)' V^{-1}(y - \mu) \sim \chi_n^2$$
(3.13)

The proof is as follows. Since V is p.d., V^{-1} is also p.d. and there exists a non-singular matrix, L, such that $L'L = V^{-1}$. The n variables defined by the transformation $z = L(y - \mu)$ are $NID(0, 1)$ since $E(z) = 0$ and

$$\text{Var}(z) = LVL' = L(L'L)^{-1} L' = LL^{-1}(L')^{-1}L' = I$$

The result then follows immediately since the quadratic form in (3.13) is equal to the sum of squares, $z'z$.

The F-distribution is defined in terms of the ratio of two independent χ^2 variates. If $z \sim \chi_n^2$ and $x \sim \chi_m^2$, then

$$F = \frac{z/n}{x/m}$$
(3.14)

is an F-distribution with (n, m) degrees of freedom.

Finally, if $z \sim N(0, 1)$ and $x \sim \chi^2_m$, and z and x are independent, the ratio

$$t = z\sqrt{m}/\sqrt{x} \tag{3.15}$$

is distributed as Student's 't' with m degrees of freedom. Note that squaring (3.15) yields a variate which follows an F-distribution with $(1, m)$ degrees of freedom.

Properties of Estimators

Suppose, for simplicity, that a model contains a single unknown parameter, ψ. If this is to be estimated, we need a rule telling us how to process the observations, $y_1, \ldots, y_n$, once they become available. Such a rule defines an *estimator* of ψ, and this estimator is a function of the observations. Once the estimator has been evaluated for a particular set of observations, it becomes an *estimate*.

A 'good' estimator should have a 'reasonably' high probability of yielding estimates which are 'reasonably' close to the true parameter value. One possible criterion is the demand that it should have minimum mean square error. The *mean square error* (MSE) of an estimator, $\hat{\psi}$, is defined by

$$\text{MSE}(\hat{\psi}) = E[(\hat{\psi} - \psi)^2] \tag{3.16}$$

If $\hat{\psi}^*$ denotes any other estimator of ψ, $\hat{\psi}$ can be said to minimise the MSE if $\text{MSE}(\hat{\psi}) \leq \text{MSE}(\hat{\psi}^*)$ for all ψ. Unfortunately this is usually an unrealistic demand since $\hat{\psi}^*$ can always be set equal to an arbitrary value within the parameter space and its MSE will then be zero for that particular value. An estimator of this kind is hardly sensible, but it can be eliminated by imposing the condition of unbiasedness. An estimator is said to be *unbiased* if

$$E(\hat{\psi}) = \psi \qquad \text{for all } \psi \tag{3.17}$$

The MSE is equal to the variance for an unbiased estimator and this leads to the concept of a *minimum variance unbiased estimator* (MVUE).

Unfortunately, the MVUE criterion has severe drawbacks as a method of assessing different estimators. It contains an element of arbitrariness, particularly with regard to unbiasedness. Thus, while the concept of an MVUE is relevant for a static regression model such as (2.1), it is of little value in (2.10), which represents one of the simplest examples of a dynamic model. The least squares estimator in (2.1) is *linear* in the observations since it may be written in the form

$$b = \sum_{t=1}^{T} w_t y_t \tag{3.18}$$

where $w_t = x_t / \Sigma x_t^2$. The weights, $w_1, \ldots, w_T$, are non-stochastic, and so the mean and variance of b may be obtained using (3.5) and (3.6). It is not difficult to show that b is unbiased. On the other hand, regressing y_t on y_{t-1} in (2.10) yields an estimator of ϕ which is biased. To insist on applying the MVUE criterion here would rule out the least squares estimator, even though it is perfectly sensible. In fact it is difficult to obtain exact expressions for both the mean and the variance of this estimator and so no criterion based on small sample considerations is particularly helpful.

1.4. Asymptotic Theory

For many estimators exact small sample results cannot be established. However, it is usually possible to determine at least the properties of an estimator *approximately*. Such approximations generally become more accurate as the sample size increases and they may be established formally by deriving a result which holds exactly in the limit as $T \to \infty$. Properties of estimators obtained on this basis are said to be asymptotic. This section sketches out these properties.

Consistency

As the sample size increases, it is desirable for an estimator to become more accurate in the sense that the probability of its being 'close' to the true value of the parameter increases. This notion is captured by the property of *consistency* which may be formally stated as follows. Consider a sequence of random variables (a_T), i.e. $a_1, a_2, \ldots, a_T \ldots$. This sequence is said to *converge in probability* to a constant, a, if

$$Pr(|a_T - a| < \epsilon) > 1 - \eta \qquad \text{for all } T > T_0, \tag{4.1}$$

where ϵ and η are arbitrarily small numbers. In other words, given ϵ and η, is is always possible to find a sample size such that the probability that a_T is outside the range $a \pm \epsilon$ is less than η.

An alternative way of expressing (4.1) is to write

$$\lim_{T \to \infty} Pr(|a_T - a| > \epsilon) = 0 \qquad \text{for any } \epsilon > 0 \tag{4.2}$$

The notation in (4.1) and (4.2) is rather awkward. If a sequence does converge in probability to a it is more common to write

$$\text{plim } a_T = a \tag{4.3}$$

This states that the *probability limit* (or 'plim') of the sequence (a_T) is a.

If (a_T) and (b_T) are sequences of random variables with probability limits a and b respectively, it is not difficult to show that

$$\text{plim}(a_T + b_T) = a + b \qquad (4.4)$$

This property is also shared by the expectation operator. However, probability limits have a number of properties which are not shared by expectations. In particular

$$\text{plim}(a_T b_T) = ab \qquad (4.5)$$

irrespective of whether or not a_T and b_T are independent. Furthermore, if $g(.)$ is a continuous function, then

$$\text{plim } g(a_T) = g(\text{plim } a_T) = g(a) \qquad (4.6)$$

The concept of a probability limit may be extended to vectors and matrices, and the properties (4.4) to (4.6) hold in these cases also. One result which is particularly important follows from the generalisation of (4.6). If A_T is a square matrix of random variables such that

$$\text{plim } A_T = A$$

where A is p.d., then

$$\text{plim } A_T^{-1} = (\text{plim } A_T)^{-1} = A^{-1} \qquad (4.7)$$

In the context of estimation theory, an estimator of a single parameter, ψ, based on T observations may be denoted by $\hat{\psi}_T$. The estimator is then said to be a *consistent* estimator of ψ if

$$\text{plim } \hat{\psi} = \psi \qquad (4.8)$$

As an example consider a random sample of T observations, $y_1, \ldots, y_T$, drawn from a probability distribution with mean μ and variance σ^2. The sample mean, $\bar{y}$, is unbiased and its variance is σ^2/T. As T gets bigger, $\text{Var}(\bar{y})$ tends to zero, indicating that the distribution of $\bar{y}$ becomes more and more concentrated around the true parameter value μ.

Consistency may be shown formally by means of *Chebyshev's inequality*. This states that for any random variable, z, with finite mean and variance, μ and ω^2 respectively, the probability of a deviation from the mean equal to k or more times the standard deviation is at most equal to $1/k^2$, i.e.

$$\text{Prob}[|\, z - \mu\,| \geq k\omega] \leq 1/k^2, \qquad \text{for any } k > 0 \qquad (4.9)$$

In the case of the sample mean, $\bar{y}$, the mean is μ and the variance σ^2/T, so that the inequality in square brackets becomes $|\bar{y} - \mu| \geq k\sigma/\sqrt{T}$. Setting $k = \epsilon\sqrt{T}/\sigma$ gives

$$\text{Prob}[|\bar{y} - \mu| \geq \epsilon] \leq \sigma^2/\epsilon^2 T, \qquad \text{for any } \epsilon > 0$$

Since $\sigma^2/\epsilon^2 T$ converges to zero as $T \to \infty$ for any $\epsilon > 0$, it follows from the definition (4.2), that $\bar{y}$ is a consistent estimator of μ.

As a second example, consider the estimation of σ^2 in the above example.

A suitable estimator is

$$s^2 = (T - 1)^{-1}\sum(y_t - \bar{y})^2 \tag{4.10}$$

and if the observations are normally distributed it can be shown that

$$(T - 1)\, s^2/\sigma^2 \sim \chi^2_{T-1} \tag{4.11}$$

Since $\mathrm{Var}(\chi^2_f) = 2f$, it follows that $\mathrm{Var}(s^2) = 2\sigma^4/(T - 1)$. Proceeding as before it may be shown that

$$\mathrm{plim}\ s^2 = \sigma^2 \tag{4.12}$$

An alternative estimator of the variance in this situation is

$$\tilde{\sigma}^2 = T^{-1}\sum(y_t - \bar{y})^2 \tag{4.13}$$

Although this estimator is biased in small samples, it is asymptotically unbiased in the sense that $\lim E(\tilde{\sigma}^2) = \sigma^2$. Given this result it is relatively straightforward to show that the estimator is consistent.

The consistency of an estimator can often be demonstrated under much weaker conditions than are implied by the above discussion. In fact, if a random sample is drawn from a parent distribution with a finite mean, μ, it can be shown that the sample mean will be a consistent estimator of μ even if the variance, σ^2, is infinite.

A final point about consistent estimators concerns the implications of (4.6). For example if $y_t \sim NID(\mu, \sigma^2)$, $\bar{y}^{-1}$ is a consistent estimator of μ^{-1}. It is *not* true, however, that $E(\bar{y}^{-1}) = \mu^{-1}$, for the simple reason that the expectation cannot be evaluated in this case.

Asymptotic Distributions

Suppose a sample of T independent observations, $y_1, \ldots, y_T$ is drawn from a normal distribution with mean μ and variance σ^2. Assume for simplicity that σ^2 is known. From the properties of the normal distribution, the sample mean, $\bar{y}$, is normally distributed with mean μ and variance, σ^2/T. Now suppose we have exactly the same situation, except that the observations no longer come from a normal distribution. In these circumstances it will not usually be possible to derive the exact distribution of $\bar{y}$. However, for a 'reasonably large' value of T, $\bar{y}$ can be taken to be *approximately* normally distributed with mean μ and variance, σ^2/T. What constitutes a 'reasonably large' sample in these circumstances depends on the form of the distribution of y_t, and the degree of approximation which can be tolerated. The *central limit theorem,* the result which forms the basis of our assertion regarding the approximate normality of $\bar{y}$, tells us nothing on this point. What it does prove formally is that $\sqrt{T}\bar{y}$ *converges in distribution* to a normal variate with mean $\sqrt{T}\mu$ and variance σ^2. In other words, as T becomes larger, the distribution of $\sqrt{T}\bar{y}$ approaches the distribution $N(\sqrt{T}\mu, \sigma^2)$. This is usually expressed by writing

$$\sqrt{T}(\bar{y} - \mu) \xrightarrow{L} N(0, \sigma^2) \tag{4.14}$$

the notation indicating that $\sqrt{T}\bar{y}$ has a *limiting normal distribution*.

Expressing the result in terms of $\sqrt{T}\bar{y}$ rather than $\bar{y}$ sometimes causes confusion. However, this is necessary in order to establish an asymptotic distribution. Suppose we have the original case where $y_t \sim N(\mu, \sigma^2)$. The variance of $\bar{y}$ is σ^2/T, but in the limit as $T \to \infty$, this goes to zero. Thus the asymptotic distribution is degenerate, all its mass being concentrated at the point $\bar{y} = \mu$. This is clearly no guide to the kind of distributional results which might be expected in finite samples. Nevertheless, although the asymptotic results do formally refer to the limiting distribution of $\sqrt{T}\bar{y}$, it is the approximation to the distribution of $\bar{y}$ which is of interest. Thus, when (4.14) holds, $\bar{y}$ is said to be *asymptotically normally distributed* and this may be written

$$\bar{y} \sim AN(\mu, \sigma^2/T) \tag{4.15}$$

The *asymptotic variance* is

$$\text{Avar}(\bar{y}) = \sigma^2/T \tag{4.16}$$

Cramér's Theorem

The following result, which is sometimes known as *Cramér's theorem*, plays an important role in the derivation of the asymptotic properties of certain estimators.

Suppose that $\eta_T = H_T\xi_T$ is an $n \times 1$ vector of random variables with a limiting multivariate normal distribution with mean μ and covariance Ω, i.e. $\xi_T \xrightarrow{L} N(\mu, \Omega)$, and H_T is an $n \times n$ matrix with the property

$$\text{plim } H_T = H$$

where H is p.d. Then

$$\eta_T \xrightarrow{L} N(H\mu, H\Omega H') \tag{4.17}$$

Example   Consider the statistic

$$\frac{\bar{y} - \mu}{s/\sqrt{T}} \tag{4.18}$$

constructed from a random sample from a non-normal distribution. The standard deviation of the parent distribution, σ, is assumed to be unknown and so is replaced by the consistent estimator, s, defined by (4.10). From the central limit theorem $\sqrt{T}(\bar{y} - \mu) \xrightarrow{L} N(0, \sigma^2)$. If $\sqrt{T}(\bar{y} - \mu)$ is taken to be the random variable, ξ_T, in Cramér's theorem, then $H_T^{-1} = s$. Since plim $s = \sigma$, it follows from (4.17) that

$$\frac{\bar{y} - \mu}{s/\sqrt{T}} \xrightarrow{L} N(0, 1) \tag{4.19}$$

This is the justification for regarding (4.18) as an *asymptotic t-ratio* which can be treated as a standard normal variate in large samples. The square root of the estimator of the asymptotic variance, (4.16),

$$\text{avar}(\bar{y}) = s^2/T \tag{4.20}$$

is an *asymptotic standard error*.

1.5. Time Series Analysis and Model Building

Some simple time series models were introduced in Section 2. This section sets out ways of characterising the properties of such models and shows how they may be extended so as to provide useful univariate models for the kind of time series typically found in economics. A more detailed discussion of these matters will be found in the companion volume, *Time Series Models* (*TSM*).

Stationarity

The disturbance term, ϵ_t, which featured in all the ARMA models of Section 2 is the simplest example of a stationary stochastic process. For any value of t, ϵ_t has zero mean and constant variance, and is uncorrelated with any other variable in the sequence. For a sequence of T terms, $\epsilon_1, \epsilon_2, \ldots, \epsilon_T$, these properties may be stated formally as:

$$E(\epsilon_t) = 0, \qquad t = 1, \ldots, T \tag{5.1a}$$

$$E(\epsilon_t^2) = \sigma^2, \qquad t = 1, \ldots, T \tag{5.1b}$$

$$E(\epsilon_t \epsilon_s) = 0, \qquad t \neq s \text{ and } t, s = 1, \ldots, T \tag{5.1c}$$

The expectation operator denotes the expected value over all possible realisations.

The properties in (5.1) define a (zero mean) 'white noise' process. The process is weakly, or covariance, stationary because it satisfies the following criteria: (i) the mean is independent of t; (ii) the variance is independent of t; and (iii) each *autocovariance*, $E(\epsilon_t \epsilon_s)$, depends only on the difference between t and s. Had a normal distribution been specified for ϵ_t, the conditions in (5.1) would have been sufficient to ensure that the process was strongly stationary. However, the distinction between weak and strong stationarity is not important in this book and the term stationarity will be employed whenever the criteria for weak stationarity are satisfied.

Now consider the first order moving average process, usually referred to as an MA(1) process, defined in (2.13). It follows from (5.1a) that

$$E(y_t) = E(\epsilon_t) + \theta E(\epsilon_{t-1}) = 0 \qquad (5.2a)$$

while from (5.1b) and (5.1c)

$$E(y_t^2) = E(\epsilon_t^2) + 2\theta E(\epsilon_t \epsilon_{t-1}) + \theta^2 E(\epsilon_{t-1}^2) = \sigma^2(1 + \theta^2) \qquad (5.2b)$$

Thus the mean and variance of the process are independent of t. Furthermore,

$$E(y_t y_{t-1}) = E\{(\epsilon_t + \theta \epsilon_{t-1})(\epsilon_{t-1} + \theta \epsilon_{t-2})\} = \theta \sigma^2 \qquad (5.2c)$$

and

$$E(y_t y_{t-\tau}) = 0, \qquad \tau = \pm 2, \pm 3, \ldots \qquad (5.2d)$$

The autocovariances therefore depend only on $\tau = t - s$ and so the model satisfies the requirements for stationarity.

In a similar way it can be shown that the MA(q) process,

$$y_t = \theta_0 + \epsilon_t + \theta_1 \epsilon_{t-1} + \cdots + \theta_q \epsilon_{t-q} \qquad (5.3)$$

is stationary. No restrictions are needed either on θ_0 or on the moving average parameters, $\theta_1, \ldots, \theta_q$. Restrictions must, however, be imposed on the parameters of an autoregressive model. For the AR(p) process, (2.12), the condition for stationarity is that the roots of the characteristic equation

$$x^p - \phi_1 x^{p-1} - \cdots - \phi_p = 0 \qquad (5.4)$$

should be less than one in absolute value. The same condition must be imposed on the general ARMA(p, q) process defined by (2.15).

For the AR(1) model, (2.10), the condition for stationarity is $|\phi| < 1$. When this condition holds, repeated substitution for lagged values of y_t yields an infinite moving average,

$$y_t = \sum_{j=0}^{\infty} \phi^j \epsilon_{t-j} \qquad (5.5)$$

This is a reflection of a more general result, namely that any stationary AR or ARMA process may be expressed as an infinite MA process.

It follows immediately from (5.1a) that $E(y_t) = 0$. As regards the variance,

$$E(y_t^2) = \sum_{j=0}^{\infty} \sum_{i=0}^{\infty} \phi^{i+j} E(\epsilon_{t-j} \epsilon_{t-i}) = \sigma^2 \sum_{j=0}^{\infty} \phi^{2j}$$

and summing the sequence 1, ϕ^2, ϕ^4, . . . as an infinite geometric progression yields

$$\text{Var}(y_t) = \sigma^2/(1 - \phi^2) \tag{5.6}$$

The autovariances may be obtained by a similar argument, although the derivation given in the next sub-section is slightly easier.

The Autocorrelation Function

The autocovariances of a stationary stochastic process are defined by

$$\gamma_\tau = E[(y_t - \mu)(y_{t-\tau} - \mu)], \qquad \tau = 0, \pm 1, \pm 2, \ldots \tag{5.7}$$

The plot of γ_τ, the autocovariance at lag τ, against τ is known as the *autocovariance* function. Since $\gamma_\tau = \gamma_{-\tau}$ negative values of τ can be ignored. In a similar way, the autocorrelations at lag τ,

$$\varrho_\tau = \gamma_\tau/\gamma_0, \qquad \tau = 0, 1, 2, \ldots \tag{5.8}$$

can be plotted against τ to yield the *autocorrelation function* (a.c.f.). Both functions contain exactly the same information on the correlation structure of the process, the only difference being that the autocorrelations are dimensionless with $\varrho_0 = 1$.

The autocorrelation function for an MA(1) process exhibits a sharp cut-off after $\tau = 1$. For an AR(1) process, however, the autocorrelations decay exponentially as shown in figure 1.3. The form of the autocorrelation function may be obtained by multiplying both sides of (2.10) by $y_{t-\tau}$ and taking expectations. Thus:

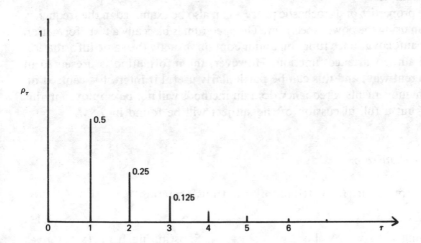

Figure 1.3   Autocorrelation Function for AR(1) Process with $\phi = 0.5$

$$E(y_t y_{t-\tau}) = \phi E(y_{t-1} y_{t-\tau}) + E(\epsilon_t y_{t-\tau}) \tag{5.9}$$

becomes

$$\gamma_\tau = \phi \gamma_{\tau-1}, \qquad \text{for } \tau = 1, 2, \ldots \tag{5.10}$$

and this implies a similar expression for the autocorrelations.

In general an MA(q) process has a cut-off in the autocorrelation function beyond lag q. On the other hand, the autocorrelation function for an AR(p) process decays gradually towards zero. It has the form of a pth order difference equation and the question of whether the decay is exponential, cyclical or oscillatory depends on the roots of the characteristic equation, (5.4). A mixed process, (2.15), has the characteristics of an AR(p) and an MA(q) and the range of patterns exhibited by the autocorrelation function can be very wide. For example, the simplest mixed model, the ARMA (1,1) process, has no less than six distinct patterns.

The sample autocorrelation at lag τ is defined as

$$r_\tau = c_\tau / c_0, \qquad \tau = 1, 2, 3, \ldots \tag{5.11}$$

where c_τ is the sample autocovariance,

$$c_\tau = T^{-1} \sum_{t=\tau+1}^{T} (y_t - \bar{y})(y_{t-\tau} - \bar{y}), \qquad \tau = 0, 1, \ldots \tag{5.12}$$

and $\bar{y}$ is the sample mean. A plot of the sample autocorrelations against τ is known as the *correlogram*. The correlogram is one of the main tools for analysing the properties of a time series, though it should be borne in mind that it is subject to sampling error and so can sometimes be misleading in small samples.

The properties of a stochastic process can also be examined in the frequency domain using the power spectrum. The spectrum is basically a transformation of the autocovariance function and it contains exactly the same information as the autocovariance function. However, the information is presented in a different way, and this can be particularly useful if interest is centred on cyclical movements. Frequency domain methods will not be employed in this book, but a full discussion of the subject will be found in *TSM*.

The Lag Operator

The lag operator, L, is defined by the transformation

$$Ly_t = y_{t-1} \tag{5.13}$$

Applying L to y_{t-1} yields $Ly_{t-1} = y_{t-2}$. Substituting from (5.13) gives $L(Ly_t) = L^2 y_t = y_{t-2}$ and so, in general,

$$L^\tau y_t = y_{t-\tau}, \qquad \tau = 1, 2, 3, \ldots \tag{5.14}$$

It is logical to complete the definition by letting L^0 have the property $L^0 y_t = y_t$ so that (5.14) holds for all non-negative integers.

The lag operator can be manipulated in a similar way to any algebraic quantity. Thus (5.5) may be expressed in the form

$$y_t = \sum_{j=0}^{\infty} (\phi L)^j \epsilon_\tau$$

and if $|\phi L| < 1$ summing 1, ϕL, $(\phi L)^2$, . . . as an infinite geometric progression yields

$$y_t = \epsilon_t / (1 - \phi L) \tag{5.15}$$

Multiplying both sides of (5.15) by $(1 - \phi L)$ gives

$$y_t - \phi y_{t-1} = \epsilon_t$$

which on re-arrangement becomes the original form of the model, (2.10).

The first difference operator,

$$\Delta y_t = y_t - y_{t-1}$$

can be used in the same way as the lag operator as $\Delta = 1 - L$. The relationship between the two operators can often be usefully exploited. For example,

$$\Delta^2 y_t = (1 - L)^2 y_t = (1 - 2L + L^2) y_t = y_t - 2y_{t-1} + y_{t-2}$$
$$\tag{5.16}$$

The general ARMA (p, q) model, (2.15), can be written in the form

$$\phi(L) y_t = \theta(L) \epsilon_t \tag{5.17}$$

where $\phi(L)$ and $\theta(L)$ are polynomials in the lag operator defined by

$$\phi(L) = 1 - \phi_1 L - \cdots - \phi_p L^p \tag{5.18}$$

and

$$\theta(L) = 1 + \theta_1 L + \cdots + \theta_q L^q \tag{5.19}$$

The stationarity condition can be expressed in terms of (5.18) by requiring that the roots of $\phi(L)$ lie *outside* the unit circle, i.e. are greater than one in absolute value, cf. (5.4). A similar condition may be imposed on the roots of $\theta(L)$ in order to ensure *invertibility*. An invertible process is one which can be expressed as an infinite autoregression; cf. (2.14).

Modelling Stationary Processes

The easiest way to construct a model for a stationary process is to estimate an autoregressive model by regressing the variable in question on its lagged values. However, it may be possible to find an ARMA model which gives just as good a fit, but contains fewer parameters. An ARMA model may be estimated by maximum likelihood, but a non-linear optimisation procedure is needed when MA terms are present. Thus there is a price to pay for parsimony. In addition, a different approach to model selection is needed. While a fairly long AR model may be fitted and subsequently simplified by dropping insignificant terms, it is better to fit a parsimonious ARMA model at the outset by choosing appropriate values of p and q; see the discussion on common factors in Section 3.6.

The basic tool for specifying suitable values of p and q is the correlogram. If the sample is reasonably large, the correlogram should display a similar pattern to that of the underlying theoretical autocorrelation function. A knowledge of the patterns of a.c.f.'s typically associated with different values of p and q can then lead the researcher to make an appropriate choice.

After estimating the chosen model, its adequacy can be assessed by testing whether the residuals are approximately random. This is diagnostic checking. The main test statistic employed is the *Box – Pierce Q-statistic,* which is defined as

$$Q = T \sum_{\tau=1}^{P} \tilde{r}_\tau^2 \tag{5.20}$$

where $\tilde{r}_\tau$ is the τth sample autocorrelation in the residuals. If the model is correctly specified, Q has a χ^2 distribution with $P - p - q$ degrees of freedom. High values of Q lead to a rejection of the hypothesis of correct specification and if the model is rejected the whole sequence of identification, estimation and diagnostic checking is repeated until a satisfactory model is obtained.

Predictions for an ARMA model can be built up recursively. Consider the ARMA(1,1) process

$$y_t = \phi y_{t-1} + \epsilon_t + \theta \epsilon_{t-1}, \qquad t = 1, \ldots, T \tag{5.21}$$

and suppose that ϕ and θ are given, and that the disturbances are known up to time T. It can be shown that the minimum mean square predictor of y_{T+1} is given by the expectation of y_{T+1}, conditional on the information at time T. If the disturbances in (5.21) are independently distributed, the conditional expectation of y_{T+1} is

$$\tilde{y}_{T+1|T} = \phi y_T + \theta \epsilon_T \tag{5.22}$$

This follows directly from writing down (5.21) for $t = T + 1$ and setting the unobserved disturbance, ϵ_{T+1}, equal to its expected value of zero. Further predictions are built up from the difference equations,

$$\tilde{y}_{T+l|T} = \phi \tilde{y}_{T+l-1|T}, \qquad l = 2, 3, \ldots \tag{5.23}$$

with (5.22) providing the starting value. In practice, ϕ and θ will be estimated, and ϵ_t will be replaced by a residual. However, the principles upon which predictions are made remain the same.

Non-Stationarity, Unit Roots and Time Trends

Most economic time series are not stationary. However, many of them can at least be approximated by stationary processes if they are differenced. If a series must be differenced d times to make it stationary, it is said to be *integrated* of order d. This is expressed by writing $y_t \sim I(d)$. The model shown in (2.11) generates a stationary series in first differences, Δy_t, but the corresponding levels, y_t, are non-stationary, hence y_t is I(1). On replacing Δ by $1 - L$ and re-arranging, (2.11) can be expressed in terms of a model for the levels, namely

$$y_t = (1 + \phi)y_{t-1} - \phi y_{t-2} + \epsilon_t \qquad (5.24)$$

This is an AR(2) process of the form (2.12), but the fact that it is non-stationary is reflected in the presence of a *unit root*. If (5.24) is written using an autoregressive polynomial in the lag operator, as in (5.18), then this polynomial may be factored as follows:

$$\phi(L) = 1 - (1 + \phi)L + \phi L^2 = (1 - \phi L)(1 - L) \qquad (5.25)$$

The roots of this polynomial are $1/\phi$ and unity. The first root lies outside the unit circle, while the unit root, which obviously lies *on* the unit circle, corresponds to the first difference operator, and cancels when this operator is applied to the series as in (2.11).

What happens if a unit root is not imposed on a model for a series when one is present? The simplest case to analyse is that of a *random walk*

$$y_t = y_{t-1} + \epsilon_t \qquad (5.26)$$

This model is a very important one in economics, but all it says is that the current observation is equal to the previous observation plus a random disturbance term. There is no parameter to estimate as there is in the AR(1) model, (2.10), since ϕ is equal to one. However, even if the series is a random walk, there is nothing to prevent us fitting an AR(1) model by regressing y_t on y_{t-1}. The consequences of doing so are that the resulting estimator is biased downwards. In practical terms, the typical estimate likely to be obtained in small samples will be well below unity, and if this point is not recognised it may well be erroneously concluded that the series is stationary. This point is pursued further in Section 2.12, and a test for a unit root is given.

Observations are sometimes 'detrended' before fitting a model. Detrending in this sense amounts to regressing the observations on time. The residuals may then have an AR model fitted to them. Such a procedure is equivalent to including a constant term and a time trend as explanatory variables when y_t is regressed on its lagged values. Thus for $p = 1$, the model is effectively

$$y_t = \alpha + \beta t + \phi y_{t-1} + \epsilon_t \tag{5.27}$$

The philosophy underlying such an approach is that the long-run movements in the series follow a deterministic path, while the short-run movements are captured by a stationary autoregression. Although this is implausible for most economic time series, the model often seems to give a reasonable fit. However, care must be taken in interpreting the results. If the series is actually generated by a random walk, the residuals obtained by regressing on time will appear to be stationary. Similarly, if an AR model is fitted with a constant and a time trend, as in (5.27), the presence of these extra variables will shift the distribution of the estimator of ϕ even further to the left, making the negative bias stronger and giving the distinct impression that no unit root is present.

ARIMA Modelling

The attraction of the ARMA(p, q) model is that it provides a parsimonious representation of a stationary stochastic process. It may be extended to encompass a much wider class of non-stationary models by differencing. If the difference operator must be applied d times before an ARMA(p, q) representation is appropriate, the variable is said to follow an *autoregressive-integrated-moving average* process of order (p, d, q). This is abbreviated as ARIMA(p, d, q). Thus (2.11) is an ARIMA(1, 1, 0) process.

ARIMA models are associated primarily with the work of Box and Jenkins (1976). They developed a model selection methodology based on three elements: identification,[1] estimation and diagnostic checking. If the model fails the diagnostic checks the whole cycle is repeated until a satisfactory model is obtained. This methodology was essentially sketched out in the earlier sub-section on modelling stationary processes. The additional feature which is now present is that the order of differencing needs to be determined. The method favoured by Box and Jenkins was to examine the correlogram for various values of d to see if it damped down sufficiently rapidly to be consistent with the behaviour of the correlogram of a stationary process.

Predictions for an ARIMA model are made by expressing it as a non-stationary ARMA model, as in (5.21), and then proceeding exactly as in the stationary case. Prediction intervals can also be calculated.

Although ARIMA models have been applied extensively to economic time series, the model selection methodology described above is subject to a

[1]Used in this context, the term 'identification' is unconnected with the concept of 'identification' or 'identifiability' referred to in Section 1.1 and defined in Section 3.6.

number of problems, particularly for the small samples which are typically found in economics. A detailed critique of the whole ARIMA approach can be found in Harvey (1989, Ch. 2).

Structural Time Series Models

A structural time series model is one which is formulated directly in terms of components of interest, such as trend, cycle and seasonal. The starting off point is to think of these components as being deterministic functions of time, in which case a regression model could be employed to model the series. However, this set up is far too rigid, and so the model is made more flexible by letting the regression parameters change stochastically over time. The mechanism by which this happens is basically a random walk, with the model cast in such a way that a degree of continuity of the dependent variable is maintained.

One of the simplest structural time series models is the *local linear trend* model

$$y_t = \mu_t + \epsilon_t \tag{5.28}$$

where ϵ_t is an irregular white noise disturbance term and μ_t is a *stochastic trend*

$$\mu_t = \mu_{t-1} + \beta_{t-1} + \eta_t \tag{5.29a}$$

$$\beta_t = \beta_{t-1} + \zeta_t \tag{5.29b}$$

in which η_t and ζ_t are also white noise disturbance terms. The level of the series is given by μ_t, while β_t is the slope. In the special case when both η_t and ζ_t have zero variance, the stochastic trend reduces to a deterministic trend and so

$$y_t = \alpha + \beta t + \epsilon_t \tag{5.30}$$

where $\alpha = \mu_0$.

An even simpler model is obtained if there is no slope since then the specification of μ_t in (5.28) is

$$\mu_t = \mu_{t-1} + \eta_t \tag{5.31}$$

This is known as the *local level* or *random walk plus noise* model. It can be made stationary by differencing once to give

$$\Delta y_t = \eta_t + (1 - L)\epsilon_t \tag{5.32}$$

The first order autocorrelation of Δy_t is

$$\varrho_1 = -1/(2 + q) \tag{5.33}$$

where q is the ratio of the variance of η_t to that of ϵ_t. The remaining autocorrelations are zero and so the autocorrelation function has the same characteristics as an MA(1) process. In fact the random walk plus noise model has as its *reduced form* an ARIMA $(0,1,1)$ model in the sense that this is a model with a single disturbance term which has the same a.c.f. as the local level model when differenced and gives the same forecasts. In the same way it can be shown that the local linear trend model has an ARIMA$(0,2,2)$ reduced form.

The statistical treatment of structural time series models is based on the Kalman filter, and is beyond the scope of this book. The main point about such models, however, is that they have a more natural interpretation than ARIMA models and hence lend themselves to a model selection strategy which is much closer to that employed for regression models in econometrics. Full details can be found in Harvey (1989).

Multivariate Time Series

The relationship between a pair of jointly stationary stochastic processes, y_{1t} and y_{2t}, is characterised by the *cross-covariance function*. If both processes have zero mean this is defined by

$$\gamma_\tau(y_1, y_2) = E(y_{1t} y_{2,t-\tau}), \qquad t = 0, \pm 1, \pm 2, \ldots \qquad (5.34)$$

The *cross-correlation function* is a dimensionless quantity obtained by dividing the cross-covariance function by the standard deviations of y_1 and y_2. Neither the cross-correlation function, nor the cross-covariance function is, in general, symmetric about $\tau = 0$.

A zero mean multivariate white noise process is defined as an $N \times 1$ vector, ϵ_t, with the following properties:

$$E(\epsilon_t) = 0 \quad , \qquad\qquad t = 1, \ldots, T \qquad\qquad (5.35a)$$

$$E(\epsilon_t \epsilon_t') = \Omega \qquad , \qquad t = 1, \ldots, T \qquad\qquad (5.35b)$$

$$E(\epsilon_t \epsilon_s) = 0 \, , \qquad\qquad t \neq s \quad , \qquad t,s = 1, \ldots, T \qquad (5.35c)$$

Clearly the cross-correlations in a bivariate white noise process are zero for $\tau \neq 0$.

The multivariate ARMA (p,q) process (2.16) may be written in the form

$$\Phi(L) \, y_t = \Theta(L)\epsilon_t \qquad\qquad (5.36)$$

where $\Phi(L)$ and $\Theta(L)$ are polynomial matrices in the lag operator defined in the same way as (5.18) and (5.19). The disturbance term, ϵ_t, is multivariate white noise and the variables in y_t are jointly stationary if the roots of the determinantal polynomial, $|\Phi(L)|$, lie outside the unit circle. Any stationary multivariate ARMA process may be written as an infinite MA process:

$$y_t = \Phi^{-1}(L)\Theta(L)\epsilon_t \tag{5.37}$$

Predictions can be made in the same way as for univariate processes. Thus for the VAR(1) model,

$$y_t = \Phi y_{t-1} + \epsilon_t \tag{5.38}$$

predictions are built up from the recursion

$$\tilde{y}_{T+l\,|\,T} = \Phi y_{T+l-1\,|\,T}, \qquad l = 1,2,\ldots \tag{5.39}$$

with $\tilde{y}_{T\,|\,T} = y_T$.

Multivariate structural time series models may also be constructed. Thus the model in (5.28) may be adapted to handle a multivariate series by letting both μ_t and ϵ_t be $N \times 1$ vectors. A further development is to let y_t depend on a reduced number of *common trends*. Thus (5.28) becomes

$$y_t = \Theta\mu_t + \epsilon_t \,, \qquad\qquad t = 1,\ldots,T \tag{5.40}$$

where the dimension of μ_t is less than N, and Θ is a conformable matrix. The attraction of a common trends model is that it is able to capture certain long-run relationships between the series.

1.6. Econometric Models

Figure 1.4 shows the links between time series models and regression models and highlights the way in which they come together to produce dynamic econometric models. In univariate time series analysis a variable is modelled

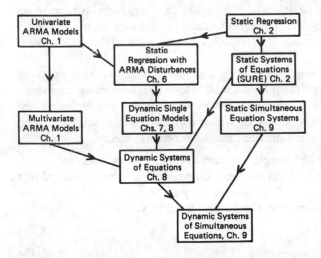

Figure 1.4 Econometric Models

in terms of its own past, while in econometrics a model is set up on the basis of a behavioural relationship suggested by economic theory. The static regression models described in Chapter 2 provide the basic framework for handling behavioural relationships. However, although such models are appropriate when the system is in equilibrium, they are unable to capture the dynamic effects associated with the adjustment from one equilibrium position to another. Hence the introduction of concepts and modelling techniques derived from univariate time series analysis.

Chapters 7 and 8 contain a detailed treatment of dynamic single equation models. There are a number of different ways of constructing such models, but whatever approach is adopted, the main problem is to determine a suitable dynamic specification. Chapter 6 is a link between Chapters 7 and 8 and Chapter 2. The models here are static, but the disturbances are assumed to follow ARMA processes. Such models provide an introduction to estimation and testing in dynamic models and so it is possible to justify studying them on purely pedagogic grounds. However, the view taken here is that the choice between static and dynamic models is dictated partly by the level of temporal aggregation in the data. If observations are available annually, rather than on a quarterly or monthly basis, it is very difficult to model dynamic effects directly. In these circumstances, a static model may be the best approximation. The ARMA disturbance term not only reflects movements in omitted variables, it also captures the effects of aggregation in what is basically a dynamic relationship.

Systems of equations are also examined in Chapters 2, 6 and 8. The static seemingly unrelated regression equation (SURE) model is introduced in Chapter 2. This can be used for modelling a set of observations over time. The observations may be on different variables or on the same variables measured for different individuals. The latter case represents a time series of cross-sections. The SURE model is extended in Chapters 6 and 8. Chapter 9 deals with simultaneous equation systems, both static and dynamic models being considered.

The relationship between time series analysis and econometrics may be viewed in a somewhat different light once the idea of multivariate time series modelling is introduced. A dynamic econometric model may be expressed as a multivariate ARMA model in which *a priori* restrictions have been imposed on the parameters on the basis of economic theory.

Example Consider a simple dynamic Keynesian model in which consumption, c, is assumed to depend on national income, y, lagged one period, and investment, i, is determined by an 'accelerator' mechanism. Adding the national income accounting identity yields:

$$c_t = \alpha y_{t-1} + \epsilon_t \qquad (6.1a)$$

$$i_t = \beta(c_{t-1} - c_{t-2}) + \eta_t \qquad (6.1b)$$

$$y_t = c_t + i_t \qquad (6.1c)$$

where ϵ_t and η_t are disturbance terms. Substituting for c_t and i_t in (6.1c) gives

$$y_t = \alpha y_{t-1} + \beta(c_{t-1} - c_{t-2}) + \xi_t$$

where $\xi_t = \epsilon_t + \eta_t$, and the three equations may now be written as a vector autoregression, (2.17), i.e.

$$\begin{pmatrix} c_t \\ i_t \\ y_t \end{pmatrix} = \begin{bmatrix} 0 & 0 & \alpha \\ \beta & 0 & 0 \\ \beta & 0 & \alpha \end{bmatrix} \begin{pmatrix} c_{t-1} \\ i_{t-1} \\ y_{t-1} \end{pmatrix} + \begin{bmatrix} 0 & 0 & 0 \\ -\beta & 0 & 0 \\ -\beta & 0 & 0 \end{bmatrix} \begin{pmatrix} c_{t-2} \\ i_{t-2} \\ y_{t-2} \end{pmatrix} + \begin{pmatrix} \epsilon_t \\ \eta_t \\ \xi_t \end{pmatrix} \quad (6.2)$$

Unrestricted, the matrices of AR coefficients, Φ_1, and Φ_2, would contain eighteen unknown parameters. In (6.2) there are only two.

The restrictions placed on (6.2) are fairly tight, and it could be argued that economic theory has no business to be so specific about the form of the dynamics. Thus in (6.1a) there is no *a priori* economic reason why c_{t-1}, c_{t-2}, y_t and y_{t-2} should not appear as explanatory variables. However, investment, whether current or lagged, could still be excluded quite reasonably on economic grounds.

Restrictions are also imposed on econometric models by the assumption that certain variables are exogenous. In a multivariate time series model all the variables are effectively endogenous. The advantage of assuming that some of the variables are exogenous is that the remaining variables can be modelled independently without any loss of information.

If the sample size is small, *a priori* restrictions are rather important, since it may be difficult to arrive at a suitable specification for a multivariate time series model on the basis of the data alone. Provided the restrictions are a reasonably accurate reflection of those in the real world, incorporating them in the model will yield a more powerful tool for forecasting. This theme is taken up and examined in the final chapter of the book. The forecasts of the endogenous variables in an econometric model are assumed to be based on predictions of the exogenous variables made on the basis of a suitable multivariate time series model. It is then argued that if a behavioural model is correctly specified, it will always forecast at least as well as a rival time series model. Indeed, this proposition is fairly obvious, although it appears that it is not always properly understood. The reason for the confusion, as well as for the quite legitimate controversy, concerns the validity of the economic theory used in constructing the model.

In the early 1970s, there appeared a number of studies comparing the forecasts from econometric models with those from 'naive' time series models. A number of these were favourable to the times series approach. One explanation for such a finding could be the shaky foundation of the economic theory upon which the econometric models were built. A second explanation concerns inadequate dynamic modelling. Most of the economic theory brought to bear on such problems is static, rather than dynamic, and this, coupled with data and computing considerations, tended to result in the construction of models which were essentially static. One of the key contributions of time series analysis has been to focus attention on the dynamic aspects of these models, and this is why the incorporation of dynamics into econometric models forms one of the principal themes of this book.

Notes

Section 2   The concept of exogeneity introduced in the section on data generation is based on the definition of 'weak exogeneity' in Engle *et al.* (1983). This point is elaborated in Section 8.8.

Section 3   Useful references for matrix algebra include Theil (1971, Ch. 1) and Johnston (1984, Ch. 4). Theil (1971, Ch. 2) also presents some of the basic statistical theory.

Section 4   The classic reference is Cramér (1946). Theil (1971, pp. 357-378) provides a review, while a more detailed account is in White (1984).

Section 5   Detrending is discussed in Nelson and Kang (1984).

Section 6   Prior beliefs in parameter values can be incorporated into an econometric model by adopting a Bayesian approach; see, for example, Leamer (1978).

Exercises

1. Consider a random sample of size T from a distribution with mean μ and variance σ^2. Show that the estimator $\hat{\mu} = 0$ has a smaller MSE than the sample mean if $T\mu^2 < \sigma^2$.

2. By substituting repeatedly for lagged values of y_t, find the coefficients in the infinite MA representation of the ARMA(1, 1) process, (5.21). Check your answer using the lag operator. State any assumptions you make.

3. Derive expressions for the variance and autocorrelations of an MA(2) model. Explain how you would predict 1, 2 and 3 periods ahead.

4. What is the effect of taking first differences in the model

    $$y_t = \alpha + \beta t + \epsilon_t$$

    where α and β are parameters? Can the resulting model be expressed as an AR process?

5. Find the mean of y_t in the model,

    $$y_t = \alpha + \phi y_{t-1} + \epsilon_t$$

    where α is a parameter and $|\phi| < 1$.

6. Is an AR(2) process stationary if $\phi_1 = 1.7$ and $\phi_2 = -0.72$?

7. Derive the autocorrelation function for the seasonal AR model

    $$(1 - \phi L)(1 - \phi^* L^4)y_t = \epsilon_t$$

    where $|\phi| < 1$ and $|\phi^*| < 1$.

2
Regression

2.1. Linear Regression Models

The starting point in the development of econometric theory is the linear multiple regression model. This may be written

$$y_t = \beta_1 x_{1t} + \beta_2 x_{2t} + \cdots + \beta_k x_{kt} + u_t, \quad t = 1, \ldots, T \quad (1.1)$$

where y_t is the tth observation on the *dependent* variable, x_{it} is the tth observation on the ith *independent* variable, u_t is a disturbance term and $\beta_1, \ldots, \beta_k$ are unknown parameters. The first independent variable, x_{1t}, will usually be a constant, i.e. $x_{1t} = 1$ for all t. In this case any systematic variation in y_t depends on the *explanatory* variables, $x_2, \ldots, x_k$.

The explanatory variables are assumed to be *exogenous*. For statistical purposes this means that they can be treated as though they were non-stochastic or *fixed* in repeated samples. As a result, the stochastic properties of the disturbances can be defined unconditionally rather than conditional on $x_2, \ldots, x_k$.

The disturbance term cannot be observed directly. By assuming that $E(u_t) = 0$ for all t, it follows that

$$E(y_t) = \beta_1 x_{1t} + \cdots + \beta_k x_{kt}, \quad t = 1, \ldots, T \quad (1.2)$$

This is the systematic part of the model.

Vector and Matrix Notation

Let $x_t = (x_{1t}, x_{2t}, \ldots, x_{kt})'$ be the $k \times 1$ vector of observations on the independent variables at time t, and let $\beta = (\beta_1, \ldots, \beta_k)'$ be the corresponding $k \times 1$ vector of regression parameters. A more concise formulation of the model in terms of *vector notation* is given by

$$y_t = x_t'\beta + u_t \ , \quad t = 1, \ldots, T \tag{1.3}$$

Rather than consider each of the T equations defined by (1.1) separately, all T sets of observations on the dependent and independent variables may be written together using *matrix notation*. Let $y = (y_1, \ldots, y_T)'$ be the $T \times 1$ vector of observations on the dependent variable, and define the $T \times k$ matrix

$$X = \begin{pmatrix} 1 & x_{21} & \cdots & x_{k1} \\ 1 & x_{22} & \cdots & x_{k2} \\ \vdots & \vdots & & \vdots \\ 1 & x_{2T} & \cdots & x_{kT} \end{pmatrix} = \begin{pmatrix} x_1' \\ x_2' \\ \vdots \\ x_T' \end{pmatrix}$$

If $u = (u_1, \ldots, u_T)'$ denotes the $T \times 1$ vector of disturbances, the complete model may be expressed as

$$y = X\beta + u \tag{1.4}$$

The Classical Assumptions

The classical linear regression model satisfies the following assumptions:

(i) the explanatory variables are fixed;
(ii) the rank of X is equal to k;
(iii) the disturbances are uncorrelated, each having zero mean and a constant, but finite, variance.

The last assumption will be denoted explicitly by writing the disturbance term as ϵ_t. In matrix notation, (1.4) becomes

$$y = X\beta + \epsilon, \tag{1.5}$$

where $\epsilon = (\epsilon_1, \ldots, \epsilon_T)'$. The properties of the disturbance term may then be expressed by writing:

$$E(\epsilon) = 0, \quad \text{Var}(\epsilon) = E(\epsilon\epsilon') = \sigma^2 I_T. \tag{1.6}$$

Note that the condition (iii) does not specify the full distribution of the disturbances, not does it assume that they are independent over time. Taking them to be uncorrelated is a weaker requirement than independence, although it does imply independence under normality.

Functional Form

The assumption of linearity may be less restrictive than appears at first sight. Consider, for example, the Cobb – Douglas production function

$$Q = AK^\beta L^\gamma \qquad (1.7)$$

where Q is quantity produced, K is capital, L is labour, and A, β and γ are parameters. From the point of view of economic theory (1.7) has a number of attractive properties, which is why it is often chosen as a basis for applied work. In particular β and γ have a direct interpretation as the elasticities of output with respect to capital and labour respectively.

Suppose that the parameters in (1.7) are to be estimated on the basis of a set of observations on Q, K and L. A stochastic formulation of the exact relationship in (1.7) must be set up and one way of doing this is to posit a disturbance term that enters *multiplicatively*. The model to be estimated is then

$$Q_t = AK_t^\beta L_t^\gamma \exp(\epsilon_t), \qquad t = 1, \ldots, T \qquad (1.8)$$

where ϵ_t is the disturbance term. This is *intrinsically linear* since a *double-log transformation* yields

$$\log Q_t = \alpha + \beta \log K_t + \gamma \log L_t + \epsilon_t, \qquad t = 1, \ldots, T \quad (1.9)$$

where $\alpha = \log A$. Although the model is non-linear in variables, it is linear in parameters. It may be cast in the form (1.1) by defining $x_{2t} = \log K_t$, $x_{3t} = \log L_t$ and $y_t = \log Q_t$.

On the other hand, suppose there were a strong *a priori* grounds for imposing an additive disturbance term on (1.7), i.e.

$$Q_t = AK_t^\beta L_t^\gamma + \epsilon_t, \qquad t = 1, \ldots, T \qquad (1.10)$$

There is no way in which (1.10) may be transformed into a linear model, and in these circumstances estimation must be carried out by the techniques of non − linear regression. This topic is pursued in Chapters 3 and 4.

The constant elasticity of substitution (CES) production function is rather more general than the Cobb − Douglas form. It is specified by the exact functional relationship

$$Q = \exp(\alpha) \left\{ (1 - \delta)L^{-\gamma} + \delta K^{-\gamma} \right\}^{-\beta/\gamma} \qquad (1.11)$$

where α, β, γ and δ are parameters. In this case, the model to be estimated will be non − linear irrespective of whether the disturbance term is multiplicative or additive. However, multiplicative disturbances are somewhat easier to handle, since taking logarithms of both sides of the equation yields

$$\log Q_t = \alpha - (\beta/\gamma)\log \left\{ (1 - \delta) L^{-\gamma} + \delta K^{-\gamma} \right\} + \epsilon_t \qquad (1.12)$$

The model is still non − linear when viewed as a whole, but for given values of γ and δ it is linear with respect to α and β. The implications for estimation are discussed in Section 4.4.

Although the logarithmic transformation is widely used, it is not the only transformation available. It is sometimes useful to let a variable enter in reciprocal form, i.e. $x_t = 1/X_t$, where X_t is the original variable. In fact, the same variable may enter an equation in several different forms, a classic example being polynomial regression where

$$y_t = \alpha + \beta_1 X_t + \beta_2 X_t^2 + \cdots + \beta_p X_t^p + \epsilon_t \qquad (1.13)$$

Qualitative Variables

The explanatory variables in a regression model may be qualitative or quantitative. Suppose that a production function is being fitted to a set of time series observations as in (1.9), but that at a certain point in time, t^*, it is known that a technological innovation was introduced. This may be handled by means of a *dummy* variable, D_t, which takes the value zero for $t < t^*$ and unity thereafter. Equation (1.9) therefore becomes

$$\log Q_t = \log A + \delta D_t + \beta \log K_t + \gamma \log L_t + \epsilon_t, \qquad t = 1, \ldots, T$$
$$(1.14)$$

For $t < t^*$, the parameter associated with the constant term in the model is $\log A$, while for $t \geq t^*$ it is $\log A + \delta$. The parameter δ therefore measures the effect of the technological innovation on production.

Note that only one dummy variable is needed in this example. As a general rule, if a qualitative variable can fall in any one of m classes, $m - 1$ dummies are needed in addition to the constant term. Alternatively the constant may be dropped and m dummy variables defined.

From the point of view of regression theory, dummy variables may be treated in exactly the same way as quantitative variables. No new issues are raised. This is not the case with qualitative dependent variables. A typical example might concern a model to explain car ownership, and the dependent variable is then unity when a family owns a car and zero otherwise. Least squares will not usually be an appropriate technique for estimating a model of this kind, and a discussion of what should be done is deferred until Section 3.4.

2.2. Least Squares Estimation

The linear model (1.1) contains k unknown regression parameters, $\beta_1, \ldots, \beta_k$, and these are to be estimated from the T sets of observations. The model contains one other unknown parameter, namely σ^2. However, the estimation of σ^2 is of secondary importance. To some extent this is also true of β_1, the parameter associated with the constant term, but for the moment all the regression parameters will be viewed in exactly the same way.

Suppose $\hat{\beta}$ is an estimator of the parameter vector β. Corresponding to this estimator are a set of T *residuals*, defined by $y_t - x_t'\hat{\beta}$, $t = 1, \ldots, T$.

The *ordinary least squares* estimator is obtained by choosing $\hat{\beta}$ such that the residual sum of squares, $\sum(y_t - x_t'\hat{\beta})^2$, is a minimum.

In order to derive an expression for the OLS estimator, the *sum of squares function*

$$S(\beta) = \sum_{t=1}^{T} (y_t - x_t'\beta)^2 \tag{2.1}$$

is defined. In the context of (2.1), β is regarded not as a vector of fixed values, but as a vector of variables. The observations, $y_1, \ldots, y_T$, are given, and the object of the exercise is to minimise $S(\beta)$ with respect to the elements of β. Although the symbol β is also used to denote the true set of parameter values, its use as an argument in $S(.)$ should not lead to any confusion.

The sum of squares function may also be expressed in matrix form as

$$S(\beta) = (y - X\beta)'(y - X\beta) \tag{2.2}$$

Differentiating with respect to β gives

$$\frac{\partial S}{\partial \beta} = -2X'(y - X\beta)$$

Since

$$\frac{\partial S}{\partial \beta \partial \beta'} = 2X'X$$

is a p.d. matrix, the least squares estimator, b, is obtained by solving the k *normal equations*,

$$X'Xb = X'y \tag{2.3}$$

Premultiplying both sides of (2.3) by the inverse of $X'X$ leads to the expression:

$$b = (X'X)^{-1}X'y \tag{2.4}$$

The relevance of the second of the classical assumptions should be apparent from this formula. Unless the matrix X is of full rank, i.e. of rank k, the cross-product matrix will be singular and there will be no unique solution to the normal equations. Having $T \geq k$ is a necessary, but not a sufficient, condition for X to be of full rank.

The Residual Sum of Squares and the Coefficient of Multiple Correlation

The OLS residuals are defined by

$$e_t = y_t - \hat{y}_t = y_t - x_t'b, \qquad t = 1, \ldots, T. \tag{2.5}$$

These residuals are orthogonal to the independent variables. If $e = (e_1, \ldots, e_T)'$, then $X'e = X'(y - Xb) = X'y - X'Xb = 0$, the last step following directly from (2.3). Using this result,

$$
\begin{aligned}
y'y &= (\hat{y} + e)'(\hat{y} + e) = (Xb + e)'(Xb + e) \\
&= b'X'Xb + e'e + 2b'X'e \\
&= b'X'Xb + e'e
\end{aligned}
\tag{2.6}
$$

This may be re-written as

$$
\sum y_t^2 = \sum \hat{y}_t^2 + \sum e_t^2
\tag{2.7}
$$

where the summation is from $t = 1$ to $t = T$. Thus the total sum of squares may be decomposed into two parts, the explained sum of squares and the residual sum of squares. This last term, which will be denoted by SSE, may be expressed as

$$
\begin{aligned}
SSE = e'e &= (y - Xb)'(y - Xb) \\
&= y'y + b'X'Xb - 2b'X'y \\
&= y'y - b'X'y
\end{aligned}
\tag{2.8}
$$

Formula (2.8) is convenient for calculation.

Similar results may be derived from working with the observations in deviation from the mean form. If the first element in x_t is the constant term, x_t may be partitioned as $x_t = (1 \; x_{*t}')'$. Similarly β and b may be partitioned as $(\beta_1, \beta_*')'$ and $(b_1, b_*')'$, where β_* and b_* are the $(k - 1) \times 1$ vectors of coefficients associated with the explanatory variables. Thus

$$
y_t = x_t'b + e_t = b_1 + x_{*t}'b_* + e_t, \qquad t = 1, \ldots, T
\tag{2.9}
$$

Summing over all observations and dividing by T gives

$$
\bar{y} = b_1 + \bar{x}_{*t}'b_*
\tag{2.10}
$$

the mean of the residuals, $\bar{e}$, being equal to zero in view of the orthogonality of X and e. Subtracting (2.10) from (2.9) leaves

$$
y_t - \bar{y} = (x_{*t} - \bar{x}_*)'b_* + e_t, \qquad t = 1, \ldots, T
\tag{2.11}
$$

The residuals therefore remain the same when the fitted equation is written in deviation from the mean form.

If the tth element in y is taken to be $y_t - \bar{y}$, and X is redefined as a $T \times (k - 1)$ matrix in which the tth row is $(x_{*t} - \bar{x}_*)'$, formulae (2.6) and (2.8) remain valid when b is replaced by b_*. This follows immediately from (2.11) which may be written in matrix form as $y = X'b_* + e$. It can also be shown that (2.4) yields the estimator b_* when X and y are in deviation from the mean form.

Expression (2.6) can now be interpreted as

$$
\sum (y_t - \bar{y})^2 = \sum (\hat{y}_t - \bar{y})^2 + \sum e_t^2
\tag{2.12}
$$

The decomposition in (2.12) is rather more useful than that in (2.7). The constant term in the regression equation cannot be regarded as 'explaining' the behaviour of y_t in any meaningful sense. It is therefore more sensible to measure 'goodness of fit' in terms of the deviations of the observations from their sample mean. This is reflected in the *coefficient of multiple correlation*

$$R^2 = 1 - \frac{\sum e_t^2}{\sum (y_t - \bar{y})^2} = \frac{\sum (\hat{y}_t - \bar{y})^2}{\sum (y_t - \bar{y})^2} \tag{2.13}$$

which lies in the range $0 \le R^2 \le 1$, and it may be interpreted as measuring the proportion of the variance of y_t explained by the regression. The closer R^2 is to unity, the better the fit of the regression model.

One objection to the use of R^2 is that it cannot decrease, and will usually increase, if additional variables are introduced into the set of regressors. The corrected R^2, $\bar{R}^2$, makes some allowance for the number of independent variables in the model. It is defined in the following way;

$$\bar{R}^2 = 1 - \frac{\sum e_t^2/(T - k)}{\sum (y_t - \bar{y})^2/(T - 1)}$$

Therefore

$$\bar{R}^2 = 1 - \{(T - 1)/(T - k)\}(1 - R^2) \tag{2.14}$$

Restricted Least Squares

It is sometimes desirable to impose constraints on the coefficients in a regression model. Thus suppose we have a Cobb–Douglas production function, (1.8), and it is felt reasonable, on *a priori* grounds, to assume constant returns to scale. This being the case, $\beta + \gamma = 1$, and such a constraint may easily be incorporated in the model by setting $\gamma = 1 - \beta$, and re-arranging (1.9) to give

$$\log(Q_t/L_t) = \alpha + \beta \log(K_t/L_t) + \epsilon_t \tag{2.15}$$

It is not usually possible to solve the problem of imposing constraints on a model quite so easily. However, a general solution may be obtained by the use of Lagrange multipliers. Suppose there are $m < k$ linear constraints. These may be written in the form

$$R\beta = r \tag{2.16}$$

where R is an $m \times k$ matrix of rank m, and r is an $m \times 1$ vector. Thus if the constraints are $\beta_1 + \beta_2 = 3$ and $\beta_2 - \beta_3 + \beta_k = 0$, they may be expressed as

$$\begin{bmatrix} 1 & 1 & 0 & 0 \dots 0 & 0 \\ 0 & 1 & -1 & 0 \dots 0 & 1 \end{bmatrix} \begin{bmatrix} \beta_1 \\ \beta_2 \\ \vdots \\ \beta_k \end{bmatrix} = \begin{bmatrix} 3 \\ 0 \end{bmatrix} \qquad (2.17)$$

The *restricted least squares* estimator of β is obtained by minimising the function

$$S(\beta, \lambda) = (y - X\beta)'(y - X\beta) - \lambda(R\beta - r) \qquad (2.18)$$

with respect to β and the $m \times 1$ vector of Lagrange multipliers, λ. This yields

$$\frac{\partial S}{\partial \beta} = -2X'y + 2X'X\beta + R'\lambda = 0 \qquad (2.19)$$

$$\frac{\partial S}{\partial \lambda} = -r + R\beta = 0 \qquad (2.20)$$

Premultiplying both sides of (2.19) by $R(X'X)^{-1}$ gives

$$-2R(X'X)^{-1}X'y + 2R\beta + R(X'X)^{-1}R'\lambda = 0$$

Since, from (2.20), $R\beta = r$, and $R(X'X)^{-1}R'$ is non-singular,

$$\lambda = -2[R(X'X)^{-1}R']^{-1}[r - R(X'X)^{-1}X'y]$$

Substituting this expression into (2.19) and premultiplying by $(X'X)^{-1}$ gives the restricted least squares estimator of β,

$$b^\dagger = b + (X'X)^{-1}R'[R(X'X)^{-1}R']^{-1}(r - Rb) \qquad (2.21)$$

If the OLS estimator actually satisfied the constraints exactly, it can be seen from (2.21) that b and $b^\dagger$ would be identical.

Except when $b = b^\dagger$, the sum of squares of the residuals associated with $b\dagger$ must exceed the sum of squares of the OLS residuals. The following result may be shown to hold

$$(y - Xb^\dagger)'(y - Xb^\dagger) = (y - Xb)'(y - Xb)$$
$$+ (r - Rb)'[R(X'X)^{-1}R']^{-1}(r - Rb); \qquad (2.22)$$

see Theil (1971, Ch. 1).

2.3. Properties of the Ordinary Least Squares Estimator

The mean and variance of the OLS estimator, (2.4), may be derived by substituting for y as given in (1.4). This yields

$$b = (X'X)^{-1}X'(X\beta + u) = \beta + (X'X)^{-1}X'u \tag{3.1}$$

If $E(u) = 0$, b is unbiased since, with X fixed,

$$E(b) = \beta + (X'X)^{-1}X'E(u) = \beta \tag{3.2}$$

The variance is then

$$\text{Var}(b) = E[(b - \beta)(b - \beta)'] = (X'X)^{-1}X'E(uu')X(X'X)^{-1} \tag{3.3}$$

If the disturbance term obeys the classical assumptions, so that the model is as in (1.5), $E(uu') = E(\epsilon\epsilon') = \sigma^2 I$ and (3.3) becomes

$$\text{Var}(b) = \sigma^2(X'X)^{-1} \tag{3.4}$$

If the disturbances are normally distributed it can be shown that b is the MVUE of β; see Section 3.4. However, if only the first two moments of the distribution of ϵ are specified, as in (1.6), a somewhat weaker result can be shown to hold. The OLS estimator is linear in the observations, and within the class of *linear* unbiased estimators it has minimum variance. The proof of this result, which is known as the Gauss–Markov theorem, is set out below.

Without knowing the form of the distribution of ϵ, very little can be said about the distribution of b in small samples. Nevertheless an asymptotic distribution for b may be derived under suitable regularity conditions. The underlying theory is presented in the last sub-section.

The Gauss–Markov Theorem

When a regression model satisfies the classical assumptions, the OLS estimator is the best linear unbiased estimator (BLUE) of β in the sense that the *covariance matrix of any other linear unbiased estimator exceeds that of b by a positive semi-definite (p.s.d.) matrix.* The proof of the theorem is as follows. Let $\hat{b} = D^*y$, where D^* is a $k \times T$ matrix which does not depend on y. Hence $\hat{b}$ is a linear estimator of β. Define $D = D^* - (X'X)^{-1}X'$, so that the estimator may be written

$$\hat{b} = [D + (X'X)^{-1}X']y$$
$$= [D + (X'X)^{-1}X'](X\beta + \epsilon)$$
$$= (DX + I)\beta + [D + (X'X)^{-1}X']\epsilon$$

If $\hat{b}$ is to be unbiased, it is necessary to have $DX = 0$. With this condition imposed, its covariance matrix becomes

$$\text{Var}(\hat{b}) = E[(\hat{b} - \beta)(\hat{b} - \beta)']$$
$$= [D + (X'X)^{-1}X']E(\epsilon\epsilon')[D' + X(X'X)^{-1}]$$
$$= \sigma^2[DD' + DX(X'X)^{-1} + (X'X)^{-1}X'D' + (X'X)^{-1}]$$

Since $DX = 0$, this expression simplifies to

$$\text{Var}(\hat{b}) = \sigma^2 DD' + \sigma^2(X'X)^{-1} \qquad (3.5)$$

Comparing (3.5) with (3.4) shows that $\text{Var}(\hat{b})$ exceeds $\text{Var}(b)$ by $\sigma^2 DD'$, which is a p.s.d. matrix.

The implications of the Gauss–Markov theorem are brought out more clearly by considering the estimation of an arbitrary linear combination of the elements of β. If w is a $k \times 1$ vector of fixed weights, the quantity to be estimated is $w'\beta$. The corresponding combination of the elements of b is unbiased, and its variance is given by

$$\text{Var}(w'b) = w'E[(b - \beta)(b - \beta)']w = \sigma^2 w'(X'X)^{-1}w \qquad (3.6)$$

Any other linear, unbiased estimator of β, $\hat{b}$, may be used to form an unbiased estimator of $w'\beta$ but, from (3.5), its variance will be

$$\text{Var}(w'\hat{b}) = \sigma^2 w'DD'w + \sigma^2 w'(X'X)^{-1}w \qquad (3.7)$$

Since DD' is p.s.d., the variance of $w'b$ cannot exceed the variance of any other linear, unbiased estimator.

As a special case, w may be chosen so that all of its elements are zero, except the ith which is unity. The above result then shows that the variance of any element in the OLS estimator cannot exceed the variance of the corresponding element in any other linear unbiased estimator of β.

It is important to appreciate that the Gauss–Markov theorem only proves that OLS is best within the class of *linear* estimators. A non-linear estimator will invariably be more time consuming to compute, but the gain in statistical efficiency may justify the extra expense. As an example, suppose that the disturbance term is known to follow a double exponential, or Laplace distribution. This distribution is symmetric and unimodal, and has a finite variance, but in large samples the variance of the OLS estimator of a given element in β is twice as large as the variance of the most efficient (non-linear) estimator; see Section 3.7.

Distribution of the OLS Estimator

The assumption that the disturbances are normally distributed enables the exact small sample distribution of the OLS estimator to be obtained. From (3.1) it will be seen that each element of b is a linear combination of normally distributed variables. Hence b has a multivariate normal distribution. Since it has already been shown that b is unbiased with covariance matrix

$\sigma^2(X'X)^{-1}$ under the classical assumptions, we may now write

$$b \sim N[\beta, \sigma^2(X'X)^{-1}] \tag{3.8}$$

If the disturbances are non-normal, the small sample distribution of b is, in general, unknown. However, if the sample size is large, b may be treated as being approximately normally distributed. This result is essentially a generalisation of the central limit theorem for a sample mean.

Consider a random sample of T observations, $y_1, \ldots, y_T$, drawn from a distribution with a mean, μ, and finite variance, σ^2. The sample mean, $\bar{y}$, is actually the OLS estimator of μ, and in Section 1.4, it was stated that the central limit theorem implies that $\sqrt{T}(\bar{y} - \mu)$ converges in distribution to a normal variate with mean zero and variance σ^2. A similar result may be demonstrated for the OLS estimator in the classical regression model, (1.5), provided that

$$\lim_{T \to \infty} T^{-1}X'X = Q \tag{3.9}$$

where Q is a p.d. matrix. This being the case, it can be shown that $\sqrt{T}(b - \beta)$ has a limiting normal distribution with a mean of 0 and a covariance matrix, $\sigma^2 Q^{-1}$. Following on from the definition in (1.4.14), b is said to be asymptotically normal with a mean of β and a covariance matrix, $\sigma^2 T^{-1}Q^{-1}$. An alternative way of expressing this result is to write

$$b \sim AN[\beta, \sigma^2(X'X)^{-1}] \tag{3.10}$$

since this is similar to (3.8). In doing this, it is to be understood that $\sigma^2(X'X)^{-1}$ is an approximation to the asymptotic covariance matrix,

$$\text{Avar}(b) = \sigma^2 T^{-1}Q^{-1} \tag{3.11}$$

The conditions embodied in (3.9) will be referred to as the *standard regularity conditions* for the explanatory variables. They are somewhat restrictive for time series regression in that they do not permit the variables to exhibit trends. As a simple illustration consider a model in which a time trend is fitted through the origin, i.e.

$$y_t = \beta x_t + \epsilon_t \tag{3.12}$$

with $x_t = t$ for $t = 1, \ldots, T$. Since

$$T^{-1}X'X = T^{-1}\sum x_t^2 = T^{-1}\sum t^2 = (T + 1)(2T + 1)/6$$

the limiting distribution of $\sqrt{T}(b - \beta)$ is degenerate. Fortunately, cases like this pose no problem from the theoretical point of view. The limiting distribution of $\sqrt{\sum x_t^2}(b - \beta)$ is $N(0, \sigma^2)$ and this provides the basis for the assertion that b will be approximately normal with a mean of β and a variance of $\sigma^2 / \sum x_t^2$. The conditions which must be imposed on the explanatory variables for this device to be used are relatively weak, and are known as

Grenander's conditions. One important feature of these conditions is that they ensure that b is consistent.

From the practical point of view, the regularity conditions are not particularly important. Unless the explanatory variables are known to have been generated in a particular way, it is impossible to check whether or not they hold for a particular sample. Imposing regularity conditions is a formal requirement needed to derive the appropriate limiting distribution. Stating that a particular estimator has a certain limiting distribution then acts as a guide indicating the approximate results which can be expected in finite samples. That the conditions could be conceived as holding as $T \rightarrow \infty$, however, is neither necessary nor sufficient for the asymptotic approximation to be a reasonable one in practice.

The discussion of OLS up to this point has been based on the assumption that the regressors are non-stochastic. As pointed out in Section 1, relaxing this assumption makes no difference to small sample properties if the disturbances are distributed independently of X. Furthermore if the standard regularity conditions are modified to

$$\text{plim } T^{-1}X'X = Q \tag{3.13}$$

the asymptotic theory goes through exactly as before. However, in some situations in econometrics, the disturbances are not distributed independently of X and/or (3.13) does not hold. Thus it cannot be taken for granted that the asymptotic properties of OLS estimators are as straightforward as in cases where the regressors are non-stochastic. Further discussion on this point can be found in the final section of this chapter and in Section 8.5.

2.4. Generalised Least Squares

Under the classical assumptions, the disturbances are uncorrelated and have constant variance. These assumptions are fairly restrictive, and a natural extension is to allow the covariance matrix of u to have a more general form. Thus (1.6) is modified to

$$E(u) = 0, \quad E(uu') = \sigma^2 V \tag{4.1}$$

where σ^2 is an unknown positive, finite parameter, and V is a $T \times T$ symmetric, p.d. matrix. The assumption of a zero mean for u is retained, as are the classical assumptions relating to the non-stochastic nature of the explanatory variables and the rank of X. Splitting up the covariance matrix into two terms, σ^2 and V, is essentially arbitrary. However, it is a natural division for many models.

The GLS Estimator and its Properties

If V is *known*, obtaining a BLUE of β is not difficult in principle. Since V

is symmetric and p.d., its inverse is also symmetric and p.d., and so there exists a non-singular $T \times T$ matrix L such that $L'L = V^{-1}$. Premultiplying both sides of (1.4) by L gives

$$Ly = LX\beta + Lu \qquad (4.2)$$

The transformed observations on the dependent and independent variables are given by the vector Ly and the matrix LX respectively. The new disturbance vector is Lu, and since L is fixed, the expectation of Lu is zero, while its covariance matrix is

$$\begin{aligned} \text{Var}(Lu) &= E(Luu'L') = \sigma^2 LVL' \\ &= \sigma^2 L(L'L)^{-1}L' = \sigma^2 I \end{aligned} \qquad (4.3)$$

The transformed disturbance vector therefore satisfies the classical assumptions, and so OLS applied to the transformed observations will yield the BLUE of β.

Replacing y and X by Ly and LX respectively in the OLS formula, (2.4), gives

$$\tilde{b} = (X'L'LX)^{-1}X'L'Ly = (X'V^{-1}X)^{-1}X'V^{-1}y \qquad (4.4)$$

This is known as the *generalised least squares* (GLS) estimator of β. Since the model obeys the classical assumptions it follows from (3.4) that

$$\text{Var}(\tilde{b}) = \sigma^2(X'L'LX)^{-1} = \sigma^2(X'V^{-1}X)^{-1} \qquad (4.5)$$

Furthermore, because $\tilde{b}$ is a linear estimator, it will have a multivariate normal distribution when the disturbances are normal.

Example 1 Consider the bivariate regression model,

$$y_t = \alpha + \beta x_t + u_t, \quad t = 1, \ldots, T \qquad (4.6)$$

in which $E(u_t) = 0$ for all t, $E(u_t u_s) = 0$ for all $t \neq s$, and $\text{Var}(u_t) = \sigma_t^2 = \sigma^2 x_t^2$ for all t. Since the variances are unequal, the disturbances are said to be heteroscedastic. However, because the disturbances are serially uncorrelated, V is diagonal. The transformation matrix, L, is also diagonal with the tth diagonal element given by $1/x_t$. The GLS estimators of α and β are therefore obtained by applying OLS to the model

$$y_t/x_t = \alpha x_t^{-1} + \beta + u_t/x_t$$

i.e. y_t/x_t is regressed on $1/x_t$.

In the above example, GLS reduces to *weighted least squares* (WLS), with the criterion to be minimised given by

$$S(\beta) = \sum_{t=1}^{T} \sigma_t^{-2}(y_t - x_t'\beta)^2$$

More generally, $S(\beta)$ is the quadratic form

$$S(\beta) = (Ly - LX\beta)'(Ly - LX\beta) = (y - X\beta)'V^{-1}(y - X\beta)$$

$$(4.7)$$

Properties of the OLS Estimator

The assumption that $E(u) = 0$ ensures that the OLS estimator, b, is unbiased. However, from (3.3), its covariance matrix is:

$$\mathrm{Var}(b) = \sigma^2(X'X)^{-1}X'VX(X'X)^{-1}$$

$$(4.8)$$

Since the GLS estimator is the BLUE of β, it follows from the Gauss—Markov theorem, that (4.8) will exceed (4.5) by a p.s.d. matrix. In general, therefore, the OLS estimator will be less efficient that GLS. The extent of the inefficiency depends on the structure of both V and X.

Example 2 Consider the model, (4.6), with $x_t = t$, for $t = 1,\ldots, T$. Figures for the variance of the GLS estimator of β divided by the variance of the corresponding OLS estimator are shown in table 2.1 for two types of heteroscedasticity. Details of the calculations will be found in Geary (1966).

Table 2.1 $\mathrm{Var}(\bar{b})/\mathrm{Var}(b)$ for Model (4.6)

T	10	20	30	40	50
$\sigma_t^2 = \sigma^2 x_t$	0.72	0.64	0.60	0.58	0.57
$\sigma_t^2 = \sigma^2 x_t^2$	0.41	0.33	0.30	0.28	0.27

Feasible GLS

In (4.6) the covariance matrix of the disturbances was completely specified up to a factor of proportionality. In other words V was known. However, setting $\sigma_t^2 = \sigma^2 x_t^2$ imposes a rather special structure on the variances, and if heteroscedasticity is to be handled in a more general fashion, greater flexibility is required. One possibility is to go to the opposite extreme and simply let V be a diagonal matrix. Unfortunately this approach is not viable, since the covariance matrix then contains T unknown parameters and these cannot be sensibly estimated from T observations. Some structure is therefore necessary, and the usual solution is to let σ_t^2 depend on a small number of unknown parameters. Estimators of these parameters can then be used to construct a *feasible* GLS estimator of β.

Example 3 Consider model (4.6) with

$$\sigma_t^2 = \delta_1 + \delta_2 x_t, \qquad t = 1, \ldots, T$$

$$(4.9)$$

where δ_1 and δ_2 are parameters. Suitable estimators, $\hat{\delta}_1$ and $\hat{\delta}_2$, may be formed from the OLS residuals by regressing e_t^2 on x_t. A feasible GLS estimator may then be based on $\hat{\sigma}_t^2 = \hat{\delta}_1 + \hat{\delta}_2 x_t$, and computed by WLS.

Serial correlation may be handled in a similar way, with the V matrix made to depend on a limited number of unknown parameters. If the parameters in a V matrix can be estimated consistently, the feasible GLS estimator will, under suitable regularity conditions, have the same asymptotic distribution as the GLS estimator; see Theil (1971, Ch. 8).

2.5. Prediction

In the context of a regression model, a *prediction* is an estimate of a future value of the dependent variable made *conditional* on the corresponding future values of the independent variables. Thus, having estimated the parameters of the model using the observations at times $t = 1, \ldots, T$, the problem is to estimate y_{T+l} given x_{T+l} for $l = 1, 2, 3, \ldots$.

Prediction in the Classical Model

If the model obeys the classical assumptions, the OLS estimator, b, is the BLUE of β. An obvious predictor is therefore

$$\tilde{y}_{T+l \mid T} = x'_{T+l} b, \qquad l = 1, 2, \ldots \tag{5.1}$$

This is the BLUE of the *fixed part* of y_{T+l}, namely $x'_{T+l}\beta$. The proof follows as a straightforward application of the Gauss–Markov theorem by setting the vector of weights, w, equal to x_{T+l}. However, $\tilde{y}_{T+l}$ cannot be regarded as a BLUE of y_{T+l} itself; it is not an unbiased estimator of y_{T+l}, since $E(\tilde{y}_{T+l \mid T}) = x'_{T+l}\beta$, and this will not, in general, be equal to y_{T+l}.

Since y_{T+l} is stochastic, the properties of $\tilde{y}_{T+l \mid T}$ as an estimator of y_{T+l} must be found in terms of the prediction error

$$e_{T+l} = y_{T+l} - \tilde{y}_{T+l \mid T}$$

$$= x'_{T+l}(\beta - b) + \epsilon_{T+l}, \qquad l = 1, 2, \ldots \tag{5.2}$$

It follows immediately from (5.2) that the expectation of e_{T+l} is zero, while its variance is given by

$$\text{Var}(e_{T+l}) = \sigma^2 \left[1 + x'_{T+l}(X'X)^{-1} x_{T+l} \right] \tag{5.3}$$

In evaluating (5.3), the cross-product terms have zero expectation as b depends only on $\epsilon_1, \ldots, \epsilon_T$ and these are assumed to be uncorrelated with the future disturbance, ϵ_{T+l}, as well as with each other.

Bearing the above results in mind, $\tilde{y}_{T+l|T}$ may be regarded as an unbiased estimator of y_{T+l} in a sense that the expectation of the associated estimation error is zero. An estimator having this property is sometimes referred to as being *unconditionally unbiased* or simply *u-unbiased*. Within the class of linear, *u*-unbiased estimators of y_{T+l}, $\tilde{y}_{T+l|T}$ is best in the sense that the variance of its estimation error cannot exceed that of any other estimator. The proof is as follows. Let $\hat{y}_{T+l|T}$ denote an estimator of y_{T+l}. If this is to be linear in the observations it must be of the form

$$\hat{y}_{T+l|T} = [x'_{T+l}(X'X)^{-1}X' + d']y, \tag{5.4}$$

where d is a $T \times 1$ vector of fixed elements. The associated estimation error is

$$\begin{aligned} y_{T+l} - \hat{y}_{T+l|T} &= \left[x'_{T+l}(X'X)^{-1}X' + d'\right](X\beta + \epsilon) \\ &\quad - x'_{T+l}\beta - \epsilon_{T+l} \\ &= d'X\beta + \left[x'_{T+l}(X'X)^{-1}X' + d'\right]\epsilon - \epsilon_{T+l} \end{aligned} \tag{5.5}$$

If this is to have zero expectation, the constraint $d'X = 0$ must be imposed. The variance of the estimation error is then

$$E\left[(y_{T+l} - \hat{y}_{T+l|T})^2\right] = \text{Var}(e_{T+l}) + \sigma^2 d'd \tag{5.6}$$

Unless $d = 0$, in which case $\hat{y}_{T+l|T} = \tilde{y}_{T+l|T}$, (5.6) will exceed (5.3).

The estimator $\tilde{y}_{T+l|T}$ is sometimes known as the *best linear unbiased predictor* (BLUP) of y_{T+l}. However, if the problem is taken to be one of minimising the MSE of the prediction error, $\tilde{y}_{T+l|T}$ is again obtained. The property of *u*-unbiasedness then emerges as a consequence of the criterion adopted, rather than as a condition imposed at the outset. The term minimum mean square linear estimator (MMSLE) may therefore be used to describe $\tilde{y}_{T+l|T}$ and in these circumstances it is often more natural to refer to (5.3) as the MSE of $\tilde{y}_{T+l|T}$. In fact this avoids any ambiguity since the MSE of the predictor can be written down in exactly the same way as the MSE of the prediction error.

When the disturbances in the model are serially correlated, (5.1) will no longer be the BLUP of y_{t+l}. If w is a $T \times 1$ vector in which the tth element is equal to $E(u_t u_{T+l})$, the BLUP of y_{T+l} is given by

$$\tilde{y}_{T+l|T} = x'_{T+l}\tilde{b} + w'V^{-1}(y - X\tilde{b}) \tag{5.7}$$

The second term on the right hand side of (5.7) is the contribution which results from taking the correlation between the realised and future disturbances into account. The original derivation of (5.7) will be found in Goldberger (1962). In most time series models, however, the predictions are built up recursively and an expression of this form is rarely used explicitly.

2.6. Recursive Least Squares

If an estimator of β in a linear regression model is calculated from the first k observations, it can be updated as each subsequent observation,

$y_{k+1}, y_{k+2}, \ldots, y_T$, is added to the data set. The updating may be based on recursive formulae which avoid repeated matrix inversions. Calculating the OLS estimator in this way has a number of attractions. Firstly, it enables the changes in the estimator to be tracked over time and secondly, it produces a set of residuals which are uncorrelated when the model satisfies the classical assumptions. These residuals may be used in conjunction with the OLS residuals to assess the suitability of the model specification.

Updating Formulae

Consider the model in its vector formulation, (1.3). The OLS estimator based on the first t observations may be written as

$$b_t = (X_t'X_t)^{-1}X_t'y_t^*, \qquad t = k, \ldots, T \tag{6.1}$$

where $X_t = (x_1, x_2, \ldots, x_t)'$ and $y_t^* = (y_1, \ldots, y_t)'$. Now suppose that an estimator has been computed from the first $t-1$ observations. This estimator is

$$b_{t-1} = (X_{t-1}'X_{t-1})^{-1}X_{t-1}'y_{t-1}^* \tag{6.2}$$

it being assumed that $t - 1 \geq k$ and that X_{t-1} is of full rank.

Once the tth observation becomes available, b_t may be obtained from b_{t-1} and y_t without the matrix inversion implied by (6.1). The cross-product matrix may be updated in a similar way. The relevant formulae are given by

$$b_t = b_{t-1} + (X_{t-1}'X_{t-1})^{-1}x_t(y_t - x_t'b_{t-1})/f_t \tag{6.3a}$$

and

$$(X_t'X_t)^{-1} = (X_{t-1}'X_{t-1})^{-1} \\ - (X_{t-1}'X_{t-1})^{-1}x_t x_t'(X_{t-1}'X_{t-1})^{-1}/f_t \tag{6.3b}$$

where

$$f_t = 1 + x_t'(X_{t-1}'X_{t-1})^{-1}x_t, \qquad t = k+1, \ldots, T \tag{6.3c}$$

Expression (6.3b) follows directly as a special case of a matrix inversion lemma given in *TSM*. If (6.3b) is substituted into (6.1), and $X_t'y_t^*$ is decomposed as

$$X_t'y_t^* = X_{t-1}'y_{t-1}^* + x_ty_t \tag{6.4}$$

a little algebraic manipulation gives (6.3a).

In the classical model, the explanatory variables are fixed and known for all time periods, and so the only random variables appearing in the updating formulae are b_{t-1} and y_t. Their role emerges more clearly if (6.3a) is rewritten as

$$b_t = b_{t-1} + (X_{t-1}'X_{t-1})^{-1}x_t\tilde{v}_t/f_t \tag{6.5}$$

where $\tilde{v}_t$ is the one-step ahead prediction error, $y_t - x_t'b_{t-1}$. This prediction error contains all the new information needed to update b_{t-1}.

A unique OLS estimator of β can only be obtained if at least k observations are available. If X_k is of full rank, b_k is given by

$$b_k = (X_k' X_k)^{-1} X_k' y_k^* = X_k^{-1} y_k^* \tag{6.6}$$

Once b_k has been computed, $b_{k+1}, \ldots, b_T$ may be obtained by repeated application of the updating formulae. No further matrix inversions are needed, and the final estimator, b_T, is identical to the OLS estimator defined by (2.4).

Recursive Residuals

A set of $T - k$ prediction errors are produced as a by-product of the OLS recursions. If the disturbances obey the classical assumptions, (1.6), these may be written

$$\tilde{v}_t = y_t - x_t' b_{t-1}$$

$$= x_t'(\beta - b_{t-1}) + \epsilon_t, \qquad t = k + 1, \ldots, T \tag{6.7}$$

and it will be seen that each one has a mean of zero and variance $\sigma^2 f_t$. The prediction errors have a further property, however, which is not immediately apparent from (6.7). Substituting for $\beta - b_{t-1}$ in (6.7) yields

$$\tilde{v}_t = \epsilon_t - x_t'(X_{t-1}' X_{t-1})^{-1} \sum_{j=1}^{t-1} x_j \epsilon_j \tag{6.8}$$

Then for all $t > s = k + 1, \ldots, T - 1$,

$$E(\tilde{v}_t \, \tilde{v}_s) = E(\epsilon_t \, \epsilon_s) - x_t'(X_{t-1}' X_{t-1})^{-1} \sum_{j=1}^{t-1} x_j E(\epsilon_j \, \epsilon_s)$$

$$- x_s'(X_{s-1}' X_{s-1})^{-1} \sum_{s=1}^{t-1} x_j E(\epsilon_j \, \epsilon_t)$$

$$+ E\left[\left\{ x_t'(X_{t-1}' X_{t-1})^{-1} \sum_{j=1}^{t-1} x_j \epsilon_j \right\} \left\{ \left(\sum_{j=1}^{s-1} x_j \epsilon_j \right)' (X_{s-1}' X_{s-1})^{-1} x_s \right\} \right]$$

$$= 0 - \sigma^2 x_t'(X_{t-1}' X_{t-1})^{-1} x_s - 0$$

$$+ \sigma^2 x_t'(X_{t-1}' X_{t-1})^{-1} X_{s-1}' X_{s-1}(X_{s-1}' X_{s-1})^{-1} x_s$$

$$= 0$$

The one-step ahead prediction errors are therefore uncorrelated. An intuitive rationale for this result is provided by (6.5). Since $\tilde{v}_t$ contains all the new information required to update the estimator, it seems reasonable to expect it to be uncorrelated with the previous prediction errors as these are incorporated in the current estimator, b_{t-1}.

The *recursive residuals* are the standardised prediction errors,

$$v_t = \bar{v}_t/f_t^{1/2}, \qquad = t + 1, \ldots, T \qquad (6.9)$$

They are uncorrelated with zero mean and constant variance, σ^2. Furthermore, since they are linear in the observations they are normally distributed when the disturbances are normal.

The recursive residuals feature in the updating formula for the residual sum of squares. This is

$$SSE_t = SSE_{t-1} + v_t^2 \qquad (6.10)$$

where

$$SSE_t = (y_t - X_t b_t)'(y_t - X_t b_t) \qquad (6.11)$$

is the sum of the squares of the OLS residuals based on the first t observations; see Brown, Durbin and Evans (1975). Since $SSE_k = 0$, it follows from (6.10) that

$$SSE_T = \sum_{t=1}^{T} e_t^2 = \sum_{t=k+1}^{T} v_t^2 \qquad (6.12)$$

Computational Aspects of the Recursions

An alternative to starting the recursions with an estimator of β based on the first k observations, is to begin at $t = 0$ with an arbitrary value of b_0, say $b_0 = 0$. The corresponding 'cross-product' matrix, which may be labelled $(X_0' X_0)^{-1}$, is set equal to $\varkappa I$, where $\varkappa$ is a large number, say 10^6. Once the first observation becomes available, the recursions can proceed. Although b_0 is arbitrary, setting $\varkappa$ equal to a large number means that its effect on estimates and prediction errors is negligible once k observations have been processed. In other words, b_k and $(X_k' X_k)^{-1}$ will be very close to the values which would have been obtained had these quantities been calculated directly. The 'estimates' $b_1, \ldots, b_{k-1}$ and the 'prediction errors', $\bar{v}_1, \ldots, \bar{v}_k$, are, however, completely arbitrary and should be discarded. Setting $b_0 = 0$ and $(X_0' X_0)^{-1} = \varkappa I$ is similar to adopting a 'diffuse prior' in Bayesian analysis. However, the term is open to some confusion here since β is a fixed parameter and the 'diffuse prior' is simply a technical device for starting the recursions.

If multicollinearity is present in the independent variables, the cross-product matrix, $X'X$, may be close to singularity. As a result the OLS estimator may be subject to inaccuracies in computation. If it is calculated recursively, the possibilities for numerical instability are even greater since rounding errors may tend to build up as the recursions proceed. One way of avoiding this problem is to adopt the QR decomposition algorithm of Gentleman (1973).

This is an efficient and numerically stable method of calculating the OLS estimate. However, its construction is such that the recursive residuals emerge as an automatic by-product.

2.7. Residuals

The residuals from a regression play an important role in detecting possible misspecifications in the model. The nature of this role is described in Section 5.2, where both graphical procedures and formal test statistics are described. In this section attention is focused on the properties of the OLS residuals when the model obeys the classical assumptions. These properties are then contrasted with those of alternative sets of residuals which are available in linear regression, and the usefulness of such residuals is examined. The final sub-section is concerned with the distribution of the residual sum of squares and the estimation of the parameter σ^2.

OLS Residuals

The $T \times 1$ vector of OLS residuals, $e = (e_1, \ldots, e_T)'$, may be expressed as a linear combination of the observations. Substituting from (2.4),

$$e = y - Xb = [I - X(X'X)^{-1}X']y = My \qquad (7.1)$$

Furthermore since the $T \times T$ matrix, M, is orthogonal to X, i.e. $MX = 0$, substituting for y yields

$$e = M(X\beta + \epsilon) = M\epsilon \qquad (7.2)$$

Thus the OLS residuals are linear combinations of the true disturbances.

If the model obeys the classical assumptions, $E(e) = M \cdot E(\epsilon) = 0$, while

$$E(ee') = M \cdot E(\epsilon\epsilon')M' = \sigma^2 M \qquad (7.3)$$

Thus although the OLS residuals have zero mean, the fact that $M \neq I$ means that, in general, they will be neither homoscedastic nor serially uncorrelated. Hence their properties do not mirror those of the true disturbances even when the model is correctly specified. Fortunately this problem becomes less important in large samples. Under the standard regularity conditions, (3.9), it can be shown that M is closely approximated by the identity matrix when T is large, and that e converges in distribution to ϵ.

The OLS residuals are uncorrelated with the elements of b. From (3.1) and (7.2).

$$E[e(b - \beta)'] = E[M\epsilon\epsilon' X(X'X)^{-1}] = \sigma^2 MX(X'X)^{-1} = 0 \qquad (7.4)$$

If the disturbances are normally distributed, e and b are independent.

LUS Residuals

If follows from (7.3) that in small samples the distribution of the OLS residuals will depend on the X matrix. This creates difficulties in constructing exact test procedures, since the distribution of any test statistic based on OLS residuals will vary with the data. It is therefore natural to ask whether it is possible to form a set of residuals which are homoscedastic and uncorrelated when the model satisfies the classical assumptions.

The OLS residuals are linear in the observations. This ensures that they are normally distributed when the disturbances are normal. If e^* denotes any other residual vector which is linear in the observations, it may be written as

$$e^* = Cy \tag{7.5}$$

where C is a matrix with T columns, in which the elements are fixed. If $CX = 0$, e^* will have zero expectation since $e^* = C(X\beta + \epsilon) = C\epsilon$. Furthermore if $CC' = I$, the residuals can be said to have a *scalar* convariance matrix since

$$E(e^*e^{*\prime}) = E[C\epsilon\epsilon'C'] = \sigma^2 CC' = \sigma^2 I$$

However, if this is to hold, C can have no more than $T - k$ rows; see Theil (1971, Ch. 5).

If C is a $(T - k) \times T$ matrix with the properties $CX = 0$ and $CC' = I$, (7.5) defines a set of $T - k$ LUS residuals. These residuals are (i) *linear;* (ii) *unbiased,* in the sense that the expectation of e^* minus the corresponding set of $T - k$ disturbances is zero; and (iii) have a *scalar* covariance matrix. If $\epsilon_t \sim NID(0, \sigma^2)$, the LUS residuals are distributed in exactly the same way, i.e. $e_t^* \sim NID(0, \sigma^2)$.

There are a number of different principles upon which the construction of LUS residuals may be based. The approach adopted by Theil (1971, Ch. 5) is to derive a vector of $T - k$ LUS residuals, which is likely to be a good estimator of a corresponding subset of $T - k$ disturbances, ϵ_1. His BLUS residuals are best in the sense that they minimise the expected sum of squares of the estimation errors, $E[(e^* - \epsilon_1)'(e^* - \epsilon_1)]$. Unfortunately, the calculations needed to obtain a set of BLUS residuals are relatively heavy and this means that they are rarely used in practice. The recursive residuals are also LUS residuals, but are much easier to compute as they emerge directly from the updating formulae in (6.3). The numerically stable OLS routine of Gentleman also yields recursive residuals and if it is felt that this algorithm should be employed simply on the basis of its merits as an OLS computational procedure, the recursive residuals are essentially a free good. In a similar manner, other sets of LUS residuals may be produced as a by-product of different algorithms; see, for example, Golub and Styan (1973).

Since $e^* = C(Xb + e) = Ce$, all the information contained in a set of LUS residuals is also contained in the corresponding OLS vector. This has important implications for testing, with a statistic based on OLS residuals being preferable, in most cases, to a corresponding statistic based on LUS residuals. The case for using a particular set of LUS residuals to detect misspecifications rests on their ability to present information in a manner which is complementary to that of the OLS residuals. Because the recursive residuals have a natural interpretation as standardised prediction errors they are particularly suitable for such a role.

The Residual Sum of Squares

The residual sum of squares, SSE, was defined in (2.8), and it was shown in (6.12) that it is identical to the sum of squares of the $T-k$ recursive residuals. It follows immediately that $E(SSE) = (T-k)\sigma^2$, and so

$$s^2 = SSE/(T-k) \tag{7.6}$$

is an unbiased estimator of σ^2.

Under the normality assumption it is apparent from (6.12) that SSE/σ^2 is the sum of $T-k$ independent χ_1^2 variates. Hence $(T-k)s^2/\sigma^2 \sim \chi_{T-k}^2$. Furthermore, because the variance of a χ^2 distribution with f degrees of freedom is $2f$,

$$\text{Var}(s^2) = 2\sigma^4/(T-k) \tag{7.7}$$

2.8. Test Statistics and Confidence Intervals

If the disturbances in a classical linear regression model are normally distributed, small sample test statistics can be derived. Similarly, exact confidence intervals may be constructed.

This section merely presents the standard results on testing within the context of the classical regression model. As such the tests may seem to be *ad hoc*. However, in Chapter 5 it is shown that all the tests presented here may be derived from general principles associated with maximum likelihood estimation. This ensures that the tests have certain desirable statistical properties.

Individual Parameters: The t-statistic

Consider β_i, the ith element in the parameter vector β. If b_i denotes the corresponding element in the OLS vector, it follows from (3.8) that

$$b_i \sim N(\beta_i, \sigma^2\zeta_i), \quad i=1,\ldots,k \tag{8.1}$$

where ζ_i denotes the ith diagonal element in $(X'X)^{-1}$.

Since σ^2 is unknown it must be estimated. Expression (7.6) gives a suitable estimator of σ^2 and it was shown in the previous section that

$$(T-k)s^2 \sim \sigma^2 \chi^2_{T-k} \tag{8.2}$$

Furthermore, in view of (7.4), s^2 and b_i are independent. Hence the statistic

$$\frac{(b_i - \beta_i)/\sigma\sqrt{\varsigma_i}}{s/\sigma} = \frac{b_i - \beta_i}{s\sqrt{\varsigma_i}}, \quad i = 1, \ldots, k \tag{8.3}$$

follows a t-distribution with $T-k$ degrees of freedom, since it is the ratio of a standard normal variate to the square root of a χ^2 variate divided by its degrees of freedom. The estimated standard deviation of b_i, $s\sqrt{\varsigma_i}$, is usually known as the *standard error*.

Hypotheses concerning specific values of the parameters may be tested using (8.3). Of particular importance is the *test of significance*, in which the null hypothesis is $H_0: \beta_i = 0$. Failure to reject this hypothesis at a particular level of significance leads to the conclusion that b_i is 'insignificant'. This suggests one of two possibilities. Either the sample evidence is consistent with $\beta_i = 0$ and so the corresponding variable should not appear in the model, or $\beta_i \neq 0$, but the size of the sample is such that β_i cannot be estimated with the degree of accuracy required to reject the null hypothesis.

Tests of significance are particularly appropriate when the data come from a controlled experiment. Unfortunately this is rarely the case in econometrics. In a regression based on time series data, tests of significance should be interpreted with great care. Time series are typically highly correlated even when there is no underlying relationship between them. This has two consequences. Firstly an explanatory variable may be 'significant', even though it has no effect on the dependent variable. Secondly, if two explanatory variables are highly correlated it may be difficult to disentangle their separate effects, even though both should properly be included in the model. Hence it is quite possible that neither will be significant on statistical grounds. The first of these points is a reflection of the problem of *spurious correlation*. The second problem is known as *multicollinearity*.

Confidence Intervals

The result (8.3) may be used to construct an exact confidence interval for β_i. Let $t_{\alpha/2}$ denote the significance value for a two-sided test based on a t-distribution with $T-k$ degrees of freedom. If $Pr(t < t_{\alpha/2}) = \alpha/2$ it follows that $Pr(-t_{\alpha/2} < t < t_{\alpha/2}) = \alpha$. Hence the probability that the interval

$$b_i \pm t_{\alpha/2}s\sqrt{\varsigma_i}, \quad i = 1, \ldots, k \tag{8.4}$$

contains the true parameter, β_i, is $1 - \alpha$. Thus (8.4) is said to be the $(1-\alpha)\%$ *confidence interval* for β_i.

In practice α is usually set at 0.05 leading to a 95% confidence interval. Unless T is very small, a useful rule of thumb is to set $t_{0.025}$ equal to two.

Linear Combinations of Parameters

In discussing the Gauss–Markov theorem, it was observed that attention is often focused on a linear combination of the parameters, $w'\beta$. From (3.6) it follows that the distribution of the unbiased estimator, $w'b$, is given by

$$w'b \sim N[w'\beta, \sigma^2 w'(X'X)^{-1}w] \qquad (8.5)$$

By the same argument used to obtain the t-statistic in (8.3), it follows that

$$\frac{w'b - w'\beta}{s\sqrt{w'(X'X)^{-1}w}} \qquad (8.6)$$

also has a t-distribution with $T-k$ degrees of freedom. Hypotheses of the form $H_0 : w'\beta = r_0$, where r_0 is a particular value, may therefore be tested using (8.6). Furthermore, confidence intervals for $w'\beta$ may be constructed along the lines of (8.4).

If w is set equal to x_{T+l} the above results may be applied to testing hypotheses and constructing confidence intervals for future expected values of y_t. However, a more relevant question concerns inferences about y_t itself. As shown in Section 5, attention then focuses on the prediction error, $y_{T+l} - x'_{T+l}b$, and it follows from the results in Section 5 that

$$y_{T+l} - x'_{T+l} b \sim N[0, \sigma^2\{1 + x'_{T+l}(X'X)^{-1}x_{T+l}\}],$$
$$l = 1,2,\dots \qquad (8.7)$$

This result may be used to test whether a new observation on y_t obeys the same model as the observations in the sample since

$$\frac{y_{T+l} - x'_{T+l}b}{s\sqrt{1 + x'_{T+l}(X'X)^{-1}x_{T+l}}}, \qquad l = 1,2,\dots \qquad (8.8)$$

has a t-distribution with $T-k$ degrees of freedom under the null hypothesis that the model is unchanged.

A $(1 - \alpha)\%$ *prediction interval* may be constructed from (8.8). This has the same form as a confidence interval but the interpretation is slightly different because y_{T+l} is stochastic.

The Subset F-test

A test of the joint significance of a subset of m ($\leq k$) variables in a regression model may be based on the F-distribution. Without any loss of generality the variables may be ordered so that the last m are those under test, i.e.

$$H_0 : \beta_{k-m+1} = \dots = \beta_k = 0 \qquad (8.9)$$

Let SSE denote the residual sum of squares, $e'e$, when the model is fitted with all k variables, and let SSE_0 be the residual sum of squares when the last m variables are omitted. When the null hypothesis is true, the statistic

$$\frac{(SSE_0 - SSE)/m}{SSE/(T-k)} = (SSE_0 - SSE)/ms^2 \qquad (8.10)$$

has an F-distribution with $(m, T-k)$ degrees of freedom.

An interesting special case arises when the model contains a constant term and the null hypothesis is that the coefficients of the other regressors are all zero. Since the constant term has no explanatory power, this test may be regarded as an overall test on the significance of the relationship as a whole. The test may be cast in terms of the coefficient of multiple correlation, R^2, by noting that $SSE_0 = \Sigma (y_t - \bar{y})^2$ and substituting from (2.13). This yields the statistic

$$\frac{R^2/(k-1)}{(1-R^2)/(T-k)} \qquad (8.11)$$

As with tests on individual coefficients, tests on subsets of parameters should be interpreted somewhat cautiously for non-experimental data. In particular an insignificant value of (8.11) tends to be the exception rather than the rule for time series data. Indeed it can be reasonably argued that the test is usually meaningless in such a context.

Analysis of Covariance

The available observations may sometimes fall naturally into two or more distinct groups. For cross-sectional data these divisions may depend on some qualitative characteristic associated with the observations. For example, the sample may be drawn from a number of different towns or countries. With time series data, the divisions may be associated with certain events, such as the outbreak of war or a change of government. However, irrespective of how the grouping arises, the basic statistical question is the same. Is the structure of the model different for different groups?

A general framework may be established by writing the complete set of observations as

$$y_j = Z_j\gamma + X_j\beta_j + \epsilon_j, \qquad j = 1,\ldots,G \qquad (8.12)$$

where $[Z_j : X_j]$ is a $T_j \times k$ matrix of observations on the explanatory variables, and $(\gamma', \beta_j')'$ is the corresponding $k \times 1$ vector of regression parameters. The $n \times 1$ parameter vector β_j is subscripted, since it is the parameters in this vector which are to be tested for equality. Any test of a hypothesis of the form

$$H_0 : \beta_1 = \ldots = \beta_G = \beta \qquad (8.13)$$

is an exercise in the *analysis of covariance*.

The disturbances are assumed to be normally distributed with a mean of zero and a variance, σ^2, which is the same for all groups. Furthermore the disturbances are independent both within and between groups. Under the restrictions imposed by (8.13) the model

$$
\begin{bmatrix} y_1 \\ \vdots \\ y_G \end{bmatrix} = \begin{bmatrix} Z_1 \\ \vdots \\ Z_G \end{bmatrix} \gamma + \begin{bmatrix} X_1 \\ \vdots \\ X_G \end{bmatrix} \beta + \begin{bmatrix} \epsilon_1 \\ \vdots \\ \epsilon_G \end{bmatrix}
\tag{8.14}
$$

is appropriate. Let the residual sum of squares be denoted by SSE_0. The unrestricted model is

$$
\begin{bmatrix} y_1 \\ y_2 \\ \vdots \\ y_G \end{bmatrix} = \begin{bmatrix} Z_1 \\ Z_2 \\ \vdots \\ Z_G \end{bmatrix} \gamma + \begin{bmatrix} X_1 & 0 & \cdots & 0 \\ 0 & X_2 & \cdots & 0 \\ & & \ddots & 0 \\ 0 & 0 & & X_G \end{bmatrix} \begin{bmatrix} \beta_1 \\ \beta_2 \\ \vdots \\ \beta_G \end{bmatrix} + \begin{bmatrix} \epsilon_1 \\ \epsilon_2 \\ \vdots \\ \epsilon_G \end{bmatrix}
\tag{8.15}
$$

and the residual sum of squares is SSE. In the special case where $n = k$, SSE is given by adding up the residual sums of squares after applying OLS to each group in turn.

Model (8.14) embodies $n(G-1)$ restrictions as compared with (8.15). If these restrictions are valid, the statistic

$$
\frac{(SSE_0 - SSE)/\{n(G-1)\}}{SSE/\{T-(k-n)-nG\}}
\tag{8.16}
$$

has an F-distribution with $(nG - n, T - k - nG + n)$ degrees of freedom. Note that $T = T_1 + \cdots + T_G$ is the total number of observations, while $(k - n) + nG = k + nG - n$ is the number of independent variables in the unrestricted model.

Example A household budget survey carried out in Kenya in 1968/9 covered three towns: Nairobi, Mombasa and Kisumu. The following model was estimated for a number of commodities:

$$
y_t = \beta_1 + \beta_2 x_{2t} + \beta_3 x_{3t} + \epsilon_t = x_t'\beta + \epsilon_t, \qquad t = 1, \ldots, T
$$

where y_t is the logarithm of expenditure on a given commodity by the tth household, x_{2t} is the logarithm of household income, and x_{3t} is the logarithm of household size. (Although the data are cross-sectional, the subscript t is used to avoid any ambiguity.) A whole range of results is reported in the *Kenya Statistical Digest* of April, 1972, but the findings for rice are particularly interesting. Estimating the above equation for each town separately and adding up the total sum of squared residuals gave

$SSE = 150.6$. Pooling the data gave $SSE_0 = 298.2$. The sample sizes in Nairobi, Mombasa and Kisumu were $T_1 = 100$, $T_2 = 86$ and $T_3 = 45$ respectively, and so the appropriate statistic for testing the equality of the regression coefficients in the three towns is

$$F = \frac{(298.2 - 150.6)/6}{150.6/222} = 36.27$$

Since the 5% significance point for an F-distribution with $(6,222)$ degrees of freedom is approximately 2.10, the calculated value is highly significant.

In terms of (8.16), $n = k$ in the above test. However, a rather different picture emerges if the test of equality is confined to β_2 and β_3. This means that when the data are pooled, the intercept terms for the three towns are allowed to differ. Introducing dummy variables into the pooled model gave the following results:

$$\hat{y}_t = -1.626 + 1.228D_{2t} - 0.860D_{3t} + 0.284x_{2t} + 0.915x_{3t},$$
$$\quad\quad\quad (0.124) \quad\quad (0.150) \quad\quad (0.068) \quad\quad (0.110)$$

$$t = 1, \ldots, T$$

where

$$D_{2t} = \begin{cases} 1 - \text{if the observation was from town 2 (Mombasa)} \\ 0 - \text{otherwise} \end{cases}$$

$$D_{3t} = \begin{cases} 1 - \text{if the observation was from town 3 (Kisumu)} \\ 0 - \text{otherwise} \end{cases}$$

The figures in parentheses are standard errors and it will be observed that both dummy variables are highly significant.

The pooled model is of the form (8.14) with the tth rows of $Z = (Z_1', \ldots, Z_G')'$ and $X = (X_1', \ldots, X_G')$ given by $(1, D_{2t}, D_{3t})$ and (x_{2t}, x_{3t}) respectively. The residual sum of squares was 156.7 and so a test of the equality of the coefficients β_2 and β_3 in the three towns is based on

$$F = \frac{(156.7 - 150.6)/6}{150.6/222} = 2.25$$

This is insignificant at the 5% level.

These results can be interpreted as follows. The hypothesis that β_2, the income elasticity of demand for rice, and β_3, the household size elasticity, are the same in all three towns cannot be rejected. However, the level of consumption of rice in the three towns appears to be different. Since $\exp(1.228) = 3.42$, the expected household consumption of rice for a given level of income and household size is 342% higher in Mombasa than in

Nairobi. On the other hand, since $\exp(-0.860) = 0.42$, rice consumption in Kisumu is only 42% of that in Nairobi.

In time series, a fundamental application of the analysis of covariance is in testing for *structural change*. Suppose that the sample period divides into two groups, with all the observations after a certain point in time falling into the second group. The hypothesis to be tested is that the complete parameter vector is the same in both periods. Stated explicitly the unrestricted model is

$$y_t = x_t'\beta_1 + \epsilon_t, \qquad t = 1, \ldots, T_1$$
$$y_t = x_t'\beta_2 + \epsilon_t, \qquad t = T_1 + 1, \ldots, T_1 + T_2$$

and the null hypothesis is $H_0 : \beta_1 = \beta_2$. Since $m = k$ and $G = 2$, the test statistic reduces to

$$\frac{(SSE_0 - SSE)/k}{SSE/(T - 2k)} \tag{8.17}$$

where SSE_0 is the sum of the residual sum of squares in each group. Under the null hypothesis of no structural change, this statistic has an F-distribution with $(k, T - 2k)$ degrees of freedom.

In order to construct (8.16) it is necessary that both T_1 and T_2 be greater than k. Indeed an assumption of this kind was implicitly made in setting up the general test statistic, (8.16). However, in testing for structural change it is not uncommon to find $T_2 \leq k$. In these circumstances a slightly different approach must be adopted. This is described in Section 5.7.

A General Test of Restrictions

In Section 2, the estimation of β was considered subject to a set of m restrictions defined by (2.16). The validity of these restrictions may be tested using the statistic

$$\frac{(SSE_0 - SSE)/m}{SSE/(T - k)} \tag{8.18}$$

where SSE_0 and SSE are the residual sums of squares for the restricted and unrestricted models respectively. Under the null hypothesis, this statistic has an F-distribution with $(m, T - k)$ degrees of freedom.

All the test statistics considered in the last sub-section are special cases of (8.18). In the case of the structural change test, for example, the constraints may be written in the form (2.16) by defining $R = [I, -I]$, $r = 0$, and $\beta = (\beta_1', \beta_2')'$. Thus if (8.18) can be shown to have an F-distribution under H_0 all the other results follow automatically. A proof is given in Theil (1971, pp. 143-144).

Heteroscedasticity-Consistent Inference

It was shown in Section 4 that if the disturbances in a regression model do not have a scalar covariance matrix, that is V is not the identity matrix, the OLS estimator is inefficient. Basing inference on a covariance matrix estimated as

$$\text{var}(b) = s^2 (X'X)^{-1} \tag{8.19}$$

is therefore inappropriate. For most of the situations typically encountered in practice, (8.19) is an underestimate of (4.8). In these circumstances the estimates of β appear to be more precise than they really are, and there is a danger that when t-tests are applied, some variables may be seen to be statistically significant when they are not.

Obtaining a consistent estimator of (4.8) would, at first sight, appear to be impossible since the expression depends on V and if this were known there would be no point in basing inference on OLS. However, in the case of disturbances which are heteroscedastic, but serially uncorrelated, it turns out that a consistent estimator of the true covariance matrix can be computed from the residuals, without even specifying a model for the heteroscedasticity. This is because the crucial component of (4.8) is not V, but rather $X'VX$, and if this is estimated by

$$X'VX = \sum e_t^2 x_t x_t' \tag{8.20}$$

it can be shown that, under standard regularity conditions, the resulting estimator of $\text{Var}(b)$

$$\text{var}^*(b) = (\sum x_t x_t')^{-1} (\sum e_t^2 x_t x_t')(\sum x_t x_t')^{-1} \tag{8.21}$$

is consistent in the sense that

$$\text{plim } T \text{ var}^*(b) = T \text{ Var}(b)$$

(Note that for a heteroscedastic situation there is usually no point in extracting a parameter σ^2 from the covariance matrix of the disturbances, and so this parameter need not figure in (4.8). It would clearly not be sensible to define such a parameter in the present context.)

2.9. Systems of Equations: Seemingly Unrelated Regression Equations

When the model in (1.1) satisfies the classical assumptions, the OLS estimator is best linear unbiased. However, it is sometimes possible to obtain a better estimator by viewing the equation as part of a *system*. This implies no contradiction with the BLUE property of OLS in a single equation, since extra information is being used in constructing the estimator.

There are basically two ways in which a gain in efficiency can occur when a single equation is considered as part of a system. The first arises when the disturbances in a particular equation are contemporaneously correlated with the disturbances in other equations. Such systems are known as *seemingly unrelated regression equations* (SURE). Secondly, models are sometimes formulated with constraints across different equations. The need to consider such equations together is rather more obvious in this case.

Seemingly Unrelated Regressions

A system of N equations may be written as

$$y_i = X_i \beta_i + \epsilon_i, \qquad i = 1, \ldots, N \tag{9.1}$$

The notation employed in (9.1) is analogous to that in (1.5) with y_i being a $T \times 1$ vector and so on. The number of independent variables for a given i in (9.1) will be denoted by k_i, and their sum, $k_1 + k_2 + \cdots + k_N$ will be denoted by k. None of the variables or parameters in the N equations need be related: the connection between the equations lies solely in the disturbance terms, which are correlated across different equations.

If the disturbances in each of the N equations obey the classical assumptions then

$$E(\epsilon_i) = 0, \qquad E(\epsilon_i \epsilon_i') = \omega_{ii} I_N \tag{9.2}$$

The correlations between disturbances in different equations may be characterised by writing

$$E(\epsilon_{it} \epsilon_{jt}) = \omega_{ij}, \qquad \text{for } i,j = 1, \ldots, N \tag{9.3}$$

All non-contemporaneous disturbances are, however, uncorrelated and so

$$E(\epsilon_{it} \epsilon_{j\tau}) = 0, \qquad \text{for } t \neq \tau \tag{9.4}$$

The information concerning the correlation structure of the disturbances may therefore be summarised by an $N \times N$ matrix Ω, the ijth element of which is equal to ω_{ij}.

The complete system may be written out in matrix terms as

$$
\begin{pmatrix} y_1 \\ y_2 \\ \vdots \\ y_N \end{pmatrix}
=
\begin{pmatrix} X_1 & 0 & \cdots & 0 \\ 0 & X_2 & \cdots & 0 \\ \vdots & \vdots & & \vdots \\ 0 & 0 & \cdots & X_N \end{pmatrix}
\begin{pmatrix} \beta_1 \\ \beta_2 \\ \vdots \\ \beta_N \end{pmatrix}
+
\begin{pmatrix} \epsilon_1 \\ \epsilon_2 \\ \vdots \\ \epsilon_N \end{pmatrix}
\tag{9.5}
$$

or more compactly as

$$y = X\beta + u \tag{9.6}$$

where y is a vector of length TN, X is a $TN \times k$ matrix and β is a vector of length k. The $TN \times 1$ vector of disturbances has a covariance matrix

$$V = E(uu') = \begin{pmatrix} E(\epsilon_1 \epsilon_1') & E(\epsilon_1 \epsilon_2') & \ldots & E(\epsilon_1 \epsilon_N') \\ E(\epsilon_2 \epsilon_1') & E(\epsilon_2 \epsilon_2') & \ldots & E(\epsilon_1 \epsilon_N') \\ \vdots & \vdots & & \vdots \\ E(\epsilon_N \epsilon_1') & E(\epsilon_N \epsilon_2') & \ldots & E(\epsilon_N \epsilon_N') \end{pmatrix} \tag{9.7}$$

For a given value of Ω, the BLUE of β is given simply by applying GLS to (9.6). Formula (4.4) implies the inversion of the matrix V which is of order TN. However, this may be avoided by first noting that the individual terms in (9.7) are all scalar matrices since

$$E(\epsilon_i \epsilon_j') = \omega_{ij} I_T, \qquad i, j = 1, \ldots, N \tag{9.8}$$

Thus V may be written as

$$V = \Omega \otimes I \tag{9.9}$$

where $\otimes$ denotes a Kronecker or tensor product. The algebra of Kronecker products is discussed briefly in the appendix.

If ω^{ij} denotes the ijth element in the inverse of Ω, it follows from the properties of Kronecker products that

$$V^{-1} = \Omega^{-1} \otimes I$$

$$= \begin{pmatrix} \omega^{11}I & \ldots & \omega^{1N}I \\ \vdots & & \vdots \\ \omega^{N1}I & \ldots & \omega^{NN}I \end{pmatrix} \tag{9.10}$$

Substituting (9.10) into the GLS formula (4.4) then yields a more tractable expression for the SURE estimator,

$$\tilde{b} = \begin{pmatrix} \omega^{11}X_1'X_1 & \omega^{12}X_1'X_2 & \ldots & \omega^{1N}X_1'X_N \\ \vdots & \vdots & & \vdots \\ \omega^{N1}X_N'X_1 & \omega^{N2}X_N'X_2 & \ldots & \omega^{NN}X_N'X_N \end{pmatrix}^{-1} \begin{pmatrix} \sum_{j=1}^{N} \omega^{1j}X_1'y_j \\ \vdots \\ \sum_{j=1}^{N} \omega^{Nj}X_N'y_j \end{pmatrix} \tag{9.11}$$

The covariance matrix of $\tilde{b}$ is simply the inverted matrix in expression (9.11); cf. (4.5).

Efficiency of the SURE Estimator

The potential gain in efficiency from using a SURE estimator depends on a number of factors. However, when the explanatory variables are pairwise orthogonal and $\omega_{ij} = \sigma^2 \varrho$ for all $i \neq j$, Zellner (1963, p. 354) has shown that the relative efficiency of the OLS estimator of a particular coefficient is given by

$$\frac{\text{Var}(\tilde{b})}{\text{Var}(b)} = \frac{(1 - \varrho)(1 - \varrho + \varrho N)}{1 - 2\varrho + \varrho N} \tag{9.12}$$

As might be expected the OLS estimator becomes more inefficient as $\varrho \to 1$. On the other hand when $\varrho = 0$, OLS is fully efficient. Indeed it is easy to see from (9.11) that the SURE and OLS estimators are identical when $\omega_{ij} = 0$ for $i \neq j$. This is only to be expected since when the disturbances are uncorrelated across equations there is nothing to connect them.

A second result to emerge from (9.12) is that for $\varrho > 0$ the gain in efficiency of the SURE estimator relative to OLS increases with the number of equations. The Monte Carlo evidence in Kmenta and Gilbert (1968) suggests that this is the case even if the explanatory variables are not orthogonal, provided that T is large.

As already noted, OLS is fully efficient when the disturbances are uncorrelated across equations. There is, however, another instance when OLS yields efficient estimators. This arises when the regressors in all N equations are identical, i.e. $X_i = \bar{X}, i = 1, \ldots, N$. The proof is as follows. In terms of (9.6), $X = I \otimes \bar{X}$ and so, using (A.8),

$$X'V^{-1}X = (I \otimes \bar{X})'(\Omega^{-1} \otimes I)(I \otimes \bar{X}) = \Omega^{-1} \otimes (\bar{X}'\bar{X}) \tag{9.13}$$

The GLS estimator is therefore

$$\tilde{b} = \{\Omega \otimes (\bar{X}'\bar{X})^{-1}\}(I \otimes \bar{X}')(\Omega^{-1} \otimes I)y$$
$$= \{I \otimes (\bar{X}'\bar{X})^{-1}\bar{X}'\}y$$

On examining this expression it will be seen that the SURE estimator in the ith equation is

$$\tilde{b}_i = (\bar{X}'\bar{X})^{-1}\bar{X}'y_i \tag{9.14}$$

for all $i = 1, \ldots, N$. In other words the OLS and SURE estimators are identical.

An Alternative Formulation of the SURE Model

An alternative way of developing the SURE estimator — which does not involve Kronecker products — is to write the N equations together as

$$y_t = X_t \beta + \epsilon_t, \qquad t = 1, \ldots, T \tag{9.15}$$

where y_t is an $N \times 1$ vector and X_t is an $N \times k$ matrix

$$X_t = \begin{pmatrix} x'_{1t} & 0 & \cdots & 0 \\ 0 & x'_{2t} & \cdots & 0 \\ \vdots & \vdots & & \vdots \\ 0 & 0 & \cdots & x'_{Nt} \end{pmatrix} \qquad (9.16)$$

where x_{it} is the $k_i \times 1$ vector of observations on the independent variables in the ith equation. The $k \times 1$ vector β is exactly as defined in (9.5), while the ϵ_t's are serially uncorrelated with mean zero and covariance matrix, $E(\epsilon_t \epsilon'_t) = \Omega$.

If the T equations in (9.15) are stacked in the usual way, the covariance matrix of the disturbances $u^* = (\epsilon'_1, \ldots, \epsilon'_T)'$ is

$$E(u^* u^{*\,\prime}) = \begin{pmatrix} \Omega & 0 & \cdots & 0 \\ 0 & \Omega & \cdots & 0 \\ \vdots & \vdots & & \vdots \\ 0 & 0 & \cdots & \Omega \end{pmatrix}$$

This may be written more concisely as $E(u^* u^{*\,\prime}) = I \otimes \Omega$. However, it is not necessary to use the algebra of Kronecker products in order to see that the GLS estimator of β is

$$\tilde{b} = \left(\sum_{t=1}^{T} X'_t \Omega^{-1} X_t \right)^{-1} \sum_{t=1}^{T} X'_t \Omega^{-1} y_t \qquad (9.17)$$

From the definition of X_t in (9.16) it is not difficult to see that (9.17) is identical to the SURE estimator given by (9.11).

Constraints across Equations

The formulation in the previous sub-section is particularly appropriate for incorporating constraints in a model. For example, suppose that in the two equation system

$$\begin{aligned} y_{1t} &= \beta_1 x_{1t} + \beta_2 x_{2t} + \epsilon_{1t} \\ y_{2t} &= \beta_3 x_{3t} + \beta_4 x_{4t} + \epsilon_{2t} \end{aligned} \qquad (9.18)$$

it is known that $\beta_2 = \beta_4$. Writing the model in the form (9.15) yields

$$\begin{pmatrix} y_{1t} \\ y_{2t} \end{pmatrix} = \begin{pmatrix} x_{1t} & x_{2t} & 0 \\ 0 & x_{4t} & x_{3t} \end{pmatrix} \beta + \begin{pmatrix} \epsilon_{1t} \\ \epsilon_{2t} \end{pmatrix} \qquad (9.19)$$

where $\beta = (\beta_1, \beta_2, \beta_3)'$. Estimating the coefficients with an allowance made for the constraint will give more efficient estimators of the elements in β even if the disturbances in the two equations are uncorrelated.

A more general method of allowing for constraints is to write them in the form (2.16). Adopting the notation of (9.6) then leads to a natural generalisation of the restricted least squares estimator, namely

$$\tilde{b}^* = \tilde{b} + (X'V^{-1}X)^{-1}R'[R(X'V^{-1}X)^{-1}R']^{-1}(r - R\tilde{b}) \quad (9.20)$$

where $\tilde{b}$ is the unconstrained GLS estimator.

A Feasible SURE Estimator

In general, Ω will be unknown and so (9.11) cannot be used directly. However, it may be estimated by applying OLS separately to each equation. If e_i denotes the $T \times 1$ vector of OLS residuals in the ith equation, an estimator of the ijth element in Ω is given by

$$\hat{\omega}_{ij} = e_i'e_j/T, \qquad i,j = 1,\ldots,N \quad (9.21)$$

Substituting for Ω in (9.11) or (9.17) then gives a *feasible* SURE estimator. The discussion at the end of Section 4 suggests that the resulting estimator of β will have the same asymptotic distribution as (9.11) under suitable conditions. The estimator of the asymptotic covariance matrix of the feasible SURE estimator is

$$\text{avar}(\tilde{b}) = (\Sigma X_t'\hat{\Omega}^{-1}X_t)^{-1} \quad (9.22)$$

Example 1 The application of Grunfeld's investment theory to data from two corporations, General Electric and Westinghouse, is a classic example of the use of the SURE technique; see Theil (1971) where the data are reproduced on p. 296. The theory states that next year's investment, y, depends on x_1 the 'market value of the firm', defined as the total value of the outstanding stock at the end-of-year stock market quotations, and the capital stock, x_2. Estimating each equation separately by OLS gives the following results

General Electric $\quad \hat{y}_1 = -10.0 + 0.027x_{11} + 0.152x_{21}$

Westinghouse $\qquad \hat{y}_2 = -0.5 + 0.053x_{12} + 0.092x_{22}$ $\qquad (9.23)$

where the second subscripts on x_1 and x_2 indicate the equation and the time subscript has been dropped for convenience.

The estimate of Ω from the OLS residuals is

$$\hat{\Omega} = \begin{bmatrix} 660.83 & 176.46 \\ 176.46 & 88.67 \end{bmatrix} \quad (9.24)$$

The correlation between the disturbances in the two equations is 0.53, which suggests that joint estimation would be appropriate. Indeed this makes sense from the theoretical point of view, since one would expect investment to be governed, to some extent, by considerations related to the economy as a whole. No such variables are specifically included in the model and so their effect must be felt through the disturbance terms.

Using the estimate of Ω in (9.24), the feasible SURE method yields

$$\hat{y}_1 = -27.7 + 0.038x_{11} + 0.139x_{21}$$
$$\hat{y}_2 = -1.3 + 0.058x_{12} + 0.064x_{22}$$

(9.25)

Incorporating the constraint that the coefficients of the explanatory variables are the same for each firm gives

$$\hat{y}_1 = -23.0 + 0.36x_{11} + 0.139x_{21}$$
$$\hat{y}_2 = 6.9 + 0.36x_{12} + 0.139x_{22}$$

(9.26)

cf. (9.19).

Example 2 Hart, Hutton and Sharot (1975) propose the following model for explaining the attendance at an English Football League match:

$$\log y_t = \alpha + \beta_1 \log x_{1t} + \beta_2 \log x_{2t} + \beta_3 \log x_{3t}$$
$$+ \beta_4 \log x_{4t} + \beta_5 \log x_{5t} + \epsilon_t$$

(9.27)

where y_t is attendance at the tth match of the season, x_1 and x_2 are the league positions of the home and away teams prior to the match, x_3 is the population of the home team's catchment area, x_4 is distance travelled by away support and x_5 is a time trend.

Equation (9.25) was estimated for four teams, Leeds, Newcastle, Nottingham Forest and Southampton. The results for Newcastle are typical:

$$\widehat{\log y_t} = 8.85 + 0.06x_{1t} - 0.08x_{2t} + 0.31x_{3t} - 0.22x_{4t} - 0.08x_{5t}$$
$$(0.84) \quad (0.12) \qquad (0.04) \qquad (0.08) \qquad (0.06) \qquad (0.33)$$

(9.28)

However, the OLS residuals had the following correlation matrix:

$$\begin{pmatrix} 1 & & & \\ 0.32 & 1 & & \\ 0.13 & 0.32 & 1 & \\ 0.14 & 0.42 & 0.12 & 1 \end{pmatrix}$$

with the teams in the order previously cited. This suggested that it would be appropriate to treat the four equations as a system. The Newcastle equation estimated by the feasible SURE method then became

$$\widehat{\log y_t} = 8.92 + 0.08x_{1t} - 0.08x_{2t} + 0.31x_{3t} - 0.24x_{4t} - 0.07x_{5t}$$
$$\phantom{\widehat{\log y_t} = } (0.64) \quad (0.09) \qquad (0.03) \qquad (0.06) \qquad (0.05) \qquad (0.03)$$

$$(9.29)$$

There are some differences in the two sets of estimates. However, the important point to note is that the estimated standard errors in (9.29) are a good deal smaller than those in (9.28). Although the standard errors quoted in (9.29) only have large sample validity they nevertheless suggest a gain in efficiency.

2.10. Multivariate Regression

Systems of equations are sometimes written in the form

$$y_t = Bx_t + \epsilon_t, \qquad t = 1, \ldots, T \tag{10.1}$$

where y_t and ϵ_t have the same interpretation as in (9.15), but B is an $N \times K$ matrix of parameters and x_t is a $K \times 1$ vector of regressors. However, unless restrictions are placed on the elements of B, a fully efficient set of estimators will be obtained simply by regressing each element of y_t on the vector x_t. Taking account of the covariances between the disturbances in different equations cannot lead to an improved estimator since each equation has exactly the same set of explanatory variables; cf. (9.14).

The *multivariate least squares* estimator of B may be written as

$$\tilde{B}' = \left[\sum_{t=1}^{T} x_t x_t' \right]^{-1} \sum_{t=1}^{T} x_t y_t' \tag{10.2}$$

The ith column of (10.2) gives the vector of OLS estimates from regressing y_{it} on x_t. Defining the $N \times T$ matrix $Y' = (y_1, \ldots, y_T)$ and the $K \times T$ matrix $\bar{X}' = (x_1, \ldots, x_T)$ leads to a more compact matrix representation of (10.2), as

$$\tilde{B}' = (\bar{X}'\bar{X})^{-1} \bar{X}' Y \tag{10.3}$$

or

$$\tilde{B} = Y'\bar{X}(\bar{X}'\bar{X})^{-1} \tag{10.4}$$

In terms of (9.14), $\tilde{B} = (b_1, \ldots, b_N)'$.

Model (10.1) may be written in the form (9.15) by defining $\beta = \text{vec}(B')$. The operator vec(.) indicates that the columns of the appropriate matrix are stacked one above the other. Thus if β_i' denotes the ith row of B, vec(B') $= (\beta_1', \ldots, \beta_N')'$. Corresponding to (9.15) therefore

$$y_t = (I \otimes x_t')\beta + \epsilon_t, \qquad t = 1, \ldots, T \tag{10.5}$$

Thus, suppose that $N = K = 2$, so that the model is

$$\begin{aligned} y_{1t} &= \beta_{11}x_{1t} + \beta_{12}x_{2t} + \epsilon_{1t} \\ y_{2t} &= \beta_{21}x_{1t} + \beta_{22}x_{2t} + \epsilon_{2t} \end{aligned} \quad , \quad t = 1, \ldots, T \quad (10.6)$$

This may be written in the form (10.5) as follows

$$\begin{bmatrix} y_{1t} \\ y_{2t} \end{bmatrix} = \begin{bmatrix} x_{1t} & x_{2t} & 0 & 0 \\ 0 & 0 & x_{1t} & x_{2t} \end{bmatrix} \begin{pmatrix} \beta_{11} \\ \beta_{12} \\ \beta_{21} \\ \beta_{22} \end{pmatrix} + \begin{bmatrix} \epsilon_{1t} \\ \epsilon_{2t} \end{bmatrix} \quad (10.7)$$

Hypothesis Testing

Hypotheses concerning elements in different rows of B may be framed in terms of the vector β in (10.5). The covariance matrix of b, the OLS estimator of β, is then given by the inverse of (9.13), i.e.

$$\text{Var}(b) = \Omega \otimes (\bar{X}'\bar{X})^{-1} \quad (10.8)$$

Suppose we wish to test $H_0 : \beta_{11} = \beta_{22}$. Any hypothesis which imposes linear restrictions on the parameters may be written in the form $w'\beta = r$; cf. Section 3. Thus

$$\text{Var}(w'\tilde{b}) = w'[\Omega \otimes (\bar{X}'\bar{X})^{-1}]w \quad (10.9)$$

For $N = 1$ this expression reduces to (3.6).

If ϵ_t follows a multivariate normal distribution, then

$$(w'b - r)/\sqrt{\text{Var}(w'b)} \sim N(0,1)$$

under H_0. However, Ω will usually be unknown, and so must be replaced by an estimator such as (9.21). In general any tests carried out on this basis will only have asymptotic validity, although if an hypothesis involves only coefficients on the *same* explanatory variable in each equation, an exact test is available. This is Hotelling's T^2-test, details of which will be found in Malinvaud (1980, pp. 230-31).

Example   Consider the hypothesis $H_0 : \beta_{11} = \beta_{22}$ in (10.6), and suppose that the sums of squares and cross-products for all variables are given by

	y_1	y_2	x_1	x_2
y_1	250			
y_2	100	500		
x_1	100	50	50	
x_2	75	150	50	100

Thus, for example, $\sum x_{1t} y_{2t} = 50$.

The multivariate least squares estimator may be computed from formula (10.4) as

$$
\tilde{B} = \begin{bmatrix} 100 & 75 \\ 50 & 150 \end{bmatrix} \begin{bmatrix} 50 & 50 \\ 50 & 100 \end{bmatrix}^{-1} = \begin{bmatrix} 100 & 75 \\ 50 & 150 \end{bmatrix} \begin{bmatrix} \dfrac{2}{50} & -\dfrac{1}{50} \\ \dfrac{1}{50} & \dfrac{1}{50} \end{bmatrix}
$$

$$
= \begin{bmatrix} 2.5 & -0.5 \\ -1 & 2 \end{bmatrix} \tag{10.10}
$$

and so $b = \text{vec}(\tilde{B}') = (2.5, -0.5, -1, 2)'$.

The hypothesis to be tested may be framed as $H_0 : w'\beta = 0$, where $w' = (1\ 0\ 0\ -1)$. Expression (10.9) may be written out as

$$
\text{Var}(w'b) = \frac{1}{50} \cdot w' \left[\begin{array}{c|c} \omega_{11} \begin{pmatrix} 2 & -1 \\ -1 & 1 \end{pmatrix} & \omega_{12} \begin{pmatrix} 2 & -1 \\ -1 & 1 \end{pmatrix} \\ \hline \omega_{21} \begin{pmatrix} 2 & -1 \\ -1 & 1 \end{pmatrix} & \omega_{22} \begin{pmatrix} 2 & -1 \\ -1 & 1 \end{pmatrix} \end{array} \right] w
$$

$$
= \frac{1}{50} (2\omega_{11} + 2\omega_{12} + \omega_{22}) \tag{10.11}
$$

as $\omega_{12} = \omega_{21}$.

The estimate of Ω, (9.21), may be obtained from the formula

$$
e'e = Y'Y - \tilde{B}X'Y \tag{10.12}
$$

cf. (2.8). Dividing through by T gives the following estimate of Ω:

$$
\hat{\Omega} = \frac{1}{50} \left[\begin{pmatrix} 250 & 100 \\ 100 & 500 \end{pmatrix} - \begin{pmatrix} 2.5 & -0.5 \\ -1 & 2 \end{pmatrix} \begin{pmatrix} 100 & 50 \\ 75 & 150 \end{pmatrix} \right]
$$

$$
= \begin{bmatrix} 0.75 & 1 \\ 1 & 5 \end{bmatrix} \tag{10.13}
$$

Substituting for the ω_{ij}'s in (10.11) gives

$$
\text{var}(w'b) = (0.75 + 10 + 2)/50 = 12.75/50 = 0.255
$$

and so the required test statistic is

$$
z = \frac{w'b - w'\beta}{\sqrt{\text{Var}(w'b)}} = \frac{0.5}{0.505} = 0.99
$$

Under $H_0 : z \sim AN(0,1)$ and since $-1.96 < 0.99 < 1.96$, the null hypothesis cannot be rejected at a (nominal) 5% level of significance.

Prediction

The BLUP of y_{T+l} is given by

$$\hat{y}_{T+l|T} = \tilde{B}x_{T+l} = (I \otimes x'_{T+l})b \qquad (10.14)$$

and so the prediction error is

$$y_{T+l} - \hat{y}_{T+l|T} = (I \otimes x'_{T+l})(\beta - b) + u_{T+l} \qquad (10.15)$$

The MSE of the prediction is therefore

$$\text{MSE}(\hat{y}_{T+l|T}) = (I \otimes x'_{T+l})\text{Var}(b)(I \otimes x_{T+l})' + \Omega$$

$$= (I \otimes x'_{T+l})[\Omega \otimes (\bar{X}'\bar{X})^{-1}](I \otimes x_{T+l})' + \Omega \qquad (10.16)$$

$$= \Omega + \Omega \otimes x'_{T+l}(\bar{X}'\bar{X})^{-1} x_{T+l}$$

$$= \Omega[1 + x'_{T+l}(\bar{X}'\bar{X})^{-1}x_{T+l}] \qquad (10.17)$$

since $x'_{T+l}(\bar{X}'\bar{X})^{-1} x_{T+l}$ is a scalar.

Constraints

The above example included a test of a restriction across the equations. Once restrictions across equations are taken to hold, the parameters in the model may no longer be efficiently estimated by OLS. The constraints must be incorporated in the estimation procedure in the manner suggested by (9.19) or (9.20).

Similarly, once different restrictions are introduced within equations, a SURE estimator will be appropriate unless, of course, Ω is diagonal.

2.11. The Method of Instrumental Variables

Suppose we have a linear model of the form

$$y_t = z'_t \delta + u_t, \qquad t = 1, \ldots, T \qquad (11.1)$$

where z_t is an $m \times 1$ vector of observations, and δ is a corresponding $m \times 1$ vector of parameters. The models considered until now have been of a similar form to (11.1), but the change in notation in (11.1) as compared with, say, (1.3) serves to indicate that the explanatory variables may be stochastic.

If the assumption that the disturbances are distributed independently of the explanatory variables is relaxed, the standard least squares estimators may lose some of their optimal properties. More seriously, if the disturbance at time t is correlated with some of the explanatory variables at time t, OLS will not, in general, be consistent.

Dynamic regression provides an important example of a situation where OLS may be inconsistent. Suppose that the disturbance term in (1.2.3) is serially correlated, i.e. $E(u_t u_{t-1}) \neq 0$. In these circumstances both y_{t-1} and u_t depend on u_{t-1}, and so $E(y_{t-1} u_t) \neq 0$. The consequences of this are examined further in Chapter 8.

A second example arises in the context of a simultaneous equations model. If an endogenous variable appears as a regressor in a particular equation, it will not in general be independent of the disturbance term, since it is itself partly determined by the dependent variable in that equation.

The Instrumental Variable Estimator

It is convenient to write (11.1) in matrix form as

$$y = Z\delta + u \tag{11.2}$$

where Z is a $T \times k$ matrix of explanatory variables. Since these variables may be stochastic, the standard regularity condition is

$$\text{plim } T^{-1} Z'Z = Q_{zz} \tag{11.3}$$

where Q_{zz} is p.d.

The OLS estimator of δ is

$$d = (Z'Z)^{-1} Z'y = \delta + (Z'Z)^{-1} Z'u \tag{11.4}$$

and if z_t and u_t are correlated it will normally be the case that

$$\text{plim } T^{-1} Z'u \neq 0 \tag{11.5}$$

Therefore d will be inconsistent, since

$$\text{plim}(d-\delta) = \text{plim}(Z'Z)^{-1} Z'u = Q_{zz}^{-1} \text{plim } T^{-1}Z'u \neq 0 \tag{11.6}$$

Note that, as a general rule, the vector plim $T^{-1} Z'u$ need only contain one non-zero element in order to render all the estimators in d inconsistent.

The consequences of (11.5) on the OLS estimator are therefore rather serious. However, a general approach to estimation problems of this kind is provided by the method of instrumental variables. Let w_t denote an $m \times 1$ vector of variables at time t. If these variables are to provide a suitable set of *instruments* for the variables in z_t, they must have two properties. Firstly they should be uncorrelated with the disturbance term in (11.1), at least in large samples. Secondly, they should be highly correlated with the explanatory variables.

Let W denote a $T \times m$ matrix in which the tth row is w_t. The standard regularity conditions, (11.3), will be replaced by two similar sets of conditions. These are

$$\text{plim } T^{-1} W' Z = Q_{wz} \qquad (11.7)$$

and

$$\text{plim } T^{-1} W' W = Q_{ww} \qquad (11.8)$$

where Q_{wz} and Q_{ww} are p.d. matrices.

Now consider the instrumental variable (IV) estimator,

$$\tilde{d} = (W' Z)^{-1} W' y \qquad (11.9)$$

The condition

$$\text{plim } T^{-1} W' u = 0 \qquad (11.10)$$

may be interpreted as saying that u_t and w_t are uncorrelated in large samples. If it holds the IV estimator is consistent since

$$\text{plim}(\tilde{d} - \delta) = \text{plim}(W' Z)^{-1} W' u = Q_{wz}^{-1} \cdot 0 = 0 \qquad (11.11)$$

As regards the asymptotic distribution of the IV estimator, assume that the disturbances are independently and identically distributed with mean zero and constant variance, σ^2, and that

$$T^{-1/2} W' u \xrightarrow{L} N(0, \sigma^2 Q_{ww}) \qquad (11.12)$$

Now consider

$$\sqrt{T}(\tilde{d} - \delta) = \left(\frac{W' Z}{T} \right)^{-1} \frac{W' u}{\sqrt{T}}$$

In view of (11.7) it follows from Cramér's theorem that

$$\sqrt{T}(\tilde{d} - \delta) \xrightarrow{L} N(0, \sigma^2 Q_{zw}^{-1} Q_{ww} Q_{wz}^{-1}) \qquad (11.13)$$

In other words $\tilde{d}$ is asymptotically normally distributed with a mean of δ and a covariance matrix

$$\text{Avar}(\tilde{d}) = \sigma^2 (Z' W)^{-1} W' W (W' Z)^{-1} \qquad (11.14)$$

Although instrumental variables would never be used in a classical regression model (except in the trivial sense that W can be set equal to Z), this case nevertheless provides some insight into the properties of the IV estimator in more general situations. To simplify matters further suppose that the model contains a single, non-stochastic explanatory variable, x, and a constant term. If an IV estimator is based on a non-stochastic instrument, it is straightforward to show that it will be unbiased with a variance given by

$$\text{Var}(\tilde{d}) = \sigma^2 \sum w_{*t}^2 \left/ \left(\sum x_{*t} w_{*t} \right)^2 \right. \qquad (11.15)$$

where x_{*t} and w_{*t} denote deviation from the mean form. The variance of the OLS estimator, d, is

$$\text{Var}(d) = \sigma^2 / \sum x_{*t}^2 \tag{11.16}$$

and if the correlation between x_t and w_t is

$$r_{xw}^2 = \frac{(\sum x_{*t} w_{*t})^2}{\sum x_{*t}^2 \sum w_{*t}^2} \tag{11.17}$$

if follows that the efficiency of $\tilde{d}$ is

$$\frac{\text{Var}(d)}{\text{Var}(\tilde{d})} = r_{xw}^2 \tag{11.18}$$

Thus the higher the correlation between x and its instrument, w, the more efficient the IV estimator. This result essentially carries over to the more general cases where IV estimation is applied to models with stochastic explanatory variables: the more highly correlated are the elements of z_t and w_t the more effective is the IV estimation procedure. On the other hand if plim $T^{-1} W'Z$ is close to a null matrix, the technique will yield very poor results.

The GIVE Estimator

The above analysis of a single variable regression model suggests that the best instrument for an explanatory variable is the one which is most highly correlated with it. However, there is no reason to restrict the choice to a single instrument. A more efficient procedure would be to take a weighted average of the possible instruments, with the weights chosen so as to maximise the correlation between this composite variable and z. Such an instrument is obtained simply by regressing z on all possible instruments. This yields the required weights. Thus if K instruments, w_{jt}^*, $j = 1, \ldots, K$, are available, the most efficient choice of instrument is given by

$$w_t' = w_t^{*\prime} (\sum w_t^* w_t^{*\prime})^{-1} \sum w_t^* z_t', \qquad t = 1, \ldots, T \tag{11.19}$$

where $w_t^* = (w_1^*, \ldots, w_K^*)'$. As formula (11.19) makes clear, the optimal instrument is given by the best linear unbiased predictor of z_t based on the set of all possible instruments.

In the general case when the model contains $m > 1$ explanatory variables, and $K > m$ possible instruments are available, the *generalised instrumental variable estimator* (GIVE) is obtained by selecting the best predictor for each element of z_t in the manner suggested above. If W^* denotes the $T \times K$ matrix of all possible instruments, this may be reduced to the $T \times m$ matrix of optimal instruments, W, by multivariate regression. Thus

$$W = W^*(W^{*\prime}W^*)^{-1}W^{*\prime}Z \tag{11.20}$$

The GIVE estimator may be expressed as

$$\tilde{d} = (Z'PZ)^{-1}Z'Py \tag{11.21}$$

where P is the projection matrix

$$P = W^*(W^{*\prime}W^*)^{-1}W^{*\prime} \tag{11.22}$$

The GIVE procedure may be extended to cases where the disturbances are correlated. Suppose that the disturbance vector has a covariance matrix given by (4.1). By defining a matrix L, such that $L'L = V^{-1}$, the observations may be transformed in the manner of (4.2) to yield

$$Ly = LZ\delta + Lu$$

The matrix of optimal instruments for LZ is

$$W = W^*(W^{*\prime}W^*)^{-1}W^{*\prime}LZ \tag{11.23}$$

and so the GIVE estimator is

$$\tilde{d} = (Z'L'PLZ)^{-1}Z'L'PLy \tag{11.24}$$

Note that

$$\text{Avar}(\tilde{d}) = \sigma^2(Z'L'PLZ)^{-1} \tag{11.25}$$

An alternative estimator is obtained by applying the same transformation to the instruments as is applied to Z. Thus W^* is replaced by LW^* in (11.23) yielding the estimator

$$\tilde{d}^\dagger = (Z'L'P_vLZ)^{-1}Z'L'P_vLy \tag{11.26}$$

where

$$P_v = LW^*(W^*V^{-1}W^{*\prime})^{-1}W^{*\prime}L' \tag{11.27}$$

This is sometimes known as the GLS analogue.

2.12. Autoregression

This section examines the distribution theory for OLS estimators when the explanatory variables, or at least some of them, are lagged values of the dependent variable.

Stable Dynamic Models

Consider a dynamic regression model of the form

$$y_t = \alpha_1 y_{t-1} + \cdots + \alpha_r y_{t-r} + x_t'\beta + \epsilon_t, \qquad t = r+1, \ldots, T \tag{12.1}$$

in which

(i) the disturbance term ϵ_t is a sequence of independent and identically distributed random variables with mean zero, variance σ^2 and finite moments of every order;

(ii) the explanatory variables are non-stochastic and are such that

$$\lim_{T \to \infty} \frac{1}{T-\tau} \sum_{t=\tau+1}^{T} x_t x_{t-\tau}$$

exists for $\tau = 0, \ldots, r$ and is non-singular for $\tau = 0$;

(iii) the roots of the AR polynomial in the lag operator,

$$\alpha(L) = 1 - \alpha_1 L - \cdots - \alpha_r L^r$$

lie outside the unit circle.

Assumptions (ii) and (iii) imply that

$$\operatorname{plim} T^{-1} \sum_{t=r+1}^{T} z_t z_t' = Q \tag{12.2}$$

where $z_t = (y_{t-1}, \ldots, y_{t-r}, x_t')'$ and Q is a p.d. matrix. This is effectively the same as the condition given earlier in (3.13). The other condition alluded to at the end of Section 3, namely that the disturbance is independent of the explanatory variables in all time periods, clearly does not hold as $E(y_t \epsilon_{t-\tau}) \neq 0$ for $\tau \geq 0$. As a result the OLS estimators of the α and β parameters will, in general, be biased in small samples and it becomes very difficult to say anything positive about small sample properties. However, following a line of argument dating back to Mann and Wald (1943), it can be shown that

$$\operatorname{plim} T^{-1} \sum z_t \epsilon_t = 0 \tag{12.3}$$

and

$$T^{-\frac{1}{2}} \sum z_t \epsilon_t \xrightarrow{L} N(0, \sigma^2 Q) \tag{12.4}$$

If we let $\gamma = (\alpha_1, \ldots, \alpha_r, \beta')'$ and denote its OLS estimator as c, then it follows from (12.2) and (12.3) that c is a consistent estimator of γ. Furthermore, Cramér's theorem, (1.4.17), may be invoked to show that $T^{\frac{1}{2}}(c - \gamma)$ has a limiting multivariate normal distribution with mean zero and covariance matrix $Q^{-1} \sigma^2 Q Q^{-1} = \sigma^2 Q^{-1}$. The practical implication of this result is that the usual least squares distribution theory holds approximately in large samples. In other words, c can be treated as being normally distributed with mean γ and covariance matrix

$$\operatorname{Avar}(c) = \sigma^2 \left(\sum z_t z_t' \right)^{-1} \tag{12.5}$$

A pure autoregressive model, such as (1.2.12), is a special case of (12.1), and the condition for dynamic stability in (iii) is then the same as the condition for stationarity given earlier in connection with (1.5.18). For a stationary AR(1) model

$$y_t = \phi y_{t-1} + \epsilon_t, \qquad |\phi| < 1, \qquad t = 2, \ldots, T \qquad (12.6)$$

the vector z_t in (12.2) is just the scalar y_{t-1} and it is not difficult to see that

$$Q = \text{plim } T^{-1} \sum y_{t-1}^2 = \sigma^2/(1 - \phi^2) \qquad (12.7)$$

This is the same as the variance of the AR(1) process as derived in (1.5.6). If $\hat{\phi}$ denotes the OLS estimator of ϕ, the variance of the limiting distribution of $T^{\frac{1}{2}}(\hat{\phi} - \phi)$ is thus $1 - \phi^2$. However, the output from a regression package will produce the following estimator for the variance of $\hat{\phi}$:

$$\text{avar}(\hat{\phi}) = s^2/(\sum y_{t-1}^2) \qquad (12.8)$$

where

$$s^2 = \sum (y_t - \hat{\phi} y_{t-1})^2/(T - 2) \qquad (12.9)$$

This is then used to construct the 't-statistic'

$$\hat{\tau} = (\hat{\phi} - \phi)/\{\text{avar}(\hat{\phi})\}^{\frac{1}{2}} \qquad (12.10)$$

which, although it does not have a t-distribution, is asymptotically $N(0,1)$; see also Section 4,6.

Unit Roots and the Dickey–Fuller Test

When the AR coefficient in (12.6) is unity, the process becomes a random walk, (1.5.26). It was observed in Section 1.5 that in small samples the OLS estimator of ϕ in this case is biased and will typically be well below unity; some evidence can be found in Table 8.5.1 of Fuller (1976). Since the underlying process is non-stationary, the asymptotic theory set out above does not apply. Indeed this should be clear from (12.7) since it makes no sense to set ϕ equal to unity. In fact it turns out that there is a limiting distribution, but it is for $T(\hat{\phi} - 1)$ rather than for $T^{\frac{1}{2}}(\hat{\phi} - 1)$. This means that convergence to the limiting distribution is much faster than for a stationary model, the intuitive reason for this being that the denominator of $\hat{\phi}$ increases at a much faster rate because the series does not hover around a constant level. The other important point about the limiting distribution is that it is not normal.

A test of the hypothesis that $\phi = 1$ can be based on the 't-statistic' of (12.10). The distribution of this statistic was tabulated by Dickey using Monte Carlo methods and is given in Table 8.5.2 of the book by Fuller (1976). Hence the test is known as the *Dickey–Fuller* test. The table is reproduced at the end of this book as Table D. The distribution of the t-statistic for ϕ changes if a constant term is included in the regression, and if a constant and a time trend are included. These statistics are denoted by $\hat{\tau}_\mu$ and $\hat{\tau}_\tau$ respectively in the Dickey–Fuller tables. A more general test which allows for certain kinds of heteroscedasticity and serial correlation in ϵ_t is given in Phillips (1987).

Another way of formulating the AR(1) model is as

$$\Delta y_t = \phi^\dagger y_{t-1} + \epsilon_t, \qquad t = 2, \ldots, T \tag{12.11}$$

where $\phi^\dagger = \phi - 1$. The parameter $\phi^\dagger$ is zero when the process is a random walk and it follows from the discussion in the previous paragraph that its estimator will tend to be negative since it is easy to see that $\hat{\phi}^\dagger = \hat{\phi} - 1$. The idea of setting up the AR(1) model in such a way that a unit root leads to a parameter being equal to zero generalises to higher order autoregressive processes. Thus the AR(p) model, (1.2.12), may be reformulated as

$$\Delta y_t = \phi^\dagger y_{t-1} + \sum_{j=1}^{p-1} \phi_j^\dagger \Delta y_{t-j} + \epsilon_t \tag{12.12}$$

where

$$\phi_j^\dagger = -\sum_{k=j+1}^{p} \phi_k, \qquad j = 1, 2, \ldots, p - 1$$

and

$$\phi^\dagger = \sum_{k=1}^{p} \phi_k - 1$$

A unit root corresponds to a value of zero for the coefficient of y_{t-1} and if the unit root is imposed, the model reduces to a $p-1th$ autoregression in Δy_t. The distribution of the 't-statistic' associated with y_{t-1} is the same as that given in the Dickey–Fuller tables for the AR(1) model, and the test for a unit root is known as the *augmented Dickey–Fuller test*. On the other hand, it can be shown that the t-statistics associated with the differenced right hand side variables in (12.12) are asymptotically standard normal.

Vector Autoregressions

The first order vector autoregressive model

$$y_t = \Phi y_{t-1} + \epsilon_t, \qquad t = 2, \ldots, T \tag{12.13}$$

has the same form as the multivariate regression model (10.1), except that the non-stochastic explanatory variables, x_t, are replaced by the vector of lagged dependent variables. The elements of Φ may therefore be estimated by multivariate least squares, that is

$$\hat{\Phi} = (\sum y_{t-1} y_{t-1}')^{-1} \sum y_{t-1} y_t' \tag{12.14}$$

and, of course, this is exactly the same as applying OLS to each equation in turn. More generally, multivariate least squares may be used to estimate any unrestricted VAR(p) model. The main drawback to such models is the large number of parameters to be estimated, since, between them, the Φ matrices contain N^2p parameters.

A generalisation of the Mann–Wald theorem suggests that, in large samples, the multivariate least squares estimator of Φ may be treated in exactly the same way as the corresponding estimator of the B matrix for the fixed regressor model, (10.1). The essential condition is that the series in y_t should be jointly stationary. This is rarely true for economic time series, and attempting to tackle the problem by taking differences is rarely satisfactory. The usual approach adopted by VAR *aficionados* is therefore to work in levels, even if some of the series are non-stationary. In this case, it is important to recognise the effect of unit roots on the distribution of the estimators; see Sims, Stock and Watson (1987).

Notes

Sections 1-5, 8 Johnston (1984), Theil (1971), Malinvaud (1980) and Mann and Wald (1943).

Section 6   Plackett (1950), Brown, Durbin and Evans (1975) and Phillips and Harvey (1974). The link between the OLS recursions and the Kalman filter is discussed in *TSM*.

Section 7   Theil (1971, Ch. 5), Koerts and Abrahamse (1969) and Phillips and Harvey (1974).

Section 8   Heteroscedasticity-consistent inference was developed by Eicker (1967) and White (1980).

Sections 9, 10 Theil (1971, Ch. 7) and Phillips and Wickens (1978, Ch. 3).

Section 11   Sargan (1958, 1961), Wickens (1969) and Bowden and Turkington (1984).

Exercises

1. Consider model (3.12) with $x_t = \varkappa x_{t-1}$ for $t = 2, \ldots, T$, with $|\varkappa| < 1$ and $x_1 \neq 0$. Is condition (3.9) satisfied? Is the OLS estimator consistent?
2. How would you estimate α and β from a set of observations on y_t and x_t if the underlying functional form is $y = \exp(\alpha + \beta/x)$? State any assumptions you make in writing down an appropriate stochastic model.
   Graph y against x for $\beta < 0$ and comment on the usefulness of this particular functional form.
3. Derive an expression for the covariance matrix of the restricted least squares estimator (2.21).
4. Show that $R^2 = b'X'Xb/y'y$, where X and y are in deviation from the mean form.
5. Does $T^{3/2}(b - \beta)$ have a limiting distribution in (3.12)?
6. If, in (1.3), Var(u_t) = $\sigma^2 h_t$ where h_t is known, derive recursions similar to those in (6.3) for the weighted least squares estimator.
7. Prove (10.12).
8. Why would you expect a low order AR model to give a relatively poor fit to a series generated by a random walk plus noise model, (5.28) and (5.31), with a small value of q?
9. An AR(2) model is fitted to a series by regressing y_t and y_{t-1} on y_{t-2}. Find an expression for the covariance matrix of the estimators of ϕ_1 and ϕ_2, if the observations are actually generated by an AR(1) process. Compare the variance of the estimator of ϕ_1 with the variance of the estimator of the AR coefficient obtained by fitting an AR(1) model.

3
The Method of Maximum Likelihood

3.1. Introduction

The method of least squares, and related techniques, such as instrumental variables, use only the first two moments of the observations. However, if, in setting up a model, the form of the distribution is specified, restricting attention to the first two moments may be statistically inefficient. The method of maximum likelihood (ML) attempts to incorporate *all* the information in a model by working with the complete distribution of the observations.

In a linear model, the Gauss–Markov theorem provides a justification for the use of ordinary least squares. The only assumptions made about the distribution of the observations concern the first two moments, and provided that attention is confined to linear estimators OLS can be shown to be best. As noted in Section 1.3, however, the same criterion cannot be applied to a dynamic model. Nor can it be applied to a non-linear model, such as (2.1.12), even though minimising the residual sum of squares has an obvious intuitive appeal, just as it does for the dynamic model (2.3.15).

If the observations in (2.1.12) and (2.3.15) are assumed to be normally distributed, the least squares estimators can be viewed as maximum likelihood estimators. Their use can then be justified in terms of statistical efficiency, provided, that is, that the sample is reasonably large. The assumption of normality also leads to stronger grounds for using OLS in the linear model. The estimator is now best within the class of all estimators, not simply those which are linear in the observations. However, once the question of specifying the complete distribution of the observations is brought into the picture, it may become more difficult to justify using OLS in certain situations. The logic of the model may be such that a normal distribution is inappropriate, even as an approximation. As an illustration, consider fitting a regression model in which the dependent variable is nominal and is defined to be zero or one. Least squares is statistically inefficient in this case, since it ignores the information that the observations are restricted to two values. The maximum likelihood estimator, on the other hand, takes the full structure of the model into account.

Viewing estimation within the least squares framework derived from classical regression has even more severe limitations. Consider the time series models introduced in Section 1.2. Although (1.2.10) and (1.2.12) can be estimated by least squares, it is not immediately apparent how to treat (1.2.13). The lagged disturbance term is unobservable, and so the unknown parameters cannot simply be estimated by regressing y_t on ϵ_{t-1}. This is typical of the kind of problem encountered in modelling time series and a more general approach is clearly needed.

The remaining parts of this section set out the principle of maximum likelihood estimation, and discuss the implications for computation. Section 2 investigates whether there are general rules for constructing minimum variance unbiased estimators of the parameters in any given model. It turns out that this is only possible in certain special cases. However, a minimum variance bound can be derived, and in Section 3 it is shown that this bound is attained by the ML estimator in large samples. This result is a fundamental one and it provides the main justification for the use of maximum likelihood in terms of statistical efficiency.

The application of ML techniques to regression models is considered in Section 4. In Section 5 it is shown how the likelihood function for a time series model may be decomposed in terms of one-step ahead prediction errors. This decomposition is the basis of ML estimation in all dynamic models.

Section 6 introduces the concept of identifiability. This is concerned with the uniqueness of estimates obtained from a particular model. Identifiability is of fundamental importance since if a model is not identified, it may not make sense. The final section considers the extent to which the ML estimator is robust to the assumption of normality. Since the discussion is carried out within the context of a linear regression model, it is also an examination of the robustness of ordinary least squares.

The Principle of Maximum Likelihood

Suppose that the sample consists of a set of observations on T random variables, $y_1, \ldots, y_T$. The statistical model specifies a distribution for $y_1, \ldots, y_T$, known as the *joint density function*. This depends on n unknown parameters in a vector $\psi = (\psi_1, \ldots, \psi_n)'$. The joint density may be denoted by $L(y_1, \ldots, y_T; \psi)$. For a discrete distribution it may be interpreted as the probability of obtaining particular values of $y_1, \ldots, y_T$.

Once the sample has been drawn, $y_1, \ldots, y_T$ become a set of fixed numbers. The expression for the joint density can then be re-interpreted as a function of ψ, where ψ is any admissible value of the parameter vector, rather than the true value. It therefore indicates the plausibility of different values of ψ, given the sample. Viewed in this way, the expression for the joint density function is called the *likelihood function,* and is denoted by $L(\psi)$.

The maximum likelihood approach to the problem of estimating ψ is to ask what value of ψ is most likely, given the observations. This leads to the following principle: the ML estimate of ψ is given by $\tilde{\psi}$, where $\tilde{\psi}$, is a value such that

$$L(\tilde{\psi}) \geq L(\hat{\psi}) \tag{1.1}$$

$\hat{\psi}$ being any other admissible estimate of ψ. The rules by which an ML *estimator* is constructed must then be such as to ensure that for any particular sample, the resulting ML *estimate* satisfies (1.1).

The classical theory of maximum likelihood estimation is based on a situation in which the T observations are drawn from the same distribution. Furthermore they are drawn independently of each other, and so the joint density function is given by

$$L(y_1, \ldots, y_T; \psi) = \prod_{t=1}^{T} p(y_t; \psi) \tag{1.2}$$

where $p(y_t; \psi)$ is the p.d.f. of y_t for $t = 1, \ldots, T$. The models encountered in econometrics rarely conform to this pattern, but the main results on the properties of ML estimators carry over in almost all cases. A full discussion of this issue is beyond the scope of this book, however, and the proofs sketched out in Sections 2 and 3 are limited to independent and identically distributed random variables.

The Likelihood Equations

In almost all the applications considered here, $L(\psi)$ is a continuous function of ψ and the ML estimator can be found by the differential calculus. As a rule, it is easier to work with the (natural) logarithm of $L(\psi)$. This raises no difficulties, since if $\tilde{\psi}$ satisfies the condition that $\log L(\tilde{\psi}) \geq \log L(\hat{\psi})$, it will also satisfy (1.1).

The $n \times 1$ vector of first derivatives, $\partial \log L(\psi)/\partial \psi$, will often be written using the differential operator, D. The advantage of this notation, $D \log L(\psi)$, is that it is easy to indicate if the derivative is to be evaluated at a certain point. Writing $D \log L(\hat{\psi})$ denotes the vector of first derivatives evaluated at $\psi = \hat{\psi}$, i.e.

$$D \log L(\hat{\psi}) = \left. \frac{\partial \log L(\psi)}{\partial \psi} \right|_{\psi = \hat{\psi}} \tag{1.3}$$

Similar notation may be used for the $n \times n$ matrix of second derivatives. Thus

$$D^2 \log L(\tilde{\psi}) = \left. \frac{\partial^2 \log L(\psi)}{\partial \psi \partial \psi'} \right|_{\psi = \tilde{\psi}} \tag{1.4}$$

indicates the Hessian of log L evaluated at the ML estimate, $\tilde{\psi}$.

The ML estimator is obtained as a solution to the likelihood equations,

$$D \log L(\psi) = 0 \tag{1.5}$$

Since there may be more than one solution to (1.5), it is important to check that a maximum has been obtained. The Hessian will be a negative definite matrix if the solution correponds to a maximum of the likelihood function, although this does not guarantee that a global, as opposed to local, maximum has been reached.

Example 1 The log−likelihood function for a sample of T independent observations from a normal distribution with mean μ and variance σ^2 is

$$\log L(\mu, \sigma^2) = -\frac{T}{2} \log 2\pi - \frac{T}{2} \log \sigma^2 - \frac{1}{2\sigma^2} \sum_{t=1}^{T} (y_t - \mu)^2 \tag{1.6}$$

In terms of the general notation, $\psi = (\mu, \sigma^2)'$ and the elements of $D \log L(\psi)$ are

$$\frac{\partial \log L}{\partial \mu} = \frac{1}{\sigma^2} \sum (y_t - \mu) \tag{1.7a}$$

and

$$\frac{\partial \log L}{\partial \sigma^2} = \frac{-T}{2\sigma^2} + \frac{1}{2\sigma^4} \sum (y_t - \mu)^2 \tag{1.7b}$$

Setting these derivatives equal to zero and solving yields

$$\tilde{\mu} = \sum_{t=1}^{T} y_t/T = \bar{y} \tag{1.8a}$$

and

$$\tilde{\sigma}^2 = \sum_{t=1}^{T} (y_t - \bar{y})^2/T \tag{1.8b}$$

These expressions are the only solutions to the likelihood equations and an examination of the matrix of second derivatives shows that they do indeed maximise log $L(\psi)$. Specifically,

$$D^2 \log L(\psi) = \begin{bmatrix} \dfrac{\partial^2 \log L}{\partial \mu^2} & \dfrac{\partial^2 \log L}{\partial \mu\, \partial \sigma^2} \\[2ex] \dfrac{\partial^2 \log L}{\partial \sigma^2\, \partial \mu} & \dfrac{\partial^2 \log L}{\partial (\sigma^2)^2} \end{bmatrix}$$

$$
= \begin{bmatrix} \dfrac{-T}{\sigma^2} & -\dfrac{1}{\sigma^4} \Sigma \ (y_t - \mu) \\[2em] -\dfrac{1}{\sigma^4} \Sigma \ (y_t - \mu) & \dfrac{T}{2\sigma^4} - \dfrac{1}{\sigma^6} \Sigma \ (y_t - \mu)^2 \end{bmatrix}
$$

(1.9)

Substituting from (1.8) yields

$$
D^2 \log L(\tilde{\psi}) = - \begin{bmatrix} \dfrac{T}{\tilde{\sigma}^2} & 0 \\[2em] 0 & \dfrac{T}{2\tilde{\sigma}^4} \end{bmatrix}
$$

(1.10)

Since $\tilde{\sigma}^2 > 0$, (1.10) is clearly negative definite and so the expressions (1.8a) and (1.8b) do indeed maximise the likelihood function.

Example 2   The p.d.f. for a standardised Cauchy variate is

$$
p(y; \psi) = \pi^{-1} \{1 + (y_t - \psi)^2\}^{-1}
$$

(1.11)

and so the log–likelihood function for a sample of T independent observations is

$$
\log L = - \sum_{t=1}^{T} \log[\pi\{1 + (y_t - \psi)^2\}]
$$

(1.12)

The ML estimator of the parameter, ψ, is given by the solution to the likelihood equation.

$$
2 \sum_{t} [(y_t - \psi)/\{1 + (y_t - \psi)^2 \}] = 0
$$

(1.13)

However, since this equation is non-linear, it is impossible to write down an explicit solution for $\tilde{\psi}$, as was done in the previous example.

Computational Aspects of Maximum Likelihood

In the second example above, the estimate must be computed by some sort of iterative procedure. This is typical of maximum likelihood estimation, since a direct solution to the likelihood equations tends to be the exception rather than the rule. The need to resort to iterative procedures is sometimes regarded as a drawback to maximum likelihood, and an alternative strategy is to look for simpler estimators which are easier to compute. In econometrics such estimators are often based on the least squares principle. However, there is no guarantee that an estimator constructed along these lines will be efficient, or even consistent.

In the last twenty years or so, the developments in computing facilities and in algorithms for carrying out non-linear optimisation have been remarkable. This has led to a shift in emphasis towards ML estimation. Since computational considerations are so important in this context, the next chapter is devoted to a review of non-linear optimisation techniques and their application in econometrics. A good grasp of this material is vital to anyone actually interested in carrying out ML estimation in practice.

The stress on maximum likelihood methodology should not be taken to imply that other methods have become redundant. The amount of computer time which can be saved by the use of a simpler estimator can often be considerable, and there is evidence to suggest that in many cases the small sample performance of a carefully chosen alternative to the ML estimator is perfectly satisfactory. Furthermore, a cruder estimation technique may be more robust when the specification is inappropriate. Nevertheless, while accepting these points, a consideration of maximum likelihood is still fundamental to any discussion of estimation. Indeed, a maximum likelihood framework provides the basis for deriving simpler estimators which retain the property of large sample efficiency. The various two-step estimators described in this book all fall within this category. By following ML principles, it is usually possible to avoid the pitfalls which have often been encountered by those attempting to construct simple, but efficient, estimators within a least squares framework.

3.2. Sufficiency and the Cramér–Rao Lower Bound

The concept of minimum variance unbiased estimation was introduced in Section 1.3. It was pointed out that it suffers from severe limitations as a criterion for assessing different estimation procedures. Nevertheless, it is a useful ideal to begin with in examining the merits of various approaches to estimation. The first part of this section considers the notion of sufficiency and the way in which it is related to minimum variance unbiased estimation. Although a link can be established, it turns out that the existence of an MVUE can be deduced from sufficiency only in certain special cases. An alternative approach to the problem is to ask whether there is a lower bound to the variance of an unbiased estimator. Showing that a particular estimator attains the lower bound is then tantamount to demonstrating that the estimator is an MVUE.

Sufficiency

Heuristically, a sufficient statistic is one which contains all the information in the sample which is relevant for the estimation of a particular parameter. To state the property formally, suppose that $\hat{\psi}$ is a statistic and that ψ^* is any other statistic which is not a function of $\hat{\psi}$. If, for each ψ^*, the conditional distribution of ψ^*, given $\hat{\psi}$, does not involve ψ, then $\hat{\psi}$ is a *sufficient statistic* for ψ. In other words if $p(\psi^*|\hat{\psi})$ does not involve ψ, $\hat{\psi}$ is sufficient.

As it stands, this definition is not particularly helpful. However, if the likelihood function can be factorised as

$$L(y_1, \ldots, y_T; \psi) = g(\hat{\psi}; \psi) \cdot k(y_1, \ldots, y_T) \tag{2.1}$$

where $g(\hat{\psi}; \psi)$ is a function of $\hat{\psi}$ and ψ alone, and $k(y_1, \ldots, y_T)$ is independent of ψ, then $\hat{\psi}$ is sufficient. In fact, under fairly general conditions, (2.1) is both a necessary and a sufficient condition for sufficiency.

A sufficient statistic, if it exists, is not unique. Any one-to-one function of a statistic which satisfies (2.1) will itself satisfy (2.1).

Example 1   For a Poisson distribution,

$$\mathrm{p}(y; \psi) = e^{-\psi}\, \psi^y/y!$$

and the likelihood function for T observations may be factorised as

$$L(\psi) = \{e^{-T\psi}\, \psi^{\Sigma y}\} \cdot \left\{ \prod_{t=1}^{T} y_t! \right\}^{-1} \tag{2.2}$$

Hence $\Sigma\, y$ or, equivalently, the sample mean is a sufficient statistic for ψ.

Example 2   The likelihood function for a random sample from an $N(0, \sigma^2)$ distribution is

$$L(\sigma^2) = (2\pi\sigma^2)^{-T/2} \cdot \exp(-\tfrac{1}{2} \Sigma\, y_t^2/\sigma^2) \tag{2.3}$$

This factors trivially into a function of σ^2 and Σy_t^2, and a term $k(y_1, \ldots, y_T)$ which is simply unity. Hence Σy_t^2 is a sufficient statistic for σ^2.

When a model contains $n > 1$ unknown parameters, the factorisation criterion generalises to define sets of *jointly* sufficient statistics.

Example 3   The exponent in the likelihood function for a random sample from an $N(\mu, \sigma^2)$ distribution may be split into two parts to yield:

$$L(\mu, \sigma^2) = (2\pi\sigma^2)^{-T/2} \cdot \exp\left[-\tfrac{1}{2} \sigma^{-2}\{ \Sigma\, (y_t - \bar{y})^2 \right.$$
$$\left. + T(\bar{y} - \mu)^2\} \right] \tag{2.4}$$

As in the previous example, $k(y_1, \ldots, y_T) = 1$, and $\bar{y}$ and $\Sigma(y_t - \bar{y})^2$ are jointly sufficient for μ and σ^2.

If the family of distributions for a sufficient statistic is *complete,* the Rao–Blackwell theorem may be used to show that a function of the sufficient statistic is an MVUE of the parameter in question; see Silvey (1975, pp. 28-33). Unfortunately there are a large number of cases where this condition does not hold.

The Cramér–Rao Lower Bound

When $n = 1$, the amount of *information* in the sample is defined by

$$I(\psi) = -E[D^2 \log L(\psi)]$$

$$= -\int D^2 \log L(\psi) \cdot L(y_1, \ldots, y_T; \psi) dy_1, \ldots, dy_T \quad (2.5)$$

Note that although $L(\psi)$ is regarded as a likelihood function for the purpose of differentiation, the expectation is taken with respect to the joint density function. The parameter, ψ, is then interpreted as the true value.

In the next sub-section it is shown that $1/I(\psi)$ is the *minimum variance bound* (MVB) for an unbiased estimator of ψ. This result extends to the case of n parameters. If $\hat{\psi}$ is an unbiased estimator of ψ, the Cramér–Rao inequality states that the covariance matrix of $\hat{\psi}$ must exceed the inverse of the information matrix by a p.s.d. matrix.

If the variance of an unbiased estimator is equal to the MVB, the estimator is said to be efficient. However, failure to attain the lower bound does not necessarily rule out an estimator on the grounds of efficiency, since, in small samples, it is quite possible that no unbiased estimator will actually reach the lower bound. In some cases it can actually be shown that an estimator is the MVUE, even though it is not efficient in the sense defined above.

·*Example 4*   If the sample consists of T independent observations from an $N(\mu, \sigma^2)$ distribution, the information matrix is obtained by taking expectations in (1.9); i.e.

$$I(\mu, \sigma^2) = -E[D^2 \log L(\mu, \sigma^2)] = \begin{pmatrix} \dfrac{T}{\sigma^2} & 0 \\ 0 & \dfrac{T}{2\sigma^4} \end{pmatrix} \quad (2.6)$$

The MVB for μ is therefore σ^2/T and this is also the variance of the sample mean, $\bar{y}$. An unbiased estimator of σ^2, s^2, was defined in (1.4.10). It follows, as a special case of the result derived in Section 2.7, that the variance of s^2 is $2\sigma^4/(T-1)$. This is greater than the MVB of $2\sigma^4/T$. However, it is impossible to find an unbiased estimator of σ^2 which does attain the lower bound, and s^2 turns out to be the MVUE.

Derivation of the Cramér–Rao Inequality*

To simplify matters assume a single unknown parameter, ψ. The joint density of T independent observations is given by $L = L(y_1, \ldots, y_T; \psi)$ as defined in (1.2). This must, by definition, satisfy the condition

$$\int \cdots \int L \cdot dy_1, \ldots, dy_T = 1 \tag{2.7}$$

Differentiating both sides of (2.7) with respect to ψ and interchanging the operations of differentiation and integration gives

$$\int \cdots \int \frac{\partial L}{\partial \psi} \, dy_1, \ldots, dy_T = 0$$

which may be written as

$$E[D \log L(\psi)] = \int \cdots \int \left(\frac{1}{L} \frac{\partial L}{\partial \psi} \right) L \, dy_1, \ldots, dy_T = 0 \tag{2.8}$$

Differentiating again and interchanging operations yields

$$\int \cdots \int \left(\left(\frac{1}{L} \frac{\partial L}{\partial \psi} \right) \frac{\partial L}{\partial \psi} + L \frac{\partial}{\partial \psi} \left(\frac{1}{L} \frac{\partial L}{\partial \psi} \right) \right) dy_1, \ldots, dy_T = 0$$

which becomes

$$\int \cdots \int \left(\left(\frac{1}{L} \frac{\partial L}{\partial \psi} \right)^2 + \frac{\partial^2 \log L}{\partial \psi^2} \right) L \, dy_1, \ldots, dy_T = 0 \tag{2.9}$$

Rearranging (2.9) then gives

$$E[\{ D \log L(\psi) \}^2] = -E[D^2 \log L(\psi)] = I(\psi) \tag{2.10}$$

If $\hat{\psi}$ denotes an unbiased estimator of ψ, then by definition

$$E(\hat{\psi}) = \int \cdots \int \hat{\psi} L \, dy_1, \ldots, dy_T = \psi \tag{2.11}$$

Differentiating (2.11) yields

$$\int \cdots \int \hat{\psi} D \log L(\psi) L \, dy_1, \ldots, dy_T = 1 \tag{2.12}$$

From (2.8), $E[D \log L(\psi)] = 0$ and so

*Indicates a more difficult section which may be omitted without loss of continuity.

$$E[\psi\ D \log L(\psi)] = \psi \cdot E[D \log L(\psi)] = 0$$

Incorporating this result into (2.12) gives

$$1 = \int \cdots \int (\hat{\psi} - \psi)\ D \log L(\psi) \cdot L\ dy_1, \ldots, dy_T$$

and so, by the Cauchy–Schwartz inequality,

$$1 \leq \left[\int \cdots \int (\hat{\psi} - \psi)^2 L\ dy_1, \ldots, dy_T \right]$$

$$\times \left[\int \cdots \int \{D \log L(\psi)\}^2 L\ dy_1, \ldots, dy_T \right] \qquad (2.13)$$

The first term on the r.h.s. of (2.13) is $E[(\hat{\psi} - \psi)^2]$. The second is the information, $I(\psi)$, defined in (2.10). Re–arranging (2.13) gives the *Cramér–Rao inequality*

$$\mathrm{Var}(\hat{\psi}) \geq 1/I(\psi) \qquad (2.14)$$

3.3. Properties of the Maximum Likelihood Estimator

It follows from the factorisation theorem, (2.1), that the ML estimator of ψ is a function of the sufficient statistic. This means that the ML estimator depends only on relevant information in the sample, although it does not necessarily mean that it uses that information in the best possible way. Nevertheless, when there exists an unbiased estimator whose variance attains the lower bound, this estimator is identical to the ML estimator.

Unfortunately the MVB is often unattainable. This was illustrated in the last example, in connection with the estimation of σ^2. Indeed in this case, the ML estimator, (1.8b), is biased. However, since $E(\tilde{\sigma}^2) = \sigma^2(T - 1)/T$, the bias becomes negligible as T becomes large. Furthermore the variance of $\tilde{\sigma}^2$ tends towards the MVB of $2\sigma^4/T$. Taken together, these results are indicative of a more general result, namely that ML estimators normally attain the Cramér–Rao lower bound in large samples.

Suppose that the information matrix, $I(\psi)$, divided by T converges to a p.d. matrix $IA(\psi)$ as $T \rightarrow \infty$, i.e.

$$IA(\psi) = \lim T^{-1}I(\psi) \qquad (3.1)$$

Then, subject to certain regularity conditions $\sqrt{T}(\hat{\psi} - \psi)$ has a limiting multivariate normal distribution with mean vector zero and covariance matrix,

$IA^{-1}(\psi)$. The same result is implied by the statement that $\tilde{\psi}$ is asymptotically normal with mean ψ and covariance matrix,

$$\mathrm{Avar}(\tilde{\psi}) = T^{-1}IA^{-1}(\psi) \tag{3.2}$$

Compare the discussion in Section 2.3. The proof is set out below for a single parameter.

Because ML estimators attain the MVB in large samples, they are said to be asymptotically efficient. Suppose that $\tilde{\psi}$ is the ML estimator of a single parameter, ψ, and that $\hat{\psi}$ is another estimator, which is asymptotically normal with mean ψ and variance, $\mathrm{Avar}(\hat{\psi})$. The *asymptotic efficiency* of $\hat{\psi}$ is given by

$$\mathrm{Eff}(\hat{\psi}) = \mathrm{Avar}(\tilde{\psi})/\mathrm{Avar}(\hat{\psi}) = T^{-1}IA^{-1}(\psi)/\mathrm{Avar}(\hat{\psi}) \tag{3.3}$$

In general, asymptotic efficiency is the only theoretical guide to the relative merits of different estimators in econometrics and time series analysis. Exact finite sample distributions are difficult to obtain, and even when they are available, a measure analogous to (3.3) is only really applicable if both estimators are normal.

Derivation of the Asymptotic Distribution of the Maximum Likelihood Estimator*

Consider a sample of T independent observations drawn from a p.d.f. containing a single unknown parameter, ψ. The likelihood function, which is of the form (1.2), may be expanded around the true value of ψ using Taylor's theorem. This yields:

$$D \log L(\tilde{\psi}) \simeq D \log L(\psi) + (\tilde{\psi} - \psi) D^2 \log L(\psi) \tag{3.4}$$

The leading term in the remainder of the expansion involves $(\tilde{\psi} - \psi)^2$, and it may be shown to be of a smaller order than $(\tilde{\psi} - \psi) \, D^2 \log L(\psi)$ when the regularity conditions are satisfied.

By definition, $D \log L(\tilde{\psi})$ is equal to zero, and so (3.4) may be rearranged to give

$$\sqrt{T}(\tilde{\psi} - \psi) \simeq \frac{-\sqrt{T} \, D \log L(\psi)}{D^2 \log L(\psi)} \tag{3.5}$$

From (1.2) it will be seen that $D \log L(\psi)$ is actually the sum of T identically distributed independent random variables, since

$$D \log L(\psi) = \sum_{t=1}^{T} \frac{\partial \log p(y_t; \psi)}{\partial \psi} = \sum_{t=1}^{T} D \log p(y_t; \psi)$$

The random variable, $D \log p(y_t; \psi)$, may be regarded as the derivative of a log−likelihood for a sample of size one, and from (2.8) and (2.10) it follows that it has zero expectation and variance $i(\psi)$ for $t = 1, \ldots, T$. The lower case notation, $i(\psi)$, indicates the information for a single observation. For the full sample

$$I(\psi) = T \cdot i(\psi) \qquad (3.6)$$

and so $D \log L(\psi)$ has zero expectation and variance $I(\psi)$. Under the regularity conditions (3.1) will hold, and so, from the Central Limit Theorem, $\xi = T^{-1/2} D \log L(\psi)/\sqrt{I(\psi)/T}$ has a limiting standardised normal distribution, i.e.,

$$\xi \xrightarrow{\ L\ } N(0, 1).$$

Substituting for $D \log L (\psi)$ in (3.5) yields

$$\sqrt{T}(\tilde{\psi} - \psi) \simeq \frac{\sqrt{I(\psi)/T}}{D^2 \log L(\psi)/T} \cdot \xi$$

Since

$$\text{plim} \left\{ \frac{\sqrt{I(\psi)/T}}{D^2 \log L(\psi)/T} \right\} = \{IA(\psi)\}^{-1/2}$$

it follows from Cramér's theorem, (1.4.17), that $\sqrt{T}(\tilde{\psi} - \psi)$ has a limiting normal distribution with mean zero and variance $IA^{-1}(\psi)$.

3.4. Maximum Likelihood Estimation of Regression Models

This section begins by examining the relationship between ML and OLS in a classical linear regression model. The results are then extended to cover the non-linear case, and in the last sub-sections the estimation of models for count data and qualitative observations is considered.

The ML estimation of linear regression models with heteroscedastic disturbances is also examined. Models of this kind represent something of a departure from the usual ML framework in that although the observations are independently distributed, they are no longer identically distributed. However, the results on asymptotic efficiency continue to hold and the properties of the ML estimators may be determined exactly as before. In a similar way, ML theory can be extended to cover systems of equations. The SURE model of Section 2.9 provides an illustration.

The Classical Linear Regression Model

The log−likelihood function for the classical linear regression model (2.1.5) with normally distributed disturbances is

$$\log L(\beta, \sigma^2) = -\frac{T}{2}\log 2\pi - \frac{T}{2}\log \sigma^2$$

$$- \frac{1}{2\sigma^2}(y - X\beta)'(y - X\beta) \tag{4.1}$$

Maximising (4.1) with respect to β and σ^2 yields the estimators

$$\tilde{\beta} = b = (X'X)^{-1}X'y \tag{4.2}$$

and

$$\tilde{\sigma}^2 = e'e/T \tag{4.3}$$

The estimator of β is identical to the OLS estimator, (2.2.4). If the log−likelihood function is written in the form

$$\log L(\beta, \sigma^2) = -\frac{T}{2}\log 2\pi - \frac{T}{2}\log \sigma^2 - \frac{1}{2\sigma^2}S(\beta) \tag{4.4}$$

where $S(\beta)$ is the sum of squares function defined in (2.2.1), the reason for this correspondence becomes clear: $\partial S(\beta)/\partial \beta = 0$ implies that $\partial \log L/\partial \beta = 0$.

The information matrix is

$$I(\beta, \sigma^2) = \begin{pmatrix} \sigma^{-2}X'X & 0 \\ 0 & T/2\sigma^4 \end{pmatrix} \tag{4.5}$$

which is an obvious generalisation of (2.6), the information matrix associated with the estimator of a population mean. It was shown in Section 2.3 that the OLS estimator of β is normally distributed with mean β and covariance matrix, $\sigma^2(X'X)^{-1}$. Hence it attains the lower bound and so is the MVUE of β. However, as in the location model, $\tilde{\sigma}^2$ is biased and s^2, the unbiased estimator, fails to attain the lower bound.

Although the MVB for σ^2 is unattainable in finite samples, both $\tilde{\sigma}^2$ and s^2 are MVB estimators in large samples. In the case of s^2, it was shown in Section 2.7 that $\text{Var}(s^2) = 2\sigma^4/(T - k)$. While this variance exceeds the MVB of $2\sigma^4/T$ in small samples, it obviously tends towards it as $T \to \infty$.

Non-Linear Regression

Some examples of non-linear regression models were given in Section 2.1. A general formulation is as follows:

$$y_t = f(x_t; \beta) + \epsilon_t, \quad t = 1, \ldots, T \tag{4.6}$$

where x_t is a $k \times 1$ vector of exogenous variables, β is an $n \times 1$ vector of parameters, and $f(x_t; \beta)$ denotes a function of x_t and β. If the disturbances are normally distributed the log−likelihood function can be written as in (4.4), with

$$S(\beta) = \sum_{j=1}^{T} \{ y_t - f(x_t;\beta) \}^2 \tag{4.7}$$

defining the sum of squares function. The non-linear (ordinary) least squares estimator of β, b, is therefore identical to the ML estimator.

Differentiating the log−likelihood function with respect to β yields

$$\frac{\partial \log L}{\partial \beta} = \sigma^{-2} \sum z_t \{ y_t - f(x_t; \beta) \} \tag{4.8}$$

where

$$z_t = \frac{\partial f(x_t; \beta)}{\partial \beta} = -\frac{\partial \epsilon_t}{\partial \beta}, \qquad t = 1, \ldots, T \tag{4.9}$$

Differentiating a second time leads to the expression

$$E\left\{ -\frac{\partial^2 \log L}{\partial \beta \, \partial \beta'} \right\} = \sigma^{-2} \sum z_t z_t' \tag{4.10}$$

The off-diagonal blocks in the information matrix, $I(\beta, \sigma^2)$, are null since

$$E\left\{ -\frac{\partial^2 \log L}{\partial \beta \, \partial \sigma^2} \right\} = E\{ \sigma^{-4} \sum z_t \epsilon_t \} = 0 \tag{4.11}$$

The result follows immediately because the elements of z_t are fixed.

Under suitable regularity conditions, therefore,

$$b \sim AN \{ \beta, \sigma^2 (\sum z_t z_t')^{-1} \} \tag{4.12}$$

The regularity conditions are similar to those imposed in the linear model. In particular the condition that $\lim T^{-1} \sum z_t z_t'$ converges to a p.d. matrix is a natural extension of (2.3.9). The large sample properties of the ML estimator of σ^2 are exactly as in the linear model with

$$\hat{\sigma}^2 \sim AN(\sigma^2, 2\sigma^4/T) \tag{4.13}$$

If normality of the disturbances is not assumed, the non-linear least squares estimator will, in general, still have the large sample distribution indicated by (4.12); cf. the discussion in Section 2.3.

Multiplicative Heteroscedasticity

Consider a regression model of the form

$$y_t = x_t' \beta + u_t, \qquad t = 1, \ldots, T \tag{4.14}$$

in which the disturbances are independently distributed about a mean of zero, but have a variance given by the expression

$$\sigma_t^2 = \exp(w_t' \delta), \qquad t = 1, \ldots, T \tag{4.15}$$

where w_t is an $r \times 1$ vector of non-stochastic, known variables, and δ is an $r \times 1$ vector of unknown parameters. The variables in w_t may, or may not be related to the elements of x_t. The parameter vectors β and δ, however, contain no elements in common. In general the first element of w_t will be unity.

The specification (4.15) is known as *multiplicative heteroscedasticity*. It encompasses a number of special cases which are of some interest. For example, if $w_t = [1, \log x_{jt}]'$ and $\delta = [\log \sigma^2, \alpha]'$

$$\sigma_t^2 = \sigma^2 x_{jt}^\alpha \tag{4.16}$$

Thus the variance is proportional to the *j*th explanatory variable raised to the power α.

The log-likelihood function is given by

$$\log L(\beta, \delta) = -\frac{T}{2} \log 2\pi - \frac{1}{2} \sum w_t' \delta$$

$$- \frac{1}{2} \sum \exp(-w_t' \delta)(y_t - x_t' \beta)^2 \tag{4.17}$$

Differentiating (4.17) with respect to β and δ yields

$$\frac{\partial \log L}{\partial \beta} = \sum x_t \exp(-w_t' \delta)(y_t - x_t' \beta) \tag{4.18}$$

and

$$\frac{\partial \log L}{\partial \delta} = -\frac{1}{2} \sum w_t + \frac{1}{2} \sum w_t \exp(-w_t' \delta)(y_t - x_t' \beta)^2 \tag{4.19}$$

Differentiating a second time, multiplying by minus one and taking expectations gives the information matrix

$$I(\beta, \delta) = \begin{pmatrix} \sum \sigma_t^{-2} x_t x_t' & 0 \\ 0 & \frac{1}{2} \sum w_t w_t' \end{pmatrix} \tag{4.20}$$

The ML estimators, $\tilde{\beta}$ and $\tilde{\delta}$, are obtained by setting the first derivatives, (4.18) and (4.19), equal to zero and solving the resulting non−linear equations; see Section 4.4 of the next chapter. Under suitable regularity conditions it can be shown that $\tilde{\beta}$ and $\tilde{\delta}$ are asymptotically normal with a covariance matrix given by the asymptotic information matrix. In view of the block diagonality of (4.20), $\tilde{\beta}$ and $\tilde{\delta}$ are independently distributed in large samples and so

$$\tilde{\beta} \sim AN[\beta, (\sum \sigma_t^{-2} x_t x_t')^{-1}] \qquad (4.21)$$

while

$$\tilde{\delta} \sim AN[\delta, 2(\sum w_t w_t')^{-1}] \qquad (4.22)$$

Dependent Variable Heteroscedasticity

If the variance of the dependent variable is proportional to the square of its expectation, the variance of the disturbance term in (4.14) may be written

$$\sigma_t^2 = \sigma^2 (x_t' \beta)^2, \qquad t = 1, \ldots, T \qquad (4.23)$$

and under the normality assumption

$$I(\beta, \sigma^2) = \begin{pmatrix} (2\sigma^2 + 1)\sum \sigma_t^{-2} x_t x_t' & (\sum \sigma_t^{-2} x_t x_t')\beta \\ \beta' \sum \sigma_t^{-2} x_t x_t' & T/2\sigma^4 \end{pmatrix} \qquad (4.24)$$

Unlike (4.20), the information matrix is not block diagonal, and so the ML estimators of β and σ^2 are not independently distributed in large samples. This has some important implications. For example, suppose an estimator is constructed by first applying OLS and then computing the WLS estimator

$$\hat{\beta} = [\sum (x_t' b)^{-2} x_t x_t']^{-1} \sum (x_t' b)^{-2} x_t y_t \qquad (4.25)$$

This has the same large sample distribution as a WLS estimator in which the observations are weighted by the true variances, $\sigma_1^2, \ldots, \sigma_T^2$; see Theil (1971, Ch. 8). Thus it is asymptotically normal with mean β and variance

$$\text{Avar}(\hat{\beta}) = [\sum \sigma_t^{-2} x_t x_t']^{-1} \qquad (4.26)$$

However, a comparison of (4.26) with the lower bound matrix obtained by inverting (4.24) shows $\hat{\beta}$ to be inefficient; see Amemiya (1973). If the disturbances in a model exhibiting this type of heteroscedasticity are normal, therefore, ML estimation is to be preferred over a feasible GLS procedure. Whether or not the normality assumption is a sensible one in the context of dependent variable heteroscedasticity is open to question. Normal variables may, in theory, be negative and the possibility of negative values for the expected value of the dependent variable could yield a strange relationship between σ_t^2 and the explanatory variables. In fact dependent variable heteroscedasticity makes much more sense if the observations are drawn from a gamma distribution

$$p(y_t) = \frac{1}{\Gamma(\lambda)} \left[\frac{\lambda}{x_t'\beta} \right]^{\lambda} y_t^{\lambda-1} \exp \left[\frac{-\lambda y_t}{x_t'\beta} \right], \quad y_t \geq 0 \qquad (4.27)$$

where $\Gamma(\lambda)$ is the gamma function and λ is a positive scalar parameter. The observations cannot be negative and properties of the gamma distribution are such that the mean of y_t is $x_t'\beta$ while its variance is given by (4.23) with $\sigma^2 = 1/\lambda$. Thus the model can still be expressed in the regression form, (4.14), although it is more natural to think of the specification in terms of the distribution of y_t rather than that of the disturbance. In fact this brings home an important point, namely that, within a maximum likelihood framework, the specification of a model is in terms of a distribution for the observations rather than for the disturbances. This point will also become apparent in the sub-sections on count data and qualitative observations.

This information matrix for observations following a gamma distribution is block diagonal with respect to β and λ, and the asymptotic variance of the ML estimator of β is given by the same expression as (4.26) and so WLS is fully efficient; again see Amemiya (1973) for details. A case of particular interest is the exponential distribution. This is a gamma distribution with λ equal to unity. The evaluation of the information matrix is relatively straightforward and is left as an exercise for the reader; see exercise 5.

Seemingly Unrelated Regressions

The SURE system was introduced in Section 2.9. Writing the model in the form (2.9.15), the joint density of the N observations at time t is given by

$$p(y_t) = (2\pi)^{-N/2} \cdot |\Omega|^{-1/2} \cdot \exp \{ -\tfrac{1}{2}(y_t - X_t\beta)'\Omega^{-1}(y_t - X_t\beta)\}$$

The log−likelihood function for all T sets of observations is therefore

$$\log L = -\frac{TN}{2} \log 2\pi - \frac{T}{2} \log |\Omega|$$

$$-\frac{1}{2} \sum_{t=1}^{T} (y_t - X_t\beta)'\Omega^{-1}(y_t - X_t\beta) \qquad (4.28)$$

Differentiating with respect to β yields

$$\frac{\partial \log L}{\partial \beta} = \sum X_t'\Omega^{-1}(y_t - X_t\beta) \qquad (4.29)$$

Compare this result with (A.3). Setting (4.29) equal to zero and rearranging gives the SURE estimator (2.9.17). However, this can only be computed if Ω is known.

Differentiating $\log L$ with respect to Ω is less straightforward. However, by making use of results (A.5) and (A.6), the derivatives of $\log L$ with respect to the elements of the inverse of Ω are readily obtainable. Thus

$$\frac{\partial \log L}{\partial \Omega^{-1}} = \frac{T}{2} \Omega - \frac{1}{2} \sum_{j=1}^{T} (y_t - X_t\beta)(y_t - X_t\beta)' \qquad (4.30)$$

a standard result on determinants having been used to set

$$-\frac{T}{2} \log |\Omega| = -\frac{T}{2} \log |\Omega^{-1}|^{-1} = \frac{T}{2} \log |\Omega^{-1}| \qquad (4.31)$$

in the likelihood function. Because of the invariance property of ML estimators, the ML estimator of Ω is equal to the inverse of the ML estimator of Ω^{-1}. Thus setting (4.30) equal to a matrix of zeros and solving will yield the ML estimators of both Ω^{-1} and Ω. In fact it is Ω which is of primary interest, and the ML estimator is given directly as

$$\tilde{\Omega} = T^{-1} \sum_{t=1}^{T} e_t e_t' \qquad (4.32)$$

where $e_t = y_t - X_t\tilde{\beta}$.

Count Data

It is not unusual to find time series consisting of *count data*. Such series record the number of events of a particular type occurring in a given interval. Examples might include the number of accidents in a factory or the number of patents taken out. Since the data must consist of non-negative integers a model based on the normal distribution is not admissible, although it might provide a reasonable approximation if the number of events observed in each time period is relatively large. For small numbers, the appropriate distribution is a Poisson or negative binomial. Models of this kind fall within the generalised linear model (GLIM) framework described by McCullagh and Nelder (1983) and they may be handled by the associated GLIM package.

If the observation at time t is drawn from a Poisson distribution with mean μ_t, its p.d.f. is

$$p(y_t) = \mu_t^{y_t} e^{-\mu_t}/y_t!, \qquad t = 1, \ldots, T \qquad (4.33)$$

When μ_t is a constant, it is easy to show that the ML estimator is just the sample mean. Our interest is in the more general case when μ_t depends on a set of k observable explanatory variables. These are related to μ_t via a *link function*. The most straightforward link function is

$$\mu_t = x_t'\beta \tag{4.34a}$$

Alternatively, since μ_t must be positive, the exponential link function

$$\mu_t = \exp(x_t'\beta) \tag{4.34b}$$

may be a better choice. The fact that the explanatory variables enter into both link functions as the linear combination, $x_t'\beta$, makes the model relatively easy to handle. The development below is in terms of (4.34a).

Given a set of independent observations the log–likelihood function is

$$\log L(y;\beta) = \sum_{t=1}^{T} y_t \log (x_t'\beta) - \sum x_t'\beta - \sum_{t=1}^{T} \log y_t! \tag{4.35}$$

Differentiating with respect to the parameter vector β gives the vector of first derivatives

$$\frac{\partial \log L}{\partial \beta} = \sum_{t=1}^{T} \frac{y_t}{x_t'\beta} x_t - \sum_{t=1}^{T} x_t \tag{4.36}$$

The likelihood equations are non–linear, but as will be seen in the next chapter, the structure of the link function leads to an easily implemented iterative algorithm in terms of WLS regression. Furthermore taking second derivatives gives

$$\frac{\partial^2 \log L}{\partial \beta \partial \beta'} = - \sum_{t=1}^{T} \frac{y_t}{(x_t'\beta)^2} x_t x_t' \tag{4.37}$$

Provided $T \geq k$ and the variables in x_t are not collinear, expression (4.37) must be negative definite for all values of β. Thus the log–likelihood is concave and the ML estimator is unique.

Multiplying (4.37) by minus one and taking expectations yields the information matrix from which

$$\text{Avar}(\beta) = \left[\sum_{t=1}^{T} \frac{1}{x_t'\beta} x_t x_t' \right]^{-1} \tag{4.38}$$

Qualitative Dependent Variables

Suppose that cross-sectional data on a sample of N households is available, and that car ownership is to be modelled in terms of a number of variables such as income, family size and geographical location. The dependent variable, y_j, is then dichotomous, since it takes a value of one if a family owns a car and a value of zero otherwise. If π_j denotes the probability of the jth family owning a car, y_j has a binomial distribution with

$$\left. \begin{array}{l} Pr(y_j = 1) = \pi_j \\[2mm] Pr(y_j = 0) = 1 - \pi_j \end{array} \right\} \quad j = 1, \ldots, N \qquad (4.39)$$

The specification of the model is completed by a link function which relates π_j to the set of k explanatory variables, x_j. The usual link function is the *logit* function

$$\pi_j = \frac{1}{1 + \exp(-x_j'\beta)} = \frac{\exp(x_j'\beta)}{\exp(x_j'\beta) + 1} \qquad (4.40)$$

where β is a $k \times 1$ vector of unknown parameters. This function has the property that π_j must be between zero and unity, irrespective of the values of x_j and β. If x_j consists of a single explanatory variable and a constant term, a plot of π_j against the explanatory variable takes the form of a logistic curve. Note that the specification in (4.40) can also be expressed in terms of the log-odds ratio

$$\log\{\pi_j/(1 - \pi_j)\} = x_j'\beta \qquad (4.41)$$

In fact the log-odds ratio is often referred to as the *logit*.

Without any loss in generality the observations may be arranged in such a way that those for households with cars are indexed $i = 1, \ldots, M$. Assuming the observations to be independent their joint density function is the product of the probabilities of each of the first M households having a car multiplied by the product of the probabilities of each of the remaining $N - M$ households not having a car. That is

$$p(y_1, \ldots, y_N) = \prod_{i=1}^{M} \pi_i \prod_{i=M+1}^{N} (1 - \pi_i)$$

Thus, with the logit link function, the log–likelihood is

$$\log L(y;\beta) = \sum_{i=1}^{M} x_i'\beta - \sum_{i=1}^{N} \log\{1 + \exp(x_i'\beta)\}. \qquad (4.42)$$

Differentiating the log–likelihood function with respect to the unknown parameters given

$$\frac{\partial \log L}{\partial \beta} = \sum_{i=1}^{M} (1 - \pi_i)x_i - \sum_{i=M+1}^{N} \pi_i x_i \qquad (4.43)$$

and then

$$\frac{\partial^2 \log L}{\partial \beta \, \partial \beta'} = -\sum_{i=1}^{N} \pi_i (1 - \pi_i) x_i x_i' \qquad (4.44)$$

As in the Poisson regression model, this matrix of second derivatives is negative definite provided that $N \geq k$ and the explanatory variables are not collinear. Hence the ML estimator is unique, and its asymptotic variance is given by multiplying the inverse of (4.44) by minus one.

When a nominal variable has more than two categories, the observations are said to be polytomous, and a multinomial distribution is appropriate. Logistic link functions can again be used to capture the relationship between the probability of an observation falling in a given category and the relevant explanatory variables.

3.5. Dependent Observations

In a time series model the observations are, by definition, dependent. This immediately raises the question of whether the standard results on the properties of the ML estimator are still valid. The theorems normally presented rest on the assumption that the observations are independently and identically distributed. This is needed in order to invoke the classical Central Limit Theorem. However, it was argued in the last section that the usual ML results carry through if the assumption of identically distributed observations is dropped. This is also, in general, the case with dependent observations and it will be assumed throughout this book that the ML estimator of a parameter vector, ψ, is asymptotically normal with a mean of ψ and a covariance matrix equal to the inverse of the information matrix.

This section is concerned with the practical question of constructing the likelihood function for a set of dependent observations. This is done by expressing the joint density function in terms of conditional densities.

Likelihood Function

When the observations are dependent, their joint density function can no longer be expressed in the form (1.2). However, it can be written down in terms of a series of conditional probability density functions. Suppose that there are only two observations. Their joint density function can be factorised as

$$p(y_2, y_1) = p(y_2 | y_1) p(y_1) \qquad (5.1)$$

where $p(y_2|y_1)$ denotes the p.d.f. of y_2, conditional on the value of the previous observation, y_1. In a similar way, the joint p.d.f. for three observations can be written as

$$p(y_3, y_2, y_1) = p(y_3|y_2, y_1)p(y_2, y_1) \qquad (5.2)$$

and, on substituting from (5.1),

$$p(y_3, y_2, y_1) = p(y_3|y_2, y_1)p(y_2|y_1)p(y_1) \qquad (5.3)$$

It should now be clear that the likelihood function for T observations can be obtained by writing the joint p.d.f. as

$$L(y;\psi) = \prod_{t=2}^{T} p(y_t|Y_{t-1})p(y_1) \qquad (5.4)$$

where Y_{t-1} denotes the set of observations up to, and including, y_{t-1}.

Many time series models are effectively specified in terms of a conditional distribution for each observation. Thus the first-order autoregressive model

$$y_t = \phi y_{t-1} + \epsilon_t, \qquad \epsilon_t \sim \text{NID}(0, \sigma^2) \qquad (5.5)$$

can also be specified by stating that the distribution of y_t, conditional on y_{t-1}, is normal with mean ϕy_{t-1} and variance, σ^2. In other words $p(y_t|y_{t-1}, \ldots, y_1)$ is $N(\phi y_{t-1}, \sigma^2)$. Given this interpretation, the log-likelihood function can be written down directly:

$$\log L(y, \phi, \sigma^2) = \frac{-(T-1)}{2} \log 2\pi - \frac{(T-1)}{2} \log \sigma^2$$

$$- \frac{1}{2\sigma^2} \sum_{t=2}^{T} (y_t - \phi y_{t-1})^2 + \log p(y_1) \qquad (5.6)$$

All that remains is to consider the treatment of the initial conditions as reflected in the distribution of y_1. If y_1 is regarded as being fixed in repeated realisations, then $p(y_1)$ does not enter into the likelihood function and the last term in (5.6) can be dropped. The ML estimator of ϕ is then linear, being given by a regression of y_t on y_{t-1}. On the other hand, if it can be assumed that $|\phi| < 1$, so that the process is stationary, the unconditional distribution of y_1 is known to be normal with mean zero and variance $\sigma^2/(1 - \phi^2)$. The likelihood function is therefore

$$\log L(y) = -\frac{T}{2} \log 2\pi - \frac{T}{2} \log \sigma^2 + \frac{1}{2} \log(1 - \phi^2)$$

$$- \frac{1}{2} \sigma^{-2}(1 - \phi^2)y_1^2 - \frac{1}{2} \sigma^{-2} \sum_{t=2}^{T} (y_t - \phi y_{t-1})^2$$

$$(5.7)$$

In this case, the ML estimator is no longer linear. Clearly this is less convenient, and so the third and fourth terms are often dropped from (5.7). The corresponding approximate ML estimator of ϕ is then linear and is the same as the estimator obtained under the assumption that y_1 is fixed. Since only one observation is involved in this simplification, the large sample properties of the estimator are not affected.

The treatment of the MA(1) model is less straightforward. The conditional distribution of y_t implied by (1.2.13) is normal with mean $\theta \epsilon_{t-1}$ and variance σ^2. The problem is that ϵ_{t-1} is not directly observable. However, if ϵ_0 is taken to be fixed and equal to zero, the full set of disturbances can be computed recursively by rearranging (1.2.13) to give

$$\epsilon_t = y_t - \theta \epsilon_{t-1}, \qquad t = 1, \ldots, T \tag{5.8}$$

with $\epsilon_0 = 0$. The likelihood function is therefore

$$\log L = -\frac{T}{2} \log 2\pi - \frac{T}{2} \log \sigma^2 - \frac{1}{2\sigma^2} \sum_{t=1}^{T} (y_t - \theta \epsilon_{t-1})^2 \tag{5.9}$$

and this must be maximised non-linearly with respect to θ. Alternatively, the sum of squares, $\Sigma \epsilon_t^2$, may be minimised. If the initial disturbance is to have the same property as the other disturbances, namely to be normal with mean zero and variance σ^2, the computation of the likelihood function is more difficult. It may be carried out *via* the prediction error decomposition; see the comments below (5.13).

Prediction Error Decomposition

The mean of the conditional distribution of y_t, $E(y_t|y_{t-1}, \ldots, y_1)$, is the optimal predictor of y_t in the sense that if minimises the prediction mean square error. The variance of the corresponding prediction error

$$v_t = y_t - E(y_t|Y_{t-1}) \tag{5.10}$$

is the same as the conditional variance of y_t, that is

$$\text{Var}(v_t) = \text{Var}(y_t|Y_{t-1}) \tag{5.11}$$

Rather than expressing the likelihood function, (5.4), in terms of the observations it can be expressed in terms of the prediction errors. This is known as the *prediction error decomposition*. This form of the likelihood function is particularly relevant for normally distributed observations and the remaining discussion will be based on this assumption. Writing

$$\text{Var}(v_t) = \sigma^2 f_t, \qquad t = 1, \ldots, T \tag{5.12}$$

where σ^2 is a parameter, the prediction error decomposition yields

$$\log L(y;\psi) = -\frac{T}{2}\log 2\pi - \frac{T}{2}\log \sigma^2 - \frac{1}{2}\sum_{t=1}^{T}\log f_t$$

$$- \frac{1}{2}\sigma^{-2}\sum_{t=1}^{T} v_t^2/f_t \qquad (5.13)$$

Thus for the AR(1) model, $f_t = 1$ for $t = 2, \ldots, T$ while $f_1 = 1/(1 - \phi^2)$. For more complicated linear time series models the prediction error decomposition form of the likelihood can be computed by casting the model in state space form and applying the Kalman filter. This approach is discussed in some detail in Harvey (1981, Ch.5) and Harvey (1989, Ch.3). It applies to structural time series models as well as ARMA models.

Considerable simplification can usually be achieved in the prediction error decomposition if it is felt that an approximation to the likelihood will be adequate. As a general rule, an approximation can be justified on theoretical grounds by making certain assumptions about the initial observations. This usually results in prediction errors with a constant variance, σ^2, and so $f_t = 1$ for all t. The log–likelihood function becomes

$$\log L = -\frac{T}{2}\log 2\pi - \frac{T}{2}\log \sigma^2 - \frac{1}{2}\sigma^{-2}\sum v_t^2 \qquad (5.14)$$

and maximising a likelihood function of this form is equivalent to minimising the sum of squares function

$$S(\psi) = \sum v_t^2 \qquad (5.15)$$

If the model contains only a single disturbance term, ϵ_t, this disturbance term will coincide with the prediction error in (5.15). Hence the sum of squares function can be written as

$$S(\psi) = \sum \epsilon_t^2 \qquad (5.16)$$

In the AR(1) model, maximising the likelihood function, (5.6), with y_1 treated as fixed leads to minimisation of a sum of squares function of the form (5.16) with the summation running from $t = 2$ to T. In the MA(1) model, with $\epsilon_0 = 0$, maximising (5.9) is equivalent to minimising (5.16) in view of the definition of ϵ_t in (5.8).

Further insight into the nature of the prediction error decomposition is obtained in cases where a model can be specified in terms of a multivariate normal distribution for the vector of observations y. Thus $y \sim N(\mu, \sigma^2 V)$, where μ is a mean vector and V is a $T \times T$ p.d. matrix. The scalar quantity σ^2 is introduced as a matter of convenience as in (2.4.1). The elements of μ may or may not be identical. Thus if $\mu = X\beta$, the generalised regression model of Section 2.4 is obtained. In general μ and V will depend on an unknown set of parameters ψ and the joint density function is

$$\log L(y;\psi) = -\frac{T}{2} \log 2\pi - \frac{T}{2} \log \sigma^2 - \frac{1}{2} \log |V|$$

$$-\frac{1}{2} \sigma^{-2}(y - \mu)' V^{-1}(y - \mu) \tag{5.17}$$

The inversion of the $T \times T$ matrix V may be time consuming and so evaluating the likelihood function directly from (5.17) may not be an attractive proposition, particularly if this has to be carried out repeatedly within a numerical optimisation procedure. The usual approach is to carry out a Cholesky decomposition of V^{-1}. If $\bar{L}$ is a lower triangular matrix with ones on the leading diagonal, V^{-1} may be factorised as

$$V^{-1} = \bar{L}'D\bar{L} \tag{5.18}$$

where $D = \text{diag}(f_1^{-1}, \ldots, f_T^{-1})$. This factorisation is unique and the $T \times 1$ vector of prediction errors defined by (5.10) is given by the transformation $v = \bar{L}y$. Thus substituting for V^{-1} in (5.17) and noting that

$$|V^{-1}| = |\bar{L}'| \cdot |D| \cdot |\bar{L}| = D = \prod_{t=1}^{T} f_t$$

leads directly to the prediction error decomposition form of the likelihood function (5.13).

Non-Linear Models

In a linear model, each observation can be expressed as a linear combination of current and past disturbances. If these are normally distributed, the full set of observations will have a multivariate normal distribution as in (5.17). In a non-linear model, on the other hand, specifying the conditional distribution of each observation to be normal no longer implies that the unconditional distribution of the observations is normal. From the point of view of constructing the likelihood function, this does not really matter. As we saw at the beginning of this section, specifying a time series model in terms of conditional distributions is a natural way to proceed and it leads directly to a likelihood function of the form (5.4). Indeed the likelihood function can be expressed in this way even if the conditional distribution of each observation is not normal. However, the assumption of normality is very common and models of this kind are referred to as being *conditionally Gaussian*.

   Example 1 The AR(1) model, (5.5), can be expressed as a linear combination of past disturbances as in (2.5.5). If these disturbances are normally distributed, the unconditional distribution of each observation is normal with mean zero and variance $\sigma^2/(1 - \phi^2)$. In fact this result was used to construct the exact likelihood of an AR(1) model in (5.7) since it enabled $p(y_1)$ to be evaluated.

By way of contrast the model

$$y_t = \phi y_{t-1}^2 + \epsilon_t, \quad \epsilon_t \sim NID(0, \sigma^2) \tag{5.19}$$

cannot be written as a linear combination of past disturbances and so is nonlinear. However, it is conditionally Gaussian since the conditional distribution of y_t is $N(\phi y_{t-1}^2, \sigma^2)$. Thus if y_1 is fixed, the likelihood function can still be written down directly as

$$\log L = -\frac{(T-1)}{2} \log 2\pi - \frac{(T-1)}{2} \log \sigma^2$$
$$- \frac{1}{2\sigma^2} \sum_{t=2}^{T} (y_t - \phi y_{t-1}^2)^2. \tag{5.20}$$

Maximising this function is, of course, equivalent to minimising a sum of squares function of the form (5.16).

Example 2 The *autoregressive conditional heteroscedastic* (ARCH) model, introduced by Engle (1982), exhibits a form of serial correlation in the variance. It is a non-linear conditionally Gaussian model in which the conditional variance depends on previous disturbances. In a simple first-order ARCH model, the conditional distribution of y_t is assumed to be normal with mean μ_t and variance

$$\text{Var}(y_t | Y_{t-1}) = h_t = \alpha_0 + \alpha_1 \epsilon_{t-1}^2 \tag{5.21}$$

where $\epsilon_t = y_t - \mu_t$, and ϵ_0 is arbitrarily assumed to be fixed and equal to zero. The mean, μ_t, may depend on a set of unknown parameters which can be estimated, along with α_0 and α_1, by maximising the likelihood function

$$\log L = -\frac{T}{2} \log 2\pi - \frac{1}{2} \sum_{t=1}^{T} \log(\alpha_0 + \alpha_1 \epsilon_{t-1}^2)$$
$$- \frac{1}{2} \sum_{t=1}^{T} \frac{(y_t - \mu_t)^2}{\alpha_0 + \alpha_1 \epsilon_{t-1}^2} \tag{5.22}$$

The properties of the ARCH model will be discussed later in Section 6.9.

Asymptotic Properties

The asymptotic properties of ML estimators, described in Section 3, continue to hold if the observations are dependent. Once the joint density function has been broken down by the prediction error decomposition, suitable expressions for $IA(\psi)$ can be obtained fairly easily.

Example 3 The asymptotic properties of ML estimators in dynamic models are generally unaffected by the treatment of the initial observations. As was pointed out above, the likelihood in the AR(1) model simplifies considerably if y_1 is fixed. From the second derivatives of log L:

$$
IA(\phi, \sigma^2) = -T^{-1}E
\begin{bmatrix}
-\sigma^{-2}\sum y_{t-1}^2 & -\sigma^{-4}\sum \epsilon_t y_{t-1} \\
-\sigma^{-4}\sum \epsilon_t y_{t-1} & -\tfrac{1}{2}\sigma^{-6}\sum \epsilon_t^2
\end{bmatrix}
$$

$$
=
\begin{bmatrix}
1/(1 - \phi^2) & 0 \\
0 & 1/2\sigma^4
\end{bmatrix}
\tag{5.23}
$$

Therefore

$$
\text{Avar}(\tilde{\phi}, \tilde{\sigma}^2) =
\begin{bmatrix}
(1 - \phi^2)/T & 0 \\
0 & 2\sigma^4/T
\end{bmatrix}
\tag{5.24}
$$

More generally, if the likelihood function is of the form (5.14), the asymptotic information matrix is block diagonal with respect to ψ and σ^2, and

$$
\text{Avar}(\tilde{\psi}) = \sigma^2 T^{-1} \left[\text{plim } T^{-1} \sum_{t=1}^{T} z_t z_t' \right]^{-1} \simeq \sigma^2 \left(\sum_{t=1}^{T} z_t z_t' \right)^{-1}
\tag{5.25}
$$

where the vector $z_t = -\partial \epsilon_t/\partial \psi$ is evaluated at the true value of ψ.

Decomposition of the Likelihood Function for Multivariate Models

The prediction error decomposition may be extended to the multivariate case where an $N \times 1$ vector is observed at each point in time. The argument goes through exactly as before with v_t being an $N \times 1$ vector of prediction errors at time t, with mean zero and covariance matrix F_t. (There is less point in extracting a scalar quantity, σ^2, in the multivariate case.) The log–likelihood may be decomposed as

$$
\log L(y_1, \ldots, y_T) = -\frac{TN}{2} \log 2\pi - \frac{1}{2} \sum_{t=1}^{T} \log |F_t|
$$

$$
-\frac{1}{2} \sum_{t=1}^{T} v_t' F_t^{-1} v_t
\tag{5.26}
$$

where $y \sim N(\mu_1, F_1)$ and $v_1 = y_1 - \mu_1$.

The Kalman filter can again be used to effect the decomposition in (5.26) provided the underlying model can be expressed in state space form. However, as in the single equation case, it is often possible to approximate log L by identifying v_t with the vector of white noise disturbances driving the process. If $\epsilon_t \sim NID(0, \Omega)$, the approximation takes the form

$$\log L = -\frac{TN}{2} \log 2\pi - \frac{T}{2} \log |\Omega| - \frac{1}{2} \sum \epsilon_t' \Omega^{-1} \epsilon_t \qquad (5.27)$$

cf. the likelihood function for the SURE system, (4.28).

Example 4   If the initial vector, y_t, in the multivariate AR(1) process, (2.12.13) is taken to be fixed, the likelihood function is of the form (5.27) with $\epsilon_t = y_t - \Phi y_{t-1}$ for $t = 2, \ldots, T$. The ML estimator is the multivariate least squares estimator of (2.12.14).

3.6. Identifiability

Identifiability is a fundamental concept in model building. If a model cannot be identified, two issues are raised. Firstly, it is reasonable to ask whether the model actually makes sense in the way is has been specified. Secondly, and this is closely related to the first point, it is important to examine what meaning, if any, can be given to the estimates computed from a model which is not identified.

For any given model, therefore, it is important to specify conditions under which the model is, or is not, identifiable. In some cases these conditions may be trivial or they may be innocuously buried in the assumptions made when the model is formulated. In other situations is may be necessary to check explicitly the conditions for identifiability whenever a model is specified. As will be seen in Chapter 9, the conditions needed for identifiability play a prominent role in the construction of simultaneous equation systems. However, questions of identifiability can arise for much simpler models, as some of the examples given in this section will show.

The Concept of Identifiability

In order to discuss the meaning of identifiability, it is important to be clear about the distinction between a *model* and a *structure*. A structure is a model in which all the parameters are assigned numerical values. Thus

$$y_t = \beta_1 x_{1t} + \beta_2 x_{2t} + \epsilon_t, \qquad t = 1, \ldots, T \qquad (6.1)$$

with $\epsilon_t \sim NID(0, \sigma^2)$ is a model, while

$$y_t = 3x_{1t} + 2x_{2t} + \epsilon_t, \qquad t = 1, \ldots, T \qquad (6.2)$$

with $\epsilon_t \sim NID(0, 4)$ is a structure of that model.

A model specifies a distribution for the endogenous variables, conditional on any exogenous variables in the system. A structure specifies the parameters of that distribution. Given this background, the following concepts may be defined.

(a) If two structures have the same density function they are said to be *observationally equivalent*.

(b) A *structure* is identifiable if there exists no other observationally equivalent structure. If a structure is not identifiable, it is said to be *underidentified*.

(c) A *model* is *identifiable* if all its possible structures are identifiable. If no structure is identifiable, the model is said to be *underidentified*.

Identifiability has an immediate bearing on estimation. If two structures have the same joint density function, the probability of generating a particular set of observations is the same for both structures. Thus there is no way of differentiating between them on the basis of the data. Even if one of the structures could be deduced from the observations, it might prove difficult to give a meaningful interpretation to the parameters. However, it will often be the case that attempts to estimate structures which are not identifiable will run into practical difficulties.

Multicollinearity

The consequences of trying to estimate a model which is not identifiable are best developed by starting with an example. Consider the linear regression model (6.1) and suppose that the observations on the explanatory variable are such that $2x_{1t} = x_{2t}$ for all $t = 1, \ldots, T$. This is the case of *extreme* or *perfect multicollinearity* and it means that the model is not identifiable. Since

$$E(y_t) = \beta_1 x_{1t} + \beta_2 x_{2t} = (\beta_1 + 2\beta_2)x_{1t}, \qquad t = 1, \ldots, T$$

the distribution of the observations is not dependent on the individual values of β_1 and β_2, but only on the linear combination $\beta_1 + 2\beta_2$. Thus if (6.2) is a structure of the model, any other structure in which β_1 and β_2 satisfy the constraint

$$\beta_1 + 2\beta_2 = 7 \qquad (6.3)$$

will be observationally equivalent. Clearly, there are an infinite number of such structures, and so (6.2) is not identifiable. Furthermore, since any structure of (6.1) is not identifiable, the model itself is underidentified.

The lack of identifiability will become apparent if any attempt is made to estimate the model by OLS. The cross-product matrix, $X'X$, is singular and so formula (2.2.4) breaks down. If an 'inverse' of $X'X$ is obtained — which is always possible because of rounding error — the multicollinearity in the model will be signalled by enormous standard errors.

If one of the regressors, say x_2, is dropped, the model becomes

$$y_t = \beta x_{1t} + \epsilon_t, \qquad t = 1, \ldots, T \qquad (6.4)$$

where $\beta = \beta_1 + 2\beta_2$. The parameter β can then be estimated by OLS. However, although there is now no technical difficulty in running the regression, the identifiability problem has not been solved insofar as β is of no direct interest, while the parameters β_1 and β_2 have some economic meaning. If sensible estimators of β_1 and β_2 are to be obtained, some *a priori* information must be found. This information may take the form of restrictions which can be imposed on the model. If it can be assumed, for example, that $\beta_2 = 3\beta_1$, then the model is no longer underidentified. The constraint effectively reduces the number of unknown parameters by one; β_1 can be estimated by regressing y_t on $x_{1t} + 3x_{2t}$, and multiplying the resulting estimate by three gives the estimate of β_2.

Provided we are not faced with perfect multicollinearity, a reparameterisation may lead to a model with parameters which can be estimated with a reasonable degree of precision. The question is whether these new parameters are of any direct interest. As an example consider the simple dynamic model.

$$y_t = \beta_0 x_t + \beta_1 x_{t-1} + \epsilon_t$$

Economic time series tend to change rather slowly over time with the result that x_t and x_{t-1} will typically be highly correlated. However, the model can be rearranged to give

$$y_t = \beta_0 \Delta x_t + \beta^\dagger x_{t-1} + \epsilon_t$$

where $\beta^\dagger = \beta_0 + \beta_1$. The multicollinearity in this second formulation is likely to be far less severe than in the first; in fact the level and first difference may hardly be correlated at all. This means that although β_1 and β_2 cannot be estimated very accurately, good estimates of β_0 and $\beta^\dagger$ are possible. Furthermore, since $\beta^\dagger$ can be interpreted as the long-run response of y_t to changes in x_t, it is of considerable interest in its own right.

Common Factors

In a dynamic model, a particular structure may not be identifiable because of a common factor. Consider the ARMA(1,1) model. Repeatedly substituting for lagged values of y_t in (1.5.21) yields

$$y_t = \sum_{j=0}^{\infty} \phi^j \epsilon_{t-j} + \sum_{j=0}^{\infty} \phi^j \epsilon_{t-j-1}, \qquad t = 1, \ldots, T \tag{6.5}$$

The first term on the right hand side of (6.5) may be split into two parts to give

$$y_t = \epsilon_t + \phi \sum_{j=0}^{\infty} \phi^j \epsilon_{t-j-1} + \theta \sum_{j=0}^{\infty} \phi^j \epsilon_{t-j-1},$$

$$= \epsilon_t + (\phi + \theta) \sum_{j=0}^{\infty} \phi^j \epsilon_{t-j-1}, \qquad t = 1, \ldots, T \tag{6.6}$$

It can be seen from (6.6) that any structure for which $\phi = -\theta$ is not identifiable, since whenever this constraint is satisfied, y_t is white noise. The two sides of (1.5.21) are said to have a common factor, and if the model is to be regarded as identifiable this possibility must be explicitly ruled out. Indeed, this is not an unreasonable course of action, since if $\phi = -\theta$, it makes little sense to regard the data as being generated by an autoregressive-moving average process. However, from the practical point of view, it is important to be aware of the consequences of common factors for estimation. In later chapters it will become apparent that estimating an autoregressive-moving average model with common factors is not unlike estimating a regression model with perfectly collinear regressors.

Identifiability and the Information Matrix

In the classical regression model with normally distributed disturbances, the ML estimator of β is given by OLS. It has already been demonstrated that the computation of the OLS estimator will tend to break down if the explanatory variables are perfectly collinear. As it happens, this is a typical feature of ML estimators whenever a structure is not identified. The computational breakdown usually stems from the singularity of the information matrix. For a linear regression model, the information matrix is (4.5) and in the example given above the failure of the standard OLS estimation formulae was a direct result of the non-invertibility of $X'X$. In the next chapter it will be shown that many of the techniques for computing ML estimators involve the inversion of the information matrix or some approximation to it. As a rule, an iterative procedure will be involved and if the algorithm does not actually break down, it will probably fail to converge. In fact, even if an algorithm which did not involve the information matrix were used, convergence problems could well be encountered because of the 'flat' likelihood function typically associated with underidentified models.

In practice, lack of identifiability is often a matter of degree rather than kind. Thus the explanatory variables in a regression model may be highly correlated without being perfectly collinear. Similarly, in the ARMA(1,1) model, (1.5.21), ϕ may be close to $-\theta$, but not exactly equal to it. In neither of these cases will the structure be underidentified. However, the information matrices will be close to singularity in both cases and the computational problems associated with structures which are truly underidentified may well be encountered. More fundamentally, the near singularity of the information matrices will be reflected in very high variances for the estimators. Because the structure is close to being underidentified, the parameters cannot be estimated with any high degree of accuracy.

Local and Global Identifiability

Although lack of identifiability is generally associated with singularity of the information matrix, this need not necessarily be so. Consider the model

$$y_t = \alpha y_{t-1} + u_t,$$
$$\qquad\qquad\qquad\qquad t = 1, \ldots, T \qquad\qquad\qquad (6.7)$$
$$u_t = \phi u_{t-1} + \epsilon_t,$$

with $|\alpha| < 1$, $|\phi| < 1$ and $\epsilon_t \sim NID(0, \sigma^2)$. This is a rather special case of a dynamic regression model with a first-order autoregressive disturbance term. Subtracting ϕy_{t-1} from both sides of (6.7) and rearranging gives

$$y_t = (\alpha + \phi)y_{t-1} - \alpha\phi y_{t-2} + \epsilon_t, \qquad t = 1, \ldots, T \qquad (6.8)$$

Assume, for simplicity, that y_1 and y_2 are fixed. The distribution of the observations $y_3, \ldots, y_T$ then depends on the disturbances $\epsilon_3, \ldots, \epsilon_T$ and the values taken by the composite parameters $\alpha + \phi$ and $\alpha\phi$. However, the values of ϕ and α can be interchanged without affecting the values of the composite parameters. Thus suppose that $\phi = 0.7$ and $\alpha = 0.2$. The joint density function of this structure will be identical to the joint density function of a structure with $\alpha = 0.7$ and $\phi = 0.2$. Hence, neither structure is identifiable. However if, for any structure, ϕ and α are restricted to lie within the immediate neighbourhood of their true value, that structure will be identifiable. Model (6.7) is therefore *locally*, but not *globally*, identifiable.

If a structure is locally identifiable it can be shown that the associated information matrix is non-singular. This has both theoretical and practical implications. On the theoretical side, local identifiability means that the standard results on the large sample properties of the ML estimator still hold. On the practical side, problems of convergence are unlikely to arise when an ML algorithm is implemented. However, the fact that a model is not globally identifiable can have other consequences. In the case of (6.7), for example, the likelihood function will, in general, be bimodal. This follows because the likelihood function for any pair of parameter values will remain unchanged if those values are interchanged. A maximum value of the likelihood function will normally be located fairly close to the true parameter values. Unless ϕ and α are identical at this maximum, another maximum will be located elsewhere.

When there is more than one maximum to the likelihood function of a model which is locally, but not globally, identifiable, it may not matter which is located if the main object of building the model is prediction. However, if the parameters have an interpretation in terms of some underlying theory, the lack of global identifiability may suggest that the specification is unsatisfactory.

3.7. Robustness

Unless there are strong *a priori* reasons to suggest otherwise, it is usually assumed that the observations in an econometric model are normally distributed. This assumption is partly justified by an appeal to the Central Limit Theorem. However, normality can rarely be taken for granted and the famous remark of Poincaré is still very apt: '. . . everyone believes in the (Gaussian) laws of errors, the experimenters because they think it is a mathematical theorem, the mathematicians because they think it is an empirical fact'.

Although it is often recognised that normality cannot be taken for granted, the assumption is still retained for pragmatic reasons. The situation is sometimes characterised by the use of the term 'quasi maximum likelihood estimator'. The OLS estimator can be regarded in this light, although the Gauss–Markov theorem provides a quite independent justification for its adoption in linear regression.

Once the assumption of normally distributed observations is cast into doubt, robustness becomes a key issue. It becomes important to ask how well the ML estimator performs when normality is assumed, but the observations are actually drawn from some other distribution. In a linear regression model this question may be answered by considering the properties of the OLS estimator. Given the relationship between the normality assumption and least squares, it seems likely that these findings will have strong implications for the kind of results to be expected in more general models.

The attention throughout this section will be focused on the linear regression model

$$y_t = x_t'\beta + u_t, \qquad t = 1, \ldots, T \tag{7.1}$$

where u_t is a sequence of independent and identically distributed random variables with p.d.f. $p(u)$. It will be assumed that $p(u)$ is symmetric about zero, but no assumption will be made about the existence of either a first or a second moment. A good deal of the literature on robustness is concerned with the location model in which the observations are distributed around a centrality parameter, ψ. This may be regarded as a regression model in which the only independent variable is the constant term, i.e. $x_t'\beta = \psi$. The OLS estimator of ψ is then the sample mean. Most of the results on the sample mean can be extended to the OLS estimator in the general model, (7.1).

After examining the performance of OLS for different distributions, the minimum absolute deviation (MAD) estimator is introduced. This estimator is less sensitive to extreme observations than OLS. The M-estimators, which are considered next, have similar properties, but are more efficient over a much wider range of distributions.

Efficiency of OLS for Non-Normal Distributions

When $p(u)$ is symmetric about zero, the OLS estimator is symmetric about β. This follows immediately from (2.3.1), since if $p(u_t) = p(-u_t)$ for all t, the joint density of $(b - \beta)$ must be identical to the joint density of $-(b - \beta)$. If the first moment of b exists, it will therefore be an unbiased estimator of β. However, the existence of the first moment cannot always be taken for granted. Consider a location model in which the observations are drawn from the standardised Cauchy distribution, (1.11). This is similar in shape to the normal distribution, except that it has fatter tails. The chances of obtaining extreme observations are therefore relatively high, and neither the mean nor the variance of the distribution is defined. As a result, the mean and variance of $\bar{y}$ are not defined. More seriously, $\bar{y}$ is not consistent. This follows immediately from the result that the mean of a sample from a Cauchy distribution has exactly the same distribution as a single observation.

Both the Cauchy and the normal distribution are members of the family of *symmetric stable* distributions. If y has a stable distribution, then for T independent observations, there exist numbers $a_T > 0$, b_T such that $a_T \Sigma y_t + b_T$ has the same distribution as y. The normal distribution is the only member of this family with a finite variance. In all the other cases, OLS leaves something to be desired as an estimation procedure.

The normal distribution is also a special case of the *'general error distribution'*. If an observation in (7.1) is drawn from such a distribution, its p.d.f. is

$$p(y_t; \beta, \phi, \theta) = [2^{1+1/\theta}\Gamma(1 + \theta^{-1})]^{-1}\phi^{-1}$$
$$\times \exp \{-\tfrac{1}{2}|(y_t - x_t'\beta)/\phi|^\theta\} \qquad (7.2)$$

where ϕ and θ are positive scalar parameters and $\Gamma(.)$ is the gamma function. The shape of the distribution is determined by θ. Setting $\theta = 2$ yields a normal distribution while the Laplace, or double exponential distribution is given by $\theta = 1$. At the other end of the scale, $\theta = \infty$ corresponds to a rectangular distribution.

Both the mean and the variance of the general error distribution are defined for all admissible values of θ. The OLS estimator is therefore unbiased, with a covariance matrix, $\sigma^2(\Sigma\, x_t x_t')^{-1}$ in which

$$\sigma^2 = 2^{2/\theta}\Gamma(3/\theta)\,|\,\Gamma(1/\theta)|^{-1}\phi^2 \tag{7.3}$$

For a given value of θ, the ML estimator of β is obtained by minimising the sum of the absolute deviations raised to the power θ; i.e.

$$S(\beta;\theta) = \sum_{t=1}^{T} |y_t - x_t'\beta|^\theta \tag{7.4}$$

This may be carried out independently of ϕ; cf. the treatment of σ^2 for a normal distribution. After some manipulation it can be shown that

$$\text{Avar}(\tilde{\beta}) = \lambda(\Sigma x_t x_t')^{-1} \tag{7.5}$$

where

$$\lambda = \frac{\Gamma(1/\theta)2^{2/\theta}}{\theta^2 \cdot \Gamma\{(2\theta - 1)/\theta\}}\,\phi^2 \quad,\quad 1 \le \theta < \infty \tag{7.6}$$

The relative efficiency of the OLS estimator is therefore characterised by the ratio λ/σ^2. Some figures are presented in table 3.1. The low efficiency for $\theta = 20$ partly reflects the situation for the rectangular distribution where the variance of the ML estimator is of $0(T^{-2})$. On the other hand, the fact that the efficiency for a Laplace distribution is only 0.5 may have more important implications in practice.

Table 3.1   Relative efficiency of OLS and MAD Estimators for a General Error Distribution

Estimator	$\theta = 1.0$	$\theta = 1.5$	$\theta = 2.0$	$\theta = 4.0$	$\theta = 20$
OLS	0.50	0.91	1.00	0.73	0.16
MAD	1.00	0.83	0.64	0.30	0.05
M-class ($c = 1.5$)	0.62	0.87	0.96	0.63	0.12

The MAD Estimator

The minimum absolute deviation estimator, $b^\dagger$, is obtained by minimising (7.4) with θ set at unity. It is therefore the ML estimator of β when the disturbances follow a Laplace distribution. Furthermore, it will be observed that in the location model, the sum of the absolute deviations is minimised by the median. The median is well known to be robust to outlying observations and so there is an obvious attraction in generalising it to regression.

Although the MAD estimator is not necessarily unique, it has a well defined asymptotic distribution. In large samples $b^\dagger$ is normal, with mean β and covariance matrix

$$\text{Avar}(b^\dagger) = \{2p(0)\}^{-2}(\Sigma\, x_t x_t')^{-1} \tag{7.7}$$

cf. Bassett and Koenker (1978). The relative efficiency of MAD for the general error distribution is indicated by the second row of figures in table 3.1 where $4\lambda p^2(0)$ is evaluated for different values of θ. The corresponding figure for the Cauchy distribution is $\pi/4 = 0.81$. This can be demonstrated for the location model by noting that $2p(0) = \sqrt{2/\pi}$ and that $\text{Avar}(\tilde{\psi}) = 2/T$; see (4.4.3).

There are a number of ways of computing the MAD estimator, the most efficient algorithms being based on linear programming. However, if a specific routine is not available, iterative weighted least squares may be used since the function to be minimised can be written as

$$S(\beta) = \sum_{t=1}^{T} w_t(y_t - x_t'\beta)^2 \tag{7.8}$$

where $w_t = |y_t - x_t'\beta|^{-1}$.

Asymptotic standard errors of a MAD estimator may be obtained by generalising known results for the median. If, in the location model, $y_{(i)}$ denotes the ith order statistic from a population with median ψ, a consistent estimator of $\{p(\psi)\}^{-1}$ is given by

$$T\{y_{(m+l)} - y_{(m-l)}\}/2l$$

where $m = (2r + 1)/2$ for r odd and l is of $0(r^d)$ with $0 < d < 1$; see Cox and Hinkley (1974, p. 470). A convenient choice of d is one half. Carrying these results over to MAD regression suggests the estimator,

$$\text{Avar}(b^\dagger) = (T/4l)^2\{r_{(m+l)} - r_{(m-l)}\}^2(\Sigma\, x_t x_t')^{-1} \tag{7.9}$$

where the $r_{(i)}$'s are ordered residuals and $r_{(m)} = 0$. Note that k residuals will be identically equal to zero as a consequence of the MAD fit.

M-Estimators

Huber (1973) has defined a class of 'M-estimators', which are obtained by minimising

$$S(\beta) = \sum_{t=1}^{T} \varrho(y_t - x_t'\beta) \tag{7.10}$$

where $\varrho(.)$ is a suitably defined function. The idea is to choose $\varrho(.)$ in such a way that the estimator is efficient over a wide range of distributions. One possibility is

$$\varrho(z) = \begin{cases} z^2/2, & |z| < c\,\sigma^*, \\ c\,|z| - c^2/2, & |z| \geq c\,\sigma^*, \end{cases} \tag{7.11}$$

where c is a constant and σ^* is a scale parameter. This estimator combines features of both OLS and MAD. In fact, it reduces to OLS if $c = \infty$, but with c set at a typical value of around one or two, outlying observations receive relatively less weight. The estimator is therefore not sensitive to extreme observations in the same way as OLS, but it remains reasonably efficient in the cases where OLS performs well. This is illustrated by the figures in table 3.1. For $c = 1.5$ and $\sigma^* = \sigma$, the relative efficiency of the M-estimator for a normal distribution is 0.96. On the other hand, its efficiency for a standardised Cauchy distribution is 0.66 for $c = 1.5$ and $\sigma^* = 1$.

In practice the scale parameter must be estimated from the data. The usual estimator, (2.7.6), is not suitable since the variance of the underlying distribution may not be finite. A robust alternative is

$$s^* = \text{median}\{|r_{(i)}|\}, \tag{7.12}$$

where $r_{(i)}$, $i = 1, \ldots, T$, are the ordered residuals.

Robust Estimation in Econometrics

Robust estimation procedures offer a viable alternative to OLS in linear regression. Furthermore, the same techniques may be employed in more general models. The use of a MAD or M-estimator in non-linear regression is straightforward, while in the multiplicative heteroscedasticity model, all that is required is a slight modification of the likelihood function in (4.17). Similar devices may be adopted in systems of equations.

The main concern is with long-tailed distributions because these are the cases where OLS is particularly unsatisfactory. Since extreme observations tend to be accommodated by the OLS fit, it is possible to remain unaware of their existence. There is a strong case for computing the MAD estimator and examining the residuals. If the form of the distribution is unclear, a sensible strategy would then be to construct a robust M-estimator.

If outliers are detected, however, it is important to ask whether they are to be considered as a purely random phenomenon, or whether they are really an indication of some misspecification in the systematic part of the model. At the simplest level it may be possible to 'explain' an outlying observation by the occurrence of a particular event. This may then be incorporated into the model by means of a dummy variable. Such an approach is clearly more appropriate than the application of a robust estimation technique, particularly if a similar event is likely to occur in the future.

Notes

Sections 1, 2 & 3 Silvey (1975) provides an excellent introduction. More detailed treatments will be found in Kendall and Stuart (1973, Vol. 2) and Cramér (1946).

Section 4 Heteroscedasticity models are described in Amemiya (1977), Goldfeld and Quandt (1972) and Harvey (1976a). Logit models are discussed in Domencich and McFadden (1975), while an example involving count data is in Hausman *et al.* (1984). A class of dynamic models for count and qualitative observations is described in Harvey (1989).

Section 6 Silvey (1975) and Rothenberg (1971).

Section 7 Robust estimators are discussed in Cox and Hinkley (1974), Huber (1973), Andrews *et al.* (1972) and Andrews (1974). Computation of the MAD estimator is treated in Schlossmacher (1973) and Armstrong and Frome (1976). Robust inference for misspecified models is discussed in White (1982).

Exercises

1. Show that the sample mean, $\bar{y}$, is a sufficient statistic for the parameter θ when: (i) $y \sim N(\theta, 1)$, (ii) $p(y) = \theta^{-1} \exp(-y/\theta)$.
2. Find the ML estimator of θ given a random sample of T observations from the exponential distribution in 1(ii). Write down its asymptotic distribution.
3. If $y \sim N(0, \sigma^2)$, find the ML estimator of σ (*not* σ^2), show that it is sufficient, and calculate its large sample variance.
4. If $p(y) = \theta^2 y \cdot \exp(-\theta y)$, show that $\bar{y}$ is a sufficient statistic for θ. Find the ML estimator of θ and its large sample variance.
5. If the observations in a dependent variable heteroscedastic regression model, (4.23), follow an exponential distribution, i.e.
   $p(y_t) = (x_t'\beta)^{-1} \cdot \exp\{-y_t/(x_t'\beta)\}$, find the information matrix and hence show that the WLS estimator is asymptotically efficient.
6. Consider the time trend model, $y_t = \alpha + \beta t + \epsilon_t$ in which $\epsilon_t \sim NID(0, \sigma^2)$. Is the estimator $\hat{\beta} = (y_T - y_1)/(T - 1)$: (i) unbiased, (ii) sufficient, (iii) consistent, (iv) efficient?
7. If θ in (7.2) is unknown, explain how you would estimate the complete set of parameters, (β', ϕ, θ) by ML.
8. Explain how you would construct an approximation to the likelihood function for the MA(2) model, $y_t = \epsilon_t + \theta_1\epsilon_{t-1} + \theta_2\epsilon_{t-2}$ with $\epsilon_t \sim NID(0, \sigma^2)$. How are the initial conditions handled?
9. Consider a SURE model, (2.9.15), with $N = 2$, and let ϱ be the correlation between ϵ_{1t} and ϵ_{2t}. *(a)* If ϱ is known, derive the ML estimators of β_1, β_2 and σ^2. (b) Prove that the ML estimator of $\beta = (\beta_1', \beta_2')'$ is unbiased, and derive its covariance matrix. (c) If ϱ is unknown, derive an expression for its ML estimator and explain briefly how you would compute ML estimates of β, ϱ and σ^2.

4
Numerical Optimisation

4.1. Introduction

In general, non-linear estimation problems are solved by *iterative* techniques. An initial estimate is obtained, and a new estimate, which (hopefully) is an 'improvement' on the original, is computed by a given rule. This process is then repeated until *convergence*. If the procedure has been successful, the final estimate should satisfy all the properties required of that particular estimation principle. The rules governing the iterative procedure provide the basis of a particular non-linear optimisation routine.

There is a wide range of algorithms available. One important way in which they differ is in the extent to which they employ partial derivatives of the function. Some routines require second derivatives, while others require only first derivatives, and some are not based on derivatives at all. However, a number of algorithms based on first derivatives offer the option of calculating these numerically. Thus there is no need to obtain the derivatives analytically, which may be difficult, and then program them, which may be expensive. Apart from the question of derivatives, algorithms differ in other ways, and the choice of a particular algorithm will depend, to some extent, on the type of function to be maximised or minimised. Ill-conditioned functions, sums of squares and problems involving optimisation with respect to only one parameter are all special cases.

Before high speed computing facilities became widely available, any form of non-linear estimation was extremely time-consuming and to be avoided at all costs. This situation has now changed dramatically, and coupled with the advances in computer technology, improved methods of carrying out non-linear optimisation have been devised. These routines are very efficient and, in addition, they avoid many of the pitfalls and difficulties inherent in non-linear estimation. This is not to imply, however, that all problems have been eliminated from non-linear optimisation. Most non-linear routines are subject to problems of execution, while the results are often liable to misinterpretation. A good deal of care is therefore required. Nevertheless, the fact that the best estimator of a parameter is non-linear should no longer be regarded as a deterrent to employing that estimator. Indeed, when faced with a new situation, there is a strong argument for basing estimation on one principle, that of maximum likelihood, rather than attempting to derive simpler formulae for alternative estimators which must then be shown to be asymptotically equivalent to the ML estimators.

Some of the general issues raised by numerical optimisation are discussed in Section 2. In particular, the iterative scheme underlying descent methods of optimisation is outlined, and this is contrasted with methods of 'direct search'. It is also pointed out that, in certain circumstances, non-linear calculations as such can be avoided by the use of a step-wise optimisation procedure. The basic Newton–Raphson algorithm is described in Section 3, while Section 4 considers ways in which this scheme may be modified for ML estimation. The methods of scoring and Gauss–Newton are introduced here, although the latter scheme has somewhat wider applicability, since it is a suitable technique for minimising any sum of squares function. In certain circumstances, linearities in the likelihood equations may be exploited by 'concentrating' the likelihood function. This technique is also described in Section 4. In Section 5, the construction of asymptotically efficient two-step estimators is considered. This material is fundamental to understanding and evaluating many of the methods which have been proposed in the literature. Finally, the question of how to compute estimates of asymptotic covariance matrices is discussed.

4.2. Principles of Numerical Optimisation

In discussing the general problem of non-linear estimation, it will be assumed that a *criterion function*, $f(\psi)$, is to be minimised with respect to the n parameters in the vector ψ. The $n \times 1$ vector of first derivatives, $\partial f(\psi)/\partial \psi$, will be denoted by $g(\psi)$ or simply g, while the $n \times n$ matrix of second partial derivatives, the Hessian, will be written as

$$\frac{\partial f(\psi)}{\partial \psi \partial \psi'} = G(\psi)$$

The generality of the discussion is not restricted by taking $f(\psi)$ as a function to be minimised, since a maximisation problem may be converted to one of minimisation simply by multiplying the criterion function by minus one.

If $g(\psi)$ and $G(\psi)$ exist and are continuous in the neighbourhood of a particular value, $\hat{\psi}$, sufficient conditions for $\hat{\psi}$ to be a local minimiser of $f(\psi)$ are that $g(\hat{\psi}) = 0$ and that $G(\hat{\psi})$ is p.d. However, these conditions do not guarantee that $\hat{\psi}$ is a global minimiser since there may be another local minimiser, $\tilde{\psi}$, such that $f(\tilde{\psi}) < f(\hat{\psi})$.

Univariate Search Techniques

Before considering the general problem of non-linear optimisation, it is worth briefly considering the one-dimensional problem, in which a function is to be minimised with respect to a single parameter only. If the function is known to contain a single minimum, then *linear search* techniques may be applicable. These methods fit a low order polynomial, and calculate where the minimum lies. The process is then repeated until convergence. Algorithms are available both with and without the requirement for programming first derivatives.

If it is felt desirable to explore the function over the whole range of values of the parameter, a *grid search* may be employed. Suppose the parameter is constrained to lie in the range $0 \le \psi \le 1$. The function may be evaluated at the points $\psi = 0$, $\psi = 0.1, \ldots, \psi = 1.0$, i.e. at 11 equally spaced points over the range of the parameter. If the minimum is found to lie at, say, $\psi = 0.7$, a 'finer' search over the interval 0.61 to 0.79 is carried out in steps of 0.01. If desired, this may be repeated until a sufficiently accurate estimate of the minimum has been obtained.

A grid search may be carried out in two-dimensional problems, but for $n \ge 3$ the technique becomes unwieldy. Linear searches are restricted to univariate problems. However, their range of application is much wider than this statement might suggest, since a line search is incorporated into most descent algorithms.

Descent Methods

Most iterative schemes are of the form

$$\psi^* = \hat{\psi} + \lambda \, d(\hat{\psi}) \tag{2.1}$$

where $\hat{\psi}$ is the current approximation to the minimum, ψ^* is the revised estimate, λ is a positive scalar known as the *step-length* and $d(\psi)$ is the *direction vector*. The direction vector is of length n, and depends on the *gradient, $g(\psi)$*.

The simplest scheme within this class is the *method of steepest descent*. In one dimension the idea can be explained simply by noting that a small change proportional to the slope multiplied by minus one will decrease the function. More generally, if the sum of squares of the changes in the elements of ψ is constrained to be a certain length, the greatest change in the function occurs when the changes in ψ are proportional to $g(\psi)$. For these changes to lead towards a minimum rather than a maximum, the constant of proportionality must be negative. Thus the direction vector is equal to $- g(\psi)$, and the step-length must be chosen so that the function does not increase at a particular iteration.

Given a suitable rule for determining λ at each iteration, it can be shown that the method of steepest descent will eventually converge. However, its rate of convergence can be extremely slow and the algorithm is rarely of practical use. A more usual choice for the direction vector is $d(\psi) = -G^{-1}(\psi)\, g(\psi)$. The rationale underlying this method, which is generally known as Newton–Raphson, is set out in the next section. However, whatever the choice of $d(\psi)$, convergence can almost invariably be speeded up by adopting an efficient line search procedure to determine λ. Once $d(\hat{\psi})$ has been evaluated, the problem is one-dimensional and the techniques referred to in the previous sub-section may be used to minimise the function

$$\phi(\lambda) = f\{\hat{\psi} + \lambda\, d(\hat{\psi})\} \qquad (2.2)$$

with respect to λ.

Stepwise Optimisation

It is sometimes possible to break down the optimisation problem in such a way that complicated non-linear calculations are avoided. Let ψ be partitioned as $\psi = (\psi_1', \psi_2')'$, and suppose that $f(\psi)$ is linear in the parameters of ψ_1 when ψ_2 is fixed, and linear in ψ_2 when ψ_1 is fixed. This suggests a *stepwise* or *zig-zag* optimisation procedure. Conditional on a value of ψ_1, $f(\psi)$ is minimised with respect to ψ_2. The value of ψ_2 obtained in this way is then held constant while $f(\psi)$ is minimised with respect to ψ_1. The function is then minimised with respect to ψ_2 conditional on this new value of ψ_1 and the process is repeated until convergence. Indeed, it can be shown that such a procedure is bound to converge; see Sargan (1964) and Oberhofer and Kmenta (1974).

Direct Search

For some objective functions it may be difficult to ascertain whether or not partial derivatives exist in the domain of interest. For other functions it may be known that partial derivatives do not exist at certain key points, or that they are ill-behaved in certain ways. When this is the case, it is imperative to seek an optimisation procedure which does not use partial derivatives and which, furthermore, does not even require the existence of partial derivatives for its theoretical justification. These requirements are satisfied by direct search methods, where the only assumption made is that $f(\psi)$ is continuous. One of the most widely used direct search algorithms is due to Powell (1964), the directions of the searches being based on the principle of 'conjugate directions'. Another useful technique is the *simplex* method of Nelder and Mead (1965). Although the algorithm does not usually converge to the exact answer, it is relatively robust. It can be applied to functions which contain discontinuous derivatives, and it normally produces a reasonably accurate answer quite efficiently. When a 'difficult' function is encountered, the simplex method has much to recommend it, even it it is only used to provide starting values for another technique.

Convergence

An iterative scheme may be regarded as having converged if: (i) $f(\psi^*)$ is close to $f(\hat{\psi})$; (ii) ψ^* is close to $\hat{\psi}$; and (iii) $g(\psi^*)$ is close to 0. 'Closeness' is generally defined in terms of a small positive scalar, $\varkappa$. Thus the first condition is taken to be satisfied if $|f(\psi^*) - f(\hat{\psi})| < \varkappa_1$. For $n > 1$, ψ and $g(\psi)$ are vectors and there are a number of different ways of specifying the last two conditions. The usual approach is to consider the second condition as being satisfied if

$$(\psi^* - \hat{\psi})'(\psi^* - \hat{\psi}) = ||\psi^* - \hat{\psi}|| < \varkappa_2$$

while the third condition is satisfied if $||g(\psi^*)|| < \varkappa_3$. Although different algorithms differ in the way in which these conditions are implemented, it is generally advisable that they be applied in one way or another. Of course, if a direct search method which does not involve first derivatives is being used, only the first two conditions are appropriate.

Achieving convergence is not always straightforward. One problem which bedevils econometric work is that the objective function is often relatively 'flat' around the optimum. This is illustrated in figure 4.1. Once at $\hat{\psi}_1$ or $\hat{\psi}_2$, the algorithm either stops or moves towards the minimum very slowly. In the latter case, a typical algorithm may well terminate before $\tilde{\psi}$, due to an upper limit on the number of iterations. The practical consequences are,

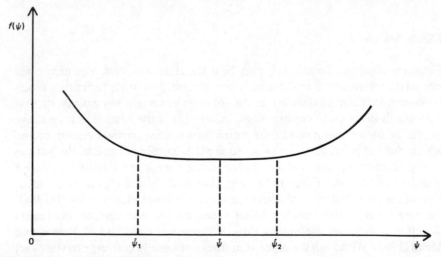

Figure 4.1 A 'Flat' Objective Function

firstly, that a good deal of computer time is likely to be burnt up to very little effect and, secondly, that different results may be obtained depending on the position of the starting values.

Although figure 4.1 provides a good illustration of the consequences of a flat objective function, such problems are normally encountered only when $f(\psi)$ depends on two or more parameters. From the statistical point of view, a flat objective function arises when a model is close to being underidentified. Thus consider the ARMA(1,1) process, (1.5.21). It was pointed out in Section 3.6 that the model is not identifiable if $\phi = -\theta$. If, on the other hand, ϕ is merely close to $-\theta$, the model is identifiable, but any pair of estimates, $\hat{\phi}$ and $\hat{\theta}$, which satisfy the constraint $\hat{\phi} + \hat{\theta} = 0$, or are near to satisfying it, will yield a value of $S(\phi, \theta)$ which is close to the minimum. Similarly, if $2x_{1t} \simeq x_{2t}$ in (3.6.1), any estimates of β_1 and β_2 which are close to satisfying (3.6.3) will be close to minimising the residual sum of squares. Since the model is linear in the parameters, the convergence problems which might be encountered in the ARMA(1,1) model will not arise here. However, the ill-conditioning of the cross-product matrix and the numerical instability of the OLS estimates are a reflection of the same underlying phenomenon. Given the multicollinearity of economic time series, and the small samples, it is perhaps not surprising that flat objective functions are the rule, rather than the exception, in non-linear estimation.

An even more serious problem arises when the objective function has more than one minimum. This situation is illustrated in figure 4.2. If the starting point is at $\hat{\psi}$, it is more than likely that a 'shortsighted' iterative procedure will converge to a *local* minimum, $\tilde{\psi}^\dagger$, rather than to the *global* minimum, $\tilde{\psi}$. One attraction of a grid search is that it will usually locate the global minimum, although if the function exhibits the type of behaviour shown in figure 4.3 even a grid search might fail. Fortunately, this kind of behaviour

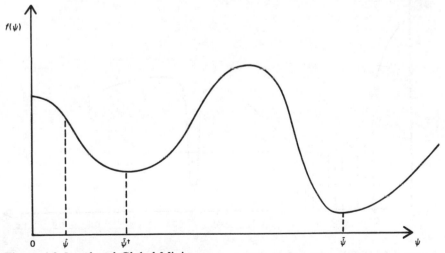

Figure 4.2 Local and Global Minima

128

THE ECONOMETRIC ANALYSIS OF TIME SERIES

is not common in statistical applications. As a result, a relatively coarse grid search can sometimes be used to provide a suitable starting value for a more refined iterative procedure. If this is not done, it is at least worth applying the optimisation procedure from a number of different starting points. This provides a check on whether a global solution has actually been obtained.

The introduction of an exogenous variable into (3.6.7) provides a simple illustration of how multiple optima can arise in econometrics. The model becomes

$$y_t = \alpha y_{t-1} + \beta x_t + u_t \tag{2.3}$$

where $u_t \sim$ AR(1), and it is now globally, as well as locally, identifiable. However, by a continuity argument, the sum of squares function will still be bimodal if the variance of x_t is sufficiently small, although the two minima will not, in general, be equal.

Numerical Evaluation of Derivatives

The first partial derivative of $f(\psi)$ with respect to the jth element of ψ, ψ_j, may be estimated from the formula

$$\{f(\hat{\psi} + h_j e_j) - f(\hat{\psi})\}/h_j, \qquad j = 1,\ldots,n \tag{2.4}$$

where the jth element of the $n \times 1$ vector e_j is unity, while all the other elements are zero. The scalar, h_j, is sometimes referred to as the step-length, although this should not be confused with the step-length, λ, defined in the iterative scheme (2.1). Each h_j must be chosen so as to be small enough for

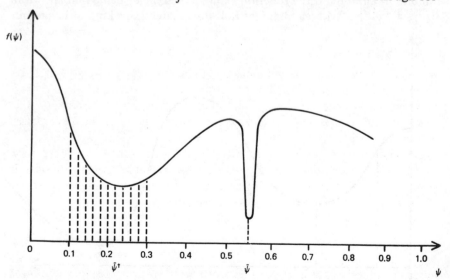

Figure 4.3 Pitfalls with a Grid Search

the difference estimates to be close to the true derivatives, but not so small that the calculated differences are dominated by rounding errors. Determining suitable value for the h_j's often requires some experimentation, and a good deal of care is needed in making a judicious choice.

The calculation of a vector of numerical derivatives from (2.4) involves n evaluations of the function. This can be quite time-consuming. Because numerical derivatives are also subject to inaccuracies, it is usually preferable to use analytic derivatives if these can be obtained reasonably easily. In many instances, however, it is not easy to obtain analytic derivatives, and hence the use of numerical derivatives is common. Indeed, it could be argued that since differentiation and computer programming are tasks which may both be time-consuming and very much open to human error, the use of numerical derivatives is, in some instances, safer as well as being more efficient.

Second derivatives may also be calculated numerically. An estimate of the ijth element in $G(\hat{\psi})$ is given by

$$\{g_j(\hat{\psi} - h_i e_i) - g_j(\hat{\psi})\}/h_i, \qquad i, j = 1, \ldots, n \tag{2.5}$$

Constrained Optimisation: The Use of Transformations

In some problems there are restrictions on the values which the parameters can take. Algorithms have been designed to handle constraints of various types and details of some of these methods will be found in Box *et al.* (1969, Ch. 5) and Dixon (1972, Ch. 6). However, simple constraints can sometimes be handled by means of transformations.

In econometrics and time series analysis, it is often desirable to impose constraints of the form:

(a) $\psi \geq k$, or
(b) $k_1 \leq \psi \leq k_2$

where k, k_1 and k_2 are known constants. The first type of constraint arises when ψ is a variance and in this case k is zero. Negative values of ψ may, however, be avoided very easily, simply by defining a new variable, θ, such that $\theta^2 = \psi$ or $\exp(\theta) = \psi$. Unconstrained optimisation may then be applied with respect to θ.

Constraining a parameter to lie within a particular range, i.e. $k_1 \leq \psi \leq k_2$, can also be handled relatively easily. One possible transformation is $\psi = k_1 + (k_2 - k_1)\sin^2 \theta$, with θ taking any value in the range $-\infty$ to ∞. If the inequality is a strict one, the transformation,

$$\psi = \frac{k_2 - k_1}{2} \frac{\theta}{1 + |\theta|} + \frac{k_2 + k_1}{2} \tag{2.6}$$

might be appropriate. In the important special case where ψ is constrained to lie within the unit circle, (2.6) simplifies to $\psi = \theta/(1 + |\theta|)$.

As a final point, note that when a grid search is to be carried out, transformations may often be applied in such a way that the role they play is exactly opposite to the one considered above. Suppose, for example, that a parameter is unconstrained, i.e. $-\infty \leq \psi \leq \infty$. It will generally be convenient to carry out a grid search over the range $(-1,1)$, for which the transformation

$$\theta = \psi/(1 + |\psi|) \tag{2.7}$$

is appropriate. Once the function has been minimised with respect to θ the required value of ψ is given by $\tilde{\psi} = \tilde{\theta}/\{1 - |\tilde{\theta}|\}$.

3. Newton–Raphson

The problems inherent in the method of steepest descent led to the consideration of new methods of optimisation. It was soon realised that approximating the function by a quadratic could form the basis of relatively efficient computational schemes. Such schemes employ second, as well as first, derivatives and the basic procedure obtained from this approach is known as *Newton–Raphson* or simply *Newton's method*.

A Taylor series expansion of $f(\psi)$ around the minimum $\tilde{\psi}$ gives

$$f(\psi) \simeq f(\tilde{\psi}) + (\psi - \tilde{\psi})g(\tilde{\psi}) + \tfrac{1}{2}(\psi - \tilde{\psi})'G(\tilde{\psi})(\psi - \tilde{\psi}) \tag{3.1}$$

Differentiating expression (3.1) with respect to ψ yields

$$g(\psi) \simeq g(\tilde{\psi}) + (\psi - \tilde{\psi})G(\tilde{\psi}) \tag{3.2}$$

However, since $g(\tilde{\psi}) = 0$, (3.2) may be rearranged to give

$$\tilde{\psi} \simeq \psi - G^{-1}(\tilde{\psi})g(\psi) \tag{3.3}$$

If $f(\psi)$ were a quadratic, ψ could be set equal to any initial estimate of $\tilde{\psi}$, and $\tilde{\psi}$ would be given exactly by the right-hand side of expression (3.3). (It is instructive to verify this by taking a simple quadratic, say $f(\psi) = \psi^2 + 4\psi + 3$, arbitrarily choosing a starting value, and then using (3.3) to calculate the minimum.) For more general functions, this will not be the case, but expression (3.3) does suggest the iterative scheme

$$\psi^* = \hat{\psi} - G^{-1}(\tilde{\psi})g(\hat{\psi}) \tag{3.4}$$

where the revised estimate, ψ^*, is expected to be closer to the minimum than the initial estimate, $\hat{\psi}$.

The evaluation of the Hessian matrix poses no problem for a quadratic function since its elements do not depend on ψ. More generally, however, an iterative scheme of the form (3.4) raises a difficulty, since it presupposes that the Hessian is evaluated at the minimum $\tilde{\psi}$, which is, of course, unknown. The solution adopted in Newton–Raphson is to evaluate the Hessian at the current estimate, $\hat{\psi}$, on the grounds that this will yield an acceptable approximation to $G(\tilde{\psi})$ if $\hat{\psi}$ is 'reasonably close' to $\tilde{\psi}$. The iterative scheme therefore becomes

$$\psi^* = \hat{\psi} - G^{-1}(\hat{\psi})g(\hat{\psi}) \tag{3.5}$$

This is sometimes written more concisely as

$$\psi^* = \hat{\psi} - G^{-1}g \tag{3.6}$$

where it is understood that G and g are evaluated at the current estimate.

Example   Consider the function

$$f(\psi) = \psi^3 - 3\psi^2 + 5, \qquad 0 \le \psi < \infty \tag{3.7}$$

The first and second derivatives are

$$g(\psi) = 3\psi(\psi - 2) \tag{3.8}$$

and

$$G(\psi) = 6(\psi - 1) \tag{3.9}$$

respectively. The function is sketched in figure 4.4.

Suppose that we decide to find the minimum by the Newton–Raphson iteration. If the starting value, $\hat{\psi}$, is chosen to be 1.500, then $g = -2.25$ and $G = 3$. Thus

$$\psi^* = 1.5000 - (-2.25)/3 = 2.2500$$

For the second iteration $\hat{\psi}$ is set equal to the previous ψ^*, 2.2500, and the revised estimate is

$$\psi^* = 2.25 - (0.16875)/7.5 = 2.0250$$

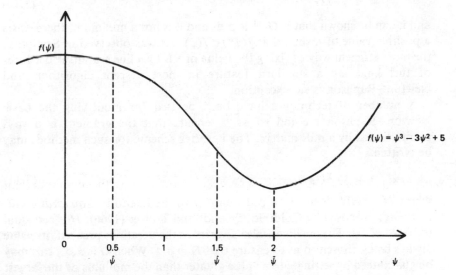

Figure 4.4   Function in Example based on (3.7)

The third iteration yields $\psi^* = 2.0003$. This is very close to the actual minimum, $\tilde{\psi}$, which is exactly equal to 2.

The above sequence seems very straightforward. However, consider what would have happened if the initial starting value had been $\hat{\psi} = 0.5$. Since $G(0.5)$ is *negative*, the effect of the first iteration is to send the estimate in the wrong direction, i.e.

$$\psi^* = 0.5 - (-2.25)/(-3) = -0.2500$$

If this process is left unchecked, the algorithm converges to the maximum at $\psi = 0$.

Safeguards and Modifications

The Newton–Raphson scheme will only progress towards a minimum if $G(\hat{\psi})$ is p.d. While it is true that the Hessian is always p.d. for a concave function, it is not true in general. If $G(\hat{\psi})$ is singular, the direction vector is not defined and the method breaks down. If G^{-1} exists, but is not p.d., the direction vector may be wrongly aligned and the value of the objective function may increase. This is precisely what happened in the example above, when the starting value was taken to be $\hat{\psi} = 0.5$.

Even if $G(\hat{\psi})$ is p.d., it is still possible for $f(\psi^*)$ to exceed $f(\hat{\psi})$. However, this represents a case of 'overshooting', and such an occurrence can always be avoided by introducing a variable step-length, λ, into the scheme. Thus (3.6) becomes

$$\psi^* = \hat{\psi} - \lambda G^{-1}g \qquad (3.10)$$

and it can be shown that if G^{-1} is p.d. and $\hat{\psi}$ is not a minimum, there exists a positive value of λ such that $f(\psi^*) < f(\hat{\psi})$. As was observed in Section 2, the most efficient way of fixing the value of λ is by a line search. Procedures of this kind are a standard feature in most descent algorithms and Newton–Raphson is no exception.

A number of techniques have been devised for modifying the basic Newton–Raphson method so as to ensure that the gradient is always premultiplied by a p.d. matrix. The iterative scheme for such methods may be written

$$\psi^* = \hat{\psi} - \lambda Hg \qquad (3.11)$$

where $H = H(\hat{\psi})$ is an $n \times n$ p.d. matrix. In the method of *quadratic hill-climbing*, proposed by Goldfeld, Quandt and Trotter (1966), H is set equal to $(G + \mu I)^{-1}$. The positive scalar μ varies as the iterations proceed, its value always being chosen so as to ensure that H is p.d. When G is n.d., this may be guaranteed by setting μ to a value greater than the modulus of the largest negative eigenvalue of G. When G is singular, any positive value of μ ensures that H is p.d. If μ is large, the iteration will be similar to the method of steepest descent. However, as the minimum is approached, G will tend to become p.d., and in this case μ may be set equal to zero, so that the method collapses to Newton–Raphson. Although quadratic hill-climbing is a useful technique in many problems, its efficiency is likely to fall markedly as n increases, since the matrix inversions and eigenvalue evaluations will impose a heavy computational burden.

Another way of carrying out an iterative scheme of the form (3.11) is to adopt an updating procedure, whereby a 'rank-one' or 'rank-two' matrix is added to a p.d. matrix at the current iteration to produce a p.d. matrix at the next iteration. If the initial Hessian matrix is not p.d., it is amended so that it is p.d. As in quadratic hill-climbing, the inverse of the matrix H will be equal to the Hessian at the minimum. A description of several of these updating methods will be found in Gill and Murray (1972). In the method they themselves propose, H is equal to $(G + D)^{-1}$ where D is a diagonal matrix. Neither G nor D is actually computed, the updating being carried out in terms of a lower triangular matrix, L, such that $L'L = H$. This method of updating is both computationally efficient and numerically stable, in that it avoids the rounding errors which are always liable to be present when a set of simultaneous equations is solved by matrix inversion.

Quasi-Newton Methods

The main advantage of *quasi-Newton*, or *variable metric*, methods is that they do not require the Hessian to be explicitly evaluated. The iterative scheme is of the form (3.11), but the initial H matrix may be any p.d. matrix. At each iteration H is updated in such a way as to yield a series of p.d. matrices which eventually converge to the inverse of the Hessian. A common choice for the starting matrix is the identity matrix. The first iteration is therefore carried out by the method of steepest descent, but the procedure gradually tends towards Newton–Raphson as the minimum is approached.

Examples of quasi-Newton algorithms include Davidson–Fletcher–Powell and the more recent programme designed by Gill, Murray and Pitfield (1972). As in the updating procedure described in the previous sub-section, the key to efficiency and numerical stability in Gill–Murray–Pitfield lies in storing H as triangular factors.

4.4. Maximisation of a Likelihood Function

Maximum likelihood estimation is usually carried out by maximising the logarithm of the likelihood function, $\log L(\psi)$, although it is often more convenient to implement a particular algorithm by considering the problem as one of minimising $\{-\log L\}$. However, whether the problem is viewed as one of maximisation or minimisation makes little difference to the discussion below.

The Newton−Raphson iteration, (3.5), for the log−likelihood function may be written

$$\psi^* = \hat{\psi} - [D^2 \log L(\hat{\psi})]^{-1}D \log L(\hat{\psi}) \tag{4.1}$$

where both the first and second derivatives are evaluated at current estimate, $\hat{\psi}$. A number of variants of (4.1) are available for ML estimation. These can sometimes exploit particular features of the problem, thereby producing a more efficient algorithm. The Gauss−Newton procedure, for example, is particularly appropriate for cases where maximising the likelihood function is equivalent to minimising a sum of squares.

The Method of Scoring

Rather than work with the matrix of second derivatives, it is sometimes more efficient to use its expectation. This yields the information matrix when multiplied by minus one and the iterative scheme in (4.1) becomes

$$\psi^* = \hat{\psi} + I^{-1}(\hat{\psi})D \log L(\hat{\psi}) \tag{4.2}$$

The procedure is known as the *method of scoring*.

The method of scoring is likely to have a slower rate of convergence than Newton−Raphson, since the information matrix is only an approximation to the Hessian. However, in many applications the information matrix has a simple form and is much easier to compute. Each iteration will therefore be performed more quickly and this may compensate for a slower rate of convergence. Furthermore, provided the model is identifiable, the information matrix will always be p.d. Some of the difficulties which may be encountered with Newton−Raphson are therefore avoided.

As with most descent methods, it will usually be advisable to introduce a variable step-length, λ, into the iterative scheme; cf. (2.1). This point should always be borne in mind as it will not be mentioned explicitly in the applications cited.

Example 1 The standardised Cauchy distribution was introduced in Example 3.1.2 and it was observed that the likelihood equation was non-linear. Differentiating $\log L$ twice with respect to ψ gives

$$\frac{\partial^2 \log L}{\partial \psi^2} = \sum_{t=1}^{T} \frac{2(y_t - \psi)^2 - 2}{\{1 + (y_t - \psi)^2\}^2} \tag{4.3}$$

and this term may be used as the basis of a Newton−Raphson iterative scheme. However, the scoring algorithm takes a much simpler form. Taking the expectation of (4.3) and using a standard result on integrals yields

$$\frac{T}{\pi} \int_{-\infty}^{\infty} \frac{2(y_t - \psi)^2 - 2}{\{1 + (y_t - \psi)^2\}^3} dy_t = -\frac{T}{2}$$

Thus $I(\psi) = T/2$ and the scoring algorithm is

$$\psi^* = \hat{\psi} + \frac{4}{T} \sum_{t=1}^{T} \frac{(y_t - \hat{\psi})}{1 + (y_t - \hat{\psi})^2} \tag{4.4}$$

Example 2 The multiplicative heteroscedasticity regression model is defined by (3.4.15). Because the information matrix, (3.4.20), is block-diagonal with a much simpler form than the Hessian, the method of scoring yields a more attractive algorithm than Newton–Raphson, i.e.

$$\beta^* = \hat{\beta} + [\Sigma \exp(-w_t'\hat{\delta}) x_t x_t']^{-1} \Sigma x_t \exp(-w_t'\hat{\delta})(y_t - x_t'\hat{\beta}) \tag{4.5a}$$

and

$$\delta^* = \hat{\delta} + [\Sigma w_t w_t']^{-1} \Sigma w_t \{\exp(-w_t'\hat{\delta})(y_t - x_t'\hat{\beta})^2 - 1\} \tag{4.5b}$$

The first iterative equation, (4.5a), reduces to WLS, while the second equation has the attraction that the matrix $\Sigma w_t w_t'$ does not depend on any unknown parameters, and so it need be inverted only once.

Example 3 The Poisson regression model was set up in Section 3.4 with a link function (4.33). Multiplying and dividing the second term on the right hand side of (4.36) by the scalar quantity $x_t'\beta$ leads to this expression becoming

$$\frac{\partial \log L}{\partial \beta} = \sum_{t=1}^{T} x_t \frac{y_t}{x_t'\beta} - \left[\sum_{t=1}^{T} \frac{1}{x_t'\beta} x_t x_t' \right] \beta$$

The inverse of the information matrix is (4.38) and so the scoring algorithm reduces to a series of WLS regressions:

$$\beta^* = \sum_{t=1}^{T} \left[\frac{1}{x_t'\hat{\beta}} x_t x_t' \right]^{-1} \sum_{t=1}^{T} \frac{1}{x_t'\hat{\beta}} x_t y_t \tag{4.6}$$

The initial estimator is simply OLS.

Gauss–Newton

The computation of estimators in econometrics and time series analysis frequently entails the minimisation of a sum of squares function of the form

$$f(\psi) = S(\psi) = \sum_t \epsilon_t^2 \tag{4.7}$$

where $\epsilon_t = \epsilon_t(\psi)$ is a 'residual' which depends on the value taken by ψ. The vector of first derivatives is

$$g(\psi) = \frac{\partial S(\psi)}{\partial \psi} = 2\sum \frac{\partial \epsilon_t}{\partial \psi} \cdot \epsilon_t \qquad (4.8)$$

while the Hessian is

$$G(\psi) = \frac{\partial^2 S(\psi)}{\partial \psi \partial \psi'} = 2\sum \left[\frac{\partial \epsilon_t}{\partial \psi} \cdot \frac{\partial \epsilon_t}{\partial \psi'} + \frac{\partial^2 \epsilon_t}{\partial \psi \partial \psi'} \cdot \epsilon_t \right] \qquad (4.9)$$

The Newton–Raphson scheme is therefore

$$\psi^* = \hat{\psi} - \left[\sum \left\{ \frac{\partial \epsilon_t}{\partial \psi} \cdot \frac{\partial \epsilon_t}{\partial \psi'} + \frac{\partial^2 \epsilon_t}{\partial \psi \partial \psi'} \cdot \epsilon_t \right\} \right]^{-1} \sum \frac{\partial \epsilon_t}{\partial \psi} \cdot \epsilon_t \qquad (4.10)$$

where all the quantities on the right-hand side of (4.10) are evaluated at the current estimate, $\hat{\psi}$. The terms in the expression for the Hessian matrix, (4.9), which involve second derivatives will, however, be small relative to the terms which involve first derivatives only. This suggests the use of the modified iterative scheme

$$\psi^* = \hat{\psi} - \left[\sum \frac{\partial \epsilon_t}{\partial \psi} \cdot \frac{\partial \epsilon_t}{\partial \psi'} \right]^{-1} \sum \frac{\partial \epsilon_t}{\partial \psi} \cdot \epsilon_t \qquad (4.11)$$

which is generally known as *Gauss–Newton*.

The above procedure may be written more concisely by defining

$$z_t = -\partial \epsilon_t / \partial \psi \qquad (4.12)$$

where z_t, like ϵ_t, is understood to depend on ψ. Substituting (4.12) into (4.11) yields

$$\psi^* = \hat{\psi} + (\Sigma z_t z_t')^{-1} \Sigma z_t \epsilon_t \qquad (4.13)$$

Writing the iterations in the form (4.13) stresses even more clearly the interpretation of Gauss–Newton as a series of OLS regressions. At each step z_t and ϵ_t are evaluated at the point $\psi = \hat{\psi}$, and $\hat{\psi}$ is then updated by means of a regression of ϵ_t on z_t.

As in Newton–Raphson, it is generally desirable to incorporate a line search into the algorithm, and a variable step length may be introduced in the manner suggested by (2.1). A slightly different scheme, due to Marquardt (1963), is based on the same principle as the quadratic hill-climbing method described in Section 3. The iterations are of the form

$$\psi^* = \hat{\psi} + (\Sigma z_t z_t' + \mu I)^{-1} \Sigma z_t \epsilon_t \qquad (4.14)$$

where μ is a non-negative scalar which may be varied with each iteration. For a large value of μ, this scheme imparts a bias in the direction of steepest descent which may be advantageous if the starting point is some distance from the minimum. Combining (4.14) with a line search produces a powerful algorithm for which strong results are available on global convergence; see Wolfe (1978, Ch. 7).

A slightly different rationalisation may be given for the Gauss–Newton iteration for the non-linear regression model, (3.4.6). A first-order Taylor series expansion of $f(x_t;\psi)$ about $\hat{\psi}$ yields

$$f(x_t;\psi) \simeq f(x_t;\hat{\psi}) + (\psi - \hat{\psi})z_t \qquad (4.15)$$

since $z_t = \partial f(x_t;\psi)/\partial \psi$. Substituting in (3.4.6) then gives

$$y_t - f(x_t;\hat{\psi}) = (\psi - \hat{\psi})z_t + \epsilon_t, \qquad t = 1,\ldots,T \qquad (4.16)$$

This again suggests the iterative scheme (4.13), in which successive estimates of ψ are obtained by regressing the residuals from the current estimate on the partial derivatives of $f(x_t ; \psi)$ and subtracting from the current estimate.

Example 4 As a specific example of a non-linear regression model, consider

$$y_t = \alpha \exp(\beta x_t) + \epsilon_t, \qquad t = 1,\ldots,T \qquad (4.17)$$

The vector of partial derivatives is given by

$$z_t = \begin{pmatrix} \exp(\beta x_t) \\ \alpha x_t \exp(\beta x_t) \end{pmatrix} \qquad (4.18)$$

Regressing the residuals, $y_t - \hat{\alpha} \exp(\hat{\beta} x_t)$, on z_t, produces 'corrections', $\Delta\hat{\alpha}$ and $\Delta\hat{\beta}$, to the original estimates. The new estimates $\alpha^* = \hat{\alpha} + \Delta\hat{\alpha}$ and $\beta^* = \hat{\beta} + \Delta\hat{\beta}$ are then used to construct residuals and their derivatives, and the process is repeated until convergence.

Example 5 In Section 3.5 it was shown that maximising the likelihood function for an MA(1) model is equivalent to minimising a sum of squares function if ϵ_0 is taken to be fixed and equal to zero. The residuals, ϵ_t, are built up recursively from (3.5.8). The first derivatives may be constructed in a similar way since

$$\frac{\partial \epsilon_t}{\partial \theta} = -\theta \frac{\partial \epsilon_{t-1}}{\partial \theta} - \epsilon_{t-1} \quad , \qquad t = 1,\ldots,T \qquad (4.19)$$

with $\partial \epsilon_0/\partial \theta = 0$. Thus, given an initial estimate, $\hat{\theta}$, ϵ_t and $\partial \epsilon_t/\partial \theta$ may be evaluated and the estimate updated by (4.11).

Berndt, Hall, Hall and Hausman (BHHH)

Gauss–Newton has two main advantages over Newton–Raphson. First, it requires only first, and not second, derivatives. Secondly, the matrix used to approximate the Hessian is either positive definite or singular, and a singular matrix can always be avoided by a modification such as (4.14).

Berndt, Hall, Hall and Hausman (1974) have proposed an algorithm which retains the advantages of Gauss–Newton while being applicable to problems more general than the minimisation of a sum of squares. They suggest approximating the Hessian by

$$\sum_{t=1}^{T} \frac{\partial \log p(y_t;\psi)}{\partial \psi} \frac{\partial \log p(y_t;\psi)}{\partial \psi'}$$

The iterative scheme for $n = 1$ is therefore

$$\psi^* = \hat{\psi} + \lambda \left[\sum_{t=1}^{T} \left\{ \frac{\partial \log p(y_t;\psi)}{\partial \psi} \right\}^2 \right]^{-1} \sum_{t=1}^{T} \frac{\partial \log p(y_t; \psi)}{\partial \psi}$$

(4.20)

where λ is the variable step-length.

Example 6 For the estimation of the location parameters for a Cauchy distribution, the BHHH scheme is

$$\psi^* = \hat{\psi} + \frac{1}{2} \left[\sum_{t=1}^{T} \frac{(y_t - \psi)^2}{\{1 + (y_t - \psi)^2\}^2} \right]^{-1} \sum_{t=1}^{T} \frac{(y_t - \psi)}{1 + (y_t - \psi)^2}$$

(4.21)

cf.(4.4).

Systems of Equations

Consider the SURE model (2.9.15). The joint density function depends on two sets of parameters, those in β and those in Ω. Each set of parameters may be estimated very easily conditional on the other set. Thus the ML estimator of Ω conditional on β is given by

$$\tilde{\Omega}(\beta) = T^{-1} \sum_{t=1}^{T} \epsilon_t \epsilon_t'$$

(4.22)

where $\epsilon_t = y_t - X_t\beta$; cf. (3.4.32). The ML estimator of β conditional on Ω is given by GLS as in (2.9.17). The step-wise optimisation procedure described in Section 2 therefore provides a natural means of computing the unconditional ML estimates. The process starts off by applying OLS to each equation in turn and using the residuals to form an estimate of Ω. A feasible GLS estimate of β is then computed and the whole process carried on until convergence.

Maximising the likelihood function for the SURE model is equivalent to minimising

$$S = T \log |\Omega| + \sum_{t=1}^{T} \epsilon_t' \Omega^{-1} \epsilon_t \qquad (4.23)$$

A criterion function of this form often emerges in more general situations, as in the prediction error decomposition of (3.5.27). However, even with Ω known, such models tend to be non-linear. Hence an optimisation technique of the type described in previous sub-sections will usually be appropriate. When Ω is unknown, the optimisation procedure adopted for the parameters other than Ω may be embedded within a stepwise algorithm of the kind described in the previous paragraph.

For a criterion function of the form (4.23), in which ϵ_t is an $N \times 1$ vector, a generalisation of the Gauss–Newton algorithm is appropriate. Conditional on Ω, the iterative scheme is

$$\psi^* = \hat{\psi} + \left[\sum_{t=1}^{T} Z_t \Omega^{-1} Z_t' \right]^{-1} \sum_{t=1}^{T} Z_t \Omega^{-1} \epsilon_t \qquad (4.24)$$

where Z_t is an $n \times N$ matrix defined by $Z_t = -\partial \epsilon_t'/\partial \psi$. The relationship of (4.24) to (4.13) on the one hand, and to (2.9.17) on the other should be apparent. The scheme may be embedded within a stepwise procedure by updating the estimate of Ω after each iteration. Such a procedure will be referred to as *multivariate Gauss–Newton*.

Concentrating the Likelihood Function

The discussion so far has assumed that the likelihood function is to be maximised with respect to all n parameters in the vector ψ using a non-linear optimisation technique. However, since there may be a heavy penalty attached to having a large number of parameters in a non-linear optimisation routine, it often pays to explore ways in which this number may be reduced. In general, this is done by recognising that the model is *linear* in a subset of parameters. This means that if the remaining parameters are held constant, ML estimates of the first set of parameters may be obtained directly, without resorting to an iterative procedure. These estimates may be substituted into the likelihood function, and the resulting *concentrated* likelihood function maximised with respect to the second set of parameters only.

Example 6 The CES production function (2.1.12), is linear with respect to two parameters, β and α, if the disturbances are multiplicative. If $\epsilon_t \sim NID(0, \sigma^2)$, ML estimation is equivalent to non-linear least squares. For given values of γ and δ, the ML estimators of β and α are given by regressing $\log Q_t$ on $-\gamma^{-1} \{\log(1-\delta)L_t^{-\gamma} + \delta^{-\gamma}K_t\}$. Maximising the concentrated likelihood function is then equivalent to minimising the residual sum of squares with respect to γ and δ. Griliches and Ringstad (1971) estimate a series of CES functions in this way using a grid search.

Example 7 In the SURE model, Ω may be concentrated out of the likelihood function using (4.22). Since

$$\sum \epsilon_t' \tilde{\Omega}^{-1} \epsilon_t = tr(\tilde{\Omega}^{-1} \sum \epsilon_t \epsilon_t') = TN \tag{4.25}$$

it follows from (4.23) that maximising the concentrated likelihood function is equivalent to minimising the generalised sum of squares function, $S = |\Omega(\beta)|$.

An important practical point to note about working with a concentrated likelihood function is that analytic first derivatives may be obtained from the original likelihood. Suppose that the parameter vector is partitioned as $\psi = (\psi_1', \psi_2')'$, and that ψ_2 is concentrated out of the likelihood function by solving

$$\frac{\partial \log L(\psi_1, \psi_2)}{\partial \psi_2} = 0 \tag{4.26}$$

to yield $\tilde{\psi}_2(\psi_1)$. Maximising the concentrated log–likelihood function, $\log L_c\{\psi_1, \psi_2(\psi_1)\} = \log L_c(\psi_1)$, will usually be accomplished more effectively if first derivatives can be employed. Using a standard result on implicit functions,

$$\frac{\partial \log L_c(\psi_1)}{\partial \psi_1} = \frac{\partial \log L(\psi_1, \psi_2)}{\partial \psi_1} + \frac{\partial \log L(\psi_1, \psi_2)}{\partial \psi_2} \cdot \frac{\partial \psi_2}{\partial \psi_1} \tag{4.27}$$

When evaluated at $\tilde{\psi}_2(\psi_1)$, the last term in (4.27) disappears because of (4.26). Hence the first derivatives of $\log L_c(\psi_1)$ may be obtained by setting $\psi_2 = \tilde{\psi}_2(\psi_1)$ in the expression for $\partial \log L(\psi_1, \psi_2)/\partial \psi_1$.

4.5. Two-step Estimators

The iterative procedures described in Section 4 are of the form

$$\psi^* = \hat{\psi} + [I^*(\hat{\psi})]^{-1} D \log L(\hat{\psi}) \tag{5.1}$$

where $I^*(\hat{\psi})$ is the information matrix, or an approximation to it, evaluated at $\psi = \hat{\psi}$. In the Newton–Raphson procedure $I^*(\psi)$ is defined as the Hessian, multiplied by minus one, while in the method of scoring it is actually equal to the information matrix. However, (5.1) defines a fairly general iterative scheme in which a variety of expressions may be used for $I^*(\psi)$. The essential point is that under standard regularity conditions, $I^*(\psi)$ is asymptotically equivalent to the information matrix in the sense that

$$\lim T^{-1} I^*(\psi) = IA(\psi) \tag{5.2}$$

A two-step estimator is constructed by evaluating the r.h.s. of (5.1) at a *consistent* estimator of ψ. In other words only one iteration is carried out, with $\hat{\psi}$ being the initial consistent estimator of ψ^* the two-step estimator. The attraction of this procedure is that the two-step estimator has the same asymptotic distribution as the ML estimator. Thus, under the usual regularity conditions, it is asymptotically efficient. As such, it will be denoted by $\tilde{\psi}^*$.

The initial estimator must be consistent in order to ensure that

$$\text{plim } T^{-1}I^*(\hat{\psi}) = IA(\psi) \tag{5.3}$$

The proof given below also requires that $\hat{\psi}$ should have a well-defined asymptotic distribution, although this is not generally necessary for the result to be true.

Example 1   Consider the problem of estimating the location parameter for a Cauchy distribution. As shown in the previous section, the scoring algorithm provides a convenient iterative scheme for finding the ML estimator. It is therefore the natural approach to adopt for finding a two-step estimator. Taking the median to be the initial consistent estimator, an asymptotically efficient estimator of ψ is given directly by (4.4).

Example 2   When maximising the likelihood function is equivalent to minimising a sum of squares function, the two-step estimator may be computed by linear regression. In the MA(1) model a consistent estimator of θ is given by

$$\hat{\theta}_c = [1 - (1 - 4r_1^2)^{1/2}]/2r_1 \tag{5.4}$$

A single iteration of Gauss−Newton, i.e. a regression of ϵ_t on $\partial \epsilon_t/\partial \theta$, then yields an asymptotically efficient estimator of θ.

Estimators formed by one iteration of (5.1) are sometimes referred to as *linearised maximum likelihood*. This conveys their method of derivation, though 'two-step' gives a better insight into their construction, and is the term adopted here. Historically, two-step estimators in econometrics have not usually been derived through (5.1), although in a single equation context, at least, most asymptotically efficient two-step estimators may be obtained as special cases of this approach. This is of some importance, since for any model, (5.1) provides the basis for constructing a two-step estimation procedure. In most cases efficiency can be established formally, but even when this is difficult to do, it will still be generally safe to assume that (5.1) is a reasonably sensible guide to estimation.

Iterating (5.1) further will usually result in an estimate which is closer to the ML solution, although this certainly cannot be guaranteed. However, iterating beyond the first round will not change the asymptotic distribution of the estimator even if continuing the process eventually produces the ML estimator.[1] Small sample properties may be improved by iterating, but this can usually be determined only by Monte Carlo experiments. It is not possible to make general statements about the small sample efficiency of two-step estimators. In some cases a two-step estimator gives essentially the same performance as the ML estimator, while in others carrying out the full ML procedure shows a clear gain.

Statistical Basis of the Two-Step Estimator*

The proof that one iteration of (5.1) yields an asymptotically efficient estimator will be given for the case of a single parameter only. A general proof may be constructed along similar lines.

A Taylor series expansion of $D \log L(\hat{\psi})$ around ψ gives

$$D \log L(\hat{\psi}) \simeq D \log L(\psi) + (\hat{\psi} - \psi)D^2 \log L(\psi) \tag{5.5}$$

Compare the result of (3.3.4). Subtracting ψ from both sides of (5.1), multiplying by $\sqrt{T}$ and substituting for $D \log L(\hat{\psi})$ from (5.5) gives

$$\sqrt{T}(\tilde{\psi}^* - \psi) \simeq \sqrt{T}(\hat{\psi} - \psi) + \sqrt{T}\frac{D \log L(\psi)}{I^*(\hat{\psi})}$$
$$+ \frac{\sqrt{T}(\hat{\psi} - \psi)D^2 \log L(\psi)}{I^*(\hat{\psi})}$$

Since $\hat{\psi}$ is a consistent estimator of ψ, (5.3) is satisfied. Furthermore $\lim\{-T^{-1}D^2 \log L(\psi)\} = IA(\psi)$, and so if $\hat{\psi}$ has a well defined asymptotic distribution, it follows from Cramér's theorem that

$$-\sqrt{T}(\hat{\psi} - \psi)D^2 \log L(\psi)/I^*(\hat{\psi})$$

has the same limiting distribution as $\sqrt{T}(\hat{\psi} - \psi)$. The limiting distribution of $\sqrt{T}(\tilde{\psi}^* - \psi)$ may therefore be determined through

$$\frac{\sqrt{T} D \log L(\psi)}{I^*(\hat{\psi})} \tag{5.6}$$

Multiplying the numerator and denominator of (5.6) by $D^2 \log L(\psi)$ and rearranging gives

$$\sqrt{T}(\tilde{\psi}^* - \psi) \simeq \frac{\sqrt{T} D \log L(\psi)}{-D^2 \log L(\psi)}\left(\frac{-D^2 \log L(\psi)}{I^*(\hat{\psi})}\right) \tag{5.7}$$

In view of (5.3), the term in parentheses has a probability limit of unity, and on comparing (5.7) with (3.3.5) it will be seen that the limiting distribution

[1]ML estimators, however, have a property known as second-order efficiency, which two-step estimators do not, in general, possess; see for example, Rothenberg (1984). Nevertheless, if *two* iterations of (5.1) are carried out from a consistent starting point, it can be shown that second order efficiency is guaranteed also. This has implications for certain three-step procedures.

of $\sqrt{T}(\tilde{\psi}^* - \psi)$ is the same as that of $\sqrt{T}(\tilde{\psi} - \psi)$, where $\tilde{\psi}$ is the ML estimator. This is the desired result.

Regression

The generalised regression model of Section 2.4 plays a prominent role in econometrics. Suppose that the elements in the matrix V depend on a finite number of parameters in a vector, δ, but are independent of the regression parameters in β. If the disturbances are normally distributed, the information matrix is block diagonal with respect to β and δ. Furthermore

$$\frac{\partial \log L(\beta, \delta)}{\partial \beta} = \sigma^{-2} X' V^{-1} (y - X\beta) \tag{5.8}$$

and so one iteration of the method of scoring for β yields

$$\beta^* = \hat{\beta} + (X'\hat{V}^{-1}X)^{-1} X'\hat{V}^{-1}(y - X\hat{\beta})$$

$$= (X'\hat{V}^{-1}X)^{-1} X'\hat{V}^{-1}y \tag{5.9}$$

where $\hat{V}$ is formed from an initial estimator of δ, $\hat{\delta}$. If $\hat{\beta}$ and $\hat{\delta}$ are consistent, (5.9) is an asymptotically efficient two-step estimator. However, it is also the expression for the feasible GLS estimator.

Example 3 In the multiplicative heteroscedasticity model, (3.4.15), a consistent estimator of δ may be obtained by regressing $\log \hat{u}_t^2$ on w_t, where $\hat{u}_t$ is the tth OLS residual. An efficient two-step estimator of β is then given by a feasible GLS regression of the form (4.5a). Less obviously, an efficient two-step estimator of δ is obtained from (4.5b).

A *three-step* estimator of β may be constructed from the two-step estimator of δ. While basing the GLS estimator of β on an efficient estimator of δ has no effect on its asymptotic distribution, it seems reasonable to suppose that its small-sample properties will be improved.

Example 4 The scoring algorithm for the Poisson regression model was given in (4.6). The two-step estimator is simply WLS applied with an initial consistent estimator given by OLS.

4.6. Test Statistics and Confidence Intervals

All the methods described in Section 3, 4 and 5 are based on the information matrix or an approximation to it. An estimator of the covariance matrix of $\tilde{\psi}$ will therefore be automatically available. If, on the other hand, a direct search is used, a numerical approximation based on (2.5) will usually be appropriate.

From the point of view of constructing asymptotically valid test statistics, all that is required is a consistent estimator of $IA(\psi)$. Thus, if avar($\tilde{\psi}$) denotes an estimator of the asymptotic covariance matrix, (3.3.2), it must satisfy the condition that

$$\text{plim } T \cdot \text{avar}(\tilde{\psi}) = IA^{-1}(\psi) \tag{6.1}$$

Asymptotic Standard Errors

An *asymptotic standard error* of any estimator, $\hat{\psi}$, is defined as a consistent estimator of the standard deviation of the limiting distribution of $\sqrt{T}(\hat{\psi} - \psi)$, divided by $\sqrt{T}$. When $\hat{\psi}$ is an ML estimator, or an estimator with the same asymptotic distribution, any approximation to avar($\tilde{\psi}$) which satisfies (6.1) yields a set of valid asymptotic standard errors.

Once valid asymptotic standard errors have been computed, the asymptotic 't-ratios',

$$\hat{\psi}_i/\sqrt{\text{avar}(\hat{\psi}_i)}, \quad i = 1,\ldots,n \tag{6.2}$$

may be constructed. It follows directly from the argument used in (1.4.19) that these are distributed as $N(0, 1)$ variables in large samples. Similarly large sample confidence intervals may also be formed.

In small samples, different methods of computing asymptotic standard errors can give conflicting results. This can happen even where an estimate can be obtained without an iterative procedure.

Example 1 For the AR(1) model it was shown in (3.5.24) that

$$\text{Avar}(\tilde{\phi}) = (1 - \phi^2)/T \tag{6.3}$$

The square root of

$$\text{avar}(\tilde{\phi}) = (1 - \tilde{\phi}^2)/T \tag{6.4}$$

therefore provides an obvious asymptotic standard error. However, if $\tilde{\phi}$ is obtained by regressing y_t on y_{t-1}, it may be more convenient to compute the asymptotic standard error as

$$s \left/ \left(\sum_{t=2}^{T} y_{t-1}^2 \right)^{1/2} \right. \tag{6.5}$$

This is the expression suggested by (2.3.17). It is perfectly valid in this context as

$$\text{plim } \left\{ Ts^2 \left/ \sum_{t=2}^{T} y_{t-1}^2 \right. \right\} = \sigma^2/\text{plim} T^{-1} \sum_{t=2}^{T} y_{t-1}^2 = 1 - \phi^2$$

The advantage over (6.4) is that hypotheses on ϕ can be tested within the standard OLS framework.

Two-Step Estimators

In a two-step procedure, an estimate of the asymptotic covariance matrix of $\tilde{\psi}^*$ is given by the inverse of $I^*(\hat{\psi})$. This must satisfy (6.1) if $\tilde{\psi}^*$ is to be asymptotically efficient; cf. (5.3). A more accurate estimate may be obtained if $I^*(\psi)$ is evaluated at $\psi = \tilde{\psi}^*$, but this will usually be less convenient.

Example 2 In Example 5.2 it was shown that an efficient estimator of θ in an MA(1) model can be constructed by regressing ϵ_t on $\partial \epsilon_t / \partial \theta$ with $\theta = \hat{\theta}_c$. An asymptotic standard error for $\tilde{\theta}^*$ may be obtained by treating the derivative of ϵ_t as though it were an explanatory variable in a standard regression model.

Notes

General treatments of numerical optimisation will be found in Wolfe (1978), Dixon (1972) and Box *et al.* (1969). In the UK the NAG collection of programs is widely available and the manual contains a discussion of the various algorithms for numerical optimisation.

Exercises

1. Suppose that the disturbances in a linear regression model have a standardised Cauchy distribution. Show that the Newton–Raphson scheme may be interpreted in terms of a series of regressions.
2. Why might the transformation $\psi = \{1 - \exp(-\theta)\}/\{1 + \exp(\theta)\}$ be useful in constrained optimisation?
3. Show that Gauss–Newton is identical to the method of scoring in a non-linear regression model.
4. What would happen to the Newton–Raphson algorithm in Example 3.1 if the starting value was $\hat{\psi} = 1.0$? Explain briefly how a quasi-Newton algorithm would work in these circumstances.
5. For the ARMA(1, 1) model, (1.5.21), show that Gauss–Newton breaks down if $\hat{\phi} = \hat{\theta} = 0$. Show that the modified scheme (4.14) avoids this problem if μ is strictly positive. Explain how you would construct an asymptotic covariance matrix for the ML estimates in this model. How would you test the hypothesis that $\phi = 0.5$?
6. Derive expressions for the first two theoretical autocorrelations, ϱ_1 and ϱ_2, in an ARMA(1, 1) model. Hence obtain expressions for calculating consistent estimators of ϕ and θ from r_1 and r_2. Show how these estimates may be used to construct an asymptotically efficient two-step estimator of (ϕ, θ).
7. Write down the scoring algorithm for the logit model given at the end of Section 3.4. What is the relationship between scoring and the Newton–Raphson algorithm in this case?

5
Test Procedures and Model Selection

5.1. Introduction

The discussion in the previous chapters has centred on the estimation of a correctly specified model. In the context of maximum likelihood, this means that the distribution of the observations on the sample space is known apart from a finite number of real parameters. The previous chapters discussed how these parameters could be estimated efficiently, but nothing was said regarding the way in which one might arrive at a suitable specification in the first place.

Before proceeding further, it is worth going back to Section 1.1 and recalling exactly what is meant by a 'correctly specified' or 'true' model in a practical context. In the real world the process by which observations are generated will almost invariably be complex. The motivation behind model construction is not to provide a description of this process, but rather to extract its main features.

Bearing this in mind, what is required is a model which is relatively simple, but has high predictive power. It is against this yardstick that a model must be assessed. The concept of a 'true' model is therefore a purely theoretical one, but it provides a basis upon which criteria for detecting misspecification may be developed. In addition it enables the consequences of inappropriate modelling to be explored and discussed in a concrete form.

Consequences of Misspecification

The consequences of adopting an inappropriate model will depend on its relationship to the true model. Three cases may be distinguished. In the first, the adopted model is *underparameterised* in the sense that it imposes invalid constraints on the true model. In the second, it is *overparameterised,* being more general than is necessary. In the third, the assumed and true models are *non-nested*: neither can be obtained as a special case of the other.

146

Overparameterisation tends to have rather different consequences from underparameterisation or the adoption of a model which is not nested within the true model. This has important implications for model selection strategies. Although no general conclusions can be drawn from the example below, the trade-off it reveals between bias and efficiency is not untypical.

Example Suppose that the true model is

$$y_t = \alpha + \beta x_t + \epsilon_t, \qquad \epsilon_t \sim NID(0, \sigma^2) \tag{1.1}$$

while in the assumed model y_t is taken to be a linear function of x_t and another variable, z_t. The consequence of regressing y_t on both z_t and x_t is to yield an estimator of β, $\hat{b}$, which is unbiased, but has a variance,

$$\text{Var}(\hat{b}) = \sigma^2 / \{\sum x_{*t}^2 (1 - r_{xz}^2)\} \tag{1.2}$$

where $x_{*t} = x_t - \bar{x}$ and r_{xz} is the correlation coefficient between x_t and z_t. Hence, $\hat{b}$ is an inefficient estimator of β since

$$\text{Eff}(\hat{b}) = \text{Var}(b)/\text{Var}(\hat{b}) = 1 - r_{xz}^2 \leq 1 \tag{1.3}$$

where b is the OLS estimator in (1.1). The estimator of the coefficient of z_t will have an expectation of zero and so any predictions made from the overparameterised model will also be unbiased. However, they will have a higher MSE than predictions from the true model. Note that overfitting can be disastrous in certain circumstances. If x_t and z_t are perfectly collinear, the model ceases to be identified (cf. the discussion in Section 3.6).

If the true model is

$$y_t = \alpha + \beta x_t + \gamma z_t + \epsilon_t, \qquad \epsilon_t \sim NID(0, \sigma^2) \tag{1.4}$$

but it is incorrectly assumed that $\gamma = 0$, the estimator of β will generally be biased. If $b^\dagger$ is the estimator obtained from regressing y_t on x_t, then

$$E(b^\dagger) = \beta + \gamma \sum x_{*t} z_{*t} / \sum x_{*t}^2 = \beta + \gamma r_{xz} \sqrt{\sum z_{*t}^2 / x_{*t}^2} \tag{1.5}$$

Thus $b^\dagger$ will be biased unless x_t and z_t are orthogonal, and this bias will persist as the sample size increases. However, if r_{xz}^2 is close to unity, the omission of z_t will have little effect on predictions.

Test Procedures

There is an important distinction to be drawn between tests of specification and tests of misspecification. This can be illustrated by model (1.4). Suppose that the only two formulations under consideration are (1.4) itself and the same model with z_t omitted. A natural way to proceed would be to estimate

(1.4) and carry out a t-test of the hypothesis that $\gamma = 0$. This is a test of *specification* and in Section 3 it is shown that a t-test of this type would, in a certain sense, be an optimal test procedure. There would be little virtue in estimating the restricted model and then using the residuals to test whether or not z_t should have been included in the regression. On the other hand, including z_t in the model might not have been an obvious possibility at the outset. Therefore y_t could have been regressed on x_t with no clear alternative in view. In such a case, it would be prudent to try and assess whether the model was adequate. If it were not, there should be some indication in the residuals. Unless x_t and z_t are orthogonal, the residuals will have non-zero expectation, and so it should be possible to detect some pattern either visually or by means of an appropriate test statistic. This would be a test of *misspecification*.

Unlike a test of specification, therefore, a test of misspecification is constructed with no clear alternative hypothesis in mind. As such, it is a procedure designed for assessing the goodness of fit of the model implied by a particular maintained hypothesis. However, although the alternative does remain rather vague, the choice of a particular test statistic is usually motivated by a suspected departure from the maintained hypothesis in some particular direction. Thus, for example, general tests against 'serial correlation' or 'heteroscedasticity' may be constructed, even though these phenomena may be modelled in a number of different ways.

Both types of test have a role to play in model building. It will be argued later that it is generally advisable to consider all possible forms of the model before any estimation is carried out, and then to plan to test the various hypotheses in a systematic fashion. Nevertheless it is not usually possible to be certain that all the alternatives have been considered, and so such a process should be supplemented by tests of misspecification.

Not all test procedures may be neatly classified as tests of specification or misspecification. Suppose that the models

$$H_1 : y_t = \beta x_t + \epsilon_t, \qquad \epsilon_t \sim NID(0, \sigma^2) \qquad (1.6)$$

and

$$H_2 : y_t = \gamma z_t + \epsilon_t, \qquad \epsilon_t \sim NID(0, \sigma^2) \qquad (1.7)$$

are under consideration as alternative explanations of the behaviour of y. These are non-nested in the sense that neither one can be obtained as a special case of the other.

There are basically two ways of approaching a non-nested problem. The first is to view it as a question of discrimination: *either H_1 or H_2* must be chosen and the choice must be based on some suitable criterion indicating goodness of fit. Alternatively the investigator may entertain two further possibilities, namely that both hypotheses may be accepted or both may be rejected. The first of these conclusions implies that there is insufficient data to separate the two hypotheses, while the second implies that neither model is satisfactory. Thus although two well-defined hypotheses are under consideration, the fact that both may be rejected suggests that the adopted procedure is, in part, a test of misspecification.

The test procedures described so far are all carried out within the sample. Hence the same observations being used to select a model are also being employed to estimate it. In general, the model which finally emerges must be regarded as being the product of a certain amount of 'data mining'. Hence its validity can really only be assessed with respect to a completely fresh set of data. This leads to the idea of *post-sample predictive testing*. The observations used in this exercise are often made available by the researcher deliberately omitting a set of points from the data used to construct the model.

Four different aspects of specification testing have therefore been distinguished, and these are discussed in the remainder of the chapter. Tests of misspecification are introduced in Section 2, with examples being drawn from linear regression. Most of these tests are based on residuals. However, because the residuals often have a natural interpretation under certain types of misspecification, graphical procedures can also play a useful role in the general process of 'diagnostic checking'.

Section 3 deals with the classical theory of hypothesis testing, and the construction of tests based on the likelihood ratio principle. Two related test procedures are discussed in Sections 4 and 5. These lead to what are commonly known as Wald and Lagrange multiplier tests, and they supplement the likelihood ratio principle in forming the basis for tests of specification. All three tests have certain desirable properties, although the justification for their use relies, in general, on large sample arguments. The choice between the three approaches rests mainly on computational considerations. The likelihood ratio approach requires that the model be estimated under both the null and alternative hypotheses, i.e. it requires estimation of both the *restricted* and *unrestricted* models. A Wald test, on the other hand, may be based on estimates from the unrestricted model, while a Lagrange multiplier statistic requires only that the model be estimated under the null. The question of which statistic is easiest to compute depends on the structure of the particular problem.

Because the Lagrange multiplier approach is based on estimation under the null hypothesis, many of the tests constructed in this way may be associated with tests of misspecification. The recognition that certain diagnostics are basically Lagrange multiplier tests provides a good deal of insight into their potential effectiveness, as well as suggesting viable generalisations. However, it is always important to distinguish the sense in which such tests are used. If a test of misspecification rejects the null hypothesis, this implies that the model is inadequate, without necessarily pointing to the more general model underlying the Lagrange multiplier interpretation.

Criteria for discriminating between models are introduced in Section 6. Although discussed primarily in the context of non-nested hypotheses, there is no reason why they should not be used in nested situations, and a number of examples of such applications are given later in the book. The remaining part of Section 6 describes test procedures applicable to the non-nested case. Section 7 deals with post-sample predictive testing, while Section 8 considers an overall strategy for model selection.

5.2. Tests of Misspecification

The purpose of constructing a model is to systematically account for as much of the variation in the observations as possible. The movements not captured by the fitted model are termed *residuals*, and if the model is reasonably adequate these residuals should be approximately random. Departures from randomness are an indication that the model is failing to pick up a systematic component in the observations, and an attempt should therefore be made to find a better model.

Residuals play an important role in procedures for detecting misspecification. Such procedures may embody a number of test statistics, since lack of randomness may manifest itself in a number of different ways. However, although test statistics provide a concise summary of the behaviour of residuals, it is generally advisable to plot the residuals. This may be done in a number of different ways, and an examination of the various plots can often prove extremely useful.

The discussion of tests of misspecification will be carried out mainly within the context of a classical linear regression model estimated by ordinary least squares. As well as being of importance in itself, this serves as a convenient vehicle for developing points of much wider applicability. The assumed model is therefore of the form (2.1.1), with the disturbances independently distributed with mean zero and variance σ^2. Since the construction of exact tests generally requires that the disturbances be normally distributed, this will be taken to hold throughout.

Residuals and Misspecification

The properties of the OLS residuals in a correctly specified model were derived in Section 2.7, where it was shown that the vector e has a multivariate normal distribution with mean vector 0 and covariance matrix $\sigma^2 M$. Thus even though the disturbances may be homoscedastic and uncorrelated, this will not, in general, be true for the OLS residuals. On the other hand, it can be shown that e converges in distribution to u as $T \to \infty$. This result holds even if the disturbance term is misspecified. In that case $E(e) = 0$ while

$E(ee') = \sigma^2 MVM'$, where $\sigma^2 V$ is the covariance matrix of u. However, in large samples e is normally distributed with zero mean and a covariance matrix given approximately by $\sigma^2 V$. Thus the OLS residuals will tend to mirror the properties of the true disturbances, even though their respective distributions are not, strictly speaking, identical.

The behaviour of the OLS residuals under structural misspecification is less obvious, but more interesting. Suppose that the assumed model is of the form (2.1.5), while the true model is

$$y = X_r \gamma_r + f + \epsilon, \qquad \epsilon \sim N(0, \sigma^2 I) \tag{2.1}$$

where X_r is a $T \times r$ matrix whose columns are a subset of the columns of X corresponding to correctly specified variables, and γ_r is an $r \times 1$ vector of parameters. This set-up covers both functional misspecification and omitted variables, depending on the composition of the elements of the $T \times 1$ vector f.

Since

$$e = My = Mf + M\epsilon \tag{2.2}$$

it follows that e will have a mean vector Mf and a covariance matrix $\sigma^2 M$. Thus the expectation of the residual vector is equal to the residual vector obtained by regressing f on X. As an example, suppose that the true model is

$$y_t = \alpha + \beta x_t + \gamma x_t^2 + \epsilon_t \tag{2.3}$$

but that the term in x_t^2 is omitted. The expectation of the residual vector will be equal to γ multiplied by the vector of OLS residuals obtained by regressing x_t^2 on x_t.

The properties of other residuals may be analysed in a similar way. The LUS residuals, (2.7.5), have $E(e^*) = Cf$ and $Var(e^*) = \sigma^2 I$ under misspecification of the type analysed in (2.1). The expectation of a LUS residual is therefore given by the corresponding vector of residuals obtained by regressing f on X.

The expectations of the residuals determine their overall pattern. This is important insofar as it gives us some insight into the likely patterns of residuals under various types of misspecification. One attraction of the recursive residuals is that their behaviour in a misspecified model is very different from that of the OLS residuals. This means that test procedures based on recursive residuals may be *complementary* to those based on OLS residuals. As an example, consider the functional misspecification which arises when x_t^2 is omitted from (2.3). Figure 5.1 shows the expectations of OLS, BLUS and recursive residuals when the data are arranged with the x_t's in ascending order and $\gamma = 3$. While the BLUS and OLS residuals show a similar pattern, that of the recursive residuals is entirely different, with all the expectations having the same sign. A heuristic argument as to why this is the case can be given with the aid of figure 5.2. Since the underlying relationship between y and x is quadratic rather than linear, the prediction errors, $\tilde{v}_t = y_t - x_t' b_{t-1}$, $t = k + 1, \ldots, T$, all tend to have the same sign.

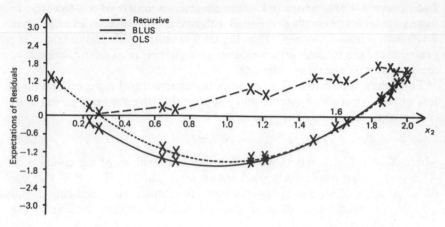

Figure 5.1   Pattern of Expectations of Residuals for Model (2.3)

Source: This figure is reproduced from Harvey and Collier (1977) with the kind permission of the *Journal of Econometrics*.

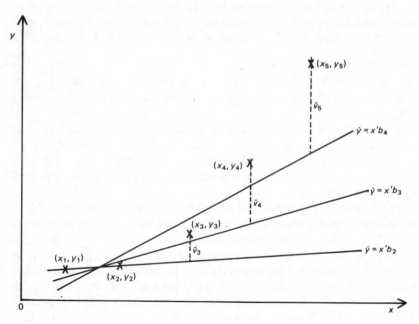

Figure 5.2   Derivation of Recursive Residuals for a Misspecified Bivariate Regression
          Model

Source: See figure 5.1.

The distinctive pattern of the recursive residuals may be exploited to yield useful test statistics as well as graphical procedures. By way of contrast, BLUS residuals tend to follow the OLS residuals more closely and hence yield little

additional information. In describing procedures for detecting misspecification, therefore, the emphasis will be primarily on OLS and recursive
residuals.

Graphical Techniques

A good deal of information may be obtained simply by plotting residuals
and examining them for some distinctive pattern. The plots may be against
time, or against one of the explanatory variables. This last type of plot may
be particularly valuable if it is suspected that the variable in question is subject
to functional misspecification.

The information contained in the residuals may also be assessed by plotting
the cumulative sum (CUSUM) and cumulative sum of squares (CUSUMSQ).
The first of these procedures is used primarily with recursive residuals, a plot
based on OLS residuals being difficult to interpret because of the constraint
that the residuals finally sum to zero. The CUSUM of recursive residuals
is defined by

$$W_t = \hat{\sigma}^{-1} \sum_{j=k+1}^{t} v_j, \quad t = k + 1, \ldots, T \tag{2.4}$$

where

$$\hat{\sigma}^2 = \Sigma(v_t - \bar{v})^2/(T - k - 1)$$

with $\bar{v}$ being the arithmetic mean of the residuals.

If the model is incorrectly specified, there may be a tendency for a
disproportionate number of recursive residuals to have the same sign. The
cumulative effect of this will then tend to show up in W_t moving away from
the horizontal axis. The functional misspecification for (2.3) provides a good
example. This type of behaviour also arises when a structural break occurs,
the point at which it happens being indicated by the beginning of a secular
increase or decrease in W_t.

Two lines drawn symmetrically above and below $W_t = 0$ provide a means
of assessing the significance of departures from the horizontal axis. The lines
are constructed in such a way that the probability of crossing either one or
both of them is equal to a given significance level. The underlying theory,
which is based on results in Brownian motion, will not be dealt with here.
However, the equation of the lines is given quite straightforwardly by

$$W = \pm \{a\sqrt{T - k} + 2a(t - k)/(T - k)^{1/2}\} \tag{2.5}$$

where $a = 0.948$ for a significance level of 5% and 0.850 for 10%.

The CUSUMSQ is based on a plot of the quantities

$$WW_t = \sum_{j=k+1}^{t} v_j^2 \Bigg/ \sum_{t=k+1}^{T} v_t^2, \quad t = k+1, \ldots, T \tag{2.6}$$

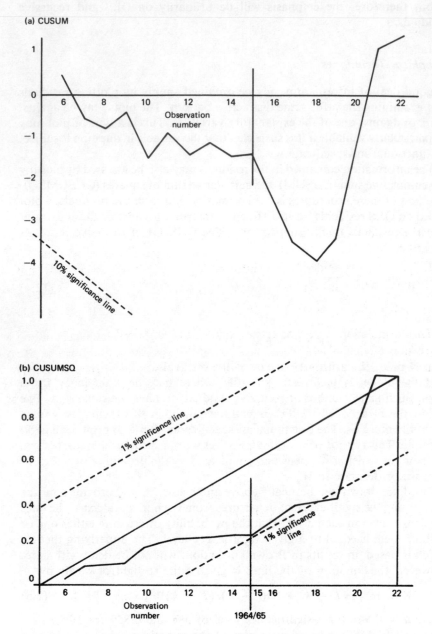

Figure 5.3 CUSUM and CUSUM of Squares of Recursive Residuals for Local
Telephone Calls

Source: This figure is reproduced from Brown, Durbin and Evans (1975) with the kind permission of the *Journal of the Royal Statistical Society* and the authors.

When the model is correctly specified, WW_t has a Beta distribution with a mean of $(t - k)/(T - k)$. This suggests drawing a pair of lines

$$WW = \pm c_0 + (t - k)/(T - k) \qquad (2.7)$$

parallel to the mean value line and rejecting H_0, the null hypothesis of correct specification, if either of the lines is crossed. The value of c_0 is determined such that the probability that either line is crossed under H_0 is equal to the desired significance level. Table C provides the required values of c_0 (see p. 365).

The CUSUMSQ plot provides a useful complement to the CUSUM plot. It may be applied with OLS as well as recursive residuals, although the test procedure just described assumes that the residuals are $NID(0, \sigma^2)$. When used with recursive residuals it should provide a means of detecting a structural break. As regards other types of misspecification, both OLS and recursive residual plots will be sensitive to variances increasing over time. However, although both the CUSUM and CUSUMSQ techniques can be used as test procedures against particular types of misspecification, they are best regarded as 'data analytic' techniques; i.e. the value of the plots lies in the information to be gained simply by inspecting them. The significance lines constructed are, to paraphrase Brown *et al.* (1975, p. 155), best regarded as *yardsticks* against which to assess the observed plots rather than as formal tests of significance.

Example Figure 5.3a reproduced from Brown *et al.* (1975, p. 159), illustrates the use of the CUSUM technique for detecting a structural break. The data relate to a model in which the growth in local telephone calls is explained in terms of four other variables and a constant term. The model shows no sign of instability up to 1964/65, but after that point the CUSUM shows a definite downward movement. This accorded with the limited prior knowledge of the data which suggested that the estimates of local telephone calls might be subject to some uncertainty. Thus the 'structural break' detected in this case really represents a break in the data series on the dependent variable. Figure 5.3b which is also reproduced from Brown *et al.* shows the plot of the CUSUM of squares, (2.6). Like the CUSUM this indicates some instability, although it is less easy to pinpoint exactly where the break occurs.

Although the CUSUM plot in figure 5.3a clearly indicates some instability beyond 1964/65, it is not formally significant. This is quite likely to be the case, even if there is a genuine structural break in the data. Thus figure 5.3a highlights the point that the CUSUM and CUSUM of squares plots contain more information than can be summarised in a single test statistic.

Test Statistics

The departures from randomness exhibited by the residuals in a misspecified model may be captured by a limited number of test statistics. Such statistics provide a compact summary of the information contained in the residuals. However, they should not be regarded as an alternative to visual checks, but rather as complementary to them.

Misspecification test statistics should have a number of desirable properties. The first is that they should be relatively easy to compute. The second is that their distribution under the null hypothesis should be known, and that significance points for this distribution should be readily available. If the distribution is known exactly, the critical region may be defined so as to yield a test of the desired size. However, for many statistics the distribution may only be derived asymptotically, in which case the actual size of the test will not be equal to the nominal size. Such tests are often termed *large sample* tests. This terminology indicates that the choice of critical region can only be justified on an asymptotic basis, in contrast to the situation for *exact* tests. However, it must be stressed that this consideration by no means precludes the use of large sample tests when the sample size is small. Choosing a test simply because its size is known exactly may not be good practice if its power characteristics are poor.

Power, of course, is a crucial aspect of any test procedure, but in diagnostic checking the issue is complicated by the fact that the researcher may have several different types of misspecification in mind. Furthermore, the alternative hypotheses implied by these misspecifications are bound to be vague. Nevertheless, a test statistic should, as a minimum requirement, exhibit a 'reasonably' high power against at least one well-defined alternative. If a test statistic exhibits high power against several types of alternative hypothesis, it is obviously useful as a general test of misspecification. Nevertheless, test statistics which are *robust* to certain classes of specification error can play a valuable complementary role, since they help to provide some indication of the direction of misspecification.

The *Durbin–Watson d-statistic* is defined by

$$d = \frac{\sum\limits_{t=2}^{T} (e_t - e_{t-1})^2}{\sum\limits_{t=1}^{T} e_t^2} \tag{2.8}$$

and this forms the basis for what is arguably the most important test of misspecification in linear regression. The d-statistic was originally constructed for use in a test against a first-order autoregressive process in the disturbances, and it will be fully described in that context in Chapter 6. For the moment, it is important to note simply that the distribution of d is centred around two when the model is correctly specified, but tends towards zero if the residuals exhibit positive serial correlation. Now, while serial correlation in the disturbances implies serial correlation in the residuals, the converse is not true. Thus although a low value of d could indicate a serially correlated disturbance term, it could also be symptomatic of some other type of misspecification. In particular, it should be clear from figure 5.1 that positive serial correlation can be expected when the functional form is inappropriate. A similar pattern may also emerge when a variable has been omitted.

Unfortunately the distribution of d depends on X, the matrix of regressors and so exact significance points cannot be tabulated. However, d is asymptotically normal with a mean of 2 and a variance of $4/T$, and this result provides the basis for a large sample test procedure.

There is no difficulty in basing an exact test on a set of LUS residuals. In the context of serial correlation, the von Neumann Ratio or the modified von Neumann Ratio is the appropriate statistic. Using recursive residuals, the *modified von Neumann Ratio* takes the form

$$\text{MVNR} = \frac{T-k}{T-k-1} \cdot \frac{\sum\limits_{t=k+2}^{T} (v_t - v_{t-1})^2}{\sum\limits_{t=k+1}^{T} v_t^2} \tag{2.9}$$

Significance points may be obtained from table B, although if the sample size is large, a satisfactory approximation is obtained from a normal distribution with mean 2 and variance $4/(T-k)$. As with the d-statistic, a one-tailed test against positive autocorrelation provides the most appropriate basis for a general test of misspecification.

In time series regression, it is natural to take the first k observations as the 'base' and to calculate recursive residuals corresponding to observations $y_{k+1}, \ldots, y_T$. However, other orderings of the data may sometimes be more appropriate. For example, if functional misspecification is suspected, it may be preferable to have the observations on a particular explanatory variable in increasing order of magnitude.

A second test statistic based on recursive residuals is given by

$$\psi = \left\{ (T-k-1)^{-1} \sum\limits_{t=k+1}^{T} (v_t - \bar{v})^2 \right\}^{-1/2} (T-k)^{-1/2} \sum\limits_{t=k+1}^{T} v_t$$

$$\tag{2.10}$$

When the model is correctly specified, ψ has a t-distribution with $T - k - 1$ degrees of freedom, a result which follows immediately from the properties of the recursive residuals. A two-sided *'recursive t-test'* may therefore be carried out. This is likely to be particularly effective in situations where the recursive residuals tend to have the same sign, as in figure 5.1. A second example concerns structural change. This is precisely the kind of misspecification against which the CUSUM of recursive residuals is effective. In fact the two procedures are closely related since $\psi = (T - k)^{-1/2} W_T$.

A Sign test provides a simple alternative to (2.10). Under the null hypothesis, the expected number of positive recursive residuals is equal to $(T - k)/2$. A critical region may therefore be constructed from the binomial distribution. However, the evidence presented in Harvey and Collier (1977) suggests that the Sign test tends to lack power compared with the t-test. Nevertheless, it is very simple and it may be more robust to non-normality.

There is no OLS counterpart to (2.10) since $\Sigma e_t = 0$. BLUS and other types of LUS residual may be used to form analogous t-statistics, but there is no obvious reason as to why they should be effective in the kind of situation just described. The great advantage of the recursive residuals is that they have a natural interpretation, and this can be exploited in deriving suitable test procedures.

A number of test statistics may be used to detect systematic patterns in the variance of the residuals. These may be termed *heteroscedasticity* tests, although heteroscedasticity in the residuals may be symptomatic of a good deal of other things besides heteroscedasticity in the disturbances.

Heteroscedasticity tests often involve some grouping of observations. Residuals which are relatively homogeneous with regard to variance are then contrasted with other groups of residuals. Thus if it is felt that there may be a tendency for the variances of the residuals to increase over time, a natural test statistic to adopt is

$$H = \sum_{t=T-m+1}^{T} e_t^2 \bigg/ \sum_{t=1}^{m} e_t^2 \qquad (2.11)$$

where $m \simeq T/3$. The purpose in dropping some observations is to accentuate any difference between the numerator and denominator of H.

High values of (2.11) indicate a rejection of the null hypothesis of correct specification, but the problem with using this statistic is that its distribution depends on the matrix of regressors, X. A large sample test may, however, be obtained by noting that mH is asymptotically χ_m^2 under the null hypothesis. This follows because the OLS residuals converge in distribution to the true disturbances and

$$\text{plim } m^{-1} \sum_{t=1}^{m} e_t^2 = \sigma^2$$

An exact heteroscedasticity test may be based on any set of LUS residuals. For recursive residuals, the statistic

$$H\dagger = \sum_{t=T-m+1}^{T} v_t^2 \bigg/ \sum_{t=k+1}^{k+m} v_t^2 \qquad (2.12)$$

has an $F_{m,\,m}$ distribution under the null hypothesis, a suitable choice of m being $(T - k)/3$.

A final method of testing for heteroscedastic residuals is provided by the CUSUMSQ plot. This may have wider applicability than (2.12), since it can still be effective in situations where the variances are not monotonically increasing.

The standardised third and fourth moments of the residuals provide information about possible non-normality of the disturbances. They are defined as

$$\sqrt{b_1} = \tilde{\sigma}^{-3} \sum e_t^3 / T$$

and

$$b_2 = \tilde{\sigma}^{-4} \sum e_t^4 / T$$

where $\tilde{\sigma}^2$ is the ML estimator, (3.4.3). These statistics are the basic measures of skewness and kurtosis, and for a normal distribution they should be centred around zero and three respectively. In large samples

$$\sqrt{b_1} \sim AN(0, 6/T)$$

and

$$b_2 \sim AN(3, 24/T)$$

when the model is correctly specified; see Bowman and Shenton (1975). A test for non-normality may therefore be based on the statistic

$$N = (T/6)b_1 + (T/24)(b_2 - 3)^2 \tag{2.13}$$

Under the null hypothesis, this statistic has a χ_2^2 distribution in large samples.

All the tests considered so far in this sub-section have been based directly on residuals. However, tests of misspecification may easily be constructed in other ways. An example is the RESET test developed by Ramsey and Schmidt (1976) in which powers of the explanatory variables are added to the regression equation and tested for significance. Thus if the maintained hypothesis were (1.1), x_t^2, x_t^3 and x_t^4 might be added to the regression and the joint significance of their coefficients tested by the usual F-statistic. The rationale for such a procedure in the context of suspected functional misspecification is obvious. However, RESET has also been proposed as a general test for specification error in regression.

The form of the test statistics described so far has been justified mainly on an intuitive basis. Given the kind of misspecification one has in mind, a reasonably sensible test statistic can often be constructed on the basis of the expected behaviour of the residuals. However, the appropriate form for such a test statistic may not always be apparent. In these circumstances, a more formal approach based on the Lagrange multiplier test principle can often prove useful. The Lagrange multiplier procedure is introduced in Section

5, and some of the examples given there show how this approach can lead to suitable tests of misspecification.

Concluding Remarks

A number of tests for checking the specification of a regression model have been suggested. As with the accompanying graphical procedures, these tests are based primarily on OLS and recursive residuals. Other LUS residuals could also be used, but there is no evidence, as yet, to indicate that they might yield additional information.

Because a whole battery of tests is being applied to the model, the results must be treated with some care. In particular, the probability of rejecting the model when it is true may be relatively high. A further conceptual problem arises when a test is carried out after a visual inspection of the residuals has suggested that such a test might be appropriate. For reasons such as these, misspecification test procedures are, strictly speaking, invalid when viewed in a classical framework, and the term 'diagnostic' is often more appropriate.

It has already been noted that a 'significant' value of a particular test statistic may be indicative of more than one type of specification error. Thus the maintained hypothesis may be rejected, but without a clear indication of where the fault lies. However, a combination of the results from several test statistics can be rather more informative. For example, the Durbin–Watson d-statistic is, amongst other things, sensitive to structural change and functional misspecification, as well as serial correlation in the disturbances. On the other hand, the recursive t-statistic has moderately high power against certain types of structural change and functional misspecification, yet is relatively robust to serial correlation in the disturbances.

All the discussion so far has assumed a normally distributed disturbance term. If this assumption is not reasonable the test procedures described may still, in general, be used, although they will have only asymptotic validity. However, difficulties may be encountered in cases where certain moments of the distribution do not exist. If the OLS estimator is inconsistent, as would, for example, be the case with a Cauchy disturbance term, none of the tests will have even asymptotic validity. When there is some doubt about the distribution of the disturbance term, the most prudent course of action is first to examine the residuals from a robust estimator such as MAD.

5.3. Classical Test Procedures: The Likelihood Ratio Test

The tests of misspecification discussed in the previous section provide a means of assessing 'goodness of fit'. No specific alternative hypothesis is entertained at the outset, although a knowledge of the power of the tests against particular alternatives is obviously useful insofar as it suggests ways of modifying the model. Tests of specification, on the other hand, employ a specific alternative hypothesis, H_1, as well as a null, H_0.

The foundations of the classical approach to hypothesis testing were laid by Neyman and Pearson. The sample space is partitioned into two regions. One is a region of acceptance, in which the data are consistent with the null hypothesis, and the other a region of rejection, known as the *critical region*. The essence of a 'good' test procedure is the choice of a critical region which is in some sense optimal.

A test procedure of the above form implies two types of error. The first, a Type I error, arises when the null hypothesis is rejected when it is true, while a Type II error is made when H_0 is incorrectly accepted. Generally speaking, the probability of a Type II error can be determined only with respect to a specific alternative hypothesis, and given such an alternative, a 'good' test should, other things being equal, make this probability small. In order that other things should be equal, the (maximum) probability of making a Type I error is fixed. This probability is termed the *significance level* or *size* of the test, and a test can then be considered optimal if it minimises the probability of making a Type II error over the complete set of parameter values associated with the alternative. Such a test is termed uniformly most powerful (UMP), since the term power is defined as $1 - Pr$(Type II Error).

The above criterion is not the only one which could be used in judging the desirability of a particular test. A natural question to ask, therefore, is whether it suggests a form for a suitable test statistic, together with an appropriate critical region. Consider first the simplest possible situation, in which the observations are drawn at random from a distribution which depends on a single parameter ψ. Furthermore, suppose that the null and alternative hypotheses each consist only of a single value of ψ, i.e. $H_0 : \psi = \psi_0$ is to be tested against $H_1 : \psi = \psi_1$. Let $L(\psi_0)$ and $L(\psi_1)$ denote the likelihood function of the sample under H_0 and H_1 respectively. The form of the most powerful test — the qualification 'uniformly' is superfluous when ψ_1 is a single point — is then determined by a fundamental result known as the *Neyman–Pearson lemma*. This states that if there exists a critical region, C, of size α and a constant x such that

$$\frac{L(\psi_0)}{L(\psi_1)} \le x \qquad \text{inside } C$$

and

$$\frac{L(\psi_0)}{L(\psi_1)} > x \qquad \text{outside } C$$

then C is most powerful critical region of size α for testing $\psi = \psi_0$ against $\psi = \psi_1$.

A proof of the Neyman–Pearson lemma may be found in almost any text on mathematical statistics, and will not be given here. However, it is worth noting the plausibility of the test suggested by the lemma: if H_0 is true, we would expect $L(\psi_0)$ to be large relative to $L(\psi_1)$ and so the ratio of the likelihoods would tend to fall outside the critical region. Conversely, if H_1 were true, $L(\psi_0)/L(\psi_1)$ would tend to be small.

Although the Neyman–Pearson lemma cases can be extended to slightly more general situations, its direct applicability to many of the situations of practical interest is limited. In fact, it is often the exception rather than the rule that a UMP test exists. Nevertheless, even in circumstances where a test satisfying the requirements for optimality cannot be constructed, the Neyman–Pearson lemma at least suggests a general method for constructing tests based on the likelihood ratio.

The Likelihood Ratio Test

The likelihood ratio (LR) takes the form

$$\lambda = \lambda(y_1,\ldots,y_T) = L(\tilde{\psi}_0)/L(\tilde{\psi}_1), \tag{3.1}$$

where $L(\tilde{\psi}_0)$ and $L(\tilde{\psi}_1)$ denote the maximised likelihood functions obtained under the null and alternative hypotheses respectively. When the alternative hypothesis holds, λ will tend to be small, which suggests setting a critical region according to the criterion $\lambda < x$, where x is determined by the desired size of the test, α. Thus when the null hypothesis is true, x is determined by the condition that

$$Pr\{\lambda < x\} = \alpha \tag{3.2}$$

What we have therefore is a sample statistic, λ, together with an indication of the form of the critical region. However, for a given size of test, a value of x which results in (3.2) being satisfied *exactly* can only be found if the small sample distribution of λ, or a monotonic function of it, is known. This is rarely the case in more complex models, with the result that testing must be carried out on the basis of large-sample approximations. Before moving on to discuss such approximations, a case where the LR principle does lead to an exact test is considered.

Example 1 Consider the problem of testing for the inclusion of a subset of $m < k$ explanatory variables in a classical linear regression model. If the disturbances are normally distributed, the maximised likelihood for the general model is

$$L(\tilde{\psi}_1) = (2\pi\tilde{\sigma}_1^2)^{-T/2} \exp(-T/2) \tag{3.3}$$

where $\tilde{\sigma}_1^2 = SSE_1/T$. The expression for $L(\tilde{\psi}_0)$ takes a similar form except that $\tilde{\sigma}_1^2$ is replaced by an estimator, $\tilde{\sigma}_0^2 = SSE_0/T$, constructed from the OLS residuals in the regression with the m explanatory variables omitted. The LR is therefore

$$\lambda = \left(\frac{\tilde{\sigma}_0^2}{\tilde{\sigma}_1^2}\right)^{-T/2} = \left(\frac{SSE_0}{SSE_1}\right)^{-T/2} \tag{3.4}$$

A critical value, x, which satisfies (3.2) cannot be obtained directly since the distribution of (3.4) is unknown. However, the distribution of

$$\lambda^* = \frac{(SSE_0 - SSE_1)/m}{SSE_1/(T - k)} \tag{3.5}$$

is known. Under H_0 it has an F-distribution with $(m, T - k)$ degrees of freedom; cf. (2.8.10). On comparing (3.5) with (3.4) it will be found that one is a monotonic function of the other, since

$$\lambda^* = (\lambda^{-2/T} - 1)(T - k)/m \tag{3.6}$$

A critical region of the form $\lambda < x$ for the LR statistic corresponds to a critical region of the form $\lambda^* > x^*$ for (3.5) and x^* may be determined such that

$$Pr\{\lambda^* > x^*\} = \alpha \tag{3.7}$$

is satisfied exactly. An exact LR test could therefore be carried out by comparing λ with a critical value, k, obtained indirectly from the F-distribution via (3.6). However, since an F-test based on λ^* will give exactly the same result, it is this statistic which is normally used.

When $m = 1$, the LR test is equivalent to the classical 't-test' of significance. This test may be shown to be UMP against a one-sided alternative, and so in this case there is a direct justification for the LR test in terms of Neyman−Pearson theory. However, when $m > 1$, a UMP test no longer exists. Nevertheless, the results for $m = 1$ at least support the notion that the LR test and the equivalent F-test are intuitively reasonable.

Example 2 A regression model is said to exhibit a structural break if the parameter vector changes at some point in time. Under such a hypothesis the model may be written as

$$y_t = x_t'\beta_1 + \epsilon_t, \qquad t = 1, \ldots, T_1$$

$$y_t = x_t'\beta_2 + \epsilon_t, \qquad t = T_1 + 1, \ldots, T$$

The null hypothesis is that $\beta_1 = \beta_2$ and so if $\epsilon_t \sim NID(0, \sigma^2)$ under both 'regimes', the LR statistic is

$$\lambda = \left(\frac{SSE_0}{SSE_1 + SSE_2}\right)^{-T/2}$$

where SSE_1, SSE_2 and SSE_0 are the residual sums of squares from the regression on the first T_1 observations, the second $T - T_1$ observations and the complete set of observations respectively.

The statistic λ is, however, a monotonic transformation of

$$\lambda^* = \frac{\{SSE_0 - (SSE_1 + SSE_2)\}/k}{(SSE_1 + SSE_2)/(T - 2k)}$$

which has an F-distribution with $(k, T - 2k)$ degrees of freedom. Hence the LR test may be based on λ^* with the upper tail of the F-distribution used to construct the critical region.

Large Sample Theory

Although the LR principle led to the construction of exact tests in the examples above, it is not generally possible to determine a suitable value for $\varkappa$ by linking the likelihood ratio to a statistic whose distribution is already known. However, provided the null hypothesis is nested within the alternative, and the conditions for the asymptotic normality and efficiency of the ML estimators are satisfied, large-sample theory provides the basis for a viable approach to LR testing.

In Example 1 above, H_0 was nested within H_1, since setting the coefficients of the m explanatory variables under test equal to zero gave the model under the null hypothesis. The restricted model is obtained from the general model with k explanatory variables by imposing a set of m *restrictions* or *constraints* on it. Such constraints take the general form

$$R\psi = r, \tag{3.8}$$

where R is an $m \times n$ matrix of full rank, and r is an $m \times 1$ vector. The values taken by the elements of R and r are specified under the null hypothesis. In Example 1, $n = k + 1$ and $\psi' = (\beta', \sigma^2)'$. The vector r is null, while if the independent variables are arranged such that it is the last m which are being tested for inclusion in the model then $R = [0_{k-m} I_m \, 0]$. The restrictions imposed by the null hypothesis need not be linear. In general, the m constraints may be written

$$r_j(\psi) = 0, \qquad j = 1, \ldots, m \tag{3.9}$$

where $r_j(\psi)$ denotes some function of ψ for which the first derivatives exist.

When the models are nested, the likelihood ratio statistic (3.1), must be less than, or equal to unity, since the value of the likelihood for the restricted model cannot exceed the likelihood for the unrestricted model.

A test of the validity of the restrictions imposed by the null hypothesis may be carried out by invoking the following result. *Subject to regularity conditions, the statistic*

$$\text{LR} = -2 \log \lambda = 2 \log L(\tilde{\psi}) - 2 \log L(\tilde{\psi}_0) \qquad (3.10)$$

is asymptotically distributed as χ_m^2 under H_0, where m is the number of restrictions needed to define the null hypothesis.

The proof of this result relies on a Taylor series expansion of $\log L(\tilde{\psi}_0)$ about $\tilde{\psi}$. This gives

$$\log L(\tilde{\psi}_0) \simeq \log L(\tilde{\psi}) + (\tilde{\psi} - \tilde{\psi}_0)' D \log L(\tilde{\psi})$$
$$+ \tfrac{1}{2} (\tilde{\psi} - \tilde{\psi}_0)' D^2 \log L(\tilde{\psi})(\tilde{\psi} - \tilde{\psi}_0)$$

The second term in the expansion is zero since $\tilde{\psi}$ is the unrestricted ML estimator, and so

$$-2 \log \lambda \simeq (\tilde{\psi} - \tilde{\psi}_0)' \{-D^2 \log L(\tilde{\psi})\}(\tilde{\psi} - \tilde{\psi}_0) \qquad (3.11)$$

Silvey (1975, p. 114) sketches out the remaining details of the proof.

Given the above result, the LR test is carried out by computing $-2 \log \lambda$, and rejecting H_0 if $-2 \log \lambda > x'$. The value of x' is chosen such that

$$Pr(\chi_m^2 > x') = \alpha, \qquad (3.12)$$

where α is the *nominal* size of the test. Unless the small sample distribution of $-2 \log \lambda$ can be determined, the true size of the test will be unknown, and it is said to be *asymptotic* rather than exact. The concept of power is subject to some ambiguity for an asymptotic test, although in any discussion which follows power will be taken to mean the probability of rejecting H_0 for a given nominal test size.

Although the LR principle can lead to UMP tests in special cases, this is not generally so. Nevertheless, it can be shown that a likelihood ratio test is *consistent*, in the sense that as the sample size increases, the probability of rejecting the null hypothesis when any particular member of the alternative holds, tends to unity. The consistency of the LR test follows from the consistency of the ML estimator. If H_0 is true, then $\lambda \to 1$ as $T \to \infty$, and so the critical region will have its boundary x' approaching one. When H_0 does not hold, the limiting value of λ will be some constant, $\bar{\lambda}$, satisfying

$$0 \le \bar{\lambda} < 1$$

Therefore $Pr\{\lambda \le x'\}$ will tend to one as $T \to \infty$.

Example 3 A natural hypothesis to test in the multiplicative heteroscedasticity model, (3.4.15), is that the variances are constant, i.e. $H_0 : \delta_2 = \cdots = \delta_r = 0$. The LR statistic is

$$\text{LR} = 2 \log L(\tilde{\beta}, \tilde{\delta}) - 2 \log L(\tilde{\beta}_0, \tilde{\delta}_0)$$
$$= T \log \tilde{\sigma}_0^2 + T - \Sigma w_t' \tilde{\delta} - \sum \exp(-w_t' \tilde{\delta})(y_t - x_t' \tilde{\beta})^2 \qquad (3.13)$$

However, when the first element in (3.4.19), the vector $\partial\log L/\partial\delta$, is evaluated at $\delta = \tilde{\delta}$ and $\beta = \tilde{\beta}$, the second and fourth terms in (3.13) cancel. The test statistic becomes

$$\text{LR} = T \log \tilde{\sigma}_0^2 - \Sigma w_t' \tilde{\delta} \tag{3.14}$$

and this is asymptotically distributed as χ^2_{r-1} under the null hypothesis of homoscedasticity.

Example 4 The maximised log-likelihood function for a SURE model is equal to a constant plus $(-T/2)\log|\Omega|$; see (3.4.28), (3.4.32) and the result in (4.4.25). Any hypothesis concerning restrictions on the covariance matrix, Ω, may therefore be tested by a statistic of the form:

$$\text{LR} = T \log\{|\tilde{\Omega}_0|/|\tilde{\Omega}|\} \tag{3.15}$$

Thus if Ω_0 is diagonal, LR is treated as a χ^2 variate with $N(N-1)/2$ degrees of freedom.

In the investment example given in Section 2.9, it follows from (2.9.24) that

$$|\tilde{\Omega}_0| = 660.83 \times 88.67 = 58{,}596$$

The unrestricted estimate of Ω should be calculated from the residuals from ML estimation. However, using the residuals from the feasible SURE estimator (2.9.25) makes little difference in large samples. On this basis Pagan and Byron (1977) report $|\Omega| = 25{,}768$. The sample size is $T = 20$ and so LR $= 16.43$. Since the LR statistic is asymptotically χ^2_1 under the null hypothesis, this is rejected quite convincingly.

5.4. Wald Tests

The form of the LR statistic implies that the model must, in general, be estimated both under the null and alternative hypotheses. Wald tests, on the other hand, may be carried out on the basis of the unrestricted model only, and so they are particularly appealing when the restricted model is difficult to estimate.

If the constraints are linear as in (3.8), the elements of the vector $R\tilde{\psi} - r$ should be 'close' to zero when the null hypothesis is true. The problem is to decide on some criterion for determining when $R\tilde{\psi} - r$ is close enough to zero to be regarded as consistent with H_0. Since

$$\sqrt{T}(\tilde{\psi} - \psi) \xrightarrow{L} N[0, IA^{-1}(\psi)]$$

it follows that

$$\sqrt{T}R(\tilde{\psi} - \psi) = \sqrt{T}(R\tilde{\psi} - r) \xrightarrow{L} N[0, R \cdot IA^{-1}(\psi) \cdot R']$$

Hence the statistic

$$T \cdot (R\tilde{\psi} - r)' \, [R \cdot IA^{-1}(\psi) \cdot R']^{-1}(R\tilde{\psi} - r) \qquad (4.1)$$

has a limiting χ_m^2 distribution. This distribution remains unchanged if the matrix $T \cdot IA(\psi)$ is replaced by any matrix, $I^*(\hat{\psi})$, with the property that plim $T^{-1} I^*(\hat{\psi}) = IA(\psi)$, where $\hat{\psi}$ is a consistent estimator of ψ. Equating $\hat{\psi}$ with the unrestricted ML estimator, $\tilde{\psi}$, gives the usual definition for the Wald statistic:

$$W = (R\tilde{\psi} - r)' \, [R \cdot I^{*-1}(\tilde{\psi}) \cdot R']^{-1}(R\tilde{\psi} - r) \qquad (4.2)$$

When the null hypothesis is false, W will tend to be large and so a natural choice of critical region is $W > \varkappa$. If the distribution of W cannot be determined exactly, a suitable value of $\varkappa$ may be obtained from χ^2 tables, and the test is an asymptotic one.

As a very simple example of a Wald test, consider an hypothesis which specifies that a single parameter, ψ, takes a particular value, ψ_0. The test statistic is then

$$W = (\tilde{\psi} - \psi_0)^2/\text{avar}(\tilde{\psi}) \qquad (4.3)$$

However, it may be more convenient to carry out an equivalent two-sided test on the statistic

$$W = (\tilde{\psi} - \psi_0)/\sqrt{\text{avar}(\tilde{\psi})} \qquad (4.4)$$

since this will have a standardised normal distribution in large samples.

Wald Tests in Regression Models

The Wald principle provides a convenient approach to the testing of restrictions in both linear and non-linear regression models. As a specific example, suppose that we wish to test the hypothesis that one of the regression coefficients in a classical linear model is equal to zero. If the coefficient is taken to be β_k, then in terms of (3.8), $R = [0 \ldots 0,1,0]$ and $r = 0$. The block of the information matrix corresponding to β is $\sigma^{-2}(X'X)$, but if σ^2 is replaced by the unbiased estimator s^2, W is the square of (2.8.3), the familiar t-statistic. The likelihood ratio approach also leads to the t-test in this case, but only after a good deal of algebraic manipulation.

More generally, the Wald statistic for testing a set of m linear constraints, $R\psi = r$, may be modified by dividing by m to give

$$(Rb - r)' \, [R(X'X)^{-1}R']^{-1}(Rb - r)/ms^2 \qquad (4.5)$$

Under the null hypothesis, (4.5) is distributed as the F-ratio with $(m, T - k)$ degrees of freedom; see Theil (1971, p. 144). After some manipulation, (4.5) becomes

$$(SSE_0 - SSE)/ms^2 \tag{4.6}$$

which is identical to the test statistic obtained from likelihood ratio considerations; cf. (3.5).

For a non-linear model, the Wald approach suggests the use of asymptotic t-ratios for testing individual coefficients. However, the justification for basing such tests on the t-distribution rests solely on the analogy with the linear case; in general, all that can be proved about the distribution of such t-statistics is that they are asymptotically normal. Asymptotic F-ratios may be employed in the same spirit.

Non-Linear Constraints

If the constraints are non-linear, a Wald test may still be constructed. A Taylor series expansion of $r_j(\tilde{\psi})$ about the true parameter, ψ, gives

$$r_j(\tilde{\psi}) \simeq r_j(\psi) + (\tilde{\psi} - \psi)' \frac{\partial r_j(\psi)}{\partial \psi} \tag{4.7}$$

If the restrictions are satisfied, then $r_j(\psi) = 0$ for $j = 1, \ldots, m$, and the Wald statistic is defined by

$$W = \{r(\tilde{\psi})\}' [\tilde{R}' I^{*-1}(\tilde{\psi}) \cdot \tilde{R}]^{-1} \{r(\tilde{\psi})\} \tag{4.8}$$

where $r(\tilde{\psi})$ is an $m \times 1$ vector in which the jth element is $r_j(\tilde{\psi})$, while $\tilde{R}$ is now a matrix of derivatives in which the jth column is $\partial r_j(\psi)/\partial \psi$ evaluated at $\psi = \tilde{\psi}$. Subject to regularity conditions, W is χ_m^2 under H_0.

Example   Consider the model

$$y_t = \beta_1 x_{1t} + \beta_2 x_{2t} + \beta_3 x_{3t} + \epsilon_t \tag{4.9}$$

The hypothesis to be tested is that $\beta_3 = \beta_1 \beta_2$, and so an LR test would be relatively unattractive since the restricted model is non-linear. However, the unrestricted model may be estimated by OLS. The Wald statistic is of the form (4.8) with $r_1(\tilde{\psi}) = b_1 b_2 - b_3$, $I^{*-1}(\tilde{\psi}) = s^2(X'X)^{-1}$, and $\tilde{R} = (b_2, b_1, - 1)'$. The use of s^2 rather than the ML estimator, $\tilde{\sigma}^2$, in the information matrix is arbitrary. Any consistent estimator of σ^2 will leave W with a χ_1^2 distribution in large samples.

One rather disturbing feature of Wald tests is that the test statistic will change if a set of non-linear restrictions is expressed in a different way. Thus in the above example, the restriction $\beta_1 \beta_2 - \beta_3 = 0$ can also be written as $\beta_1 - \beta_3/\beta_2 = 0$, provided that $\beta_2 \neq 0$, or as $\beta_2 - \beta_3/\beta_1 = 0$, provided that $\beta_1 = 0$; see Gregory and Veall (1985). The different test statistics may lead to different conclusions.

5.5. The Lagrange Multiplier Test

As with the Wald test, the Lagrange multiplier (LM) procedure is applicable to testing nested hypotheses. It also leads to a test statistic with the same asymptotic distribution as the LR statistic under the null hypothesis, and it is consistent. The distinguishing feature of the LM test is that it only entails the estimation of the restricted model.

Let $\tilde{\psi}_0$ denote the ML estimator of ψ in the restricted model. If the restrictions are valid, $\tilde{\psi}_0$ will be 'close' to the unrestricted estimator, $\tilde{\psi}$, and so the partial derivatives in the vector $D \log L(\tilde{\psi}_0)$ will also be 'close' to zero. On the other hand if H_0 is not true, there is no reason to believe that this will be the case.

A procedure for testing whether $D \log L(\tilde{\psi}_0)$ is close to zero may be developed by first taking a Taylor series expansion around $\tilde{\psi}$, i.e.

$$D \log L(\tilde{\psi}_0)' \simeq D \log L(\tilde{\psi})' + (\tilde{\psi}_0 - \tilde{\psi})' D^2 \log L(\tilde{\psi}) \qquad (5.1)$$

Since $\tilde{\psi}$ is the unrestricted ML estimator, $D \log L(\tilde{\psi}) = 0$, and so (5.1) reduces to

$$D \log L(\tilde{\psi}_0)' \simeq (\tilde{\psi}_0 - \tilde{\psi})' D^2 \log L(\tilde{\psi}) \qquad (5.2)$$

Now consider the test statistic

$$\text{LM} = \{D \log L(\tilde{\psi}_0)\}' I^{-1}(\tilde{\psi}_0)\{D \log L(\tilde{\psi}_0)\} \qquad (5.3)$$

Substituting from (5.2) yields

$$\text{LM} = (\tilde{\psi}_0 - \tilde{\psi})' D^2 \log L(\tilde{\psi}) I^{-1}(\tilde{\psi}_0) D^2 \log L(\tilde{\psi})(\tilde{\psi}_0 - \tilde{\psi})$$

However, under H_0, $T^{-1} I(\tilde{\psi}_0)$ has the same probability limit as $- T^{-1} D^2 \log L(\tilde{\psi})$. For a large sample, therefore, the distribution of the LM statistic, (5.3), will be the same as the distribution of

$$-(\tilde{\psi}_0 - \tilde{\psi})' D^2 \log L(\tilde{\psi})(\tilde{\psi}_0 - \tilde{\psi})$$

when the null hypothesis is true. This expression is exactly the same as that given in (3.11) for the LR statistic, and so LM has a χ_m^2 distribution under H_0.

Expression (5.3) is the usual definition of the LM statistic. However, $I(\tilde{\psi}_0)$ may be replaced by any matrix, $I^*(\tilde{\psi}_0)$, which is asymptotically equivalent in the sense implied by (4.5.3), under the null hypothesis. This will not affect the distribution in large samples, and any statistic of the form

$$\{D \log L(\tilde{\psi}_0)\}' I^{*-1}(\tilde{\psi}_0)\{D \log L(\tilde{\psi}_0)\} \qquad (5.4)$$

will be referred to as a *Lagrange multiplier statistic*. A critical region for the test is then found with respect to the χ_m^2 distribution in exactly the same way as for the LR statistic.

The use of the term 'Lagrange multiplier' in this context is not obvious from the above argument. However, given a set of restrictions of the form (3.9), a restricted likelihood function may be defined by

$$\log L^* = \log L + \sum_{j=1}^{m} \lambda_j r_j(\psi) \tag{5.5}$$

where the λ_j's are Lagrange multipliers. Maximising $\log L^*$ with respect to ψ implies

$$D \log L(\tilde{\psi}_0) + \tilde{R}\tilde{\lambda} = 0,$$

or

$$D \log L(\tilde{\psi}_0) = -\sum \lambda_j \frac{\partial r_j(\psi)}{\partial \psi} = -\tilde{R}\tilde{\lambda} \tag{5.6}$$

where $\tilde{R}$ is the $n \times m$ matrix of derivatives and $\tilde{\lambda}$ is the $m \times 1$ vector of Lagrange multipliers, evaluated at $\psi = \tilde{\psi}_0$. Substituting for $D \log L(\tilde{\psi}_0)$ in (5.3) yields the alternative form of the LM statistic,

$$\text{LM} = \tilde{\lambda}' \tilde{R}' \cdot I^{-1}(\tilde{\psi}_0) \cdot \tilde{R}\tilde{\lambda} \tag{5.7}$$

A third form for the LM statistic has been suggested by Breusch and Pagan (1980). If $\tilde{\psi}_0$ is updated by a single iteration of the method of scoring as defined by (4.4.2), then

$$D \log L(\tilde{\psi}_0) = I(\tilde{\psi}_0) \cdot (\psi^* - \tilde{\psi}_0)$$

Substituting this expression in (5.3) then gives

$$\text{LM} = (\psi^* - \tilde{\psi}_0)' I(\tilde{\psi}_0)(\psi^* - \tilde{\psi}_0) \tag{5.8}$$

which may be interpreted as a test of the 'hypothesis' $\psi^* = \tilde{\psi}_0$.

This form of the statistic may be easier to evaluate than (5.3) in certain circumstances. If it is the case that an alternative procedure such as Gauss–Newton or Newton–Raphson is more readily applied, then as with (5.4) it is appropriate to write (5.8) with $I(\tilde{\psi}_0)$ replaced by $I^*(\tilde{\psi}_0)$.

Testing Subsets of Parameters

In many problems the restrictions under test involve only a subset of the parameters. Thus if ψ is partitioned as

$$\psi = \begin{pmatrix} \psi^{(1)} \\ \psi^{(2)} \end{pmatrix}$$

only the $m \times 1$ vector $\psi^{(2)}$ is subject to constraints imposed by the null hypothesis. An important special case is

$$H_0 : \psi^{(2)} = 0$$

Partitioning the information matrix conformably with $\psi^{(1)}$ and $\psi^{(2)}$ yields

$$I(\psi) = \begin{pmatrix} I_{11} & I_{12} \\ I_{21} & I_{22} \end{pmatrix} \tag{5.9}$$

Let $D_j \log L(\psi)$ denote the vector of partial derivatives of $\log L(\psi)$ with respect to $\psi^{(j)}$ for $j = 1,2$. From (5.6) it follows that $D_1 \log L(\tilde{\psi}_0) = 0$ since the parameters in $\psi^{(1)}$ do not enter into the restrictions. The LM statistic is therefore

$$\text{LM} = [0' \ D_2 \log L(\tilde{\psi}_0)'] \begin{pmatrix} I_{11} & I_{12} \\ I_{21} & I_{22} \end{pmatrix}^{-1} \begin{pmatrix} 0 \\ D_2 \log L(\tilde{\psi}_0) \end{pmatrix}$$

and using the formula for a partitioned inverse this becomes

$$\text{LM} = \{D_2 \log L(\tilde{\psi}_0)\}' [I_{22} - I'_{21} I_{11}^{-1} I_{12}]^{-1} \{D_2 \log L(\tilde{\psi}_0)\} \tag{5.10}$$

Note that all the components of the information matrix are evaluated at $\psi = \tilde{\psi}_0$.

If $I_{12} = I_{21} = 0$ under H_0, the information matrix $I(\tilde{\psi}_0)$ is block diagonal and expression (5.10) reduces to

$$\text{LM} = D_2 \log L(\tilde{\psi}_0)' \cdot I_{22}^{-1}(\tilde{\psi}_0) \cdot D_2 \log L(\tilde{\psi}_0) \tag{5.11}$$

This formulation of the LM statistic is particularly convenient in generalised regression models where the parameters in $\psi^{(2)}$ determine the form of the disturbance covariance matrix. Provided the expectation of the dependent variable is independent of the elements of $\psi^{(2)}$, the information matrix will be block diagonal and (5.11) may be applied.

Example The LR test for constant variance in the multiplicative heteroscedascity model was obtained in Section 3. For the derivation of the LM statistic, it is convenient to partition the parameter vector as $\psi^{(1)} = \beta$ and $\psi^{(2)} = \delta$ even though the first parameter in δ, $\log \sigma^2$, is not restricted by the null hypothesis. This takes advantage of the block diagonality of the information matrix and the LM statistic is given by

$$\text{LM} = \left(\frac{\partial \log L}{\partial \delta} \right)' \left(-E\left(\frac{\partial^2 \log L}{\partial \delta \ \partial \delta} \right) \right)^{-1} \left(\frac{\partial \log L}{\partial \delta} \right)$$

This expression is evaluated at $\tilde{\delta}_0 = (\log \tilde{\sigma}_0^2 \ 0 \ldots 0)'$, where $\tilde{\sigma}_0^2$ is the ML estimator of σ^2 in the OLS regression. From (3.4.19)

$$\frac{\partial \log L}{\partial \delta} = \tfrac{1}{2} \sum w_t v_t$$

where $v_t = \{ (y_t - x'_t b)^2 / \tilde{\sigma}_0^2 \} - 1$. Thus

$$\text{LM} = (\Sigma w_t v_t)'(\Sigma w_t w_t')^{-1}(\Sigma w_t v_t)/2 \qquad (5.12)$$

and this will be asymptotically χ^2_{r-1} under H_0.

An alternative form of the LM statistic is given by observing that in the classical linear regression model the formula for R^2, (2.2.13), may be expressed as:

$$R^2 = \frac{\Sigma \hat{y}_t^2 - T\bar{y}^2}{\Sigma y_t^2 - T\bar{y}^2} = \frac{b'X'Xb - T\bar{y}^2}{y'y - T\bar{y}^2} = \frac{y'X(X'X)^{-1}X'y - T\bar{y}^2}{y'y - T\bar{y}^2}$$

$$(5.13)$$

The last two steps follow from (2.2.6) and (2.2.4) respectively. Bearing this in mind, and noting that $\Sigma v_t = 0$, the statistic

$$\text{LM*} = \frac{T(\Sigma w_t v_t)'(\Sigma w_t w_t')^{-1}(\Sigma w_t v_t)}{\Sigma v_t^2} \qquad (5.14)$$

is equal to TR^2 where R^2 is the coefficient of multiple correlation obtained from regressing v_t on w_t. Since plim $T^{-1}\Sigma v_t^2 = 2$, LM* has the same asymptotic distribution as LM.

One attraction of the LM statistic in this context is that it is appropriate for a wide range of heteroscedastic formulations. It can be shown that (5.12) is the LM statistic for any model in which σ_t^2 is a function of $w_t'\delta$. Thus, for example, in the model

$$\sigma_t^2 = \delta_1 + \delta_2 x_{2t}^2 + \ldots + \delta_k x_{kt}^2$$

an LM test of $H_0 : \delta_2 = \delta_3 = \ldots = \delta_k = 0$ is carried out via (5.12) or (5.14) with $w_t = (1 \; x_{2t}^2 \ldots x_{kt}^2)'$. This suggests that an LM test based on (5.12) or (5.14) may be useful as a general test for heteroscedasticity.

A final point to note is that the LM* test is relatively robust to departures from the assumption of normally distributed disturbances; see Koenker (1981).

The LM Test in Least Squares Problems

In Section 3.5 it was observed that for many models, maximising the likelihood is equivalent to minimising a sum of squares function. From the definition of the likelihood function in (3.5.14)

$$\partial \log L(\psi, \sigma^2)/\partial\psi = \sigma^{-2}\Sigma z_t \epsilon_t$$

where $z_t = z_t(\psi) = -\partial\epsilon_t/\partial\psi$, the vector ψ denoting all the parameters apart from σ^2. Since σ^2 will never be subject to constraints in this type of model, the block diagonality of the information matrix may be exploited via (5.11). Replacing

$$I^*(\psi) = E\left[\left(\frac{\partial \log L}{\partial \psi}\right)\left(\frac{\partial \log L}{\partial \psi'}\right)\right] = \sigma^{-4}E(\Sigma \epsilon_t^2 \, z_t z_t')$$

by the asymptotically equivalent expression $\sigma^{-2}\Sigma z_t z_t'$ and evaluating at $\psi = \tilde{\psi}_0$ in (5.3), gives

$$\tilde{\sigma}_0^{-2}(\Sigma z_t \epsilon_t)'(\Sigma z_t z_t)^{-1}(\Sigma z_t \epsilon_t) \tag{5.15}$$

where both ϵ_t and z_t are evaluated at $\psi = \tilde{\psi}_0$ and $\tilde{\sigma}_0^2 = T^{-1}\Sigma \epsilon_t^2(\tilde{\psi}_0)$.

When the model contains a constant term, the sum of the residuals will be identically equal to zero. In view of the definition of the coefficient of multiple correlation in (5.13), the statistic (5.15) may be written

$$\text{LM}^* = TR^2 \tag{5.16}$$

This result will still be approximately true even if the model does not contain a constant term. In all cases a valid LM test may be carried out simply by regressing $\epsilon_t(\tilde{\psi}_0)$ on $z_t(\tilde{\psi}_0)$ and testing TR^2 as a χ^2 variate with m degrees of freedom.

Example The demand for money in an economy depends on real national income and the rate of interest. Konstas and Khouja (1969) adopt the functional form

$$y_t = \beta_1 x_{1t} + \beta_2(x_{2t} - \gamma)^{-1} + \epsilon_t \tag{5.17}$$

where x_{1t} is real national income, x_{2t} is the rate of interest, and y_t is real money demand. A positive value of γ implies the existence of a liquidity trap: once the rate of interest has fallen to $x_2 = \gamma$, further increases in the money supply cannot lower it further because the additional money is all held as speculative balances.

Konstas and Khouja attempted to carry out an LR test of the hypothesis that $\gamma = 0$. Unfortunately, as Spitzer (1976) observed, the test was misleading as their algorithm failed globally to maximise the likelihood function. The LM approach avoids this difficulty because when $\gamma = 0$ the model is *linear*. Regressing y on x_1 and x_2^{-1} yields a set of residuals which may then be regressed against x_1, x_2^{-1} and x_2^{-2}. If R^2 is the coefficient of determination from the second regression, an LM test of the liquidity trap may be based on the statistic TR^2 which is taken to be χ_1^2 under H_0. In carrying out this test, Breusch and Pagan (1980) find a value of $\text{LM}^* = 11.47$. This indicates a rejection of the null hypothesis that there is no liquidity trap, a result which agrees with Spitzer's LR test.

In terms of the notation of (5.15), $\psi = (\beta_1, \beta_2, \gamma)'$

$$z_{1t} = -\partial \epsilon_t / \partial \beta_1 = x_{1t} \tag{5.18a}$$

$$z_{2t} = -\partial \epsilon_t / \partial \beta_2 = (x_{2t} - \gamma)^{-1} \tag{5.18b}$$

and

$$z_{3t} = -\partial \epsilon_t / \partial \gamma = \beta_2 (x_{2t} - \gamma)^{-2} \qquad (5.18c)$$

These derivatives are all evaluated at $\gamma = 0$ in constructing the LM test statistic. Although the expression for z_{3t} implies the use of the regressor $b_2 x_{2t}^{-2}$, the omission of b_2 makes no difference to the value of R^2.

The Modified LM Test

Suppose we wish to test the hypothesis that a subset of m parameters in a classical linear regression model are zero. Both the LR and Wald principles lead to the F-statistic defied by (3.5). The LM statistic, (5.16), however, is based on the R^2 obtained by taking the residuals from the OLS regression on the restricted model and regressing them on the complete set of independent variables. Suppose the vector of residuals from this second regression is denoted by e^*, while the original OLS residuals are e_0. The explained sum of squares in the second regression is then $e_0' e_0 - e^* {}' e^*$ and so

$$R^2 = (e_0' e_0 - e^* {}' e^*) / e_0' e_0$$

However

$$e^* = Me_0 = M \left\{ y - X \begin{pmatrix} b_0 \\ 0 \end{pmatrix} \right\} = My = e \qquad (5.19)$$

since $M = I - X(X'X)^{-1}X'$ and $MX = 0$. Thus the residuals obtained from regressing e^* on e_0 are identical to those obtained from regressing y on X. Hence $e^* {}' e^* = e'e$ and so the LM test statistic is given by

$$\text{LM} = TR^2 = T(e_0' e_0 - e'e)/e_0' e_0 = T(SSE_0 - SSE)/SSE_0 \qquad (5.20)$$

This is a monotonic function of the classical F-statistic, (2.8.18), and so the LM principle leads to the standard F- and t-tests just as the LR and Wald approaches do.

The way in which the LM statistic may be modified to produce an exact test for the linear model suggests that similar modifications may be useful for least squares problems in general. In terms of the Gauss–Newton scheme, (4.4.13), $\epsilon_t(\tilde{\psi}_0)$ is regressed on $z_t(\tilde{\psi}_0)$ and hypotheses regarding the validity of any restrictions are tested using the standard F- and t-statistics. Such tests will be termed *modified* LM tests. The F-tests are based not on TR^2 but on

$$\text{LM } F = \frac{T - n}{m} \cdot \frac{R^2}{1 - R^2} \qquad (5.21a)$$

The critical region is based on an F-distribution with $(m, T - n)$ degrees of freedom.

Example A test of $\gamma = 0$ in (5.17) may be carried out by regressing the OLS residuals from the restricted model on x_1, x_2^{-1} and x_2^{-2}, and examining the t-statistic associated with x_2^{-2}. A one-sided test may be carried out very easily using this approach. This would seem to be appropriate, since the liquidity trap hypothesis implies $\gamma > 0$.

Because (5.17) is linear under the null hypothesis, the modified LM test can be carried out on the basis of only one regression. Since the OLS residuals in the restricted model are given by $y_t - z_t'\hat{\psi}_0$, where $\hat{\psi}_0 = (b_1, b_2, 0)'$, the first iteration of Gauss–Newton yields

$$\psi^* = (\Sigma z_t z_t')^{-1} \Sigma z_t y_t$$

Thus the test may be carried out directly by regressing y_t on x_{1t}, x_{2t}^{-1} and x_{2t}^{-2} and examining the t-statistic associated with x_{2t}^{-2}.

Apart from being convenient to carry out, the modified LM test is attractive for the following reasons. Firstly, the results for the linear regression model suggest that the true significance levels for modified LM tests might be reasonably close to their nominal values when an exact test is not available. A second point relates to the question of power, which in this context means the probability of rejecting the null hypothesis for a given *nominal* test size. In terms of (5.15) the modification to the LM statistic amounts to replacing $\bar{\sigma}_0^2$ by $\bar{\sigma}_1^2$. This last statistic is constructed from the residuals obtained from the revised estimates given by one iteration of Gauss–Newton. Thus the modified LM statistic is given by

$$\text{LM}\dagger = TR^2/(1 - R^2), \tag{5.21b}$$

and this must be greater than, or equal to, (5.20). Hence the 'power' of the standard LM test cannot exceed the power of a similar test based on the modified statistic, LM$\dagger$. While this statement is no longer strictly true when the modified LM test is based on the F-distribution as in (5.21a), any reduction in power is likely to be small. On the other hand, dividing by $1 - R^2$ could make an enormous difference.

Comparison between the Wald, LR and LM Procedures

In comparing the three classical test procedures, there are essentially two issues at stake. The first is computational convenience, and the second is power.

As regards power, the first point to note is that all three statistics are asymptotically equivalent in the sense that they give the same result if the data are generated by the null or a local alternative. A sequence of local alternatives for the parameters under test is such that

$$H_1 : \psi^{(2)} = \psi_0^{(2)} + T^{-\frac{1}{2}}\delta$$

for some vector δ. The source of the asymptotic equivalence of the test statistics can be explained as follows. If a single parameter is under test, the likelihood may be as in figure 5.4. The Wald test is based upon the horizontal distance between ψ_0 and ψ, the LR test is based upon the vertical distance, and the LM test is based on the slope of the likelihood at ψ_0. Each is a reasonable measure of the distance between H_0 and H_1. When L is a quadratic function they all give the same test, and when the true value of ψ is equal to, or close to, ψ_0, the likelihood function will be approximately quadratic for large samples.

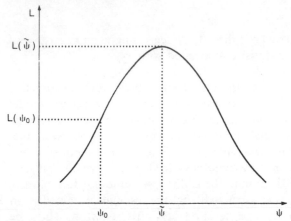

Figure 5.4   Typical Likelihood Function for a Single Parameter

The fact that the three tests are asymptotically equivalent by no means supports the notion that the three tests will have similar power in small samples. Unfortunately the question of power in small samples is difficult to resolve analytically, although some progress has been made by Rothenberg (1984). However, for a regression model with a general p.d. covariance matrix, as in (2.4.1), it can be shown that the test statistics obey the inequality

$$W \geq \mathrm{LR} \geq \mathrm{LM} \tag{5.22}$$

see Berndt and Savin (1977) and Breusch (1979a). Thus whenever the LM test rejects the null, the Wald and LR tests will also reject. However, this does not mean that the Wald test is more powerful than the LR and LM tests, since it also has a higher probability of rejection under the null. Thus a proper power comparison of the tests requires that they be corrected in some way so as to be of the same size; see, for example, the results in Evans and Savin (1982).

As regards computational convenience, the LR statistic is very simple to construct but suffers from the disadvantage that it requires ML estimates for both the restricted and unrestricted models. This suggests that as far as computer time is concerned, the LM and Wald tests are both preferable, the choice being dependent on whether the restricted or unrestricted model is easiest to estimate.

As a final point it is perhaps worth stressing what should by now be obvious, namely that the computation of the test statistics given by all three approaches is, in principle, straightforward, if testing, like estimation, is approached in an ML framework. The main point in examining the form of a test statistic in a particular case is to determine whether it can be transformed into a statistic whose exact distribution under H_0 is known.

5.6. Non-Nested Models

So far the discussion has been confined to testing nested hypotheses. In such cases the restricted model is a special case of the unrestricted model. However, this need not always be so. A problem which frequently arises is when the models specified under two hypotheses are non-nested, in that one cannot be obtained as a special case of the other. In these circumstances the conventional approaches are no longer applicable.

There are two ways of tackling this problem. The first is to choose between the two models on the basis of some appropriate criterion. This is termed *discrimination*, and a simple example of such a procedure would be choosing between linear regression models on the basis of R^2. Alternatively, the problem may be approached within a framework which relies on considerations similar to those in classical hypothesis testing. One possibility is to embed the competing models within a more general model. Each hypothesis may then be tested separately as a set of restrictions in the general case. On the other hand, Cox has suggested another method in which a test of significance is carried out on one of the models using a statistic similar to the LR statistic. If the roles of the two models are reversed, however, a different test statistic is usually obtained.

While only two outcomes are possible if the problem is taken as one of discrimination, the hypothesis testing approach leads to four. This is because both models can be accepted or rejected.

Discrimination

Suppose H_1 and H_2 denote two hypotheses concerning the distribution of a variable, y. One possible way of discriminating between the models would be to compare the maximised values of their respective likelihood functions.

However, it would seem desirable to make some allowance for n, the number of parameters estimated. The *Akaike Information Criterion* (AIC) attempts to make such a correction, the decision rule being to select the model for which

$$\text{AIC} = -2 \log L(\tilde{\psi}) + 2n \qquad (6.1)$$

is a minimum.

The AIC is used for testing nested as well as non-nested hypotheses. In doing so it breaks away from conventional procedures which test whether a parameter is 'significant' using a test the size of which is essentially arbitrary. Thus the emphasis is on comparing the 'goodness of fit' of various models with an appropriate allowance made for parsimony. This has a good deal of appeal in problems where the specification is based primarily on pragmatic considerations.

In the case of regression models with white noise disturbances, a comparison of the likelihood functions reduces to a comparison of the residual sum of squares. When the competing models contain the same number of parameters, therefore, the AIC decision rule leads to the selection of the model for which R^2 is greatest. However, when the number of parameters differs, an adjustment must be made. A number of criteria which are different from those already considered have been suggested. The best known is probably $\bar{R}^2$ which was defined in (2.2.14).

Example 1   In comparing the linear and log-linear production functions, (2.1.9) and (2.1.10), we are faced with the immediate problem that while one of the specifications concerns y_t itself, the second is an hypothesis relating to the distribution of $\log y_t$. Hence the maximised likelihoods cannot be compared directly. However, the joint distribution of $y_1, \ldots, y_T$, in (2.1.9) may be obtained by a change of variables. Thus

$$p(y_1, \ldots, y_T; \alpha, \beta) = |J| \cdot p(\log y_1, \ldots, \log y_T; \alpha, \beta) \quad (6.2)$$

where the Jacobian, J, is a $T \times T$ diagonal matrix in which the tth diagonal element is given by $\partial \log y_t / \partial y_t = 1/y_t$. The maximised log–likelihood function is therefore

$$\log L = -\tfrac{1}{2} T(\log 2\pi + 1) - \tfrac{1}{2} T \log \tilde{\sigma}_M^2 - \Sigma \log y_t \qquad (6.3)$$

where $\tilde{\sigma}_M^2$ is the ML estimator of σ^2 based on regressing $\log Q_t$ on $\log K_t$ and $\log L_t$. Since both the additive and multiplicative models contain the same number of parameters, the AIC decision rule is to accept the additive model if $T \log \tilde{\sigma}_A^2$ is less than $T \log \tilde{\sigma}_M^2 + 2 \Sigma \log y_t$.

Embedding within a General Model

If the competing models are embedded within a general model, then H_1 and H_2 may each be tested separately. A Wald or LR test will usually be appropriate for this purpose.

A general procedure for carrying out such tests was suggested by Cox (1961, 1962) and further developed by Atkinson (1970). If $p_1(y_1, \ldots, y_T; \psi_1)$ and $p_2(y_1, \ldots, y_T; \psi_2)$ are the p.d.f.'s under H_1 and H_2 respectively, the p.d.f. of the general model can be made proportional to

$$\{p_1(y_1, \ldots, y_T; \psi_1)\}^{\lambda} \{p_2(y_1, \ldots, y_T; \psi_2)\}^{1-\lambda}$$

Tests of the two hypotheses may then be carried out as tests on λ. However, although this procedure is straightforward in theory, the calculations involved may be relatively heavy.

In many cases there is no need to resort to the general procedure outlined above. For example, suppose the two hypotheses concern linear regression models of the form:

$$H_1 : y_t = x_t'\beta + \epsilon_t \tag{6.4}$$

$$H_2 : y_t = z_t'\gamma + \epsilon_t \tag{6.5}$$

where x_t and β are $n_1 \times 1$ vectors and x_t and γ are $n_2 \times 1$ vectors. These may be embedded within the more general model

$$y_t = x_t'\beta + z_t'\gamma + \epsilon_t \tag{6.6}$$

A significant F-statistic in a test of the hypothesis that $\gamma = 0$ leads to a rejection of H_1, while H_2 is rejected if the estimate of β is significant. Of course, if z_t and x_t contain some elements in common, these are only included once in the general model, and are not involved in the test procedures. Further development along these lines can be found in Mizon and Richard (1986).

Example 2   Consider again the problem of multiplicative versus additive disturbances. Both (2.1.9) and (2.1.10) may be embedded within a more general model by means of the Box–Cox transform,

$$y^{(\lambda)} = \begin{cases} (y^\lambda - 1)/\lambda, & 0 < \lambda \leq 1 \\ \log y & , \quad \lambda = 0 \end{cases} \tag{6.7}$$

The general model is

$$y_t^{(\lambda)} = \{AK_t^\beta L_t^\gamma\}^{(\lambda)} + \epsilon_t \tag{6.8}$$

Setting $\lambda = 1$ yields (2.1.10) while (2.1.9) is obtained with $\lambda = 0$.
Since $\epsilon_t \sim NID(0, \sigma^2)$, the joint density function is

$$\log L(y_1, \ldots, y_T; \alpha, \beta, \sigma^2, \lambda) = -\tfrac{1}{2} T \log 2\pi - \tfrac{1}{2} T \log \sigma^2$$
$$-\tfrac{1}{2}\sigma^{-2} \sum [y_t^{(\lambda)} - \{AK_t L_t\}^{(\lambda)}]^2 + (\lambda - 1)\sum \log y_t \tag{6.9}$$

The last term in (6.9) is the determinant of the Jacobian which results from transforming $y_t^{(\lambda)}$ to y_t; cf. (6.3).

The parameter σ^2 may be concentrated out of the likelihood function, leaving non-linear optimisation to be carried out with respect to α, β and λ. The hypotheses H_1 and H_2 can then be conveniently tested by setting up a confidence interval around $\tilde{\lambda}$.

It is quite possible that the above procedure will fail to reject both models. This simply means that the sample is insufficiently large to allow a definite conclusion to be drawn. On the other hand, if both models are rejected, this should not necessarily imply acceptance of the more general model, particularly if $\lambda \neq 0, 1$ yields a model for which the theoretical interpretation is unclear.

The Cox Procedure

The method developed by Cox is based on a modification of the Neyman–Pearson likelihood ratio. Let $L_1(\psi_1)$ and $L_2(\psi_2)$ denote the likelihood functions under H_1 and H_2 respectively. A test of the hypothesis H_1 is then based on

$$T_1 = \{\log L_1(\tilde{\psi}_1) - \log L_2(\tilde{\psi}_2)\}$$
$$- E_{\tilde{\psi}_1}\{\log L_1(\tilde{\psi}_1) - \log L_2(\tilde{\psi}_2)\} \qquad (6.10)$$

This statistic compares the observed difference of log–likelihoods with an estimate of the difference to be expected when H_1 is true. If H_1 is true, T_1 should be close to zero, whereas under H_2 it will tend to be negative. A large sample test may be based on the normal distribution. The test is one-sided, a general formula for deriving the asymptotic variance of T_1 being given by Cox (1962). This must be estimated consistently from the data.

In carrying out a test based on T_1 only, the hypotheses are being considered unsymmetrically with H_2 serving only to indicate the type of alternative for which high power is required. However, the roles of the hypotheses may be interchanged, and a second test statistic, T_2, calculated. This takes the form

$$T_2 = \{\log L_2(\tilde{\psi}_2) - \log L_1(\tilde{\psi}_1)\}$$
$$- E_{\tilde{\psi}_2}\{\log L_2(\tilde{\psi}_2) - \log L_1(\tilde{\psi}_1)\} \qquad (6.11)$$

In general T_1 and T_2 will be different functions of the observations. As with the embedding procedure, the application of T_1 and T_2 raises the possibility that both or neither of the hypotheses will be rejected.

Example 3   When H_1 and H_2 relate to non-nested linear models of the form (6.4) and (6.5), Pesaran (1974) has shown that the Cox procedure is relatively straightforward to apply. Let $\tilde{\sigma}_1^2$ and $\tilde{\sigma}_2^2$ be the estimated variances from H_1 and H_2 respectively; let e_{21} be the vector of OLS residuals in the regression of $x_t' b$ on z_t and let e_{121} be the vector of OLS residuals in the regression of e_{21} on x. Finally let $\tilde{\sigma}_{21}^2 = \tilde{\sigma}_1^2 + T^{-1} e_{21}' e_{21}$. The statistic (6.10) is then given by $T_1 = (T/2)\log(\tilde{\sigma}_2^2/\tilde{\sigma}_{21}^2)$ while a consistent estimate of its asymptotic variance is given by $\mathrm{avar}(T_1) = (\tilde{\sigma}_1^2/\tilde{\sigma}_{21}^4) e_{121}' e_{121}$. Thus the statistic

$$N_1 = T_1/\sqrt{\mathrm{avar}(T_1)}$$

is asymptotically $N(0, 1)$ when H_1 is true, and a significant negative value of N_1 implies a rejection of H_1 against H_2. A similar statistic, N_2, may be constructed for testing H_2 against H_1.

5.7. Post-Sample Predictive Testing

The aim of the test procedures described in the preceding sections is to select an appropriate model from the data. Once a suitable model has been identified, its parameters are then estimated using the same set of data. The only way in which the adequacy of the chosen model may then be assessed is by its ability to make accurate predictions *outside* the sample period. It is therefore important to retain a subset of the available observations for post-sample predictive testing.

Suppose that a dynamic model of the form (2.12.1) has been estimated. Given values of the exogenous variables, x_t, predictions may be generated for the dependent variable over the whole of the post-sample period, $t = T + 1$ to $T + l$. Various plots of the prediction errors, $e_{T+j|T}$, $j = 1, \ldots, l$ can be constructed, one possibility being the CUSUM

$$W_\tau^\dagger = s^{-2} \sum_{j=1}^{\tau} e_{T+j|T}, \qquad \tau = 1, \ldots, l \tag{7.1}$$

Formal tests may also be carried out, the most important being based on a comparison of the sum of squares of the post-sample prediction errors with the residual sum of squares from the fitted model.

The Post-Sample Goodness of Fit Test

The basic post-sample predictive test may be applied to any static or dynamic model including those with non-linearities and moving average disturbances. However, attention will be focused on the dynamic model, (2.12.1). Let $\psi = (\alpha_1, \ldots, \alpha_r, \beta')'$ and suppose that $\epsilon_t \sim NID(0, \sigma^2)$. If ψ is known, the prediction errors

$$\epsilon_{T+j \mid T} = y_{T+j} - \alpha_1 y_{T+j-1} - \cdots - \alpha_r y_{T+j-r} - x'_{T+j}\beta,$$

$$j = 1, \ldots, l \quad (7.2)$$

will be $NID(0, \sigma^2)$ and if σ^2 is known the statistic

$$\xi^\dagger(l) = \sigma^{-2} \sum_{j=1}^{l} \epsilon^2_{T+j \mid T} \quad (7.3)$$

will have a χ^2_l distribution.

When ψ is estimated, the variance of each prediction error, $\epsilon_{T+j \mid T}(\tilde{\psi}) = e_{T+j \mid T}$, consists of two parts. The first part is σ^2, the variance of the random term in the model, while the second part arises from the estimation of ψ. However, if this second term is of $0(T^{-1})$, which is almost invariably the case, it becomes small relative to σ^2 when the sample size is large. Therefore, if $\hat{\sigma}^2$ denotes a consistent estimator of σ^2, the statistic

$$\xi(l) = \hat{\sigma}^{-2} \sum_{j=1}^{l} e^2_{T+j \mid T} \quad (7.4)$$

is asymptotically χ^2_l. A significant value of $\xi(l)$ may indicate one of two things: *either* that the observations in the sample and post-sample periods are generated by different models, *or* that the model fitted to the sample observations is misspecified. The first of these conclusions implies a structural break, but if the division into sample and post-sample observations were essentially arbitrary this would seem unlikely. In general, the conclusion to be drawn from a significant value of $\xi(l)$ is that the chosen model is in some sense inadequate.

Example Davidson *et al.* (1978, p. 675) report the following equation for the UK consumption function:

$$\hat{y}_t = 509 + 0.75 y_{t-1} + 0.18 x_t + 68 D_t^0 - 812 Q_{1t}$$
$$\phantom{\hat{y}_t = 509 +} (0.11) \phantom{y_{t-1} +} (0.08) (49) (63)$$

$$+ 32 Q_{2t} - 169 Q_{3t}$$
$$ (46) \phantom{Q_{2t}} (26)$$

$$R^2 = 0.990, \quad d = 2.1, \quad \xi(20) = 190$$

where y is consumers' expenditure, x is personal disposable income, D^0 is a dummy variable allowing for the effect of the 1968 budget and the introduction of VAT in 1973, and Q_1, Q_2 and Q_3 are seasonal dummies. The high R^2 indicates a close fit to the data, while the Durbin–Watson statistic, although not strictly speaking valid because of the lagged dependent variable, nevertheless gives no hint of misspecification. However twenty observations were retained for past sample predictive testing, and the value of $\xi(20)$ is such that the model is convincingly rejected.

Post-Sample Predictive Tests in the Classical Regression Model

Since the variance of each prediction error, $e_{T+j\,|\,T}$, will be greater than σ^2, the size of a test based on $\xi(l)$ will tend to exceed the nominal significance level. However, in the classical linear regression model, an exact test is available. If $X_T^{(l)} = (x_{T+1}, \ldots, x_{T+l})'$ and $y_T^{(l)} = (y_{T+1}, \ldots, y_{T+l})'$, the $l \times 1$ vector of post-sample predictions is given by $\tilde{y}_T^{(l)} = X_T^{(l)}{}' b$, where b is the OLS estimator of β in (2.1.5). For normally distributed disturbance, it follows from (1.3.13) that

$$(y_T^{(l)} - \tilde{y}_T^{(l)})' \{ I + X_T^{(l)}(X'X)^{-1}X_T^{(l)}{}' \}^{-1}(y_T^{(l)} - \tilde{y}_T^{(l)})/\sigma^2$$

has a χ_l^2 distribution. Therefore, if s^2 is the unbiased estimator of σ^2 from the first T observations,

$$\xi^*(l) = (y_T^{(l)} - \tilde{y}_T^{(l)})' \{ I + X_T^{(l)}(X'X)^{-1}X_T^{(l)}{}' \}^{-1}(y_T^{(l)} - \tilde{y}_T^{(l)})/ls^2 \tag{7.5}$$

follows an F-distribution with $(l, T - k)$ degrees of freedom when the model is correctly specified and the parameters, including σ^2, remain constant throughout time. It will be observed that the crucial difference between $\xi(l)$ and $\xi^*(l)$ is that the latter allows for the estimation of β through the matrix term $X_T^{(l)}(X'X)^{-1}X_T^{(l)}{}'$.

The test statistic (7.5) may be written in two alternative forms. The first is

$$\xi^*(l) = (SSE^* - SSE)/ls^2 \tag{7.6}$$

where SSE and SSE^* are the residual sums of squares from regressions on the first T and $T + l$ observations respectively. Expression (7.6) forms the basis for the 'Chow test'. This is the usual test for a structural change in the vector of regression coefficients when the number of observations occurring after the hypothesised break is less than, or equal to, k. A proof of the equivalence of (7.5) and (7.6) will be found in Chow (1960).

Further insight into the test statistic may be obtained by noting that the numerator of (7.6) is equal to the sum of squares of the recursive residuals computed at $t = T + 1, T + 2, \ldots, T + l$. This follows immediately from the residual sum of squares recursion, (2.6.10). Hence

$$\xi^*(l) = \frac{\displaystyle\sum_{j=1}^{l} v_{T+j}^2/l}{\displaystyle\sum_{t=k+1}^{T} v_t^2 /(T - K)} \tag{7.7}$$

The fact that (7.7) has an F-distribution for a correctly specified model follows from the properties of recursive residuals. As a corollary to this derivation, it is possible to show a further result, namely that a sequence of Chow tests are mutually independent. Suppose there are p such statistics, $\xi(l_1), \ldots, \xi(l_p)$, defined over the consecutive post-sample periods $t = T + 1$ to $T + l_1$ for $\xi(l_1)$, $t = T + l_1 + 1$ to $T + l_1 + l_2$ for $\xi(l_2)$ and so on. These statistics can be written as

$$\xi^*(l_i) = \frac{\displaystyle\sum_{t=T_{i-1}+1}^{T_i} v_t^2/l_i}{\displaystyle\sum_{t=k+1}^{T_{i-1}} v_t^2/(T_{i-1}-k)} , \qquad i = 1, \ldots, p$$

where $T_i = T + l_1 + l_2 + \ldots + l_i$. If both the numerators and denominators in the $\xi^*(l_i)$'s are divided by σ^2, they may be expressed as

$$\xi(l_i) = \frac{z_i/l_i}{\displaystyle\sum_{j=0}^{i-1} z_j/(T_{i-1}-k)} , \qquad i = 1, \ldots, p$$

where z_0 is SSE/σ^2. It follows from the properties of recursive residuals that $z_0, \ldots, z_p$ are independent chi-square variates with degrees of freedom $T - k, l_1, l_2, \ldots, l_p$ respectively, and this makes it possible to invoke a lemma in Hogg and Tanis (1963, p. 436) from which it follows that the $\xi^*(l_i)$'s are mutually independent. The practical importance of this result is that it makes it possible to assess the overall significance level of a sequence of Chow tests.

The original formulation of the post-sample predictive test statistic in (7.5) is based on the errors arising from predictions made with an estimator constructed from the first T observations. That the quadratic form involving these quantities may be re-expressed in terms of a series of one-step ahead prediction errors based on updating that estimator is certainly not obvious. Nevertheless it is extremely useful, since the independence of the one-step ahead prediction errors suggests that they may be used to construct other tests. Thus if σ^2 is estimated from the sample observations, the CUSUM and CUSUMSQ procedures may be carried out using the recursive residuals from $t = T + 1$ to $t = T + l$. The same set of post-sample recursive residuals may be subjected to a Sign test, or a t-test based on the statistic,

$$\sum_{j=1}^{l} v_{T+j}/s\sqrt{l} \tag{7.8}$$

With the exception of the Sign test, the powers of the various post-sample prediction tests hinge on the estimation of σ^2. If σ^2 were known for the true model, then the χ^2 test, (7.3), could be carried out and there would be few qualifications regarding its effectiveness. However, σ^2 will not generally be known. It must be estimated, and if the model is inappropriate, s^2 will tend to overestimate σ^2. Hence the denominator as well as the numerator of (7.5) will be inflated with a consequent loss in power. The t-test based on (7.8) suffers from the same drawback. A Sign test or, alternatively, a Wilcoxon test, may therefore be more attractive in certain circumstances.

5.8. A Strategy for Model Selection

A number of alternative approaches for testing the specification of a model have been discussed. In this section an attempt is made to bring these various components together and develop an overall strategy for model selection. All the different test procedures have a role to play in such an approach, and if used correctly they are complementary rather than competitive. However, before proceeding a word of caution is in order. The issues raised by the problem of model selection are extremely complex, and it would be foolish to pretend that there is a generally acceptable solution which can be applied in most cases. What follows should therefore be regarded as no more than an outline of what seems to me to be a reasonably sensible and systematic approach.

In many areas, particularly in economics, models are constructed on a somewhat haphazard basis. A typical approach is to begin by formulating the simplest model consistent with the theory of the subject in question. This model is then estimated. If it is a regression model, the researcher may well be tempted to proceed no further if he obtains a 'high' R^2, say over 0.9. However, a high R^2 may be obtained very easily with time series data, even when the variables in question are totally unrelated. Assuming that the researcher is sophisticated enough to appreciate this point, he will supplement his consideration of R^2 with some tests of misspecification. Should one or more of these tests be 'significant' he will reject his model, but the direction in which the model is subsequently revised will be essentially arbitrary.

The *ad hoc* approach to specification testing described above is avoided by imposing some structure on the problem at the outset. The various alternative formulations suggested by theory are first delineated and a systematic procedure for testing the hypotheses implicit in them is determined. All the available *a priori* knowledge is used to set up a decision framework *before* any estimation is carried out. Specification testing may then proceed, the starting point being the most *general* model, or models, under consideration.

The theory underlying this systematic approach is dealt with in the next sub-section. However, it is extremely rare, in practice, for a researcher to be able to enumerate confidently all the possible models he is prepared to consider. For this reason tests of misspecification still play an important part in any overall specification strategy. Nevertheless, their role is to complement the tests of specification, rather than to provide the basis for an alternative strategy.

Testing Ordered Hypotheses

Given a set of possible model specifications, the most obvious structure to look for is one of *nesting*. Consider the three models

(0) $y_t = \beta_1 x_{1t} + \epsilon_t$

(1) $y_t = \beta_1 x_{1t} + \beta_2 x_{2t}^{-1} + \epsilon_t$ $\qquad\qquad$ (8.1)

(2) $y_t = \beta_1 x_{1t} + \beta_2 (x_{2t} - \gamma)^{-1} + \epsilon_t$

The last of these is the demand for money equation, (5.17). However, model (1) is nested within model (2), while (0) is, in turn, nested within (1). The hypotheses implicit in this nest form a uniquely ordered set and this enables a *sequential testing procedure* to be carried out. The hypotheses are tested in increasing order of restrictiveness, with the sequence indicated by

$$H_1 : \gamma = 0$$
$$H_0 : \gamma = 0, \ \beta_2 = 0$$

$\qquad\qquad\qquad\qquad\qquad\qquad\qquad\qquad\qquad$ (8.2)

The first test is of the null hypothesis $\gamma = 0$ against the alternative $\gamma \neq 0$. The second test sets $\beta_2 = 0$ against $\beta_2 \neq 0$. This is a test for the inclusion of x_{2t}^{-1} in the regression model, but it is only carried out if the first test does not reject the null hypothesis that $\gamma = 0$. If $H_1 : \gamma = 0$ is rejected, all succeeding hypotheses (i.e. $H_0 : \gamma = 0, \ \beta_2 = 0$) are rejected as well.

The tests employed in a sequential procedure may be based on the Wald, LR or LM principles. If it were felt desirable to estimate the most general model in (8.1), then a test of $\gamma = 0$ could, following the Wald principle, be based on the relevant asymptotic t-ratio. It would, however, be equally valid to employ the LR statistic, although there is no guarantee that it would give the same result. If the hypothesis were not rejected, then a test of $\beta_2 = 0$ would be carried out straightforwardly using a t-test from a linear regression based on model (1). The sequential test procedures used in the study by Mizon (1977a) are all based on tests derived from the Wald or LR principles. However, in example (8.1), an LM test of $\gamma = 0$ has considerable appeal since it renders estimation of the non-linear model, (2), unnecessary.

The sequential testing procedure starts from the most general, or *maintained*, hypothesis and tests hypotheses in increasing order of restrictiveness. Approaching the problem in this way yields a procedure with certain optimal properties with regard to power; see Anderson (1971, pp. 34–43, 116–134, 270–276). However, an alternative strategy, which is often used in practice, is to start from the most restricted model. In the case of (8.1), this would mean starting at (0) and treating the hypotheses in reverse order. Such an approach has obvious computational advantages if the more general models in the nest are highly non-linear. However, even if the full testing framework is specified at the beginning, the test statistics will not, in general, be independent, and this makes the analysis of statistical power difficult. Indeed, one of the main reasons for testing the hypotheses in increasing order of restrictiveness is that the incremental test statistics are all independent in large samples.

Suppose the hypotheses in (8.2) are tested using Wald statistics, W_1 for H_1 and W_0 for H_0. W_1 and W_0 will be asymptotically χ_1^2 and χ_2^2 respectively, but the important result is that the incremental statistic, $W_0 - W_1$, is asymptotically χ_1^2 and is distributed independently of W_1 in large samples. Thus if the two hypotheses in (8.2) are tested at the 5% level of significance, the nominal significance level of the most restricted hypothesis, (0), against the maintained, (2), will be $1 - (0.95)^2 = 0.0975$.

Non-Nested Hypotheses

The sequential testing procedure is obviously inapplicable when some of the models under consideration are non-nested. However, problems of non-nestedness also arise when there is no natural ordering of hypotheses. Consider model (1) in (8.1). There are two possible sequences for testing the 'significance' of the estimates of β_1 and β_2. In the first, a t-test is carried out on the estimate of β_2 in a regression based on (1). This is followed by a t-test on the estimate of β_1 in a regression of y_t on x_{1t} only. The second sequence, which may be formalised as $H_1 : \beta_1 = 0$, $H_0 : \beta_1 = 0$, $\beta_2 = 0$, treats the parameters the other way round. If x_{1t} and x_{2t}^{-1} are strongly correlated, the chances of the two testing sequences yielding conflicting inferences are quite high. One approach may suggest that y_t depends only on x_{1t} while in the other it depends only on x_{2t}. These two models are non-nested.

The above considerations lead to what Mizon (1977b) has called an *exhaustive test procedure*. Optimal sequential testing procedures are applied to all possible orderings of the complete set of hypotheses. An appropriate method is then used to discriminate between the preferred hypotheses from all the orderings.

Tests of Misspecification

The scheme set out so far has avoided the use of misspecification. By first considering the various options available before any estimation or testing is carried out, an overall structure is imposed on the problem. A series of tests of specification are then carried out within this framework. However, although this approach is very attractive, there has never been any suggestion that rules out the use of tests of misspecification. It is rarely the case that the researcher can be certain at the outset that his most general models are in fact adequate. He may not become aware of certain formulations until recognition of the shortcomings of the proposed models forces him to revise his initial preconceptions. Tests of misspecification and other diagnostic checking procedures clearly play a key role in this process. However, they are a *supplement* to the formal procedure, rather than an alternative.

Post-Sample Predictive Testing and Model Evaluation

The strategy outlined so far employs a number of procedures all of which are based on the sample. They may therefore be regarded as a means of arriving at a specification which is *internally valid,* in the sense that it provides a good fit to the data in the sample. However, it is now important to determine whether the model is *externally valid,* i.e. does it perform well outside the sample period? This leads to the tests based on prediction, and it is particularly important that they be applied when tests of misspecification have led to some revision of the hypotheses entertained. That being the case, the preferred model will, to some extent, be the product of data mining. The 'good fit' obtained is merely the final result of a series of experimental specifications suggested by the data themselves.

The aim of post-sample predictive testing is to provide an independent check on the specification suggested by the sample. However, if the post-sample test rejects the null hypothesis of correct specification, it is not altogether clear what the next step should be. The route most likely to be taken is to return to the sample data, and attempt to find a model which will satisfy the post-sample predictive test. This cycle could be repeated several times, and while the end result may be a perfectly satisfactory model, the procedure as a whole could be open to a charge of data mining. The post-sample predictive test is effectively being used in the same way as a conventional test of misspecification, and it no longer serves the purpose of providing an independent assessment of the adequacy of the fitted model.

A failure to reject the preferred model on the basis of its performance over the prediction period will often mean that the model is accepted. However, in doing this it is important to be aware of the shortcomings of such criteria. In particular, if the fit in the sample is relatively poor, the estimate of the error variance, σ^2, will be inflated. This will tend to weaken the standard post-sample predictive tests such as (7.6). It was suggested in Section 7 that the Wilcoxon and Sign tests might be more effective in certain circumstances, but even they would fail if the prediction errors were approximately random.

Thus suppose a variable is omitted from a regression equation, and that this variable is uncorrelated with the variables included. Neither within-sample nor post-sample tests are likely to detect the omission. Thus, unless there is some absolute standard for determining whether the size of the prediction errors is acceptable, there are no statistical grounds on which the model may be deemed unsatisfactory. The model is therefore likely to be retained until it is challenged by an alternative specification. This leads to the adoption of a criterion such as

$$s_p^2(l) = \sum_{j=1}^{l} e_{T+j|T}^2 / l \tag{8.3}$$

as a measure of post-sample goodness of fit. Comparing different models on the basis of (8.3) is more meaningful than a within-sample comparison based on s^2 or R^2.

Notes

Section 2   Ramsey (1969) discusses the properties of residuals generally. Tests involving recursive residuals are described in Harvey and Phillips (1974), Brown, Durbin and Evans (1975) and Harvey and Collier (1977). Harrison and McCabe (1979) give exact and bounds tests for heteroscedasticity based on OLS residuals.

Sections 3, 4 and 5   Silvey (1975), Breusch and Pagan (1979, 1980), Harvey and Phillips (1980b), Engle (1984), Jarque and Bera (1980).

Section 6   Sargan (1964), Akaike (1973), Seber (1978, pp. 359-370), Box and Cox (1964).

Sections 7 and 8   Gadd and Wold (1964), Harvey (1976b), Leamer (1978), Mizon (1977a, 1977b), Hendry and Richard (1983).

Exercises

1. Prove (1.2) and (1.3), and comment on the interpretation of (1.3).
2. The CES production function was defined in (2.1.12). Given a multiplicative disturbance term, dividing through by L_t and taking logarithms yields,

   $$\log q_t = \alpha + (\beta - 1)\log L_t - \beta\gamma^{-1} \log(1 - \delta + \delta k_t^{-\gamma}) + \epsilon_t$$

   where $q_t = Q_t/L_t$ and $k_t = K_t/L_t$. When $\gamma = 0$, the Cobb–Douglas form is obtained. If $\epsilon_t \sim NID(0, \sigma^2)$ show that the modified LM test of $\gamma = 0$ may be based on the t-statistic obtained by regressing $\log q_t$ on $\log L_t$, $\log k_t$ and $(\log k_t)^2$. [Hint: Taylor Series of term involving k_t.]
3. The VES function is

   $$Q = e^\alpha K^{\beta(1 - \gamma\delta)} \lceil L + (\gamma - 1)K \rceil^{\beta\gamma\delta}$$

   where α, β, γ and δ are parameters; see Revankar (1971). If the disturbances are multiplicative, construct a test of $\gamma = 1$ using a similar approach to that employed in Question 2 above. If the test rejected the null hypothesis, explain how you would proceed to estimate the model.

4. How would you construct a Wald test of $H_0 : \delta_2 = \cdots = \delta_r$ in the multiplicative heteroscedasticity model (3.4.15); cf. (3.14) and (5.12)?
5. Construct an LR test for the inclusion of an equation in a SURE system.
6. How would you carry out a Wald test of $H_0 : \beta_2 = \beta_4$ in (2.9.18)?
7. Construct a modified LM test of the hypothesis $\gamma = 1$ in (8.1).
8. How would you carry out an LM test of $\theta = 0$ in the ARMA (1, 1) model, (1.5.21)? Compare this test with the Wald and LR tests.
9. Consider a set of T independent observations on a Bernoulli random variable which takes on the values

$$y_t = \begin{cases} 1 & \text{, with probability } \pi \\ 0 & \text{, with probability } 1 - \pi \end{cases}$$

Find the ML estimator of π and show that it is a sufficient statistic.

   Construct Wald, LM and LR test statistics for testing $H_0: \pi = \pi_0$ against $H_1 : \pi \neq \pi_0$. What is the asymptotic distribution of these test statistics? Explain why this distribution follows immediately from the central limit theorem in the case of the Wald and LM tests. Is it possible to construct exact tests based on these statistics in this case?

6
Regression Models with
Serially Correlated
Disturbances

6.1. First Order Autoregressive Disturbances

The classical linear regression model was introduced in Chapter 2. Written in vector notation it has the form

$$y_t = x_t'\beta + u_t, \qquad t = 1, \ldots, T \tag{1.1}$$

with the symbols defined as in (2.1.3). A key assumption in the classical model is that the disturbances are uncorrelated. However, in dealing with time series regression this may not always be reasonable. If the disturbance term is regarded as being made up of a number of omitted variables, then in a time series context it seems more than likely that it will exhibit serial correlation since relatively few time series are random.

The traditional method of handling serially correlated disturbances is to model them by a stationary AR(1) process,

$$u_t = \phi u_{t-1} + \epsilon_t, \qquad |\phi| < 1 \tag{1.2}$$

Although such a model is not unreasonable for economic data, its main attraction lies in its ease of estimation. However, with modern computing facilities this is no longer a major consideration, and there is no reason why a general ARMA(p, q) disturbance should not be entertained. Such models are considered from Section 4 onwards, but from the point of view of exposition it is convenient to restrict attention to (1.2) initially.

Generalised Least Squares

The easiest way of carrying out GLS estimation is to find a matrix, L, with the property that $L'L = V^{-1}$. This may be used to transform the

191

observations in the manner described in Section 2.4, and the GLS estimator is then obtained by applying OLS. For a given V matrix — which in this case amounts to a given value of ϕ — this procedure yields the BLUE of β.

The V matrix may be readily constructed given the autocovariance properties of the AR(1) process. Since $E(u_t u_{t-\tau}) = \sigma^2 \phi^\tau / (1 - \phi^2)$, it follows that the ijth element of V is given by $\phi^{|i-j|}/(1 - \phi^2)$ for $i, j = 1, \ldots, T$. Inverting this matrix yields

$$V^{-1} = \begin{bmatrix} 1 & -\phi & 0 & \ldots & 0 & 0 \\ -\phi & 1 + \phi^2 & -\phi & \ldots & 0 & 0 \\ \vdots & \vdots & \vdots & \vdots \vdots \vdots & \vdots & \vdots \\ 0 & 0 & 0 & \ldots & 1 + \phi^2 & -\phi \\ 0 & 0 & 0 & \ldots & -\phi & 1 \end{bmatrix} \quad (1.3)$$

and it is not difficult to verify that the $T \times T$ matrix

$$L = \begin{bmatrix} \sqrt{1 - \phi^2} & 0 & 0 & \ldots & 0 & 0 \\ -\phi & 1 & 0 & \ldots & 0 & 0 \\ \cdot & -\phi & 1 & \ldots & & \cdot \\ \vdots & \vdots & \vdots & \vdots \vdots \vdots & \vdots & \vdots \\ 0 & 0 & 0 & \ldots & 1 & 0 \\ 0 & 0 & 0 & \ldots & -\phi & 1 \end{bmatrix} \quad (1.4)$$

has the desired property $L'L = V^{-1}$. The transformed observations are therefore

$$y_1^* = \sqrt{1 - \phi^2}\, y_1, \qquad x_1^* = \sqrt{1 - \phi^2}\, x_1 \quad (1.5)$$

$$y_t^* = y_t - \phi y_{t-1}, \qquad x_t^* = x_t - \phi x_{t-1}, \qquad t = 2, \ldots, T \quad (1.6)$$

For a given value of ϕ, regressing y_t^* on x_t^* for $t = 1, \ldots, T$, gives the GLS estimator of β.

Because the first observation is handled in a slightly different way from the remaining observations, it is often dropped from the computations. Thus OLS is based only on the $T - 1$ quasi-differences defined by (1.6). This is sometimes referred to as the *Cochrane–Orcutt* transformation. The rationale behind this transformation may be seen directly by multiplying (1.1) by ϕ at time $t - 1$. This yields

$$\phi y_{t-1} = \phi x_{t-1}' \beta + \phi u_{t-1}$$

Subtracting from (1.1) with u_t set equal to $\phi u_{t-1} + \epsilon_t$ then gives

$$y_t - \phi y_{t-1} = (x_t - \phi x_{t-1})' \beta + \epsilon_t \quad (1.7)$$

The effect of dropping the first observation depends crucially on the structure of the explanatory variables. Under the regularity conditions generally imposed for deriving asymptotic properties, it can be shown that the effect of omitting (1.5) is negligible in large samples. On the other hand it is always possible to find sets of explanatory variables for which the efficiency of the Cochrane–Orcutt system is very low. Maeshiro (1976) reports a series of calculations for a model with a constant term and a single explanatory variable equal to US real GNP. For all positive values of ϕ, the GLS estimator computed by the Cochrane–Orcutt transformation was actually less efficient than OLS. Furthermore its performance worsened the higher the value of ϕ; with $\phi = 0.98$ the variance of the Cochrane–Orcutt estimator of the coefficient of the explanatory variable was twice that of the OLS estimator.

Chipman (1979) provides analytic evidence on the above point. For the time trend model

$$y_t = \alpha + \beta t + u_t, \qquad t = 1, \ldots, T \tag{1.8}$$

he is able to show that the minimum efficiency of the Cochrane–Orcutt estimator is 0.54. On the other hand, the minimum efficiency of OLS is higher at 0.75. Unfortunately the actual efficiency is a complicated function of ϕ and T, and the interested reader should refer to Chipman's paper for further details. However, a heuristic rationale for the poor performance of Cochrane–Orcutt in this particular case is obtained by noting that the transformed explanatory variable is $x_t^* = t - \phi(t - 1)$. When ϕ is close to one, $x_t^* \simeq 1$ and this is almost perfectly collinear with the constant term, $1 - \phi$. Hence the estimates of both α and β will be relatively imprecise.

Further discussion of the relative efficiency of the Cochrane–Orcutt transform with respect to both the full GLS transform and OLS will be found in Section 2. For the moment, however, the main point to note is a tendency for the Cochrane–Orcutt transformation to yield unsatisfactory results when one of the explanatory variables is trending.

Two-Step and Iterative Procedures

Since ϕ will not, in general, be known, it must be estimated. If a consistent estimator of ϕ can be found, a feasible GLS estimator of β may be constructed. Subject to regularity conditions of the type described in Chapter 2, the feasible GLS estimator may be shown to have the same large sample distribution as the GLS estimator proper.

There are basically two methods of estimating ϕ. The first is based on the OLS residuals, and is given by the regression of e_t on e_{t-1}, i.e.

$$\hat{\phi} = \sum_{t=2}^{T} e_t e_{t-1} \bigg/ \sum_{t=2}^{T} e_{t-1}^2 \tag{1.9}$$

The second approach, due to Durbin (1960), consists of regressing y_t on y_{t-1}, x_t and x_{t-1}. The coefficient of y_{t-1} then provides the required estimate. The rationale behind this may be seen by rearranging (1.7). This yields

$$y_t = \phi y_{t-1} + x_t'\beta - x_{t-1}'(\phi\beta) + \epsilon_t, \qquad t = 1, \ldots, T \qquad (1.10)$$

Both of the above estimators of ϕ can be shown to be consistent under fairly general conditions. The inclusion of the first observation, (1.5), is immaterial as regards the asymptotic properties of the estimator of β, but as indicated in the previous sub-section this could be quite important in practice. If the first observation is omitted, the feasible GLS estimator based on (1.9) is known as two-step Cochrane–Orcutt. However, the nature of this estimation procedure lends itself naturally to iteration. Having computed a feasible GLS estimator of β, a new set of residuals may be used to construct another estimator of the form (1.9). This is then used to compute another feasible GLS estimator, and the process is repeated until convergence. The *Cochrane–Orcutt iterative procedure,* as it is called, implies no improvement as far as asymptotic properties are concerned, although it may have a significant effect in small samples. Similar considerations hold for an iterative procedure based on the full GLS transform.

Maximum Likelihood Estimation

If the disturbances in (1.1) are normally distributed, the log–likelihood function is of the form (3.5.13), but with y_t replaced by $y_t - x_t'\beta$. However, as in the case of the time series AR(1) model, considerable simplification results if y_1 is taken to be fixed. Conditional on β, the ML estimator of ϕ is then given by a straightforward regression of $y_t - x_t'\hat{\beta}$ on $y_{t-1} - x_{t-1}'\hat{\beta}$. This suggests that if the ML estimator of β, conditional on ϕ, is also linear, a stepwise optimisation procedure is likely to be computationally effective. Now, maximising the approximate log–likelihood function is equivalent to minimising the residual sum of squares function

$$S(\beta; \phi) = \sum_{t=2}^{T} \{ (y_t - x_t'\beta) - \phi(y_{t-1} - x_{t-1}'\beta) \}^2$$

$$= \sum_{t=2}^{T} \{ y_t - \phi y_{t-1} - (x_t - \phi x_{t-1})'\beta \}^2$$

and using the definition (1.6) this becomes

$$S(\beta; \phi) = \sum_{t=2}^{T} (y_t^* - x_t^{*'}\beta)^2 \qquad (1.11)$$

The conditional ML estimator of β is therefore identical to the Cochrane–Orcutt estimator. The iterative Cochrane–Orcutt procedure can now be interpreted as a stepwise algorithm for computing the ML estimators of β and ϕ when y_1 is regarded as fixed.

By a similar argument to the one employed above, the full GLS esimator is given implicitly when the exact likelihood function is decomposed in terms of prediction errors as in (3.5.13). Thus, conditional on ϕ, the ML estimator of β is obtained by applying OLS to the complete set of transformed observations, (1.5) and (1.6), while the conditional ML estimator of ϕ is obtained by solving a certain cubic equation; see Beach and MacKinnon (1978).

Since the GLS estimator is the MVUE of β, the two-step estimator is asymptotically efficient under the normality assumption. Furthermore, because the OLS estimator of β is consistent, the estimator (1.9) is an asymptotically efficient estimator of ϕ.

Asymptotic Distribution of the ML Estimator

The large sample properties of the ML estimators of β, ϕ and σ^2 are unaffected by the treatment of the initial conditions. The simplest approach is to take y_1 as fixed. Taking the expectation of the matrix of second derivatives of log L yields a block diagonal matrix. The ML estimator of β is therefore distributed independently of the estimators of ϕ and σ^2. These in turn have exactly the same asymptotic distribution as in an AR(1) time series model; see (3.5.23). Thus, asymptotically, $(\tilde{\beta}', \tilde{\phi}, \tilde{\sigma}^2)'$ has a multivariate normal distribution with mean $(\beta', \phi, \sigma^2)'$ and covariance matrix

$$\text{Avar}(\tilde{\beta}, \tilde{\phi}, \tilde{\sigma}^2) = \begin{bmatrix} \sigma^2(X'V^{-1}X)^{-1} & 0 & 0 \\ 0 & (1 - \phi^2)/T & 0 \\ 0 & 0 & 2\sigma^4/T \end{bmatrix} \quad (1.12)$$

6.2. Comparison of Estimators

All the procedures described in the previous sections yield estimators with identical large sample properties. Nevertheless their behaviour in small samples can be very different. This section reviews some of the evidence on small sample properties. Before this is done, however, the effect of applying OLS when the disturbances are autocorrelated is considered in some detail. Two issues are examined. The first is the extent to which OLS is inefficient, while the second concerns the implications of making inferences when the autocorrelation in the disturbances is ignored.

Efficiency of OLS

If the value of the AR parameter, ϕ, is known, the OLS estimator of β cannot be more efficient than the GLS estimator. This follows directly from the Gauss–Markov theorem. Furthermore, if ϕ is unknown, any consistent estimator of ϕ will lead to a feasible GLS estimator of β with the same asymptotic distribution as the GLS estimator proper. Thus a comparison between OLS and GLS for given values of ϕ provides a sensible measure of the relative efficiency of OLS in practice, provided that the sample size is reasonably large. On the other hand if T is small, it is quite possible for OLS to yield a more efficient estimator of β than a method which 'allows' for serial correlation. If, for example, ϕ is close to zero the additional source of variation arising from the need to estimate ϕ may more than offset any loss in efficiency incurred by taking ϕ to be equal to zero. Unfortunately there is little analytic evidence available on this point, although the relative small-sample efficiency of OLS in certain circumstances does emerge quite clearly in Monte Carlo results. This sub-section therefore concentrates on examining the extent to which OLS is likely to be inefficient in large samples.

A single regressor model

$$y_t = \beta x_t + u_t, \qquad t = 1, \ldots, T \tag{2.1}$$

is relatively straightforward to analyse, and provides a good deal of insight into the factors affecting the performance of OLS. If u_t is an AR(1) process of the form, (1.2), the GLS estimator is obtained by applying OLS to the transformed observations, (1.5) and (1.6). Therefore

$$\text{Var}(\bar{b}) = \sigma^2 \left[(1 - \phi^2)x_1^2 + \sum_{t=2}^{T} (x_t - \phi x_{t-1})^2 \right]^{-1} \tag{2.2}$$

The variance of the Cochrane–Orcutt estimator is given by an expression of the form (2.2), but with the term involving x_1 omitted.

The variance of the OLS estimator of β may be obtained by evaluating the general expression (2.4.8). Thus

$$\text{Var}(b) = \sigma^2 \varkappa \left/ \left[(1 - \phi^2)\left(\sum_{t=1}^{T} x_t^2 \right)^2 \right] \right. \tag{2.3}$$

where

$$\varkappa = (1 - \phi^2)X'VX = \sum_{t=1}^{T} x_t^2 + 2 \sum_{i=1}^{T-1} \sum_{t=1}^{T-i} \phi^i x_t x_{t+i} \tag{2.4}$$

Now suppose that x_t itself is generated by a stationary AR(1) process of the form

$$x_t = \bar{\phi} x_{t-1} + \xi_t \tag{2.5}$$

where $\xi_t \sim NID(0, \bar{\sigma}^2)$. Then

$$\text{plim } x/\Sigma x^2 = 1 + 2\phi\bar{\phi} + 2(\phi\bar{\phi})^2 + 2(\phi\bar{\phi})^3 + \cdots$$

$$= 2/(1 - \phi\bar{\phi}) - 1 = (1 + \phi\bar{\phi})/(1 - \phi\bar{\phi})$$

and so

$$\text{Avar}(b) = T^{-1} \text{ plim } T \text{ Var}(b) = \frac{1}{T} \frac{\sigma^2}{\bar{\sigma}^2} \frac{(1 - \bar{\phi}^2)(1 + \phi\bar{\phi})}{(1 - \phi^2)(1 - \phi\bar{\phi})} \tag{2.6}$$

For the GLS estimator

$$\text{Avar}(\tilde{b}) = \sigma^2 T^{-1} \left[\text{plim}(\Sigma x_t^2 - 2\phi\Sigma x_t x_{t-1} + \phi^2 \Sigma x_{t-1}^2)/T \right]^{-1}$$

$$= \frac{1}{T} \frac{\sigma^2}{\bar{\sigma}^2} \frac{(1 - \bar{\phi}^2)}{1 + \phi^2 - 2\phi\bar{\phi}} \tag{2.7}$$

irrespective of whether the full or Cochrane—Orcutt transform is carried out. The asymptotic efficiency of OLS is

$$\text{Eff}(b) = \frac{\text{Avar}(\tilde{b})}{\text{Avar}(b)} = \frac{(1 - \phi^2)(1 - \phi\bar{\phi})}{(1 + \phi\bar{\phi})(1 + \phi^2 - 2\phi\bar{\phi})} \tag{2.8}$$

For $\phi = 0.9$ and $\bar{\phi} = 0.8$, $\text{Eff}(b) = 0.03$.

The above results suggest that the performance of OLS may be very poor in certain circumstances. As an alternative case, however, suppose that $x_t - 1$ for $t = 1,\ldots,T$, rather than being generated by (2.5). Then

$$x = T + 2(T - 1)\phi + 2(T - 2)\phi^2 + \ldots + 2\phi^{T-1}$$

$$= \{T(1 - \phi^2) - 2\phi(1 - \phi^T)\}/(1 - \phi)^2$$

and on evaluating Avar $(\tilde{b})$ and Avar (b), it will be found that $\text{Eff}(b) = 1$. The efficiency of OLS in these circumstances is actually a reflection of a more general result, namely that for polynomial or trigonometric regressors OLS is asymptotically efficient for all values of ϕ.

Inferences Based on OLS

Although the true covariance matrix of the OLS estimator is given by (2.4.8), this formula will not, of course, be used in practice. Estimating Var(b) in the usual way may give a misleading picture of the accuracy of the procedure.

As an example, consider model (2.1) with x_t generated by the AR(1) process (2.5). The variance of the OLS estimator will be estimated by

$$\text{var}(b) = s^2/\Sigma x_t^2 \tag{2.9}$$

and

$$T^{-1} \text{ plim } T \text{ var}(b) = T^{-1} \text{ plim } s^2/\text{plim } \Sigma x^2/T$$

$$= T^{-1} \frac{\sigma^2}{1-\phi^2} \frac{(1 - \bar{\phi}^2)}{\bar{\sigma}^2} \tag{2.10}$$

A comparison of (2.10) with (2.6) shows that, in large samples, the ratio of the estimated variance to the true variance will be about $(1 - \phi\bar{\phi})/(1 + \phi\bar{\phi})$ on average. If both x_t and u_t exhibit positive serial correlation therefore, the analysis indicates that (2.9) will tend to *underestimate* the true variance.

Small-Sample Properties

The results shown in table 6.1 are taken from a series of Monte Carlo experiments carried out by Harvey and McAvinchey (1978). They show the estimated root mean square error (RMSE) of a number of estimators in relation to the estimated RMSE of the full ML estimator. The model examined was

$$y_t = \beta_1 + \beta_2 x_t + u_t, \qquad t = 1,\ldots,T \tag{2.11}$$

with u_t generated by an AR(1) process. Two forms for the explanatory variable were considered. In the first, x_t displayed a strong upward *trend*, being generated by a process of the form

$$x_t = \exp(0.04t) + \xi_t, \qquad t = 1,\ldots,T \tag{2.12}$$

where $\xi_t \sim NID(0, 0.0009)$. In the second, x_t was *stationary* and random. The summary statistics reported in table 6.1 are based on two hundred independent replications for each model.

The design of the Monte Carlo experiments in Harvey and McAvinchey (1978) is exactly the same as that used by Beach and MacKinnon (1978). Unfortunately the Beach–MacKinnon study had been restricted to a comparison of full ML with iterative Cochrane–Orcutt. They had found that when the explanatory variable was trending, Cochrane–Orcutt could give very inefficient estimators of β. This point was confirmed by Harvey and McAvinchey as the results presented for $\phi = 0.6$ and $T = 20$ show. However, the main motive behind the Harvey–McAvinchey study was to extend the Beach–McKinnon results to include two-step estimators. Using the same initial consistent estimator of ϕ, (1.9), feasible GLS estimates of β were computed using the full transformation, (1.4), and Cochrane–Orcutt.

Several conclusions emerged from this exercise. Firstly, the two-step estimator of β based on the full transformation appears to be as efficient as full ML in small samples. Secondly, the results for the two-step Cochrane–Orcutt estimator show that it is quite possible that iterating a particular procedure until convergence will result in a deterioration in small-sample properties. Thirdly, the results for trending data and $T = 20$ show the

Table 6.1 Ratio of RMSEs of OLS, Cochrane–Orcutt and Two-Step Estimators to Full ML for $\phi = 0.6$*

| | Two-Step Estimators | | | | | Iterative Cochrane–Orcutt | | | OLS | |
| | Full Transform | | | Cochrane–Orcutt | | | | | | |
Model	β_1	β_2	ϕ	β_1	β_2	β_1	β_2	ϕ	β_1	β_2
Trending Data $T = 20$	99.8	100.0	101.0	113.0	109.2	183.9	133.5	100.9	103.3	103.9
$T = 100$	100.0	100.0	100.5	102.5	100.0	102.5	100.0	100.3	102.0	100.0
Stationary Data $T = 20$	100.0	100.9	105.3	109.6	100.5	112.4	99.8	100.0	100.0	115.7
$T = 100$	100.0	100.5	103.0	103.4	100.5	103.4	100.5	100.7	100.0	152.1

*Estimated by Monte Carlo Experiments using 200 Replications.

two-step Cochrane–Orcutt estimators of both β_1 and β_2 having a significantly higher RMSE than the corresponding estimators based on the full transformation. This lends support to the argument advanced in Section 1 around (1.7) and (1.8). However, the results for $T = 100$ lead to a fourth conclusion, namely that the effect of the Cochrane–Orcutt approximation is relatively unimportant for moderately large samples.

The main conclusion to emerge from table 6.1 — and this is supported by the results not reproduced here — is that a significant loss in efficiency may be incurred if the Cochrane–Orcutt transformation is used in small samples. However, this does not necessarily constitute an argument for the use of full ML estimation. As the results for the two-step estimators show, the key feature of a successful estimation procedure is the use of the full GLS transform.

The results in table 6.1 also shed some light on the small sample performance of OLS. This estimator was included in the simulations as a yardstick by which to judge the other estimators, and within this framework its performance for trending data is particularly striking. In fact the relatively high efficiency of OLS in these circumstances is perhaps not surprising in view of the result noted at the close of the sub-section on the efficiency of OLS. The performance of OLS for stationary data is, however, less impressive. This is what one would be led to expect from (2.8). However, this asymptotic formula does imply that OLS is much more inefficient than it typically is for a moderately sized sample. For $T = 100$, the estimated efficiency of OLS is $(100/152.1)^2 = 0.81$. By way of contrast, evaluating (2.8) for $\phi = 0.6$ and $\bar{\phi} = 0.0$ gives $\text{Eff}(b) = 0.47$.

6.3. Testing for First Order Autoregressive Disturbances

In Chapter 5 the construction of tests of specification based on the LR, Wald and LM principles was discussed. These procedures may all be applied to the problem of testing for an AR(1) disturbance term in (1.1), i.e. testing the null hypothesis $H_0 : \phi = 0$ against the alternative $H_1 : \phi \neq 0$. In order to simplify matters it will be assumed that y_1 is fixed. The remaining observations will be taken to be normally distributed.

If it is felt desirable to estimate the unrestricted model by an iterative procedure, such as Cochrane–Orcutt, a Wald test may be carried out quite easily. In terms of (5.3.8), $\psi = (\beta',\phi)'$, $R = (0 \ldots 1)'$ and $r = 0$. The Wald statistic (5.4.2) is therefore

$$W = \tilde{\phi}^2/\text{avar}(\tilde{\phi}) = \tilde{\phi}^2/\{(1 - \tilde{\phi}^2)/T\} \tag{3.1}$$

and under H_0 this will have a χ_1^2 distribution. However, it will generally be preferable to base the test on $\tilde{\phi}/\sqrt{\text{avar}(\tilde{\phi})}$ since this is $AN(0,1)$ under H_0, and allows a one-sided test to be carried out. A slightly more convenient form of the test is given by noting that it is asymptotically equivalent to a t-test in the final regression of $y_t - x_t'\tilde{\beta}$ on $y_{t-1} - x_{t-1}'\tilde{\beta}$; cf. Example 4.6.1.

The need to estimate the unrestricted model may, however, be regarded as a disadvantage from the computational viewpoint. Because the restricted model is linear in this case, it may be estimated simply by OLS. This suggests a test based on the LM principle. For an AR(1) time series model it follows from (5.5.16) that the appropriate LM statistic is Tr_1^2, where r_1 is the first-order sample autocorrelation. Using exactly the same argument the LM principle in the regression case leads to a test statistic based on the first-order autocorrelation in the OLS residuals. A one-sided test may be carried out by treating r_1 as being normally distributed with mean 0 and variance $1/T$ in large samples.

In the time series AR(1) model a test of $\phi = 0$ is not usually based on r_1, but rather on the von Neumann Ratio. This statistic is a monotonic transformation of r_1 but its exact significance points have been tabulated. Unfortunately an exact test based on OLS residuals cannot be constructed in the same way, since the residuals will not, in general, be independently and identically distributed.

The Durbin–Watson d-statistic

Apart from a factor of $T/(T - 1)$, the Durbin–Watson statistic

$$d = \frac{\sum\limits_{t=2}^{T} (e_t - e_{t-1})^2}{\sum\limits_{t=1}^{T} e_t^2} \tag{3.2}$$

is identical to the von Neumann Ratio, since the mean of the OLS residuals must be zero. However, the vector of OLS residuals is defined by $e = Mu$, where $M = I - X(X'X)^{-1}X'$. Although $E(e) = 0$ when $u \sim N(0,\sigma^2 I)$, the covariance matrix is given by $E(ee') = \sigma^2 M$ and so will not, in general, be scalar. Since the distribution of e depends on the set of regressors X, the distribution of d also depends on X. Therefore, exact significance points for d cannot be tabulated once and for all. However, as the sample size increases the effect of the regressors becomes less important. In fact, since $r_1 \sim AN(0,1/T)$ and

$$d \simeq 2(1 - r_1) \tag{3.3}$$

it is not difficult to see that $d \sim AN(2,4/T)$. The approximation in (3.3) arises because of the treatment of end points and these are unimportant in large samples.

The range of the d-statistic is $[0, 4]$, and again this ties in with its relationship with r_1 as given by (3.3). Furthermore, when the residuals are positively autocorrelated, r_1 is greater than zero and the value of d will tend to be low. On the other hand, d tends towards 4 for negative serial correlation. A one-sided test against positive serial correlation — the most common alternative — will therefore be based on a critical region for which the null is rejected when d falls *below* a certain value. Thus with $T = 100$, the critical region for a large sample one-sided test at the 5% level of significance comprises all values of d less than $2 - 1.64(0.2) = 1.67$.

Although the asymptotic distribution of d is independent of the regressors, the behaviour of the d-statistic for different regressors can vary quite markedly in small samples. A test based on the asymptotic distribution could therefore be misleading in certain circumstances. Hence the small sample distribution of d is of some interest. Although this distribution depends on X it may nevertheless be computed. In matrix terms, the d statistic is

$$d = \frac{e'Ae}{e'e} = \frac{u'MAMu}{u'Mu} \tag{3.4}$$

where A is a fixed $T \times T$ matrix defined in Durbin and Watson (1950). The expression on the far right-hand side of (3.4) is a quadratic form in normal variables, and the exact distribution of such a statistic may be found numerically using the method of Imhof or Pan Jie-Jan; see Durbin and Watson (1971) and Koerts and Abrahamse (1969). However, from the point of view of carrying out a test, all that is required is the appropriate significance point. Thus for a one-tailed test against positive serial correlation it is necessary to compute a value d^*, such that

$$Pr(d < d^*) = \alpha$$

where α is the size of the test. A procedure carried out on this basis may be referred to as the *exact Durbin–Watson test*.

The Bounds Test

Although the exact significance point for the d-statistic varies with X, it is subject to an upper and a lower bound. These bounds, denoted respectively by d_U and d_L, were tabulated by Durbin and Watson in 1950. The critical values for a one-sided test at the 0.05 and 0.01 levels of significance are given in tables A.1 and A.2 (see pp. 361 – 362). Although these points apply to a test against positive serial correlation, a test against negative serial correlation may be carried out in exactly the same way using the statistic $4 - d$. The critical values d_U and d_L depend on k as well as T. It is important to note not only that k includes the constant term, but that a constant term must be included in the regression in order for the bounds to be valid.

The bounds test is carried out as follows. If $d < d_L$, the null hypothesis is rejected; if $d > d_U$ it is not rejected; while if $d_L \leq d \leq d_U$ the test is inconclusive. If the test is inconclusive, one might resort to calculating d^* numerically by one of the methods referred to above. Alternatively the Beta or $a + bd_U$ approximations may be used. Although these methods are unable to give d^* exactly, they will usually give a value accurate enough for most practical purposes. This is a small price to pay in view of the fact that they are relatively inexpensive compared with the Imhof or Pan Jie-Jan algorithms. Further details of these approximate procedures will be found in Durbin and Watson (1951, 1971).

A totally different reaction to an inconclusive bounds test would simply be to treat it as a rejection of the null hypothesis. For economic data, which is typically 'slowly changing' this may not imply a particularly big increase in the size of the Type I error. The reason is that for this type of regressor, d^* is close to d_U. On the other hand this is less likely to be the case when first differences have been taken, and when k is large the bounds may be very wide. Nevertheless there is still a strong argument for going ahead and actually estimating a more general model. Any 'losses' incurred are likely to be much higher if the restricted model is accepted when it is inadequate.

Tests Based on LUS Residuals*

The problem of the inconclusive region in the bounds test may be by-passed by using LUS residuals. A test may then be based directly on the von Neumann Ratio. However, such tests will be less effective than the exact Durbin–Watson procedure. Given d^*, a test based on the d-statistic is uniformly the most powerful invariant against a one-sided alternative in the neighbourhood of $\phi = 0$. This theoretical evidence in favour of basing a test on OLS residuals is supported by the Monte Carlo results reported in Koerts and Abrahamse (1969) and Phillips and Harvey (1974). Thus a test against AR(1) disturbances using LUS residuals can only be justified on computational grounds. Since the computations involved in obtaining a set of BLUS residuals are of a similar order to those needed to compute d^* exactly the case for using them is very weak. Recursive residuals, on the other hand, are relatively easy to obtain and in Section 5.2 it was argued that a modified von Neumann Ratio statistic based on them would play an important role in any battery of misspecification tests. However, against an AR(1) alternative such a test is less attractive overall as compared with a Durbin–Watson procedure which utilises the Beta or $a + bd_U$ approximation.

Robustness of Other Test Statistics

It was pointed out in Section 5.2 that serial correlation in the residuals does not necessarily imply serial correlation in the disturbances. Therefore although

Table 6.2 Estimated Powers of Tests for $y_t = \alpha + \beta t + u_t$ with AR(1) Disturbances, based on 200 Replications

ϕ	0.5		0.8	
T	30	60	30	60
MVNR	0.78	0.96	0.94	1.00
$D-W$	$0.68-0.79$	$0.95-0.97$	$0.93-0.94$	$1.00-1.00$
CUSUM	0.16	0.24	0.34	0.50
ψ	0.15	0.18	0.34	0.36
CUSUMSQ	0.15	0.17	0.29	0.36
H†	0.14	0.12	0.35	0.42
H	0.08	0.08	0.06	0.12

the Durbin–Watson procedure is formally a test against an AR(1) disturbance term, it may well be indicative of other types of misspecification besides serial correlation. Indeed, it was in this spirit that it was proposed in Section 5.2 as a general test of misspecification, as was the von Neumann Ratio based on recursive residuals.

Bearing these considerations in mind it is important to consider supplementary statistics, which provide some indication of the nature of the misspecification when a significant d-statistic or von Neumann Ratio is obtained. Several tests were proposed in Section 5.2, and table 6.2 presents estimates of their respective powers for various values of ϕ. The results, taken from Harvey and Phillips (1976), refer to model (2.11) with $x_t = t$. Apart from the von Neumann Ratio (with recursive residuals) and d-statistic, the tests are relatively robust to a moderate level of serial correlation such as $\phi = 0.5$. They are less robust when $\phi = 0.8$.

6.4. Higher Order Autoregressive Disturbances

An AR(p) disturbance term,

$$u_t = \phi_1 u_{t-1} + \ldots + \phi_p u_{t-p} + \epsilon_t \tag{4.1}$$

provides a natural extension of the model considered so far. The AR(p) model is rather more flexible than the AR(1) model, and specifying the disturbance in this way permits a wide variety of behavioural patterns to be represented. For example, pseudo-cyclical movements can often be modelled by an AR(2) process. In fact, it can be shown that any stationary stochastic process can be approximated to any degree of accuracy if p is made sufficiently large. Thus specifying an autoregressive process of sufficiently high order can be made the basis for a non-parametric approach to estimating the regression coefficients.

Higher order autoregressive representation is also important in the context of seasonal data. Just as seasonal effects need to be taken into account in modelling univariate time series, so they must be allowed for in specifying the form of the disturbance term in regression analysis. In economics, observations are generally available on a monthly or quarterly basis. This suggests the use of twelfth or fourth order processes. As in univariate time series analysis, these effects may be compounded with lower order autoregressive effects, so that in the quarterly case, for example, a typical specification for the disturbance might be

$$(1 - \phi_1 L)(1 - \phi_4 L^4)u_t = \epsilon_t \qquad (4.2)$$

The seasonal effect is captured by the fourth-order coefficient, ϕ_4, while the serial correlation from one quarter to the next is accounted for by the first-order term. Combining the two processes leads to an eventual AR(5) specification, albeit with certain constraints on the parameters.

Maximum Likelihood Estimation

Methods for estimating regression models with AR(p) disturbances may be derived by generalising the results for the first-order case. As with the AR(1) model, a unified approach is obtained by working with the likelihood function. The form of the GLS estimator then emerges quite naturally.

If $\epsilon_t \sim NID(0, \sigma^2)$, the full log–likelihood function may be decomposed as

$$\log L(y) = \sum_{t=p+1}^{T} \log l(y_t \mid y_{t-1}, \ldots, y_1) + \log L(y_1, \ldots, y_p);$$

cf. (3.5.4). This becomes

$$\log L(y;\phi,\beta,\sigma^2) = -\tfrac{1}{2} T \log 2\pi - \tfrac{1}{2} T \log \sigma^2 - \tfrac{1}{2} \log |V_p|$$

$$- \tfrac{1}{2} \sigma^{-2} (y_p - X_p \beta)' V_p^{-1} (y_p - X_p \beta)$$

$$- \tfrac{1}{2} \sigma^{-2} \sum_{t=p+1}^{T} \{(y_t - x_t'\beta) - \phi_1(y_{t-1} - x_{t-1}'\beta) -$$

$$\ldots - \phi_p(y_{t-p} - x_{t-p}'\beta)\}^2 \quad (4.3)$$

where V_p denotes the covariance matrix of $y_p = (y_1, \ldots, y_p)'$, and $X_p = (x_1, \ldots, x_p)'$.

Maximising (4.3) with respect to β gives the GLS estimator for a given value of $\phi = (\phi_1, \ldots, \phi_p)'$. The form taken by this estimator is implicitly given by the last two terms in the expression. If L_p defines a $p \times p$ matrix with the property $L_p' L_p = V_p^{-1}$, the first p transformed observations are given by

$$y_p^* = L_p \, y_p \quad \text{and} \quad X_p^* = L_p X_p \tag{4.4}$$

The remaining $T - p$ transformed observations are effectively defined by the last term in (4.3) to be

$$
\begin{aligned}
y_t^* &= y_t - \phi_1 \, y_{t-1} - \cdots - \phi_p \, y_{t-p} \\
x_t^* &= x_t - \phi_1 \, x_{t-1} - \cdots - \phi_p \, x_{t-p}
\end{aligned}
\quad , \quad t = p + 1, \ldots, T \tag{4.5}
$$

The transformed observations have a scalar covariance matrix and so the application of OLS yields the GLS estimator of β. The independence of the disturbances corresponding to the first p transformed observations follows by definition, while in the case of (4.5), it should be clear by analogy with (1.7) that

$$y_t^* = x_t^* \beta + \epsilon_t, \qquad t = p + 1, \ldots, T \tag{4.6}$$

The computation of L_p may be carried out by the Cholesky decomposition; cf. Section 1.3. The full GLS transform for $p = 1$ depends on (1.5) which is a special case of (4.4). The matrix L_p is simply a scalar taking the value $\sqrt{1 - \phi^2}$.

Given a method for computing the GLS estimator, the likelihood function may be concentrated with respect to ϕ. Substituting the conditional ML estimator

$$
\begin{aligned}
\tilde{\sigma}^2(\phi) &= T^{-1}(y - X\tilde{b})' V^{-1}(y - X\tilde{b}) \\
&= T^{-1} \sum_{t=1}^{T} (y_t^* - x_t^{*\prime} \tilde{b})^2
\end{aligned}
\tag{4.7}
$$

into (4.3) yields

$$\log L_c(y;\phi) = -\tfrac{1}{2} T \log 2\pi - \tfrac{1}{2} T \log \tilde{\sigma}^2(\phi) + \tfrac{1}{2} \log | V_p^{-1}(\phi) | - \tfrac{1}{2} T \tag{4.8}$$

The function (4.8) may be maximised by a general numerical optimisation procedure, possibly incorporating constraints to ensure stationarity. However, a simplification of the ML procedure is obtained by taking y_p to be *fixed*. This allows a straightforward stepwise optimisation approach since the third and fourth terms in the log−likelihood function, (4.3), disappear. If $\hat{u}_t = y_t - x_t' \hat{\beta}$ denotes the tth residual from an estimator of β, the ML estimator of ϕ, conditional on $\hat{\beta}$, is given by a linear regression of $\hat{u}_t$ on $\hat{u}_{t-1}, \ldots, \hat{u}_{t-p}$. The form of the GLS estimator also simplifies somewhat since fixing y_p effectively removes the first p transformed observations, (4.4). The resulting transformation, based only on (4.5), is therefore a direct generalisation of Cochrane−Orcutt, and the stepwise optimisation procedure, involving successive estimation of β and ϕ, is the natural analogue of the Cochrane−Orcutt iterative procedure. However, given the undesirable properties exhibited by the Cochrane−Orcutt transformation for certain types of data, it may be advisable to base GLS estimation on the full transform, even though the estimation of ϕ is simplified. From the computational point of view this makes very little difference since the Cholesky decomposition of a $p \times p$ matrix should not be particularly time consuming. Furthermore, the extra computation is to some extent justified insofar as the Cholesky decomposition acts as a check on the stationarity of the AR process; when the process is non-stationary V_p will not be p.d. and the factorisation of V_p^{-1} breaks down. As a final point, V_p^{-1} need not be specifically computed since an estimate of it emerges directly from the inverse of the cross-product matrix in the regression of $\hat{u}_t$ on its lagged values.

Two-Step Estimators

Given an estimate of ϕ, a feasible GLS estimator of β may be computed using either the full transform or the approximation based on (4.5). Provided the estimator of ϕ is consistent, both estimators of β may be shown to have the same asymptotic distribution as the GLS estimator based on the true value of ϕ, subject, of course, to the usual conditions on the explanatory variables. However, insofar as the findings for the AR(1) model may be generalised, there is a strong argument for using the full GLS transform in small samples.

A consistent estimator of ϕ may be obtained from the OLS residuals by a regression of the type described in the previous sub-section. This is rather convenient, since it makes it very easy to carry out tests of significance on the parameters in ϕ . In fact, it follows directly from the material presented in Section 5.5, that an 'F-test' of the hypothesis $\phi = 0$ represents a straightforward application of the modified LM procedure.

Asymptotic Distribution of Estimators

All the procedures considered in this section yield estimators of both β and ϕ which have identical large sample properties. Hence they may all be regarded as variants of what is sometimes termed autoregressive least squares.

The asymptotic covariance matrix of ML estimators of β, ϕ and σ^2 takes exactly the same form as (1.12) but with $(1 - \phi^2)/T$ replaced by the general expression $T^{-1}V_p^{-1}$.

6.5. Moving Average and Mixed Disturbances

A general specification for the disturbance term in a regression model is the ARMA(p, q) model

$$u_t = \phi_1 u_{t-1} + \cdots + \phi_p u_{t-p} + \epsilon_t + \theta_1 \epsilon_{t-1} + \cdots + \theta_q \epsilon_{t-q}$$

$$(5.1)$$

An MA model is, of course, a special case of the ARMA model with $p = 0$. However, in terms of their statistical treatment it is convenient to consider ARMA and MA models together. Both give rise to estimation problems which do not occur with pure autoregressive disturbances.

An MA specification is plausible for a number of reasons. ARMA disturbances are perhaps even more important, firstly, because aggregation of a number of variables generally leads to an ARMA process, and, secondly, because any stationary stochastic process can be represented reasonably parsimoniously by an ARMA model.

As in the case of a pure time series model, the likelihood function for a regression model with ARMA disturbances simplifies considerably if certain assumptions are made about the initial values. This permits a straightforward decomposition of the likelihood in terms of prediction errors, and maximising the likelihood function is then equivalent to minimising a conditional sum of squares function (3.5.16). On the other hand, it may be felt that a full ML approach is desirable. A detailed discussion of full ML for ARMA disturbances is beyond the scope of this book, but in *TSM* a method based on the Kalman filter is proposed.

Approaching estimation from an ML viewpoint effectively solves the problem of obtaining a GLS estimator. It is shown below that an approximation similar to Cochrane–Orcutt can be based on transformed observations built up from simple recursive formulae.

Approximate Maximum Likelihood Estimation

The principles underlying the CSS approach to estimating a regression model with ARMA disturbances may be developed by considering the case of an MA(1) disturbance term

$$u_t = \epsilon_t + \theta \epsilon_{t-1} \tag{5.2}$$

This embodies all the difficulties which are not encountered in the pure AR case, and the generalisation to other ARMA models is relatively straightforward.

If ϵ_0 is taken to be fixed and equal to zero, maximising the likelihood function is equivalent to minimising the conditional sum of squares. For a given value of θ, the residual is obtained by a recursion having exactly the same form as (3.5.8), i.e.

$$\epsilon_t = (y_t - x_t'\beta) - \theta \epsilon_{t-1}, \qquad t = 1, \ldots, T \tag{5.3}$$

with $\epsilon_0 = 0$. Minimising the sum of squares of these residuals with respect to β and θ may be carried out very easily by Gauss–Newton. The derivatives are computed from the recursions

$$\frac{\partial \epsilon_t}{\partial \beta} = -x_t - \theta \frac{\partial \epsilon_{t-1}}{\partial \beta}, \qquad t = 1, \ldots, T \tag{5.4}$$

with $\partial \epsilon_0 / \partial \beta = 0$, and

$$\frac{\partial \epsilon_t}{\partial \theta} = -\theta \frac{\partial \epsilon_{t-1}}{\partial \theta} - \epsilon_{t-1}, \qquad t = 1, \ldots, T \tag{5.5}$$

with $\partial \epsilon_0 / \partial \phi = 0$. As with autoregressive disturbances, the information matrix in this model is block diagonal, as

$$\text{plim} \frac{1}{T} \sum_{t=1}^{T} \frac{\partial \epsilon_t}{\partial \beta} \frac{\partial \epsilon_t}{\partial \theta} = 0 \tag{5.6}$$

This suggests a modified optimisation procedure whereby the Gauss–Newton scheme is broken down into two separate regressions. The first consists of regressing ϵ_t on $\partial \epsilon_t / \partial \beta$ while the second, which corresponds directly to the iterative procedure in the pure time series model, is a regression of ϵ_t on $\partial \epsilon_t / \partial \theta$. Although the function to be minimised is unchanged, this modified scheme should be more efficient computationally. It is worth noting that defining a Gauss–Newton scheme for an AR(1) disturbance term and then modifying it in this way leads directly to Cochrane–Orcutt. However, there is a difference, in that for the MA(1) model a simple regression of ϵ_t on $\partial \epsilon_t / \partial \theta$ does not yield the ML estimator of θ conditional on β. On the other hand regressing ϵ_t on its derivatives with respect to β does yield an approximation to the GLS estimator. This therefore implicitly defines the equivalent of the Cochrane–Orcutt transform for the MA model.

The link between the Gauss–Newton recursion and GLS may be established as follows. Conditional on a value of θ, the sum of squares function, $S = S(\beta)$, is minimised when

$$\frac{\partial S}{\partial \beta} = 2 \sum_{t=1}^{T} \frac{\partial \epsilon_t}{\partial \beta} \epsilon_t = 0 \tag{5.7}$$

Repeatedly substituting in (5.3) and (5.4) yields

$$\epsilon_t = \sum_{j=0}^{t-1} (-\theta)^j (y_{t-j} - x'_{t-j} \beta) \tag{5.8}$$

and

$$\frac{\partial \epsilon_t}{\partial \beta} = -\sum_{j=0}^{t-1} (-\theta)^j x_{t-j} \tag{5.9}$$

respectively. Substituting from (5.8) and (5.9) into (5.7) gives

$$\sum_{t=1}^{T} x_t^*(y_t^* - x_t^{*\prime}\beta) = 0 \tag{5.10}$$

where

$$y_t^* = \Sigma(-\theta)^j y_{t-j} \quad \text{and} \quad x_t^* = \Sigma(-\theta)^j x_{t-j} = -\partial\epsilon_t/\partial\beta$$

Therefore, given the assumptions made for the initial value of the disturbance term, the GLS estimator of β is obtained by regressing y_t^* on x_t^*. This is identical to the estimate obtained by regressing ϵ_t on $\partial\epsilon_t/\partial\beta$ and subtracting the result from the current estimate of β. Note that the transformed dependent variable, y_t^*, can be obtained from a recursion with a similar form to (5.3), i.e.

$$y_t^* = y_t - \theta y_{t-1}^*, \qquad t = 1, \ldots, T \tag{5.11}$$

with $y_0^* = 0$.

Two-Step Estimators

A consistent estimator of β is given by OLS. A consistent estimator of θ is given by (4.5.4), where r_1 is now the first-order autocorrelation in the OLS residuals. From these starting values, asymptotically efficient estimators of both β and θ are produced by a single iteration of Gauss–Newton.

In view of (5.6), an alternative method for calculating an efficient estimator of β is simply to regress ϵ_t on $\partial\epsilon_t/\partial\beta$. This is equivalent to regressing y_t^* on x_t^* and so it can be regarded as a feasible GLS estimator. It is directly comparable with the two-step Cochrane–Orcutt estimator in the AR(1) case.

6.6. Tests Against Serial Correlation

The serial correlation tests described in Section 3 were constructed on the assumption that the disturbances followed an AR(1) process. However, in view of (3.3), a test procedure based on a statistic having the form of the von Neumann Ratio will be relatively effective against any disturbance term which exhibits strong first-order autocorrelation, irrespective of the form of the underlying stochastic process. Thus, for example, the probability that the Durbin–Watson test will reject the null hypothesis of white noise disturbances will be relatively high for an AR(2) process,

$$u_t = \phi_1 u_{t-1} + \phi_2 u_{t-2} + \epsilon_t \tag{6.1}$$

unless ϕ_1 is close to zero. In a similar way the test will also be effective against an MA(1) disturbance term. Indeed, in this case, the LM test is identical to the LM test against an AR(1) alternative.

As a general rule, therefore, a 'significant' value of a test statistic such as the Durbin–Watson should not necessarily be taken as an indication of an AR(1) disturbance term. Assuming that the structural part of the equation is correctly specified, the possibility of modelling the disturbance by a more general ARMA process should always be explored.

Although tests against AR(1) disturbances are effective against a wide variety of alternatives, they are nevertheless limited. In particular they may be totally inadequate when dealing with seasonal data, or when strong cyclical effects are present.

Testing for Seasonal Effects

Faced with quarterly observations, a reasonable model for the disturbance term may be

$$u_t = \phi_4 u_{t-4} + \epsilon_t, \qquad |\phi_4| < 1 \tag{6.2}$$

This is an AR(4) model but with ϕ_1, ϕ_2 and ϕ_3 constrained to be zero. Since successive observations in (6.2) are independent, any test based on the first-order autocorrelation of the residuals will obviously be completely inappropriate. As might be expected, the Lagrange multiplier principle suggests a test based on r_4, both for (6.2) and for the corresponding MA(4) seasonal process. Under the null hypothesis $r_4 \sim AN(0, T^{-1})$.

If an exact small sample test is required, a natural statistic to adopt is the generalisation of the Durbin–Watson d-statistic

$$d_4 = \frac{\sum\limits_{t=5}^{T} (e_t - e_{t-4})^2}{\sum\limits_{t=1}^{T} e_t^2} \tag{6.3}$$

Wallis (1972) presents upper and lower significance points for carrying out a bounds tests based on d_4. The test procedure is essentially the same as in the first-order case, except that two tables are presented for d_4, depending on whether or not seasonal dummies are included in the regression. When the test is inconclusive, an approximation to the exact significance point may be obtained by a Beta or $a + bd_u$ approximation. Alternatively the exact probability value of d_4 may be obtained at the outset by the method of Imhof or Pan Jie-Jan.

When using quarterly data it will usually be advisable to compute both d_1 and d_4. Statistically significant values of these statistics may then indicate that both first and fourth order autocorrelation effects should be allowed for in the estimation procedure. However, some care should be taken in interpreting what is meant by 'statistically significant' in this context. Suppose the exact significance points are computed for d_1 and d_4 at the 5% level, and the null hypothesis of white noise disturbances is rejected if either of the test statistics is 'significant'. The size of the Type I error of this test procedure will then be greater than 0.05.

Portmanteau Tests

The Q-statistic, (1.5.20), may be used to test the assumption of white noise disturbances. The fact that the autocorrelations are constructed from OLS residuals makes no difference to the large sample distribution of Q, which is asymptotically χ^2_P under the null hypothesis. The modified statistic,

$$Q^* = T(T + 2) \sum_{\tau=1}^{P} (T - \tau)^{-1} r_\tau^2 \tag{6.4}$$

also has this distribution under the null, but the available evidence suggests that it is a better approximation.

The Q and Q^* statistics form the basis for 'portmanteau' tests since they are designed to pick up departures from randomness indicated by the first P residual autocorrelations. The alternative hypothesis might seem to be rather vague, but in fact the Q-test can be derived as the LM test against an AR(P) or an MA(P) process. However, there remains the problem of how to choose P. Too small a value of P may result in a failure to detect a process where high-order lags are important. On the other hand, too large a value of P may result in a test with a low power since the effect of the dominant autocorrelations is diluted by a series of autocorrelations close to zero.

Neither version of the portmanteau test is exact. Furthermore, the distribution of Q is difficult to compute since it cannot be expressed as a quadratic form in normal variables; cf. (3.4). An alternative approach is to construct a test statistic by generalising the d-statistic. Schmidt has suggested the statistic

$$d_{1,2} = \left[\sum_{t=2}^{T} (e_t - e_{t-1})^2 + \sum_{t=3}^{T} (e_t - e_{t-2})^2 \right] \bigg/ \sum_{t=1}^{T} e_t^2 \tag{6.5}$$

Since $d_{1,2}$ may be expressed as a quadratic form in normal variables, its small sample distributions can be found by the method of Imhof or Pan Jie-Jan. A bounds test may also be developed, and the appropriate significance points are tabulated in Schmidt (1972). This approach could be generalised further, but it is not clear whether tests carried out on this basis would have desirable properties. The Q-statistic may at least be rationalised as the appropriate statistic for carrying out an LM test against an AR(P) or MA(P) alternative. This provides a sounder basis for constructing a test statistic than the requirement that its distribution be known exactly in small samples.

Tests when the Disturbance Term is Modelled as an ARMA Process

When a regression model has been estimated with a particular ARMA disturbance term, it will usually be desirable to carry out diagnostic checks on the specification. Insofar as the model has been estimated by a straightforward extension of a method used to fit an ARMA time series model, no new issues are raised. Thus the large sample distribution of the CSS residuals is unaffected by the addition of β to the parameter set, and the null hypothesis that the disturbances are serially independent can be tested by treating the Box–Pierce Q-statistic as having a χ^2 distribution with $P - p - q$ degrees of freedom.

6.7. Prediction

Given future values of the explanatory variables, the dependent variable in a regression model with ARMA disturbances, (5.1), may be predicted recursively. Multiplying both sides of (1.1) by the AR polynomial, $\phi(L)$ yields

$$
\begin{aligned}
y_t &= \phi_1 y_{t-1} + \cdots + \phi_p y_{t-p} + (x_t - \phi_1 x_{t-1} - \cdots - \phi_p x_{t-p})'\beta \\
&\quad + \epsilon_t + \theta_1 \epsilon_{t-1} + \cdots + \theta_q \epsilon_{t-q} \\
&= x_t'\beta + \phi_1(y_{t-1} - x_{t-1}'\beta) + \cdots + \phi_p(y_{t-p} - x_{t-p}'\beta) \\
&\quad + \epsilon_t + \cdots + \theta_q \epsilon_{t-q}
\end{aligned}
\tag{7.1}
$$

This equation forms the basis for the recursive calculation of the optimal predictors of future values of y_t. Setting future disturbances equal to their expected value of zero yields:

$$
\begin{aligned}
\tilde{y}_{T+l|T} &= \phi_1 \tilde{y}_{T+l-1|T} + \cdots + \phi_p \tilde{y}_{T+l-p|T} \\
&\quad + (x_{T+l} - \phi_1 x_{T+l-1} - \cdots - \phi_p x_{T+l-p})'\beta \\
&\quad + \tilde{\epsilon}_{T+l|T} + \cdots + \theta_q \tilde{\epsilon}_{T+l-q|T}, \qquad l = 1, 2, \ldots
\end{aligned}
\tag{7.2}
$$

where

$$
\tilde{y}_{T+j|T} = \begin{cases} \tilde{y}_{T+j|T} & \text{for } j > 0 \\ y_{T+j} & \text{for } j \le 0 \end{cases}
$$

$$\tilde{\epsilon}_{T+j\,|T} = \begin{cases} 0 & j > 0 \\ \epsilon_{T+j} & j \leq 0; \end{cases}$$

cf. (1.5.22). The ϵ_t's themselves are obtained recursively, as in (5.3).

Mean Square Error of Predictions

If β, ϕ and θ are known, the MSEs of predictions may be obtained in exactly the same way as for a time series ARMA model; see *TSM* (Section 6.4). Thus

$$\text{MSE}(\tilde{y}_{T+l\,|T}) = (1 + \psi_1^2 + \cdots + \psi_{l-1}^2)\sigma^2 \tag{7.3}$$

where ψ_j is the coefficient of ϵ_{t-j} in the MA representation of the ARMA process. For an AR(1) model it follows from (1.5.5) that

$$\text{MSE}(\tilde{y}_{T+l\,|T}) = \{1 + \phi^2 + \cdots + \phi^{2(l-1)}\}\sigma^2$$

$$= \sigma^2(1 - \phi^{2l})/(1 - \phi^2) \tag{7.4}$$

When β is unknown, the predictions in the regression model are subject to an additional source of variation as compared with the pure time series case. This arises from the estimation of β. The effect may be illustrated for AR(1) disturbances. Here, predictions are computed from the recursion

$$\tilde{y}_{T+l\,|T} = \phi\tilde{y}_{T+l-1\,|T} + (x_{T+l} - \phi x_{T+l-1})'\tilde{b}, \qquad l = 1, 2, \ldots \tag{7.5}$$

where $\tilde{b}$ is the GLS estimator of β and $\tilde{y}_{T|T} = y_T$. Repeated substitution for predicted values of y_t gives

$$\tilde{y}_{T+l\,|T} = (x_{T+l} - \phi^l x_T)'\tilde{b} + \phi^l y_T \tag{7.6}$$

$$= x'_{t+l}\tilde{b} + \phi^l \tilde{u}_T \tag{7.7}$$

where $\tilde{u}_T = y_T - x'_T\tilde{b}$. The last expression shows how the predictor of $\tilde{y}_{T+l}$ is made up of two components: one the BLUE of $E(y_{T+l})$, and the other the BLUP of u_{T+l}.

The true value of y_{T+l} is given by

$$y_{T+l} = x'_{T+l}\beta + u_{T+l}$$

$$= x'_{T+l}\beta + \sum_{j=0}^{l-1} \phi^j \epsilon_{T+l-j} + \phi^l(y_T - x'_T\beta)$$

$$= (x_{T+l} - \phi^l x_T)'\beta + \sum_{j=0}^{l-1} \phi^j \epsilon_{T+l-j} + \phi^l y_T \tag{7.8}$$

Subtracting (7.8) from (7.6) gives

$$y_{T+l} - \tilde{y}_{T+l\,|T} = \sum_{j=0}^{l-1} \phi^j \epsilon_{T+l-j} + (x_{T+l} - \phi^l x_T)'(\beta - \tilde{b}) \tag{7.9}$$

The two components in (7.9) are independent, and so the MSE of the prediction error consists of a contribution from the estimation error, $\beta - \tilde{b}$, plus a contribution from future values of the disturbance term, i.e.

$$
\begin{aligned}
\mathrm{MSE}(\tilde{y}_{T+l|T}) &= E(y_{T+l} - \tilde{y}_{T+l|T})^2 \\
&= \sigma^2 \frac{1 - \phi^{2l}}{1 - \phi^2} \\
&= \sigma^2 (x_{T+l} - \phi^l x_T)'(X'V^{-1}X)^{-1}(x_{T+l} - \phi^l x_T)
\end{aligned}
$$

$$(7.10)$$

Estimation of ARMA Parameters*

The fact that the parameters in ϕ and θ will generally need to be estimated raises additional problems in the computation of the MSE, although the actual predictions, $\tilde{y}^*_{T+l|T}$, are obtained exactly as in the case when ϕ and θ are known. Baillie (1979) has considered this problem and has evaluated the asymptotic mean square error (AMSE) of predictions made for regression models with AR disturbances. In the case of AR(1) disturbances

$$
\begin{aligned}
\mathrm{AMSE}(\tilde{y}^*_{T+l|T}) &\simeq \sigma^2 \frac{1 - \phi^{2l}}{1 - \phi^2} \\
&+ \sigma^2(x_{T+l} - \phi^l x_T)'(X'V^{-1}X)^{-1}(x_{T+l} - \phi^l x_T) \\
&+ \frac{\sigma^2}{T} l^2 \phi^{2(l-1)}
\end{aligned}
$$

$$(7.11)$$

terms of $0(T^{-1})$ having been excluded from the formula. The first two terms in (7.11) give the MSE of $\tilde{y}_{T+l|T}$ when ϕ is known while the last term arises because of the estimation of ϕ. Thus the AMSE depends on three things: the unknown disturbances $\epsilon_{T+1}, \ldots, \epsilon_{T+l}$, the error in estimating β, and the error in estimating ϕ. However, it must be stressed that the justification for simply adding up these components is not as simple as might seem at first sight.

The most important question raised by expression (7.11) concerns the likely relative importance of the three components in practice. If T is large the last term will become relatively small. However, the extent to which the first term dominates the second will depend very much on the future values of x_t. If these fall outside the range of the sample x_t's the error arising from the estimation of β could be very large. Furthermore, as l increases the first term in (7.11) tends towards a constant value of $\sigma^2/(1 - \phi^2)$. If the explanatory variables are trending the contribution from the second term could well exceed that of the first term even if T is relatively large.

Some useful evidence on the likely order of magnitude of the three terms in (7.11) is given in the paper by Baillie (1979). He considers an equation estimated by Hendry on the relationship between UK imports and income. The model contained a constant term and quarterly dummy variables in addition to income, and ϕ was estimated as 0.53. The sample size was 46. For a one period ahead forecast ($l = 1$) the proportion of the total AMSE accounted for by each of the three terms in (7.11) was 0.860, 0.121 and 0.019 respectively. For $l = 4$ the corresponding figures were 0.748, 0.248 and 0.004. Thus the contribution from the estimation of ϕ is small, and for $l = 4$ it could quite happily be ignored. The estimation of β, however, becomes increasingly important as the lead time increases.

The OLS predictor is simply $\tilde{y}_{T+l|T} = x'_{T+l}b$. This ignores any serial correlation in the disturbances, both in estimation and prediction, and the MSE is given by

$$\text{MSE}(\tilde{y}_{T+l|T}) = \sigma^2/(1 - \phi^2)$$
$$+ \sigma^2 x'_{T+l}(X'X)^{-1}X'VX(X'X)^{-1}x_{T+l}$$

However, the relative inefficiency of the OLS predictor decreases as the lead time increases, since the disturbance term becomes more difficult to predict even though the form of the underlying process is known. This point is illustrated in Baillie's results where the MSE for the OLS predictor exceeds the AMSE of the BLUP by 140% for $l = 1$ and by 55% for $l = 4$.

6.8. Systems of Equations

The SURE system introduced in Section 2.9 may be extended to allow the disturbances to follow a vector ARMA process. Using the notation of (2.9.15), such a model may be written as

$$y_t = X_t\beta + u_t, \qquad t = 1, \ldots, T \tag{8.1a}$$

$$u_t = \Phi_1 u_{t-1} + \cdots + \Phi_p u_{t-p} + \epsilon_t + \Theta_1 \epsilon_{t-1} + \cdots + \Theta_q \epsilon_{t-q} \tag{8.1b}$$

where $\epsilon_t \sim NID(0, \Omega)$. Since the explanatory variables in all the equations are fixed, estimation and testing may be carried out by a straightforward extension of the methods appropriate for dealing with a multivariate ARMA time series model.

Estimation

Given the specification of the vector ARMA disturbance term, the computation of ML estimates is, in principle, straightforward. By making appropriate assumptions about the initial observations and disturbances, maximisation of the likelihood reduces to minimisation of the multivariate conditional sum of squares function

$$S = \Sigma \, \epsilon_t' \Omega^{-1} \epsilon_t + T \log |\Omega| \tag{8.2}$$

The residuals are evaluated from the recursion

$$\epsilon_t = (y_t - X_t\beta) - \cdots - \Phi_p(y_{t-p} - X_{t-p}\beta)$$
$$- \Theta_1 \epsilon_{t-1} - \cdots - \Theta_q \epsilon_{t-q}, \qquad t = p+1, \ldots, T \tag{8.3}$$

and the derivatives of these residuals with respect to $\Phi_1, \ldots, \Phi_p, \Theta_1, \ldots, \Theta_q$ and β may be used to minimise (8.2) by the multivariate Gauss–Newton procedure described in Section 4.4. However, because the explanatory variables are fixed, the ML estimator of β is distributed independently of the ML estimators of the ARMA parameters. The block diagonality of the information matrix can therefore be exploited by breaking each iteration down into two parts, one based on a SURE regression of ϵ_t and $\partial \epsilon_t / \partial \beta'$ and the other based on a SURE regression of ϵ_t on its derivatives with respect to the elements of $\Phi_1, \ldots, \Theta_q$. For given values of $\Phi_1, \ldots, \Phi_p, \Theta_1, \ldots, \Theta_q$, and Ω, the first SURE regression, ϵ_t on $\partial \epsilon_t / \partial \beta'$, yields the GLS estimator of β when subtracted from the initial estimates. An estimator of the asymptotic covariance matrix of $\tilde{\beta}$ is directly available since

$$\text{Avar}(\tilde{\beta}) = \left[\sum_{t=p+1}^{T} \frac{\partial \epsilon_t'}{\partial \beta} \, \Omega^{-1} \, \frac{\partial \epsilon_t}{\partial \beta'} \right]^{-1} \tag{8.4}$$

For a vector MA(1) disturbance term, the recursion in (8.3) is

$$\epsilon_t = (y_t - X_t\beta) - \Theta \epsilon_{t-1}, \qquad t = 1, \ldots, T \tag{8.5}$$

with $\epsilon_0 = 0$; cf. (3.5.8). The matrix of derivatives with respect to β is given by a recursion which is a direct generalisation of (5.4), i.e.

$$\frac{\partial \epsilon_t}{\partial \beta'} = -X_t - \Theta \frac{\partial \epsilon_{t-1}}{\partial \beta'}, \qquad t = 1, \ldots, T \tag{8.6}$$

with $\partial \epsilon_0 / \partial \beta' = 0$. The derivatives with respect to θ are obtained by generalising (4.4.19).

Matters are simplified considerably if the disturbance term is assumed to follow a pure autoregressive process. In the first order case, when $u_t = \Phi u_{t-1} + \epsilon_t$, the recursion (8.3) becomes

$$\epsilon_t = y_t - \Phi y_{t-1} - (X_t - \Phi X_{t-1})\beta \tag{8.7}$$

and so

$$\frac{\partial \epsilon_t}{\partial \beta'} = -(X_t - \Phi X_{t-1}), \qquad t = 2, \ldots, T \tag{8.8}$$

Conditional on Φ, the GLS estimator of β is given directly by a SURE regression of $y_t - \Phi y_{t-1}$ on $X_t - \Phi X_{t-1}$. At the same time, the recursions for estimating Φ are simplified considerably. If $\hat{u}_t$ denotes the tth residual vector at a particular iteration, the ith row in Φ is estimated by an OLS regression of the ith element in $\hat{u}_t$ on the complete vector $\hat{u}_{t-1}$. Following the argument in Examples of Section 3.5 these estimates will be the ML estimates of Φ conditional on β. Thus for an AR(1) disturbance term the multivariate Gauss–Newton scheme is a stepwise optimisation procedure. It could have been derived as a natural generalisation of Cochrane–Orcutt since subtracting Φy_{t-1} from both sides of (8.1) gives

$$y_t - \Phi y_{t-1} = (X_t - \Phi X_{t-1})\beta + \epsilon_t, \qquad t = 2,\ldots,T \qquad (8.9)$$

Conditional on Φ and Ω, the GLS estimator of β in (8.9) is given by a SURE regression of $y_t - \Phi y_{t-1}$ on $X_t - \Phi X_{t-1}$.

Asymptotically efficient two-step estimators of β may be constructed in much the same way as for single equation models. The first step is to obtain consistent estimators of the ARMA parameters and Ω from the OLS residuals. These estimators are then used to construct a two-step estimator of β by carrying out a SURE regression of ϵ_t on $\partial \epsilon_t / \partial \beta'$. As in the single equation model, it will usually be more convenient to carry out the second step in a slightly different way. Thus in the MA(1) case, a transformed set of observations on the dependent variables may be obtained from the recursion of the form (8.5), i.e.

$$y_t^\dagger = y_t - \Theta y_{t-1}^\dagger, \qquad t = 1,\ldots,T \qquad (8.10)$$

with $y_0^\dagger = 0$. A SURE regression of $y_t^\dagger$ on $-\partial \epsilon_t / \partial \beta'$ then yields the two-step estimator of β directly; there is no need to subtract from the initial OLS estimates.

For an AR(1) disturbance term, the two-step procedure is particularly appealing. The estimator, $\hat{\Phi}$, obtained from the OLS residuals is not only consistent, but asymptotically efficient. Furthermore, the second step is simply a SURE regression of $y_t - \hat{\Phi} y_{t-1}$ on $X_t - \hat{\Phi} X_{t-1}$.

Example Pagan and Byron (1977) estimate the investment model of Section 2.9, under the assumption that the disturbances are generated by a vector MA(1) process. Both the unrestricted MA(1) model and the seemingly unrelated MA(1) process in which $\Theta_{12} = \Theta_{21} = 0$ are considered. In the latter case they report

$$\hat{y}_1 = 0.041 x_{11} + 0.132 x_{21}$$
$$\hat{y}_2 = 0.048 x_{12} + 0.065 x_{22} \qquad (8.11)$$

with

$$\tilde{\Theta} = \begin{bmatrix} 0.638 & 0 \\ 0 & 0.647 \end{bmatrix} \quad \text{and} \quad |\tilde{\Omega}| = 13189.$$

The LR statistic for testing $H_0 : \Theta_{11} = \Theta_{22} = 0$ is

$$\text{LR} = 20 \log \frac{25768}{13189} = 13.40$$

This is significant at the 1% level, since under H_0, LR is asymptotically distributed as χ^2 with two degrees of freedom.

Common Regressors

In the multivariate regression model, described in Section 2.10, the explanatory variables in each equation are identical. As a result OLS applied to each equation separately will give fully efficient estimators of the regression parameters when the disturbances are normally distributed and serially independent. However, once serial correlation is introduced into the model, asymptotically efficient estimators of the parameters can no longer be constructed by considering each equation in isolation.

The above point may be illustrated by a relatively simple example. Suppose that the disturbance term, u_t, follows a vector AR(1) process in which Φ is diagonal. The transformed system, corresponding to (8.9), may be written as

$$y_{it} - \phi_i y_{i,t-1} = (x_t - \phi_i x_{t-1})' \beta_i + \epsilon_i,$$

$$i = 1,\ldots, N, \quad t = 2,\ldots,T \qquad (8.12)$$

where ϕ_i is the ith diagonal element of Φ. However, unless the value of ϕ_i is the same in all the equations, the regressors in (8.12) will be different. Thus even with Φ known, the estimation of the model must, in general, be carried out within the SURE framework developed in this section. It will often be convenient to cast the model in the form (2.10.5) for this purpose.

6.9. ARCH Disturbances

The idea of serial correlation in the variance was introduced in Example 2 of Section 3.5. Effects of this kind are quite plausible for many economic time series, particularly those concerned with prices. The ARCH process described there can easily be incorporated in a regression framework by assuming that the distribution of y_t conditional on the information at time $t - 1$ is normal with mean $x_t'\beta$ and variance, h_t, where h_t depends on past disturbances. Thus a regression model with a first-order ARCH disturbance could be expressed as

$$y_t = x_t'\beta + \epsilon_t \qquad (9.1a)$$

where, conditional on the information at time $t - 1$, ϵ_t is normally distributed with mean zero and variance

$$h_t = \alpha_0 + \alpha_1 \epsilon_{t-1}^2 \qquad (9.1b)$$

It is shown below that the disturbances in (9.1a), the ϵ_t's, are white noise, in the sense that they are uncorrelated with mean zero and constant variance. It therefore follows from the Gauss–Markov theorem that OLS is BLUE and its variance is estimated consistently by (2.8.19). However, although the disturbances are uncorrelated, they are not independent of each other. Hence OLS is inefficient. A fully efficient estimator which takes account of the dependence in variance can be constructed by maximum likelihood.

The likelihood function is of the form given in (3.5.22) with μ_t set equal to $x_t' \beta$. An explicit expression for the information matrix can be obtained and it can be shown that it is block diagonal with respect to the regression parameters, β, and the ARCH parameters, α_0 and α_1; see Engle (1982). The method of scoring appears to be a viable estimation procedure.

The first order ARCH model of (9.1b) can be generalised to a pth order ARCH model

$$h_t = \alpha_0 + \alpha_1 \epsilon_{t-1}^2 + \cdots + \alpha_p \epsilon_{t-p}^2 \qquad (9.2)$$

A further extension is the generalised ARCH, or GARCH model, proposed by Bollerslev (1986). In this model, the conditional variance of ϵ_t depends on the conditional variance in previous time periods as well as on lagged disturbances. The simplest GARCH model is

$$h_t = \alpha_0 + \alpha_1 \epsilon_{t-1}^2 + \gamma h_{t-1} \qquad (9.3)$$

The estimation of GARCH models proceeds along similar lines to the basic ARCH model of (9.1b).

Properties of ARCH

In order to examine the properties of the ARCH model we again consider (9.1) with β set equal to zero so that y_t is conditionally Gaussian with mean zero and variance $\alpha_0 + \alpha_1 y_{t-1}^2$. The essential device for evaluating the mean, variance and covariances of y_t is the law of iterative expectations. As applied to y_t itself, this means that the unconditional mean can be obtained by repeatedly taking conditional expectations starting at time $t - 1$, that is

$$E(y_t) = \underset{0}{E} \ \cdots \ \underset{t-2}{E} \ \underset{t-1}{E} (y_t) \qquad (9.4)$$

Since $\underset{t-1}{E}(y_t)$, the conditional expectation of y_t at time $t - 1$, is zero, it is clear that the unconditional expectation of y_t is also zero. In the case of the variance this operation is somewhat less trivial. By assumption

$$\underset{t-1}{E}(y_t^2) = \alpha_0 + \alpha_1 y_{t-1}^2$$

and so

$$\begin{aligned}
\underset{t-2}{E} \ \underset{t-1}{E}(y_t^2) &= \alpha_0 + \alpha_1 \underset{t-2}{E}(y_{t-1}^2) \\
&= \alpha_0 + \alpha_1 (\alpha_0 + \alpha_1 y_{t-2}^2) \\
&= \alpha_0 + \alpha_1 \alpha_0 + \alpha_1^2 y_{t-2}^2
\end{aligned}$$

Repeating this process by taking conditional expectations at time $t - 3$, $t - 4$ and so on gives

$$E(y_t^2) = \alpha_0 (1 + \alpha_1 + \ldots + \alpha_1^{t-1}) + \alpha_1^t y_0^2 \qquad (9.5)$$

If t is large and $|\alpha_1| < 1$,

$$\text{Var}(y_t) = \alpha_0/(1 - \alpha_1) \qquad (9.6)$$

The autocovariances can all be shown to be zero using conditional expectations since, for $\tau \geq 1$,

$$\underset{t-\tau}{E} (y_t y_{t-\tau}) = y_{t-\tau} \underset{t-\tau}{E} (y_t) = 0 \qquad (9.7)$$

Although the ARCH observations are uncorrelated, this is not true of the squared observations. Thus serial correlation shows up not in the correlogram of y_t, but in the correlogram of the squares of y_t. Assuming finite kurtosis, which requires $3\alpha_1^2 < 1$, the theoretical a.c.f. is such that the τth autocorrelation is α_1^τ. Thus it has the same form as the a.c.f. of an AR(1) process.

Testing for ARCH

The standard test procedure for AR(1) disturbances is based on the first-order sample autocorrelation in the residuals; see the discussion in Section 3. In a similar way, a test for first-order ARCH disturbances may be based on the first-order autocorrelation between the *squares* of the residuals, rsq_1. A large sample test may then be carried out by treating $\sqrt{T}.rsq_1$ as having an N(0,1) distribution under the null hypothesis.

The rationale for basing a test for first-order ARCH on rsq_1 is the LM principle. Thus there is a direct parallel with tests for AR(1) disturbances carried out using r_1. Bearing in mind that the information matrix in the ARCH regression model is block diagonal, the derivation of the LM test for ARCH can be simplified by treating the disturbances as though they were observable. Thus we effectively take the model as written in (9.1) but set $\beta = 0$ so that $\epsilon_t = y_t$. The likelihood function is as in (3.5.22) with $\mu = 0$ and differentiating with respect to $\alpha = (\alpha_0, \alpha_1)'$ yields

$$\frac{\partial \log L}{\partial \alpha} = \frac{1}{2} \sum_t \frac{\partial h_t}{\partial \alpha} \frac{1}{h_t} \left(\frac{y_t^2}{h_t} - 1 \right) \qquad (9.8)$$

Differentiating a second time gives the Hessian matrix

$$\frac{\partial^2 \log L}{\partial \alpha \partial \alpha'} = -\frac{1}{2} \sum_t \frac{1}{h_t^2} \frac{\partial h_t}{\partial \alpha} \frac{\partial h_t}{\partial \alpha'} \left(\frac{y_t^2}{h_t} - 1 \right)$$

$$+ \sum_t \left(\frac{y_t^2}{h_t} - 1 \right) \frac{\partial}{\partial \alpha} \left[\frac{1}{2h_t} \frac{\partial h_t}{\partial \alpha'} \right] \qquad (9.9)$$

Simply taking expectations of (9.9) is not easy. However, it is possible to take the expectation of the tth term in the expression conditional on the information at time $t - 1$. If this is done, expression (9.9) simplifies dramatically: the second term on the right-hand side disappears, since $E(y_t^2 \mid Y_{t-1}) = h_t$ and the remaining part of the term is fixed at time $t - 1$, while the part of the first term in parentheses is unity. Multiplying by minus one yields

$$I^*(\alpha) = \frac{1}{2} \sum_t \frac{1}{h_t^2} \frac{\partial h_t}{\partial \alpha} \frac{\partial h_t}{\partial \alpha'} \tag{9.10}$$

This is not, strictly speaking, the information matrix, since it has been obtained as the sum of a set of conditional expectations and the information matrix is the unconditional expectation of the Hessian. However, $T^{-1} I^*(\alpha)$ is a consistent estimator of the asymptotic information matrix, and $I^*(\alpha)$ is by far the most convenient expression with which to construct test statistics.

The general form of the LM test is as in (5.5.4). Letting w_t denote the derivative of h_t with respect to the vector α, that is

$$w_t = \partial h_t / \partial \alpha = (1 \ y_{t-1}^2)'$$

and noting that, under the null hypothesis $H_0 : \alpha_1 = 0$, h_t is estimated by

$$h_t = \tilde{\alpha}_0 = \tilde{\sigma}^2 = \Sigma y_t^2 / T$$

the information matrix to be used in the construction of the test statistic is, in the notation of (5.5.4),

$$I^*(\tilde{\psi}_0) = \frac{1}{2\tilde{\sigma}^2} \Sigma w_t w_t' \tag{9.11}$$

Similarly, under the null hypothesis, the score vector is

$$\frac{\partial \log L}{\partial \alpha} = \frac{1}{2\tilde{\sigma}^2} \Sigma w_t v_t, \tag{9.12a}$$

where

$$v_t = y_t^2 / \tilde{\sigma}^2 - 1 \tag{9.12b}$$

Putting these expressions together yields a test statistic which has the same form as the LM test for multiplicative heteroscedasticity given in (5.5.12). Furthermore, by an argument similar to the one used to obtain the TR^2 test statistic in (5.5.14), the LM test statistic for ARCH is

$$LM^* = T.rsq_1^2$$

and this is asymptotically χ_1^2 under the null hypothesis that there are no first-order ARCH effects.

The ARCH test easily generalises to testing for a Pth order ARCH process of the form (9.2). The test statistic in this case is the Q statistic, or the Q^* statistic (6.4) with r_τ replaced by rsq_τ. This test statistic has a χ_P^2 distribution under the null; see McLeod and Li (1983). Again, there is a parallel with testing for serial correlation where, as noted below (6.4), the portmanteau test is the LM test against an AR(P) or an MA(P) disturbance term.

Notes

Section 2   Griliches and Rao (1969).
Section 5   Pierce (1971a), Harvey and McAvinchey (1982).
Section 6   Pierce (1971b), Ljung and Box (1978). Durbin (1969) describes a test based on the cumulative periodogram.
Section 7   Box and Jenkins (1976, Ch. 5, pp. 267–69).
Section 8   Monte Carlo evidence on various systems estimators will be found in Kmenta and Gilbert (1970).

Exercises

1. Consider the AR(1) model, (1.2.10), with $|\phi|<1$ and $\epsilon_t \sim NID(0,\sigma^2)$ and show that the LM principle leads to a test based on the first order sample autocorrelation, r_1. Show that similar reasoning leads to a test based on the corresponding sample autocorrelation for the OLS residuals in a linear regression model.

2. Compare the Gauss–Newton, Newton–Raphson and method of scoring procedures for model (1.1), (1.2). How are these related to the Cochrane–Orcutt iterative procedure?

3. (a) For the single regressor model (2.1) with $x_t = 1$ for $t = 1,\dots,T$, show that for a given value of ϕ in the range $0<\phi<1$,

$$\frac{\text{Var}(\tilde{b}^\dagger)}{\text{Var}(b)} = \frac{T(1 - \phi^2) - 2\phi(1 - \phi^T)}{T^2(1 - \phi)^2} \cdot \frac{(T - 1)(1 - \phi)}{(1 + \phi)} \geq T/(T - 1)$$

where $\tilde{b}^\dagger$ is the Cochrane–Orcutt approximation to GLS.
   (b) Repeat the above calculations with $x_t = 1$ for t odd and $x_t = 0$ for t even. Comment on the results.

4. For model (2.1) with $x_t = 1$, determine whether the usual estimator of the variance of the OLS estimator, b, will tend to underestimate or overestimate the true variance in large samples.

5. Consider an AR(2) model

$$y_t = \phi_1 y_{t-1} + \phi_2 y_{t-2} + \epsilon_t, \qquad \epsilon_t \sim NID(0, \sigma^2)$$

Explain: (a) how you would test the hypothesis $\phi_1 = \phi_2 = 0$ using LR and Wald statistics; (b) how you would test the hypothesis $\phi_2 = 0$ using LR, Wald and LM statistics. How would you apply these tests if the AR(2) process were a disturbance term in a regression model?

6. The following is a sequence of residuals from a regression on two exogenous variables and a constant term: $+1.4$, $+1.6$, $+0.4$, -0.9, -0.2, -0.6, $+0.1$, -1.9, -0.7, $+0.2$, $+1.8$, $+1.2$, $+0.4$, -0.5, -1.2, -1.1. Test the hypothesis that the disturbances are serially independent against the alternative that they

are positively autocorrelated using the Durbin–Watson test. State any assumptions you make and comment on the significance of your findings.

Carry out a large sample test of the same hypothesis based on r_1, the first order autocorrelation in the residuals.

7. Consider the model (1.1), in which the disturbance term follows an ARMA(1, 1) process

$$u_t = \phi u_{t-1} + \epsilon_t + \theta \epsilon_{t-1}$$

(a) Show that under certain simplifying assumptions, maximising the likelihood function is equivalent to minimising a sum of squares function. Hence show how maximum likelihood estimates may be obtained by the Gauss–Newton procedure. Write down expressions for any derivatives employed in this procedure. Indicate briefly how you would test the hypothesis that $\theta = 0$ within this framework.

(b) Suppose that $x_{T+1}^{+}\tilde{\beta} = 10$ and $x_{T+2}^{+}\tilde{\beta} = 11$, $y_T - x_T^{+}\tilde{\beta} = 2.0$ and $e_T = 1.0$, where e_T is the maximum likelihood residual corresponding to ϵ_T. Obtain predictions for y_{T+1} and y_{T+2} given that $\phi = \theta = 0.5$.

8. Show that the portmanteau test based on OLS residuals may be derived as an LM test against either an AR(P) or an MA(P) disturbance term.

9. Formulate LR, Wald and LM statistics for testing that the disturbance vector in a SURE model is serially uncorrelated against the alternative that it is generated by a vector AR(1) process. If the AR matrix, Φ, is taken to the diagonal how would this affect the estimation and test procedures?

10. (i) Explain how you would extend the Gauss–Newton algorithm in (4.4.17) if the disturbance term were generated by an AR(1) process, (1.2). (ii) How are the estimators distributed in large samples? (iii) Discuss any modifications you might consider making to the Gauss–Newton algorithm.

7
Dynamic Models I

7.1. Introduction

The regression models considered up to this point have been *static*, in the sense that the dependent variable is taken to be a function of a set of explanatory variables observed at the same point in time. A *dynamic* model, on the other hand, involves non-contemporaneous relationships between variables. A simple example of such a model is therefore

$$y_t = \delta x_{t-3} + u_t \tag{1.1}$$

In this case the effect of a change in x is only felt on y after three time periods have elapsed. However, (1.1) does not really capture the spirit of a dynamic model since once x begins to influence y its full effect is immediately realised. If, on the other hand, several lagged values of x are included in the model, any change in the level of x will work its way through to y in stages. Thus suppose that

$$y_t = 0.4x_{t-1} + 1.0x_{t-2} + 0.6x_{t-3} + u_t \tag{1.2}$$

If x_t is running at a constant level, i.e. $x_t = \bar{x}$, then

$$E(y_t) = 0.4\bar{x} + 1.0\bar{x} + 0.6\bar{x} = 2\bar{x}$$

An increase in the level of x, from $\bar{x}$ to $\bar{x} + 1$, clearly increases the expected value of y by 2 units. However, this is accomplished gradually. There is no immediate change in the expected value of y, but after one and two time periods respectively, 20% and 70% of the adjustment will have taken place. The full effect is realised when three time periods have elapsed.

The model in (1.2) is known as a *distributed lag*. Such a model may be written more generally as

$$y_t = \delta_0 x_t + \delta_1 x_{t-1} + \ldots + \delta_m x_{t-m} + u_t \tag{1.3}$$

where $\delta_0, \ldots, \delta_m$ are the *lag coefficients*. These determine the way in which y will respond to a change in x. Models of this kind are important in econometrics since there are many situations where it is plausible to assume that the effect of a change in an explanatory variable takes time to work through to the dependent variable. A capital appropriation in a given quarter, for example, may result in capital expenditure in several subsequent quarters, as real investment in buildings and machinery cannot be realised instantaneously. Similarly, there will be time delays of some sort before changes in prices and output are induced by a change in the money supply.

In principle, a finite distributed lag model of the form (1.3) causes no new estimation problems. If $u_t \sim NID(0, \sigma^2)$, OLS will yield efficient estimators of all the parameters, while if u_t is subject to serial correlation or heteroscedasticity it may be handled by the GLS techniques already introduced. However, if the object of the analysis is to obtain reasonably precise estimates of the lag coefficients, such an approach may be unsatisfactory. The reason is that economic time series are typically slowly changing and so the x_t's on the right hand side of (1.3) are likely to be highly correlated with each other. This multicollinearity makes it difficult to determine the lag structure very precisely.

There are a number of ways of tackling this problem. However, they all have the same objective, which is to impose some *a priori* structure on the form of the lag, thereby reducing the number of parameters to be estimated. One approach, originally suggested by Almon (1965), is to approximate the pattern of lag coefficients by a polynomial of a fairly low degree. An alternative approach, which fits more naturally into a time series framework, is to represent the lag structure by the ratio of two polynomials in the lag operator. This is known as a *rational distributed lag*. Approximating the lag structure in this way is motivated by the same principle which leads a stationary stochastic process to be modelled by a mixed ARMA process.

One of the simplest examples of a rational lag structure is the *Koyck* or *geometric* distributed lag. In this model the coefficients are constrained to decline exponentially as the length of the lag increases. Thus, in terms of (1.3), $\delta_j = \beta\alpha^j$, $j = 0, 1, 2, \ldots, m$, where β and α are parameters and $0 < \alpha < 1$. By imposing this constraint, a more parsimonious model is obtained since $m + 1$ lag coefficients are represented by only two parameters. Although the lag length, m, could take any value, it is actually most convenient to set it equal to infinity. This will not, in general, involve any serious distortion in a finite lag structure since the implied lag coefficients will tend to be very small for high values of j. However, from the technical point of view an infinite lag structure is far easier to handle. The model may be written as

$$y_t = \beta \sum_{j=0}^{\infty} \alpha^j x_{t-j} + u_t \tag{1.4}$$

and multiplying both sizes of (1.4) at time $t - 1$ by α, subtracting from (1.4) and rearranging gives

$$y_t = \alpha y_{t-1} + \beta x_t + v_t \qquad (1.5)$$

where

$$v_t = u_t - \alpha u_{t-1} \qquad (1.6)$$

The simple form of equation (1.5) is very appealing, although the simplicity is, to some extent, illusory. If the disturbance term in (1.4) is white noise, v_t will be serially correlated and OLS will *not* be an appropriate estimation technique. However, provided the problem is approached within a maximum likelihood framework, rather than on an *ad hoc* basis, there is no difficulty in constructing efficient estimators of α and β.

By defining the polynomial

$$D(L) = \delta_0 + \delta_1 L + \delta_2 L^2 + \ldots + \delta_m L^m \qquad (1.7)$$

model (1.3) may be expressed in the form

$$y_t = D(L)x_t + u_t \qquad (1.8)$$

For the Koyck model,

$$\begin{aligned} D(L) &= \beta(1 + \alpha L + \alpha^2 L^2 + \alpha^3 L^3 + \ldots) \\ &= \beta\{1 + \alpha L + (\alpha L)^2 + (\alpha L)^3 + \ldots\} \\ &= \beta/(1 - \alpha L) \end{aligned} \qquad (1.9)$$

Thus (1.4) is indeed a member of the rational lag family since $D(L)$ is equal to the ratio of two polynomials in the lag operator. (Although the numerator is simply β.) More generally we may define

$$B(L) = \beta_0 + \beta_1 L + \ldots + \beta_s L^s \qquad (1.10)$$

$$A(L) = 1 - \alpha_1 L - \alpha_2 L^2 - \cdots - \alpha_r L^r \qquad (1.11)$$

A general rational distributed lag structure is then given by setting $D(L) = B(L)/A(L)$. If u_t is assumed to be generated by an ARMA(p, q) process, the resulting model,

$$y_t = \frac{B(L)}{A(L)} x_{t-v} + \frac{\theta(L)}{\phi(L)} \epsilon_t \qquad (1.12)$$

is known as a *transfer function*. The first term on the right hand side of (1.12) encompasses the *systematic dynamics* of the model, while the second term reflects the *disturbance dynamics*. If there is a delay before any change in x_t is felt in y_t, then v is a positive integer.

Augmenting the right hand side of a regression equation with lagged values of the explanatory variables is not the only way of making the model dynamic. An alternative approach is to introduce lagged values of the dependent variable into the regression. A simple example of such a model is:

$$y_t = \alpha y_{t-1} + \beta x_t + u_t \qquad (1.13)$$

where α and β are parameters and u_t is a disturbance term. There are a number of reasons why a model may be cast directly in this form. However, the important point to note for the moment is the close similarity between (1.13) and (1.5). This implies that if $|\alpha| < 1$, (1.13) has an implicit rational lag structure. By substituting repeatedly for lagged values of y_t, or by writing the model as

$$(1 - \alpha L)y_t = \beta x_t + u_t \tag{1.14}$$

and multiplying both sides by $1/(1 - \alpha L)$, it will be seen that (1.13) is equivalent to

$$y_t = \beta \sum_{j=0}^{\infty} \alpha^j x_{t-j} + \sum_{j=0}^{\infty} \alpha^j u_{t-j} \tag{1.15}$$

The systematic part of (1.15) is therefore a Koyck distributed lag, but the model differs from (1.14) in that the disturbance term depends on the same parameter, α, as does the lag structure itself.

The duality between stochastic difference equations and transfer function models persists in more general cases. Provided a lagged dependent variable model is stable, its mean path, i.e. $E(y_t)$, will be a rational distributed lag function of the explanatory variable or variables. Defining $A(L)$ and $B(L)$ as in (1.11) and (1.10) respectively leads to the following general formulation for a single explanatory variable:

$$A(L)y_t = B(L)x_t + u_t \tag{1.16}$$

The model is *stable* if the roots of $A(L)$ lie outside the unit circle. Provided that this condition is met, the lag structure is given by $B(L)/A(L)$, and so the systematic dynamics may be deduced from the corresponding results derived for (1.12). As with the transfer function model, u_t may be modelled by an ARMA(p, q) process.

Estimation of Dynamic Regression Models

If the disturbance term in a stochastic difference equation is a white noise process, the Mann–Wald result of Section 2.12 is applicable. The parameters in $A(L)$ and $B(L)$ of (1.16) will be estimated consistently by OLS and if u_t is normally distributed these estimators will be asymptotically efficient. However, if u_t is serially correlated, OLS may not even be consistent. Thus consider (1.13) and suppose that $E(u_t u_{t-1}) \neq 0$. Let $z_t = (y_{t-1}, x_t)'$. The OLS estimator of α and β may then be written

$$\begin{bmatrix} a \\ b \end{bmatrix} = \begin{bmatrix} \alpha \\ \beta \end{bmatrix} + \left[\frac{\Sigma z_t z_t'}{T} \right]^{-1} \frac{\Sigma z_t u_t}{T} \tag{1.17}$$

If plim $T^{-1} \Sigma x_t^2$ is a positive number, $T^{-1} \Sigma z_t z_t'$ converges to a p.d. matrix.

The estimators a and b will therefore be consistent if plim $T^{-1}\Sigma z_t u_t = 0$. Since x is exogenous, plim $T^{-1}\Sigma x_t u_t = 0$ by definition, but because u_t and u_{t-1} are correlated

$$\text{plim } T^{-1}\Sigma y_{t-1} u_t \neq 0 \qquad (1.18)$$

Expression (1.18) captures the basic difficulty with this model, namely that one of the regressors is correlated with the disturbance term, and from (1.17) it will be seen that this is sufficient to render the OLS estimators of both α and β inconsistent.

The Koyck distributed lag model, (1.4), may be transformed to (1.5), which is very similar to (1.13). However if the disturbance term in (1.4) is white noise, the disturbance term in the transformed model is generated by an MA(1) process. Thus regressing y_t on y_{t-1} and x_t will *not* yield consistent estimators of the parameters in the model.

In a classical regression model the OLS estimator remains unbiased (and consistent) even though the disturbances are serially correlated. Once a lagged dependent variable is introduced into a model, either directly as in (1.13) or by a transformation as in (1.5), serial correlation has more serious consequences. Furthermore, attempting to overcome these problems by constructing a feasible GLS estimator will not, in general, be successful. Fortunately these problems are not difficult to overcome provided that estimation is approached within a maximum likelihood framework rather than on an *ad hoc* basis. This point is worth stressing since in econometrics there has, in the past, been a tendency to approach estimation from a least squares point of view. This is not usually a successful strategy in dynamic models insofar as it rarely leads to fully efficient estimators. In addition the argument that such procedures have the compensating advantage of simplicity is not generally valid since two-step maximum likelihood estimators are usually very easy to compute while still being fully efficient.

Partial Adjustment and Adaptive Expectations

Although the systematic part of the stochastic difference equation, (1.13), is a Koyck distributed lag, the structure of the disturbance term in (1.15) places the model in a different class from (1.4). The decision as to which formulation is appropriate in a given situation will depend on a number of factors. These include pragmatic considerations such as ease of estimation and goodness of fit. More fundamentally, however, both formulations may be rationalised in terms of a behavioural theory. The transfer function specification, (1.4), can be derived from a theory of adaptive expectations, while the stochastic difference equation (1.13) arises as a consequence of a process of partial adjustment.

The adaptive expectations hypothesis is best described in a specific context. Suppose we are dealing with the estimation of an agricultural supply function in which quantity, y, is related to price, x. A farmer must make his decisions regarding how much of a given crop to plant before he knows the price the crop will actually fetch on the market. Thus he will plan production on the basis of *expected* price in the next time period. It may therefore be reasonable to write

$$y_t = \beta x_{t+1}^* + u_t \qquad\qquad (1.19)$$

where u_t is a disturbance term which represents factors such as the weather, as well as individual differences between farmers in the way they react to a particular expected price.

Since x_{t+1}^* is not directly observable, a reasonable hypothesis concerning the manner in which expectations are generated must be formulated. One possibility is to put

$$x_{t+1}^* = x_t^* + \gamma(x_t - x_t^*), \qquad 0 < \gamma < 1 \qquad\qquad (1.20)$$

This is the *adaptive expectations* hypothesis, and it states that decision makers revise their expectations on the basis of the discrepancy between their prediction of the current value of x_t and the actual outcome. The parameter γ measures the extent to which they react to this discrepancy.

Rearranging (1.20) and rewriting it using the lag operator gives

$$(1 - \alpha L)x_{t+1}^* = (1 - \alpha)x_t \qquad\qquad (1.21)$$

where $\alpha = 1 - \gamma$. Thus expectations are an exponentially weighted moving average of past values of the series since

$$x_{t+1}^* = \frac{(1 - \alpha)}{1 - \alpha L} x_t = (1 - \alpha) \sum_{j=0}^{\infty} \alpha^j x_{t-j}$$

Substituting for x_{t+1}^* in (1.19) yields

$$y_t = \beta(1 - \alpha) \sum_{j=0}^{\infty} \alpha^j x_{t-j} + u_t$$

which is of the same form as (1.4).

The *partial adjustment* mechanism operates in a slightly different way. Suppose that y_t^* the *desired* level of y at time t, is related to x by the equation

$$y_t^* = \beta x_t \qquad\qquad (1.22)$$

In an economic context x_t might be income and y_t^* desired expenditure. Alternatively x_t may be the price of a good, while y_t^* is the quantity the firm wishes to produce at that price. In both cases, however, there are plausible reasons why the adjustment to the desired level cannot take place immediately. In the first example, the consumer is likely to take time to adjust to a new set of spending habits associated with his new income, while in the second example the firm may not be able to switch production very easily from one good to another, or undertake the investment required to increase production.

Because of these rigidities only a partial adjustment is possible and this may be modelled by a *reaction function* of the form

$$y_t = y_{t-1} + \gamma(y_t^* - y_{t-1}) + u_t \qquad (1.23)$$

where $0 < \gamma \le 1$. Thus (1.23) asserts that in the current period the consumer or firm only moves part of the way towards the optimal position, the speed of adjustment being determined by the parameter γ.

Combining (1.22) and (1.23) gives

$$y_t = (1 - \gamma)y_{t-1} + \beta\gamma x_t + u_t \qquad (1.24)$$

which is a stochastic difference equation of the form (1.13).

Model Selection

The choice between a transfer function model and a stochastic difference equation cannot always be resolved on the basis of *a priori* theory in the way suggested above. In a situation where very little information regarding a suitable specification is available, both a transfer function, (1.12), and a stochastic difference equation, (1.16), represent valid ways of approaching dynamic modelling. There is, however, some divergence in the literature regarding the appropriate way to proceed. The strategy adopted by Box and Jenkins (1976) is based on the transfer function formulation, and a suitable dynamic specification is reached by using techniques similar to those employed in the identification of an ARMA time series model. Econometricians, on the other hand, have tended to favour stochastic difference equations, at least in macroeconomics.

At one time the predilection of econometricians for stochastic difference equations could be attributed to pragmatic motives. If the disturbance term in (1.16) is a normally distributed white noise process, OLS is the appropriate estimation technique. However, while ease of estimation might have been a sensible criterion for model selection ten or fifteen years ago, this is no longer the case now. If a particular specification is felt to be appropriate, there seems to be general agreement that the correct course of action is to attempt to estimate it by maximum likelihood.

The fundamental reasons for the differences in the literature concern specification. These differences are a reflection of different attitudes to model building, which stem mainly from the type of problems under consideration. In the examples considered by Box and Jenkins (1976, Ch. 11), the explanatory variable is an input to a physical system. The observations are generated by a controlled experiment, and so the question of whether other explanatory variables should be included in the model does not arise. In econometrics the problem is to estimate a behavioural relationship from non-experimental data. Thus specification takes on two dimensions. As well as determining the dynamics of the model, there is also the more fundamental question of which variables should be included in the model in the first place. This favours an approach in which the first stage in model selection is to estimate a very general model. If such an approach is adopted, there are important technical reasons for preferring to work within the framework of a stochastic difference equation. These points are discussed in detail in Section 5 of the next chapter.

There are two other reasons why stochastic difference equations have been favoured in econometrics. The first is that generalisation to systems of equations, and in particular to systems of simultaneous equations, is somewhat easier. Secondly, economic theory sometimes suggests *a priori* constraints on the model specification because of long-run solutions. These constraints are generally easier to handle within a stochastic difference equation framework.

The next section describes ways in which the systematic dynamics of a model may be characterised. This material is common to both transfer functions and stochastic difference equations. The same could be said of the material on seasonality in Section 6. However, the bulk of the chapter is concerned with the estimation and testing of transfer function models. The last section is devoted to polynomial, or Almon, distributed lags. This represents an alternative approach to approximating the lag structure in a model of the form (1.8). Hence it fits more naturally into this chapter than the next, which is primarily concerned with stochastic difference equations. However, from the point of view of specification, the polynomial distributed lag possesses some of the advantages of the stochastic difference equation, insofar as it is relatively easy to move from a general specification to a more specific one.

7.2. Systematic Dynamics

The systematic dynamics of a model concern the behaviour of the *mean path* of y_t. This is defined as the expected value of y_t, conditional on the current and past values of the exogenous variables. For both the transfer function (1.12), and the stochastic difference equation, (1.16), the mean path is given by

$$\bar{y}_t = E(y_t) = A^{-1}(L)B(L)x_t \tag{2.1}$$

Hence the systematic dynamics for the two classes of model can be considered together.

The nature of the expected response of y to changes in x depends on the pattern of lag coefficients implied by the polynomial ratio $B(L)/A(L)$. Thus the first step in an examination of the systematic dynamics of the model is the derivation of the lag coefficients. Once this has been done, the properties of the lag may be characterised by summary statistics, such as the mean lag, and by various multipliers.

Throughout the discussion it will be assumed that the model is *stable*. This will be the case if the roots of the polynomial $A(L)$ lie outside the unit circle. An *equilibrium* solution is then possible since if x_t is constant at $\bar{x}$, the mean path of y_t is also constant at $\bar{y}$, where

$$\bar{y} = \frac{\beta_0 + \beta_1 + \cdots + \beta_s}{1 - \alpha_1 - \cdots - \alpha_r} \bar{x} = \frac{B(1)}{A(1)} \bar{x} \tag{2.2}$$

Note that setting $L = 1$ in the lag polynomials $A(L)$ and $B(L)$ has the effect of reducing them to the sums of their respective coefficients.

Derivation of the Lag Coefficients

In the geometric lag model, the relationship between the ratio $\beta/(1 - \alpha L)$ and the lag coefficients emerges as a consequence of the result on summing a geometric series. This approach may be extended to cases where $r > 1$. Suppose that

$$\bar{y} = \frac{2.0}{1 - 0.8L + 0.15L^2} x_t$$

The roots of $A(L)$ are obtained by factorising it as

$$A(L) = (1 - 0.5L)(1 - 0.3L)$$

Both roots are real and distinct, and so expanding the ratio $B(L)/A(L)$ in partial fractions yields

$$\frac{B(L)}{A(L)} = 2\left\{ \frac{0.5}{0.2} \frac{1}{1 - 0.5L} - \frac{0.3}{0.2} \frac{1}{1 - 0.3L} \right\}$$

Each of the terms in this expression may be treated as the sum of an infinite number of terms in geometric progression. Therefore

$$D(L) = 2\left(2.5 \sum_{j=0}^{\infty} 0.5^j L^j - 1.5 \sum_{j=0}^{\infty} 0.3^j L^j \right)$$

$$= 2 \sum_{j=0}^{\infty} \{2.5(0.5)^j - 1.5(0.3)^j\} L^j$$

and so $\delta_0 = 2$, $\delta_1 = 1.6$, $\delta_2 = 0.98$ and so on. The same technique may be applied even if the numerator polynomial, $B(L)$, is of a higher order.

An alternative method of obtaining the lag coefficients is based on equating coefficients of powers of L in the expression

$$B(L) = A(L)D(L)$$

This gives

$$\delta_j = \sum_{i=1}^{\min(j,r)} \alpha_i \delta_{j-i} + \beta_j, \qquad 1 \le j \le s \tag{2.3a}$$

$$\delta_j = \sum_{i=1}^{\min(j,r)} \alpha_i \delta_{j-i}, \qquad j > s \tag{2.3b}$$

Note that in all cases $\delta_0 = \beta_0$.

In the numerical example above, the lag coefficients emerge as follows:

$$\delta_0 = 2.0$$

$$\delta_1 = 0.8(2.0) = 1.6$$

$$\delta_2 = 0.8(1.6) - 0.15(2.0) = 0.98$$

and so on. Thus the weights are determined by a second-order difference equation from $j = 2$ onwards. In this example the roots of $A(L)$ are real. However with complex roots, the possibility of the lag coefficients following a damped cyclical pattern arises. This implies that certain of the δ_j's will be negative, a situation which may, in some cases, be ruled out by prior considerations.

Total, Interim and Impact Multipliers

The concept of a multiplier is defined within the context of an equilibrium solution to the model. Suppose that x_t is constant at a level $\bar{x}$, so that the equilibrium solution, $\bar{y}$, is given by (2.2). If this level increases by unity, i.e. from $\bar{x}$ to $\bar{x} + 1$, the new equilibrium solution will be

$$\bar{y}^* = \frac{B(1)}{A(1)}(\bar{x} + 1) = \bar{y} + \frac{B(1)}{A(1)}$$

This reflects a rise in the level of the mean path from $\bar{y}$ to $\bar{y} + B(1)/A(1)$. The change is known as the *total multiplier*, and since

$$B(1)/A(1) = D(1) = \sum_{j=0}^{\infty} \delta_j \tag{2.4}$$

it may be interpreted as the sum of the lag coefficients.

The new equilibrium solution, $\bar{y}^*$, represents the long-run effect of a unit increase in $\bar{x}$. At the other extreme is the immediate effect on $\bar{y}_t$. The increase in $\bar{y}_t$ induced by a unit increase in $\bar{x}$ is known as the *impact multiplier*, and this is simply equal to δ_0.

The efffect of a unit change in $\bar{x}$ after J time periods is measured by the Jth *interim multiplier*,

$$\delta_J^* = \sum_{j=0}^{J} \delta_j, \qquad J = 0, 1, 2, \ldots \qquad (2.5)$$

It is sometimes convenient to standardise the interim multipliers by dividing through by the total multiplier. The resulting quantities,

$$\delta_J^\dagger = \delta_J^*/\delta_\infty^*, \qquad J = 0, 1, 2 \ldots \qquad (2.6)$$

then give the proportion of the total change completed after J time periods.

Example 1   The pattern of interim multipliers for the Koyck lag, (1.4), with $\alpha = 0.5$ is shown implicitly in figure 7.1. The diagram traces out the mean path of y_t resulting from a unit change in x_t at the time $t = \tau$. Since the lag is infinite, the new equilibrium level of y is only approached asymptotically.

Example 2   Consider a model in which the systematic part is

$$\bar{y}_t = 0.6\bar{y}_{t-1} - 0.4\bar{y}_{t-2} + 1.2x_t$$

The roots of the polynomial $A(L) = 1 - 0.6L + 0.4L^2$ are complex with the result that the pattern of lag coefficients shows a damped cyclical movement. This is illustrated in figure 7.2(a). Figure 7.2(b) shows the interim multipliers. The initial response in $\bar{y}_t$ is to overshoot the new equilibrium level. Thereafter a gradual adjustment takes place by a series of cyclical movements.

Mean and Median Lags

When all the lag coefficients are non-negative, the *mean* or average *lag* is defined as

$$\text{Mean lag} = \sum_{j=0}^{\infty} j\delta_j \bigg/ \sum_{j=0}^{\infty} \delta_j \qquad (2.7)$$

Higher order moments may also be defined although these are not often employed. However, another summary statistic which does often prove useful is the *median lag*. This gives the number of time periods it takes for 50% of the total adjustment to be completed.

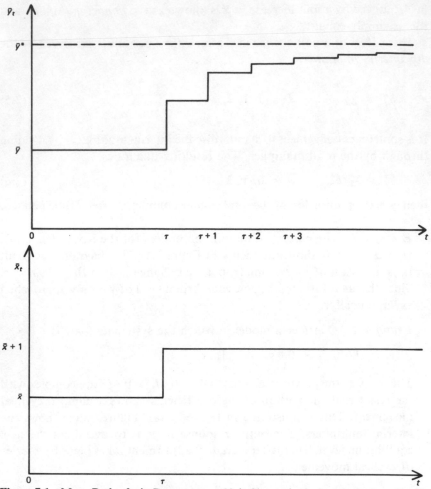

Figure 7.1 Mean Path of y in Response to a Unit Change in the Level of x for a Koyck Distributed Lag

Example 3   In the finite distributed lag model

$$\bar{y}_t = 0.2x_{t-2} + 0.4x_{t-3} + 0.1x_{t-4} \tag{2.8}$$

the impact multiplier is 0, the total multiplier 0.7, and

$$\text{mean lag} = \frac{0.2 \times 2 + 0.4 \times 3 + 0.1 \times 4}{0.7} = 2.86$$

The standardised interim multipliers at $J = 2$ and $J = 3$ are 0.29 and 0.86 respectively. The median lag is therefore given by[1]

---

[1]There is a case for adding 0.5 to the median lag. This would ensure that the mean and median lags were identical for a symmetric pattern of lag coefficients.

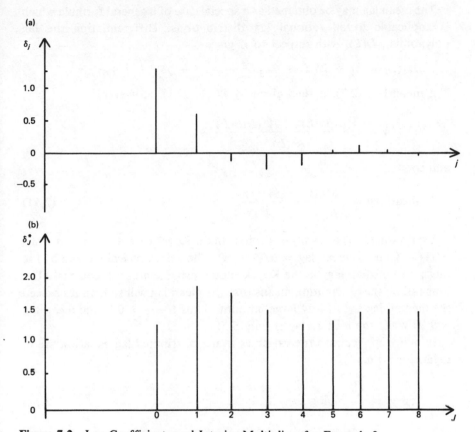

Figure 7.2 Lag Coefficients and Interim Multipliers for Example 2

$$\text{median lag} = 2.0 + \frac{0.50 - 0.29}{0.86 - 0.29} = 2.37$$

Example 4 Consider the Koyck distributed lag model, (1.4). The total multiplier is $\beta/(1 - \alpha)$ while the standardised interim multipliers are

$$\delta_J^\dagger = 1 - \alpha^{J+1}, \qquad J = 0, 1, \ldots \qquad (2.9)$$

The median lag is obtained by finding a value of J such that $\delta_J^\dagger = 0.5$. Solving the equation

$$1 - \alpha^{J+1} = 0.5$$

gives the following expression:

$$\text{median lag} = (\log \alpha)^{-1} \log 0.5 - 1 \qquad (2.10)$$

This will be negative if $\alpha < 0.5$, in which case it may be sensible to round it to zero.

The mean lag may be obtained as a special case of a general formula which is applicable to all rational lag distributions. Differentiating the lag polynomial, $D(L)$, with respect to L gives

$$D'(L) = \delta_1 + 2\delta_2 L + 3\delta_3 L^2 + \cdots + j\delta_j L^{j-1} + \cdots$$

The mean lag, (2.7), is then given by $D'(1)/D(1)$. However,

$$D'(L) = \frac{A(L)B'(L) - A'(L)B(L)}{A^2(L)}$$

and so

$$\text{mean lag} = \frac{B'(1)}{B(1)} - \frac{A'(1)}{A(1)} \tag{2.11}$$

Expression (2.11) is readily evaluated. In the Koyck case $A'(1) = -\alpha$ while $B'(1) = 0$ and so mean lag $= \alpha/(1 - \alpha)$. The values typically taken by the mean and median lags in the Koyck model provide a useful contrast. The long tail on the distribution means that the mean lag will sometimes exceed the median lag by a fairly large amount. Thus for $\alpha = 0.9$, the mean lag is 9.00 while the median lag is only 5.58.

In many applications the variables in the distributed lag equation are in logarithms, i.e.

$$\log y_t = \sum_{j=0}^{\infty} \delta_j \log x_{t-j} + u_t \tag{2.12}$$

A 1 per cent increase in the level of x will mean that after J periods the percentage increase in the mean path of y will be

$$100 \sum_{j=0}^{J} \delta_j \log 1.01 \simeq \sum_{j=0}^{J} \delta_j$$

since $\log 1.01 \simeq 0.00995 \simeq 0.01$. Thus the interim and total multipliers in a double log model may be interpreted as giving percentage increases in the level of y when x changes by 1 per cent.

7.3. Estimation of Transfer Function Models with Independent Disturbances

This section examines the way in which ML estimation of a transfer function model may be carried out when the disturbances are normally distributed white noise. Attention is focused on the geometric distributed lag

$$y_t = \beta \sum_{j=0}^{\infty} \alpha^j x_{t-j} + \epsilon_t, \qquad t = 1, \ldots, T \qquad (3.1)$$

with $\epsilon_t \sim NID(0, \sigma^2)$. Although this is a very simple model, it embodies all the important features present in more general formulations.

The first sub-section considers an instrumental variable estimator of the parameters in the geometric distributed lag. Although it is not efficient, the IV estimator is consistent and easy to compute. It therefore provides a suitable initial estimate for a two-step or iterative ML procedure. The ML estimator is then developed and its properties examined. The section closes by showing how the results may be extended to more general models, including those with several explanatory variables.

IV Estimation

The transformed equation for the geometric distributed lag model is (1.5). However, as indicated in Section 1, the OLS estimators of both α and β will be inconsistent, because the disturbance term, v_t, is correlated with y_{t-1}. This may be shown formally by noting that

$$\text{plim } T^{-1} \Sigma \, y_{t-1} v_t = \text{plim } T^{-1} \Sigma \, y_{t-1}(\epsilon_t - \alpha \epsilon_{t-1})$$

$$= 0 - \alpha \text{ plim } T^{-1} \Sigma \, (\alpha y_{t-2} + \beta x_{t-1} + \epsilon_{t-1}) \, \epsilon_{t-1}$$

$$= -\alpha \sigma^2 \qquad (3.2)$$

The parameters may be estimated consistently by constructing an IV estimator in which x_{t-1} is used as an instrument for y_{t-1}. In terms of the notation of Section 2.11, $z_t = (y_{t-1}, x_t)'$ and $w_t = (x_{t-1}, x_t)'$ and so the estimator may be written as

$$\begin{bmatrix} \tilde{a} \\ \tilde{b} \end{bmatrix} = (\Sigma w_t z_t')^{-1} \, \Sigma w_t y_t$$

$$= \begin{bmatrix} \Sigma x_{t-1} y_{t-1} & \Sigma x_{t-1} x_t \\ \Sigma x_t y_{t-1} & \Sigma x_t^2 \end{bmatrix}^{-1} \begin{bmatrix} \Sigma x_{t-1} y_t \\ \Sigma x_t y_t \end{bmatrix} \qquad (3.3)$$

Since x is exogenous, x_{t-1} is, by definition, uncorrelated with v_t since it is independent of both ϵ_t and ϵ_{t-1}. Furthermore, it is not necessary to place particularly restrictive conditions on x in order to ensure that plim $T^{-1} \Sigma w_t z_t'$ is positive definite, and so the conditions necessary for consistency are easily satisfied.

The structure of the model ensures that x_{t-1} will show a reasonably high degree of correlation with y_{t-1}. The actual correlation depends on a number of factors including the value of α and the nature of the process generating x_t. However, the IV estimator will not, in general, be asymptotically efficient. Furthermore, even though it is consistent, it is quite conceivable that its small sample performance will be poorer than that of OLS. In fact the Monte Carlo results reported in the Appendix to Dhrymes (1971) indicate that in small samples OLS is 'a remarkably good estimator' when α is large, say around 0.9, and the x_t sequence exhibits strong positive autocorrelation. This point should be borne in mind in constructing initial estimates for an ML procedure.

Maximum Likelihood Estimation

Maximising the likelihood function of (3.1) is equivalent to minimising the sum of squares function

$$S(\alpha, \beta) = \sum_{t=1}^{T} \left(y_t - \beta \sum_{j=0}^{\infty} \alpha^j x_{t-j} \right)^2 \tag{3.4}$$

However, this poses an immediate problem, since the right hand side of (3.4) contains an infinite number of explanatory variables. Furthermore, $x_0, x_{-1}, x_{-2}, \ldots$, are, in any case, assumed to be unobservable.

One approach to the problem is to decompose the infinite lag on x into two parts, one observable and the other unknown. Equation (3.1) then becomes

$$y_t = \beta \sum_{t=0}^{t-1} \alpha^j x_{t-j} + \alpha^t \left\{ \beta \sum_{j=0}^{\infty} \alpha^j x_{-j} \right\} + \epsilon_t$$

$$= \beta x_t^* + \alpha^t \xi + \epsilon_t, \qquad t = 1, \ldots, T \tag{3.5}$$

The term $\xi = E(y_0)$ represents the unobservable component in the model. There are two ways of dealing with it, the first of which is simply to set $\xi = 0$. The estimation problem then reduces to an exercise in non-linear least squares, minimising

$$S(\alpha, \beta) = \sum_{j=1}^{T} (y_t - \beta x_t^*)^2 \tag{3.6}$$

with respect to α and β. There are a number of ways of going about this, but since (3.6) is linear in β for a given value of α, carrying out a direct search over the interval $0 \leq \alpha \leq 1$ is one possibility. Note that x_t^* may be built up recursively from the relationship

$$x_t^* = \alpha x_{t-1}^* + x_t, \qquad t = 1, \ldots, T, \tag{3.7}$$

with $x_0^* = 0$.

The second way of dealing with ξ is to treat it as an unknown parameter which is to be estimated along with α and β. As before, the likelihood function may be concentrated with respect to α and a grid search carried out. In other words, for a given value of α, y_t is regressed on x_t^* and α^t to yield a residual sum of squares which forms the criterion function to be minimised.

Both methods of handling the unobservable component in (3.5) have disadvantages. Although the second solution makes full use of all the available information, adding extra parameters to a model is not usually regarded as desirable. On the other hand setting $\xi = 0$ may cause considerable distortion, particularly if x_t is non-stationary.

A third solution, which is, to some extent, a compromise between the first two, is to write the model as

$$y_t = \beta \sum_{j=0}^{t-2} \alpha^j x_{t-j} + \alpha^{t-1}\left(\beta \sum_{j=0}^{\infty} \alpha^j x_{1-j}\right) + \epsilon_t$$

$$= \beta x_t^\dagger + \alpha^{t-1}\xi_1 + \epsilon_t, \qquad t = 2, \ldots, T \qquad (3.8)$$

Apart from x_1, all the lagged values of x_t in ξ_1 are unobservable. However, because $\xi_1 = E(y_1)$, it seems reasonable to replace it by y_1. The parameters in the model may then be estimated by non-linear least squares in much the same way as before. If ϵ_1 were fixed and equal to zero, this procedure would be identical to full ML.

The construction of the likelihood function may be approached from a completely different direction if the transformed model, (1.5), is taken as the starting point. A set of prediction errors may be computed from the recursion,

$$\epsilon_t = y_t - \alpha y_{t-1} - \beta x_t + \alpha \epsilon_{t-1}, \qquad t = 2, \ldots, T \qquad (3.9)$$

Taking y_1 to be fixed provides a theoretical justification for setting $\epsilon_1 = 0$ and, from the prediction error decomposition of Section 3.5, maximising the likelihood function is equivalent to minimising the sum of squares function,

$$S(\alpha,\beta) = \sum_{t=2}^{T} \epsilon_t^2 \qquad (3.10)$$

The recursion in (3.9) is similar to the recursion used to construct the residual function in an ARMA time series model. It was argued in Section 3.5 that setting pre-sample values of y_t equal to zero is not a good way of approximating the likelihood function. This consideration is even more important in the present context because of the presence of the explanatory variable. Thus only $T - 1$ residuals are computed in (3.9), thereby avoiding the need to set any pre-sample values equal to zero. However, if we were prepared to set y_0 (and ϵ_0) equal to zero a full set of T residuals could be obtained. On substituting repeatedly for lagged values of ϵ_t, it can be seen that the T residuals obtained in this way are identical to the T residuals obtained from (3.5) with $\xi = 0$. Similarly, replacing ξ_1 by y_1 in (3.8) leads to a set of $T - 1$ residuals which are identical to the residuals obtained from (3.9). This correspondence is not surprising, since the assumption that ϵ_1 is fixed and equal to zero is implicit in both (3.9) and (3.8).

Unless full ML estimation is contemplated, therefore, the most satisfactory approach is by (3.8) or (3.9). Although these will yield identical sum of squares functions, the recursive equation (3.9) is more convenient since it implicitly includes the recursion for $x_t^{\dagger}$; cf. (3.7). Furthermore the derivatives of ϵ_t may also be computed recursively. Differentiating (3.9) with respect to α and β yields

$$\frac{\partial \epsilon_t}{\partial \alpha} = -y_{t-1} + \epsilon_{t-1} + \alpha \frac{\partial \epsilon_{t-1}}{\partial \alpha}, \qquad t = 2, \ldots, T \qquad (3.11)$$

and

$$\frac{\partial \epsilon_t}{\partial \beta} = -x_t + \alpha \frac{\partial \epsilon_{t-1}}{\partial \beta}, \qquad t = 2, \ldots, T \qquad (3.12)$$

Both derivatives are equal to zero for $t = 1$ since $\epsilon_1 = 0$. The ease with which analytic derivatives may be obtained suggests that they be exploited in a Gauss–Newton optimisation procedure.

Asymptotic Properties of the ML Estimator

The three ML estimators discussed above differ in the assumptions made about starting values. However, these differences are unimportant in large samples, and all three procedures yield estimators with the same asymptotic distribution. On examining (3.8) it will be apparent that we are essentially dealing with a classical regression model, since $x_t^{\dagger}$ is fixed and the disturbances are white noise. The asymptotic efficiency of the ML estimator therefore follows immediately from standard results.

One minor problem concerns the regularity conditions which must be imposed on x_t in order that the ML estimators of α and β have a well defined asymptotic distribution. To see what this entails, consider the definition of the asymptotic information matrix in (3.5.25). On examining (3.11) and (3.12), it will be seen that this involves the evaluation of terms containing y_t and ϵ_t as well as x_t. However, (3.12) may be written as

$$(1 - \alpha L) \frac{\partial \epsilon_t}{\partial \beta} = -x_t, \qquad t = 2, \ldots, T \qquad (3.13)$$

and relaxing the assumption that y_1 is fixed, yields

$$z_{2t} = - \frac{\partial \epsilon_t}{\partial \beta} = \frac{x_t}{1 - \alpha L} = \sum_{j=0}^{\infty} \alpha^j x_{t-j} \qquad (3.14)$$

Similarly,

$$z_{1t} = - \frac{\partial \epsilon_t}{\partial \alpha} = \frac{-(y_{t-1} - \epsilon_{t-1})}{1 - \alpha L} = \frac{-\beta \sum_{j=0}^{\infty} \alpha^j x_{t-j-1}}{1 - \alpha L}$$

$$= - \beta \sum_{j=0}^{\infty} (j + 1) \alpha^j x_{t-j-1} \qquad (3.15)$$

These formulae make it possible to write down an expression for the asymptotic information matrix which involves only x_t, α and β. Any conditions which must be imposed on x_t may therefore be obtained explicitly.

An Efficient Two-Step Estimator

An asymptotically efficient two-step estimator of α and β may be based on a single iteration of the Gauss–Newton scheme. The first step is to estimate α and β consistently, say by the method of instrumental variables. These estimates are then used to compute the residual function, ϵ_t, and its derivatives, using (3.9), (3.11) and (3.12) respectively. Regressing ϵ_t on its derivatives and subtracting the resulting coefficients from the initial estimates then yields the two-step estimator.

Although consistent initial estimates of α and β are necessary for the two-step estimator to be asymptotically efficient, there is a case for using OLS rather than instrumental variables at the first stage. This arises because OLS appears to have rather better small sample properties than the IV estimator, even though it is inconsistent. However, it must be stressed that if OLS were used as the basis for a two-step procedure, the resulting estimator would not, in general, be asymptotically efficient. A thorough Monte Carlo study is therefore needed before such an estimator can be recommended.

Estimation of a General Rational Lag Structure

The principles of estimation established for the geometric lag extend quite naturally to the more general model

$$y_t = \frac{B(L)}{A(L)} x_t + \epsilon_t, \qquad t = 1, \ldots, T \qquad (3.16)$$

with $\epsilon_t \sim NID(0, \sigma^2)$. Multiplying through by $A(L)$ gives

$$A(L)y_t = B(L)x_t + A(L)\epsilon_t \tag{3.17}$$

and so the prediction errors may be evaluated from the recursion,

$$\epsilon_t = y_t - \alpha_1 y_{t-1} - \cdots - \alpha_r y_{t-r} - \beta_0 x_t - \cdots - \beta_s x_{t-s}$$
$$+ \alpha_1 \epsilon_{t-1} + \ldots + \alpha_r \epsilon_{t-r}, \qquad t = t^* + 1, \ldots, T \tag{3.18}$$

where $t^* = \max(s, r)$ and $\epsilon_t = 0$ for $t = t^* + 1 - r, \ldots, t^*$. The sum of squares function is then minimised with respect to $\alpha_1, \ldots, \alpha_r, \beta_0, \ldots, \beta_s$, with or without the use of analytic derivatives. Although t^* residuals are 'lost' by starting the recursion at $t = t^* + 1$, no distortion is introduced by setting pre-sample values of y_t or x_t equal to zero.

A two-step estimation procedure could be based on the Gauss–Newton scheme as before. Consistent estimators of the parameters may be obtained by an IV estimator which uses $x_t, x_{t-1}, \ldots, x_{t-r-s}$ as the set of instruments.

Several Explanatory Variables*

The discussion so far has been restricted to the case of a single regressor. However, there is no difficulty in extending the model to include additional variables which are not dynamic. Adding a second explanatory variable to (3.1) yields

$$y_t = \beta_1 \sum_{j=0}^{\infty} \alpha^j x_{1,t-j} + \beta_2 x_{2t} + \epsilon_t \tag{3.19}$$

The transformed equation is

$$y_t = \alpha y_{t-1} + \beta_1 x_{1t} + \beta_2 x_{2t} - \alpha\beta_2 x_{2,t-1} + \epsilon_t - \alpha\epsilon_{t-1},$$
$$t = 2, \ldots, T \tag{3.20}$$

and a recursive expression for the residuals, together with corresponding formulae for the derivatives may be built up in the same way as before.

The estimation problem becomes more complex if there is a dynamic relationship between x_2 and y. Suppose that the lag structure for x_2 is again of the Koyck form, so that (3.19) becomes

$$y_t = \beta_1 \sum_{j=0}^{\infty} \alpha_1^j x_{1,t-j} + \beta_2 \sum_{j=0}^{\infty} \alpha_2^j x_{2,t-j} + \epsilon_t$$
$$= \frac{\beta_1 x_{1t}}{1 - \alpha_1 L} + \frac{\beta_2 x_{2t}}{1 - \alpha_2 L} + \epsilon_t \tag{3.21}$$

The residuals may be computed from the recursion

$$\epsilon_t = y_t - (\alpha_1 + \alpha_2) y_{t-1} + \alpha_1 \alpha_2 y_{t-2} - \beta_1 x_{1t} + \alpha_2 \beta_1 x_{1,t-1}$$
$$- \beta_2 x_{2t} + \alpha_1 \beta_2 x_{2,t-1} + (\alpha_1 + \alpha_2) \epsilon_{t-1} - \alpha_1 \alpha_2 \epsilon_{t-2},$$
$$t = 3, \ldots, T \tag{3.22}$$

This is started at $t = 3$ in order to avoid setting any pre-sample values of y_t equal to zero. For a more general model,

$$y_t = \frac{B_1(L)}{A_1(L)} x_{1t} + \frac{B_2(L)}{A_2(L)} x_{2t} + \epsilon_t \tag{3.23}$$

such an approach implies the loss of t^* residuals where $t^* = \max(s_1 + r_2, s_2 + r_1, r_1 + r_2)$. However, this is preferable to the alternative strategy of setting pre-sample values of the observations equal to zero. Nevertheless, this second approach is the one adopted by Box and Jenkins (1976, p. 389). They write (3.21) in the form

$$y_t = \beta_1 x_{1t}^* + \beta_2 x_{2t}^* + \epsilon_t \tag{3.24}$$

and suggest that x_{1t}^* and x_{2t}^* be computed from the recursion

$$x_{it}^* = \alpha_i x_{i,t-1}^* + x_{it}, \qquad t = 1,\ldots,T \tag{3.25}$$

with $x_{i,0}^* = 0$ for $i = 1, 2$; cf. (3.7). For a single explanatory variable, this is the estimation procedure in which ξ of expression (3.5) is set equal to zero.

7.4. Serial Correlation

In the general transfer function model, (1.12), the disturbance term is assumed to be generated by an ARMA(p, q) process. The $p + q$ parameters of this process must therefore be estimated along with the parameters of the rational distributed lag. It is shown below how the method of maximum likelihood may be applied to a geometric distributed lag with AR(1) disturbances. Estimation of (1.12) raises no new issues of principle. Testing is considered in the final sub-section.

Estimation

Consider (1.4) with disturbances generated by an AR(1) process (6.1.2), i.e.

$$y_t = \frac{\beta x_t}{1 - \alpha L} + \frac{\epsilon_t}{1 - \phi L} \tag{4.1}$$

Multiplying by $(1 - \alpha L)(1 - \phi L)$ gives the transformed equation, and this leads to the following recursion for the residuals:

$$\epsilon_t = y_t - (\alpha + \phi) y_{t-1} + \alpha\phi y_{t-2} - \beta x_t + \beta\phi x_{t-1} + \alpha\epsilon_{t-1},$$
$$t = 3,\ldots,T \tag{4.2}$$

with $\epsilon_2 = 0$. Recursive expressions for the analytic derivatives are also available. As before, these may be exploited in a Gauss–Newton procedure, although for more complicated models there is an argument for evaluating the derivatives numerically if programming time is at a premium.

Minimising the residual sum of squares function is equivalent to maximising the likelihood function when the disturbances are normally distributed and y_1 and y_2 are fixed. However, this last assumption is relatively unimportant, and minimising the sum of squares is a reasonable approximation to ML. An explicit expression for the information matrix may be derived in much the same way as when the disturbances are independent. However, the important point to note is that the ML estimator of ϕ is independent of the ML estimators of α and β in large samples. In other words the information matrix has the same block diagonal form exhibited by the information matrix of a static regression model with AR(1) disturbances; cf. (6.1.12). One implication of this is that the lag structure will be estimated consistently even if the disturbance term is misspecified.

Test Procedures

The block diagonality of the information matrix in a transfer function model means that all the test procedures discussed in the previous chapter can be applied in large samples. Thus a large sample test against an AR(1), or MA(1), disturbance term may be based on the Durbin–Watson d-statistic. If an ARMA disturbance term has been fitted to the model, the Box–Pierce Q-statistic may be used. This will have a χ^2 distribution with $P - p - q$ degrees of freedom under the null hypothesis, provided that P is sufficiently large.

7.5. Model Selection

Finding efficient estimates of the parameters in a transfer function model (1.12) is primarily a matter of computation. However, actually arriving at a suitable specification is a far more difficult task, requiring a good deal of skill and judgement. Box and Jenkins (1976, Ch. 11) approach the problem in the same spirit as in univariate time series model building, pursuing the overall strategy of identification, estimation and diagnostic checking. In the absence of any *a priori* knowledge of the system, this is a sensible strategy, although there are a number of different ways of handling the most difficult aspect of the problem, which is identification.

The identification procedure consists of three main stages. The first is to obtain some idea of the shape of the lag structure. This entails computing rough estimates of a finite number of the lag coefficients, $\delta_0, \delta_1, \delta_2, \ldots, \delta_m$. Given these estimates, the second stage is to find a suitable approximation to the lag polynomial, $D(L)$, in terms of the ratio, $B(L)/A(L)$. This means assigning numbers to r and s, the orders of the polynomials in the rational lag structure, as well as determining the extent of any delay, v. Finally, a suitable ARMA(p, q) process must be found for the disturbance term.

Estimates of the parameters in $A(L)$ and $B(L)$ may be derived from the lag coefficients, and these estimates may be used as starting values in an ML algorithm. An ARMA(p, q) model may then be identified from the residual autocorrelations as discussed in Section 1.5. Having chosen suitable values of r, s, v, p and q, the full model is estimated by ML. The residuals resulting from this procedure provide the basis for diagnostic checking of the model. As indicated in Section 4, the main test statistic is the Box–Pierce Q-statistic, although this could be supplemented by tests based on the Lagrange multiplier principle and by graphical procedures.

In univariate modelling it is important to consider the possibility of common factors in the ARMA polynomials $\phi(L)$ and $\theta(L)$. The same question arises in a transfer function model, but with respect to the rational lag polynomials, $A(L)$ and $B(L)$, as well as the ARMA polynomials in the disturbance term. However, it was demonstrated in Section 3.6 that one aspect of common factors, or near common factors, is the large standard errors associated with the estimates. The implications of this point are summarised by Box and Jenkins (1976, p. 387) as follows: 'In practice we shall be dealing with estimated coefficients which may be subject to rather large errors, so that only approximate factorization can be expected, and considerable imagination may need to be exerted to spot a possible factorization.' Another pertinent point concerns the possible instability of ML algorithms. Difficulties in convergence may well be experienced in these circumstances, thereby giving an early indication of an over-parameterised model.

Determining the Shape of the Lag Structure*

The first stage in the identification procedure is to obtain rough estimates of the lag coefficients δ_0, δ_1,...,δ_m. The *direct* approach is to fix the maximum lag length, m, at a suitable high value and to regress y_t on x_t, x_{t-1},...,x_{t-m}. The main difficulty with this procedure is in determining a suitable value for m. The sequence of x_t's will typically be slowly changing, and so setting m too high could result in very imprecise estimates. On the other hand, including too few lagged values of x_t could give a totally false impression of the shape of the lag distribution. Some experimentation with different values of m will therefore be necessary.

It is possible to circumvent the need to run several regressions with different lag lengths by *pre-whitening* the explanatory variable. Suppose x_t can be modelled by an ARIMA process,

$$\varphi_x(L)\, x_t = \theta_x(L)\xi_t \tag{5.1}$$

where ξ_t is white noise and $\varphi_x(L) = \Delta^d\phi_x(L)$. Applying the transformation $\varphi_x(L)/\theta_x(L)$ to both sides of (1.8) gives

$$y_t^* = D(L)x_t^* + u_t^* \qquad (5.2)$$

where $y_t^* = \theta_x^{-1}(L)\varphi_x(L)y_t$, $u_t^* = \theta_x^{-1}(L)\varphi_x(L)u_t$ and $x_t^* = \theta_x^{-1}(L)\varphi_x(L)x_t$. The advantage of working with (5.2) as opposed to (1.8) is that when y_t^* is regressed on $x_t^*,\ldots,x_{t-m}^*$, the cross-product matrix of the explanatory variables is approximately diagonal. Therefore

$$d_j^* \simeq \sum_{t=m+1}^{T} (x_{t-j}^* - \bar{x}^*)(y_t^* - \bar{y}^*) \Big/ \sum_{t=m+1}^{T} (x_{t-j}^* - \bar{x}^*)^2,$$

$$j = 0,\ldots,m \qquad (5.3)$$

No matrix inversions are required and the coefficients remain the same if m is increased. In the time series literature, d_j^* is normally expressed as the ratio of the cross-covariance between x_t^* and y_t^* at lag j to the variance of x_t^*.

Although pre-whitening has some computational attractions it suffers from the disadvantage that x_t must be modelled as an ARIMA process. Furthermore, there are no statistical reasons for preferring (5.2) to (1.8). If u_t is white noise, OLS applied to (1.8) will, in the absence of any restrictions on $D(L)$, yield the BLUE of δ. On the other hand, (5.3) will be inefficient. Only if x_t and u_t are generated by *identical* ARIMA processes will u_t^* be white noise. Applying OLS to the transformed model, (5.2), is then equivalent to computing a GLS estimator for (1.8).

Example   If x_t follows an AR(1) process with parameter ϕ_x, the pre-whitening transformation is $x_t^* = x_t - \phi_x x_{t-1}$. Applying the same transformation to y_t yields a disturbance term of the form

$$u_t^* = u_t - \phi_x u_{t-1}$$

If $u_t \sim NID(0, \sigma^2)$, u_t^* will follow an MA(1) process. Only if u_t is an AR(1) process with $\phi = \phi_x$ will (5.3) be efficient.

When the model contains more than one explanatory variable, pre-whitening is no longer a viable alternative to the direct approach. The only other possibility is to employ a spectral estimator. This has a good deal to recommend it, but a full discussion of the technique is beyond the scope of this book.

Identification of a Rational Lag Structure*

Once the shape of the lag coefficients has been determined, suitable rational lag structures may be considered. As an example, suppose that the estimated coefficients take the values shown in figure 7.3.

The first point to note is that both $\hat{\delta}_0$ and $\hat{\delta}_1$, are very close to zero. This suggests that there is a delay of two time periods, i.e. $\nu = 2$. The next problem is to find polynomials $A(L)$ and $B(L)$ such that the pattern exhibited by the

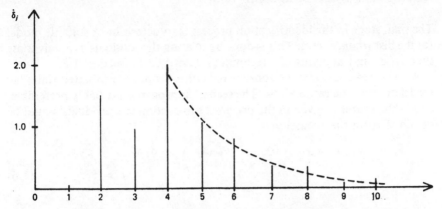

Figure 7.3 Estimated Lag Coefficients for Rational Lag Structure in (7.5.4)

estimated lag coefficients is captured by a relatively small number of parameters. On examining figure 7.3 it will be observed that $\hat{\delta}_2$, $\hat{\delta}_3$ and $\hat{\delta}_4$ appear to follow no set pattern, but that from $\hat{\delta}_4$ onwards there is the suggestion of an exponential decline. It will be recalled that exponential decline is a characteristic of the geometric distributed lag, (1.4), and so setting $r = 1$ would seem to be an appropriate course of action. The irregular behaviour of the first three coefficients in the lag distribution may be accommodated by setting $s = 3$.

These results suggest that the rational lag structure

$$\frac{B(L)L^2}{A(L)} = \frac{\beta_0 L^2 + \beta_1 L^3 + \beta_2 L^4}{1 - \alpha L} \tag{5.4}$$

should provide a suitable approximation to $D(L)$. Preliminary estimates of the parameters in $A(L)$ and $B(L)$ may be obtained by equating coefficients of powers of L in the expression

$$(1 - \alpha L)D(L) = \beta_0 L^2 + \beta_1 L^3 + \beta_2 L^4$$

This yields

$$\delta_2 = \alpha\delta_1 + \beta_0$$
$$\delta_3 = \alpha\delta_2 + \beta_1$$
$$\delta_4 = \alpha\delta_3 + \beta_2$$
$$\delta_j = \alpha\delta_{j-1}, \qquad j \geq 5 \tag{5.5}$$

The parameter α may be estimated by

$$\hat{\alpha} = \hat{\delta}_5/\hat{\delta}_4 = 1.2/2 = 0.6$$

Substituting estimated values for α, δ_2, δ_3 and δ_4, and setting $\delta_1 = 0$ then gives

$$\hat{\beta}_0 = \hat{\delta}_2 = 1.5$$
$$\hat{\beta}_1 = \hat{\delta}_3 - \hat{\alpha}\hat{\delta}_2 = 1.0 - 0.6(1.5) = 0.1$$
$$\hat{\beta}_2 = \hat{\delta}_4 - \hat{\alpha}\hat{\delta}_3 = 2.0 - 0.6(0.1) = 1.94$$

Identification of the Disturbance Term*

The final stage in the identification process is to determine a suitable model
for the disturbance term. This is done by treating the residuals as a univariate
time series and applying the techniques described in Section 1.5.

A set of residuals may be constructed either from the estimated finite lag
model or from the rational lag. The second approach is probably preferable,
and in the example given in the previous sub-section the residuals would be
obtained from the recursion,

$$\hat{u}_t = \hat{\alpha}\hat{u}_{t-1} + y_t - \hat{\alpha}y_{t-1} - \hat{\beta}_0 x_{t-2} - \hat{\beta}_1 x_{t-3} - \hat{\beta}_2 x_{t-4},$$

$$t = 5,\ldots,T \quad (5.6)$$

7.6. Trend and Seasonality

Dynamic models may contain trend and seasonal components. This section
discusses how such components may be interpreted and how they relate to
certain statistical techniques.

Differencing and Stochastic Trends

Variables are often differenced before a transfer function model is
constructed. This is done so that the two series can be regarded as being jointly
stationary, and a suitable model identified on the basis of the cross-correlation
function. However, if the true model is in terms of levels, differencing will
introduce an additional MA term into the disturbance. For example, taking
first differences in the model

$$y_t = \beta x_t + \epsilon_t, \qquad t = 1,\ldots,T \tag{6.1}$$

gives

$$\Delta y_t = \beta \Delta x_t + v_t, \qquad t = 2,\ldots,T \tag{6.2}$$

where v_t is the non-invertible MA(1) process,

$$v_t = \epsilon_t - \epsilon_{t-1}, \qquad t = 2,\ldots,T \tag{6.3}$$

This strict non-invertibility is a characteristic feature of 'over-differencing'.

The issue of differencing is thus subject to a good deal of confusion. There
are circumstances in which it is appropriate to model a relationship between
variables in differences, but this is not done because the variables in question
are non-stationary. Rather the issue is whether the disturbance term in the
levels model is non-stationary. As a rule the aim of econometric modelling
is to find a relationship between levels of the variables, in other words to have

a stationary disturbance term. Unfortunately this is not always possible, since sometimes variables which might enter into a model are difficult to measure. If these omitted variables are non-stationary, then so is the disturbance term. The structural time series modelling framework outlined in Section 1.5 offers a direct interpretation of this point, and can be of considerable help in model specification. For example, consider the following transfer function model for sales[1] constructed by Box and Jenkins (1976, pp. 409-412)

$$\Delta y_t = 0.035 + \frac{4.82\Delta x_{t-3}}{1 - 0.72L} + (1 - 0.54L)\epsilon_t \tag{6.4}$$

where x_t is an explanatory variable. This model can be regarded as the reduced form of the structural time series model[2]

$$y_t = \mu_t + \{4.82/(1 - 0.72L)\} x_{t-3} + \epsilon_t \tag{6.5a}$$

$$\mu_t = \mu_{t-1} + 0.035 + \eta_t \tag{6.5b}$$

where $\text{Var}(\eta_t)/\text{Var}(\epsilon_t) = (1 + \theta)^2/\theta = (1 - 0.54)^2/0.54 = 0.392$; see the discussion surrounding (1.5.33). The interpretation of (6.5) is that the explanatory variable is only able to explain some of the movements in the level of sales and so a *stochastic trend* component, μ_t, is introduced in order to account for the remaining movements. An example of the direct modelling of a stochastic trend in econometrics can be found in Harvey *et al.* (1986). It should be noted that although a structural model with a stochastic trend is consistent with a model in differences, state space methods allow it to be handled directly in levels.

Seasonality

A deterministic seasonal component may be incorporated into a transfer function model by introducing a set of dummy variables. The model takes the form

$$y_t = A^{-1}(L)B(L)x_t + \sum_{i=1}^{s} \gamma_i z_{it} + u_t \tag{6.6}$$

where the z_{it}'s and γ_i's are the seasonal dummies and their respective coefficients, and s is the number of 'seasons'. A model of this kind poses no new problems as regards estimation and specification. Note, however, that if a constant term is included in the model, then only $s - 1$ dummy variables are needed or the z_{it}'s must be defined in such a way that the seasonal effects sum to zero over a year.

In some situations, the seasonal pattern may change over time. This can be handled within the framework of structural time series models by letting the

[1,2]In writing the models in this way, the estimated parameters are being treated as though they were known.

seasonal coefficients be stochastic. The development follows along similar lines to the stochastic trend; see Harvey (1989). The reduced form of a model with stochastic trend and seasonality will typically involve variables which have been subject to seasonal differencing, that is $\Delta_s y_t = y_t - y_{t-s}$.

Seasonal Adjustment

Most seasonal adjustment procedures yield a series of observations which can be approximated by a weighted average of the original observations. If the superscript (a) denotes an adjusted series,

$$y_t^a = \sum_{j=-m}^{n} w_j y_{t-j} \tag{6.7}$$

where the w_j's are weights; see *TSM* (Ch. 3). A transformation of this kind is known as a moving average filter, and the filter itself may be expressed as a polynomial in the lag operator by writing

$$S(L) = \sum_{j=-m}^{n} w_j L^j \tag{6.8}$$

Suppose that two time series, y_t and x_t, are subject to seasonal adjustment. The filters employed need not be the same and so

$$y_t^a = S_y(L) y_t \quad \text{and} \quad x_t^a = S_x(L)x_t \tag{6.9}$$

If the relationship between the unadjusted variables is a dynamic model of the form (3.16), substituting from (6.9) implies the following model for the adjusted variables:

$$y_t^a = S_x^{-1}(L)S_y(L)D(L) x_t^a + S_y(L) u_t \tag{6.10}$$

There are two points to note about (6.10). The first is that by subjecting the variables to different adjustment procedures, the systematic dynamics are altered. The lag function becomes $S_y(L)D(L)/S_x(L)$, and in general this will be two-sided. It may therefore appear that y_t^a depends on future as well as well as past values of x_t^a. When the model is static, the effect of different seasonal filters is to introduce a spurious dynamic element into the relationship.

If the variables are adjusted in the same way, i.e. $S_y(L) = S_x(L)$, the lag structure is preserved. However, a second feature of (6.10), namely the change in the disturbance term, remains. If u_t is white noise, $S_y(L)u_t$ will be autocorrelated. Least squares will no longer be efficient, and it becomes necessary to make some allowance for serial correlation in the estimation procedure.

7.7. Prediction and Forecasting

Optimal predictions of future values of y_t in a transfer function model may be computed recursively. The required expression is obtained by multiplying (1.12) by $A(L)\phi(L)$ to yield

$$\phi(L)A(L)y_t = \phi(L)B(L)x_{t-v} + A(L)\theta(L)\epsilon_t \tag{7.1}$$

and rearranging so that only y_t appears on the left-hand side.

Example 1 For the geometric distributed lag, (3.1),

$$\tilde{y}_{t+l\,|\,T} = \alpha\,\tilde{y}_{T+l-1\,|\,T} + \beta x_{T+l} + \tilde{\epsilon}_{T+l\,|\,T} - \alpha\,\tilde{\epsilon}_{T+l-1\,|\,T},$$
$$l = 1, 2, \ldots, \tag{7.2}$$

where $\tilde{y}_{T+l\,|\,T}$ and $\tilde{\epsilon}_{T+l\,|\,T}$ are defined in (6.7.2).

There is no problem in extending these results to handle models cast in differenced form. If the model is

$$\Delta^d y_t = \frac{B(L)}{A(L)} \Delta^d x_{t-v} + \frac{\theta(L)}{\phi(L)} \epsilon_t \tag{7.3}$$

expression (7.1) is modified to

$$\phi(L)A(L)\,\Delta^d y_t = \phi(L)B(L)\,\Delta^d x_{t-v} + A(L)\theta(L)\epsilon_t \tag{7.4}$$

Example 2 If y_t and x_t in (3.1) are replaced by Δy_t and Δx_t, predictions are computed from the recursion

$$\tilde{y}_{T+l\,|\,T} = (1 + \alpha)\tilde{y}_{T+l-1\,|\,T} - \alpha\,\tilde{y}_{T+l-2\,|\,T} + \beta x_{T+l} - \beta x_{T+l-1}$$
$$+ \tilde{\epsilon}_{T+l\,|\,T} - \alpha\,\tilde{\epsilon}_{T+l-1\,|\,T} \tag{7.5}$$

MSE of Predictions

Suppose that the following assumptions hold: (i) the parameters in $A(L)$, $B(L)$, $\phi(L)$ and $\theta(L)$ are known; and (ii) future values of x_t are known. The MSE of $\tilde{y}_{T+l\,|\,T}$ may then be obtained by a straightforward extension of the result given in (6.7.3). If differences have been taken, ψ_j is the jth power of L in the polynomial

$$\Psi(L) = \theta(L)/(\Delta^d \phi(L)) \tag{7.6}$$

Example 3 In example 2 above, $\Psi(L) = 1/(1 - L)$. Therefore,

$$\Psi(L) = L\Psi(L) + 1$$

and so

$$\psi_j = \psi_{j-1} + 1, \qquad j = 1, 2, \ldots$$

with $\psi_0 = 0$. Hence

$$\text{MSE}(\tilde{y}_{T+l|T}) = \sigma^2 l, \qquad l = 1, 2, \ldots, \tag{7.7}$$

Assumption (i) will not hold in practice. The parameters will be replaced by their ML estimates, while the disturbances are set equal to the residuals. However, the additional contribution to the MSE will be of $0(1/T)$.

MSE of Forecasts*

The assumption that future values of x_t are known will not usually be reasonable. Nevertheless, the evaluation of the MSE conditional on future x_t's is still very useful. The user of the model will often have a particular scenario in mind with regard to future values of the exogenous variables. The conditional MSE is then a relevant piece of information, since it enables the user to gauge the accuracy of the model's predictions given his particular view of the world.

On the other hand, in making unconditional predictions or *forecasts*, some account must be taken of the error in predicting future values of x_t. One way of predicting these values is to build an ARIMA model of the form

$$\phi_x(L)\Delta^d x_t = \theta_x(L)\zeta_t \tag{7.8}$$

where $\zeta_t \sim NID(0, \sigma_\zeta^2)$ and ζ_t and ϵ_t are independent. The MSE of $\tilde{y}_{T+l|T}$, the best predictor of y_{T+l} at time T, can be derived by first substituting from (7.8) into (7.3). This yields

$$y_t = \frac{B(L)\theta_x(L)L^v}{A(L)\phi_x(L)\Delta^d} \zeta_t + \frac{\theta(L)}{\phi(L)\Delta^d} \epsilon_t = K(L)\zeta_t + \Psi(L)\epsilon_t \tag{7.9}$$

and at time $t = T + l$,

$$y_{T+l} = \sum_{j=0}^{\infty} x_j \zeta_{T+l-j} + \sum_{j=0}^{\infty} \psi_j \epsilon_{T+l-j}, \qquad l = 1, 2, \ldots \tag{7.10}$$

where x_j is the coefficient of L^j in the polynomial $K(L)$. If both ϵ_t and ζ_t are assumed to be normally distributed, the minimum mean square estimator (MMSE) of y_{T+l} will be linear in the observations and, in view of the representation in (7.9), it will also be linear in the disturbances. It will therefore be of the form

$$\hat{y}_{T+l|T} = \sum_{j=0}^{\infty} x_{j+l}^* \zeta_{T-j} + \sum_{j=0}^{\infty} \psi_{j+l}^* \epsilon_{T-j} \tag{7.11}$$

where the x_j^* and ψ_j^* are the weights to be determined.

Subtracting (7.11) from (7.10), squaring and taking expectations gives

$$E\{(y_{T+l} - \hat{y}_{T+l|T})^2\} = \sigma_\zeta^2 \sum_{j=0}^{l-1} x_j^2 + \sigma^2 \sum_{j=0}^{l-1} \psi_j^2$$

$$+ \sigma_\zeta^2 \sum_{j=0}^{\infty} (x_{l+j} - x_{l+j}^*)^2$$

$$+ \sigma^2 \sum_{j=0}^{\infty} (\psi_{l+j} - \psi_{l+j}^*)^2 \qquad (7.12)$$

This expression is minimised by setting $x_{l+j}^* = x_{l+j}$ and $\psi_{l+j}^* = \psi_{l+j}$. The MMSE of y_{T+l} is therefore

$$\tilde{y}_{T+l|T} = \sum_{j=0}^{\infty} x_{l+j} \zeta_{T-j} + \sum_{j=0}^{\infty} \psi_{l+j} \epsilon_{T-j}, \qquad l = 1, 2, \dots \quad (7.13)$$

and this is identical to the predictor which is built up recursively by forecasting future values of x_t from (7.8) and substituting these forecasts in expressions like (7.2) and (7.5). The MSE of this predictor, conditional on the parameters in both (7.3) and (7.8), is given by

$$\text{MSE}(\tilde{y}_{T+l|T}) = \sigma_\zeta^2 \sum_{j=0}^{l-1} x_j^2 + \sigma^2 \sum_{j=0}^{l-1} \psi_j^2 \qquad (7.14)$$

where x_j is the coefficient of L^j in the polynomial $K(L)$.

Example 4 In the sales model, (6.4), constructed by Box and Jenkins, the exogenous variable, x, is a *leading indicator* since it is known with certainty three time periods in advance of y. The forecast function is

$$\tilde{y}_{T+l|T} = 1.72\tilde{y}_{T+l-1|T} - 0.72\tilde{y}_{T+l-2|T} + 0.0098$$

$$+ 4.82\hat{x}_{T+l-3|T} - 4.82\hat{x}_{T+l-4|T} + \tilde{\epsilon}_{T+l|T}$$

$$- 1.26\tilde{\epsilon}_{T+l-1|T} + 0.39\tilde{\epsilon}_{T+l-2|T}, \qquad l = 1, 2, \dots$$

$$(7.15)$$

However, for $l \le 3$, the values of $\hat{x}_t$ appearing in (7.15) are known with certainty and so the MSE is given by (6.7.3). The weights are obtained from (7.6) by equating coefficients in the expression

$$\Psi(L)(1 - L) = 1 - 0.54L$$

On expanding this becomes

$$\psi_0 + (\psi_1 - \psi_0)L + (\psi_2 - \psi_1)L^2 + \cdots = 1 - 0.54L$$

Hence $\psi_0 = 1$, while $\psi_1 - \psi_0 = -0.54$, implying that $\psi_1 = 0.46$. Thereafter $\psi_j = \psi_{j-1} = 0.46$, and so, for example,

$$\text{MSE}(\bar{y}_{T+3|T}) = \sigma^2(1 + 0.46^2 + 0.46^2) = 1.42\sigma^2$$

For making predictions beyond $l = 3$, forecasts of future values of x_t are needed. Box and Jenkins fit the model

$$\Delta x_t = (1 - 0.32L)\zeta_t$$

and so from (7.13),

$$K(L) = \frac{4.82(1 - 0.32L)L^3}{(1 - 0.72L)(1 - L)}$$

Therefore

$$(1 - 0.72L)(1 - L)K(L) = 4.82(1 - 0.32L)L^3$$

Equating coefficients in powers of L yields $x_3 = 4.82$, $x_4 = 6.75$ and so on.

Leading Indicators*

There are basically two reasons for constructing a dynamic regression model for the variable y_t. The first is to obtain an understanding of the behaviour of the system, and to relate this to the theory of the subject. The second is to obtain better forecasts.

If the goal of model building is forecasting, the exercise can only be judged successful if, by relating y to x, improved forecasts are obtained. The yardstick against which improvements are judged is the accuracy of forecasts derived from a univariate model for y. Such a model must be a serious contender, since if the bivariate model is of the form (7.3) and $\Delta^d x_t$ is modelled by an ARMA process, y_t must have an ARIMA representation. This follows because $\Delta^d y_t$ is the sum of two independent ARMA processes; cf. *TSM* (Ch. 2). The question of whether there is any gain in forecasting performance from constructing a bivariate model is therefore a pertinent one.

Nelson (1975) was the first to establish one of the basic results in this area. For a correctly specified model he was able to show that when x is forecast, the one-step ahead prediction error variance of y cannot exceed that which would result from forecasting y on the basis of its past history alone. This result may be generalised to forecasts l steps ahead. However, it does not answer the question of when the forecasts from the bivariate model are actually better. One obvious case is when some values of x are known in advance of observing y. This corresponds to the pure delay model, where v is positive.

When there is a pure delay in the model, x is said to be a leading indicator of y. However, Pierce (1975) provides a more general definition of this term. Let $\Delta(l)$ denote the reduction in the MSE of the forecast l periods ahead, when y is modelled in terms of present and past values of x. Then x is a *leading indicator* of y whenever $\Delta(l)$ is strictly positive. Pierce then proceeds to establish conditions under which x is a leading indicator in this sense. In other words, he establishes conditions under which there is a gain in forecasting accuracy from utilising the information contained in x. The pure delay model emerges only as a special case of a leading indicator.

The extent to which x is useful in predicting y is measured by the *predictive-R^2*. This is a scale free quantity defined by

$$R_\dagger^2 = \Delta(1)/\sigma_\dagger^2 \tag{7.16}$$

where $\sigma_\dagger^2$ is MSE of one-step ahead predictions in the univariate model for y. A positive value of $R_\dagger^2$ indicates that x is a leading indicator for y. However, if the transfer function model is misspecified, it is quite conceivable that $R_\dagger^2$ will be less than zero. In these circumstances, a 'naive' univariate model is actually giving better forecasts than a dynamic regression model. This is something which has often been observed in practice.

7.8. Polynomial Distributed Lags

An alternative approach to modelling a distributed lag is to approximate its structure by a polynomial. The lag is assumed to be finite, with a maximum lag length of m, and so the basic model is

$$y_t = \sum_{\tau=0}^{m} \delta_\tau x_{t-\tau} + u_t, \qquad t = m + 1, \ldots, T \tag{8.1}$$

Rather than attempting to estimate all $(m + 1)$ coefficients, it is assumed that they lie on a polynomial of degree $n < m$. If this supposition is valid, the systematic part of (8.1) will depend on only $n + 1$ parameters, and by imposing the appropriate structure, more efficient estimators of the lag coefficients will be obtained.

Let $P(\tau)$ be a polynomial of degree n which is a continuous function of τ. This depends on $n + 1$ coefficients, $\gamma_0, \ldots, \gamma_n$, and is defined by

$$P(\tau) = \sum_{i=0}^{n} \gamma_i \tau^i \tag{8.2}$$

Under the polynomial lag hypothesis, the lag coefficients in (8.1) are defined by

$$\delta_\tau = P(\tau) \tag{8.3}$$

for the integers $\tau = 0, 1, \ldots, m$. Note that $\delta_0 = P(0) = \gamma_0$.

A simple illustration should convey the flavour of the approach. Suppose that $P(\tau)$ is a second degree polynomial,

$$P(\tau) = 2 + 5\tau - \tau^2 \tag{8.4}$$

The maximum lag length is five, and the six lag coefficients in (8.1) are obtained by evaluating (8.4) at $\tau = 0, \ldots, 5$. The pattern of the coefficients is shown in figure 7.4. However, because the coefficients all lie on a second degree polynomial, the lag structure depends on only three parameters $\gamma_0 = 2$, $\gamma_1 = 5$ and $\gamma_2 = -1$.

Estimation

Expressions (8.2) and (8.3) imply that

$$\delta_\tau = \sum_{i=0}^{n} \gamma_i \tau^i, \qquad \tau = 0, \ldots, m \tag{8.5}$$

Substituting into (8.1) yields

$$y_t = \sum_{\tau=0}^{m} \left(\sum_{i=0}^{n} \gamma_i \tau^i \right) x_{t-\tau} + u_t$$

$$= \sum_{i=0}^{n} \gamma_i w_{it} + u_t, \qquad t = m+1, \ldots, T \tag{8.6}$$

where

$$w_{it} = \sum_{\tau=0}^{m} \tau^i x_{t-\tau}, \qquad i = 0, \ldots, n \tag{8.7}$$

Note that when τ is zero, τ^i is also zero for $i \neq 0$, but is unity for $i = 0$. If (8.1) obeys the classical assumptions, OLS applied to (8.6) will yield the BLUE of $\gamma = (\gamma_0, \ldots, \gamma_n)'$. An estimator of $\delta = (\delta_0, \ldots, \delta_m)'$ may then be constructed directly from (8.5). This estimator, denoted by d, is the BLUE of δ, a result which follows directly from the Gauss–Markov theorem.

The covariance matrix of d may be obtained most easily by writing the transformation (8.5) in matrix terms as

$$\delta = S\gamma \tag{8.8}$$

where S is an $(m+1) \times (n+1)$ matrix defined by $S = (s_0, \ldots, s_m)'$, where

$$s_0 = (1, 0, \ldots, 0)'$$

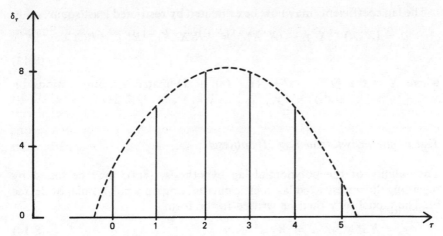

Figure 7.4   Lag Coefficients Based on Second Degree Polynomial (7.8.4)

and

$$s_\tau = (\tau^0, \tau^1, \ldots, \tau^n)', \qquad \tau = 1, \ldots, m \tag{8.9}$$

If W is the $(T - m + 1) \times (n + 1)$ matrix of transformed observations, (8.7), then

$$E[(d - \delta)(d - \delta)'] = \sigma^2 S(W'W)^{-1}S' \tag{8.10}$$

Thus if $u_t \sim NID(0, \sigma^2)$, d will have a multivariate normal distribution with a mean of δ and a covariance matrix, (8.10).

An alternative approach is obtained by recognising that constraining the m lag coefficients to lie on an nth degree polynomial is equivalent to imposing a set of $(m - n)$ linear restrictions on the model. These may be written

$$R\delta = 0 \tag{8.11}$$

where R is an $(m - n) \times (m + 1)$ matrix. Differencing a polynomial reduces its degree by one. The $(n + 1)$th difference of (8.5) is therefore zero and so

$$\Delta^{n+1}\delta_\tau = 0, \qquad \tau = n + 1, \ldots, m \tag{8.12}$$

Since $\Delta^{n+1} = (1 - L)^{n+1}$, each row of R consists of the coefficients of L in the difference polynomial $(1 - L)^{n+1}$. For a second degree polynomial such as (8.4), each row of R is equal to $(1, -3, 3, -1)$, and (8.12) becomes

$$\delta_\tau = 3\delta_{\tau-1} - 3\delta_{\tau-2} + \delta_{\tau-3}, \qquad \tau = n + 1, \ldots, m$$

Thus, taking the figures in (8.4), the coefficient at lag 5 is

$$\delta_5 = 3(6) - 3(8) + 1(8) = 2$$

This agrees with the direct calculation.

The lag coefficients may now be estimated by restricted least squares, i.e.

$$d = (X'X)^{-1}X'y - (X'X)^{-1}R' \{ R(X'X)^{-1}R' \}^{-1} R(X'X)^{-1}X'y$$

(8.13)

where X is the $(T - m + 1) \times (m + 1)$ matrix of observations on $x_t, \ldots, x_{t-m}$, and $y = (y_{m+1}, \ldots, y_T)'$; cf. (2.2.21).

Test of the Polynomial Lag Hypothesis

The validity of the polynomial lag hypothesis, (8.3), may be tested by regarding the unrestricted lag coefficients as lying on a polynomial of degree m. The model may then be written in the form

$$y = XS^*\gamma^* + u = W^*\gamma^* + u$$

(8.14)

where S^* is an $(m + 1) \times (m + 1)$ matrix defined by (8.8). This may be partitioned as $S^* = [S \colon S^\dagger]$ where S is the $(m + 1) \times (n + 1)$ matrix introduced earlier. In a similar way γ^* and W^* are partitioned as $\gamma^* = (\gamma', \gamma^{\dagger'})'$ and $W^* = [W \colon W^\dagger]$ respectively. Expression (8.14) may then be written as

$$y = XS\gamma + X^\dagger S^\dagger \gamma^\dagger + u = W\gamma + W^\dagger \gamma^\dagger + u$$

(8.15)

If $u_t \sim NID(0, \sigma^2)$, a subset F-test may be used to test the hypothesis $H_0 : \gamma^\dagger = 0$. This is obviously a test of the validity of a polynomial lag of degree n. However, in practice it is unnecessary to estimate the unrestricted model in the form (8.14). The residual sum of squares from regressing y on W^* is

$$
\begin{aligned}
e^{*\prime}e^* &= u' \{ I - W^*(W^{*\prime}W^*)^{-1}W^{*\prime} \} u \\
&= u' \{ I - XS^*(S^{*\prime}X'XS^*)^{-1}S^{*\prime}X' \} u \\
&= u' \{ I - X(X'X)^{-1}X' \} u
\end{aligned}
$$

(8.16)

Thus $e^{*\prime}e^*$ is identical to the residual sum of squares from regressing y on X, a result which is hardly surprising since taking the lag coefficients to lie on a polynomial of degree $(m + 1)$ imposes no restrictions on the original model. The subset F-test, (2.8.18), is therefore carried out by computing the residual sum of squares from the OLS regression of y on X and comparing this with the residual sum of squares from the polynomial distributed lag model. The resulting statistic has an F-distribution with $(m - n, T - 2m - 1)$ degrees of freedom.

The test may be carried out without actually estimating the restricted model. In the previous sub-section it was shown that the polynomial distributed lag formulation imposes $(m - n)$ linear restrictions of the form $R\delta = 0$. If d is the unrestricted OLS estimator of δ, the validity of these restrictions may be tested using the statistic

$$\frac{d'R'\{R(X'X)^{-1}R'\}^{-1}Rd}{s^2(m-n)} \tag{8.17}$$

where s^2 is the unbiased estimator of σ^2 in (8.1). Under $H_0 : R\delta = 0$, (8.17) has an F-distribution with $(m - n, T - 2m - 1)$ degrees of freedom; cf. (5.4.5). The null hypothesis being tested is the same as that in the test discussed above, as $R\delta = 0$ and $\gamma^\dagger = 0$ are equivalent. A little algebraic manipulation reveals that the two statistics are, in fact, identical.

Testing the Polynomial Lag Specification

Given the maximum lag m, testing the validity of a polynomial of a given degree is straightforward. When n is unknown, this suggests carrying out a series of tests in the manner described in Section 5.8. We first test for a polynomial of degree $m - 1$. If this hypothesis is not rejected, we test for a polynomial of degree $m - 2$ and so on.

Although the above procedure is optimal in the sense defined in Section 5.8, it does hinge on prior specification of the length of the lag, m. It may therefore be prudent to carry out the procedure with a number of different values of m, possibly using the AIC or $\bar{R}^2$ as a final check on the goodness of fit of the preferred specification in each series of tests.

Polynomial Distributed Lags and the Rational Lag Structure*

Although the polynomial and rational lag formulations have traditionally been viewed as alternatives, Pagan (1978) has pointed out that they are related. Consider a rational lag model of the form (1.12). The lag associated with such a model will normally be infinite. However, suppose that for comparability with (8.1) it is decided that the underlying lag distribution should be finite with a maximum lag of m. This leads to a *finite rational distributed lag* formulation. The recurrence relations (2.3) are still assumed to hold, but only for $\delta_0, \ldots, \delta_s$. Thereafter, $\delta_\tau = 0$. The relationship between this model and the polynomial distributed lag then emerges as follows. If $A(L) = (1 - L)^{n+1}$ and $B(L)$ is of order n, the estimates of $\delta_0, \ldots, \delta_m$ will be identical to those obtained by a polynomial distributed lag estimator in which the approximating polynomial is of degree n. The rationale behind this result follows almost immediately from (8.12). On examining the recurrence relations (2.3a) and (2.3b) it will be seen that (2.3a) imposes no constraints on the lag structure since for the $n + 1$ equations there are $n + 1$ unknown parameters $\beta_0, \ldots, \beta_n$. However, the relations (2.3b) impose $m - n$ constraints, and these constraints are identical to those in (8.12).

The restrictions imposed on the model therefore correspond exactly to those imposed by the polynomial distributed lag.

Example In (8.4), the corresponding finite rational distributed lag model is

$$y_t = \frac{(2 - 4L^2)}{(1 - L)^3} x_t + u_t \qquad (8.18)$$

Perhaps the most important implication of this result concerns the interpretation of estimates of rational distributed lag models in which the roots of $A(L)$ lie close to, or on, the unit circle.

Notes

Section 1 Expectations models are developed further in the literature on 'rational expectations'; see, for example, Wallis (1980) and Lucas and Sargent (1981).

Sections 3 and 4 Maddala and Rao (1971), Pesaran (1973), and Schmidt (1975).

Section 5 The treatment here differs from that in Box and Jenkins (1976, Ch. 11) in that more stress is placed on the 'direct approach' to model identification. Box and Jenkins place much more emphasis on the role of the cross-correlation function; see Haugh and Box (1977) as well. In addition, differencing is seen primarily as a way of achieving joint stationarity. Further discussion on 'over-differencing' will be found in Plosser and Schwert (1977).

Section 6 Wallis (1974), Harvey (1989, Ch.7).

Section 8 Polynomial lags were introduced by Almon (1965), and are sometimes known as 'Almon' lags. Specification is considered in Godfrey and Poskitt (1975) and Sargan (1980b).

Exercises

1. Find the mean and median lags in (1.1).
2. Explain how you would construct an efficient two-step estimator in a model of the form (3.1) with $s = 0$ and $r = 2$.
3. Consider (1.4) with an MA(1) disturbance term. Explain how you would compute consistent estimates of α, β and the MA parameter θ. Derive recursive expressions for ϵ_t and its derivatives, and explain how you would compute efficient estimators of all three parameters by least squares regression. How would you test the hypothesis that $\theta = 0$ on the basis of this regression?
4. Construct an LM test of the hypothesis that $\phi = 0$ in (4.1). Show that it is equivalent to a test based on the DW statistic in large samples.
5. A regression of y_t on $x_t, x_{t-1}, \ldots, x_{t-6}$ produced the following coefficients:

$$d_0 = 2.00, d_1 = 0.80, d_2 = -0.72, d_3 = 0.64, d_4 = -0.58, d_5 = -0.52,$$
$$d_6 = -0.46.$$

Explain why a rational distributed lag with $r = s = 1$ might be an appropriate way of modelling the relationship between x and y. Compute preliminary estimates of the parameters in such a model and indicate how you would proceed to identify a suitable model for the disturbance term.

6. How would you estimate the model

$$\Delta_4 \, y_t = (1 - \alpha L)^{-1} \Delta_4 \, x_t + u_t$$

if u_t was generated by the seasonal ARMA process, (6.4.2)?

7. If the explanatory variable in (3.16) is modelled by the ARIMA(1, 1, 0) process

$$\Delta x_t = 0.6 \Delta x_{t-1} + \zeta_t$$

and $r = s = 1$ with $\tilde{\alpha} = 0.3$, $\tilde{\beta} = 2.0$, find an expression for the forecast function and compute $\text{MSE}(\tilde{y}_{T + l|T})$ for $l = 1, 2$ and 3.

8. Given that

$$\Sigma x_t^2 = 50 \qquad\qquad \Sigma x_t \, x_{t-1} = 48 \qquad\qquad \Sigma x_t \, y_t = 10.2$$

$$\Sigma x_t \, y_{t-1} = 10 \qquad\qquad \Sigma x_{t-1} \, y_t = 9.9 \qquad\qquad \Sigma x_{t-1} \, y_{t-1} = 9.8$$

where all summations are from $t = 2$ to T, calculate consistent estimates of α and β in (1.4), showing why the method you have chosen does, in fact, yield consistent estimates. State any assumptions you make. Find the time taken for the overall change in y resulting from a change in x to be 90% complete.

9. Find the total multiplier and average lag in a polynomial distributed lag in which, in (8.2), $n = 2$, $\gamma_0 = 1.2$ and $\gamma_1 = -0.2$.

8
Dynamic Models II: Stochastic Difference Equations

8.1. Introduction

In modelling dynamic relationships, econometricians have tended to favour stochastic difference equations over transfer functions. There are cases where this preference reflects a strong prior belief in a partial adjustment theory of behaviour. However, as a general rule, economic theory cannot be relied upon to provide any firm guidance on this matter. Given that a model is only an approximation to reality, questions of model specification are, to a large extent, determined on pragmatic grounds.

The advantages of a stochastic difference equation formulation only really become apparent when the model contains more than one explanatory variable. Suppose that y depends on k explanatory variables, and that the influence of each of these variables is felt through a geometric distributed lag. Such a relationship could be modelled by the 'multiple input' transfer function

$$y_t = \sum_{i=1}^{k} \frac{\beta_i x_{ti}}{1 - \alpha_i L} + \frac{\epsilon_t}{1 - \phi L} \tag{1.1}$$

Although the disturbance term in (1.1) has been specified as an AR(1) process it could, in principle, be any ARMA process. However, assuming it to be an AR(1) process is a convenient simplification in the argument that follows.

As it stands, (1.1) is highly non-linear, and contains $2k + 2$ unknown parameters. Furthermore, in constructing the sum of squares function, kr residuals are 'lost' if setting pre-sample values of x and y to zero is to be avoided; cf. Section 7.3. However, matters are simplified considerably by imposing the constraints $\alpha_i = \alpha$, $i = 1, \ldots, k$ and $\phi = \alpha$. On rearranging this gives the stochastic difference equation,

$$y_t = \alpha y_{t-1} + \sum_{i=1}^{k} \beta_i x_{ti} + \epsilon_t \qquad (1.2)$$

There are two attractions to (1.2), the first obvious, the second less so. The obvious attraction concerns estimation. If ϵ_t is normally distributed, OLS will be fully efficient. The second point in favour of a formulation like (1.2), however, is more fundamental. It is much easier, within a stochastic difference equation framework, to adopt a model selection procedure which moves from the general to the specific. Such an approach is particularly appropriate when there is uncertainty regarding the explanatory variables to be included in the model. The technical aspects of model specification are discussed in some detail in Section 5.

The price paid for imposing the restrictions leading to (1.2) is a less flexible lag structure. However, this can, to some extent, be compensated for by adding lagged values of the x_i's. If (1.2) is extended to include each explanatory variable lagged one period, the model will contain the same number of unknown parameters as (1.1). This may, or may not, give a better approximation to the underlying dynamic structure. However, the advantages of (1.2) with regard to estimation and specification still remain.

Autoregressive Distributed Lag and ARMAX Models

Equation (1.2) may be generalised to

$$A(L)y_t = \sum_{i=1}^{k} B_i(L)x_{ti} + \epsilon_t \qquad (1.3)$$

where $A(L)$ is a polynomial in the lag operator defined by (7.1.11), and $B_i(L)$ is a polynomial of order s_i defined as in (7.1.10) for $i = 1,\ldots,k$. A necessary condition for stability is that the roots of $A(L)$ should be outside the unit circle. Such a model is sometimes known as an *autoregressive distributed lag*, and the precise specification is given by the abbreviation $AD(r, s_1,\ldots,s_k)$. Using this terminology (7.1.13) is $AD(1, 0)$.

The specification of the disturbance term in (1.3) may be extended to allow it to follow any ARMA process. There are, however, some advantages in restricting attention to pure AR processes, and these advantages will become apparent in Section 5. On the other hand, an MA specification for the disturbance term does have a certain appeal. Such a model may be written in the form

$$A(L)y_t = \sum_{i=1}^{k} B_i(L)x_{ti} + \theta(L)\epsilon_t \qquad (1.4)$$

and referred to as ARMAX $(r, s_1,\ldots, s_k, q)$. Any transfer function may be expressed as an ARMAX model with restrictions on the lag polynomials. For example, (7.3.16) has $A(L) = \theta(L)$.

The properties of the disturbance term are irrelevant as regards the systematic dynamics of the model. As was indicated in Section 7.1, the material on transfer functions is directly applicable to stochastic difference equations. Thus the mean path of y_t in (1.3), or (1.4), is given by

$$E(y_t) = \sum_{i=1}^{k} \frac{B_i(L)x_{ti}}{A(L)}$$

and the systematic dynamics may be deduced by regarding the model as a special case of a transfer function.

Example 1   Consider the model

$$y_t = \alpha y_{t-1} + \beta_1 x_{t1} + \beta_2 x_{t2} + u_t \tag{1.5}$$

The expected effect of a change in the vector $x_t = (x_{t1}, x_{t2})'$ may be assessed additively. Thus the impact multiplier, the immediate effect of a unit change in both x_1 and x_2, is simply $\beta_1 + \beta_2$. After one time period this increases to $(\beta_1 + \beta_2)(1 + \alpha)$ and so on.

Seasonality and Prediction

The systematic dynamics of a stochastic difference equation can be deduced from the properties of the corresponding transfer function model. Thus the material of the previous section is directly relevant. In a similar way, the treatment of seasonality and the handling of predictions essentially follows from what has gone before.

It was argued in Section 7.6 that dynamic relationships should, wherever possible, be estimated using series which have not been seasonally adjusted. This conclusion continues to hold for models formulated as stochastic difference equations. By and large the same techniques for introducing deterministic and stochastic seasonal components into the model are appropriate, and seasonal differencing and seasonal dummies are widely used. In addition, seasonal effects are often introduced into the lag structure itself in a stochastic difference equation, e.g.

$$y_t = \alpha y_{t-1} + \beta_0 x_t + \beta_4 x_{t-4} + \epsilon_t \tag{1.6}$$

Seasonality could also be introduced into a transfer function model in this way, although the approach seems to be a more natural one within the context of a stochastic difference equation. When there is no option but to use seasonally adjusted data, it should be borne in mind that seasonal effects may still be present.

Predictions from a stochastic difference equation can be made recursively, since the model is already in a form corresponding to (7.7.1). The MSE of a prediction may be deduced by casting the model in transfer function form. Consider the general formulation, (1.4). If the parameters in the model are known, the prediction MSE is the same as the MSE of a prediction from the time series model, $y_t = A^{-1}(L)\theta(L)\epsilon_t$.

Example 2 The predictions of future values of y_t in the model

$$y_t = \alpha y_{t-1} + \beta x_t + \epsilon_t \qquad (1.7)$$

are made directly from the recursion

$$\tilde{y}_{T+l|T} = \alpha \tilde{y}_{T+l-1|T} + \beta x_{T+l}, \qquad l = 1, 2, \ldots \qquad (1.8)$$

with $\tilde{y}_{T|T} = y_T$. The transfer function formulation of (1.7),

$$y_t = \frac{\beta x_t}{1 - \alpha L} + \frac{\epsilon_t}{1 - \alpha L}$$

implies that for given values of α and β the MSE of $\tilde{y}_{T+l|T}$ is identical to the MSE of the l-step ahead predictor in an AR(1) time series model. Thus formula (6.7.4), with ϕ replaced by α, is applicable in this case.

8.2. Estimation

The main issues which arise in estimating stochastic difference equations can be discussed with respect to the simple model introduced in (7.1.13)

$$y_t = \alpha y_{t-1} + \beta x_t + u_t, \qquad t = 2, \ldots, T \text{ with } |\alpha| < 1 \qquad (2.1)$$

The extensions to the more general model, (7.1.16), are straightforward and will not be discussed explicitly.

OLS and Instrumental Variables

The simplest way to estimate α and β in (2.1) is to regress y_t on y_{t-1} and x_t. If the disturbance term is white noise and x_t is non-stochastic, the result of Section 2.12, based on the Mann–Wald theorem, applies. Thus a model of the form (2.1) may be treated in exactly the same way as a classical regression model, provided the sample size is large. Thus if a and b denote the OLS estimators of α and β respectively,

$$\begin{bmatrix} a \\ b \end{bmatrix} \sim AN \left[\begin{pmatrix} \alpha \\ \beta \end{pmatrix}, \sigma^2 \begin{pmatrix} \Sigma y_{t-1}^2 & \Sigma y_{t-1} x_t \\ \Sigma y_{t-1} x_t & \Sigma x_t^2 \end{pmatrix}^{-1} \right] \qquad (2.2)$$

If, in addition to being white noise, u_t is normally distributed, the OLS estimator is the ML estimator. It is therefore asymptotically efficient.

Although OLS has very desirable properties when u_t is white noise, it becomes less attractive in the presence of serial correlation. If $E(u_t u_{t-1}) \neq 0$, u_t and y_{t-1} will be correlated even in large samples, cf. (7.1.18). As was noted in Section 7.1, the result of this is that OLS is no longer consistent.

The IV solution to problems of this kind was discussed in Section 7.3, and the results established there are directly applicable in this case as well. The IV estimator of (2.1) is identical to the estimator introduced for the Koyck distributed lag. Thus taking x_{t-1} as an instrument for y_{t-1} leads to estimators of α and β which are consistent.

ML Estimation with AR(1) Disturbances

Suppose that the disturbances in (2.1) follow a stationary AR(1) process as defined by (6.1.2). If y_1 and y_2 are fixed, the joint density of $y_3, \ldots, y_T$ is determined by $\epsilon_3, \ldots, \epsilon_T$. For given values of α, β and ϕ, a set of $T - 2$ residuals is defined by

$$\epsilon_t = y_t - \alpha y_{t-1} - \beta x_t - \phi(y_{t-1} - \alpha y_{t-2} - \beta x_{t-1}),$$

$$t = 3, \ldots, T \quad (2.3)$$

and ML estimation is carried out by minimising the sum of squares function

$$S(\alpha, \beta, \phi) = \sum_{t=3}^{T} \epsilon_t^2 \quad (2.4)$$

A natural algorithm for minimising $S(\alpha, \beta, \phi)$ is Gauss–Newton, particularly as analytic first derivatives are readily available. Differentiating (2.3) with respect to α, β and ϕ gives

$$\frac{\partial \epsilon_t}{\partial \alpha} = -(y_{t-1} - \phi y_{t-2}) \quad (2.5)$$

$$\frac{\partial \epsilon_t}{\partial \beta} = -(x_t - \phi x_{t-1}) \quad (2.6)$$

$$\frac{\partial \epsilon_t}{\partial \phi} = -(y_{t-1} - \alpha y_{t-2} - \beta x_{t-1}), \quad t = 3, \ldots, T \quad (2.7)$$

respectively. Note that the last derivative is equal to $-u_{t-1}$ when α and β are set at their true values.

A Cochrane–Orcutt procedure could also be adopted by minimising (2.4). This would be applied in much the same way as in Chapter 6, with α and β being estimated for a given value of ϕ, and ϕ being estimated conditional on

α and β. For a fixed regressor model, it was shown that Cochrane–Orcutt is equivalent to Gauss–Newton in large samples. However, this equivalence no longer holds for a model with a lagged dependent variable, the reason being that

$$\text{plim } T^{-1} \sum \frac{\partial \epsilon_t}{\partial \alpha} \frac{\partial \epsilon_t}{\partial \phi} \neq 0 \tag{2.8}$$

The Cochrane–Orcutt scheme will eventually converge as it is a stepwise optimisation procedure. However, it is arguably less attractive than Gauss–Newton insofar as information about the structure of the model is suppressed.

There are a number of ways of obtaining starting values for an iterative ML procedure in this model. One possibility is to estimate α and β by the method of instrumental variables, and then compute an estimate of ϕ from the residuals in the usual way; cf. (6.1.9). This has the advantage that the estimates of all three parameters will be consistent. On the other hand, OLS may be more attractive in practice, even though it is inconsistent. Note that the Gauss–Newton iterations cannot be started by setting all three parameters equal to zero. On examining (2.5) and (2.7), it can be seen that this would invite immediate disaster in view of the perfect multicollinearity between $\partial \epsilon_t / \partial \alpha$ and $\partial \epsilon_t / \partial \phi$.

Asymptotic Properties

Under suitable conditions the ML estimator of $\psi = (\alpha, \beta, \phi)'$ is asymptotically normally distributed with a mean of ψ and a covariance matrix equal to the inverse of the asymptotic information matrix, $IA(\psi)$, divided by T. A formal demonstration of this result will be found in Hatanaka (1974). All that will be done here is to derive an expression for Avar($\tilde{\psi}$). This may be carried out most easily by using the first derivatives, (2.5) to (2.7), in formula (3.5.25). As is usual in this type of problem, the ML estimator of σ^2 is distributed independently of the other estimators in large samples with a variance of $2\sigma^4/T$. It can therefore be ignored in any discussion of the large sample properties of the ML estimator of ψ.

The terms which only involve derivatives with respect to α or β are relatively easy to evaluate. Thus, for example,

$$\text{plim } \frac{1}{T} \sum \left(\frac{\partial \epsilon_t}{\partial \beta} \right)^2 = q_x^2 \tag{2.9}$$

where

$$q_x^2 = \text{plim } T^{-1} \sum (x_t - \phi x_{t-1})^2 \tag{2.10}$$

Similar expressions may be obtained for the other elements in the 2×2 sub-matrix in the top left hand corner of $IA(\alpha, \beta, \phi)$. The terms q_y^2 and q_{xy} are defined in the same way as q_x^2 with y interpreted as y_{t-1}. Note that these definitions imply that certain assumptions must be imposed on the sequence of x_t's.

The remaining terms in $IA(\psi)$ may be evaluated as follows:

$$\text{plim } \frac{1}{T}\sum \left(\frac{\partial \epsilon_t}{\partial \phi}\right)^2 = \text{plim } \frac{1}{T}\sum u_{t-1}^2 = \frac{\sigma^2}{1 - \phi^2} \tag{2.11}$$

$$\text{plim } \frac{1}{T}\sum \frac{\partial \epsilon_t}{\partial \phi}\frac{\partial \epsilon_t}{\partial \beta} = 0 \tag{2.12}$$

and

$$\text{plim } \frac{1}{T}\sum \frac{\partial \epsilon_t}{\partial \alpha}\frac{\partial \epsilon_t}{\partial \phi} = \frac{\sigma^2}{1 - \alpha\phi} \tag{2.13}$$

The last of these expressions is evaluated by noting that $y_t = \{\beta x_t + u_t\}/(1 - \alpha L)$ and so

$$\text{plim } \frac{1}{T}\sum u_t y_{t-j} = \frac{\sigma^2 \phi^j}{1 - \phi^2}(1 + \alpha\phi + \alpha^2\phi^2...) = \frac{\sigma^2}{1 - \phi^2}\frac{\phi^j}{1 - \alpha\phi} \tag{2.14}$$

Using this result for $j = 0$ and $j = 1$ then gives

$$\text{plim } \frac{1}{T}\sum \frac{\partial \epsilon_t}{\partial \phi}\frac{\partial \epsilon_t}{\partial \alpha} = \text{plim } T^{-1}\sum (y_{t-1} - \phi y_{t-2})u_{t-1}$$

$$= \frac{\sigma^2}{1 - \phi^2}\frac{1 - \phi^2}{1 - \alpha\phi} = \frac{\sigma^2}{1 - \alpha\phi}$$

The full asymptotic covariance matrix is

$$\text{Avar}(\tilde{\psi}) = T^{-1}IA^{-1}(\alpha, \beta, \phi)$$

$$= T^{-1}\begin{bmatrix} \sigma^{-2}q_y^2 & \sigma^{-2}q_{xy} & (1 - \alpha\phi)^{-1} \\ \sigma^{-2}q_{xy} & \sigma^{-2}q_x^2 & 0 \\ (1 - \alpha\phi)^{-1} & 0 & (1 - \phi^2)^{-1} \end{bmatrix}^{-1} \tag{2.15}$$

The crucial feature of (2.15) as compared with (6.1.12) is the appearance of the term $1/(1 - \alpha\phi)$. Thus, when a lagged dependent variable appears in a model, its estimated coefficient is not independent of the coefficient of the AR process driving the disturbance term. One implication of this point has already been noted in discussing ML iterative procedures. However, the consequences of the result are far more important in the context of two-step estimation and testing for serial correlation.

Two-Step Estimators

Given initial consistent estimators of α, β and ϕ, one iteration of Gauss–Newton will yield a set of asymptotically efficient estimators; see Section 4.5. A feasible Aitken estimator, based on a regression of $y_t - \hat{\phi}y_{t-1}$ on $y_{t-1} - \hat{\phi}y_{t-2}$ and $x_t - \hat{\phi}x_{t-1}$, where $\hat{\phi}$ is consistent, will *not*, however, be fully efficient. This is basically because of the term $(1 - \alpha\phi)^{-1}$ in the information matrix which establishes a link between y_{t-1} and the disturbance.

Hatanaka (1974) was the first to point out how an efficient two-step estimator might be obtained for this model. His estimator may be constructed as follows:

(i) Estimate α and β consistently using the method of instrumental variables. Denoting these estimators by $\hat{\alpha}$ and $\hat{\beta}$, form the residuals $\hat{u}_t = y_t - \hat{\alpha}y_{t-1} - \hat{\beta}x_t$, and estimate ϕ by regressing $\hat{u}_t$ on $\hat{u}_{t-1}$. Denote this estimator by $\hat{\phi}$.

(ii) Regress $y_t - \hat{\phi}y_{t-1}$ on $y_{t-1} - \hat{\phi}y_{t-2}$, $x_t - \hat{\phi}x_{t-1}$ and $\hat{u}_{t-1}$. The two-step estimators of α and β are given directly by the regression coefficients of $y_{t-1} - \hat{\phi}y_{t-2}$ and $x_t - \hat{\phi}x_{t-1}$ respectively. If $\phi^\dagger$ denotes the regression coefficient of $\hat{u}_{t-1}$, the two-step estimator of ϕ is equal to $\hat{\phi} + \phi^\dagger$.

Hatanaka refers to this estimator as the *residual adjusted Aitken estimator*. It is the presence of $\hat{u}_{t-1}$ in the second stage regression which differentiates it from the feasible Aitken estimator, and ensures asymptotic efficiency.

Unfortunately, the form of the residual adjusted Aitken estimator does not make its relationship to Gauss–Newton immediately apparent. Given $\hat{\alpha}$, $\hat{\beta}$ and $\hat{\phi}$ as in (i) above, one iteration of Gauss–Newton involves regressing ϵ_t on the three derivatives, (2.5) to (2.7). However, if ϵ_t is split up into three parts,

$$\epsilon_t = (y_t - \phi y_{t-1}) - \beta(x_t - \phi x_{t-1}) - \alpha(y_{t-1} - \phi y_{t-2}) \quad (2.16)$$

it will be observed from (2.5) and (2.6) that it may be written

$$\epsilon_t = (y_t - \phi y_{t-1}) + \beta \cdot \partial\epsilon_t/d\beta + \alpha \cdot \partial\epsilon_t/\partial\alpha \quad (2.17)$$

Now $\partial\epsilon_t/\partial\beta$ and $\partial\epsilon_t/\partial\alpha$ are regressors in the Gauss–Newton iteration, and when a regressor is identical to the dependent variable, its estimated coefficient will be unity while all the other coefficients are zero; see, for example, Theil (1971, p. 549). Given this, it follows almost immediately that the two-step Gauss–Newton estimator is identical to Hatanaka's residual adjusted Aitken estimator.

*Treatment of the 'First Observation'**

In Section 6.1, the full GLS transformation was contrasted with the Cochrane–Orcutt transform. It was argued there that omitting the first set of transformed observations, as is done in Cochrane–Orcutt, can have an adverse effect on small sample properties. The same argument applies in dynamic models, and it therefore seems reasonable to define the likelihood function with only y_1 regarded as being fixed. This means that y_2 is taken to be normally distributed with a mean of $y_2 - \alpha y_1 - \beta x_2$ and a variance of $\sigma^2/(1 - \phi^2)$. The set of residuals given in (2.3) are therefore augmented by

$$\epsilon_2 = \sqrt{1 - \phi^2}\,(y_2 - \alpha y_1 - \beta x_2) \tag{2.18}$$

and the sum of squares function, (2.4), is redefined to include ϵ_2.

Unfortunately, the way in which y_2 is handled introduces a determinantal term into the likelihood. The function to be minimised is therefore

$$S^*(\alpha, \beta, \phi) = S(\alpha, \beta, \phi)/|1 - \phi^2|^{1/T} \tag{2.19}$$

However, it was argued in Section 6.1 that the inclusion of the determinant in the likelihood function is usually unimportant in practice. It therefore seems reasonable to construct an estimator based on minimising the sum of squares, $S(\alpha, \beta, \phi)$. This simplifies matters considerably since the Gauss–Newton algorithm can again be applied and the structure of the two-step estimator remains the same. The derivatives of (2.18) are

$$\frac{\partial \epsilon_2}{\partial \alpha} = -\sqrt{1 - \phi^2} \cdot y_1 \tag{2.20}$$

$$\frac{\partial \epsilon_2}{\partial \beta} = -\sqrt{1 - \phi^2} \cdot x_2 \tag{2.21}$$

and

$$\frac{\partial \epsilon_2}{\partial \phi} = -\phi(y_2 - \alpha y_1 - \beta x_2)/\sqrt{1 - \phi^2} \tag{2.22}$$

respectively.

Given the evidence from the fixed regressor model it would seem advisable to include ϵ_2 in both ML and two-step estimation procedures, *particularly when one or more of the exogenous variables is subject to a trend.* The only relevant Monte Carlo work for the lagged dependent variable model is provided, somewhat incidentally, in an article by Maddala and Rao (1973). They examine an ML estimator for (2.1) with AR(1) disturbances and, with US GNP data used for x_t, find that ML is in many cases inferior to OLS on an MSE comparison; see Maddala and Rao (1973, Table V, p. 767).

The estimates they used did not allow for the first set of transformed observations implicit in (2.18), and since GNP data is trending, the poor results for the ML estimator exactly parallel those for the Cochrane–Orcutt procedure in the fixed regressor case.

Estimation of ARMAX Models

In more general formulations of stochastic difference equation models, the disturbances are generated by an ARMA(p, q) process. However, the main principles involved in estimating such models can be illustrated by taking (2.1) and allowing the disturbance term to follow an MA(1) process. The model in question,

$$y_t = \alpha y_{t-1} + \beta x_t + \epsilon_t + \theta \epsilon_{t-1} \qquad (2.23)$$

falls within the class of ARMAX models defined in (1.4).

If y_1 is assumed to be fixed and ϵ_1 is assumed to be zero, maximising the likelihood function is equivalent to minimising the sum of squares function

$$S(\alpha, \beta, \theta) = \sum_{t=2}^{T} \epsilon_t^2 \qquad (2.24)$$

where

$$\epsilon_t = y_t - \alpha y_{t-1} - \beta x_t - \theta \epsilon_{t-1}, \qquad t = 2, \ldots, T \qquad (2.25)$$

with $\epsilon_1 = 0$. As is usual with MA disturbances, the derivatives of the residuals may be obtained recursively. In this case

$$\frac{\partial \epsilon_t}{\partial \alpha} = -y_{t-1} - \theta \frac{\partial \epsilon_{t-1}}{\partial \alpha} \qquad (2.26)$$

$$\frac{\partial \epsilon_t}{\partial \beta} = -x_t - \theta \frac{\partial \epsilon_{t-1}}{\partial \beta} \qquad (2.27)$$

$$\frac{\partial \epsilon_t}{\partial \theta} = -\epsilon_{t-1} - \theta \frac{\partial \epsilon_{t-1}}{\partial \theta} \qquad (2.28)$$

All three derivatives are evaluated by setting them equal to zero for $t = 1$.

The analytic derivatives can be exploited in an iterative ML scheme such as Gauss–Newton. However, from the theoretical point of view the most interesting aspect of (2.26) to (2.28) lies in the construction of a two-step estimator. Initial consistent estimators of α and β can be obtained by the method of instrumental variables, as in Section 7.3, and the residuals used to construct a consistent estimator of θ using (4.5.4). Asymptotically efficient estimators of all three parameters can then be obtained by regressing ϵ_t on (2.26) to (2.28) and subtracting the resulting coefficients from the corresponding initial estimates. This procedure exactly parallels the residual adjusted Aitken estimator in that it is based on a single iteration of Gauss–Newton. However, its small-sample properties have yet to be investigated.

The Effect of Misspecification

It was pointed out earlier that applying OLS to (2.1) in the presence of serially correlated disturbances generally yields inconsistent estimators of α and β. However, while underparameterising the disturbance term can lead to inconsistency, overparameterisation can lead to inefficiency, even in large samples. This may at first sight seem surprising, since for a fixed regressor model, carrying out estimation on the assumption that the disturbances follow, say, an AR(1) process when they are really white noise has no effect on the asymptotic efficiency of the ML estimators of β. Once again it is the structure of the information matrix which differentiates a lagged dependent variable model from one with fixed regressors.

Consider (2.1), and suppose that the disturbance term is white noise. If the model is estimated by ML under the assumption that $u_t \sim AR(1)$, the large sample covariance matrix of $(\tilde{\alpha}, \tilde{\beta}, \tilde{\phi})$ is given by

$$\text{Avar}(\tilde{\alpha}, \tilde{\beta}, \tilde{\phi}) = \frac{\sigma^2}{T} \begin{bmatrix} q_y^2 & q_{xy} & \sigma^2 \\ q_{xy} & q_x^2 & 0 \\ \sigma^2 & 0 & \sigma^2 \end{bmatrix}^{-1} \tag{2.29}$$

This expression is obtained by setting ϕ equal to zero in (2.15).

For $\tilde{\alpha}$,

$$\text{Avar}(\tilde{\alpha}) = \frac{\sigma^2}{T} \cdot \frac{q_x^2}{q_y^2 q_x^2 - q_{xy}^2 - \sigma^2 q_x^2} \tag{2.30}$$

but if $u_t \sim NID(0, \sigma^2)$, the OLS estimator is asymptotically efficient. The large sample variance of the OLS estimator of α is given by the top left hand element of (2.2). Using the notation of (2.15) this becomes

$$\text{Avar}(a) = \frac{\sigma^2}{T} \cdot \frac{q_x^2}{q_x^2 q_y^2 - q_{xy}^2} \tag{2.31}$$

On comparing (2.30) with (2.31) it will be seen that

$$\text{Avar}(\tilde{\alpha}) \geq \text{Avar}(a) \tag{2.32}$$

The equality only holds if $q_x^2 = 0$, in which case x_t would be a constant term.

8.3. Testing for Serial Correlation

In a static regression model, tests of randomness appropriate for an observable time series may be applied directly to the OLS residuals. As a rule these tests will only have asymptotic validity, although in certain special cases the exact distribution of a test statistic can be derived. The same tests may be used when a transfer function model is estimated under the assumption that the disturbances are normally distributed white noise. However, the non-linear nature of the estimation problem means that small-sample results are unavailable. Thus, a valid test for AR(1) disturbances may be carried out with the Durbin–Watson d-statistic, but only on the basis of its asymptotic distribution. This is equivalent to calculating the first order sample autocorrelation coefficient from the residuals and taking it to be normally distributed with a mean of zero and a variance of $1/T$.

Given the above results, it might seem reasonable to suppose that the tests described in Sections 6.3 and 6.6 are applicable when a stochastic difference equation is estimated by OLS. However, in general, this turns out not to be the case. The lagged dependent variable affects the test statistic in such a way that the usual distribution theory fails to hold, even in large samples. The net result is that the tests against serial correlation are not, in general, as powerful as they might be.

The Durbin h-Test

Although model (2.1) contains only one lagged value of the dependent variable, it encompasses all the difficulties described above. Suppose the hypothesis to be tested is that the disturbances follow an AR(1) process. As in the classical model, rejection of this hypothesis may be an indication of a more complicated disturbance process or even of a more fundamental equation misspecification. However, the point at issue here is to derive a test which is valid in the sense that the distribution of the test statistic is known, at least asymptotically, under the null hypothesis.

By suitably modifying the d-statistic to allow for the influence of the lagged dependent variable, Durbin (1970) was able to obtain a suitable test procedure. This is based on the 'h-statistic',

$$h = (1 - \tfrac{1}{2} d) \sqrt{\frac{T}{1 - T \cdot \operatorname{avar}(a)}} \tag{3.1}$$

where $\operatorname{avar}(a)$ is the estimated variance of the OLS estimator of α. Under the null hypothesis, $h \sim AN(0, 1)$, and a test for positive serial correlation at the 5% level would take $h > 1.645$ as the critical region.

Since $d \simeq 2(1 - r_1)$, where r_1 is the first order autocorrelation of the OLS residuals, the h-statistic may be expressed as

$$h \simeq r_1 \sqrt{\frac{T}{1 - T \cdot \text{avar}(a)}} \tag{3.2}$$

This implies that r_1 is asymptotically normal with a mean of zero and a variance of $\{ 1 - T \cdot \text{Avar}(a) \} / T$. In the static regression and transfer function models, on the other hand, $r_1 \sim AN(0, 1/T)$. The distribution of r_1 is therefore more concentrated when a lagged dependent variable is present, at least in large samples. This implies that taking r_1 to have a variance of $1/T$ will result in a test in which the actual size is smaller than the nominal size. Hence we find the potential loss in power.

Derivation of the h-Statistic and Some Alternatives

The rationale behind the h-statistic becomes clear once it is recognised that it can be derived using the Lagrange Multiplier principle. The log–likelihood function for (2.1) with AR(1) disturbances is

$$\log L(\alpha, \beta, \phi) = - \frac{T}{2} \log 2\pi - \frac{T}{2} \log \sigma^2 - \frac{1}{2\sigma^2} S(\alpha, \beta, \phi) \tag{3.3}$$

where $S(\alpha, \beta, \phi)$ is defined in (2.4). The theory surrounding formula (5.5.10) is directly appropriate, with $\psi^{(1)} = (\alpha, \beta)'$ and $\psi^{(2)} = \phi$. Thus, using (2.7),

$$\frac{\partial \log L}{\partial \phi} = D_2 \log L (\psi) = - \sigma^{-2} \sum \frac{\partial \epsilon_t}{\partial \phi} \cdot \epsilon_t$$

$$= \sigma^{-2} \sum u_{t-1} (u_t - \phi u_{t-1}) \tag{3.4}$$

where $u_t = y_t - \alpha y_{t-1} - \beta x_t$. Under the null hypothesis, $H_0 : \phi = 0$, expression (3.4) is evaluated as

$$D_2 \log L(\tilde{\psi}_0) = \hat{\sigma}^{-2} \sum \hat{u}_{t-1} \hat{u}_t \tag{3.5}$$

where $\hat{u}_t$ denotes the tth OLS residual from the regression of y_t on y_{t-1} and x_t, and $\hat{\sigma}^2 = T^{-1} \sum \hat{u}_t^2$ is the ML estimator of σ^2.

The information matrix for the unrestricted model is given in (2.15). Partitioning in accordance with (5.5.9) and evaluating at $\phi = 0$ yields

$$I_{22} - I_{21}' I_{11}^{-1} I_{12} = T - T^2 \text{ avar}(a) \tag{3.6}$$

The vector $I_{12} = (T, 0)'$ effectively picks out the top left-hand element of

I_{11}^{-1}. This is a consistent estimator of the asymptotic variance of the OLS estimator of α when the null hypothesis is true; cf. (2.2).

Substituting (3.5) and (3.6) into the expression for the LM statistic given in (5.5.10) gives

$$\text{LM} = \frac{(\hat{\sigma}^{-2} \sum \hat{u}_t \hat{u}_{t-1})^2}{T - T^2 \text{ avar}(a)} = r_1^2 \left\{ \frac{T}{1 - T \cdot \text{avar}(a)} \right\} \tag{3.7}$$

Under H_0, LM is asymptotically χ_1^2. However, the square root is identical to (3.2), thereby justifying a test procedure in which the critical region for the h-statistic is based on a standardised normal distribution.

Since maximising the log–likelihood function, (3.3), is equivalent to minimising the sum of squares function, (2.4), the LM test statistic can also be expressed in the TR^2 form of (5.5.16). The derivatives of ϵ_t are given by (2.5) to (2.7). These may be evaluated under the restriction that $\phi = 0$. In terms of the notation of Section 5.5 this yields $z_{t1} = y_{t-1}$, $z_{t2} = x_t$ and $z_{t3} = \hat{u}_{t-1}$. An LM test of $\phi = 0$ is therefore obtained by regressing $\hat{u}_t$ on y_{t-1}, x_t and $\hat{u}_{t-1}$, and treating the statistic TR^2 as χ_1^2. Alternatively, a test of significance may be carried out on the coefficient of $\hat{u}_{t-1}$. This last approach was suggested by Durbin (1970), although within the framework of Section 5.5 it will be recognised as a modified LM test. The most convenient way to carry out the test is with reference to the t-distribution, although the test is, of course, only valid asymptotically.

The modified LM test can be used with a one-sided or a two-sided alternative. The former will usually be most appropriate, with the null hypothesis being rejected against the alternative of positive serial correlation when the t-ratio is greater than a particular critical value.

The Monte Carlo results reported in Spencer (1975) suggest that the actual size of the modified LM test will be close to the nominal size even for a sample as small as twenty. However, this does not appear to be the case for the h-statistic. In his experiments Spencer found that in only three cases out of twenty-seven did the expected proportion of rejections *not* differ significantly from the proportion expected. Furthermore, the h-test suffers from an important practical disadvantage. If $T \cdot \text{avar}(a) \geq 1$, the h-statistic cannot be computed and the test breaks down. Spencer found that the proportion of such cases was relatively high, particularly for small values of T and α.

A General Test of Misspecification

The portmanteau test, described in Section 6.6, provides a useful check on the goodness of fit in a classical regression model. It is also valid for a transfer function model with white noise disturbances. However, for the reasons already given, it is not appropriate to use it with the residuals from a stochastic difference equation.

The portmanteau test may be rationalised in terms of an LM test against an AR(P) or MA(P) disturbance term. Given that an effective test against AR(1) disturbances has just been derived using the LM principle, it seems natural to employ the same approach in developing an overall test for goodness of fit.

Suppose that model (2.1) has been estimated by OLS, and that it is required to test the assumption of white noise disturbances against the alternative, $u_t \sim$ MA(P). The unrestricted model is ARMAX(1, 0, P), with a residual function

$$\epsilon_t = y_t - \alpha y_{t-1} - \beta x_t - \theta_1 \epsilon_{t-1} - \cdots - \theta_P \epsilon_{t-P} \qquad (3.8)$$

The derivatives for the ARMAX(1, 0, 1) model are given in (2.26) to (2.28) and it is not difficult to see that the derivatives for (3.8) with respect to α, β and $\theta_1, \ldots, \theta_P$ have a similar form. Evaluating these derivatives under the null hypothesis that $\theta_1 = \cdots = \theta_P = 0$ gives

$$\frac{\partial \epsilon_t}{\partial \alpha} = -y_{t-1}, \quad \frac{\partial \epsilon_t}{\partial \beta} = -x_t \quad \text{and} \quad \frac{\partial \epsilon_t}{\partial \theta_j} = -\hat{u}_{t-j}, \quad j = 1, \ldots, P$$

where $\hat{u}_t$ is the tth OLS residual in the regression of y_t on y_{t-1} and x_t. The modified LM procedure therefore consists of regressing $\hat{u}_t$ on y_{t-1}, x_t and $\hat{u}_{t-1}, \ldots, \hat{u}_{t-P}$. The LM test is based on TR^2 from the same regression, and is, of course, asymptotically equivalent. Exactly the same test procedure is obtained if the alternative hypothesis is taken to be $u_t \sim$ AR(P).

In the general case, the underlying model is of the form (1.3). Extending the model to include an MA(P) disturbance term then leads to the ARMAX model, (1.4), and a test analogous to the one described in the previous paragraph may be summarised as follows. *Add P lagged OLS residuals, $\hat{u}_{t-1}, \ldots, \hat{u}_{t-P}$, to the set of regressors and carry out an F-test of joint significance.* Although the formal justification for this procedure is a test for an MA(P), or equivalently AR(P), disturbance term, its main use is likely to be in the context of diagnostic checking. As such it will be referred to as the *goodness of fit F-test*, and denoted by $Q^\dagger(P, T^\dagger)$, where $T^\dagger$ denotes the sample size after making an appropriate correction for the loss in degrees of freedom.

Given the above derivation, the form of the modified LM test for any higher order AR or MA process should be clear. For example, a test for fourth-order autocorrelation may be obtained by adding $\hat{u}_{t-4}$ to the set of regressors and testing it for significance. As in the first-order case a one-sided critical region will often be appropriate.

An Estimated ARMA Disturbance Term*

The LM approach also enables valid tests to be constructed when a stochastic difference equation is estimated with an ARMA(p, q) disturbance term. The general principle may be stated as follows: write down an expression for the ϵ_t in the unrestricted model; find expressions for the derivatives of ϵ_t with respect to all the parameters of the model; evaluate ϵ_t and its derivatives under the null hypothesis; regress ϵ_t on all its derivatives and carry out an F-test of joint significance on the coefficients associated with the derivatives of the parameters which are set equal to zero under H_0. Test statistics of this kind can easily be brought into a computer program constructed within an ML framework. However, it is interesting to examine one or two special cases.

Example 1 Suppose that model (2.1) is estimated with an AR(1) disturbance term and it is required to test the hypothesis that $u_t \sim$ AR(2). The residual function in the unrestricted model is given by

$$\epsilon_t = y_t - \alpha y_{t-1} - \beta x_t - \phi_1(y_{t-1} - \alpha y_{t-2} - \beta x_{t-1})$$
$$- \phi_2(y_{t-2} - \alpha y_{t-3} - \beta x_{t-2}) \tag{3.9}$$

The derivatives of ϵ_t, evaluated under the restriction $\phi_2 = 0$, are

$$\frac{\partial \epsilon_t}{\partial \alpha} = -(y_{t-1} - \tilde{\phi}_1 y_{t-2})$$

$$\frac{\partial \epsilon_t}{\partial \beta} = -(x_t - \tilde{\phi}_1 x_{t-1})$$

$$\frac{\partial \epsilon_t}{\partial \phi_1} = -(y_{t-1} - \tilde{\alpha} y_{t-2} - \tilde{\beta} x_{t-1}) = -\tilde{u}_{t-1}$$

$$\frac{\partial \epsilon_t}{\partial \phi_2} = -\tilde{u}_{t-2} \tag{3.10}$$

where $\tilde{\alpha}$, $\tilde{\beta}$ and $\tilde{\phi}_1$ are the ML estimators. The modified LM test of the hypothesis $H_0: \phi_2 = 0$ is then carried out by regressing $\tilde{u}_t$ on the four derivatives given in (3.10), and testing $\partial \epsilon_t / \partial \phi_2$ for significance. If $\tilde{\alpha}$, $\tilde{\beta}$ and $\tilde{\phi}_1$ are calculated by the Gauss–Newton scheme described in Section 2, the first three derivatives in (3.10) are immediately available.

Example 2 Consider the ARMAX model, (2.23) and let the alternative hypothesis be that the disturbance term follows an ARMA(1,1) process. The residual function is

$$\epsilon_t = y_t - \alpha y_{t-1} - \beta x_t - \phi(y_{t-1} - \alpha y_{t-2} - \beta x_{t-1}) - \theta \epsilon_{t-1}$$

$$(3.11)$$

Under the null hypothesis that $\phi = 0$, the derivatives are evaluated as

$$\frac{\partial \epsilon_t}{\partial \alpha} = -y_{t-1} - \tilde{\theta} \frac{\partial \epsilon_{t-1}}{\partial \alpha}$$

$$\frac{\partial \epsilon_t}{\partial \beta} = -x_t - \tilde{\theta} \frac{\partial \epsilon_{t-1}}{\partial \beta}$$

$$\frac{\partial \epsilon_t}{\partial \theta} = -\epsilon_{t-1} - \tilde{\theta} \frac{\partial \epsilon_{t-1}}{\partial \theta}$$

and

$$\frac{\partial \epsilon_t}{\partial \phi} = -\tilde{u}_{t-1} - \tilde{\theta} \frac{\partial \epsilon_{t-1}}{\partial \phi} \qquad (3.12)$$

while

$$\epsilon_t = \tilde{u}_t - \tilde{\theta} \epsilon_{t-1} \qquad (3.13)$$

On comparing the first three derivatives of (3.12) with (2.26) to (2.28), it will be observed that they are automatically available as a by-product of the ML computations for the restricted model. Similarly, (3.13) is given directly as the dependent variable in the final Gauss–Newton iteration. Thus all that is entailed in the modified LM test is the addition of $\partial \epsilon_t / \partial \phi$ to the set of regressors, followed by a test of significance on its estimated coefficient.

A goodness of fit test, analogous to the one described in the previous subsection, may be obtained by considering a more general model in which the order of *either* the AR *or* the MA component is increased by P. However, except for the case when the fitted model is assumed to have white noise disturbances, the test statistics will be different.

8.4. Model Selection

The methodology which has been built up for determining the specification of stochastic difference equations is somewhat different from that which surrounds transfer functions. In modelling transfer functions, a suitable specification is achieved by the cycle of identification, estimation and diagnostic checking. The most appropriate methodology for specifying a stochastic difference equation, on the other hand, is to begin with a very general specification and then 'test down' until a more specific model is obtained. However, any model which is seriously entertained must satisfy various diagnostic checking procedures.

Since economic time series typically change rather slowly, including a large number of lags in a model may lead to numerical instability because of the resulting multicollinearity. It is often advisable, therefore, to rearrange (1.3) as follows:

$$y_t = \alpha y_{t-1} + \sum_{j=1}^{r-1} \alpha_j^\dagger \, \Delta y_{t-j} + \beta x_t + \sum_{j=0}^{s-1} \beta_j^\dagger \, \Delta x_{t-j} + \epsilon_t \qquad (4.1)$$

where a single explanatory variable, x_t, has been assumed for simplicity and

$$\alpha_j^\dagger = - \sum_{k=j+1}^{r} \alpha_k \,, \qquad j = 1, 2, \ldots, r - 1$$

$$\alpha = \sum_{k=1}^{r} \alpha_k$$

$$\beta_j^\dagger = - \sum_{k=j+1}^{s} \beta_k \,, \qquad j = 0, 1, 2, \ldots, s - 1$$

and

$$\beta = \sum_{k=0}^{s} \beta_k$$

By casting the model in levels and differences, a formulation of this kind separates out long-run and short-run effects. The total multiplier is given by

$$D(1) = \beta/(1 - \alpha) \qquad (4.2)$$

Note that, in a stable model, $|\alpha| < 1$.

Subtracting y_{t-1} from both sides of (4.1) leads to the dependent variable being Δy_t. The coefficient of y_{t-1} is then equal to $\alpha - 1$ and the total multiplier is equal to β divided by minus this coefficient. A further modification is to have x_{t-1}, rather than x_t, appearing as the levels explanatory variable in the model. The lag on this variable then corresponds to the lag on the level of the dependent variable, and the model may be written as

$$\Delta y_t = (\alpha - 1) y_{t-1} + \sum_{j=1}^{r-1} \alpha_j^\dagger \, \Delta y_{t-j} + \beta_0 \Delta x_t$$

$$+ \beta x_{t-1} + \sum_{j=1}^{s-1} \beta_j^\dagger \, \Delta x_{t-j} + \epsilon_t \qquad (4.3)$$

The relevance of this formulation will become apparent in the next section when the idea of steady state solutions is developed. For the moment we concentrate on model selection, and observe that since the dynamics in both (4.2) and (4.3) are captured by the differenced variables, they are particularly amenable to a general to specific model selection strategy. The higher order lags will often have the smallest coefficients and it is natural to begin by testing them for significance, and gradually moving down to the lower order lags.

Note that other rearrangements of the equation are also possible. For example, the levels variables can appear as y_{t-r} and x_{t-s}, while the remaining terms are in differences.

The main feature of the general to specific methodology is the abandonment of any attempt to identify a suitably parsimonious model at the outset. Instead, there is deliberate 'overfitting'. One of the reasons for this stems primarily from the fact that stochastic difference equations typically contain several explanatory variables. In these circumstances it becomes difficult to identify a suitable model by any of the techniques described in Section 5 of the previous chapter. Furthermore, the decision as to whether or not a particular explanatory variable should be included in the model can only really be made if it is included in the model in the first place.

There is a second reason why overfitting is more popular in stochastic difference equations than in transfer functions, and in a sense this is more fundamental than the reason already given. Consider a transfer function model in which $r = s = 1$, i.e.

$$y_t = \frac{(\beta_0 + \beta_1 L) x_t}{(1 - \alpha L)} + \epsilon_t \tag{4.4}$$

A specification of this kind can lead to computational problems arising from common factors. This happens irrespective of the form of the disturbance term, and so for simplicity it has been assumed to be white noise. In the development that follows it will be convenient to reparameterise the numerator of the rational lag in (4.4) by defining γ and β such that $\beta(1 - \gamma L) = \beta_0 + \beta_1 L$. Maximising the likelihood function of (4.4) is equivalent to minimising a sum of squares function in which the residuals are computed recursively from

$$\epsilon_t = \alpha \epsilon_{t-1} + y_t - \alpha y_{t-1} - \beta x_t + \beta \gamma x_{t-1}, \qquad t = 2, \ldots, T \tag{4.5}$$

with $\epsilon_1 = 0$. The derivatives of (4.5) with respect to α and γ are

$$\frac{\partial \epsilon_t}{\partial \alpha} = \epsilon_{t-1} - y_{t-1} + \alpha \frac{\partial \epsilon_{t-1}}{\partial \alpha} \tag{4.6a}$$

and

$$\frac{\partial \epsilon_t}{\partial \gamma} = -\beta x_{t-1} + \alpha \frac{\partial \epsilon_{t-1}}{\partial \gamma} \qquad (4.6b)$$

Now suppose that there is a common factor in (4.4), i.e. $\gamma = \alpha$. Imposing this restriction in (4.5) implies that

$$\epsilon_t = y_t - \beta x_t \qquad (4.7)$$

This is also apparent from (4.4). Using (4.7), it will be seen that when $\alpha = \gamma$, $\partial \epsilon_t / \partial \alpha$ and $-\partial \epsilon_t / \partial \gamma$ are identical. A Gauss—Newton iterative scheme will therefore break down due to multicollinearity. Furthermore, any other iterative scheme will probably also run into difficulties since $\alpha = \gamma$ implies singularity of the information matrix.

The above argument may be summarised by saying that when the lag structure of a transfer function is overparameterised, problems are likely to arise due to lack of identifiability. In a stochastic difference equation, on the other hand, the existence of common factors in the lag structure will not generally imply that the model is underidentified. Thus starting with a very general model will not usually lead to the kind of problem described in the previous paragraph. The movement to a more specific formulation then proceeds by a search for common factors in the lag structure. Once a set of common factors has been extracted, further simplification will be possible if it turns out that some of the factors have a root of zero.

The common factor approach to dynamic specification has been developed by Sargan (1964, 1980a), and applied by Hendry and Mizon (1978) and Mizon and Hendry (1980). In order to avoid any possible confusion with the multivariate technique of 'factor analysis', the common factor method is often referred to as 'COMFAC analysis'. The full procedure is described in some detail in the sub-section below, but there is no loss in continuity in moving directly to the sub-section on a strategy for model selection.

COMFAC Analysis*

The essential point behind COMFAC analysis is the integration of systematic and disturbance dynamics. Thus serial correlation in the disturbances is taken as a reflection of a particular structure imposed on the systematic dynamics of the equation. This is best explained by means of a simple example.

Consider the model

$$y_t = \alpha y_{t-1} + \beta_0 x_t + \beta_1 x_{t-1} + \epsilon_t, \qquad t = 2, \ldots, T \qquad (4.8)$$

with $|\alpha| < 1$. This may be rewritten as

$$(1 - \alpha L) y_t = (\beta_0 + \beta_1 L) x_t + \epsilon_t \qquad (4.9)$$

and a common factor will be present if $\beta_0 (1 - \alpha L) = \beta_0 + \beta_1 L$.

The existence of such a common factor implies that the parameters in (4.8) are subject to the restriction

$$\alpha \beta_0 + \beta_1 = 0 \qquad (4.10)$$

However, in contrast to the transfer function, (4.1), which has exactly the same systematic dynamics as (4.8), no computational problems arise when (4.10) holds. Estimation of (4.8) may still be carried out by OLS, and the only consequence of ignoring the restriction in (4.10) is a loss in efficiency.

If the common factor restriction is imposed on the model, it may be rearranged by dividing both sides of (4.9) by $(1 - \alpha L)$. This gives

$$y_t = \beta_0 x_t + u_t \qquad (4.11)$$

where $u_t = \epsilon_t / (1 - \alpha L)$. The original dynamic model is therefore reduced to a static one in which the disturbance term follows a stationary AR(1) process,

$$u_t = \alpha u_{t-1} + \epsilon_t \qquad (4.12)$$

Thus although serial correlation may be regarded as a 'nuisance' in static regression, it may actually represent a simplification when viewed in the wider context of dynamic regression.

By starting from (4.8) it is possible to test two hypotheses, one of which is nested within the other. The first hypothesis concerns the validity of the common factor restriction, (4.10). If this restriction is accepted, the hypothesis of a zero root, i.e. $\alpha = 0$, may be tested. Failure to reject this second hypothesis leads to a static regression model with white noise disturbances. A model with three parameters is therefore reduced to a model with only one. This is an example of a *simplification search,* and as was argued in Section 5.8, an approach of this kind is generally preferable to one in which a very restricted model is taken as the starting point.

The common factor framework may be generalised as follows. In the stochastic difference equation, (1.3), the orders of the polynomials $A(L)$, $B_1(L)$, . . . , $B_{k-1}(L)$ and $B_k(L)$ are r, s_1, . . . , s_{k-1} and s_k respectively. These polynomials can therefore have at most l common roots, where $l = \min(r, s_1, \ldots, s_k)$. If there are actually $p \leq l$ common roots, there exists a polynomial $\phi(L)$ of order p which is common to $A(L)$, $B_1(L)$, . . . , $B_k(L)$. The polynomials may therefore be factorised as $A(L) = \phi(L)A^*(L)$, $B_1(L) = \phi(L)B_1^*(L)$, . . . , $B_k(L) = \phi(L)B_k^*(L)$, and the model becomes

$$A^*(L)y_t = \sum_{i=1}^{k} B_i^*(L)x_{ti} + \phi^{-1}(L)\epsilon_t \qquad (4.13)$$

The net result is that the number of parameters in the model is reduced by kp, while the disturbance term becomes an AR(p) process.

The test procedure implemented in Sargan's COMFAC algorithm is based on a series of Wald tests. The reason for this is that estimation of the unrestricted model is relatively easy. If $\epsilon_t \sim NID(0, \sigma^2)$, the ML estimates are given by OLS, and these estimators are used as the basis for a series of common factor tests. Unfortunately, the form of the Wald statistics is rather complicated, in general, and a full discussion is beyond the scope of this book. However, in the case of the simple model introduced in (4.8), the derivation of the common factor test is straightforward, and this provides a useful illustration of the technique underlying the whole approach.

A common factor is present in (4.8) when the constraint (4.10) holds. In terms of the notation of Section 5.4, this may be written

$$r(\psi) = \alpha\beta_0 + \beta_1 = 0 \tag{4.14}$$

where $\psi = (\alpha, \beta_0, \beta_1)'$. The derivatives of $r(\psi)$ with respect to α_1, β_0 and β_1 are $\partial r(\psi)/\partial\alpha = \beta_0$, $\partial r(\psi)/\partial\beta_0 = \alpha$ and $\partial r(\psi)/\partial\beta_1 = 1$. The complete vector of derivatives may therefore be written as

$$\partial r(\psi)/\partial\psi = (\beta_0, \alpha, 1)' \tag{4.15}$$

Expressions (4.14) and (4.15) may be evaluated using the OLS estimates in (4.5) and can then be used to construct the Wald statistic, (5.4.8). The matrix $I^*(\tilde{\psi})$ can then be set equal to $s^2(\Sigma z_t z_t')^{-1}$ where $z_t = (y_{t-1}, x_t, x_{t-1})'$. Under $H_0: r(\psi) = 0$, W has a χ_1^2 distribution in large samples, but when no common factor is present it tends to become large.

Example 1 Godfrey (1973) applied the above test procedure using the data published in Durbin and Watson (1951). The model considered by Durbin and Watson was

$$y_t = \delta + \beta_1 x_{1t} + \beta_2 x_{2t} + u_t \tag{4.16}$$

where y is the logarithm of consumption of spirits per head, x_1 is the logarithm of real income per head and x_2 is a relative price index. The data refer to the UK over the period 1870–1938, and when (4.16) was estimated by OLS the DW statistic obtained was 0.249. This is obviously highly significant, and it could be taken to imply that the appropriate course of action is to estimate the model with an AR(1) disturbance term. However, a more general dynamic specification is a model of the form (4.8). Estimating such a model by OLS in deviation from the mean form gave

$$\hat{y}_t = 0.947y_{t-1} + 0.717x_{1t} - 0.744x_{1,t-1} - 0.892x_{2t}$$

$$+ 0.824x_{2,t-1} \tag{4.17}$$

The question now is whether the restrictions implied by fitting (4.16) with an AR(1) disturbance term are consistent with the estimates of the unrestricted model displayed in (4.17).

Since the model contains two explanatory variables there are two restrictions of the form (4.14). These are evaluated as:

$$r_1(\tilde{\psi}) = (0.717)(0.947) - 0.744 = -0.065$$

$$r_2(\tilde{\psi}) = (-0.898)(0.947) - 0.824 = -0.026$$

Differentiating $R(\psi) = \{r_1(\psi), r_2(\psi)\}'$ with respect to the parameters in ψ, in the order in which they appear in (4.17) yields

$$\frac{\partial R(\psi)}{\partial \psi} = \begin{bmatrix} 0.717 & 0.947 & 1.0 & 0 & 0 \\ -0.898 & 0 & 0 & 0.947 & 1.0 \end{bmatrix}$$

when evaluated at the estimates in (4.17). This matrix together with the estimated covariance matrix in (4.17) gave

$$W = (-0.065, -0.026) \begin{bmatrix} 0.302 \times 10^{-2} & -0.158 \times 10^{-4} \\ -0.158 \times 10^{-4} & 0.536 \times 10^{-3} \end{bmatrix}$$

$$\times \begin{pmatrix} -0.065 \\ -0.026 \end{pmatrix} = 2.702$$

Under the null hypothesis that the restrictions are valid $W \sim \chi_2^2$ in large samples. Since the critical value for a χ_2^2 variate at the 10% level of significance is 4.61, the test supports the notion that estimating the static regression model, (4.16), with an AR(1) disturbance term is an appropriate course of action.

The last aspect of the COMFAC procedure is the way in which a series of common factor tests are carried out. Having decided on the most general dynamic specification, a series of nested hypotheses are mapped out. The overall test procedure is then executed in the way described in Section 5.8. The first test is for one common factor. If this is not rejected, a test for two common factors is carried out, and so on. The procedure terminates when an hypothesis is rejected.

Example 2   The study by Mizon and Hendry (1980) is concerned with the specification of a model for Canada relating expenditure on consumer durables (y) to real income (x_1) and relative price (x_2). The observations are quarterly and so a reasonable specification for a general model is to take four period lags on all variables, i.e.

$$\log y_t = \delta_0 + \sum_{j=1}^{3} \delta_j Q_{jt} + \sum_{j=1}^{4} \alpha_j \log y_{t-j} + \sum_{j=0}^{4} \beta_{1j} \log x_{1,t-j}$$

$$+ \sum_{j=0}^{4} \beta_{2j} \log x_{2,t-j} + \epsilon_t \qquad (4.18)$$

The model also includes a constant and three seasonal dummies.

The results of COMFAC are shown in table 8.1. It is the incremental values of the Wald statistics which are used in the test procedure, since these are independent of each other. Thus, for example, a test for two common factors is based on

$$W_2^* = W_2 - W_1$$

i.e.

$$W_2^* = 1.24 - 0.47 = 0.77$$

If each of these tests is carried out at the 1% level of significance, the overall probability of a Type I error is $1 - (0.99)^4 = 0.0394$. Since $Pr(\chi_2^2 > 9.21) = 0.01$, it is clear from the table that the hypothesis of three common factors cannot be rejected, whereas four can be. The above results suggest that a convenient simplification of (4.18) might be to include c, y and p with one period lags, and to allow the disturbance term to follow an AR(3) process. However, this was not the model which Mizon and Hendry finally adopted. On examining the estimates in the unrestricted model, (4.18), it was found that the coefficients of y_{t-2} and x_{t-2} were far larger than the corresponding coefficients at $t-1$. Furthermore, the restricted model yielded a value of s markedly larger than that in the unrestricted model, and a likelihood ratio test indicated a rejection of the common factor restrictions which COMFAC had suggested were data admissible. These findings point very strongly to the view that the results of a COMFAC analysis should not be accepted uncritically, insofar as they suggest a particular specification. However, there is no doubt that COMFAC has a valuable role to play in *rejecting* models which impose invalid common factor restrictions.

Table 8.1 COMFAC Analysis for Model (4.15)

		Direct Tests		Incremental Tests
No. of common factors (i)	Degrees of freedom	Value of test statistic (W_i)	Degrees of freedom	Value of test statistic (W_i^*)
1	2	0.47	2	0.47
2	4	1.24	2	0.77
3	6	6.09	2	4.85
4	8	32.01	2	25.92

Source: Mizon and Hendry (1980)

A Strategy for Model Selection

Any specification which is being seriously entertained must be subject to diagnostic checks. The modified LM test developed in Section 3 is particularly appropriate for this purpose. However, although a test based on $Q^{\dagger}(m, T^{\dagger})$ is formally a test against an AR(m) or an MA(m) disturbance term, a rejection of the null hypothesis should not be interpreted as evidence *for* such a specification. It was emphasised in earlier chapters that serial correlation in the residuals need not be symptomatic of serial correlation in the disturbances. A more fundamental problem, such as an omitted variable, may lie at the heart of the problem. This is still the case in dynamic regression, although the matter is now further complicated by the consideration that serial correlation in the residuals may also be a reflection of an inappropriate specification of the systematic dynamics. As an example, suppose that the true model is (4.8). The residuals which emerge from regressing y_t on x_t will tend to be serially correlated, but unless the restriction in (4.10) is valid, extending the model to include an AR(1) disturbance term will not be an appropriate course of action.

When the disturbance term in a stochastic difference equation is modelled as an ARMA(p, q) process, the LM test against an ARMA($p + m, q$) process provides the basis for a convenient diagnostic check. Of course, all the points made in the previous paragraph are still relevant.

The residual sum of squares, or alternatively s^2, provides a useful measure of *goodness of fit*. It is worth recalling from (4.3) that any stochastic difference equation in which the dependent variable is in levels may be re-arranged so that the dependent variable is in first differences. Reformulating the model in this way makes no difference to s^2. However, the coefficient of multiple correlation now gives the proportion of the variance of first differences explained by the model and such a measure is arguably more appropriate for time series regression. Indeed, this statistic can also be computed when the dependent variable is in levels, being given by

$$R_D^2 = 1 - SSE \bigg/ \sum_{t=2}^{T} (\Delta y_t - \overline{\Delta y})^2 \tag{4.19}$$

where $\overline{\Delta y}$ is the mean of first differences.

Once a model has been selected, it should be validated against post-sample observations. This can be done using the $\xi(l)$ statistic defined in (5.7.4). However, in an autoregressive distributed lag model, OLS is the appropriate estimation technique and it therefore seems reasonable to adopt some of the procedures proposed in Section 5.7 for classical regression. In particular, $\xi(l)$ may be replaced by the Chow statistic, $\xi^*(l)$. A test based on the F-distribution will only have asymptotic validity, but because the prediction errors in $\xi^*(l)$ are 'standardised' — see (5.7.7) — the size of the test should be reasonably close to the nominal significance level.

Bearing the above points in mind, a general strategy for dynamic model selection is to proceed in the following way.

(i) Estimate a general model in which the dynamics are of a relatively high order. Examine the coefficients in order to gain some idea of which lags are likely to be important, and retain the value of s^2. This provides a yardstick against which the goodness of fit of more restricted models may be assessed.

(ii) Formulate a more restricted model than the one just estimated, using any prior economic theory to suggest a suitable specification for the dynamics. (The role played by economic theory in this context is discussed in the next section.) The model so specified should, however, be consistent with the estimated general model. Thus a large coefficient in the general model would not be arbitrarily set equal to zero.

In the absence of any prior economic theory, COMFAC analysis may be used to develop a more parsimonious model.

(iii) Check the estimated restricted model for consistency with the general model. Large discrepancies between estimated parameters and/or a substantial increase in s^2 imply that some change in specification might be appropriate.

At the same time, diagnostic checks based on LM tests may be carried out. These procedures may be supplemented by the less formal graphical procedures described in Section 5.2.

(iv) A particular specification may be regarded as acceptable if: (a) it satisfies any prior constraints imposed by economic theory; (b) it is consistent with the most general model estimated; (c) it passes the diagnostic checks; (d) it compares favourably with other models in terms of goodness of fit; and (e) it satisfies the post-sample predictive tests of Section 5.7.

8.5. Error Correction Models and Co-Integration

The above strategy is not without its problems. In particular, it can become very cumbersome if the possibility of a large number of explanatory variables, coupled with high order lags is entertained. The next section shows how the notion of a steady state can be incorporated in a dynamic model. This aids interpretation of the properties of the model and provides a framework within which restrictions from economic theory can be imposed. The concept of co-integration is then introduced, and is shown to have important statistical implications for dynamic models. In particular, it turns out that there are circumstances when the OLS estimators of certain parameters in equations of the form (4.3) are not asymptotically normal. However, these complications potentially offer some consolation in that they suggest the possibility of a two-stage model-building strategy, with the initial stage focusing on long-run relationships between variables and the second stage concentrating on short-run dynamics.

The Steady State and Error Correction

The equilibrium solution of (4.1) is the mean path of y_t when x_t is constant. This is simply

$$\bar{y}_t = D(1)\bar{x} \qquad (5.1)$$

as in (7.2.2). As a concept, the static equilibrium embodied in the above equation is somewhat limited since most economic variables grow over time. Of much more importance is the idea of a *steady-state* relationship between variables which are evolving over time.

Suppose that x_t is stationary in first differences. In other words it is integrated of order one, that is $x_t \sim I(1)$, and it can be expressed as

$$\Delta x_t = g_x + \eta_t \qquad (5.2)$$

where η_t is a stationary process with a mean of zero. If x_t is in logarithms, as is usually the case, then g_x is the average growth rate. Suppose also that y_t is $I(1)$, but with a mean of g_y. Models of the form (5.2) are not unreasonable for many macroeconomic time series as they are capable of reproducing the kind of evolutionary behaviour often observed in practice. Now suppose that there is a relationship between x_t and y_t, so that although they are both non-stationary, they tend to keep together in the long run. More specifically, they obey an equation of the form

$$y_t = \nu_0 + \nu x_t + u_t \qquad (5.3)$$

where ν_0 and ν are parameters and u_t is a zero mean stationary disturbance term. Again if y_t and x_t are in logarithms, ν can be interpreted as the *long-run elasticity* of y with respect to x. Furthermore, on taking first differences in (5.3), followed by expectations, the following relationship is seen to hold between the growth rates in the two series:

$$g_y = \nu g_x \qquad (5.4)$$

Finally, if capital letters are used to denote antilogarithms the underlying long-run relationship in (5.3) may be thought of as

$$Y = KX^\nu \qquad \text{with } K = \exp(\nu_0) \qquad (5.5)$$

Now return to the general dynamic model as expressed in equation (4.3), but with a constant term, δ, included. The contributions from the two levels variables may be written together as

$$(\alpha - 1)y_{t-1} + \beta x_{t-1} = (\alpha - 1)\{y_{t-1} - D(1)x_{t-1}\}$$

leading to

$$\Delta y_t = \delta + \sum_{j=1}^{r-1} \alpha_j^\dagger \Delta y_{t-j} + \beta_0 \Delta x_t + \sum_{j=1}^{s-1} \beta_j^\dagger \Delta x_{t-j}$$

$$+ (\alpha - 1)\{y_{t-1} - D(1)x_{t-1}\} + \epsilon_t \qquad (5.6)$$

The differenced variables are stationary, and it can be seen from (5.2) that the mean of Δx_t is g_x, while, from (5.4), the mean of Δy_t is νg_x. Thus if equation (5.6) is rearranged so that, on redefining $t-1$ as t, y_t appears on the left hand side, it is seen to be consistent with the long-run equation, (5.3), with

$$\nu = D(1) \tag{5.7a}$$

and

$$\nu_0 = \left\{\delta + \left(\nu \sum_{j=1}^{r-1} \alpha_j{}^\dagger - \nu + \beta_0 + \sum_{j=1}^{s-1} \beta_j{}^\dagger\right) g_x\right\} / (1 - \alpha) \tag{5.7b}$$

In the special case when $r = s = 1$,

$$\nu_0 = \{\delta + (\beta_0 - \nu)g_x\}/(1 - \alpha) \tag{5.8}$$

Example 1 In the model for consumer durables in Canada referred to in Section 4, Mizon and Hendry (1980) estimated the general model (4.15) as a first step in their model selection procedure. In steady-state growth, the long-run solution for the model is of the form

$$y = K_j \, x_1^{\nu(1)} \, x_2^{\nu(2)}, \qquad j = 0, 1, 2, 3 \tag{5.9}$$

where

$$v(i) = \frac{\beta_{i0} + \beta_{i1} + \beta_{i2} + \beta_{i3} + \beta_{i4}}{1 - \alpha_1 - \alpha_2 - \alpha_3 - \alpha_4}, \qquad i = 1, 2$$

and $\log K_j$ takes a different value in each quarter depending on the estimated coefficient of the corresponding seasonal dummy. In other words the steady-state equation corresponding to (5.3) contains three seasonal dummy variables in addition to the constant term. From the results in table II of their paper,

$$v(1) = \frac{0.93}{0.71} = 1.3 \quad \text{and} \quad v(2) = \frac{-0.39}{0.71} = -0.55$$

Thus the long-run income elasticity of demand for consumer durables is 1.3, while the price elasticity of demand is -0.55. These values are reasonable on the basis of prior knowledge: the share of consumer durables in total expenditure tends to go up with rising income, while a negative price elasticity is consistent with a downward sloping demand curve.

The long-run relationship in the model is captured by the term in curly brackets in (5.6) involving the levels variables, y_{t-1} and x_{t-1}. If this levels term were omitted, all the variables would be in first differences and only short-run effects would be picked up. A model of this kind might be regarded as a reasonable approximation to (5.6), particularly if α is close to unity. However, as long as α is less than one, a model in first differences is inadequate from the point of view of both estimation and forecasting. The levels term in (5.6) plays a crucial role in the working of the model. Suppose that y starts to increase more rapidly than is consistent with the steady-state solution, perhaps because of a series of large positive disturbances. The net result is that the term in curly brackets becomes positive, since y_{t-1} has drifted above the steady-state growth path. However, because $\alpha - 1$ is negative, the overall effect is to slow down the short-term growth in y, thereby forcing y_t back towards its long-run growth path. For this reason, the levels term in (5.6) is said to be an error correction mechanism, and the model as a whole is referred to as an *error correction model* or ECM.

Economic Theory and Restrictions on the Long Run

In Example 1, prior economic knowledge was helpful insofar as it suggested a reasonable range of values for the long-run parameters. However, economic theory may sometimes suggest more precise constraints on these parameters. In order to simplify the exposition, assume that $r = s = 1$, so that the model is just

$$y_t = \delta + \alpha y_{t-1} + \beta_0 x_t + \beta_1 x_{t-1} + \epsilon_t, \quad |\alpha| < 1 \tag{5.10}$$

The rearrangement corresponding to (5.6) is then

$$\Delta y_t = \delta + \beta_0 \Delta x_t + (\alpha - 1)\{y_{t-1} - \nu x_{t-1}\} + \epsilon_t \tag{5.11}$$

where ν, the long-run elasticity, is

$$\nu = (\beta_0 + \beta_1)/(1 - \alpha) \tag{5.12}$$

In some situations it may be reasonable to specify a particular value for ν, ν^*, on the basis of economic theory. The error correction term,

$$z^*_{t-1} = y_{t-1} - \nu^* x_{t-1} \tag{5.13}$$

then appears as an observable explanatory variable in (5.11) and estimation can be carried out by running OLS. Furthermore, because all the variables in this regression are stationary, the estimators will be asymptotically normal and the usual standard errors will be asymptotically valid. Unfortunately, testing for the validity of the restriction in the error correction term is less straightforward. The obvious approach is to include x_{t-1} as an additional regressor. This is equivalent to estimating the original unrestricted model, but its advantage is that the coefficient of x_{t-1} is $\alpha + \beta_0 + \beta_1 - \nu$, which is zero when $\nu = \nu^*$. The complication arises because, as shown in the next sub-section, the t-statistic for the coefficient of x_{t-1} does not have an asymptotic standard normal distribution.

The most common prior restriction that is placed on ν is that it is unity. The error correction term is then simply $z_t = y_t - x_t$. Models of this kind have been found to be appropriate in a variety of applications, including wage-price models (Sargan 1964), the demand for money (Hendry 1980) and the consumption function (Davidson *et al.*, 1978). The error correction model of the consumption function is particularly interesting in that it provides a reconciliation of short-run and long-run behaviour. The empirical evidence available for most countries shows that over a prolonged period of time, the relationship between consumption, y, and personal disposable income, x, is of the form:

$$y = Kx \tag{5.14}$$

Thus the long-run elasticity of income with respect to consumption is unity and the proportion of income consumed (the 'average propensity to consume') remains constant at a value of K. However, a key feature of the Keynesian consumption function is that the marginal propensity to consume (the increase in consumption induced by an additional unit of income) should be less than the average propensity to consume, whereas in (5.14), they are the same. The error correction model takes account of this apparent contradiction by having a steady-state solution of the form (5.14), coupled with a marginal propensity to consume (MPC) which is considerably less than K in the short run.

Example 2 In their study of the UK consumption function, Davidson *et al.* (1978, p. 684) estimated the model

$$\Delta_4 y_t = 0.49\Delta_4 x_t - 0.17\Delta_1\Delta_4 x_t$$
$$(0.04) (0.05)$$

$$-0.06\,(y_{t-4} - x_{t-4}) + 0.01\,\Delta_4 D_t^0 \tag{5.15}$$
$$(0.01) (0.004)$$

$$R^2 = 0.71, \quad s = 0.0067, \quad DW = 1.6, \quad \xi(20) = 80.7$$

where the observations on consumption and income are quarterly, seasonally unadjusted and measured in £ million at 1970 prices. The dummy variable, D_t^0, allows for the effect of the 1968 budget and the introduction of VAT in 1973.

A number of features differentiate this model from (5.11). In the first place, first differences are replaced by fourth differences, and the variables in the error correction term appear with a lag of four periods rather than one. However, this is simply a reflection of the fact that the observations are quarterly. The annual growth rates are now measured by the fourth differences of logarithms and the theory goes through exactly as before. In particular, the error correction term, $(y_{t-4} - x_{t-4})$, comes in to alter the short-run consumption decision whenever the proportion of income consumed strays from the steady-state value, K, implied by (5.14).

A second feature of (5.15) is the introduction of the regressor $\Delta_1\Delta_4 x_t$. Ignoring the dummy variable, the model implies that consumers plan to spend the same as they did in the corresponding quarter of the previous year, modified by a proportion of their annual change in income ($+0.49\,\Delta_4 x_t$), and by whether the change itself is increasing or decreasing ($-0.17\,\Delta_1\Delta_4 x_t$). These factors determine the short-run consumption decision. Expressing them in levels implies that y_t depends partly on the linear combination

$$(0.49 - 0.17) x_t - 0.17 (-x_{t-1}) = 0.32 x_t + 0.17 x_{t-1}$$

The immediate effect of a unit change in x (the impact elasticity) is 0.32. This rises to 0.49 after one quarter but remains constant for the next two quarters. In the short run, therefore, the marginal propensity to consume (MPC) is around one half. This contrasts with a long run MPC of between 0.8 and 0.9, obtained from a direct examination of the data.

The third feature of (5.15) which differentiates it from (5.11) is the absence of a constant term. This was specifically excluded from the estimated model, since to have left it in would have resulted in relatively imprecise estimates due to multicollinearity; this arises because the error correction term shows very little variation when the observations all lie close to the steady-state growth path. However, in a later paper, Hendry and von Ungern-Sternberg (1980) found that $(y_{t-4} - x_{t-4})$ retained its significance if seasonal dummies were added to the model.

The last point to note about (5.15) is that the post-sample predictive test statistic, $\xi(20)$ is significant at the 1% level. This suggests that some change in the specification is necessary, and in a later part of their paper Davidson *et al.* extend their model to allow for inflation effects. However, the basic dynamic structure of (5.15) remains unchanged. Hendry and von Ungern-Sternberg (1980) take the development one step further by allowing for changes in liquid assets.

Co-Integration

Two series, y_t and x_t, are said to be *co-integrated* of order d, b, denoted as $\mathrm{CI}(d, b)$, if (i) they are both $I(d)$; and (ii) there is a linear combination of them which is $I(d - b)$ where $b > 0$. The definition extends to several series; see Engle and Granger (1987).

The idea behind co-integration can most easily be explained by considering the case of $d = b = 1$. Both series are non-stationary, and it is generally true that an arbitrary linear combination, $y_t - ax_t$, where a is a constant, will also be non-stationary. However, because the series are co-integrated, there must be a values of a such that $y_t - ax_t$ is $I(0)$ rather than $I(1)$. In other words, the long-run movements cancel out. Thus there is some kind of steady-state relationship between the variables. In the case of $a = 1$, the steady-state relationship is such that y_t and x_t cannot drift too far apart.

A steady-state relationship between two $I(1)$ variables was posited in equation (5.3). Thus the series y_t and x_t are $\mathrm{CI}(1,1)$ and it can be seen from (5.3) that setting the constant a equal to ν yields a stationary linear combination, z_t, that is

$$z_t = y_t - \nu x_t = \nu_0 + u_t \tag{5.16}$$

The implications of co-integration can be explored within the context of a multivariate model, in which both y_t and x_t are taken to be endogenous, or within the context of a single equation ECM of the form (5.6). Various ways in which co-integrating restrictions can be incorporated in multivariate models are discussed in Engle and Granger (1987) and Harvey (1989). However, the issues raised are beyond the scope of the present book, and the main focus of attention here is on single-equation ECM's where co-integration of y_t and x_t has important implications for both estimation and specification.

The steady-state relationship between y_t and x_t in the ECM, (5.6), is given by (5.3). At first sight it might seem inappropriate to apply OLS to this equation since the disturbance term depends on differences of the explanatory variable, x_t. However, the fact that x_t is $I(1)$, while the disturbance term is stationary, means not only that the OLS estimator of the long-run elasticity, ν, is consistent, but that it converges more rapidly to its limiting distribution than is usually the case; see Stock (1987). This suggests that it might be a relatively accurate estimator of ν in practice. Thus, having estimated ν in this way, a further possibility is to construct the error correction term

$$\hat{z}_{t-1} = y_{t-1} - \hat{\nu}x_{t-1} \tag{5.17}$$

and use it as an explanatory variable in the full ECM. This is essentially what was done in the previous sub-section except that there the value of ν was predetermined rather than being estimated. It transpires that, because of the rapid convergence of $\hat{\nu}$, the OLS estimators of the short-run parameters in the model have the usual asymptotic normal distribution. Thus tests can be carried out on them in exactly the same way as if ν were known.

The above results suggest a *two-stage modelling strategy* which may be formalised as follows. *Stage One:* estimate the long-run parameters by running a static regression in levels; test the null hypothesis of no co-integration by a Dickey–Fuller test for a unit root in the residuals, or by one of the other methods described in Engle and Granger (1987, p. 268); hence find a set of explanatory variables which form a co-integrating relationship with the dependent variable. *Stage Two:* use the error correction term, $\hat{z}_{t-1}$, that is the residuals from the static regression, as an explanatory variable and estimate the short-run dynamics; test down to find a parsimonious dynamic structure. Applications of this strategy can be found in Engle and Granger (1987) and Hall (1986).

Unfortunately the two-stage procedure is not without its drawbacks. Although the OLS estimators in what is sometimes termed the *co-integrating regression* converge very rapidly to their limiting distributions, these distributions are not normal and they depend strongly on the other parameters in the full model. Furthermore, the evidence presented in Stock (1987) and Banerjee *et al.* (1986) shows that the bias in the estimators can be substantial, particularly in small samples. Thus inferences may be very misleading, and erroneous decisions may be made regarding variables to be included or restrictions to be imposed. At the second stage the bias in the estimators carries over to the error correction term and may adversely affect the small-sample properties of the short-run parameters. The conclusion is that the two-stage procedure is perhaps best viewed as an initial data exploratory tool, rather than as a formal modelling procedure.

Non-standard distribution theory also applies when the long-run parameters are estimated from the full model. In general, co-integration of the series implies non-linear restrictions on the parameters. However, if there is only one explanatory variable, the appropriate estimator of the long-run parameter, ν, can be computed by first applying OLS to the ECM in the form (4.3) and then dividing minus the coefficient of y_{t-1} by the coefficient of x_{t-1}. The asymptotic distribution of the estimator obtained in this way is not the same as that of the corresponding estimator obtained from the co-integrating regression, and the available Monte Carlo evidence suggests that its small-sample bias, is, in general, less severe. On the other hand, the rapid convergence of the estimators of the long-run parameters means that the estimators of the short-run parameters have the same asymptotic normal distributions irrespective of whether they are computed directly or by the two-stage procedure.

8.6. Systems of Equations

Systems of regression equations were analysed in Sections 2.9 and 6.9. However, these models were static. A dynamic system is characterised by the appearance of lagged dependent variables among the regressors in some or all of the equations. As might be expected, this raises similar issues to those involved in the single equation case.

Following the approach adopted in Section 6.9, the full model may be written as

$$y_t = Z_t \gamma + u_t, \qquad t = 1,\ldots,T \tag{6.1}$$

where y_t and u_t are $N \times 1$ vectors as in (2.9.15). The matrix Z_t is defined in the same way as X_t in (2.9.16), the difference in notation serving to indicate that some of the regressors are lagged dependent variables. For the same reason the symbol γ, rather than β, is used to denote the parameter vector.

Example 1 Consider the two equation system,

$$\left.\begin{array}{l} y_{1t} = \alpha_1 y_{1,t-1} + \beta_1 x_{1t} + u_{1t} \\ y_{2t} = \alpha_2 y_{2,t-1} + \alpha_2^* y_{1,t-2} + \beta_2 x_{2t} + u_{2t} \end{array}\right\} \quad t = 1,\ldots,T \tag{6.2}$$

where x_{1t} and x_{2t} are exogenous. The matrix Z_t for (6.2) is defined by

$$Z_t = \begin{bmatrix} y_{1,t-1} & x_{1t} & 0 & 0 & 0 \\ 0 & 0 & y_{2,t-1} & y_{1,t-2} & x_{2t} \end{bmatrix} \tag{6.3}$$

while the corresponding vector of parameters is

$$\gamma = (\alpha_1, \beta_1, \alpha_2, \alpha_2^*, \beta_2)' \tag{6.4}$$

An alternative way of writing models of this kind is as follows:

$$y_t = A_1 y_{t-1} + \ldots + A_r y_{t-r} + B_0 x_t + \ldots + B_s x_{t-s} + u_t,$$
$$t = 1, \ldots, T \tag{6.5}$$

This is a generalisation of (2.10.1) with x_t denoting a $K \times 1$ vector of exogenous variables, $A_1, \ldots, A_r$ denoting $N \times N$ matrices of parameters, and $B_0, \ldots, B_s$ denoting $N \times K$ matrices of parameters. Model (6.2) may be expressed in the notation of (6.5) by writing it as:

$$\begin{pmatrix} y_{1,t} \\ y_{2,t} \end{pmatrix} = \begin{bmatrix} \alpha_1 & 0 \\ 0 & \alpha_2 \end{bmatrix} \begin{pmatrix} y_{1,t-1} \\ y_{2,t-1} \end{pmatrix} + \begin{bmatrix} 0 & 0 \\ \alpha_2^* & 0 \end{bmatrix} \begin{pmatrix} y_{1,t-2} \\ y_{2,t-2} \end{pmatrix}$$

$$+ \begin{bmatrix} \beta_1 & 0 \\ 0 & \beta_2 \end{bmatrix} \begin{pmatrix} x_{1t} \\ x_{2t} \end{pmatrix} + \begin{pmatrix} u_{1t} \\ u_{2t} \end{pmatrix}, \quad t = 1, \ldots, T \tag{6.6}$$

Note that the parameter matrices in (6.6) are subject to restrictions, in that certain variables are excluded from each of the equations. This will often be the case with a model developed in the form (6.5). In fact (6.2) is rather extreme, since the equations contain no explanatory variables in common, except insofar as y_1 appears in each with a different lag.

In the discussion below, estimation and testing procedures will be developed using (6.1). Other aspects of dynamic systems are best considered in terms of (6.5). It is therefore useful to be able to work with both representations.

Systematic Dynamics*

The dynamic properties of the system, (6.5), are derived by generalising the results of Section 7.2. Consider first the case when $r = s = 1$, i.e.

$$y_t = A y_{t-1} + B x_t + u_t \tag{6.7}$$

This model reduces to (7.1.13) when $N = 1$, and it is instructive to compare the results below with the corresponding results obtained in the single equation case.

Repeated substitution for lagged values of y_t in (6.7) gives

$$y_t = \sum_{j=0}^{\infty} A^j B x_{t-j} + \sum_{j=0}^{\infty} A^j u_{t-j} \tag{6.8}$$

This representation is valid only if $\lim A^j = 0$ as j tends to infinity.

A necessary and sufficient condition for this to happen is that the roots of the determinantal equation,

$$| A - \lambda_i I | = 0 \tag{6.9}$$

are less than one in absolute value. A similar assumption is needed if (6.7) is to have an equilibrium solution. If x_t is constant at $\bar{x}$,

$$E(y_t) = \bar{y} = \left[\sum_{j=0}^{\infty} A^j \right] B\bar{x} \tag{6.10}$$

Writing (6.10) as an equilibrium solution pre-supposes that the infinite sum of A^j's converges. In fact it can be shown that

$$\sum_{j=0}^{\infty} A^j = (I - A)^{-1} \tag{6.11}$$

This is a matrix generalisation of the standard result for summing an infinite geometric progression.

The matrix $(I - A)^{-1}B$ is generally referred to as the *matrix of total multipliers*, although the term *dynamic multipliers* is also used by some writers. This gives the total effect on the mean path of y_t of a unit change in the level of all the variables in x. On the other hand, the immediate effect of a unit change in x is given by B, the *matrix of impact multipliers*. These concepts are completely analogous to those developed for the single equation case. Finally, matrices of interim multipliers may be defined. The operation in (6.8) enables the mean path of y to be expressed as an infinite distributed lag in x. Thus

$$\bar{y}_t = E(y_t) = \sum_{j=0}^{\infty} D_j x_{t-j}$$

where

$$D_j = A^j B, \quad j = 0, 1, \dots \tag{6.12}$$

By analogy with (7.2.6), the *matrix of Jth interim multipliers* is defined as

$$D_J^* = \sum_{j=0}^{J} D_j \tag{6.13}$$

Thus, for example, after two time periods the mean path of y will have changed by $(I + A + A^2) B$ in response to a unit change in all the elements of x.

In the general case, (6.5), these formulae are best developed using the lag operator. Defining the matrix polynomials in the lag operator,

$$A(L) = I - A_1 L - \dots - A_r L^r \tag{6.14}$$

and

$$B(L) = B_0 + B_1 L + \ldots + B_s L^s \tag{6.15}$$

(6.5) may be expressed as

$$A(L)y_t = B(L)x_t + u_t \tag{6.16}$$

The system will be *stable* if the roots of the determinantal polynomial $|A(L)|$ lie outside the unit circle; cf. *TSM* (Section 2.6). If this condition holds, the polynomial matrix $A(L)$ is non-singular, and the system may be expressed in the form

$$y_t = D(L)x_t + u_t \tag{6.17}$$

where $D(L)$ is an infinite matrix polynomial in the lag operator defined by

$$D(L) = A^{-1}(L)B(L) \tag{6.18}$$

cf. (6.12). The interim multipliers, (6.13), can be obtained by solving (6.18). The equilibrium solution of the system is given by

$$\bar{y} = D(1)\bar{x} \tag{6.19}$$

where $D(1)$, the matrix of total multipliers, may be evaluated from the expression

$$D(1) = A^{-1}(1)B(1)$$

Example 2 In (6.6)

$$D(1) = \begin{bmatrix} 1 - \alpha_1 & 0 \\ -\alpha_2^* & 1 - \alpha_2 \end{bmatrix}^{-1} \begin{bmatrix} \beta_1 & 0 \\ 0 & \beta_2 \end{bmatrix}$$

$$= \frac{1}{(1 - \alpha_1)(1 - \alpha_2)} \begin{bmatrix} \beta_1(1 - \alpha_2) & 0 \\ \beta_1\alpha_2^* & \beta_2(1 - \alpha_1) \end{bmatrix} \tag{6.20}$$

A change in x_2 will not therefore affect the mean path of y_1. On the other hand, a unit increase in x_1, with x_2 held constant, will eventually raise the level of y_2 by $\beta_1\alpha_2^*/(1 - \alpha_1)(1 - \alpha_2)$.

Estimation*

If $u_t \sim NID(0,\Omega)$, the estimation of (6.1) reduces to a straightforward application of the SURE technique. The fact that the model is dynamic has no implications for the asymptotic efficiency of any of the estimators already considered. Furthermore, if each equation in the system contains the same set of explanatory variables, OLS applied to each equation in turn will be fully efficient. A situation of this kind arises if no restrictions are placed on the matrices of parameters in (6.5).

The introduction of serial correlation into the disturbances complicates matters. The issues which arise are essentially the same as those noted for the single equation case. However, provided estimation is approached within an ML framework, it is not difficult to ensure asymptotic efficiency.

In the single equation model, the main points concerning estimation were established with respect to an AR(1) disturbance term. For the system (6.1), a vector AR(1) process will be assumed for u_t. Once this case has been sorted out, the theory of estimating models with more general ARMA disturbance terms can be deduced by drawing on the material presented in Section 6.8.

Maximising the likelihood function for (6.1) with an AR(1) disturbance term is equivalent to minimising the function

$$S(\Phi, \gamma) = \sum_t \epsilon_t' \Omega^{-1} \epsilon_t + T \log | \Omega | \tag{6.21}$$

The residuals are defined by

$$\epsilon_t = u_t - \Phi u_{t-1} = y_t - Z_t \gamma - \Phi(y_{t-1} - Z_{t-1}\gamma) \tag{6.22}$$

and a suitable way of minimising (6.21) is by the multivariate Gauss–Newton algorithm. The relevant vectors of derivatives are

$$\frac{\partial \epsilon_t}{\partial \gamma'} = -(Z_t - \Phi Z_{t-1}) \tag{6.23}$$

and

$$\frac{\partial \epsilon_t}{\partial \phi'} = -u'_{t-1} \otimes I_N \tag{6.24}$$

where $\phi = \text{vec}(\Phi)$.

A stepwise optimisation procedure can also be used to compute the ML estimator. Such a procedure was suggested in connection with the fixed regressor system of Section 6.8, and it was pointed out that this was a natural generalisation of the Cochrane–Orcutt scheme for a single equation. However, while an iterative stepwise procedure is a valid method of computing ML estimates in the dynamic model, a recognition of the fact that the information matrix is no longer block diagonal with respect to Φ and γ may lead to a preference for multivariate Gauss–Newton. (The discussion in Hendry and Tremayne (1976) is relevant here.) A more important point is that a two-step estimator of γ based on the generalisation of Cochrane–Orcutt will not, in general, be asymptotically efficient in the dynamic case. This situation exactly parallels that in the single equation model and the solution is essentially the same: given initial consistent estimates of γ, Φ and Ω, one iteration of multivariate Gauss–Newton will yield asymptotically efficient estimators of Φ and γ.

The *two-step estimation* procedure may therefore be summarised as follows:

(i) Compute a consistent estimator of γ, $\hat{\gamma}$, by applying the method of instrumental variables to each equation in turn. Compute estimates, $\hat{\Phi}$ and $\hat{\Omega}$, from the residual vectors, $\hat{u}_1, \ldots, \hat{u}_T$.

(ii) Carry out a SURE regression, (2.9.17), of $\hat{u}_t - \hat{\Phi}\hat{u}_{t-1}$ on $Z_t - \hat{\Phi} Z_{t-1}$ and $\hat{u}_{t-1} \otimes I_N$. Let the estimated coefficients in this regression be denoted by $\gamma^\dagger$ and $\Phi^\dagger$. The two-step estimators are then given by $\gamma^* = \hat{\gamma} + \gamma^\dagger$ and $\Phi^* = \hat{\Phi} + \Phi^\dagger$. Alternatively, take $y_t - \hat{\Phi}y_{t-1}$ as the vector of dependent variables, in which case γ^* is given directly by the vector of regression coefficients.

Some Monte Carlo evidence on the small sample performance of the two-step estimator is given in Spencer (1979). He compares this estimator with a number of other procedures which are known not to be fully efficient in large samples. Taken as a whole, his results are very favourable to the two-step procedure.

Testing for Serial Correlation*

The LM principle may be used to derive an asymptotically valid test for serial correlation when the system of equations is estimated under the assumption that $u_t \sim NID(0, \Omega)$. If the alternative hypothesis is that u_t follows a vector AR(1) process, the resulting test may be regarded as a generalisation of the procedures developed by Durbin for the single equation case; see Section 3.

The unrestricted model — i.e. with a vector AR(1) disturbance term — is the same as that considered in the previous section. The log–likelihood function is

$$\log L = \frac{TN}{2} \log 2\pi - \frac{T}{2} \log |\Omega| - \tfrac{1}{2}\sum \epsilon_t' \Omega^{-1} \epsilon_t$$

Let $\psi = (\gamma', \phi')'$, where $\phi = \text{vec}(\Phi)$. Because the information matrix is block diagonal with respect to ψ and Ω, the LM statistic for testing any hypothesis regarding the elements of ψ is of the form (5.5.4). However, a test of the null hypothesis $H_0 : \Phi = 0$ against the alternative $H_1 : \Phi \neq 0$ is a standard example of a subset test. In terms of the notation of (5.5.10)

$$D_2 \log L(\psi_0) = \frac{\partial \log L}{\partial \phi} = - \sum \frac{\partial \epsilon_t'}{\partial \phi} \Omega^{-1}\epsilon_t \tag{6.25}$$

Under the null hypothesis, $\bar{\psi}_0 = (\hat{\gamma}', 0')'$ where $\hat{\gamma}$ is the SURE estimator of γ. Using (6.22) and (6.24), expression (6.25) becomes

$$D_2 \log L(\bar{\psi}_0) = - \sum (\hat{u}_{t-1} \otimes \Omega^{-1}) \hat{u}_t \tag{6.26}$$

where $\hat{u}_t = y_t - Z_t \hat{\gamma}$.

The matrix $I_{22} - I_{21}' I_{11}^{-1} I_{12}$ must also be computed in order to evaluate the LM statistic, (5.5.10). This matrix is the asymptotic covariance matrix of the ML estimator of Φ evaluated at $\Phi = 0$ and $\gamma = \hat{\gamma}$. It can be estimated as follows. In large samples the information matrix for ψ is given by

$$I^*(\psi) = \sum \frac{\partial \epsilon_t'}{\partial \psi} \Omega^{-1} \frac{\partial \epsilon_t}{\partial \psi'} \tag{6.27}$$

where the elements of $\partial \epsilon_t / \partial \psi'$ are given by (6.23) and (6.24). Inverting $I^*(\psi)$ and evaluating at $\Phi = 0$, $\gamma = \hat{\gamma}$ gives a suitable estimator of the matrix in question. Under H_0 the LM statistic will be asymptotically χ^2 with N^2 degrees of freedom. If the alternative hypothesis is modified to Φ being a diagonal matrix, the calculations involved will be simplified somewhat, and the resulting LM statistic will be tested as a χ^2_N variate. The reduction in degrees of freedom may make this test more appealing, particularly if it is used in a diagnostic checking capacity.

The LM test can, in principle, be extended to situations where the alternative hypothesis is a higher order AR or MA process. Furthermore, when the model is estimated with a vector ARMA disturbance term, tests of goodness of fit may be developed using a similar methodology to that employed in the single equation case.

Identification*

When a dynamic system is estimated with a vector ARMA disturbance term, problems of identification can arise due to common factors. However, with pure AR disturbances, difficulties of this kind are unlikely. In the vector AR(1) case, Sargan (1972) has shown that a sufficient condition for the model to be globally identified is that the system should contain at least N exogenous variables which do not become redundant when lagged (i.e. constant terms and certain dummy variables are not included). This condition is not particularly stringent. The reasoning underlying Sargan's condition can be sketched out for a simple model as follows. Consider the model (6.7), with the disturbances generated by a vector AR(1) process. Subtracting Φy_{t-1} from both sides of the model yields

$$y_t = (\Phi + A)y_{t-1} - \Phi A y_{t-2} + B x_t - \Phi B x_{t-1} + \epsilon_t \tag{6.28}$$

If the model contained no exogenous variables, the values of Φ and A would be interchangeable. This is precisely the situation highlighted in (3.6.7). In that case the introduction of an exogenous variable is sufficient to ensure the global identifiability of all the parameters in the model.

Model (6.28) may be written as

$$y_t = A_1^* y_{t-1} + A_2^* y_{t-2} + B_0^* x_t + B_1^* x_{t-1} + \epsilon_t \tag{6.29}$$

The restrictions in (6.28) imply that $B_1^* = -\Phi B$ and $B_0^* = B_0$. Taken together these imply:

$$B_1^* + \Phi B_0^* = 0$$

These equations can be solved for Φ if B_0^* has full column rank. Since $B_0^* = B_0$, this implies that B_0 should have full column rank, and unless B_0 is subject to restrictions, the condition that $k \geq N$ is sufficient to ensure that this is the case. Once Φ is identifiable, it follows that A is identifiable also.

8.7. Causality

The concept of cause and effect is fundamental in any science. However, when it is not possible to conduct a controlled experiment, it becomes very difficult to produce convincing evidence that a cause and effect relationship actually exists. This is almost invariably the case in economics, and as a result the traditional approach in econometrics has been to set up a model on the basis of prior economic theory. Not only is a cause and effect relationship assumed to hold but, furthermore, the direction of causality is also taken to be known.

Suppose, for simplicity, that a system contains only two variables, x and y. Given that a cause and effect relationship can be in only one direction, say from x to y, the only question that remains is whether such a relationship actually exists. The most common approach to answering this question is to regress y_t on x_t and test the coefficient of x_t for 'significance'. However, a high correlation between two sets of non-experimental observations does not constitute evidence for a relationship between the underlying variables. Furthermore, the problem of spurious correlation remains even if some dynamic structure is imposed on the model by taking y to depend on current and past values of x. Thus even though it is assumed at the outset that y cannot cause x, there is no way in which a causal relationship from x to y can be established on the basis of the data alone.

Given the limitations imposed by non-experimental data, it is not unreasonable to take the view that fitting a regression model is primarily an exercise in measurement. That a relationship exists is not actually questioned, but is taken for granted on the basis of economic theory. In these circumstances, tests of significance are no longer used to judge whether or not a relationship exists between two variables. What is of most importance is the measured effect of one variable on another. While this approach underlies a good deal of econometric model building, it suffers from the disadvantage that an inordinate amount of faith is placed in prior knowledge from economic theory. Furthermore, it means that certain untestable features are being brought into a model, thereby violating an important principle of scientific research.

The need to examine the assumptions underlying an econometric model estimated from non-experimental time series data has led to the development of the concept of *causality*. The idea of causality dates back to Wiener, but was first formalised by Granger (1969). Two basic rules are taken to apply. The first is that the future cannot predict the past. Thus strict causality can only occur with the past causing the present or future. Secondly, it is assumed that it is only meaningful to discuss causality for a group of stochastic variables. A variable x is then said to 'cause' a variable y if taking account of past values of x enables better predictions to be made for y, all other things being equal. This notion of causality is a purely statistical one, and it does *not* correspond to any acceptable definition of cause and effect in the philosophical sense. Instead, it refers to the more limited concept of *predictability*. An acknowledgement of the view that causality is too strong a word in this context is offered by the qualified term *Granger causality*.

Granger's Definition of Causality

The essence of Granger's concept of causality is that x causes y if taking account of past values of x leads to improved predictions for y. However, in order to make this concept operational, it is necessary to be more precise about the way in which predictions are generated, and the way in which their accuracy is measured. In his definition, Granger restricts attention to unbiased least squares predictions, and measures the accuracy of such predictions by the variance of the one-step ahead prediction error. The full definition, which is given below, may therefore be characterised by the phrase: 'reduction in forecasting variance with respect to a given information set'.

Definition Let U be an information set including all past and present information, and let $\bar{U}$ denote the same set, but excluding present information. Similarly, let X denote all past and present information on the variable x, i.e. $X = (x_\tau, \tau \le t)$, and let $\bar{X}$ be the past information alone, i.e. $\bar{X} = (x_\tau, \tau < t)$. The variable x is then said to *cause y* if the one step ahead predictor of y, $\hat{y}$, based on all past information has a smaller mean square error than the predictor of y based on all past information excluding x. More precisely, x causes y if

$$\text{MSE}(\hat{y}|\bar{U}) < \text{MSE}(\hat{y}|\bar{U} - \bar{X}) \tag{7.1}$$

Similarly, x causes y *instantaneously* if

$$\text{MSE}(\hat{y}|U) < \text{MSE}(\hat{y}|U - X) \tag{7.2}$$

However, as Granger and Newbold (1977, p. 255) observe, the occurrence of instantaneous causality may partly be a function of the data, insofar as a time lag would exist if observations could be taken sufficiently close together in time.

As it stands, Granger's definition of causality is non-operational, insofar as U represents *all* available information. In dealing with this problem,

Granger suggests replacing all the information in the universe with the concept of 'all relevant information'. Once this is done, however, the notion that causality may be determined on purely statistical grounds is no longer valid since *a priori* theory must play a key role in deciding what constitutes relevant information. Nevertheless, these requirements may be regarded as being fairly minimal.

Given the above definitions, a complete classification of the patterns of causality has three dimensions: (a) whether x causes y; (b) whether y causes x; and (c) whether instantaneous causality exists. This leads to $2^3 = 8$ basic outcomes. These are listed in table 8.2, together with a scheme of notation. Thus, for example, $x \Rightarrow y$ indicates that x causes y instantaneously, with no feedback.

In addition to these symbols, the statement 'does not cause' may be represented by '$\not\rightarrow$'.

Tests of Causality

In order to simplify matters it will be assumed that the relevant information set, U, consists only of information on the two variables x and y. A statistical framework for characterising causality may then be developed by assuming that (x_t, y_t) is a bivariate time series which is linear, covariance stationary and purely non-deterministic.

The autoregressive representation of such a process is of the form

$$\Pi(L) \begin{bmatrix} y_t \\ x_t \end{bmatrix} = \begin{bmatrix} \epsilon_t \\ \eta_t \end{bmatrix} \tag{7.3}$$

where $(\epsilon_t, \eta_t)'$ is a bivariate white noise process with a mean of zero and covariance matrix, Ω, and $\Pi(L)$ is a 2×2 matrix polynomial in the lag operator, i.e.

$$\Pi(L) = \Pi_0 + \Pi_1 L + \ldots + \Pi_r L^r + \ldots \tag{7.4}$$

Table 8.2 Patterns of Causality

Description	Notation
(1) Instantaneous causality only	$(x - y)$
(2) x causes y only and not instantaneously	$(x \rightarrow y)$
(3) ....instantaneously	$(x \Rightarrow y)$
(4) y causes x only and not instantaneously	$(x \leftarrow y)$
(5) ....instantaneously	$(x \Leftarrow y)$
(6) Feedback, not instantaneously	$(x \leftrightarrow y)$
(7) Feedback and instantaneous causality	$(x \Leftrightarrow y)$

Setting Π_0, the leading term in (7.4), equal to the identity matrix implies no loss in generality.

Expression (7.3) may be rewritten in terms of scalar polynomials as

$$\begin{bmatrix} \pi_{11}(L) & \pi_{12}(L) \\ \pi_{21}(L) & \pi_{22}(L) \end{bmatrix} \begin{pmatrix} y_t \\ x_t \end{pmatrix} = \begin{pmatrix} \epsilon_t \\ \eta_t \end{pmatrix} \tag{7.5}$$

When $\pi_{21}(L) = 0$, the system depicted by (7.5) is characterised by *unidirectional causality* since, to the extent that a relationship exists, the direction of causality can only be from x to y.

Stated formally, the tests set out below are tests of the hypothesis that y does not cause x, irrespective of whether or not there is instantaneous causality or causality from x to y. If there is causality from x to y, and the hypothesis that y does not cause x is rejected, the relationship may be characterised by 'feedback'. Tests of unidirectional causality are sometimes referred to as tests of exogeneity (of x.). However, this concept of exogeneity does not correspond precisely to the definition given towards the end of Section 1.2. The use of the term exogenous in this context is therefore best avoided; see Engle *et al.* (1983).

(i) *The 'Direct' Test*   The second line of (7.5) may be written out as

$$\pi_{21}(L)y_t + \pi_{22}(L)x_t = \eta_t \tag{7.6}$$

Bearing in mind that setting $\Pi_0 = I$ implies that the leading terms in $\pi_{21}(L)$ and $\pi_{22}(L)$ are zero and one respectively, expression (7.6) may be rearranged in such a way that x_t is equal to a linear combination of past values of x_t and y_t. The hypothesis that y causes x can then be examined by regressing x_t on $y_{t-1}, \ldots, y_{t-m}, x_{t-1}, \ldots, x_{t-n}$ and testing the joint significance of the lagged values of y. If $\pi_{21}(L) = 0$, it can be seen from (7.6) that x_t will be determined solely by η_t and its own past values.

In adopting this approach, it is important to ensure that the specification is adequate so that the disturbance term in the regression of x_t on lagged values of x_t and y_t is close to being white noise. This means choosing suitable values of m and n. The value of n is particularly important, since omitting relevant lagged values of x could inflate the coefficients of the lagged y's.

(ii) *Sims' Test*   Sims' test is based on the following theorem. *When $(y, x)'$ has an autoregressive representation, y can be expressed as a distributed lag function of current and past x with a residual which is not correlated with any values of x, past or future, if, and only if, y does not cause x in Granger's sense.* A practical test procedure may therefore be based on a regression of y_t on past and future values of x_t. The regression model is effectively

$$y_t = \sum_{\tau = -m}^{n} \gamma_\tau x_{t-\tau} + w_t \tag{7.7}$$

with n and m sufficiently large to exclude any expected non-negligible coefficients. A test that y does not cause x is then a test of the null hypothesis, $H_0 : \gamma_{-1} = \gamma_{-2} = \ldots = \gamma_{-m} = 0$. However, in implementing this procedure, it is important to take account of any serial correlation in the disturbance term, w_t, since otherwise the results of the F-test could be misleading. One possibility is to fit a suitable ARMA model to the disturbances and apply generalised least squares. In his 1972 paper, however, Sims preferred to simplify matters by assuming a particular structure for the disturbances *a priori*. He effectively took w_t to be generated by an AR(2) process with $\phi_1 = 1.5$ and $\phi_2 = -0.5625$, and so GLS was carried out by multiplying each variable in the regression by $1 - 1.5L + 0.5625L^2$. Such an approach is often referred to as *ad hoc filtering*. A second way of avoiding the need to build a model for the disturbance term, is to fit an autoregressive disturbance term of an arbitrarily high order. This is effectively a non-parametric approach, and it would seem preferable to *ad hoc* filtering since in some cases the pre-chosen filter may not result in the transformed disturbances being even approximately white noise.

(ii) *Geweke's Test* One difficulty with Sims' procedure is the need to treat serial correlation in the disturbances. It was suggested above that one possibility is to estimate the regression by a non-parametric procedure. Either a time domain or a spectral approach could be adopted, but assuming that w_t can be approximated by an AR(P) process leads to a convenient modification of Sims' test.

By defining suitable polynomials in the lag operator, (7.7) may be expressed as

$$y_t = \gamma(L)x_t + \phi^{-1}(L)\zeta_t \tag{7.8}$$

where ζ_t is assumed to be white noise. Multiplying (7.8) through by the AR polynomial, $\phi(L)$, gives

$$\phi(L)y_t = \phi(L)\gamma(L)x_t + \zeta_t \tag{7.9}$$

This suggests regressing y_t on $y_{t-1}, \ldots, y_{t-p}$ together with m future values of x_t and $n + p$ past values. The hypothesis that y does not cause x can then be tested by computing the F-statistic for the future values of x_t.

Tests for the Direction of Causality

The test procedures described in the previous sub-section can be used in a more general framework to test the *direction* of causality. In Sims (1972) the relationship between GNP and the money supplied is examined. The regressions were carried out using quarterly US data from 1947 to 1969 with both GNP and the money supply measured in logarithms. All variables were subject to the *ad hoc* filter referred to in the description of Sims' test above. The values of n and m in (7.7) were set equal to eight and four respectively.

Two definitions of money supply were used by Sims: MB — currency plus reserves adjusted for changes in reserve requirements; and MI — currency plus demand deposits. However, as can be seen from the results in table 8.3, the way in which the money supply is defined makes little difference to results. When GNP(y) is regressed on the money supply (x), the future values of x are clearly insignificant. On the other hand, regressing money supply on GNP leads to F-statistics which are significant at the 5% level. Sims (1972, p. 540) summarises his conclusion as follows. 'The main empirical finding is that the hypothesis that causality is unidirectional from money to income agrees with post-war US data, whereas the hypothesis that causality is unidirectional from income to money is rejected.'

Table 8.3 F-Tests on Four Future Quarters Coefficients

Regression Equation	F
GNP on MI	0.36
GNP on MB	0.39
MI on GNP	4.29*
MB on GNP	5.89*

*Significant at 5% level for an F-distribution with (4, 60) degrees of freedom.
Source: Sims (1972, p. 547).

An alternative approach to assessing the pattern of causality between two variables is to *pre-whiten* both series. Given that $(y_t, x_t)'$ has the vector autoregressive representation, (7.3), it can be shown that x_t and y_t each have representations as univariate ARMA processes. The disturbances in these processes constitute the pre-whitened series, and the cross-correlations between them can be expected to yield information on the causality patterns between x and y since they are the components of x and y which cannot be predicted from their own past.

If x_t^* and y_t^* denote the pre-whitened series, the theoretical cross-correlations are defined by

$$\varrho_\tau(x^*, y^*) = E[(y_t^* - \mu_y^*)(x_{t-\tau}^* - \mu_x^*)]/(\sigma_{x^*}\sigma_{y^*}),$$

$$\tau = 0, \pm 1, \pm 2, \ldots \quad (7.10)$$

These cross-correlations characterise the various causality patterns. The essential features, corresponding to the three dimensional classification noted earlier, are as follows:

(a) $\varrho_\tau(x^*, y^*) \neq 0$ for some $\tau > 0$ indicates $x \to y$
(b) $\varrho_\tau(x^*, y^*) \neq 0$ for some $\tau < 0$ indicates $y \to x$
(c) $\varrho_0(x^*, y^*) \neq 0$ indicates instantaneous causality.

The sample cross-correlations, $r_\tau(x^*, y^*)$, are calculated from the residuals obtained by fitting suitable ARMA models to x_t and y_t. The patterns of causality can then be assessed by examining the sample cross-correlation function. Under the null hypothesis that x and y are not causally related, the sample cross-correlations of the residuals are independently and normally distributed with mean zero and variance $1/T$ when the sample size is large.

A test that there is some sort of causal relationship between x and y can be based on the statistic

$$U = T \sum_{\tau = -n}^{m} r_\tau^2(x^*, y^*) \tag{7.11}$$

where m and n are chosen so as to include any expected non-negligible cross-correlations. Under the null hypothesis that x and y are not causally related, U is asymptotically χ^2 with $m + n + 1$ degrees of freedom. This test procedure is used in Pierce (1977) in order to assess the evidence for causal relationships between certain economic time series. By and large Pierce concluded that the evidence for causal relationships was not very strong, a result which has led to some debate as to whether the pre-whitening approach is really appropriate.

8.8. Exogeneity*

The ability to treat a regression model within a single equation framework depends on the exogeneity of the explanatory variables, x_t. Efficient estimation of the parameters requires that no information on these parameters is lost by conditioning on the explanatory variables. In other words, the explanatory variables may be treated as though they are fixed in repeated samples, even though they may be generated by a stochastic mechanism in the same way as y_t. If this condition is satisfied, the explanatory variables are said to be weakly exogenous. For purposes of prediction, stronger conditions must be placed on the explanatory variables. Specifically, there must be no feedback between them and the dependent variable. If this condition holds, the explanatory variables are said to be strongly exogenous. Strong exogeneity implies weak exogeneity, but not *vice versa*.

A formal definition of weak exogeneity requires that we are able to conceive of a joint probability density function for $y = (y_1, \ldots, y_T)'$ and $X = (x_1, \ldots, x_T)'$. Writing this function in terms of conditional distributions as in (3.5.4) gives

$$L(y, X; \lambda) = \prod_{t=1}^{T} p(y_t, x_t | Y_{t-1}, X_{t-1}; \lambda) \tag{8.1}$$

where λ denotes the full set of parameters upon which the joint p.d.f. of y and X depends. Suppose that the model may be reparameterised in terms of a new set of parameters, $\theta^\dagger$, which may be partitioned as $\theta^\dagger = (\theta', \theta'_x)'$ where θ and θ_x are *variation-free* in the sense that for any specific admissible value of θ_x, θ can take any value in its parameter space and *vice versa*. Suppose also that the *parameters of interest* are a function only of θ. The explanatory variables, x_t, are *weakly exogenous* for θ over the sample period, if the joint p.d.f. in (8.1) can be factored as

$$L(y, X; \theta^\dagger) = \left\{ \prod_{t=1}^{T} p(y_t | Y_{t-1}, X_t; \theta) \right\}$$

$$\times \left\{ \prod_{t=1}^{T} p(x_t | X_{t-1}, Y_{t-1}; \theta_x) \right\} \tag{8.2}$$

This being the case, the marginal distribution of x_t, the second term on the right hand side of (8.2), can be ignored as it contains no information on the parameters of interest. Inference on θ can be based on the conditional distribution of y_t, which is the first term on the right hand side of (8.2), that is

$$L(y | X; \theta) = \prod_{t=1}^{T} p(y_t | Y_{t-1}, X_t; \theta) \tag{8.3}$$

Constructing the likelihood function from (8.3) is equivalent to regarding the explanatory variables as being fixed in repeated samples.

In order to be able to concentrate exclusively on a single equation for prediction purposes, the distribution of x_t must be independent of past values of y_t. Thus

$$p(x_t | Y_{t-1}, X_{t-1}; \theta_x) = p(x_t | X_{t-1}; \theta_x), \qquad t = 1, \ldots, T \tag{8.4}$$

If this is the case, then, in the terminology of the previous section, Y_{t-1} does not *Granger cause* x_t. When (8.4) holds, x_t is *strongly exogenous* with respect to θ.

Example Consider the following bivariate model for y_t and a single explanatory variable, x_t:

$$y_t = \phi_{11} y_{t-1} + \phi_{12} x_{t-1} + \epsilon_{1t} \tag{8.5a}$$

$$x_t = \phi_{22} x_{t-1} + \epsilon_{2t} \tag{8.5b}$$

where, conditional on Y_{t-1} and X_{t-1}, the disturbance vector $(\epsilon_{1t}, \epsilon_{2t})'$ has a multivariate normal distribution with mean zero and p.d. covariance matrix

$$\Sigma = \begin{bmatrix} \sigma_{11} & \sigma_{12} \\ \sigma_{12} & \sigma_{22} \end{bmatrix}$$

A single equation for y_t can be formulated by conditioning on current as well as past values of the explanatory variable. Making use of standard results on the properties of the multivariate normal distribution enables one to assert that, by conditioning on current values of x_t, y_t is normally distributed with mean

$$
\begin{aligned}
E(y_t | Y_{t-1}, X_t; \theta) &= \phi_{11} y_{t-1} + \phi_{12} x_{t-1} \\
&\quad + (\sigma_{12}/\sigma_{22})(x_t - \phi_{22} x_{t-1}) \\
&= \phi_{11} y_{t-1} + (\sigma_{12}/\sigma_{22}) x_t + \{\phi_{12} - (\phi_{22}\sigma_{12}/\sigma_{22})\} x_{t-1}
\end{aligned}
$$

$$(8.6a)$$

and variance

$$\mathrm{Var}(y_t | Y_{t-1}, X_t; \theta) = \sigma_{11} - \sigma_{12}^2/\sigma_{22} \tag{8.6b}$$

This leads to the autoregressive distributed lag model

$$y_t = \phi y_{t-1} + \delta_0 x_t + \delta_1 x_{t-1} + \epsilon_t \tag{8.7}$$

where the parameters ϕ, δ_0, δ_1 and σ^2 are related to the original parameters *via* equations (8.6a) and (8.6b). The two sets of parameters, $\theta = (\phi, \delta_0, \delta_1, \sigma^2)$ and $\theta_x = (\phi_{22}, \sigma_2^2)$ are variation-free. The equation for x_t remains as specified in (8.5b), and by the properties of the multivariate normal distribution ϵ_{2t} and ϵ_t are independently distributed of each other; hence the factorisation in (8.2) is possible.

As can be seen from equation (8.5b), the distribution of x_t does not depend on past values of y_t and so (8.4) is satisfied. Hence x_t is strongly exogenous with respect to the parameters of interest in θ.

It is difficult to test directly whether the explanatory variables are weakly exogenous without specifying the general multivariate model. This is unfortunate since one of the main reasons for working with a single equation is to avoid the need to specify a general model. Exogeneity can, however, be tested indirectly since if it does not hold, the model is unlikely to be stable and this is likely to show up when it is subjected to diagnostic checking. Further details on exogeneity and testing for exogeneity can be found in Engle, Hendry and Richard (1983) and Engle (1984).

Notes

Section 3   Breusch and Pagan (1980), Godfrey (1978b), Kenward (1976), Kiviet (1986).

Section 6   Pagan and Byron (1977), Hatanaka (1976).

Exercises

1. (a) If $\alpha = 0.6$ and $\beta = 2$ in (2.1) find the total multiplier, the mean lag and the median lag.

   (b) In (7.1.16), $B(L) = \beta_0 + \beta_1 L$ and $A(L) = 1 - \alpha L$. Find an expression for the coefficients in the polynomial $D(L) = B(L)/A(L)$.

   (c) If the disturbance term in (7.1.16) follows an AR(1) process, explain how you would compute ML estimates of the parameters.

   (d) Calculate the total multiplier and the mean lag if $\beta_0 = 2$, $\beta_1 = 3$ and $\alpha = 0.5$.

2. Determine the mean lag in (1.6).

3. Suppose that (2.1) is estimated with an AR(1) disturbance term. Construct a general test of misspecification analogous to the one described in Section 4.

4. Suppose that (1.7) is estimated by OLS. How would you test this specification against the alternative (7.4.1)?

5. Show that Durbin's estimator of ϕ compared from (6.1.10) is: (i) consistent, (ii) asymptotically efficient.

6. Show that the h-statistic in (3.1) is the LM statistic for testing against an MA(1) disturbance.

7. Using the estimates in table 8.1, show that K_1 in (5.9) is equal to $\exp(-2.17 - 2.21g_1 - 1.55g_2)$ where g_1 and g_2 are the annual growth rates of x_1 and x_2 respectively.

8. Derive an expression for the mean lag in equation (5.10).

9. Suppose that a consumption function is estimated on the basis of equation (5.11) with $\nu = 1$. Show that an increase in the growth rate of income implies a decrease in the long-run average propensity to consume. Is this what you would expect?

10. Consider the system

$$y_t = Ay_{t-1} + B_0 x_t + B_1 x_{t-1} + u_t$$

Find an expression for (i) the matrix of total multipliers; (ii) the matrix of interim multipliers after two time periods.

11. Calculate the interim multipliers in (5.14) up to a lag of 8 and comment on the pattern. Find the total multiplier, the mean lag and the median lag.

12. Under what circumstances would the ARMAX model, (1.4), be underidentified?

9
Simultaneous Equation Models

9.1. Introduction

In the dynamic model introduced towards the end of the previous chapter, the explanatory variables in each equation consisted of observations on exogenous variables together with observations on *lagged* values of the endogenous variables. However, in econometric problems, it often makes sense to suppose that an endogenous variable is also affected by *current* values of the other endogenous variables in the system. Although instantaneous feedback as such is unlikely to occur, the time interval between observations means that the system must effectively be treated as a simultaneous one.

The model of Section 8.6 may be extended to allow for simultaneity by the introduction of an $N \times N$ matrix, Γ. Thus (8.6.5) becomes

$$\Gamma y_t = A_1 y_{t-1} + \ldots + A_r y_{t-r} + B_0 x_t + \ldots + B_s x_{t-s} + u_t \qquad (1.1)$$

Apart from Γ, the notation is the same as in (8.6.5) with u_t a disturbance vector with mean zero and covariance matrix Ω. It will be assumed throughout that u_t has a multivariate normal distribution.

An interesting special case arises when the equations can be arranged in such a way that Γ is triangular. Consider a three equation system in which

$$\Gamma = \begin{bmatrix} 1 & 0 & 0 \\ \gamma_{21} & 1 & 0 \\ \gamma_{31} & \gamma_{32} & 1 \end{bmatrix} \qquad (1.2)$$

The first endogenous variable y_1 depends only on the exogenous variables and past values of the endogenous variables. The second variable, y_2, depends on the current value of y_1 but there is no instantaneous feedback from y_2 to y_1. Similarly, y_3 depends on the current values of both y_2 and y_1, but there is no feedback from y_3 to y_1 and y_2.

A system in which Γ is triangular and Ω is diagonal is said to be *recursive*. Such a model is to be contrasted with an *interdependent* system. Suppose the matrix, (1.2), is modified to

313

$$\Gamma = \begin{bmatrix} 1 & 0 & \gamma_{13} \\ \gamma_{21} & 1 & 0 \\ \gamma_{31} & \gamma_{32} & 1 \end{bmatrix} \qquad (1.3)$$

This model exhibits instantaneous feedback, since the current value of y_3 now influences y_1 directly through γ_{13}. Furthermore since y_{2t} depends on y_{1t}, the current value of y_3 also affects the current value of y_2. Hence y_{1t}, y_{2t} and y_{3t} are determined simultaneously.

This chapter is primarily concerned with systems which are interdependent, although some attention is paid to recursive models insofar as they represent special features. In particular it is shown that the assumption of recursiveness can simplify estimation considerably.

The Reduced Form

The equations in (1.1) give the *structural form* of the model. Pre-multiplying both sides of (1.1) by Γ^{-1} leads to the *reduced form*:

$$y_t = \Gamma^{-1}A_1 y_{t-1} + \ldots + \Gamma^{-1}A_r y_{t-r} + \Gamma^{-1}B_0 x_t + \ldots$$
$$+ \Gamma^{-1}B_s x_{t-s} + \Gamma^{-1}u_t$$
$$= \Pi_1^+ y_{t-1} + \ldots + \Pi_r^+ y_{t-r} + \Pi_0 x_t + \ldots + \Pi_s x_{t-s} + v_t \quad (1.4)$$

The $N \times N$ matrices Π_i^+, $i = 1,\ldots,r$ and the $N \times K$ matrices Π_j, $j = 0,\ldots,$ s contain the reduced form parameters, while v_t is the reduced form disturbance. Given the properties of the structural disturbance term, u_t, it follows that

$$E(v_t) = E(\Gamma^{-1}u_t) = \Gamma^{-1}E(u_t) = 0$$

and

$$E(v_t v_t') = \Gamma^{-1}E(u_t u_t')\,\Gamma^{-1'} = \Gamma^{-1}\Omega\Gamma^{-1'}$$

Furthermore the linear transformation from u_t to v_t means that a normal distribution for the structural disturbances implies normality for the reduced form disturbances.

The reduced form represents a solution to the simultaneity of the structural equations. Given a particular realisation of the disturbances, together with a set of values for the exogenous and lagged endogenous variables, (1.4) solves for the values of the current endogenous variables. However, on comparing (1.4) with (8.6.5) it will be seen that the reduced form is exactly the kind of model considered in Section 8.6. Thus all the theory developed there is directly applicable to (1.4). In particular, the systematic dynamics may be derived, and the predictions of future values obtained, using material which has already been presented. Furthermore, since the reduced form is just the solved version of the structural form, the systematic dynamics and predictions derived for (1.4) are also directly applicable to (1.1). Suppose the total multipliers for (1.1) are required. The matrix of total multipliers for (1.4) is

$$(I - \Pi_1^+ - \cdots - \Pi_r^+)^{-1}(\Pi_0 + \cdots + \Pi_s)$$

Substituting structural for reduced form parameters gives the matrix of total multipliers in terms of (1.1), i.e.

$$(I - \Gamma^{-1}A_1 - \cdots - \Gamma^{-1}A_r)^{-1}(\Gamma^{-1}B_0 + \cdots + \Gamma^{-1}B_s)$$

$$= (\Gamma - A_1 - \cdots - A_r)^{-1}(B_0 + \cdots + B_s)$$

More generally the systematic dynamic properties may be explored by converting the reduced form to the *final form,* in which y_t is expressed in terms of current and lagged values of the exogenous variables only; cf. (8.6.17).

The reduced form coefficients may be estimated directly. If we ignore the way in which it was derived, the system in (1.4) appears simply as a linear dynamic model in which the disturbances are normally distributed with mean vector zero and an unknown covariance matrix. Since the explanatory variables in each equation are the same, the ML estimators are given by applying OLS to each equation in turn. Given a set of estimates, predictions for future values of y_t may be computed straightforwardly. Furthermore, this whole approach generalises to models in which v_t is assumed to be generated by a multivariate ARMA process.

The fact that the reduced form may be estimated directly, immediately raises the question: why do we need to consider methods of estimating the structural form? There are two reasons, although they are closely related. The first is that economic theory is framed in terms of the structural equations. The numerical values of the structural parameters are therefore of interest in their own right, and indeed part of the motivation for estimating a model is to test economic hypotheses. Furthermore, economic theory will impose *a priori* restrictions on the structural form. Such restrictions play a vital role in setting up a simultaneous equation model, since without them it becomes impossible to obtain meaningful estimates of the structural parameters. However, the restrictions also have implications for prediction. This leads to the second reason for being interested in the structural form. If sufficient restrictions are placed on the structural form, the reduced form will be subject to restrictions as well. Ignoring these restrictions will then lead to inefficient estimators of the reduced form parameters, and hence inefficient predictions. Thus although it may be convenient to base prediction on the *unrestricted reduced form* (URF), this will not be desirable insofar as it leads to a loss in efficiency. However, this argument presupposes that any restrictions placed on the structural form are valid. Fortunately, the validity of the restrictions is a testable proposition, the appropriate methodology being described in Section 5.

Identifiability

In the previous paragraph is was observed that restrictions must be placed
on the structural equations in order to obtain meaningful estimates. This is
an issue of identifiability, a concept which was touched on in the first chapter,
and then explored more thoroughly within a statistical framework in Section
3.6. The question of identifiability is central in any consideration of a
simultaneous equation system, and Section 2 gives a discussion of the problem
in the context of a static model,

$$\Gamma y_t = B x_t + u_t, \qquad t = 1, \ldots, T \tag{1.5}$$

The reduced form of (1.5) is

$$y_t = \Pi x_t + v_t, \qquad t = 1, \ldots, T \tag{1.6}$$

where $\Pi = \Gamma^{-1}B$ and $v_t = \Gamma^{-1}u_t$. The distribution of the endogenous
variables is determined by the reduced form, the expected value of y_t
depending on the NK parameters in Π, and its variance depending on the
$N(N + 1)/2$ parameters in the covariance matrix of v_t. The covariance
matrix of the disturbance term in the structural form likewise contains
$N(N + 1)/2$ distinct parameters. However, the matrices B and Γ can contain
up to $N^2 + NK$ parameters between them. Therefore, unless restrictions are
placed on some of the elements in B, Γ and Ω, the structural form will contain
N^2 more parameters than the reduced form. In Section 2 it is shown that
at least N^2 restrictions must be placed on the structural form if every
equation is to be identifiable. If more than N^2 restrictions are imposed on
the structural form, the reduced form will also be subject to restrictions, and
it is in these circumstances that there is likely to be a gain in basing predictions
on estimates of the reduced form parameters derived from the structural
parameters.

Most of the restrictions on the structural form are obtained from *a priori*
theory. However, N restrictions are given simply as a result of *normalisation*.
One endogenous variable in each structural equation is usually regarded as
the dependent variable, and so its coefficient may be arbitrarily set at unity.
Thus the matrix Γ must have a one in each of its N columns. Since the
endogenous variables in the reduced form have already been implicitly
normalised, the minimum number of restrictions which must be provided
by economic theory is not N^2, but $N^2 - N$. In general, these restrictions
are imposed by setting certain parameters in B and Γ equal to zero, and it
is this form of restriction which is emphasised in the text. Constraining a
parameter to be zero is equivalent to excluding the corresponding variable
from the equation in question.

Estimation

The complete set of equations in the structural form may be estimated jointly by a *full information* procedure. Alternatively attention may be focused on a single equation within the system and a *limited information* approach employed. A limited information estimator takes no account of any *a priori* restrictions on the other equations within the system. It will therefore be less efficient than the corresponding full information estimator, except in certain special cases. However, if there is some uncertainty surrounding the specification of the model as a whole, a limited information estimator may be more attractive. Its failure to incorporate all the prior information will probably be a virtue if that 'information' is of dubious validity. Thus a contrast between full information and limited information methods essentially involves a trade-off between robustness and efficiency.

Maximum likelihood estimation is considered in Section 3. The method appropriate for the model as a whole is known as *full information maximum likelihood* (FIML). Although it is straightforward to set up the likelihood function, the likelihood equations are highly non-linear. This is also true for the *limited information maximum likelihood* (LIML) estimator. Although calculating these estimators does not present an insurmountable problem with modern computing facilities, there is still a good case for employing estimators which are easier to handle computationally. The *two-stage least squares* (2SLS) and *three-stage least squares* (3SLS) estimators are both relatively straightforward to compute, and under fairly general conditions they can be shown to have the same large sample properties as the LIML and FIML estimators respectively. Both 2SLS and 3SLS can be regarded as instrumental variable procedures, and they are derived within this framework in Section 4.

In developing both the 2SLS and 3SLS estimators it is convenient to have a notation for individual equations. Bearing in mind that certain variables will be excluded from each equation for reasons of identifiability, the ith equation in (1.5) may be written as:

$$y_{it} = z_{it}' \, \delta_i + u_{it}, \qquad \begin{aligned} t &= 1, \ldots, T, \\ i &= 1, \ldots, N \end{aligned} \qquad (1.7)$$

The vector z_i contains only the exogenous and endogenous variables, other than the dependent variable, which have not been excluded from the equations. Let k_i denote the number of included exogenous variables, and let n_i denote the number of included endogenous variables, including the dependent variable. Define $m_i = n_i + k_i - 1$. Then z_i and the corresponding vector of parameters, δ_i, are both length m_i for $i = 1, \ldots, N$. The number of variables excluded is $K + N - k_i - n_i$, $i = 1, \ldots, N$.

Outline of Remainder of Chapter

As already indicated, Sections 2 to 5 concentrate on developing particular features of (1.1) which arise purely because of the simultaneity aspect. Sections 6 and 7 bring these results together with those of earlier chapters to examine the dynamic case. This model, (1.1), is the most general considered in the book, and it forms the basis for modern econometric model building. In the last section, it is contrasted with three other approaches to model building. These approaches are based on estimation of an unrestricted reduced form, a multivariate ARMA model, and a set of univariate ARMA models. The amount of prior information incorporated in each model diminishes in moving from (1.1) to the univariate ARMA models, and the main purpose of Section 8 is to examine the implications of these different approaches for prediction and control.

9.2. Identifiability

This section considers the problem of identifiability within the context of a static simultaneous equation model, (1.5). A heuristic introduction is first given in terms of a simple demand and supply model. The discussion is then widened and rules for identification are derived within the general framework established in Section 3.6. A consideration of the dynamic model, (1.1), is delayed until Section 6.

Demand and Supply

A demand and supply model was introduced in Chapter 1. Assuming that the market always clears, the model reduces to a system of just two behavioural equations as in (1.2.7). Adding a disturbance term to each equation yields the stochastic specification

$$S : q_t = \gamma_{11} p_t + \beta_{11} + \beta_{12} x_{2t} + \epsilon_{1t},$$
$$D : q_t = \gamma_{21} p_t + \beta_{21} \qquad\qquad + \epsilon_{2t},$$
$$t = 1, \dots, T$$

(2.1a)

(2.1b)

where $(\epsilon_{1t} \epsilon_{2t})' \sim NID(0, \Omega)$. No restrictions are placed on the covariance matrix, Ω, and an equation can only be identified if restrictions are placed on the coefficients of the variables themselves.

As it stands, (2.1) is simply a stochastic version of the deterministic specification in (1.2.7). In figure 1.1 it was shown that assigning different values to x_2 effectively traces out the demand curve. The introduction of a disturbance term into (2.1) means that this is no longer strictly the case, although as figure 9.1 shows the observations will be close to the underlying demand curve. This suggests that the demand curve can still be sensibly

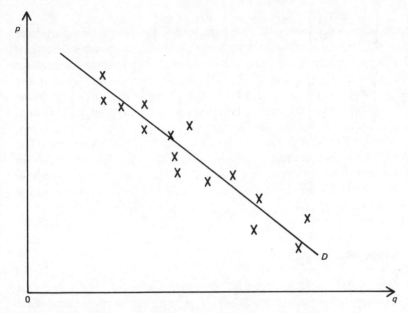

Figure 9.1 Path Generated by Model (2.1)

estimated, although as we shall see later, an OLS regression of q_t on p_t will not be an appropriate way of achieving this objective.

The crucial feature of (2.1) is the exclusion of x_2 from the demand equation. No restrictions have been placed on the supply equation, however, and the observations themselves are unable to provide sufficient information to enable meaningful estimates of the parameters to be constructed. Of course if x_2 were excluded from the supply equation, but included in the demand equation, the situation would be reversed. This leaves the question of what happens if x_2 is excluded from neither equation. In a sense the answer is obvious. Since both the supply and demand equations have exactly the same specification, there is no way in which it is possible to discriminate between them on the basis of the sample information. Hence neither equation is identifiable.

It is instructive to relate these findings to the reduced form. Treating the supply and demand equations as a pair of simultaneous equations in p and q, we can solve out to obtain expressions for p and q in terms of the exogenous variables only, i.e.

$$q_t = \pi_{11} + \pi_{12} x_{2t} + v_{1t} \qquad (2.2a)$$
$$p_t = \pi_{21} + \pi_{22} x_{2t} + v_{2t} \qquad , \qquad t = 1, \ldots, T \qquad (2.2b)$$

In the matrix notation of (1.5),

$$\Gamma = \begin{bmatrix} 1 & -\gamma_{11} \\ 1 & -\gamma_{21} \end{bmatrix} \quad \text{and} \quad \beta = \begin{bmatrix} \beta_{11} & \beta_{12} \\ \beta_{21} & \beta_{22} \end{bmatrix} \tag{2.3}$$

so that

$$\Pi = \begin{bmatrix} \pi_{11} & \pi_{12} \\ \pi_{21} & \pi_{22} \end{bmatrix} = \begin{bmatrix} 1 & -\gamma_{11} \\ 1 & -\gamma_{21} \end{bmatrix}^{-1} \begin{bmatrix} \beta_{11} & \beta_{12} \\ \beta_{21} & \beta_{22} \end{bmatrix}$$

Thus,

$$\pi_{11} = \frac{\gamma_{11}\beta_{21} - \gamma_{21}\beta_{11}}{\gamma_{11} - \gamma_{21}} \tag{2.4a}$$

$$\pi_{21} = \frac{\beta_{21} - \beta_{11}}{\gamma_{11} - \gamma_{21}} \tag{2.4b}$$

$$\pi_{12} = \frac{\gamma_{11}\beta_{22} - \gamma_{21}\beta_{12}}{\gamma_{11} - \gamma_{21}} \tag{2.4c}$$

$$\pi_{22} = \frac{\beta_{22} - \beta_{12}}{\gamma_{11} - \gamma_{21}} \tag{2.4d}$$

The joint distribution of p_t and q_t is determined through the reduced form equations (2.2). However, while there are only $KN = 4$ reduced form parameters, the number of structural parameters in B and Γ totals six, i.e. $KN + N(N - 1)$. It can be seen from (2.4) that an infinite number of structural form parameters will be consistent with a particular set of values for the π_{ij}'s.

In model (2.1), a restriction is introduced as β_{22} is set equal to zero. On examining (2.4c) and (2.4d) it will be seen that this implies

$$\pi_{12}/\pi_{22} = \gamma_{21} \tag{2.5}$$

Thus there is only one value of γ_{21} which is consistent with the values of π_{12} and π_{22}. Similarly, only one value of β_{21} is consistent with the reduced form parameters, since from (2.4a) and (2.4b),

$$\pi_{11} - \gamma_{21}\pi_{21} = \beta_{21}$$

and from (2.5)

$$\beta_{21} = \pi_{11} - \pi_{21}\pi_{12}/\pi_{22} \tag{2.6}$$

However, it is not difficult to see that there are still an infinite number of values of γ_{11}, β_{11} and β_{12} consistent with any set of values for the reduced form parameters.

We can now move on to bring out the implications of identifiability for estimation. The reduced form parameters can be estimated consistently by applying OLS to each equation in (2.2). Expressions (2.5) and (2.6) suggest that consistent estimators of γ_{21} and β_{21} can be constructed from the reduced form estimators. However, because an infinite set of values of the supply equation parameters can be associated with any set of values for the reduced form parameters, it is not possible to obtain consistent estimators of these parameters from the reduced form estimators. In terms of figure 9.1, this means that for a given value of x_2 we can sketch in a supply curve with any slope and intercept we care to choose, and there will be nothing in the data to contradict our particular choice.

The discussion of identifiability in Section 1 implied that for all the equations in the structural form to be identifiable, at least $N(N - 1)$ restrictions would have to be found. For (2.1), $N = 2$ and so if the model as a whole is to be identifiable at least one more restriction must be imposed. One possibility is to set $\beta_{12} = 0$. However, if this were done x_2 would not appear anywhere in the system and so neither equation would be identifiable. An alternative possibility is to set $\beta_{11} = 0$, so that the model becomes

$$S : q_t = \gamma_{11} p_t \qquad + \beta_{12} x_{2t} + \epsilon_{1t} \qquad\qquad (2.7a)$$

$$D : q_t = \gamma_{21} p_t + \beta_{21} \qquad\qquad + \epsilon_{2t} \quad , \quad t = 1, \ldots, T \qquad (2.7b)$$

Equations (2.4a) and (2.4b) may then be rearranged to give

$$\gamma_{11} = \pi_{11} / \pi_{21} \qquad\qquad\qquad (2.8)$$

while β_{12} may similarly be expressed in terms of the reduced form parameters only; cf. (2.5) and (2.6). Thus only one set of values of the supply equation parameters will be consistent with a given set of reduced form parameters and so the equation is identifiable.

The restriction that $\beta_{11} = 0$ implies that the supply curve passes through the origin. This may not be an unreasonable assumption although it is not very common for a priori restrictions to be imposed on the constant term. Figure 9.2 shows why a restriction of this kind is effective in identifying an equation. In order to illustrate the point in two dimensions the structural form is taken to be

$$S : q_t = \gamma_{11} p_t \qquad + \epsilon_{1t} \qquad\qquad (2.9a)$$

$$D : q_t = \gamma_{21} p_t + \beta_{21} + \epsilon_{2t} \qquad\qquad (2.9b)$$

The observations are clustered around a single point and while the demand curve is no longer identifiable, an estimate of γ_{11} is given by the slope of the line marked S.

The motivation behind the introduction of (2.7) was the desire to have a structural form with the same numbers of parameters as the reduced form. Thus $N(N - 1) = 2$ parameters were set equal to zero. However, had the

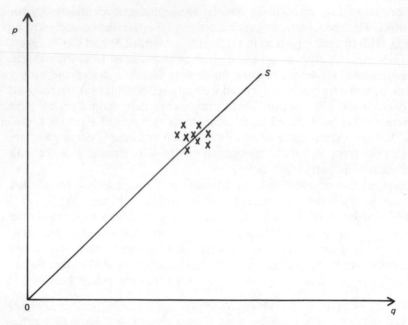

Figure 9.2   Data Generated by Model (2.9)

two parameters set equal to zero been in the same equation, it would no longer have been the case that the model as a whole was identifiable. Thus consider the model

$$S : q_t = \gamma_{11} p_t \qquad\qquad\qquad\quad + \epsilon_{1t} \qquad\qquad (2.10a)$$

$$D : q_t = \gamma_{21} p_t + \beta_{21} + \beta_{22} x_{2t} + \epsilon_{2t} \qquad\qquad (2.10b)$$

Although there are two restrictions on the structural form they both serve to identify the same equation, namely the supply curve. On comparing (2.10) with (2.9) it will be apparent that one restriction is quite sufficient for this purpose. The supply curve in (2.10) is therefore said to be *overidentified*, whereas in (2.9) it is *exactly identified*. The fact that the supply curve is overidentified in (2.10), however, is of no consolation to the demand curve: this is still *underidentified*.

Conditions for Identifiability

The concept of identifiability was defined quite precisely in Section 3.6 in terms of the joint density function of the endogenous variables; a structure of a model is identifiable if and only if no other structure is observationally equivalent. When the observations are generated by a simultaneous equation model, their distribution is determined by the reduced form. If the disturbances in (1.5) are normally distributed and independent the model may be written as

$$\Gamma y_t = B x_t + \epsilon_t \tag{2.11}$$

where $\epsilon_t \sim NID\ (0,\ \Omega)$. If follows that $y_t \sim NID\ (\Gamma^{-1} B x_t,\ \Gamma^{-1} \Omega \Gamma^{-1\prime})$.

Thus any two structures which have reduced forms in which both the expected value of y_t and its covariance matrix are identical will be observationally equivalent.

A class of observationally equivalent structures may be defined by pre-multiplying (2.11) by a non-singular matrix F. This yields

$$F \Gamma y_t = F B x_t + F \epsilon_t \tag{2.12}$$

The reduced form of (2.12) is

$$y_t = (F\Gamma)^{-1} F B x_t + (F\Gamma)^{-1} F \epsilon_t$$
$$= \Gamma^{-1} B x_t + \Gamma^{-1} \epsilon_t$$

This is precisely the same as the reduced form of (2.11).

It was argued earlier that identifiability of a structural form can only be achieved if restrictions are placed on the parameters of the model. Thus although (2.12) is observationally equivalent to (2.11) it will only be a *model admissible* structure if it satisfies the same *a priori* restrictions as does (2.11). If, for example, B has a zero in a certain position, FB must also have a zero in exactly the same position. If it does not, it cannot be considered as a structure of the model with which we are concerned. A particular structure of (2.11) will therefore be identifiable if the constraints on the model imply that (2.12) can only be model admissible if F is equal to the identity matrix. Since this argument holds for all structures of (2.11), this condition is also a necessary and sufficient one for the identifiability of the model itself. What is therefore needed is a set of rules which tell us the conditions under which the only transformation matrix consistent with an admissible structure is the identity matrix. As will be shown below these rules can be established for one equation at a time, and the identifiability of the system as a whole determined from the identifiability of each individual equation. However, in a limited information approach, attention is focused on a single equation, and the identifiability of the other equations need never be considered.

Throughout this sub-section it will be assumed that the only way in which restrictions can be imposed on the model is by setting certain coefficients in B and Γ equal to zero. More generally, it is possible to impose restrictions by considering linear combinations of the parameters in an equation. Thus, in the context of model (2.1) it can be shown that the restriction $\gamma_{11} = \beta_{12}$ is sufficient to ensure the identifiability of the supply equation. Restrictions of this kind will not be considered explicitly here. Nor will a great deal of attention be paid to restrictions on the Ω matrix, although in the next sub-section it is shown that the identifiability of a recursive model is guaranteed by taking Ω to be diagonal. However, in the remainder of the section it is supposed that Ω is unrestricted.

Consider a single equation in the model (2.11). Without any loss of generality, this can be taken to be the first equation, and it may be written as

$$\sum_{i=1}^{N} \gamma_{1i} y_{it} = \sum_{j=1}^{K} \beta_{1j} x_{jt} + \epsilon_{1t} \tag{2.13}$$

The normalisation rule implies that one of the γ_{1i}'s must be set equal to unity. In order for the equation to be identifiable a certain number of variables must be excluded from (2.13). When this has been done, the equation will contain $n_1 \leq N$ endogenous variables and $k_1 \leq K$ exogenous variables. Another specification of this equation will only be model admissible if it includes the same set of exogenous and endogenous variables.

Let the first row of the matrix F be denoted by $(1 \; f')$, where f is an $(N-1) \times 1$ vector. Setting the first element equal to unity is done simply to comply with the normalisation requirement. The first rows of the matrices $F\Gamma$ and FB in (2.12) are given by $(1 \; f')\Gamma$ and $(1 \; f')B$ respectively. The vector, f, will be deemed admissible if $(1 \; f')\Gamma$ and $(1 \; f')B$ obey the same restrictions as the first rows of Γ and B. If the only admissible f is the null vector, the equation is identifiable. In other words what is being asked is whether it is possible to reproduce the characteristics of the first equation in the model by a linear combination of the other equations.

Some examples should make these concepts clearer as well as suggesting some possible rules for identification.

Example 1   In (2.9) the Γ matrix is subject to no restrictions, apart from normalisation, but B is $B = [0 \; \beta_{21}]'$. Since $N = 2$, f is a scalar and so

$$(1 \; f)B = f\beta_{21} \tag{2.14}$$

The model for the supply equation (2.9a) contains the *a priori* restriction that $\beta_{11} = 0$. The transformation in (2.14) is therefore only admissible if $f = 0$. Hence (2.9a) is identifiable.

Example 2   Now consider a three equation system:

$$y_{1t} + \gamma_{12} y_{2t} + \gamma_{13} y_{3t} = \beta_{11} x_{1t} + \qquad\qquad + \beta_{13} x_{3t} + \epsilon_{1t}$$

$$y_{2t} + \gamma_{23} y_{3t} = \qquad\qquad \beta_{22} x_{2t} + \beta_{23} x_{3t} + \epsilon_{2t}$$

$$\gamma_{31} y_{1t} + \qquad y_{3t} = \qquad\qquad \beta_{32} x_{2t} \qquad\qquad + \epsilon_{3t}$$

$$\tag{2.15}$$

In examining the identifiability of the first equation, all we need to consider is the second element in $(1\ f')\,B$. If there exists an $f \neq 0$ such that this element is zero, no structure of the equation will be identifiable, since it will always be possible to find an observationally equivalent structure. Let g and h denote the two elements in f, i.e. $f' = (g\ h)$. The question is whether it is possible to satisfy the equation

$$g\beta_{22} + h\beta_{32} = 0 \qquad\qquad (2.16)$$

with either g or h, or both, taking a non-zero value. The answer is obviously in the affirmative, since all that needs to be done is to set $g/h = -\beta_{32}/\beta_{22}$.

Excluding one variable from an equation is obviously not sufficient to ensure identifiability in this case. However, suppose that x_3 is excluded as well, i.e. $\beta_{13} = 0$. The matrix FB will only satisfy the same restrictions as B if g and h can be chosen such that both (2.16) and the equation

$$g\beta_{23} = 0 \qquad\qquad (2.17)$$

are satisfied. However, unless $\beta_{23} = 0$, this implies that g must be zero and unless $\beta_{32} = 0$ it follows from (2.16) that $h = 0$. Therefore the only admissible f vector is $f = 0$ and so the equation is now identifiable. Specifying that β_{23} and β_{32} be non-zero is obviously rather pedantic insofar as the specification of the model states that the corresponding variables are indeed included in the relevant equations.

These examples suggest a rule for identifiability, namely that at least $N-1$ variables must be excluded from the equation in question. Indeed this ties in with some of the earlier discussion, since if $N - 1$ variables are excluded from each equation, the total number of restrictions in the structural form is $N(N - 1)$. The structural form therefore contains the same number of parameters as the reduced form. However, while the requirement that $N-1$ variables be excluded from an equation will usually ensure identifiability, there are cases where it is not enough.

Example 3 Suppose a minor amendment is made to the three equation model in Example 2. Including x_3 in the third equation means that the model is now written as

$$y_{1t} + \gamma_{12}y_{2t} + \gamma_{13}y_{3t} = \beta_{11}x_{1t} + \qquad\qquad + \epsilon_{1t}$$

$$y_{2t} + \gamma_{23}y_{3t} = \qquad \beta_{22}x_{2t} + \beta_{23}x_{3t} + \epsilon_{2t}$$

$$\gamma_{31}y_{1t} + \qquad y_{3t} = \qquad \beta_{32}x_{2t} + \beta_{33}x_{3t} + \epsilon_{3t}$$

$$\qquad\qquad (2.18)$$

Equation (2.17) now becomes

$$g\beta_{23} + h\beta_{33} = 0 \tag{2.17}'$$

In general, equations (2.16) and (2.17)' will only both be satisfied by setting $g = h = 0$. However, if

$$\beta_{22}\beta_{33} - \beta_{32}\beta_{23} = 0$$

it is possible to find non-zero values of g and h which solve the equations provided that

$$g/h = -\beta_{32}/\beta_{22} = -\beta_{33}/\beta_{23}$$

Such possibilities must therefore be specifically excluded in stating conditions which are both necessary and sufficient to ensure the identifiability of an equation.

Now consider the general case of (2.12). The $N \times (N + K)$ matrix $[\Gamma \vdots B]$ may be partitioned as

$$[\Gamma \vdots B] = \begin{bmatrix} 1, -\gamma_1' & \vdots & 0' & \vdots & \beta_1' & \vdots & 0' \\ \hline \bar{\Gamma}_1 & \vdots & \Gamma_1 & \vdots & \bar{B}_1 & \vdots & B_1 \end{bmatrix} \begin{matrix} \} & 1 \\ \} & N-1 \end{matrix} \tag{2.19}$$

$$\underbrace{}_{n_1} \quad \underbrace{}_{N-n_1} \quad \underbrace{}_{k_1} \quad \underbrace{}_{K-k_1}$$

The first row in (2.19) corresponds to the first equation in the model. The variables have been arranged in such a way that the coefficients corresponding to the n_1 endogenous variables included in the first equation appear in the first n_1 columns. The next set of $N - n_1$ columns contains the coefficients of the endogenous variables excluded from the first equation. The remaining K columns are arranged on a similar basis.

The first row in (2.19) shows the coefficients for the first equation in the model, the notation (γ_1, β_1) being the same as that employed later in the chapter in (4.3). However, the important point about the first row of (2.19) in the present context is that it contains two null row vectors. These correspond to the coefficients of the excluded variables. If the row vector $(1\ f')[\Gamma \vdots B]$ is to be subject to the same restrictions as the first row of (2.19), the vector f must satisfy the two sets of equations, $f'\Gamma_1 = 0$ and $f'B_1 = 0$. These may be written jointly as

$$f'[\Gamma_1 \vdots B_1] = 0 \tag{2.20}$$

The two equations (2.16) and (2.17)' represent a special case of (2.20).

The matrix $[\Gamma_1 \vdots B_1]$ is of order $(N - 1) \times (N - n_1 + K - k_1)$. Unless $N - n_1 + K - k_1 \geq N - 1$, it will always be possible to find an $f \neq 0$ such that (2.20) is satisfied. This argument holds for any equation in the model and so the condition

$$N - n_i + K - k_i \geq N - 1, \qquad i = 1, \ldots, N \qquad (2.21)$$

is *necessary* for the ith equation to be identifiable. This is usually referred to as the *order condition*.

Although the order condition is necessary for identification it is not sufficient. It is only possible to be certain that $f = 0$ is a unique solution to (2.20) if $[\Gamma_1 \vdots B_1]$ includes an $(N - 1) \times (N - 1)$ sub-matrix which is non-singular. This is equivalent to demanding that $[\Gamma_1 \vdots B_1]$ has full row rank. If this condition — the *rank condition* — is met the equation must be identified. Hence it is both necessary and sufficient.

To check the identifiability of an equation, the order condition is first examined. The inequality (2.21) may be interpreted as saying that the number of excluded variables must be at least as great as $N - 1$. Alternatively a rearrangement of (2.21) yields

$$K \geq n_i + k_i - 1 = m_i, \qquad i = 1, \ldots, N \qquad (2.22)$$

This has the interpretation that the number of exogenous variables in the system must be greater than or equal to the number of explanatory variables in the ith equation. If the order condition is not satisfied the equation is under-identified, and there is no need even to consider the rank condition. If it is satisfied, the rank condition may be examined. The first step is to construct the $(N - 1) \times (N - n_i + K - k_i)$ matrix $[\Gamma_i \vdots B_i]$, which is made up of parameters in Γ and B corresponding to variables *not* included in the ith equation. The equation is then identified if at least one of the $(N - 1) \times (N - 1)$ sub-matrices of $[\Gamma_i \vdots B_i]$ is non-singular. In (2.18)

$$[\Gamma_1 \vdots B_1] = \begin{bmatrix} \beta_{22} & \beta_{23} \\ \beta_{32} & \beta_{33} \end{bmatrix}$$

and so the rank condition for the first equation is

$$\beta_{22}\beta_{33} - \beta_{23}\beta_{32} \neq 0 \qquad (2.23)$$

This is exactly what emerged in the discussion below (2.17)′. A similar condition may be derived for the second and third equations. In model (2.15), however, the third equation is overidentified and

$$[\Gamma_3 \vdots B_3] = \begin{bmatrix} \gamma_{12} & \beta_{11} & \beta_{13} \\ 1 & 0 & \beta_{23} \end{bmatrix}$$

Any one of the following three conditions is therefore sufficient to ensure identifiability:

$$\begin{vmatrix} \gamma_{12} & \beta_{11} \\ 1 & 0 \end{vmatrix} = -\beta_{11} \neq 0 \qquad (2.24a)$$

$$\begin{vmatrix} \gamma_{12} & \beta_{13} \\ 1 & \beta_{23} \end{vmatrix} = \beta_{23}\gamma_{12} - \beta_{13} \neq 0 \qquad\qquad (2.24b)$$

or

$$\begin{vmatrix} \beta_{11} & \beta_{13} \\ 0 & \beta_{23} \end{vmatrix} = \beta_{11}\beta_{23} \neq 0 \qquad\qquad (2.24c)$$

The difficulty in applying the rank condition in practice is that it may require more *a priori* knowledge than is normally available. This point is highlighted by (2.23). There may be economic reasons to suggest that $\beta_{22}/\beta_{23} = \beta_{32}/\beta_{33}$, and if this is the case the first equation is clearly not identifiable. On the other hand if economic theory has nothing to say about the relationship between these parameters, identifiability can only be established by default. If the equation is not, in fact, identifiable this may or may not become apparent in the process of estimating the model. For example, in computing the FIML estimator the algorithm may fail to converge due to the singularity of the information matrix at the true parameter values.

A further point about the rank condition is that it can only be established if we are prepared to specify the complete model. In limited information estimation the researcher may be unable, or unwilling, to fulfil this requirement. Fortunately, the order condition is usually sufficient to ensure identifiability, and although it is important to be aware of the rank condition, a failure to verify it will rarely result in disaster.

Restrictions on Disturbances*

Throughout the discussion of the previous sub-section Ω was taken to be unrestricted. However, placing constraints on the form of Ω can aid identifiability in much the same way as can constraints on B and Γ.

If Ω is specified to be diagonal, the observationally equivalent structures given by (2.12) will only be model admissible if $F\Omega F'$ is also diagonal. However, constraining Ω to be diagonal is not sufficient to ensure identifiability by itself. This is basically because Ω is symmetric and so contains only $N(N - 1)/2$ distinct off-diagonal terms. More formally, if the model, (2.12), is normalised by setting the N diagonal terms in Ω equal to unity, the diagonality restriction implies $\Omega = I$. If the matrix F is then chosen as any orthogonal matrix, this restriction will be preserved. However, the structure of the model is clearly altered since $F\Gamma$ and FB need not be the same as Γ and B.

If Ω is specified to be diagonal at least $N(N - 1)/2$ further restrictions are needed to ensure identifiability of the model as a whole. In a recursive model — cf. (1.2) — the assumption of a triangular Γ matrix imposes this number of constraints and every equation in the model can be shown to be identifiable.

9.3. Maximum Likelihood Estimation

The joint distribution of the observations $y_1, \ldots, y_T$ in the reduced form of (2.11), is given by

$$\log L = -\frac{TN}{2} \log 2\pi - \frac{T}{2} \log |\Gamma^{-1}\Omega\Gamma^{-1\prime}|$$

$$-\frac{1}{2} \sum_{t=1}^{T} (y_t - \Pi x_t)' \Gamma' \Omega^{-1} \Gamma (y_t - \Pi x_t) \qquad (3.1)$$

as $E(v_t v_t') = \Gamma^{-1}\Omega\Gamma^{-1\prime}$. Since $\Pi = \Gamma^{-1}B$, the model may be expressed entirely in terms of the structural parameters. Within the last term in (3.1)

$$(y_t - \Pi x_t)' \Gamma' = (\Gamma y_t - \Gamma\Pi x_t)' = (\Gamma y_t - B x_t)'$$

while

$$-\frac{T}{2} \log |\Gamma^{-1}\Omega\Gamma^{-1\prime}| = T \log |\Gamma| - \frac{T}{2} \log |\Omega|$$

This follows from a standard result on determinants. Thus (3.1) becomes

$$\log L = -\frac{TN}{2} \log 2\pi + T \log |\Gamma| - \frac{T}{2} \log |\Omega|$$

$$-\frac{1}{2} \sum_{t=1}^{T} (\Gamma y_t - B x_t)' \Omega^{-1} (\Gamma y_t - B x_t) \qquad (3.2)$$

If $\Gamma = I$, the system collapses to the multivariate regression model, (2.10.1). However, if some elements of B are specified to be zero the model is best handled within a SURE framework. The complications in ML estimation of a simultaneous system (i.e. $\Gamma \neq I$) arise because of the inclusion of the determinant of Γ in (3.2). The derivatives of $\log |\Gamma|$ with respect to the non-zero elements in Γ depend on elements in Γ^{-1}, and so although differentiating the last term in (3.2) with respect to Γ is straightforward, the likelihood equations will be highly non-linear.

There are a number of approaches to computing the full information maximum likelihood (FIML) estimator in the simultaneous equation model. They will not be described in detail here. However, two points are worth noting. Firstly, the covariance matrix, Ω, may be concentrated out of the likelihood function in the same way as in the SURE model; thus

$$\tilde{\Omega}(\Gamma, B) = T^{-1} \sum_{t=1}^{T} (\Gamma y_t - B x_t)(\Gamma y_t - B x_t)'$$

$$= T^{-1} \sum_{t=1}^{T} \epsilon_t \epsilon_t' \qquad (3.3)$$

and substituting for Ω in (3.2) yields the concentrated log−likelihood function

$$\log L_c(\Gamma, B) = -\frac{TN}{2}(\log 2\pi + 1) + T \log |\Gamma| - \frac{T}{2}\log |\tilde{\Omega}| \qquad (3.4)$$

cf. (4.4.25). Secondly, analytic expressions for the derivatives of log L with respect to B and Γ may be obtained. A derivation of the relevant formulae is beyond the scope of this book, but the interested reader may refer to Phillips and Wickens (1978), Hendry (1976) or Rothenberg and Leenders (1964) for further details. However, one interesting point to note is that deriving expressions for first and second derivatives enables a *two-step estimator* to be constructed. The initial consistent estimators needed to ensure asymptotic efficiency can be obtained relatively easily using the two-stage least squares method outlined in the next section.

The ML estimators of B and Γ can be shown to have the usual properties under regularity conditions. An expression for the covariance matrix of the asymptotic distribution of $\tilde{\Gamma}$ and $\tilde{B}$ will not be given here. However, in the next section the three-stage least squares (3SLS) estimator will be derived. Unless Ω is subject to *a priori* restrictions, the 3SLS estimator has the same large sample distribution as the ML estimator, and so the properties established for the estimator are directly applicable for FIML.

Recursive Systems

Recursive systems were introduced in Section 1. Although it is arguable whether such systems should really be regarded as simultaneous equation models, they represent an interesting special case within the context of ML estimation.

A recursive system has two characteristics. Firstly the matrix Γ can be arranged in such a way that it is triangular, and so the determinant of Γ is equal to the product of the elements on the (main) diagonal. In view of the normalisation rule all these elements are unity and so $|\Gamma| = 1$. The second term in the log−likelihood function, (3.2), is therefore zero.

The second characteristic of a recursive system is the diagonality of Ω. This simplifies the third term in (3.2). More importantly, it enables the last term in (3.2) to be split up into separate terms for each equation. In the notation of (1.7) the ith element in the vector $\Gamma y_t - B x_t$ is given by $y_{it} - z_{it}' \delta_i$, and so (3.2) may be written

$$\log L = -\frac{TN}{2}\log 2\pi - \frac{T}{2}\sum_{i=1}^{N} \log \omega_{ii}$$

$$-\frac{1}{2}\sum_{i=1}^{N}\sum_{t=1}^{T} \omega_{ii}^{-1} (y_{it} - z_{it}' \delta_i)^2$$

$$= \sum_{i=1}^{N} \left\{ -\frac{T}{2} \log 2\pi - \frac{T}{2} \log \omega_{ii} - \frac{1}{2\omega_{ii}} \sum_{t=1}^{T} (y_{it} - z_{it}'\delta_i)^2 \right\} \quad (3.5)$$

where ω_{ii} is the ith diagonal element in Ω. The log–likelihood function is the sum of N log–likelihood functions corresponding to the individual structural equations. The full ML estimators of $\delta_1, \ldots, \delta_N$ are therefore given by applying OLS separately to each equation in the system.

Limited Information Maximum Likelihood

The limited information maximum likelihood (LIML) procedure is appropriate for estimating a single equation in a system. Data is assumed to be available for all exogenous variables in the system, but no *a priori* information on the specification of other equations in the system is employed.

The theory underlying the traditional derivation of LIML is relatively complicated; see Theil (1971). An equivalent way of formulating LIML is as follows. Let the equation of interest be the first one as in (2.13). This may be written as

$$y_{1t} = \gamma_1' y_{1t}^* + \beta_1' x_{1t} + \epsilon_{1t} , \qquad t = 1, \ldots, T \qquad (3.6)$$

where γ_1 and β_1 are respectively $(n_1 - 1) \times 1$ and $k_1 \times 1$ vectors of unknown parameters, and y_{1t}^* and x_{1t} are corresponding vectors of endogenous and exogenous variables. The reduced form for the endogenous variables included in (3.6) can be written as

$$y_{1t}^* = \Pi_1 x_t + v_{1t} , \qquad t = 1, \ldots, T \qquad (3.7)$$

where v_{1t} is the $(n_1 - 1) \times 1$ vector of reduced form disturbances. Taken together, equations (3.6) and (3.7) embody the information available for a limited information equation; the first equation contains the *a priori* restrictions imposed by economic theory, while the second does not. Hence the application of ML to (3.6) and (3.7) together yields the LIML estimator of (γ_1', β_1').

The LIML estimator may be regarded as the application FIML to (3.6) and (3.7). Writing these equations as

$$\begin{bmatrix} 1 & -\gamma_1 \\ 0 & I \end{bmatrix} \begin{bmatrix} y_{1t} \\ y_{1t}^* \end{bmatrix} = \begin{bmatrix} \beta_1' & 0 \\ & \Pi_1 \end{bmatrix} \begin{bmatrix} x_{1t} \\ x_{2t} \end{bmatrix} + \begin{bmatrix} \epsilon_{1t} \\ v_{1t} \end{bmatrix}$$

is analogous to the formulation of the full model in (2.11) and the likelihood function is as in (3.2). However, since the Jacobian is unity, that is

$$\begin{vmatrix} 1 & -\gamma_1' \\ 0 & I \end{vmatrix} = 1 \qquad (3.8)$$

the term log $|\Gamma|$ disappears from the likelihood function and the ML estimator can be computed by treating (3.6) and (3.7) as a SURE system. Given consistent starting values, iterating the feasible SURE estimator to convergence yields LIML. A consistent estimator of Π_1 is obtained simply by applying OLS to (3.7). A consistent estimator of γ_1 and β_1 is given by the two-stage least squares (2SLS) estimator described in the next section. In fact 2SLS and LIML have the same asymptotic properties and so the case for using LIML must rest primarily on its having better small sample properties.

9.4. Two-Stage and Three-Stage Least Squares

In developing the two-stage and three-stage least squares estimation procedures it is convenient to write the model, (2.11) in the form

$$y_{it} = z_{it}'\delta_i + \epsilon_{it}, \qquad i = 1,\ldots, N, \quad t = 1,\ldots,T \qquad (4.1)$$

where z_i is an $m_i \times 1$ vector consisting of the $n_i - 1$ endogenous variables and k_i exogenous variables considered to be explanatory variables in the ith equation. The $m_i \times 1$ vector δ_i consists of the corresponding parameters. Thus it is supposed that identifiability restrictions are imposed by excluding variables from each equation. Any equation which is to be estimated will be taken as satisfying the order condition, $K \geq m_i$. In discussing distributional theory it will be implicitly assumed that any relevant rank condition is also fulfilled.

The equations in (4.1) may be written in matrix form as

$$y_i = Z_i\delta_i + \epsilon_i, \qquad i = 1,\ldots, N \qquad (4.2)$$

where y_i and ϵ_i are $T \times 1$ vectors and Z_i is a $T \times m_i$ matrix for $i = 1,\ldots,$ N. The relationship between (4.2) and (4.1) is the same as the relationship between the vector and matrix formulations of the classical regression model, and so an explicit definition of y_i, Z_i and ϵ_i is unnecessary; cf. (2.1.3) and (2.1.4).

When it is necessary to differentiate between endogenous and exogenous regression variables, (4.2) will be written as

$$y_i = Y_i\gamma_i + X_i\beta_i + \epsilon_i, \qquad i = 1,\ldots, N \qquad (4.3)$$

where Y_i is a $T \times (n_i - 1)$ matrix of observations on the endogenous variable and X_i is a $T \times k_i$ matrix of observations on the exogenous variables. In terms of the notation of (4.1), $Z_i = [Y_i : X_i]$ and $\delta_i = (\gamma_i', \beta_i')'$ for $i = 1,\ldots, N$.

The purpose of this section is to obtain estimators which are simpler than LIML and FIML while retaining desirable statistical properties. One obvious candidate is OLS. However, although FIML collapses to a set of OLS regressions in the special case of a recursive system, OLS will not be an appropriate estimation technique for an interdependent system. When an equation contains endogenous variables one of the critical assumptions of the classical regression model is violated, as these variables will, in general, be correlated with the disturbance term. As a result OLS will not even be consistent. This is precisely the situation highlighted at the beginning of Section 2.11. The IV estimator was introduced there as an appropriate method of handling the problem and it turns out that this technique can be effectively employed in the present context. However, before considering these matters the OLS estimator is placed in perspective by examining its performance in a specific case.

Ordinary Least Squares

In discussing the identifiability of model (2.1) it was remarked, in passing, that simply regressing q_t on p_t would not be an appropriate way of estimating the demand curve. Even though the demand curve is identifiable, OLS is inconsistent as can be seen by evaluating its probability limit for γ_{21}, the slope of the demand curve.

The OLS estimator of γ_{21} is

$$c_{21} = \frac{\Sigma(p_t - \bar{p})(q_t - \bar{q})}{\Sigma(p_t - \bar{p})^2}$$

$$= \gamma_{21} + \frac{\Sigma(p_t - \bar{p})(\epsilon_{2t} - \bar{\epsilon}_2)}{\Sigma(p_t - \bar{p})^2}$$

Hence

$$\text{plim } c_{21} = \gamma_{21} + \frac{\text{Cov}(p_t, \epsilon_{2t})}{\text{Var}(p_t)}$$

As p is an endogenous variable, determined by the market, random shifts in the demand curve, due to ϵ_{2t}, affect p_t and imply that $\text{Cov}(p_t, \epsilon_{2t})$ is non-zero.

In order to evaluate $\text{Cov}(p_t, \epsilon_{2t})$ consider the reduced form equation (2.2b). Since x_2 is exogenous it follows immediately that

$$\text{Cov}(p_t, \epsilon_{2t}) = \text{Cov}(v_{2t}, \epsilon_{2t})$$

where

$$v_{2t} = (\epsilon_{2t} - \epsilon_{1t})/(\gamma_{11} - \gamma_{21})$$

$$\therefore \quad \text{Cov}(p_t, \epsilon_{2t}) = (\omega_{22} - \omega_{12})/(\gamma_{11} - \gamma_{21})$$

Meanwhile,

$$\text{Var}(p_t) = \text{Var}(v_{2t}) = (\omega_{11} + \omega_{22} - 2\omega_{12})/(\gamma_{11} - \gamma_{21})^2$$

Therefore

$$\text{plim } c_{21} - \gamma_{21} = (\gamma_{11} - \gamma_{21}) \cdot \frac{(\omega_{22} - \omega_{12})}{\omega_{11} + \omega_{22} - 2\omega_{12}} \neq 0 \qquad (4.4)$$

This quantity measures the 'inconsistency' of c_{21}. It is sometimes referred to as simultaneous equation bias.

If $\omega_{12} = 0$ the disturbances are independent and (4.4) simplifies to

$$\text{plim } c_{21} - \gamma_{21} = (\gamma_{11} - \gamma_{21}) \cdot \frac{\omega_{22}}{\omega_{11} + \omega_{22}} \tag{4.5}$$

On the basis of a *a priori* economic theory $\gamma_{11} > 0$ and $\gamma_{21} < 0$. Therefore the large sample bias in c_{21} is unambiguously positive, implying that the estimated curve will be too flat.

Two-Stage Least Squares

The difficulty with applying OLS to (4.1) arises because of the endogenous variables appearing on the right hand side of the equation. The idea underlying 2SLS is to first 'purge' the endogenous variables of their stochastic component, and then to regress y_{it} on z_{it}. The purged observations are obtained by applying OLS to the reduced form equations: hence the name two-stage least squares.

The notation of (4.3) is most appropriate for describing the procedure. The $n_i - 1$ reduced form equations corresponding to the endogenous variables on the right hand side of (4.3) may be written

$$Y_i = X\Pi_i' + V_i, \qquad i = 1, \ldots, N \tag{4.6}$$

where Π_i' is a $K \times (n_i - 1)$ matrix of reduced form coefficients, X is a $T \times K$ matrix of observations on all the exogenous variables, and V_i is a $T \times (n_i - 1)$ matrix of reduced form disturbances. These equations are a standard example of a multivariate regression model, and as shown in Section 2.10, OLS applied to each equation in turn is fully efficient. The matrix of OLS estimators may be written as

$$P_i' = (X'X)^{-1}X'Y_i \tag{4.7}$$

The predicted values of the observations in Y_i are therefore given by

$$\hat{Y}_i = XP_i' = X(X'X)^{-1}X'Y_i \tag{4.8}$$

The 2SLS estimator of δ_i is given by regressing y_i on $\hat{Y}_i$ and X_i. An explicit expression for the estimator is:

$$\tilde{d}_i = \begin{bmatrix} \tilde{c}_i \\ \tilde{b}_i \end{bmatrix} = \begin{bmatrix} \hat{Y}_i'\hat{Y}_i & \hat{Y}_i'X_i \\ X_i'\hat{Y}_i & X_i'X_i \end{bmatrix}^{-1} \begin{bmatrix} \hat{Y}_i'y_i \\ X_i'y_i \end{bmatrix} \tag{4.9}$$

On substituting for $\hat{Y}_i$ from (4.8) and noting that $X(X'X)^{-1}X'X_i = X_i$, this becomes

$$\tilde{d}_i = \begin{bmatrix} \tilde{c}_i \\ \tilde{b}_i \end{bmatrix} = \begin{bmatrix} Y_i' X(X'X)^{-1}X'Y_i & Y_i'X_i \\ X_i'Y_i & X_i'X_i \end{bmatrix}^{-1}$$

$$\times \begin{bmatrix} Y_i' X(X'X)^{-1}X'y_i \\ X_i'y_i \end{bmatrix} \tag{4.10}$$

The 2SLS estimator can also be derived by the method of instrumental variables. This is perhaps a more natural approach to adopt since it places the estimator within a more general framework. This is important, since the IV approach provides a more fruitful way of extending 2SLS to more complicated situations.

A set of instruments are needed for the endogenous variables in (4.3). However, the problem falls more easily into the framework established in Section 2.11, if we look for a set of instruments for all the variables in the equation. The argument will therefore be conducted in terms of (4.1); cf. (2.11.1).

The exogenous variables in the system as a whole provide suitable candidates for the instrumental variables. They are, by definition, uncorrelated with the structural disturbances. On the other hand, they will be highly correlated with the endogenous variables through the reduced form. Sufficient instruments will exist provided that $K \geq m_i$, but, of course, this is just the usual order condition for identifiability. When the equation in question is exactly identified $K = m_i$, and the IV estimator is simply

$$\tilde{d}_i = (X'Z_i)^{-1}X'y_i, \qquad i = 1, \ldots, N \tag{4.11}$$

In the more general case where the equation is overidentified an optimal set of m_i instruments must be constructed. The GIVE procedure, (2.11.20), suggests the following instruments:

$$W_i = X(X'X)^{-1}X'Z_i, \qquad i = 1, \ldots, N \tag{4.12}$$

The GIVE estimator of δ_l is

$$\tilde{d}_i = (W_i'Z_i)^{-1}W_i'y_i \tag{4.13}$$

On substituting for W_i from (4.12) this becomes

$$\tilde{d}_i = (Z_i'X(X'X)^{-1}X'Z_i)^{-1}Z_i'X(X'X)^{-1}X'y_i, \qquad i = 1, \ldots, N \tag{4.14}$$

As the notation suggests, (4.14) is identical to the 2SLS estimator, (4.10). This can be shown by observing that the matrix of instruments in (4.12) decomposes into two parts:

$$W_i = [XP_i' \vdots X_i] = [\hat{Y}_i \vdots X_i] \tag{4.15}$$

where $\hat{Y}_i$ is the matrix of predicted values of Y_i obtained from the reduced form; cf. (4.8). The second part of W_i simply states that the exogenous variables in the equation are used as their own instruments. Substituting $Z_j = [\,Y_i \vdots X_i]$ and (4.15) into (4.13) gives the 2SLS estimator (4.10) when $\hat{Y}_i$ is replaced by the expression on the right hand side of (4.8).

The results given for the large sample properties of GIVE estimators suggest that $\tilde{d}_i$ will be asymptotically normally distributed with a mean of δ_i and a covariance matrix

$$\text{Avar}(\tilde{d}_i) = \sigma_i^2 [\, Z_i' X (X' X)^{-1} X' Z_i]^{-1} \tag{4.16}$$

where $\sigma_i^2 = \omega_{ii} = \text{Var}(\epsilon_{it})$ for $i = 1, \ldots, N$. However, in order for this result to hold the conditions (2.11.8) and (2.11.9) must be satisfied. This can be shown to be the case if

$$\text{plim } T^{-1} X' X = Q \tag{4.17}$$

where Q is a p.d. matrix.

Three-Stage Least Squares

Two-stage least squares is a limited information procedure which can be used to estimate any identifiable equation in isolation from the other equations in the system. Three-stage least squares, on the other hand, is a method for estimating the system as a whole. Hence it is an alternative to FIML.

The N individual equations in (4.2) can be expressed in the form of a single equation by writing

$$\begin{bmatrix} y_1 \\ \vdots \\ y_N \end{bmatrix} = \begin{bmatrix} Z_1 & & 0 \\ & \ddots & \\ 0 & & Z_N \end{bmatrix} \begin{bmatrix} \delta_1 \\ \vdots \\ \delta_N \end{bmatrix} + \begin{bmatrix} \epsilon_1 \\ \vdots \\ \epsilon_N \end{bmatrix} \tag{4.18}$$

or, in more compact notation,

$$y = Z\delta + \epsilon \tag{4.19}$$

An IV approach can again be used. However, the covariance matrix of the disturbances in (4.19) is

$$E(\epsilon\epsilon') = \Omega \otimes I_T \tag{4.20}$$

and so it is first necessary to transform the observations. Let L be a non-singular $N \times N$ matrix such that

$$L'L = \Omega^{-1} \tag{4.21}$$

and define $\bar{L} = L \otimes I_T$. The disturbances in the transformed model,

$$\bar{L}y = \bar{L}Z\delta + \bar{L}\epsilon \tag{4.22}$$

have a scalar covariance matrix since

$$E(\bar{L}\epsilon\epsilon'\bar{L}') = (L \otimes I_T)(\Omega \otimes I_T)(L \otimes I_T)'$$
$$= L\,\Omega\,L' \otimes I_T$$
$$= I_{NT}$$

As in 2SLS the exogenous variables can be used to form the instruments in each equation. Let

$$\bar{X} = \begin{bmatrix} X & 0 & \cdots & 0 \\ 0 & X & \cdots & 0 \\ \vdots & \vdots & \ddots & \vdots \\ 0 & 0 & \cdots & X \end{bmatrix} = I \otimes X$$

The optimal set of instruments for the GIVE estimator are constructed from a multivariate regression of $\bar{L}Z$ on $\bar{X}$, i.e.

$$\bar{W} = \bar{X}(\bar{X}'\bar{X})^{-1}\bar{X}'\bar{L}Z$$

The GIVE estimator is then

$$\tilde{d} = (\bar{W}'\bar{Z})^{-1}\bar{W}'\bar{y}$$

where $\bar{Z} = \bar{L}Z$ and $\bar{y} = \bar{L}y$. This can be rewritten in the same way as (2.11.24), i.e.

$$\tilde{d} = (Z'\bar{L}'\bar{P}\bar{L}Z)^{-1}Z'\bar{L}'\bar{P}\bar{L}y \qquad (4.23)$$

where $\bar{P} = \bar{X}(\bar{X}'\bar{X})^{-1}\bar{X}'$. On substituting for $\bar{X}$ and $\bar{L}$, and rearranging, it will be found that

$$\bar{L}'\bar{P}\bar{L} = \Omega^{-1} \otimes X(X'X)^{-1}X' \qquad (4.24)$$

Since Ω will, in general, be unknown, it must be replaced by an appropriate estimator. The usual procedure is to apply 2SLS to each individual equation in turn and to estimate Ω from the residuals, i.e.

$$\hat{\Omega} = T^{-1} \sum_{t=1}^{T} e_t e_t' \qquad (4.25)$$

where the ith element in the $N \times 1$ vector e_t is $e_{it} = y_{it} - z_{it}' \tilde{d}_i$. Substituting (4.24) into (4.23) and replacing Ω by $\hat{\Omega}$ yields the three-stage least squares estimator,

$$\tilde{d} = [Z'\{\hat{\Omega}^{-1} \otimes X(X'X)^{-1}X'\}Z]^{-1}Z'\{\hat{\Omega}^{-1} \otimes X(X'X)^{-1}X'\} y$$

$$(4.26)$$

The asymptotic properties of $\tilde{d}$ may be established on the basis of the general results for IV estimators. Subject to the relevant conditions, which may be verified in much the same way as for 2SLS, the 3SLS estimator is asymptotically normally distributed with a mean of δ and a covariance matrix,

$$\text{Avar}(\tilde{d}) = [Z'(\Omega^{-1} \otimes X(X'X)^{-1}X')Z]^{-1} \qquad (4.27)$$

cf. (2.11.25). Note that replacing Ω by the consistent estimator, $\hat{\Omega}$, has no effect on the asymptotic distribution of $\tilde{d}$.

There are two special cases where 3SLS collapses to 2SLS applied separately to each equation. These are

    (i) when Ω is diagonal; and
    (ii) when every equation in the system is exactly identified.

Classes of IV Estimators: LIVE and FIVE*

The instruments defined in (4.12) may be replaced by the instruments

$$W_i^\dagger = [X\hat{\Pi}_i \vdots X_i], \qquad i = 1, \ldots, N \tag{4.28}$$

where $\hat{\Pi}_i$ is a consistent estimator of Π_i. An IV estimator of δ_i constructed using $W_i^\dagger$ will have the same asymptotic properties as the 2SLS estimator. Estimators which take this form are known as *limited information instrumental variables efficient* (LIVE) estimators. The corresponding *full information instrumental variables efficient* (FIVE) estimator uses a matrix of instrumental variables defined by

$$W^\dagger = (\hat{\Omega}^{-1} \otimes I_T)\bar{W} \tag{4.29}$$

where $\bar{W}$ is the matrix

$$\bar{W} = \begin{bmatrix} W_1^\dagger & 0 & \ldots & 0 \\ 0 & W_2^\dagger & \ldots & 0 \\ \vdots & \vdots & \ddots & \vdots \\ 0 & 0 & & W_N^\dagger \end{bmatrix} \tag{4.30}$$

and the $W_i^\dagger$'s are as defined in (4.28). The 3SLS estimator is a special case in which each $W_i^\dagger$ is the 2SLS matrix of instruments defined in (4.12). However, as long as all the reduced form coefficients in $\bar{W}$ are estimated consistently and Ω is estimated consistently, any FIVE estimator will have the same asymptotic distribution as 3SLS.

The LIVE and FIVE procedures are of particular importance in large systems where the size of K means that the construction and inversion of the matrix $X'X$ becomes unmanageable. In these circumstances 2SLS, and hence 3SLS, is no longer a viable proposition. Further discussion will be found in Brundy and Jorgenson (1971).

k-Class Estimators

A useful way of looking at the principal single equation estimators is within the k-class framework developed by Theil. Using the notation of (4.10), the k-class estimator of δ_i is

$$\begin{bmatrix} \hat{c}_i \\ \hat{d}_i \end{bmatrix} = \begin{bmatrix} Y_i' Y_i - k \hat{V}_i' \hat{V}_i & Y_i' X_i \\ X_i' Y_i & X_i' X_i \end{bmatrix}^{-1} \begin{bmatrix} Y_i - k \hat{V}_i \\ X_i \end{bmatrix} y_i \qquad (4.31)$$

where $\hat{V}_i$ is the matrix of OLS residuals from the reduced form regression involving the included endogenous variables, that is, from (4.8),

$$\hat{V}_i = Y_i - \hat{Y}_i = M Y_i \qquad (4.32)$$

where $M = I - X(X'X)^{-1}X'$. The scalar k can be fixed or stochastic.

(a) If $k = 0$, it can be seen immediately that the estimator corresponds to OLS.

(b) If $k = 1$, then

$$Y_i' Y_i - \hat{V}_i' \hat{V}_i = Y_i' Y_i - Y_i' M Y_i = Y_i X(X'X)^{-1}X' Y_i$$

and

$$Y_i - \hat{V}_i = Y_i - MY_i = X(X'X)^{-1}X' Y_i$$

and so the estimator is 2SLS.

(c) For any fixed value of k, (4.31) can be interpreted as an IV estimator with the matrix of instruments for the endogenous variables being

$$W_i = Y_i - k \hat{V}_i \qquad (4.33)$$

This may be verified directly by writing down the IV estimator and noting that $\hat{V}_i' Y_i = Y_i' M Y_i = Y_i' M M Y_i = \hat{V}_i' \hat{V}_i$.

(d) Finally, if k is stochastic and equal to the smallest root, μ, of the determinantal equation

$$| y_i' M_i y_i - \mu \, y_i' M \, y_i | = 0 \qquad (4.34)$$

where $M_i = I - X_i(X_i'X_i)^{-1}X_i'$, then the k-class estimator is the LIML estimator. This is the traditional definition of LIML. Further details may be found in Theil (1971) or Schmidt (1976).

FIML as an IV Estimator*

The FIML procedure can be placed within the IV framework; see, for example, Hausman (1975), Hendry (1976) or Phillips and Wickens (1978, pp. 333-335). The estimator has the form of a FIVE estimator, with the estimates of the reduced form parameters computed from estimates of the structural form parameters, i.e. $\hat{\Pi} = \hat{\Gamma}^{-1}\hat{B}$. If this procedure is iterated to convergence, with $\hat{\Omega}$ updated after each iteration, the resulting estimators of B and Γ are FIML estimators.

An obvious way to start off the FIML iteration would be to compute the initial estimates of the Π_i's from the reduced form as in 2SLS, and then to estimate Ω from (4.25). The first FIVE estimator is then 3SLS. Further iteration does not affect asymptotic efficiency since all that is required to ensure this is that the reduced form parameters are estimated consistently. However, if the procedure is iterated to convergence, the reduced form parameters will be perfectly consistent with the structural parameters. In this sense FIML makes use of all the over-identifying restrictions in the model, whereas 3SLS uses only some. Since FIML does truly utilise all the *a priori* information in the model it might reasonably be expected to have more desirable properties than 3SLS in small samples.

9.5. Testing the Validity of Restrictions on the Model

A key feature of the specification of a simultaneous equation model is the imposition of *a priori* restrictions on the parameters. If more than $N(N-1)$ restrictions are placed on the structural form the reduced form must also be subject to restrictions. Hence a gain in predictive efficiency can reasonably be expected from an estimator based on the structural form, as opposed to an estimator based on the unrestricted reduced form.

The validity of any restrictions over and above those needed to exactly identify each equation in the model can be tested. However, the test can be regarded as a test of the validity of the model only in a rather limited sense: it is testing whether it is reasonable to over-identify some of the equations. While a rejection of the null hypothesis can be taken as evidence that some restrictions on the model are invalid, a failure to reject does not constitute evidence that the model as a whole is reasonable.

The material below is divided into two sections, the first dealing with tests on the model as a whole and the second dealing with tests in a single equation.

Tests on the Model

Consider the multivariate regression model,

$$y_t = Bx_t + \epsilon_t, \qquad t = 1, \ldots, T \tag{5.1}$$

with $\epsilon_t \sim NID\,(0, \Omega)$; cf. (2.10.1). If restrictions are placed on the parameters of B, the model must be estimated as a SURE system. However, if the restrictions are valid, taking account of them in the estimation procedure should lead to a gain in predictive efficiency. When the model is estimated both with and without the restrictions, an LR test of the validity of the restrictions may be carried out. The test statistic is of the form (5.3.15).

In the static simultaneous equation model (2.11), the log−likelihood function of the *unrestricted reduced form* (URF) is given by

$$\log L = \frac{-TN}{2} \log 2\pi - \frac{T}{2}\log |\Sigma| - \frac{1}{2} \sum_{t=1}^{T} v_t'\Sigma^{-1}v_t \qquad (5.2)$$

where $v_t = y_t - \Pi x_t$ and $\Sigma = E(v_t v_t')$. This has exactly the same form as the likelihood function of (5.1) and, as in that case, the maximised likelihood function depends on the estimated covariance matrix, which for (5.2) is denoted by $\tilde{\Sigma}$. The maximised log−likelihood function for the restricted model is obtained by substituting the ML estimator of Ω,

$$\tilde{\Omega} = T^{-1} \sum_{t=1}^{T} (\tilde{\Gamma}y_t - \tilde{B}x_t)(\tilde{\Gamma}y_t - \tilde{B}x_t)' \qquad (5.3)$$

into (3.2) to yield

$$\log L = \frac{-TN}{2} (\log 2\pi + 1) - \frac{T}{2}\log |\tilde{\Gamma}^{-1}\tilde{\Omega}\tilde{\Gamma}^{-1'}|$$

Hence the LR test statistic is

$$\text{LR} = T \log \{|\tilde{\Sigma}_0|/|\tilde{\Sigma}|\} \qquad (5.4)$$

where $\tilde{\Sigma}_0 = \tilde{\Gamma}^{-1}\tilde{\Omega}\tilde{\Gamma}^{-1'}$ is the ML estimator of the disturbance covariance matrix in the restricted reduced form. The unrestricted reduced form will only be a more general model if some of the structural equations are overidentified. Thus under the null hypothesis that the over-identifying restrictions on the structural form are valid, (5.4) will be asymptotically χ_R^2 where

$$R = \sum_{i=1}^{N} (K - m_i) = NK - \sum_{i=1}^{N} m_i \qquad (5.5)$$

Maximum likelihood estimation of the URF may be carried out by N OLS regressions. While this is straightforward enough, FIML should ideally be used to estimate the structural equations. However, the test procedure is still valid if Γ, B and Σ are estimated by 3SLS.

Tests on Single Equations

The over-identifying restrictions on a single equation in the system may be tested within a limited information framework. In some ways this is more attractive than testing all the over-identifying restrictions in the system as a whole. Attention can be focused on one equation, and the results are not conditional on the specification of the rest of the model.

If the equation is estimated by 2SLS, the following test statistic is appropriate:

$$\frac{T - K}{K - m_i} \frac{(y_i - Y_i \tilde{c})'(M_i - M)(y_i - Y_i \tilde{c})}{(y_i - Y_i \tilde{c})'M(y_i - Y_i \tilde{c})} \tag{5.6}$$

where $M_i = I - X_i(X_i' X_i)^{-1} X_i'$ and $M = I - X(X'X)^{-1}X'$. This has the form of the F-statistic for testing for the inclusion of a subset of parameters in a classical linear regression model. Thus

$$(y_i - Y_i \tilde{c})'M(y_i - Y_i \tilde{c})$$

is the residual sum of squares obtained by regressing $y_i - Y_i \tilde{c}$ on X. However, it will be observed that $K - m_i$ is used as a divisor rather than $K - k_i$.

Under the null hypothesis that the model is correctly specified, the distribution of this statistic can be approximated by an F-distribution with $(K - m_i, T - K)$ degrees of freedom; see the Monte Carlo evidence in Basmann (1960). A high value of the statistic will lead to a rejection of the null hypothesis in favour of the alternative that some of the excluded exogenous variables should have been included in the equation.

9.6. Dynamic Models

The general form of a dynamic linear simultaneous equation model was given in (1.1) as

$$\Gamma y_t = A_1 y_{t-1} + \cdots + A_r y_{t-r} + B_0 x_t + \cdots + B_s x_{t-s} + u_t \tag{6.1}$$

More complicated models, which are non-linear in parameters, may also be constructed. However, the development here is restricted to (6.1); the additional technical problems raised by the introduction of non-linearities are not considered explicitly.

The first point to be explored in connection with (6.1) concerns its dynamic properties, and the relationship between a model of this kind and the basic time series models examined in Chapter 1. An explicit link is found to connect these different classes of model, and the implications of this for forecasting are discussed in the final section of the chapter. The other topic dealt with in the final section is control, and the relationship between the forecasting and control functions of the dynamic simultaneous equation model are placed in some kind of perspective.

Estimation, and the question of identifiability, are considered in the later parts of this section. The assumption that the disturbances in (6.1) are serially uncorrelated makes a significant difference from the technical point of view, and this case is considered first.

Dynamic Properties

As pointed out in Section 1, the systematic dynamics of a simultaneous equation model may be derived from the reduced form (1.4). However, the reduced form equations can be rearranged so that each endogenous variable is expressed in terms of current and lagged values of the exogenous variables only. This is known as the final form. Let $A(L)$ be the matrix polynomial

$$A(L) = \Gamma - A_1 L - \ldots - A_r L^r \tag{6.2}$$

and define $B(L)$ in terms of $B_0, \ldots, B_s$ in a similar way; cf. (8.6.15). Model (6.1) may then be written as

$$A(L)y_t = B(L)x_t + u_t \tag{6.3}$$

and pre-multiplying by $A^{-1}(L)$ yields the *final form*

$$y_t = A^{-1}(L)B(L)x_t + A^{-1}(L)u_t \tag{6.4}$$

This is directly comparable with the operation in (8.6.18), and the matrices of interim multipliers may be deduced directly from $A^{-1}(L)B(L)$.

Subtracting the mean path, $\bar{y}_t$, from both sides of (6.4) gives

$$y_t - \bar{y}_t = A^{-1}(L)u_t \tag{6.5}$$

The vector $y_t - \bar{y}_t$ gives the deviations of the observations from their mean path and this represents the stochastic part of the model. If u_t is specified to be a particular multivariate ARMA process,

$$\Phi_u(L)u_t = \Theta_u(L)\epsilon_t \tag{6.6}$$

the stochastic properties of the model are available immediately since $y_t - \bar{y}$ is governed by the multivariate ARMA process

$$y_t - \bar{y}_t = A^{-1}(L)\Phi_u^{-1}(L)\Theta_u(L)\epsilon_t \tag{6.7}$$

Further insight into the properties of the model may be obtained by writing

$$A^{-1}(L) = A^*(L)/|A(L)|$$

where $A^*(L)$ is the adjoint matrix of $A(L)$. Substituting in (6.4) gives the *final equations*,

$$y_t = \frac{A^*(L)B(L)}{|A(L)|}x_t + \frac{A^*(L)}{|A(L)|}u_t \tag{6.8}$$

Note that $|A(L)|$ is just a scalar polynomial. Thus the equations in (6.8) may be regarded as a set of N transfer functions. However, they are subject to two special characteristics. Assuming no cancellation of common factors, the denominator polynomials are the same, firstly for every exogenous variable and disturbance term, and secondly for every equation. The first of these constraints is a feature of stochastic difference equations, and it suggests writing the system in (6.8) as

$$|A(L)|y_t = A^*(L)B(L)x_t + A^*(L)u_t \qquad (6.9)$$

This is sometimes known as the *autoregressive final form*. Each equation in (6.9) is a stochastic difference equation of the kind considered in Chapter 8. However, in all N equations the coefficients of the lagged values of the dependent variable are the same. This 'remarkable result', as it was called by Kendall, implies a common pattern of dynamic behaviour for the endogenous variable in the system.

Example Consider the dynamic supply and demand model, (1.2.8), with a white noise disturbance term attached to each equation. The system may be expressed in the form (6.3) by writing

$$\begin{bmatrix} 1 & -\gamma_{11}L \\ 1 & -\gamma_{21} \end{bmatrix} \begin{bmatrix} q_t \\ p_t \end{bmatrix} = \begin{bmatrix} \beta_{11} & 0 \\ \beta_{21} & \beta_{22} \end{bmatrix} \begin{bmatrix} 1 \\ x_t \end{bmatrix} + \begin{bmatrix} \epsilon_{1t} \\ \epsilon_{2t} \end{bmatrix} \qquad (6.10)$$

Since $|A(L)| = -\gamma_{21} + \gamma_{11}L$, the autoregressive final form is:

$$(-\gamma_{21} + \gamma_{11}L) \begin{bmatrix} q_t \\ p_t \end{bmatrix} = \begin{bmatrix} -\gamma_{21}\beta_{11} + \gamma_{11}\beta_{21}L & \gamma_{11}\beta_{22}L \\ \beta_{21} - \beta_{11} & \beta_{22} \end{bmatrix} \begin{bmatrix} 1 \\ x_t \end{bmatrix}$$

$$+ \begin{bmatrix} -\gamma_{21} & \gamma_{11}L \\ -1 & 1 \end{bmatrix} \begin{bmatrix} \epsilon_{1t} \\ \epsilon_{2t} \end{bmatrix} \qquad (6.11)$$

Alternatively,

$$q_t = (\gamma_{11}/\gamma_{21})q_{t-1} + \{\beta_{11} - \gamma_{11}\beta_{21}/\gamma_{21}\}$$
$$- (\gamma_{11}\beta_{22}/\gamma_{21})x_{t-1} + \epsilon_{1t} - (\gamma_{11}/\gamma_{21})\epsilon_{2,t-1} \qquad (6.12a)$$
$$p_t = (\gamma_{11}/\gamma_{21})p_{t-1} + \{(\beta_{11} - \beta_{21})/\gamma_{21}\}$$
$$- (\beta_{22}/\gamma_{21})x_t + (\epsilon_{1t} - \epsilon_{2t})/\gamma_{21} \qquad (6.12b)$$

The coefficients attached to the lagged dependent variables are identical. That they satisfy the dynamic stability condition, $|\gamma_{11}/\gamma_{21}| < 1$, follows immediately from the condition for stability in a cobweb model, (1.2.9).

*Stochastic Exogenous Variables**

If the exogenous variables are taken to be stochastic, rather than fixed, the random behaviour in the endogenous variables emanates from two sources. Consider the model (6.1), (6.6) and suppose that x_t is generated by a multivariate ARMA process,

$$\Phi_x(L)x_t = \Theta_x(L)\xi_t \tag{6.13}$$

where ξ_t is a vector of serially uncorrelated disturbances with mean zero and covariance matrix Ω_x. The complete vector of observations $(y_t'x_t')'$ can now be regarded as being generated by a multivariate ARMA process

$$\begin{bmatrix} A(L) & B(L) \\ 0 & \Phi_x(L) \end{bmatrix} \begin{bmatrix} y_t \\ x_t \end{bmatrix} = \begin{bmatrix} \bar{\Theta}_u(L) & 0 \\ 0 & \Theta_x(L) \end{bmatrix} \begin{bmatrix} \epsilon_t \\ \xi_t \end{bmatrix} \tag{6.14}$$

where $\bar{\Theta}_u(L) = \Phi_u^{-1}(L)\Theta_u(L)$ on the assumption that u_t has an MA representation for all t, s. Substituting (6.1) into the final form, together with (6.6), yields

$$y_t = \frac{B(L)\Theta_x(L)}{A(L)\Phi_x(L)} \xi_t + \frac{\Theta_u(L)}{A(L)\Phi_x(L)} \epsilon_t \tag{6.15}$$

and so y_t is a stochastic process driven by the innovations in the disturbance term and the explanatory variables. It can be shown to have a multivariate ARMA representation, since it is itself the sum of two multivariate ARMA processes.

A multivariate ARMA process can be decomposed into a set of seemingly unrelated univariate ARMA processes. Therefore if (6.13) does hold, it will be possible to represent each endogenous variable in the dynamic simultaneous equation model, (6.1), by a univariate ARMA process. This result is of some importance in understanding the relationship between the forecasts produced by econometric models and those produced by 'naive' time series methods.

Not all exogenous variables can reasonably be regarded as being generated by stochastic processes. For example, policy variables, such as the tax rate or the rate of interest, typically show step changes. Other exogenous variables also behave in such a way that an ARMA representation would be inappropriate. An extreme example is a dummy variable used to measure the effect of some external event such as a change in government. Rather less extreme is the behaviour of a variable like the price of oil, which is subject to rapid changes in a short period of time due to price fixing by the OPEC cartel.

Bearing the above considerations in mind, it is useful to divide the exogenous variables into two groups. At the risk of oversimplification these may be labelled '*deterministic*' and '*stochastic*'. The deterministic variables will be denoted by x_1, and the stochastic variables by x_2. Thus $x_t = (x'_{1t} \; x'_{2t})'$ and, corresponding to this division, the polynomial matrix $B(L)$ may be partitioned as $[B_1(L) \; \vdots \; B_2(L)]$. The final equations, (6.8), therefore become:

$$y_t = \frac{A^*(L)B_1(L)}{|A(L)|} x_{1t} + \frac{A^*(L)B_2(L)}{|A(L)|} x_{2t} + \frac{A^*(L)}{|A(L)|} u_t \qquad (6.16)$$

If x_{2t} is generated by a multivariate ARMA process, it follows from the argument above that y_t may be expressed in the form

$$y_t = \frac{A^*(L)B_1(L)}{|A(L)|} x_{1t} + u_t^\dagger \qquad (6.17)$$

where $u_t^\dagger$ is generated by a multivariate ARMA process, the form of which depends on both u_t and x_{2t}. However, as in the case of (6.14) it follows that $u_t^\dagger$ may be decomposed into a vector of univariate ARMA processes. This implies that each endogenous variable has a transfer function representation in which only the elements of x_1 appear as explanatory variables; cf. (6.8). Alternatively, because of the common factor $|A(L)|$ in (6.16), a set of stochastic difference equations with ARMA disturbance terms might present a better specification.

9.7. Estimation and Identification of Dynamic Models

If the disturbance term in (6.1) is white noise, the fact that the model is dynamic raises no difficulties beyond those encountered in the static case. The lagged endogenous variables may be classified with the exogenous variables as *predetermined*. All the results of Sections 2 to 5 carry over directly with the predetermined variables playing exactly the same role as the exogenous variables in the static model.

Example Writing the supply and demand model of (6.10) in the format of (6.1) yields:

$$\begin{bmatrix} 1 & 0 \\ 1 & -\gamma_{21} \end{bmatrix} \begin{pmatrix} q_t \\ p_t \end{pmatrix} = \begin{bmatrix} 0 & \gamma_{11} \\ 0 & 0 \end{bmatrix} \begin{pmatrix} q_{t-1} \\ p_{t-1} \end{pmatrix}$$

$$+ \begin{bmatrix} \beta_{11} & 0 \\ \beta_{21} & \beta_{22} \end{bmatrix} \begin{pmatrix} 1 \\ x_t \end{pmatrix} + \begin{bmatrix} \epsilon_{1t} \\ \epsilon_{2t} \end{bmatrix} \qquad (7.1)$$

The order condition for a dynamic model is that the number of *predetermined* variables in the system must be greater than, or equal to, the number of explanatory variables included in that equation. The second equation in (7.1) — the demand equation — contains $m_2 = 3$ explanatory variables. This is exactly equal to the number of predetermined variables appearing in the system and so the equation is exactly identified. The rank condition is, of course, trivial in this case since the model contains only two behavioural equations.

The supply equation has no current endogenous variables appearing as explanatory variables and it is automatically identifiable. The fact that both equations are identifiable is in accordance with the heuristic reasoning of Section 1.2.

Although the treatment of dynamic simultaneous equation models is straightforward when the disturbances are serially uncorrelated, a number of new issues arise once this assumption is relaxed. The resulting complications can, to a certain extent, be anticipated on the basis of the material presented in the previous chapter.

Identification

Consider the dynamic model, (6.1), and let $F(L)$ be any non-singular $N \times N$ polynomial matrix in the lag operator, i.e.

$$F(L) = F_0 + F_1 L + \ldots + F_m L^m \tag{7.2}$$

A class of observationally equivalent structures is then defined by

$$F(L)A(L)y_t = F(L)B(L)x_t + F(L)u_t \tag{7.3}$$

since the final form is given by (6.4) irrespective of the specification of $F(L)$; cf. (2.12). As in the static case, (7.3) is said to be model admissible if it satisfies the same *a priori* restrictions as (6.1). If the only way of obtaining a model admissible structure is by setting $F(L) = I$, then (6.1) is identifiable.

The assumption that the disturbance terms in the model are serially uncorrelated effectively constrains the coefficients of the lag operator in $F(L)$ to be zero. Thus $F(L) = F$, where F is an $N \times N$ matrix of the type considered in Section 2, and so the question of identifiability can be handled as in the static case. Once the assumption that the disturbances are serially uncorrelated is relaxed, the sort of identifiability questions raised in the context of multivariate ARMA models become relevant. As might be expected, MA and mixed disturbance terms are more difficult to handle than pure AR disturbances. Indeed for a vector AR(1) specification of u_t, Sargan's condition, which was stated in Section 8.6, is directly applicable. Thus, if the system contains at least N exogenous variables which do not become redundant when lagged, the AR coefficient matrix, Φ, is globally identifiable. The conventional static criteria may then be applied to the identifiability of the remaining parameters in the model. The conditions developed for more complicated cases by Hannan (1970), Sargan (1972), Deistler (1976), and others will not, however, be described in this book. Instead, attention will be

focused on the approach adopted by Hatanaka (1975). Here, the problem
is viewed in a rather different way.

Hatanaka argues that the dynamic specification of a model will, in general,
be determined empirically. He therefore assumes: (i) that the orders of the
lags on the endogenous and exogenous variables are not known *a priori*; and
(ii) that the disturbance term is known only to be a stationary process. Within
this framework, he shows that it is possible to derive a simple order condition
for identifiability in terms of the exclusion of exogenous variables from an
equation.

Consider the first equation in (6.1). This may be written as

$$y_t' \alpha(L) = x_t' \beta(L) + u_t \tag{7.4}$$

where $\alpha(L)$ is an $N \times 1$ vector polynomial in the lag operator and $\beta(L)$ is
a $k \times 1$ vector polynomial. It is assumed that none of the variables in x_t
is redundant when lagged. Thus, for example, x_t must contain no constant
terms or seasonal dummies. Variables of this kind will typically be found
in an econometric model, but within this context they are simply ignored.

The only relevant *a priori* information in (7.4) is whether or not a variable
is excluded from the equation. Excluding a variable in this way means not
only that the current values do not appear, but also that lagged values are
inadmissible. Thus if a variable in y_t or x_t is excluded from the equation,
the corresponding element in $\alpha(L)$ or $\beta(L)$ will be zero. The $N \times (N + K)$
polynomial matrix $[A(L) \vdots B(L)]$ may then be partitioned as

$$[A(L) \vdots B(L)] = \begin{bmatrix} 1, & -\alpha_1(L)' & \vdots & 0' & \vdots & \beta_1'(L) & \vdots & 0' \\ \hline A_1(L) & & \vdots & A_1(L) & \vdots & B_1(L) & \vdots & B_1(L) \end{bmatrix} \tag{7.5}$$

The notation in (7.5) is analogous to that in (2.19), and the implications
for identifiability are similar. The *rank condition* states that the rank of
$[A_1(L) \vdots B_1(L)]$ must be $N - 1$. The *order condition*, which is a
generalisation of (2.21), is that the number of excluded *exogenous* variables
is greater than or equal to, the number of included endogenous variables
minus one. It is important to note that with serially uncorrelated disturbances
the classical order condition would emerge in terms of excluded predetermined
variables, albeit with a different definition of exclusion.

Maximum Likelihood Estimation

The system of equations defined by (6.1) may be written more compactly
by defining $w_t = (y_t', y_{t-1}', \ldots, y_{t-r}', x_t', \ldots, x_{t-s}')'$ and
$A = [\Gamma \vdots -A_1 \vdots \ldots \vdots -A_r \vdots -B_0 \vdots \ldots \vdots -B_s]$. Then

$$Aw_t = u_t, \qquad t = \tau, \ldots, T \tag{7.6}$$

where $\tau = \max(r + 1, s + 1)$.

Suppose that the disturbances are normally distributed and follow a vector AR(1) process, i.e.

$$u_t = \Phi u_{t-1} + \epsilon_t \tag{7.7}$$

where $\epsilon_t \sim NID(0, \Omega)$. The equations in (7.6) then become

$$Aw_t - \Phi A w_{t-1} = \epsilon_t, \qquad t = \tau + 1, \ldots, T \tag{7.8}$$

The logarithm of the joint distribution of $\epsilon_{\tau+1}, \ldots, \epsilon_T$ is given by

$$p(\epsilon_{\tau+1}, \ldots, \epsilon_T) = \frac{-(T - \tau)N}{2} \log 2\pi - \frac{(T - \tau)}{2} \log |\Omega|$$

$$- \frac{1}{2} \sum_{t=\tau+1}^{T} \epsilon_t' \Omega^{-1} \epsilon_t \tag{7.9}$$

Under the assumption that the initial observations, $y_1, \ldots, y_\tau$ are fixed, the log–likelihood function is given by

$$\log L = - \frac{(T - \tau)N}{2} \log 2\pi - (T - \tau) \log |\Gamma| - \frac{(T - \tau)}{2} \log |\Omega|$$

$$- \frac{1}{2} \sum_{t=\tau+1}^{T} (Aw_t - \Phi A w_{t-1})' \Omega^{-1} (Aw_t - \Phi A w_{t-1})$$

$$\tag{7.10}$$

since the Jacobian of the transformation from $\epsilon_{\tau+1}, \ldots, \epsilon_T$ to $y_{\tau+1}, \ldots, y_T$ is

$$\frac{\partial(\epsilon_{\tau+1}, \ldots, \epsilon_T)}{\partial(y_{\tau+1}, \ldots, y_T)} = \begin{vmatrix} \Gamma & & & & & \\ -\Phi\Gamma & \Gamma & & & 0 & \\ & -\Phi\Gamma & \Gamma & & & \\ & & \ddots & \ddots & & \\ & & & \ddots & \ddots & \\ 0 & & & & \ddots & \cdot\Gamma \\ & & & & \cdot & -\Phi\Gamma & \Gamma \end{vmatrix}$$

$$= |\Gamma|^{T-\tau}$$

The ML estimators of Ω and Φ, conditional on A, are given by expressions analogous to (5.3) and (2.10.2) respectively. The likelihood function may therefore be concentrated with respect to A, and then maximised by a numerical optimisation procedure. As in the static case, analytic derivatives may be derived and these may be incorporated within an appropriate algorithm. Furthermore if initial consistent estimators are available, these derivatives may be used to construct asymptotically efficient two-step estimators.

Testing for Serial Correlation*

Consider a test of the null hypothesis $H_0 : \Phi = 0$ in (7.7). The fact that the model is both dynamic and interdependent means that any test statistic constructed on an intuitive basis is almost certain to be invalid. However, a valid test procedure can be based on the LM principle. An expression for the test statistic is given by Breusch (1979b). Unfortunately this expression is rather complicated, but Breusch suggests an alternative approach which is likely to be more practical. This is based on the form of the LM statistic given in (5.5.8). Writing the test statistic in this way implies that it can be computed as a Wald statistic based on the estimates obtained by one step of Newton–Raphson or the method of scoring. The initial estimates are computed under the null hypothesis which means that Φ is set equal to 0.

Formulating the LM test in this way fits very neatly into the two-step estimation framework. The derivatives needed to compute a two-step estimator are the same as those needed to compute the LM statistic. However, the starting values are different. If the two-step estimator is to be efficient, the initial estimators of A and Φ must be consistent estimators of the parameters in the unrestricted model.

Estimation of a Single Equation

In Section 4, the 2SLS estimator was derived within an IV framework. This approach may be extended to handle serially correlated disturbances, the simplest assumption being that an AR(1) process is appropriate.

The ith equation in (6.1) may be written as

$$y_{it} = z_{it}'\delta_i + u_{it}, \qquad i = 1,\ldots,N, \qquad t = 1,\ldots,T \qquad (7.11)$$

The notation is similar to that adopted in (4.1) except that z_i now includes lagged values of both exogenous and endogenous variables. The disturbance term is assumed to follow a stationary AR(1) process,

$$u_{it} = \phi_i u_{i,t-1} + \epsilon_t \qquad (7.12)$$

and so (7.11) may be transformed to

$$y_{it} - \phi_i y_{i,t-1} = (z_{it} - \phi_i z_{i,t-1})'\delta_i + \epsilon_{it}$$

$$i = 1,\ldots,N, \quad t = 2,\ldots,T \qquad (7.13)$$

Given ϕ_i, a suitable set of instruments is obtained by regressing $z_{it} - \phi_i z_{i, t-1}$ on x_{it}^*, $x_{i, t-1}^*$ and x_t, where x_{it}^* is a vector containing the predetermined variables, including lagged values, in the ith equation. In the notation of Section 2.11, $w_t^* = (x_{it}^{*\prime}, x_{it-1}^{*\prime}, x_t')'$, while the matrix L is as defined in (6.1.4) but with the first row deleted. Furthermore, conditional on δ_i, an estimator of ϕ_i may be obtained in the usual way, simply by regressing the residuals on their lagged values. This suggests a stepwise optimisation procedure in which ϕ_i is estimated by regression and δ_i is estimated by instrumental variables. The GIVE estimator is obtained on convergence.

9.8. Forecasting, Prediction and Control

It is possible to distinguish three motives for building an econometric model. These are: (a) forecasting; (b) prediction and policy evaluation; and (c) control. The forecasting aspect of econometric modelling ties in closely with time series analysis, while the theory surrounding the third function, control, is derived mainly from the engineering literature. Naturally the relative importance of forecasting, prediction and control depends on the particular application of the model. Furthermore, there is considerable overlap between all three. However, by classifying the roles of a model in this way, it is possible to gain some insight, not only into the role of econometrics as such, but also into its role in relation to time series analysis and control engineering. The aim of this final section, therefore, is to develop some kind of overall perspective.

Forecasting from a dynamic simultaneous equation model of the form (1.1) may be viewed as a generalisation of the process described in Section 7.7. Predictions of future values of the exogenous variables are made in some kind of systematic fashion, and unconditional predictions of the endogenous variables are then derived from the model. These are the forecasts of the endogenous variables, and they may be compared directly with forecasts made by any other method. Such methods may range from fitting 'naive' time series models to consulting the stars, although within the context of this book it is clearly the first of these methods which is the more interesting.

Prediction differs from forecasting in that the predictions are made conditional on future values of the exogenous variables. This does not necessarily imply that these future values are known, although from the theoretical point of view it is convenient to evaluate the accuracy of such predictions on this basis. The essential feature of prediction in practice is that it embodies certain assumptions about the future time paths of the exogenous variables. Thus the user of the model is free to bring his own views and prejudices into the forecasting process. However, these views and prejudices are made *explicit* in the declared values of future exogenous variables.

There is a further aspect to prediction. In many situations, the user of the model can actually manipulate some of the exogenous variables. Thus, for example, in the case of a macroeconomic model, the government is able to set a variable such as the rate of indirect taxation equal to whatever value it chooses. A variable which can be manipulated in this way is known as a *control variable* or *instrument*. Assigning a particular set of values to the control variables in the model then represents a *policy*. The effect of the policy on the endogenous variables may then be assessed from the model, conditional on the remaining, uncontrolled, exogenous variables. This exercise may be repeated with different policies and different assumptions about the uncontrolled variables.

Policy evaluation is an important aspect of econometric model building. However, a rather different approach to problems of this kind has been developed by control engineers. They assume at the outset that any policy objectives are well defined. This implies two things: firstly, that there should be *target* values for both endogenous and control variables, and secondly, that penalties can be assigned when these targets are not met and that these penalties can be combined in an overall *loss function*. The *theory of optimal control* is concerned with methods of deriving rules for finding values of the control variables which minimise this loss function.

There is an increasing awareness of the potential of optimal control in econometrics, and this is reflected in a growing literature on economic applications. Chow (1975) gives a review of some of these applications as well as providing an excellent introduction to the subject as a whole. The material presented in the later part of this section is merely intended to give a brief review of the main concepts involved.

The different uses to which a model may be put represents only one aspect of the discussion in this section. A second theme concerns the role of *a priori* assumptions derived from economic theory. This issue was raised right at the beginning of the first chapter. The discussion below draws on the material presented in Section 5 to compare the forecasting performance of simultaneous equation models, single equation models and time series models. By comparing the models within a unified framework the trade-off between robustness and efficiency becomes clear.

The assumptions used in the construction of a model also have implications for policy evaluation and control. Again the treatment below attempts to place the various models in perspective, and to explore the relationship between different strands of the literature.

Prediction

Predictions of future values of the endogenous variables in a dynamic simultaneous equation model, (1.1), are made from the reduced form.

Consider a simple example in which $r = 1$ and the disturbances are serially uncorrelated, i.e.

$$\Gamma y_t = A y_{t-1} + B x_t + \epsilon_t \tag{8.1}$$

Given that future values of the exogenous variables are known, the value of s has no bearing on the discussion below, and both current and past values of the exogenous variables can conveniently be included in x_t.

The reduced form can then be written

$$y_t = \Pi_1 y_{t-1} + \Pi x_t + v_t \tag{8.2}$$

where $\Pi_1 = \Gamma^{-1} A$ and $\Pi = \Gamma^{-1} B$. The optimal predictions are obtained from the recursive expression:

$$\tilde{y}_{T+l|T} = \Pi_1 \tilde{y}_{T+l-1|T} + \Pi x_{T+l}, \qquad l = 1, 2, \ldots \tag{8.3}$$

where $\tilde{y}_{T|T} = y_T$. This may be solved to yield

$$\tilde{y}_{T+l|T} = \Pi_1^l y_T + \sum_{j=0}^{l-1} \Pi_1^j \Pi x_{T+l-j}, \qquad l = 1, 2, \ldots \tag{8.4}$$

Conditional on the parameters in Π_1 and Π, the MSE of $\tilde{y}_{T+l|T}$ is given by

$$\text{MSE}(\tilde{y}_{T-l|T}) = \sum_{j=0}^{l-1} \Pi_1^j \, \Omega \Pi_1^{\prime j}, \qquad l = 1, 2, \ldots \tag{8.5}$$

In practice, Π_1 and Π will be unknown. They must therefore be estimated, and the usual procedure is to derive the estimators from the structural form. If $\tilde{\Gamma}$, $\tilde{A}$ and $\tilde{B}$ denote the estimators of the structural parameters in (8.1), obtained by an efficient full information procedure such as 3SLS or FIML, then

$$\tilde{\Pi}_1 = \tilde{\Gamma}^{-1} \tilde{A} \quad \text{and} \quad \tilde{\Pi} = \tilde{\Gamma}^{-1} \tilde{B} \tag{8.6}$$

These estimators are used in constructing the optimal predictor of y_{T+l} from (8.3). It is important to stress that $\tilde{\Pi}$ and $\tilde{\Pi}_1$ will not, in general, be the same as the estimators obtained by applying OLS directly to the reduced form. These estimators represent the first stage of 3SLS. However, they are inefficient insofar as they fail to make use of any over-identifying restrictions in the model. As a rule, A, B and Γ contain a large number of zeros and this information can only be incorporated in the estimators of the reduced form parameters if they are derived from the structural form. The exception is when every equation in the system is exactly identified, for in that case the structural and reduced forms contain the same number of parameters; cf. the discussion in Section 5.

Replacing Π and Π_1 by estimates results in an increase in the predictive MSE. Under standard regularity conditions it can be shown that the additional term which must be added to (8.5) is of $0(T^{-1})$. However, the results in

Schmidt (1974, 1977) suggest that the contribution made by this term can be relatively large in small samples. Over-identifying restrictions on the structural form will therefore tend to have a significant impact on predictive efficiency. In the static case these gains may be assessed more precisely since a theoretical analysis of the problem is less complex. Reference should be made to Goldberger, Nagar and Odeh (1961).

Forecasting

The analysis of the previous sub-section was based on the assumption that future values of the exogenous variables are known. In forecasting, on the other hand, the concern is with unconditional or *ex ante* prediction. Future values of the exogenous variables must themselves be predicted and so the dynamic structure of the exogenous variables is now critical, whereas in conditional prediction it is irrelevant. This should be apparent from the results cited in Section 7.7. It will be assumed throughout this sub-section that future values of the exogenous variables are forecast by modelling them as a multivariate ARIMA process.

In the discussion of predictive efficiency in the previous sub-section, the main emphasis was on the *a priori* restrictions incorporated in the structural form, but not incorporated in the reduced form. However, in both cases one piece of *a priori* knowledge was taken for granted: the distinction between endogenous and exogenous variables. If this distinction cannot be made, predictions must be made on the basis of a time series model.

Suppose that the exogenous variables are generated by a multivariate ARMA process. Both the endogenous and exogenous variables can then be considered as being generated by a multivariate ARMA process of the form (6.13). However, because of the assumed exogeneity certain assumptions are embodied in (6.13). These are, firstly, that the autoregressive polynomial matrix is block triangular and, secondly, that the disturbance terms, $\bar{\theta}_u(L) \, \epsilon_t$ and $\Theta_x(L) \, \xi_t$, are uncorrelated. If the assumption of exogenous x's were dropped, the complete vector $(y_t', x_t')'$ could still be modelled as a multivariate ARMA process but without the restrictions. Alternatively, attention might be restricted to modelling only y_t as a multivariate ARMA process as suggested by (6.15). In the latter case a generalisation of the analysis in Section 7.7 would imply that, in general, this will involve a loss in predictive efficiency when compared with predictions made from the reduced form with the exogenous variables forecast from a multivariate ARMA model. However, this assumes that the variables in x_t really are exogenous. If this is not the case, the time series model may perform better. Again there is a trade-off between robustness and efficiency.

A multivariate time series model still embodies some *a priori* assumptions insofar as it treats the variables as being jointly determined. A univariate model, however, considers each variable in isolation, thereby invoking no *a priori* knowledge whatsoever. As was pointed out in Section 6, a set of variables generated by a multivariate ARMA process can be modelled individually. Predictions can then be constructed from these models, although if the multivariate model is correctly specified this will normally involve a loss in efficiency.

If the exogenous variables do indeed follow a multivariate ARMA process, modelling the variables in y_t as univariate ARMA processes is quite consistent with the dynamic econometric model (1.1). Forecasting on this basis comes bottom of the following hierarchy:

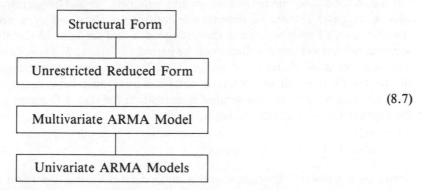

(8.7)

The extent to which *a priori* information is incorporated in the model specification decreases as one moves down the hierarchy. If the *a priori* information is valid, the forecasts of the endogenous variables derived from the structural form of an econometric model will normally be the best available. Conversely, forecasts obtained from fitting individual ARMA processes will be the least efficient. However, if the economic theory underlying the specification of the structural form is based on invalid premises, it is conceivable that a forecast from a univariate ARMA model might yield better results. The crucial point, though, is that were this to happen, it would be an indictment of the economic theory rather than the econometric methodology.

One qualification must be made to the above statement. Dynamic economic theory is not well-developed and is rarely definitive. The dynamic specification of an econometric model is therefore largely an empirical matter. In this respect, econometric methodology is of critical importance. Even if the economic theory relating to the inclusion and exclusion of variables is basically correct, an inappropriate specification of the dynamic structure may lead to a very poor forecasting performance. In these circumstances it is possible that a 'naive' time series model could outperform an econometric model. However, the rapid development of the dynamic aspects of econometric model building over the last ten years has made this occurrence less likely. A comparison of the predictive performance of a dynamic econometric model with a set of univariate time series models will be found in Prothero and Wallis (1976). On p. 485 they summarise their results as follows:

Overall, the econometric approach, which makes the inter-relationships between the variables quite explicit, provides a better-fitting representation than the univariate time series approach,... [and] we conclude that to take account of the specific interdependence of economic variables, whether or not these variables can be individually represented as ARIMA processes, provides a more fruitful approach to model building.

Control

Let the vector of exogenous variables in an econometric model be partitioned as $x_t = (x_{1t}' \, x_{2t}')'$, where x_{1t} denotes the control variables and x_{2t} denotes the uncontrolled variables. Both the endogenous and the control variables are assumed to have target values over the period $t = 1, \ldots, T$. These targets will be denoted by $y_t^\dagger$ and $x_{1t}^\dagger$, $t = 1, \ldots, T$. In order to assess the impact of deviations from these targets a lost function must be constructed. Mathematically, the most convenient specification for such a function is as the expectation of a quadratic form, i.e.

$$W = E \sum_{t=1}^{T} (\dot{y}_t' \, \dot{x}_{1t}') Q_t (\dot{y}_t' \, \dot{x}_{1t}')' \tag{8.8}$$

where Q_t is a matrix of weights, and a dot indicates a deviation from the target value, i.e. $\dot{y}_t = y_t - y_t^\dagger$ and $\dot{x}_t = x_t - x_t^\dagger$. If the expectation were not taken in (8.8) the stochastic nature of y_t would mean that the loss function was a random variable. Note that if the model assumed to be generating the endogenous variables is dynamic, as in (1.1), the expectation in (8.8) is conditional on the initial values $y_0, \ldots, y_{1-r}$.

The optimal control problem is to minimise the loss function, (8.8), subject to the econometric model (1.1). This means finding a rule for determining the optimal values of the control variables, $x_{11}^0, x_{12}^0, \ldots, x_{1T}^0$. If the econometric model were deterministic, i.e. $u_t \equiv 0$ for all t, the time path of x_1 could be determined at the outset. However, in the usual case, where y_t is stochastic, a feedback rule is needed. This incorporates the observations currently available and so the optimal values of the control variables evolve over time. There are a number of ways of deriving the *feedback equation*. These will not be described here, but the book by Chow (1975) provides an excellent reference. The solution takes the form

$$x_{1t}^0 = G_t z_{t-1} + g_t \tag{8.9}$$

where $z_t = (y_t, y_{t-1}, \ldots, y_{t-r+1}, x_t, x_{t-1}, \ldots, x_{t-s+1})'$ and G_t is a matrix, the elements of which depend on the structural parameters of the econometric model and the weights in the loss function. The vector g_t also depends on these quantities, together with the target values of y_t and x_{1t}, and the actual values of x_{2t}.

Although taking the loss function to be a quadratic form permits an elegant solution to the problems of optimal control, it does pose a number of conceptual problems. In the first place, a positive deviation from a target is assigned the same cost as a negative deviation. Secondly, the function is additive so that an expectation is taken for the *sum* of functions of variables in different periods. Both of these properties may be restrictive in certain circumstances.

In a macroeconomic application the variables entering the loss function will be indicators of economic performance. These indicators are traded off against each other in a way that reflects the preferences of the policy makers. Since the economic indicators may include variables such as the level of unemployment and the rate of increase of prices, it is clear that these preferences will be determined by political, as well as economic, considerations. Within this framework the loss function is sometimes referred to as a *welfare function*.

It may not always be easy for the policy makers to formulate their preferences in the precise manner needed for an optimal control calculation to be made. One way of attempting to cope with this uncertainty is to determine the solutions to a number of related loss functions. The desirability of various strategies can then be assessed with regard to their implications for optimal control. Somewhat related to this observation is the point that the recommendations from an optimal control solution may not be the end of an analysis. It may also be desirable to take account of the dynamic behaviour implied by that solution. If the feedback equation settles down into a steady-state solution,

$$x^0_{1t} = \bar{G}z_{t-1} + \bar{g}, \qquad t = 1, \ldots, T \tag{8.10}$$

this is relatively easy to do. Substituting from (8.10) into the reduced form, (1.4), and rearranging enables the dynamic behaviour of the endogenous variables to be assessed using the methods already developed.

Notes

Section 6   Wallis (1977), Zellner and Palm (1974).
Section 7   On estimation see Hendry (1971, 1976), Pagan and Byron (1977), Chow and Fair (1973), Reinsel (1979) and Sargan (1961). A large sample test against serial correlation in single equations is given in Godfrey (1978a); the test in Harvey and Phillips (1980a) is exact.
Section 8   Econometric and time series models are compared in Nelson (1972), Prothero and Wallis (1976) and McNees (1980).

Exercises

1. What is the relationship between the final equations, (6.8), and the reduced form in the static model, (1.5)?
2. Models (2.7) and (2.10) both incorporate two restrictions. Show that the latter implies restrictions on the reduced form whereas the former does not.
3. Construct an estimator of γ_{11} in (2.9a) from the OLS estimates of the reduced form and show that it is consistent. Show that it is identical to the 2SLS estimator. Repeat the exercise for (2.10a) and comment.
4. Prove (8.5).
5. Show that 3SLS collapses to 2SLS applied to each equation in turn when (i) Ω is diagonal or (ii) every equation is exactly identified.
6. Derive the autoregressive final form for the Keynesian model, (1.6.1).
7. In his comments on the paper by Prothero and Wallis (1976, pp. 487–490), Dr O.D. Anderson said: 'No one doubts that...econometric model building...ought to be the obvious choice to back in a bout between an adult and an infant — univariate time series analysis.' He continued: '...what econometric modelling will have to compete with very soon is multivariate time series analysis. I do not see how it can hope to cope then.' Comment.
8. Show that 3SLS is a special case of a FIVE estimator.

Appendix on Matrix Algebra

Differentiation

Differentiation of linear functions and quadratic forms play an important role in the derivation of estimators.

Let a and x be $n \times 1$ vectors and consider the linear function, $a'x = \Sigma a_i x_i$. Since $\partial(a'x)/\partial x_i = a_i$, $i = 1, \ldots, n$, differentiating $a'x$ with respect to the complete vector x may be expressed as

$$\frac{\partial(a'x)}{\partial x} = a \qquad (A.1)$$

Alternatively, differentiating with respect to the transpose of x yields

$$\frac{\partial(a'x)}{\partial x'} = a' \qquad (A.2)$$

For the quadratic form $x'Ax$

$$\frac{\partial(x'Ax)}{\partial x} = (A + A')x \qquad (A.3)$$

$$\frac{\partial(x'Ax)}{\partial x \, \partial x'} = A + A' \qquad (A.4)$$

while

$$\frac{\partial(x'Ax)}{\partial A} = xx' \qquad (A.5)$$

Finally

$$\frac{\partial \log |A|}{\partial A} = (A')^{-1}, \qquad \text{if } |A| > 0 \tag{A.6}$$

Further details and more results can be found in Magnus and Neudecker (1988).

Kronecker Products

Consider the $m \times n$ matrix $A = \{a_{ij}\}$ and the $p \times q$ matrix B. The Kronecker (or tensor) product of A and B (in that order) is the $mp \times nq$ matrix.

$$A \otimes B = \begin{bmatrix} a_{11}B & a_{12}B & \cdots & a_{1n}B \\ a_{21}B & a_{22}B & \cdots & a_{2n}B \\ \vdots & \vdots & & \vdots \\ a_{m1}B & a_{m2}B & \cdots & a_{mn}B \end{bmatrix} \tag{A.7}$$

The basic result on the multiplication of two Kronecker products is:

$$(A \otimes B)(C \otimes D) = AC \otimes BD \tag{A.8}$$

Given (A.8) the following results are easily established:

$$(A \otimes B)^{-1} = A^{-1} \otimes B^{-1} \text{ if A and B are square and non-singular} \tag{A.9}$$

$$(A \otimes B)' = A' \otimes B' \tag{A.10}$$

$$A \otimes (B + C) = A \otimes B + A \otimes C \tag{A.11}$$

$$A \otimes (B \otimes C) = A \otimes B) \otimes C \tag{A.12}$$

Furthermore, it can be shown that, if A is $n \times n$ and B is $m \times m$,

$$|A \otimes B| = |A|^n |B|^m \tag{A.13}$$

and

$$\text{tr}(A \otimes B) = (\text{tr}A)(\text{tr}B) \tag{A.14}$$

Tables

Table A.1   Lower and Upper Bounds of the 5% Points of the Durbin–Watson Test Statistic[a]

T	k = 2 d_L	k = 2 d_U	k = 3 d_L	k = 3 d_U	k = 4 d_L	k = 4 d_U	k = 5 d_L	k = 5 d_U	k = 6 d_L	k = 6 d_U
15	1.08	1.36	0.95	1.54	0.82	1.75	0.69	1.97	0.56	2.21
16	1.10	1.37	0.98	1.54	0.86	1.73	0.74	1.93	0.62	2.15
17	1.13	1.38	1.02	1.54	0.90	1.71	0.78	1.90	0.67	2.10
18	1.16	1.39	1.05	1.53	0.93	1.69	0.82	1.87	0.71	2.06
19	1.18	1.40	1.08	1.53	0.97	1.68	0.86	1.85	0.75	2.02
20	1.20	1.41	1.10	1.54	1.00	1.68	0.90	1.83	0.79	1.99
21	1.22	1.42	1.13	1.54	1.03	1.67	0.93	1.81	0.83	1.96
22	1.24	1.43	1.15	1.54	1.05	1.66	0.96	1.80	0.86	1.94
23	1.26	1.44	1.17	1.54	1.08	1.66	0.99	1.79	0.90	1.92
24	1.27	1.45	1.19	1.55	1.10	1.66	1.01	1.78	0.93	1.90
25	1.29	1.45	1.21	1.55	1.12	1.66	1.04	1.77	0.95	1.89
26	1.30	1.46	1.22	1.55	1.14	1.65	1.06	1.76	0.98	1.88
27	1.32	1.47	1.24	1.56	1.16	1.65	1.08	1.76	1.01	1.86
28	1.33	1.48	1.26	1.56	1.18	1.65	1.10	1.75	1.03	1.85
29	1.34	1.48	1.27	1.56	1.20	1.65	1.12	1.74	1.05	1.84
30	1.35	1.49	1.28	1.57	1.21	1.65	1.14	1.74	1.07	1.83
31	1.36	1.50	1.30	1.57	1.23	1.65	1.16	1.74	1.09	1.83
32	1.37	1.50	1.31	1.57	1.24	1.65	1.18	1.73	1.11	1.82
33	1.38	1.51	1.32	1.58	1.26	1.65	1.19	1.73	1.13	1.81
34	1.39	1.51	1.33	1.58	1.27	1.65	1.21	1.73	1.15	1.81
35	1.40	1.52	1.34	1.58	1.28	1.65	1.22	1.73	1.16	1.80
36	1.41	1.52	1.35	1.59	1.29	1.65	1.24	1.73	1.18	1.80
37	1.42	1.53	1.36	1.59	1.31	1.66	1.25	1.72	1.19	1.80
38	1.43	1.54	1.37	1.59	1.32	1.66	1.26	1.72	1.21	1.79
39	1.43	1.54	1.38	1.60	1.33	1.66	1.27	1.72	1.22	1.79
40	1.44	1.54	1.39	1.60	1.34	1.66	1.29	1.72	1.23	1.79
45	1.48	1.57	1.43	1.62	1.38	1.67	1.34	1.72	1.29	1.78
50	1.50	1.59	1.46	1.63	1.42	1.67	1.38	1.72	1.34	1.77
55	1.53	1.60	1.49	1.64	1.45	1.68	1.41	1.72	1.38	1.77
60	1.55	1.62	1.51	1.65	1.48	1.69	1.44	1.73	1.41	1.77
65	1.57	1.63	1.54	1.66	1.50	1.70	1.47	1.73	1.44	1.77
70	1.58	1.64	1.55	1.67	1.52	1.70	1.49	1.74	1.46	1.77
75	1.60	1.65	1.57	1.68	1.54	1.71	1.51	1.74	1.49	1.77
80	1.61	1.66	1.59	1.69	1.56	1.72	1.53	1.74	1.51	1.77
85	1.62	1.67	1.60	1.70	1.57	1.72	1.55	1.75	1.52	1.77
90	1.63	1.68	1.61	1.70	1.59	1.73	1.57	1.75	1.54	1.78
95	1.64	1.69	1.62	1.71	1.60	1.73	1.58	1.75	1.56	1.78
100	1.65	1.69	1.63	1.72	1.61	1.74	1.59	1.76	1.57	1.78

Source: This table is taken from Durbin and Watson (1951) with the kind permission of *Biometrika*, the publisher, and the authors.

[a]The value of k at the head of each pair of columns is the number of elements of the parameter vector, and it is assumed that one of these elements is a constant term. See Section 6.3 for details.

Table A.2   Lower and Upper Bounds of the 1% Points of the Durbin–Watson Test Statistic[a]

T	d_L (k=2)	d_U (k=2)	d_L (k=3)	d_U (k=3)	d_L (k=4)	d_U (k=4)	d_L (k=5)	d_U (k=5)	d_L (k=6)	d_U (k=6)
15	0.81	1.07	0.70	1.25	0.59	1.46	0.49	1.70	0.39	1.96
16	0.84	1.09	0.74	1.25	0.63	1.44	0.53	1.66	0.44	1.90
17	0.87	1.10	0.77	1.25	0.67	1.43	0.57	1.63	0.48	1.85
18	0.90	1.12	0.80	1.26	0.71	1.42	0.61	1.60	0.52	1.80
19	0.93	1.13	0.83	1.26	0.74	1.41	0.65	1.58	0.56	1.77
20	0.95	1.15	0.86	1.27	0.77	1.41	0.68	1.57	0.60	1.74
21	0.97	1.16	0.89	1.27	0.80	1.41	0.72	1.55	0.63	1.71
22	1.00	1.17	0.91	1.28	0.83	1.40	0.75	1.54	0.66	1.69
23	1.02	1.19	0.94	1.29	0.86	1.40	0.77	1.53	0.70	1.67
24	1.04	1.20	0.96	1.30	0.88	1.41	0.80	1.53	0.72	1.66
25	1.05	1.21	0.98	1.30	0.90	1.41	0.83	1.52	0.75	1.65
26	1.07	1.22	1.00	1.31	0.93	1.41	0.85	1.52	0.78	1.64
27	1.09	1.23	1.02	1.32	0.95	1.41	0.88	1.51	0.81	1.63
28	1.10	1.24	1.04	1.32	0.97	1.41	0.90	1.51	0.83	1.62
29	1.12	1.25	1.05	1.33	0.99	1.42	0.92	1.51	0.85	1.61
30	1.13	1.26	1.07	1.34	1.01	1.42	0.94	1.51	0.88	1.61
31	1.15	1.27	1.08	1.34	1.02	1.42	0.96	1.51	0.90	1.60
32	1.16	1.28	1.10	1.35	1.04	1.43	0.98	1.51	0.92	1.60
33	1.17	1.29	1.11	1.36	1.05	1.43	1.00	1.51	0.94	1.59
34	1.18	1.30	1.13	1.36	1.07	1.43	1.01	1.51	0.95	1.59
35	1.19	1.31	1.14	1.37	1.08	1.44	1.03	1.51	0.97	1.59
36	1.21	1.32	1.15	1.38	1.10	1.44	1.04	1.51	0.99	1.59
37	1.22	1.32	1.16	1.38	1.11	1.45	1.06	1.51	1.00	1.59
38	1.23	1.33	1.18	1.39	1.12	1.45	1.07	1.52	1.02	1.58
39	1.24	1.34	1.19	1.39	1.14	1.45	1.09	1.52	1.03	1.58
40	1.25	1.34	1.20	1.40	1.15	1.46	1.10	1.52	1.05	1.58
45	1.29	1.38	1.24	1.42	1.20	1.48	1.16	1.53	1.11	1.58
50	1.32	1.40	1.28	1.45	1.24	1.49	1.20	1.54	1.16	1.59
55	1.36	1.43	1.32	1.47	1.28	1.51	1.25	1.55	1.21	1.59
60	1.38	1.45	1.35	1.48	1.32	1.52	1.28	1.56	1.25	1.60
65	1.41	1.47	1.38	1.50	1.35	1.53	1.31	1.57	1.28	1.61
70	1.43	1.49	1.40	1.52	1.37	1.55	1.34	1.58	1.31	1.61
75	1.45	1.50	1.42	1.53	1.39	1.56	1.37	1.59	1.34	1.62
80	1.47	1.52	1.44	1.54	1.42	1.57	1.39	1.60	1.36	1.62
85	1.48	1.53	1.46	1.55	1.43	1.58	1.41	1.60	1.39	1.63
90	1.50	1.54	1.47	1.56	1.45	1.59	1.43	1.61	1.41	1.64
95	1.51	1.55	1.49	1.57	1.47	1.60	1.45	1.62	1.42	1.64
100	1.52	1.56	1.50	1.58	1.48	1.60	1.46	1.63	1.44	1.65

Source: This table is taken from Durbin and Watson (1951) with the kind permission of *Biometrika*, the publisher, and the authors.

Table B   5%, 1%, and 0.1% Points of the Modified Von Neumann
Ratio[a]

Degrees of Freedom	5%	1%	0.1%	5%	1%	0.1%
	One-tailed test against positive autocorrelation			One-tailed test against negative autocorrelation		
2	0.025	0.001	0.000	3.975	3.999	4.000
3	0.252	0.052	0.005	4.142	4.427	4.493
4	0.474	0.170	0.037	3.827	4.295	4.496
5	0.598	0.292	0.095	3.571	4.076	4.378
6	0.701	0.386	0.163	3.413	3.881	4.233
7	0.790	0.464	0.228	3.299	3.731	4.095
8	0.861	0.537	0.285	3.206	3.618	3.973
9	0.922	0.601	0.339	3.131	3.524	3.871
10	0.975	0.657	0.390	3.069	3.445	3.784
11	1.020	0.708	0.438	3.016	3.378	3.710
12	1.060	0.753	0.482	2.970	3.319	3.645
13	1.096	0.795	0.523	2.930	3.268	3.587
14	1.128	0.832	0.561	2.895	3.222	3.535
15	1.157	0.866	0.597	2.863	3.181	3.488
16	1.183	0.898	0.630	2.835	3.144	3.445
17	1.207	0.927	0.661	2.809	3.110	3.406
18	1.228	0.954	0.691	2.785	3.079	3.370
19	1.249	0.979	0.718	2.764	3.051	3.337
20	1.267	1.003	0.744	2.774	3.025	3.306
21	1.285	1.024	0.769	2.725	3.000	3.277
22	1.301	1.045	0.792	2.708	2.978	3.250
23	1.316	1.064	0.814	2.692	2.957	3.225
24	1.330	1.082	0.834	2.677	2.937	3.201
25	1.344	1.100	0.854	2.663	2.918	3.179
26	1.356	1.116	0.873	2.650	2.901	3.157
27	1.368	1.131	0.891	2.638	2.884	3.137
28	1.380	1.146	0.908	2.626	2.868	3.118
29	1.390	1.160	0.925	2.615	2.854	3.100
30	1.400	1.173	0.940	2.605	2.839	3.083

[a]See Section 5.2 for details.

Degrees of Freedom	5%	1%	0.1%	5%	1%	0.1%
	One-tailed test against positive autocorrelation			One-tailed test against negative autocorrelation		
31	1.410	1.186	0.955	2.595	2.826	3.066
32	1.419	1.198	0.970	2.585	2.813	3.051
33	1.428	1.209	0.984	2.576	2.801	3.036
34	1.437	1.221	0.977	2.567	2.789	3.021
35	1.445	1.231	1.010	2.559	2.778	3.007
36	1.452	1.241	1.022	2.351	2.767	2.994
37	1.460	1.251	1.034	2.544	2.757	2.982
38	1.467	1.261	1.045	2.536	2.747	2.969
39	1.474	1.270	1.057	2.529	2.738	2.957
40	1.480	1.279	1.067	2.522	2.729	2.946
41	1.487	1.287	1.078	2.516	2.720	2.935
42	1.493	1.295	1.088	2.510	2.711	2.925
43	1.499	1.303	1.097	2.504	2.703	2.914
44	1.504	1.311	1.107	2.498	2.695	2.904
45	1.510	1.318	1.116	2.492	2.687	2.895
46	1.515	1.325	1.125	2.487	2.680	2.885
47	1.520	1.332	1.133	2.482	2.673	2.876
48	1.525	1.339	1.142	2.477	2.666	2.868
49	1.530	1.346	1.150	2.472	2.659	2.859
50	1.535	1.352	1.158	2.467	2.653	2.851
51	1.540	1.358	1.165	2.462	2.646	2.843
52	1.544	1.364	1.173	2.458	2.640	2.835
53	1.548	1.370	1.180	2.453	2.634	2.828
54	1.552	1.376	1.187	2.449	2.628	2.820
55	1.557	1.381	1.194	2.445	2.623	2.813
56	1.561	1.387	1.201	2.441	2.617	2.806
57	1.564	1.392	1.207	2.437	2.612	2.799
58	1.568	1.397	1.214	2.433	2.606	2.793
59	1.572	1.402	1.220	2.429	2.601	2.786
60	1.575	1.407	1.226	2.426	2.596	2.780

Source: This table is taken from Press and Brooks (1969) with kind permission of the authors.

Table C   Significance Values for the CUSUM of Squares Test

	α				
n	0.10	0.05	0.025	0.01	0.005
1	0.40000	0.45000	0.47500	0.49000	0.49500
2	0.35044	0.44306	0.50855	0.56667	0.59596
3	0.35477	0.41811	0.46702	0.53456	0.57900
4	0.33435	0.39075	0.44641	0.50495	0.54210
5	0.31556	0.37359	0.42174	0.47692	0.51576
6	0.30244	0.35522	0.40045	0.45440	0.48988
7	0.28991	0.33905	0.38294	0.43337	0.46761
8	0.27828	0.32538	0.36697	0.41522	0.44819
9	0.26794	0.31325	0.35277	0.39922	0.43071
10	0.25884	0.30221	0.34022	0.38481	0.41517
11	0.25071	0.29227	0.32894	0.37187	0.40122
12	0.24325	0.28330	0.31869	0.36019	0.38856
13	0.23639	0.27515	0.30935	0.34954	0.37703
14	0.23010	0.26767	0.30081	0.33980	0.36649
15	0.22430	0.26077	0.29296	0.33083	0.35679
16	0.21895	0.25439	0.28570	0.32256	0.34784
17	0.21397	0.24847	0.27897	0.31489	0.33953
18	0.20933	0.24296	0.27270	0.30775	0.33181
19	0.20498	0.23781	0.26685	0.30108	0.32459
20	0.20089	0.23298	0.26137	0.29484	0.31784
21	0.19705	0.22844	0.25622	0.28898	0.31149
22	0.19343	0.22416	0.25136	0.28346	0.30552
23	0.19001	0.22012	0.24679	0.27825	0.29989
24	0.18677	0.21630	0.24245	0.27333	0.29456
25	0.18370	0.21268	0.23835	0.26866	0.28951
26	0.18077	0.20924	0.23445	0.26423	0.28472
27	0.17799	0.20596	0.23074	0.26001	0.28016
28	0.17533	0.20283	0.22721	0.25600	0.27582
29	0.17280	0.19985	0.22383	0.25217	0.27168
30	0.17037	0.19700	0.22061	0.24851	0.26772
31	0.16805	0.19427	0.21752	0.24501	0.26393
32	0.16582	0.19166	0.21457	0.24165	0.26030
33	0.16368	0.18915	0.21173	0.23843	0.25683
34	0.16162	0.18674	0.20901	0.23534	0.25348
35	0.15964	0.18442	0.20639	0.23237	0.25027
36	0.15774	0.18218	0.20387	0.22951	0.24718
37	0.15590	0.18003	0.20144	0.22676	0.24421
38	0.15413	0.17796	0.19910	0.22410	0.24134
39	0.15242	0.17595	0.19684	0.22154	0.23857
40	0.15076	0.17402	0.19465	0.21906	0.23589

Note: Enter the table at $n = \frac{1}{2}(T - k) - 1$. The level of significance for a one-sided test is α; for a two-sided test it is 2α.

n	α				
	0.10	0.05	0.025	0.01	0.005
41	0.14916	0.17215	0.19254	0.21667	0.23310
42	0.14761	0.17034	0.19050	0.21436	0.23081
43	0.14611	0.16858	0.18852	0.21212	0.22839
44	0.14466	0.16688	0.18661	0.20995	0.22605
45	0.14325	0.16524	0.18475	0.20785	0.22377
46	0.14188	0.16364	0.18295	0.20581	0.22157
47	0.14055	0.16208	0.18120	0.20383	0.21943
48	0.13926	0.16058	0.17950	0.20190	0.21735
49	0.13800	0.15911	0.17785	0.20003	0.21534
50	0.13678	0.15769	0.17624	0.19822	0.21337
51	0.13559	0.15630	0.17468	0.19645	0.21146
52	0.13443	0.15495	0.17316	0.19473	0.20961
53	0.13330	0.15363	0.17168	0.19305	0.20780
54	0.13221	0.15235	0.17024	0.19142	0.20604
55	0.13113	0.15110	0.16884	0.18983	0.20432
56	0.13009	0.14989	0.16746	0.18828	0.20265
57	0.12907	0.14870	0.16613	0.18677	0.20101
58	0.12807	0.14754	0.16482	0.18529	0.19942
59	0.12710	0.14641	0.16355	0.18385	0.19786
60	0.12615	0.14530	0.16230	0.18245	0.19635
62	0.12431	0.14316	0.15990	0.17973	0.19341
64	0.12255	0.14112	0.15760	0.17713	0.19061
66	0.12087	0.13916	0.15540	0.17464	0.18792
68	0.11926	0.13728	0.15329	0.17226	0.18535
70	0.11771	0.13548	0.15127	0.16997	0.18288
72	0.11622	0.13375	0.14932	0.16777	0.18051
74	0.11479	0.13208	0.14745	0.16566	0.17823
76	0.11341	0.13048	0.14565	0.16363	0.17604
78	0.11208	0.12894	0.14392	0.16167	0.17392
80	0.11079	0.12745	0.14224	0.15978	0.17188
82	0.10955	0.12601	0.14063	0.15795	0.16992
84	0.10835	0.12462	0.13907	0.15619	0.16802
86	0.10719	0.12327	0.13756	0.15449	0.16618
88	0.10607	0.12197	0.13610	0.15284	0.16440
90	0.10499	0.12071	0.13468	0.15124	0.16268
92	0.10393	0.11949	0.13331	0.14970	0.16101
94	0.10191	0.11831	0.13198	0.14820	0.15940
96	0.10192	0.11716	0.13070	0.14674	0.15783
98	0.10096	0.11604	0.12944	0.14533	0.15631
100	0.10002	0.11496	0.12823	0.14396	0.15483

Source: This table is taken from Durbin (1969) with the kind permission of *Biometrika* and the author.

Table D　　Empirical Cumulative Distribution of $\hat{\tau}$

Sample Size	Probability of a Smaller Value							
	0.01	0.025	0.05	0.10	0.90	0.95	0.975	0.99
				$\hat{\tau}$				
25	−2.66	−2.26	−1.95	−1.60	0.92	1.33	1.70	2.16
50	−2.62	−2.25	−1.95	−1.61	0.91	1.31	1.66	2.08
100	−2.60	−2.24	−1.95	−1.61	0.90	1.29	1.64	2.03
250	−2.58	−2.23	−1.95	−1.62	0.89	1.29	1.63	2.01
300	−2.58	−2.23	−1.95	−1.62	0.89	1.28	1.62	2.00
∞	−2.58	−2.23	−1.95	−1.62	0.89	1.28	1.62	2.00
				$\hat{\tau}_\mu$				
25	−3.75	−3.33	−3.00	−2.62	−0.37	0.00	0.34	0.72
50	−3.58	−3.22	−2.93	−2.60	−0.40	−0.03	0.29	0.66
100	−3.51	−3.17	−2.89	−2.58	−0.42	−0.05	0.26	0.63
250	−3.46	−3.14	−2.88	−2.57	−0.42	−0.06	0.24	0.62
500	−3.44	−3.13	−2.87	−2.57	−0.43	−0.07	0.24	0.61
∞	−3.43	−3.12	−2.86	−2.57	−0.44	−0.07	0.23	0.60
				$\hat{\tau}_\tau$				
25	−4.38	−3.95	−3.60	−3.24	−1.14	−0.80	−0.50	−0.15
50	−4.15	−3.80	−3.50	−3.18	−1.19	−0.87	−0.58	−0.24
100	−4.04	−3.73	−3.45	−3.15	−1.22	−0.90	−0.62	−0.28
250	−3.99	−3.69	−3.43	−3.13	−1.23	−0.92	−0.64	−0.31
500	−3.98	−3.68	−3.42	−3.13	−1.24	−0.93	−0.65	−0.32
∞	−3.96	−3.66	−3.41	−3.12	−1.25	−0.94	−0.66	−0.33

This table was constructed by David A. Dickey using Monte Carlo methods. Standard errors of the estimates vary, but most are less than 0.02. The table is reproduced from Fuller (1976) by kind permission of the publishers.

Answers to Selected Exercises

Chapter 1. — **4.** Δy_t follows a non-invertible MA(1) process.
 5. $\alpha/(1 - \phi)$.
 6. Yes; roots of (5.4) are -0.8 and -0.9.

Chapter 2. — **1.** $\Sigma x_t^2 = x_1^2/(1 - x^2)$. Therefore Var($b$) is of $0(1)$, (3.9) does not hold and b is not consistent.
 2. Regress log y_t on $1/x_t$.

Chapter 3. — **2.** $\bar{y}$, $\bar{y} \sim AN(\theta, \theta^2/T)$.
 3. Avar($\tilde{\sigma}$) = $\sigma^2/2T$.
 5. The exponential distribution is a special case of the gamma distribution; see Amemiya (1973).
 6. (i) Yes; (ii) No; (iii) Yes; (iv) No.
 7. Zeckhauser and Thompson (1970).
 8. CSS with $\epsilon_0 = \epsilon_{-1} = 0$.

Chapter 5. — **5.** LR is χ^2 with $N - 1$ degrees of freedom.
 7. Regress y on x, z and z log z and carry out a t-test on z log z.

Chapter 6. — **3.** (a) See Kadiyala (1968). (b) C−O now better.
 7. (ii) $\tilde{y}_{T+1|T} = 11.5$; $\tilde{y}_{T+2|T} = 11.75$.

Chapter 7. — **2.** IV estimation with x_{t-1} and x_{t-2} as instruments for y_{t-1} and y_{t-2} respectively, followed by one iteration of Gauss−Newton.
 3. Estimate α and β by instrumental variables and estimate θ from the residuals; cf. exercise (4.6).
 5. $\hat{\alpha} = -0.9$, $\hat{\beta}_0 = 2.0$, $\hat{\beta}_1 = 2.6$.
 8. IV estimators, $\tilde{b} = 0.096$, $\tilde{\alpha} = 0.540$.

Chapter 8. — **1.** (a) 5, 1.50, 0.36. (b) $\delta_j = \delta^{j-1}(\alpha\beta_0 + \beta_1)$ for $j \geq 1$, $\delta_0 = \beta_0$. (d) 10, 1.6.

    4. LM test of $H_0 : \alpha = \phi$ in (4.2). Regress (4.3) on its derivatives evaluated under H_0 and test TR^2 as χ_1^2.

    9. See Davidson *et al.* (1979, p. 681).

    10. (i) $(1 - A)^{-1} (B_0 + B_1)$. (ii) $A^2 B_0 + AB_1$.

Chapter 9. — **1.** Same.

    2. $\gamma_{11} = \pi_{11}/\pi_{21} = \pi_{12}/\pi_{22}$.

    3. The estimator is known as indirect least squares; see Johnston (1984, p. 442).

References

Akaike, H. (1973) 'Information theory and an extension of the maximum likelihood principle', in B. N. Petrov and F. Csaki (eds), *2nd International Symposium on Information Theory*, Budapest, Akademini Kiado, pp. 267-281.

Almon, S. (1965) 'The distributed lag between capital appropriations and expenditures', *Econometrica*, 33, pp. 178-196.

Amemiya, T. (1973) 'Regression analysis when the variance of the dependent variable is proportional to the square of its expectation', *Journal of the American Statistical Association,* 68, pp. 928-934.

Amemiya, T. (1977) 'A note on a heteroscedastic model', *Journal of Econometrics,* 6, pp. 365-370.

Anderson, T.W. (1971) *The Statistical Analysis of Time Series,* John Wiley.

Andrews, D.F. (1974) 'A robust method for multiple linear regression', *Technometrics,* 16, pp. 523-531.

Andrews, D.F., Bickel, P.J., Hampel, F.R., Huber, P.J., Rogers, W.H. and Tukey, J.W. (1972) *Robust Estimates of Location,* Princeton University Press.

Armstrong, R.D. and Frome, E.L. (1976) 'A comparison of two algorithms for absolute deviation curve fitting', *Journal of the American Statistical Association,* 71, pp. 328-330.

Atkinson, A.C. (1970) 'A method for discriminating between models', *Journal of the Royal Statistical Society,* B, 32, pp. 323-344.

Baillie, R.T. (1979) 'The asymptotic mean squared error of multistep prediction from the regression model with autoregressive errors', *Journal of the American Statistical Association,* 74, pp. 175-184.

Banerjee, A., Dolado, J.J., Hendry, D.F. and Smith, G.W. (1986) 'Exploring equilibrium relationships in econometrics through static models: some Monte Carlo evidence', *Oxford Bulletin of Economics and Statistics,* 48, pp. 253-277.

Basmann, R.L. (1960) 'On finite sample distributions of generalized classical linear identifiability test statistics', *Journal of the American Statistical Association,* 55, pp. 650-659.

Bassett, G. and Koenker, R. (1978) 'Asymptotic theory of least absolute error regression', *Journal of the American Statistical Association,* 73, pp. 618-622.

Beach, C.M. and MacKinnon, J.G. (1978) 'A maximum likelihood procedure for regression with autocorrelated errors', *Econometrica,* 46, pp. 51-58.

Berndt, E.K., Hall, B., Hall, R.E. and Hausman, J.A. (1974) 'Estimation and inference in non-linear structural models', *Annals of Economic and Social Measurement,* 3, pp. 653-665.

Berndt, E.R. and Savin, N.E. (1977) 'Conflict among criteria for testing hypotheses in the multivariate regression model', *Econometrica,* 45, pp. 1263-1278.

Bollerslev, T. (1986) 'Generalized autoregressive conditional heteroscedasticity', *Journal of Econometrics,* 31, pp. 307-327.

Bowden, R.J. and Turkington, D.A. (1984) *Instrumental Variables*, Cambridge University Press.

Bowman, K.O. and Shenton, L.R. (1975) 'Omnibus test contours for departures from normality based on $\sqrt{b_1}$ and b_2', *Biometrika*, 62, pp. 243-250.

Box, G.E.P. and Cox, D.R. (1964) 'An analysis of transformations', *Journal of the Royal Statistical Society*, B, 26, pp. 211-252.

Box, M.J., Davies, D. and Swann, W.H. (1969) *Non-Linear Optimization Techniques*, Oliver and Boyd.

Box, G.E.P. and Jenkins, G.M. (1976) *Time Series Analysis: Forecasting and Control*, revised edition, Holden-Day.

Breusch, T.S. (1979a) 'Conflict among criteria for testing hypotheses: extensions and comments', *Econometrica*, 47, pp. 203-207.

Breusch, T.S. (1979b) *Indirect Calculation of Lagrange Multiplier Test Statistics with Application to Testing for Autocorrelation in Dynamic Simultaneous Equations Systems*, University of Southampton Discussion Paper.

Breusch, T.S. and Pagan, A.R. (1979) 'A simple test for heteroscedasticity, and random coefficient variation', *Econometrica*, 47, pp. 1287-1294.

Breusch, T.S. and Pagan, A.R. (1980) 'The Lagrange multiplier test and its applications to model specification in econometrics', *Review of Economic Studies*, XLVII, pp. 239-253.

Brown, R.L., Durbin, J. and Evans, J.M. (1975) 'Techniques for testing the constancy of regression relationships over time (with discussion)', *Journal of the Royal Statistical Society*, B, 37, pp. 149-192.

Brundy, J.M. and Jorgenson, D.W. (1971) 'Efficient estimation of simultaneous equations by instrumental variables', *Review of Economics and Statistics*, 53, pp. 207-224.

Chipman, J.S. (1979) 'Efficiency of least squares estimation of linear trend when residuals are autocorrelated', *Econometrica*, 47, pp. 115-128.

Chow, G.C. (1960) 'Tests for equality between sets of coefficients in two linear regressions', *Econometrica*, 28, pp. 591-605.

Chow, G.C. (1975) *Analysis and Control of Dynamic Economic Systems*, John Wiley.

Chow, G.C. and Fair, R.C. (1973) 'Maximum likelihood estimation of linear equation systems with auto-regressive residuals', *Annals of Economic and Social Measurement*, 2, pp. 17-28.

Cox, D.R. (1961) 'Tests of separate families of hypotheses', *Proceedings of the Fourth Berkeley Symposium*, I.

Cox, D.R. (1962) 'Some further results on separate families of hypotheses', *Journal of the Royal Statistical Society*, B, 38, pp. 45-53.

Cox, D.R. and Hinkley, D.V. (1974) *Theoretical Statistics*, Chapman and Hall.

Cramer, H. (1946) *Mathematical Methods of Statistics*, Princeton University Press.

Davidson, J., Hendry, D.F., Srba, F. and Yeo, S. (1978) 'Econometric modelling of the aggregate time-series relationship between consumers' expenditure and income in the United Kingdom', *Economic Journal*, 88, pp. 661-692.

Deistler, M. (1976) 'The identifiability of linear econometric models with autocorrelated errors', *International Economic Review*, 17, pp. 26-45.

Dhrymes, P.J. (1970) *Distributed Lags: Problems of Formulation and Estimation*, Holden-Day.

Dickey, D.A. and Fuller, W.A. (1979) 'Distribution of the estimators for autoregressive time series with a unit root', *Journal of the American Statistical Association*, 74, pp. 427-431.

Dixon, L.C.W. (1972) *Nonlinear Optimisation*, English Universities Press.

Domencich, T. and McFadden, D. (1975) *Urban Travel Demand: A Behavioural Analysis,* North-Holland.

Durbin, J. (1960) 'Estimation of parameters in time-series regression models', *Journal of the Royal Statistical Society,* B, 22, pp. 139-153.

Durbin, J. (1969) 'Tests for serial correlation in regression analysis based on the periodogram of least-square residuals', *Biometrika,* 56, pp. 1-15.

Durbin, J. (1970) 'Testing for serial correlation in least squares regression when some of the regressors are lagged dependent variables', *Econometrica,* 38, pp. 410-421.

Durbin, J. and Watson, G.S. (1950) 'Testing for serial correlation in least squares regression, I', *Biometrika,* 37, pp. 409-428.

Durbin, J. and Watson, G.S. (1951) 'Testing for serial correlation in least squares regression, II', *Biometrika,* 38, pp. 159-178.

Durbin, J. and Watson, G.S. (1971) 'Testing for serial correlation in least squares regression, III', *Biometrika,* 58, pp. 1-19.

Eicker, F. (1967) 'Limit theorems for regressions with unequal and dependent errors', in *Proceedings of the Fifth Berkeley Symposium in Mathematical Statistics and Probability,* Vol. 1, University of California Press, pp. 59-82.

Engle, R.F. (1982) 'Autoregressive conditional heteroscedasticity with estimates of the variance of UK inflation', *Econometrica,* 50, pp. 987-1007.

Engle, R.F. (1984) 'Wald, likelihood ratio and Lagrange multiplier tests in econometrics', in Z. Griliches and A.D. Intriligator (eds), *Handbook of Econometrics,* North-Holland.

Engle, R.F. and Granger, C.W.J. (1987) 'Co-integration and error correction: representation, estimation and testing', *Econometrica,* 35, pp. 251-276.

Engle, R.F., Hendry, D.F. and Richard, J.F. (1983) 'Exogeneity', *Econometrica,* 51, pp. 277-304.

Evans, G.B.A. and Savin, N.E. (1982) 'Conflict among the criteria revisited: the W, LR and LM tests', *Econometrica,* 50, pp. 737-748.

Friedman, M. (1953) 'The methodology of positive economics', in *Essays in Positive Economics,* University of Chicago Press, pp. 3-43.

Fuller, W.A. (1976) *Introduction to Statistical Time Series,* John Wiley.

Fuller, W.A. (1985) 'Nonstationary autoregressive time series', in E.J. Hannan, P.R. Krishnaiah, M.M. Rao, (eds), *Time Series in the Time Domain,* North-Holland, pp. 1-23.

Gadd, A. and Wold, H. (1964) 'The Janus quotient: a measure for the accuracy of prediction', in H. Wold (ed.), *Economic Model Building,* North-Holland.

Geary, R.C. (1966) 'A note on residual heterovariance and estimation efficiency in regression', *American Statistician,* October, pp. 30-31.

Gentleman, W.M. (1973) 'Least squares computation by Givens transformations without square roots', *Journal of the Institute of Mathematics and Its Applications,* 12, pp. 329-336.

Gill, P.E. and Murray, W. (1972) 'Quasi-Newton methods for unconstrained optimization', *Journal of the Institute of Mathematics and Its Applications,* 9, pp. 91-108.

Gill, P.E., Murray, W. and Pitfield, R.A. (1972) 'The implementation of two revised quasi-Newton algorithms for unconstrained optimization', *National Physical Laboratory Report, NAC 11.*

Godfrey, L.G. (1973) 'A note on the treatment of serial correlation', *Canadian Journal of Economics,* 6, pp. 567-573.

Godfrey, L.G. (1978a) 'A note on the use of Durbin's *h* test when the equation is estimated by instrumental variables', *Econometrica,* 46, pp. 225-228.

Godfrey, L.G. (1978b) 'Testing against general autoregressive and moving average error models when the regressors include lagged dependent variables', *Econometrica*, 46, pp. 1293-1302.

Godfrey, L.G. and Poskitt, D.S. (1975) 'Testing the restrictions of the Almon lag technique', *Journal of the American Statistical Association*, 70, pp. 105-108.

Goldberger, A.S. (1962) 'Best linear unbiased prediction in the generalised linear regression model', *Journal of the American Statistical Association*, 57, pp. 369-375.

Goldberger, A.S., Nagar, A.L. and Odeh, H.S. (1961) 'The covariance matrices of reduced-form coefficients and of forecasts for a structural econometric model', *Econometrica*, 29, pp. 556-573.

Goldfeld, S.M. and Quandt, R.E. (1972) *Nonlinear Methods in Econometrics*, North-Holland.

Goldfeld, S.M., Quandt, R.E. and Trotter, H.F. (1966) 'Maximisation by quadratic hill-climbing', *Econometrica*, 34, pp. 541-551.

Golub, G.H. and Styan, G.P.H. (1973) 'Numerical computations for univariate linear models', *Journal of Statistical Computation and Simulation*, 2, pp. 253-274.

Granger, C.W.J. (1969) 'Investigating causal relations by econometric models and cross-spectral methods', *Econometrica*, 37, pp. 424-438.

Granger, C.W.J. and Newbold, P. (1977) *Forecasting Economic Time Series*, Academic Press.

Gregory, A.W. and Veall, M.R. (1985) 'Formulating Wald tests of nonlinear restrictions', *Econometrica*, 6, pp. 1465-1468.

Griliches, Z. and Rao, P. (1969) 'Small sample properties of several two-stage regression methods in the context of autocorrelated errors', *Journal of the American Statistical Association*, 64, pp. 253-272.

Griliches, Z. and Ringstad, V. (1971) *Economics of Scale and the Form of the Production Function*, North-Holland.

Hall, S.G. (1986) 'An application of the Granger and Engle two-step estimation procedure to United Kingdom aggregate wage data', *Oxford Bulletin of Economics and Statistics*, 48, pp. 229-239.

Hannan, E.J. (1970) *Multiple Time Series*, John Wiley.

Harrison, M.J. and McCabe, B.P.M. (1979) 'A test for heteroscedasticity based on ordinary least squares residuals', *Journal of the American Statistical Association*, 74, pp. 474-499.

Hart, R.A., Hutton, J. and Sharot, T. (1975) 'A statistical analysis of association football attendances', *Applied Statistics*, 24, pp. 17-27.

Harvey, A.C. (1976a) 'Estimating regression models with multiplicative heteroscedasticity', *Econonometrica*, 44, pp. 461-465.

Harvey, A.C. (1976b) 'An alternative proof and generalisation of a test for structural change', *The American Statistician*, 30, pp. 122-123.

Harvey, A.C. (1980) 'On comparing regression models in levels and first differences', *International Economic Review*, 21, pp. 707-720.

Harvey, A.C. (1981) *Time Series Models*, Philip Allan and Humanities Press.

Harvey, A.C. (1989) *Forecasting, Structural Time Series Models and the Kalman Filter*, Cambridge University Press.

Harvey, A.C. and Collier, P. (1977) 'Testing for functional misspecification in regression analysis', *Journal of Econometrics*, 6, pp. 103-119.

Harvey, A.C. and McAvinchey, I.D. (1978) *The Small Sample Efficiency of Two-Step Estimators in Regression Models with Autoregressive Disturbances*, Discussion Paper No. 78-10, University of British Columbia, April.

Harvey, A.C. and McAvinchey, I.D. (1982) 'On the relative efficiency of various estimators of regression models with moving average disturbances', in G. Charatsis (ed.), *Proceedings of European Meeting of the Econometric Society*, Athens, 1979, North-Holland.

Harvey, A.C.. Henry, B., Peters, S. and Wren-Lewis, S. (1986) 'Stochastic trends in dynamic regression models: an application to the output–employment equation', *Economic Journal*, 96, pp. 975-985.

Harvey, A.C. and Phillips, G.D.A. (1974) 'A comparison of the power of some tests for heteroscedasticity in the general linear model', *Journal of Econometrics*, 2, pp. 307-316.

Harvey, A.C. and Phillips, G.D.A. (1976) *Testing for Stochastic Parameters in Regression Models*, Paper presented at the European Meeting of the Econometric Society, Helsinki.

Harvey, A.C. and Phillips, G.D.A. (1980a) 'Testing for serial correlation in simultaneous equation models', *Econometrica*, 48, pp. 747-759.

Harvey, A.C. and Phillips, G.D.A. (1980b) 'Testing for heteroscedasticity in simultaneous equation models', *Journal of Econometrics*, 15, pp. 311-340.

Hatanaka, M. (1974) 'An efficient two-step estimator for the dynamic adjustment model with autoregressive errors', *Journal of Econometrics*, 2, pp. 199-220.

Hatanaka, M. (1975) 'On the global identification of the dynamic simultaneous equations model with stationary disturbances', *International Economic Review*, 16, pp. 545-554.

Hatanaka, M. (1976) 'Several efficient two-step estimators for the dynamic simultaneous equation models with autoregressive disturbances', *Journal of Econometrics*, 4, pp. 189-204.

Haugh, L.D. and Box, G.E.P. (1977) 'Identification of dynamic regression (distributed lag) models connecting two time series', *Journal of the American Statistical Association*, 72, pp. 121-130.

Hausman, J.A. (1975) 'An instrumental variable approach to full information estimators for linear and certain nonlinear econometric models', *Econometrica*, 43, pp. 727-738.

Hausman, J.A., Hall, B.H. and Griliches, Z. (1984) 'Econometric models for count data with an application to the patents-R & D relationship', *Econometrica*, 52, pp. 909-938.

Hendry, D.F. (1971) 'Maximum likelihood estimation of systems of simultaneous regression equations with errors generated by a vector autoregressive process', *International Economic Review*, 12, pp. 257-272.

Hendry, D.F. (1976) 'The structure of simultaneous equations estimators', *Journal of Econometrics*, 4, pp. 51-88.

Hendry, D.F. (1980) 'Predictive failure and econometric modelling in macroeconomics: the transactions demand for money', in P. Ormerod (ed.), *Modelling the Economy*, Heinemann Educational Books.

Hendry, D.F. and Mizon, G.E. (1978) 'Serial correlation as a convenient simplification not a nuisance: a comment on a study of the demand for money by the Bank of England', *Economic Journal*, 88, pp. 549-563.

Hendry, D.F. and Richard, J.-F. (1983) 'The econometric analysis of economic time series', *International Statistical Review*, 51, pp. 111-164.

Hendry, D.F. and Tremayne, A. (1976) 'Estimating systems of dynamic reduced form equations with vector autoregressive errors', *International Economic Review*, 17, pp. 463-471.

Hendry, D.F. and von Ungern-Sternberg, T. (1980) 'Liquidity and inflation effects on consumers' expediture', in A.S. Deaton (ed.), *Essays in the Theory and Measurement of Consumers' Behaviour*, Cambridge University Press.

Hogg, R.V. and Tanis, E.A. (1963) 'An iterated procedure for testing the equality of several experimental distributions', *Journal of the American Statistical Association*, 58, pp. 435-443.

Huber, P.J. (1973) 'Robust regression: asymptotics, conjectures and Monte Carlo', *Annals of Statistics,* 1, pp. 799-821.

Jarque, C.M. and Bera, A.K. (1980) 'Efficient tests for normality, homoscedasticity and serial independence of regression residuals', *Economics Letters,* 6, pp. 255-259.

Johnston, J. (1984) *Econometric Methods,* 3rd edition, McGraw-Hill.

Jorgenson, D.W. (1966) 'Rational distributed lag functions', *Econometrica,* 34, pp. 135-149.

Kadiyala, K.R. (1968) 'A transformation used to circumvent the problem of autocorrelation', *Econometrica,* 36, pp. 93-96.

Kendall, M.G. and Stuart, A. (1973) *The Advanced Theory of Statistics,* Vol. II, Charles Griffin.

Kenward, L.R. (1976) 'A new test for residual randomness in a class of dynamic autocorrelated econometric models', *Canadian Journal of Statistics,* C, 4, pp. 51-64.

Kiviet, J.F. (1986) 'On the rigour of some misspecification tests for modelling dynamic relationships', *Review of Economic Studies,* 53, pp. 241-261.

Kmenta, J. and Gilbert, R.F. (1968) 'Small sample properties of alternative estimators of seemingly unrelated regressions', *Journal of the American Statistical Association,* 63, pp. 1180-1200.

Kmenta, J. and Gilbert, R.F. (1970) 'Estimation of seemingly unrelated regressions with autoregressive disturbances', *Journal of the American Statistical Association,* 65, pp. 186-197.

Koenker, R. (1981) 'A note on studentising a test for heteroscedasticity', *Journal of Econometrics,* 17, pp. 107-111.

Koerts, J. and Abrahamse, A.P.J. (1969) *On the Theory and Application of the General Linear Model,* Rotterdam University Press.

Konstas, P. and Khouja, M. (1969) 'The Keynesian demand for money function', *Journal of Money, Credit and Banking,* 1, pp. 765-777.

Leamer, E. (1978) *Specification Searches,* John Wiley.

Ljung, G.M. and Box, G.E.P. (1978) 'On a measure of lack of fit in time series models', *Biometrika,* 66, pp. 297-303.

Lucas. R.E.J. and Sargent, T.J. (eds), (1981) *Rational Expectations and Econometric Practice,* George Allen and Unwin.

McCullagh, P. and Nelder, J.A. (1983) *Generalised Linear Models,* Chapman and Hall.

McLeod, A.I. and Li, W.K. (1983) 'Diagnostic checking ARMA time series models using squared-residual autocorrelations', *Journal of Time Series Analysis,* 4, pp. 269-273.

McNees, S. (1980) 'The accuracy of macroeconometric models and forecasts of the US economy', in P.A. Ormerod, *Economic Modelling,* Heinemann.

Maddala, G.S. and Rao, A.S. (1971) 'Maximum likelihood estimation of Solow's and Jorgenson's distributed lag models', *Review of Economics and Statistics,* 53, pp. 80-88.

Maddala, G.S. and Rao, A.S. (1973) 'Tests for serial correlation in regression models with lagged dependent variables and serially correlated errors', *Econometrica,* 41, pp. 761-774.

Maeshiro, A. (1976) 'Autoregressive transformation, trended independent variables and autocorrelated disturbance terms', *Review of Economics and Statistics,* 58, pp. 497-500.

Magnus, J.R. and Neudecker, H. (1988) *Matrix Differential Calculus,* John Wiley.

Malinvaud, E. (1980) *Statistical Methods of Econometrics,* 3rd edition, North-Holland.

Mann, H.B. and Wald, A. (1943) 'On the statistical treatment of linear stochastic difference equations', *Econometrica*, 11, pp. 173-220.

Marquardt, D.W. (1963), 'An algorithm for least squares estimation of nonlinear parameters', *Journal of Society of Industrial Applied Mathematics*, 11, pp. 431-441.

Mizon, G.E. (1977a) 'Inferential procedures in nonlinear models: an application in a UK industrial cross-section study of factor substitution and returns to scale', *Econometrica*, 45, pp. 1221-1242.

Mizon, G.E. (1977b) 'Model selection procedures', in M.J. Artis and A.R. Nobay (eds), *Studies in Modern Economic Analysis*, Basil Blackwell.

Mizon, G.E. (1984) 'The encompassing approach in econometrics', in D.F. Hendry and K.F. Wallis (eds), *Econometrics and Quantitative Economics,* Blackwell.

Mizon, G.E. and Hendry, D.F. (1980) 'An empirical and Monte Carlo analysis of tests of dynamic specification', *Review of Economic Studies,* XLVII, pp. 21-45.

Mizon, G.E. and Richard, J.-F. (1986) 'The encompassing principle and its application to testing non-nested hypotheses', *Econometrica,* 54, pp. 657-678.

Nelder, J.A. and Mead, R. (1965) 'A simplex method for function minimization', *Computer Journal,* 5, pp. 308-313.

Nelson, C.R. (1972), 'The prediction performance of the FRB—MIT—PENN model of the US economy', *American Economic Review,* LXII, pp. 902-917.

Nelson, C.R. (1975) 'Rational expectations and the predictive efficiency of economic models', *The Journal of Business* (University of Chicago), July, pp. 331-343.

Nelson, C.R. and Kang, H. (1984) 'Pitfalls in the use of time as an explanatory variable', *Journal of Business and Economic Statistics,* 2, pp. 73-82.

Oberhofer, W. and Kmenta, J. (1974) 'A general procedure for obtaining maximum likelihood estimates in generalized regression models', *Econometrica,* 42, pp. 579-590.

Pagan, A.R. (1978) 'Rational and polynomial lags: the finite connection', *Journal of Econometrics,* 8, pp. 247-254.

Pagan, A.R. and Byron, R.P. (1977) 'A synthetic approach to the estimation of models with autocorrelated disturbance terms', in R. Bergstrom (ed.), *Stability and Inflation,* John Wiley.

Pesaran, M.H. (1973) 'The small sample problem of truncation remainders in the estimation of distributed lag models with autocorrelated errors', *International Economic Review,* 14, pp. 120-131.

Pesaran, H. (1974) 'On the general problem of model selection', *Review of Economic Studies,* 41, pp. 153-171.

Phillips, G.D.A. and Harvey, A.C. (1974) 'A simple test for serial correlation in regression analysis', *Journal of the American Statistical Association,* 69, pp. 935-939.

Phillips, P.C.B. and Wickens, M.R. (1978) *Exercises in Econometrics,* Vols. 1 and 2, Philip Allan.

Phillips, P.C.B. (1986) 'Understanding spurious regressions in econometrics', *Journal of Econometrics,* 33, pp. 311-340.

Phillips, P.C.B. (1987) 'Time series regression with a unit root', *Econometrica,* 55, pp. 277-302.

Phillips, P.C.B. and Durlauf, S.N. (1986) 'Multiple time series regression with integrated processes', *Review of Economic Studies,* 53, pp. 473-495.

Pierce, D.A. (1971a) 'Least squares estimation in the regression model with autoregressive-moving average errors', *Biometrika,* 58, pp. 299-312.

Pierce, D.A. (1971b) 'Distribution of the residual autocorrelations in the regression model with autoregressive-moving average errors', *Journal of the Royal Statistical Society,* B, 33, pp. 140-146.

Pierce, D.A. (1975) 'Forecasting in dynamic models with stochastic regressors', *Journal of Econometrics*, 3, pp. 349-374.

Pierce, D.A. (1977) 'Relationships — and the lack thereof — between economic time series, with special reference to money and interest rates', *Journal of the American Statistical Association*, 72, pp. 11-22.

Plackett, R.L. (1950) 'Some theorems in least squares', *Biometrika*, 37, pp. 149-157.

Plosser, C.I. and Schwert, G.W. (1977) 'Estimation of a non-invertible moving average process: the case of overdifferencing', *Journal of Econometrics*, 6, pp. 199-224.

Popper, K.F. (1959) *The Logic of Scientific Discovery*, Hutchinson.

Powell, M.J.D. (1964) 'An efficient method for finding the minimum of a function of several variables without calculating derivatives', *Computer Journal*, 7, pp. 155-162.

Press, S.J. and Brooks, R.B. (1969) *Testing for Serial Correlation in Regression*, Report No. 6911, Center for Mathematical Studies in Business and Economics, University of Chicago.

Prothero, D.L. and Wallis, K.F. (1976) 'Modelling macroeconomic time series (with discussion)', *Journal of the Royal Statistical Society*, Series A, 139, pp. 468-500.

Ramsey, J.B. (1969) 'Tests of specification error in the general linear model', *Journal of the Royal Statistical Society*, B, 31, pp. 250-271.

Ramsey, J.B. and Schmidt, P. (1976) 'Some further results on the use of OLS and BLUS residuals in specification error tests', *Journal of the American Statistical Association*, 71, pp. 389-90.

Reinsel, G. (1979) 'FIML estimation of the dynamic and simultaneous equations model with ARMA disturbances', *Journal of Econometrics*, 9, pp. 263-282.

Revankar, N.S. (1971) 'A class of variable elasticity of substitution production functions', *Econometrica*, 39, pp. 61-71.

Rothenberg, T.J. and Leenders, C.T. (1964) 'Efficient estimation of simultaneous equation systems', *Econometrica*, 32, pp. 57-76.

Rothenberg, T.J. (1971) 'Identification in parametric models', *Econometrica*, 39, pp. 577-591.

Rothenberg, T.J. (1984) 'Approximating the distributions of econometric estimators and test statistics', in Z. Griliches and M.D. Intriligator (eds), *Handbook of Econometrics*, Vol. 2, North-Holland.

Rothenberg, T.J. (1988) 'Approximate power functions for some robust tests of regression coefficients', *Econometrica*, 56, pp. 997-1020.

Sargan, J.D. (1958) 'The estimation of economic relationships using instrumental variables', *Econometrica*, 26, pp. 393-415.

Sargan, J.D. (1961) 'The maximum likelihood estimation of economic relationships with autoregressive residuals', *Econometrica*, 29, pp. 414-426.

Sargan, J.D. (1964) 'Wages and prices in the United Kingdom: a study in econometric methodology', in P.E. Hart, G. Mills and J.K. Whitaker (eds), *Econometric Analysis for National Economic Planning*, Butterworth, pp. 25-54.

Sargan, J.D. (1972) *The Identification and Estimation of Sets of Simultaneous Stochastic Equations*, LSE Discussion Paper No. A1, LSE Econometrics Programme.

Sargan, J.D. (1980a) 'Some tests of dynamic specification for a single equation', *Econometrica*, 48, pp. 879-897.

Sargan, J.D. (1980b) 'The consumer price equation in the post-war British economy: an exercise in equation specification testing', *Review of Economic Studies*, XLVII, pp. 113-135.

Schlossmacher, E.J. (1973) 'An iterative technique for absolute deviations curve fitting', *Journal of the American Statistical Association*, 68, pp. 857-859.

Schmidt, P. (1972) 'A generalization of the Durbin–Watson test', *Australian Economic Papers*, 11, pp. 203-209.

Schmidt, P. (1974), 'The asymptotic distribution of forecasts in an econometric model', *Econometrica*, 42, pp. 303-309.

Schmidt, P. (1975) 'The small sample effects of various treatments of truncation remainders in the estimation of distributed lag models', *Review of Economics and Statistics*, 57, pp. 387-389.

Schmidt, P. (1976) *Econometrics*, Marcel Dekker.

Schmidt, P. (1977) 'Some small sample evidence on the distribution of dynamic simulation forecasts', *Econometrica*, 45, pp. 997-1006.

Silvey, S.D. (1975) *Statistical Inference,* Chapman and Hall.

Sims, C.A. (1972) 'Money, income and causality', *American Economic Review,* 62, pp. 540-552.

Sims, C.A. (1980) 'Macroeconomics and reality', *Econometrica*, 48, pp. 1-48.

Sims, C.A., Stock, J.H. and Watson, M.W. (1987) *Inference in Linear Time Series Models with Some Unit Roots*, Working Paper in Economics E-87-1, Hoover Institution, Stanford University.

Spencer, B.G. (1975) 'The small sample bias of Durbin's tests for serial correlation', *Journal of Econometrics,* 3, pp. 249-254.

Spencer, D.E. (1979) 'Estimation of a dynamic system of seemingly unrelated regressions with autoregressive disturbances', *Journal of Econometrics,* 10, pp. 227-241.

Spitzer, J.J. (1976) 'The Keynesian demand for money function revisited', *Journal of Monetary Economics*, 2, pp. 381-387.

Stock, J.H. (1987) 'Asymptotic properties of least squares estimators of cointegrating vectors', *Econometrica*, 55, pp. 1035-1056.

Theil, H. (1971) *Principles of Econometrics,* John Wiley.

Wallis, K.F. (1972) 'Testing for fourth order autocorrelation in quarterly regression models', *Econometrica*, 40, pp. 617-636.

Wallis, K.F. (1974) 'Seasonal adjustment and relations between variables', *Journal of the American Statistical Association,* 69, pp. 18-31.

Wallis, K.F. (1977) 'Multiple time series analysis and the final form of econometric models', *Econometrica*, 45, pp. 1481-1497.

Wallis, K.F. (1980) 'Econometric implications of the rational expectations hypothesis', *Econometrica*, 48, pp. 49-73.

White, H. (1980) 'A heteroscedasticity-consistent covariance matrix estimator and a direct test for heteroscedasticity', *Econometrica*, 48, pp. 817-838.

White, H. (1982) 'Maximum likelihood estimation of misspecified models', *Econometrica*, 50, pp. 1-26.

White, H. (1984) *Asymptotic Theory for Econometricians,* Academic Press.

Wickens, M.R. (1969) 'The consistency and efficiency of generalized least squares in simultaneous equation systems with autocorrelated errors', *Econometrica*, 37, pp. 651-659.

Wolfe, M.A. (1978) *Numerical Methods for Unconstrained Optimization,* Van Nostrand Reinhold.

Zeckhauser, R. and Thompson, M. (1970) 'Linear regression with non-normal error terms', *Review of Economics and Statistics,* 52, pp. 280-287.

Zellner, A. (1963), 'Estimators for seemingly unrelated regression equations: some exact finite sample results,' *Journal of the American Statistical Association,* 58, pp. 977—992.

Zellner, A. and Palm, F. (1974) 'Time series analysis and simultaneous equation econometric models', *Journal of Econometrics*, 2, pp. 17-54.

Subject Index

Adaptive expectations, 229-30
Akaike Information Criterion (AIC), 177-8
Analysis of covariance, 61-4
ARMAX models, 265-6, 273-4, 278-80
Asymptotic theory, 21-2
  asymptotic distributions, 21-2, 47
  asymptotic normality, 22
  asymptotic standard error, 23, 144
  asymptotic t-ratio, 23, 144
  asymptotic variance and covariance, 22, 47
  consistency, 19-21, 65, 77
  convergence in probability, 19
  efficiency, 94
  regularity conditions (*see* Explanatory variables)
Autocorrelation function, 25-6, 28, 32, 201, 221
Autocovariance, 23-5
Autoregressive conditional heteroscedasticity (ARCH), 109, 219-23
  ARCH disturbances, 219-23
  generalised ARCH, 220
  information matrix, 220
  processes, 109
  testing for, 221-3
Autoregressive distributed lag, 265-8, 311
Autoregressive disturbances in dynamic regression:
  estimation, 245-6, 268-73, 348-50
  tests, 275-8
Autoregressive disturbances in static regression models:
  comparison of estimators, 195-200
  generalised least squares, 191-3, 205-7
  ML estimation, 194-5, 205-7
  ordinary least squares, 196-200
  systems of equations, 216-19
  two-step estimators, 193-4, 207
  (*see also* Autoregressive-moving average disturbances, Autoregressive processes, Prediction, Serial correlation tests

Autoregressive-moving average disturbances:
  dynamic regression, 228-9, 245-6, 279-80
  static regression, 208-10
  systems, 216-19
  (*see also* Autoregressive-moving average processes; Prediction; Serial correlation tests)
Autoregressive-moving average (ARMA) processes, 12-13
  autocorrelation function, 25
  estimation, 28, 105, 107
  integrated (ARIMA) processes, 30-2, 247-8, 254-6
  prediction, 28, 30, 352-6
Autoregressive processes, 11-12, 81-2
  autocorrelation function, 25
  estimation, 105, 109, 144-5
  stationarity, 11-12, 24
  (*see also* Autoregressive disturbances; Autoregressive-moving average processes; Multivariate autoregressive-moving average processes)

Berndt, Hall, Hall and Hausman algorithm, 137-8
Best linear unbiased estimator (BLUE), 45-6, 51, 67, 220
Best linear unbiased predictor (BLUP), 52
Binomial distribution, 103
Box–Cox transformation, 179
Box–Pierce Q-statistic (*see under* Q-statistic)

Cauchy distribution, 88, 117-18, 120, 134-5, 138, 141
Causality, 303-9
  Granger causality, 304-5
Central limit theorem, 190
CES production function, 39, 140
Characteristic equation, 24
Chebyshev's inequality, 20
Chi-square distribution, 17
Cholesky decomposition, 15, 108, 206-7

Chow test, 183-4, 288
Cobweb, 10-11, 344
Cochrane–Orcutt:
  generalisations, 206, 208-10
  iterative procedure, 194, 198-200, 268
  transformation, 192-3, 197, 198-200
  two-step estimator, 194, 198-200
Coefficient of multiple correlation,
  43, 61, 288
Co-integration, 289, 294-6
COMFAC analysis, 283-7, 289
Common factors, 114, 247, 283-9
Common trends models, 33
  (see also Co-integration)
Conditional sum of squares, 208
Conditionally Gaussian models, 108-9
Confidence intervals, 59, 143-5
Conjugate directions, 125
Constrained optimisation, 129-30
Constraints (see Restrictions)
Consumption function, 293-4
Control theory, 352, 356-7
  control variable, 352
  feedback equation, 356
  loss function, 352, 356-7
  policy instrument (see above, control
    variable)
  welfare function (see above,
    loss function)
Convergence, 122, 126-8
Correlation (see Coefficient of multiple
  correlation)
Correlogram, 26, 28, 30, 221
Count data, 100, 101-2
Covariance matrix, definition of, 16
Cramér–Rao inequality, 92-3
Cramér–Rao lower bound, 91
Cramér's theorem, 22-3, 77, 80
Criterion function, 123-6
Cross-correlation function, 32, 250, 308-9
Cross-sectional observations, 1, 102
CUSUM (of recursive residuals), 153-5
CUSUM of squares (CUSUMSQ), 153-5

Data admissibility, 6
Data coherency, 6
Data generation process, 13-14
Davidon–Fletcher–Powell algorithm, 133
Detrending, 29, 36
Diagnostic checking (see Model selection)
Dickey–Fuller test, 81-2, 295
Differencing, 12, 30-1, 83, 250-1, 253, 291
  first difference operator, 26-7
  seasonal differencing, 252, 293
Differentiation of vectors and matrices,
  15, 359-60
Direct search, 125-6
Direction vector, 124, 132
Discrimination (see Non-nested models)

Distributed lags, 225-57
  estimation, 238-46, 258-60
  geometric (Koyck), 226-7, 229-31, 237-43,
    253
  lag coefficients, 226, 233-4
  polynomial (Almon), 226, 257-62
  rational, 226, 248-9, 261-2
  (see also Dynamic properties;
    Stochastic difference equations,
    Transfer functions)
Dummy variables, 40, 63, 251, 291, 293
Durbin h-test, 275-7
Durbin–Watson d-statistic, 156-7, 201-4,
  210-11, 246, 275
  bounds test, 202-3
  exact test, 202
Dynamic properties, single equations,
  7-8, 227-8, 232-8
  equilibrium solution, 7-8, 232, 289
  impact, interim and total multipliers,
    234-5, 266, 281, 298, 315
  long-run dynamics, 281, 289-91, 292-4,
    295
  mean and median lags, 235-8
  mean path, 233, 266
  short-run dynamics, 281, 289, 291, 295
  stability, 81
  steady-state solution, 282, 289-92, 294-5
Dynamic properties, systems of equations,
  8-11, 297-9, 314-15, 342-6
  autoregressive final form, 344
  final equations, 343
  final form, 315, 343
Dynamic regression models, 79-83
  (see also Distributed lags; Stochastic
    difference equations; Transfer
    functions)

Encompassing, 7
Endogenous variables, 8, 313
Error correction mechanism, 289-92, 295-6
Exogenous variables, 8, 13-14, 37, 46-8,
  309, 345-6
  Granger causality, 310
  strong exogeneity, 309-11
  testing for exogeneity, 311
  weak exogeneity, 36, 309-11
  (see also Explanatory variables)
Expectation operator, 15-16
Explanatory variables, 37, 102, 281, 289,
  292, 309
  Grenander's conditions, 48
  standard regularity conditions, 47-8
  (see also Exogenous variables)
Exponential distribution, 100

F-distribution, 17
F-tests:
  analysis of covariance, 62-4
  restrictions, general test for, 64-5
  structural change, 64, 163
  subset F-test, 60-1, 162-3, 260-1

Forecasting, 14, 253-7, 351, 354-6
(*see also* Prediction)
Full information maximum likelihood
(FIML), 317, 329-30, 331
Functional form, 38-40

Gamma distribution, 100
Gauss–Markov theorem, 45-6, 84, 116,
220
Gauss–Newton, 135-7
applications, 208-9, 242, 269, 272-3
multivariate, 138-9, 217
General error distribution, 116-18
Generalised Instrumental Variable
Estimator (GIVE) (*see* Instrumental
variables)
Generalised least squares (GLS), 48-51, 67,
191-3, 206-7, 209-10
Generalised linear model (GLIM), 101
Generalised regression model, 107
Gill–Murray–Pitfield algorithm, 133
Grenander's conditions (*see* Explanatory
variables)
Grid search, 124, 127-8, 241

Hessian matrix, 15, 123, 130-2, 138
Heteroscedasticity, estimation, 49-50,
65, 82-3
dependent variable heteroscedasticity,
99-100
multiplicative heteroscedasticity, 98-9,
120, 135, 143
tests, 158-9, 165-6, 171-2
(*see also* Autoregressive conditional
heteroscedasticity)

Identifiability (identification), 5-6, 111-16
convergence of optimisation routines,
127-8
dynamic models, 282-3, 302-3
information matrix, 114-15
local and global, 115-16
rank and order conditions, 327-8, 348
simultaneous equation models,
316, 318-28, 346-8
tests, 340-2
Identification (*see* Identifiability and/or
Model selection)
Information matrix, 91, 100, 102, 114-15,
134-5
Instrumental variables, 75-9, 339
dynamic models, 239-40, 267-8, 350-1
FIVE and LIVE, 338
GIVE, 78-9, 335-7, 351
GLS analogue, 79
(*see also* Two-stage least squares; Three-
stage least squares)
Integrated series, 29, 289

Joint density function, 85-6

k-class estimators, 338-9
Kalman filter, 32, 107, 111, 208
Kronecker products, 360
Kurtosis, 159, 221

Lagged dependent variable (*see* Stochastic
difference equations)
Lag operator, 26-7
polynomials in the lag operator, 27, 227
Lagrange multiplier tests, 169-77, 190
AR and ARMA disturbances, 201, 207,
212, 276-80, 301-2
ARCH effects, 221-2
least squares, 172-4
modified test, 174-5
multiplicative heteroscedasticity, 222
Laplace (double exponential) distribution
117-18
Leading indicator, 255-7
Least absolute error (LAE) estimator
(*see* Minimum absolute deviation
estimator)
Likelihood ratio test, 162-4, 175-7, 190,
219, 341
Limited information maximum likelihood
(LIML), 317, 331-2, 339
Line (linear) search, 124, 137
Linearised maximum likelihood, 141
(*see also* Two-step estimators)
Link function, 102-3, 135
Local and global minima, 127-8
Local level model, 31-2
(*see also* Random walk plus noise
model)
Local linear trend model, 31-2
Logarithmic transformation, 290
Logistic curve, 103
Logit model, 103
Long-tailed distributions (*see* Robustness)

Mann–Wald theorem, 80, 83
Marquardt's algorithm, 136-7
Maximum likelihood estimation:
computation, 88-9, 133-40
concentrated likelihood function, 139-40
dependent observations, 104-11
dynamic models, 240-3, 268-73, 299-301,
348-50
likelihood equations, 86-8
properties of ML estimators, 93-5
'quasi' ML estimator, 116
regression, 95-104
simultaneous equation systems,
329-32, 348-50
Mean path (*see* Dynamic properties)
Mean square error, 18
Median, 118-20
M-estimators, 119-20
Minimum absolute deviation (MAD)
estimator, 118-19, 120

Minimum mean square estimator
  (MMSE), 52
Minimum variance bound (see Cramér–
  Rao lower bound)
Minimum variance unbiased estimator
  (MVUE), 18-19
Misspecification:
  consequences, 146-7, 150-3
  tests, 147-60, 187-8
Model selection, 5
  ARMA models, 30-1
  diagnostic checking, 148-9, 278, 280-1,
    288-9
  dynamic models, 231-2, 246-50, 260-1,
    280-9
  economic theory, 6
  exhaustive test procedure, 187
  goodness of fit, 6, 43, 288
  ordered hypothesis, 186-7
  post-sample predictive testing, 6-7, 149,
    181-5, 188-9, 287-9
  sequential testing procedure, 186-7
  structural models, 32
  tests of specification and mis-
    specification, 147-50
  (see also Misspecification; Non-nested
    models; Tests)
Moving average disturbances (see
  Autoregressive-moving average
  disturbances)
Moving average processes, 12, 24
  estimation, 106, 137, 141, 145
  invertibility, 27, 250
Multicollinearity, 59, 112-13, 127, 226, 281
Multinomial distribution, 104
Multipliers (see Dynamic properties)
Multivariate autoregressive-moving
  average disturbances, 216-17, 299-301
Multivariate autoregressive-moving
  average processes, 12-13, 82-3, 111,
  354-6
Multivariate regression, 72-5, 82

Negative binomial distribution, 101
Newton–Raphson, 130-3, 134
Neyman–Pearson lemma, 161
Non-linear:
  models, 108-9
  regression, 96-7, 120, 137, 139, 172-4
  optimisation, 28
Non-nested models, 146, 148-9, 177-81, 187
Non-normality, 159
Non-stationarity, 29-30, 250-1, 290
Normal distribution, 16-18, 101
  multivariate, 17, 107
  standard, 17
Normal equations, 41
Normalisation, 316
Numerical evaluation of derivatives,
  128-9

Objective function (see Criterion function)
Omitted variables, 147, 150-3, 288
Ordinary least squares, 40-1, 44-8, 65,
  120, 135, 220, 289, 292, 295-6
  asymptotic properties, 48
  correlated and/or heteroscedastic
    disturbances, 50, 196-200
  dynamic models, 228-9, 240, 267-8
  lagged dependent variables, 79-83
  multivariate, 83
  non-normality, 117-18
  prediction, 51-2
  recursions, 52-6
  simultaneous equation models, 330-1,
    333-4
Outliers, 120
Overfitting, 146-7, 247, 274-5, 282
Overparameterisation (see Overfitting)

Parsimony, 5, 7, 28, 295
Partial adjustment, 229-31
Poisson distribution, 90, 101
  Poisson regression model, 104, 135
Portmanteau tests, 212-13, 277-8
Post-sample predictive testing (see Model
  selection)
Power, 175-6
Predetermined variables, 346
Prediction:
  ARMA models, 28-9
  ARMA disturbances, 213-16
  dynamic regression, 253-7, 266-7
  ex ante and ex post, 14
  minimum mean square predictor, 28
  optimal predictor, 106
  prediction error variance, 106
  prediction mean square error, 106
  static regression, 51-2
  systems, 75, 352-4
  (see also Forecasting)
Prediction error decomposition, 106-11, 208
Predictive-R^2, 257
Pre-whitening, 247-8, 308-9

Q-statistic, 28, 212-13, 223, 247
Quadratic hill-climbing, 132-3, 136
Qualitative variables, 40, 100, 102-4
  (see also Dummy variables)
Quasi-Newton methods, 133

Random walk, 29-30, 81-2
Random walk plus noise model, 31-2, 83
  (see also Local level model)
Rational distributed lags (see Distributed
  lags; Transfer functions)
Realisation, 13
Rectangular distribution, 118
Recursive residuals (see Residuals)
Recursive system of equations, 313, 330-1
Recursive t-test, 157-8

Reduced form, 314-15, 331, 339
  unrestricted reduced form (URF),
    315, 341, 355
Regression model:
  classical assumptions, 31, 38, 309
  deviation from mean form, 42
  estimation, 40-51
  multivariate, 73-7
  tests, 58-65
  vector and matrix notation, 37-8
RESET test, 159
Residual adjusted Aitken estimator, 271
Residuals, 150-60
  BLUS, 57, 151-2, 158, 203
  LUS, 57-8, 151, 157-8, 203
  misspecified models, 150-3
  OLS, 41, 56, 150-3, 203
  recursive, 54-5, 153-5, 157-9, 184, 203
Residual sum of squares, 42, 288
  distribution, 58
  recursion, 55-6
Restricted least squares, 43-4, 260
Restrictions, 43-4, 64, 69-70, 129-30, 164,
    260-1, 315, 340-2
  identifiability, 113, 316, 318-29
  non-linear, 168, 296
Robustness, estimators, 116-21
  tests, 156, 203-4

Scoring algorithm, 134-5, 220
Search techniques (see Conjugate
    direction; Grid search; Line search;
    Simplex method)
Seasonal effects:
  adjustment, 31, 252
  dummy variables, 251, 291
  modelling, 205, 251-2, 266-7
  stochastic seasonality, 252
  tests, 211-12
Seemingly unrelated regression equations,
    33, 65-72, 100-1, 138-9, 140-1, 166,
    190, 299, 332
Serial correlation tests, dynamic models,
    246, 275-80, 301-2
  simultaneous equation models, 350
  static regression, 200-4
Sign test, 158, 184-5, 188
Simplex method, 125
Simultaneous equation bias, 334
Skewness, 159
Specification (see Model selection)
Spurious correlation, 59
State space form, 107, 251
Stationarity, 12, 23-5, 27-9, 83
Steady-state solution (see Dynamic
    properties)
Steepest descent, 124, 133
Step-length, 124, 132, 134

Stepwise optimisation, 125, 218
Stochastic difference equations, 227-31,
    264-311
  estimation, 267-75
  misspecification, 274-5
  tests, 275-89
  (see also Dynamic properties;
    Model selection)
Structural change tests, 64, 163-4
  (see also Chow test; Model selection;
    Post-sample predictive testing)
Structural time series models, 31-2, 107,
    251
  multivariate, 33
  reduced form, 32
  (see also Local linear trend model;
    Local level model; Random walk
    plus noise model)
Structure (of a model), 111-12
Sufficiency, 89, 90-1, 93, 190
Sum of squares function, 41, 107, 109, 135
Symmetric stable distributions, 117

t-distribution, 18
Tests:
  consistency, 165
  critical region, 161
  exact and large sample, 156, 165
  non-nested, 179-81
  uniformly most powerful (UMP),
    161-3, 165, 203
  (see also Lagrange multiplier tests;
    Likelihood ratio tests; Model selection;
    Wald tests)
Three-stage least squares (3SLS), 317-18,
    336-8
Three-step estimators, 142-3
Time series models, 11-13, 23-36, 255-7,
    354-6
  (see also Autoregressive processes;
    Autoregressive-moving average processes;
    Multivariate ARMA processes)
Transfer functions, 227
  estimation, 238-45
  model selection, 231-2, 246-50, 264-5
  prediction, 253-7
Transformations, 129-30
t-tests, 58-9, 65, 81-2, 292
  (see also asymptotic t-ratio
    under Asymptotic theory)
Trend:
  deterministic, 30-1
  stochastic, 31, 250-1, 252
Two-stage least squares (2SLS),
    317-18, 332, 334-6, 339

Two-step estimators, 140-3, 145
  dynamic regression, 228-9, 243-4, 271,
    300-1
  simultaneous equations, 330
  static regression with ARMA
    disturbances, 193-4, 207, 210, 218

Unbiasedness, 18, 52
Underparameterisation, 146-7
Unit roots, 29-30, 83
  testing for, 81-2
Updating formulae, 53-4

Variable metric (*see* Quasi–Newton
  methods)
Vector autoregressive-moving average
  processes (*see* Multivariate
  autoregressive-moving average
  processes)

von Neumann Ratio, 157, 203-4

Wald tests, 149, 166-9, 175-7, 190
  regression, 167-8, 200-1, 285-7
  non-linear constraints, 168
Weighted least squares, 49-50, 83, 100, 102,
  119, 135
White noise, 23
  multivariate, 32
Wilcoxon test, 188

Zig-zag optimisation (*see* Stepwise
  optimisation)

Author Index

Abrahamse, A.P.J., 83, 202, 203
Akaike, H., 189
Almon, S., 226, 262
Amemiya, T., 99, 100, 121
Anderson, O.D., 358
Anderson, T.W., 186
Andrews, D.F., 121
Armstrong, R.D., 121
Atkinson, A.C., 179

Baillie, R.T., 215, 216
Banerjee, A., 295
Basmann, R.L., 342
Bassett, G., 119
Beach, C.M., 195, 198
Bera, A.K., 189
Berndt, E.R., 137, 138, 176
Bollerslev, T., 220
Bowden, R.J., 83
Bowman, K.O., 159
Box, G.E.P., 30, 189, 223, 231, 245, 246, 247, 251, 255, 262
Box, M.J., 129, 145
Breusch, T.S., 170, 173, 176, 189, 311, 350
Brown, R.L., 55, 83, 154, 155, 189
Brundy, J.M., 338
Byron, R.P., 166, 218, 311, 357

Chipman, J.S., 193
Chow, G.C., 352, 356, 357
Collier, P., 158, 189
Cox, D.R., 119, 121, 177, 179, 180, 189
Cramér, H., 36, 121

Davidson, J., 182, 292
Deistler, M., 347
Dhrymes, P.J., 240
Dickey, D.A., 81, 368
Dixon, L.C.W., 129, 145
Domencich, T., 121
Durbin, J., 55, 83, 189, 194, 202, 223, 275, 277, 285, 301, 312

Eicker, F., 83
Engle, R.F., 36, 109, 189, 220, 294, 295, 306, 311
Evans, G.B.A., 176
Evans, J.M., 55, 83, 189

Fair, R.C., 357
Friedman, M., 5, 6
Frome, E.L., 121
Fuller, W.A., 81, 368

Gadd, A., 189
Geary, R.C., 50
Gentleman, W.M., 55, 57
Geweke, J., 307
Gilbert, R.F., 68, 223
Gill, P.E., 133
Godfrey, L.G., 262, 285, 311, 357
Goldberger, A.S., 52, 354
Goldfeld, S.M., 121, 132
Golub, G.H., 57
Granger, C.W.J., 294, 295, 304, 305, 306
Gregory, A.W., 168
Griliches, Z., 140, 223

Hall, B., 137, 138
Hall, R.E., 137, 138
Hall, S.G., 295
Hannan, M.J., 347
Harrison, M.J., 189
Hart, R.A., 71
Harvey, A.C., 31, 32, 83, 107, 121, 158, 189, 198, 203, 204, 223, 251, 252, 262, 295, 357
Hatanaka, M., 269, 271, 311, 348
Haugh, L.D., 262
Hausman, J.A., 121, 137, 138, 339
Hendry, D.F., 189, 216, 283, 286, 287, 291, 292, 294, 300, 311, 330, 339, 357
Hinkley, D.V., 119, 121
Hogg, R.V., 184
Huber, P.J., 119, 121
Hutton, J., 71

Imhof, P., 202, 211

Jarque, C.M., 189
Jenkins, G.M., 30, 223, 231, 245,
246, 247, 251, 255, 262
Johnston, J., 36, 83
Jorgenson, D.W., 338

Kang, H., 36
Kendall, M.G., 121, 344
Kenward, L.R., 311
Khouja, M., 173
Kiviet, J.F., 311
Kmenta, J., 68, 125, 223
Koenker, R., 119, 172
Koerts, J., 83, 202, 203
Konstas, P., 173

Leamer, E., 36, 189
Leenders, C.T., 330
Li, W.K., 223
Ljung, G.M., 223
Lucas, R.E.J., 262

McAvinchey, I.D., 198, 223
McCabe, B.P.M., 189
McCullagh, P., 101
McFadden, D., 121
MacKinnon, J.G., 195, 198
McLeod, A.I., 223
McNees, S., 357
Maddala, G.S., 262, 272
Maeshiro, A., 193
Magnus, J.R., 360
Mallnvaud, E., 73, 83
Mann, H.B., 80, 83
Marquardt, D.W., 136
Mead, R., 125
Mizon, G.E., 7, 179, 186, 187,
189, 283, 286, 287, 291
Murray, W., 133

Nagar, A.L., 354
Nelder, J.A., 101, 125
Nelson, C.R., 36, 256, 357
Neudecker, H., 360
Newbold, P., 304
Neyman, J., 161

Oberhofer, W., 125
Odeh, H.S., 354

Pagan, A.R., 166, 170, 173, 189,
218, 261, 311, 357
Palm, F., 357
Pan Jie-Jan, 202, 211
Pearson, E.S., 161
Pesaran, H., 180, 262
Phillips, G.D.A., 83, 189, 203, 204, 357
Phillips, P.C.B., 82, 83, 330, 339

Pierce, D.A., 223, 257, 309
Pitfield, R.A., 133
Plackett, R.L., 83
Plosser, C., 262
Popper, K.F., 5
Poskitt, D.S., 262
Powell, M.J.D., 125
Prothero, D.L., 355, 357, 358

Quandt, R., 121, 132

Ramsey, J.B., 159, 189
Rao, A.S., 262, 272
Rao, P., 223
Reinsel, G., 357
Revankar, N.S., 189
Richard, J-F., 179, 189, 311
Ringstad, V., 140
Rothenberg, T.J., 121, 142, 176, 330

Sargan, J.D., 83, 125, 189, 262, 283, 285,
292, 302, 347, 357
Sargent, T.J., 262
Savin, N.E., 176
Schlossmacher, E.J., 121
Schmidt, P., 159, 212, 262, 339, 354
Schweppe, F., 121
Schwert, G.W., 262
Seber, G.A.F., 189
Sharot, T., 71
Shenton, L.R., 159
Silvey, S.D., 91, 121, 189
Sims, C.A., 83, 306, 307, 308
Spencer, B.G., 277
Spencer, D.E., 301
Spitzer, J.J., 173
Stock, J.H., 83, 295
Stuart, A., 121
Styan, G.P.H., 57

Tanis, E.A., 184
Theil, H., 36, 44, 51, 57, 64, 70, 83, 99,
271, 331, 338, 339
Tremayne, A., 300
Trotter, H.F., 132
Turkington, D.A., 83

Veall, M.R., 168
von Ungern-Sternberg, T., 294

Wald, A., 80, 83
Wallis, K.F., 211, 262, 355, 357, 358
Watson, G.S., 202, 285
Watson, M.W., 83
White, H., 36, 83, 121
Wickens, M.R., 83, 330, 339
Wiener, H., 304
Wold, H., 189
Wolfe, M.A., 15, 137, 145

Zellner, A., 68, 357